UMBIA ELECTRIC RAILWAY

JG LINES IN CANADA AND THE U.S.A.

avily, other electric railways thus : •••••)

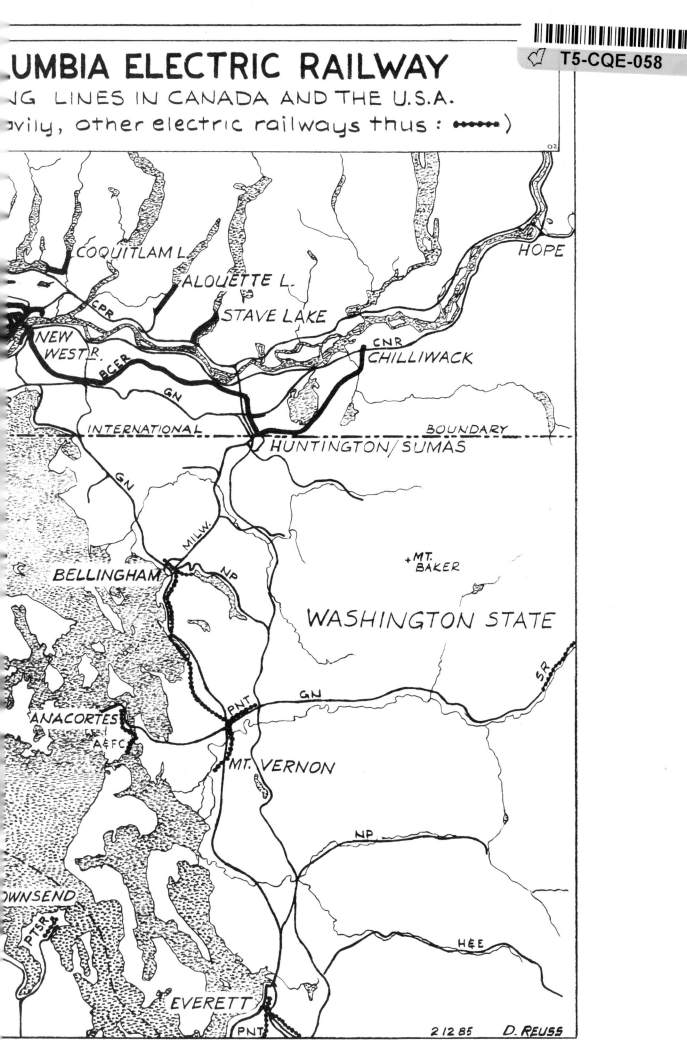

COQUITLAM L.

ALOUETTE L.

STAVE LAKE

HOPE

CPR

NEW WEST R.

BCER

CNR CHILLIWACK

GN

INTERNATIONAL   BOUNDARY

HUNTINGTON/SUMAS

GN

MILW.

NP

+MT. BAKER

BELLINGHAM

WASHINGTON STATE

S R

GN

PNT

ANACORTES

A&FC

MT. VERNON

NP

OWNSEND

PTSR

H&E

EVERETT

PNT

2 12 85   D. REUSS

THE STORY OF THE
B.C.Electric
RAILWAY COMPANY

HENRY EWERT

WHITECAP BOOKS

Canadian Cataloguing in Publication Data

Canadian Cataloguing in Publication Data

Ewert, Henry, 1937-
    The Story of the B.C. Electric Railway

    Bibliography: p.
    ISBN 0-920620-54-X

    1. British Columbia Electric Company — History.
2. Street-railroads — British Columbia — Vancouver
— History. 3. Street-railroads — British Columbia
— New Westminster — History. 4. Street-railroads
— British Columbia — Nanaimo — History. 5.
Street-railroads — British Columbia — Victoria —
History. I. Title.
TF727.B5E84 1986   388.4'6'097113   C86-091140-3

Published by Whitecap Books Ltd., 1086 W. 3rd St.
North Vancouver, B.C.
Telephone: (604) 980-9852

Designed by Michael Kluckner.

Printed by D. W. Friesen & Sons,
Altona, Manitoba, Canada

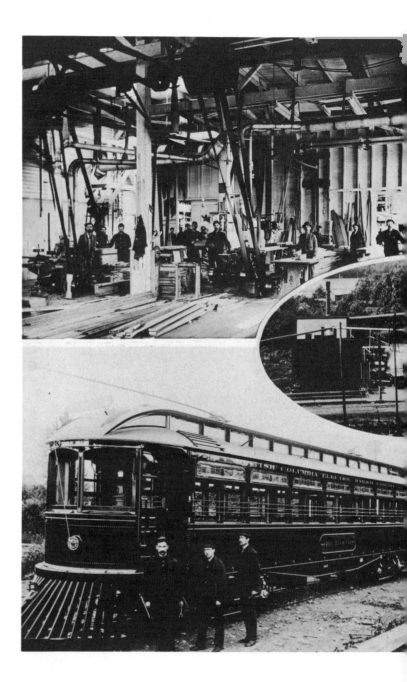

(Frontspiece)
It's a 1909 morning on Park Row (Queen's Park in the background) as conductor D.H. Miller and motorman Al Hudson bring car 39 (formerly W. & V. Tramway 17) down into New Westminster. (Peggy Webb collection)

(Title Pages)
A four-car Chilliwack train settles in at Sullivan in May of 1923.

TO GEOFF MEUGENS,
whose electric interurban enthusiasts
association, started in the 1930's,
is still a vehicle to inspire our hopes
for the ideal transportation.

(Above)
*The company's car shops at New
Westminster in operation.
(Peggy Webb collection)*

(Pages 8&9)
*New Westminster's interurban
depot in 1926, already canopied
and displaying more bus than
interurban, 1224. The twin tracks
at centre left sweep down Eighth
Street into Columbia. Notice that
no track was laid to the right,
toward the barn. (B.C. Hydro)*

Introduction

Evidence of the B. C. Electric's magnificent street cars and interurban coaches has almost entirely disappeared. Memories of their empire remain, but those by their very nature seldom trade in details of their peregrinations and their fundamental importance in a "new" land. The year of Expo 86, set in Vancouver, as well as Vancouver's hundredth birthday, affords an occasion for looking back at how we once travelled to work, to play, and home again.

This volume sets down in year-by-year fashion an account of the tribulations and triumphs, the decisions and their outcomes, as the British Columbia Electric Railway strove to provide quality transportation, and survive to grow. Not treated is the B. C. Electric's leadership and success in the role of hydro-electric and gas producer and supplier.

The story is purely chronological from 1917 to the end, in contrast with the compartmentalized treatment accorded the various systems until 1905, and the separation into two strands of the Vancouver Island and lower mainland operations during the eleven hectic years between 1906 and 1916.

Table of Contents

List of Maps

Preface

It has been a long time since street cars dominated our downtown streets and interurban trams threaded t
way out to the suburbs and beyond. To my friend Henry and me, and the thousands who rode them, they a
not forgotten. Who can ever forget riding the number 10 or 11 cars to the big, crowded loop at Stanley
on a hot summer's Sunday? The cars seemed to possess a quality which causes them to linger with affec
in our memories.

The street cars and trams were imposing and efficient. They were also colourful. Although they no long
grace our cities and landscapes, they are fully deserving of the dignity and respect a book confers on th

This volume appropriately fills a significant void and appears at an opportune time.
It celebrates the British Columbia Electric Railway's street cars and trams not only
in the year of Vancouver's centenary, but also in conjunction with Expo 86, the
World's Fair dedicated to transportation and technology.

Long may our former, much-loved means of transit live, even if only in our memories!

JIM PATTISON

JIM PATTISON
Chairman, Expo 86 Corporation

Acknowledgements

This book could never have been fashioned without the influence and support over a period of many years of two men central to the appreciation of electric railway transportation in British Columbia: V.L. Sharman, once interurban motorman on B. C. Electric's District 2, today corporate secretary, B.C. Transit (a B. C. Electric successor) and Ernie Les Plant, B. C. Electric Kitsilano shops mainstay between 1943 and 1954, and rail enthusiast and railfan organizer extraordinaire.

The meticulous drawings and maps by David Reuss wrested countless hours from his precious pastoral and family time; indeed, so did his day to day encouragement and inspiration. Each of the following was absolutely essential to the book, providing indispensable enrichment: George Bergson, Ted Clark, Bob Dillabough, Geoff Meugens, Barrie Sanford, and Bob Webster.

In Vancouver, the Public Affairs Division of B. C. Hydro, a B. C. Electric successor corporation, headed by Peter McMullan, Manager Editorial Services, provided more assistance than any researcher has a right to expect. Bill Chatterton, Publications Supervisor, was always ready to help, and Graham MacDonell, Publications Editor, enthusiastically and energetically spent countless hours of his own time tracking down details and clearing the way for research to occur.

In Victoria's B. C. Hydro offices, Lily Flynn, Administrative Services Supervisor, threw herself unhesitatingly into this project.

Railway Manager Gerry Stevenson of B. C. Hydro Rail (another B. C. Electric successor) invariably came up cheerfully with answers and information.

The staffs of the following institutions and organizations were unstinting in their willingness to participate and assist: Provincial Archives of British Columbia, Victoria, particularly archivist David Mattison; British Columbia Provincial Museum, Victoria, particularly Monte Wright; Museum of Science and Technology, Ottawa, particularly Ian Jackson; University of British Columbia Library, Vancouver; British Columbia Forest Museum, Duncan, particularly Varick Wagner; British Columbia Transit, particularly Diane Hughes; Burnaby Village Museum, particularly Jennifer Pride and Jim Wolf; Chilliwack Museum & Historical Society, particularly Barb Townley; Irving House Historic Centre, New Westminster; Mission Museum; New Westminster Public Library, particularly Jos Halvorson; North Shore Museum and Archives, particularly June Thompson; Vancouver Archives; Vancouver Public Library; Victoria Archives; and Victoria Public Library.

Each of the following persons has contributed in a major way to a better understanding of the B. C. Electric's mission: Cliff Banner, Ed Banning, Doug Barbour, Jack Berry, Bill Boston, Lloyd Brice, Mrs. J. L. Corson, Tom Cronk, Jimmy Donald, Jack Elliott, Percy Enefer, Bill Gibbs, Norm Gidney, Sr., Ronald A. Greene, Fred Hall, Ken Hodgson, Frank Horne, Jack Lobban, Miss Hilda McGillivray, Phil Magnall, Arthur Miller, Charles Murdoch, Douglas Parker, Don Payne, Rick Percy, John Reuss, Miss Nell Ross, John Sikora, Bob Straw, Nelson Tate, and Norman W. Williams.

That so many eagerly contributed and made suggestions, wrote letters and made telephone calls, was one of the great joys in preparing this volume.

Incredibly, the mammoth task of typing the manuscript was despatched by Mrs. Betty Blair with her usual aplomb and good humour.

To Michael Burch, Whitecap Books, I tender the most special thanks for making a book about B. C. Electric's street cars and interurbans possible; furthermore, the ministrations of editor Elaine Jones were unfailingly apt and encouraging.

I am deeply grateful to my mother and father for teaching me to value my environment and for exposing me to the thrill of travel. Finally, the tolerance and concern of Dianna and her magical supply of freshly-brewed German coffee ensured the existence of the necessary work ethic and a focussed anxiety.

I

From the Beginning to 1897:

Dreams and Nightmares

The completion of the Canadian Pacific Railway to Vancouver on the shores of the Pacific Ocean began dreams and stimulated growth, just as almost everyone expected it would. The promise of a link with long-settled, well-populated eastern Canada had hustled an isolated British Columbia into confederation with the four-year-old Dominion of Canada in 1871, but sixteen years was surely a frustrating wait for a promised lifeline.

But when it finally arrived, the C.P.R. brought unbounded optimism and enthusiastic industry, though few would have dared predict that within twenty-five years, the areas of British Columbia's coast most profoundly affected by the railway would possess an extraordinary street car and interurban system, one of surpassing variety, scope, service, and fascination — the British Columbia Electric Railway.

Vancouver, the great ocean port to be, had been incorporated little more than thirteen months when the C.P.R.'s inaugural transcontinental passenger train arrived in Vancouver from Montreal on May 23, 1887. Three weeks later, the C.P.R.'s trans-Pacific steamship service began with the arrival in Vancouver — from Yokohama — of the chartered S.S. *Abyssinia*, with freight, mail, newspapers, and just over a hundred passengers.

Although the Vancouver area had been settled as early as 1862, acquiring the unofficial name of Gastown by 1867, and the official one of Granville Townsite in 1870, its population of 5,000 hardly impressed the 15,000 residents of British Columbia's capital city, Victoria. On Vancouver Island, Victoria had almost every reason to feel comfortable. Incorporated in 1862 — it had begun life as the Hudson's Bay Company's Fort Victoria in 1843 — and capital of the province of British Columbia since 1868, Victoria had since August 1886 been connected by the Esquimalt and Nanaimo Railway with Nanaimo, 72 miles up-island from Victoria.

New Westminster, however, fewer than a dozen miles southeast of Vancouver, had cause for concern. Though incorporated in 1860, on the heels of the great Fraser River gold rush, making it the first incorporated municipality in the whole of British territory west of the Great Lakes, its

population had taken these twenty-seven years to equal that of Vancouver. Like Vancouver, New Westminster was an ocean port, but it was situated along the north bank of the Fraser River some fifteen miles from the ocean, reason enough for the C.P.R. to lay an 8.2-mile branch from its main line at Westminster Junction (Coquitlam today) into New Westminster by 1887.

All four cities lusted eagerly after a credibility-giving street car system, and only Nanaimo, incorporating its Nanaimo Electric Tramway Company in 1891, would find itself unable to follow through. But which of the three would be first? And how extraordinary that a new method of moving people (street cars on rails, with overhead trolley, had begun operating successfully hardly a year earlier, first in Detroit, then in Windsor, Ontario, on May 28, 1886) should be grasped at so precipitously by these brash, fresh-faced British Columbia cities!

Victoria

"We notice," editorialized the November 10, 1888 issue of the *Victoria Standard,* "that our sister city Vancouver, with its usual energy and promptitude when any scheme for the advancement of her interests are concerned, has virtually passed the by-law giving permission to open a street railway in that city, and it is to be hoped that the council of this city will lose no time in following the example set."

Ten days later, an agreement was signed between five prominent Victoria citizens — headed by Captain James Douglas Warren — and the City of Victoria, authorizing the former to put a street car service into operation. Captain Warren's bid was one of two in Victoria, but his success there was not duplicated in Vancouver, where his application to run street cars was rejected in favour of that of the Vancouver Street

Railways Company. On April 6, 1889, the National Electric Tramway and Lighting Company Limited was incorporated by an Act of British Columbia's provincial legislature; and just over a month later, on May 16, the following notice appeared in Victoria newspapers: "TENDERS are invited up to noon of Friday the 7th inst., under Seal, for the construction of FIVE MILES, more or less, of STREET TRAMWAY, in the city of Victoria. Particulars can be learned on application at the office of the Company, between the hours of two and four o'clock daily. The lowest or any tender not necessarily accepted. H. F. Heisterman, Sec." It was Heisterman, now a member of the National's Board of Directors — and secretary-treasurer — who had proposed the rival bid for operating street cars in Victoria.

The initial authorized capital for the National Electric Tramway and Lighting Company was $250,000. Street cars were not to exceed a speed of ten miles an hour over the two routes to be laid, one from the fountain (where Douglas and Government streets and Hillside Avenue converge), south on Douglas to Yates Street, west on Yates, south on Government to Superior, and then west to the outer wharf area via Superior, St. Lawrence, and Erie streets; and the second route from the north end of Store Street (at Rock Bay bridge), south on Store to Johnson Street, east to Government, then south to Fort Street (sharing the last two of these three blocks with the other street car line), and well east on Fort past the city's schools to Richmond Road, the site of Royal Jubilee Hospital, which would open in the following year on May 20. On June 17, four first-class sixteen-foot street cars (termed "passenger coaches" in the press) were ordered by telegraph from car builder Patterson & Corbin of St. Catharines, Ontario; rails were already on the way by sailing ship around Cape Horn from Antwerp, Belgium.

Construction of the car barn and power house, to contain a 110 horsepower steam engine and two Thomson-Houston generators, began on September 2, on the west side of Store Street at the Rock Bay bridge. A month later, rails had been laid on James Bay bridge (today's Government Street in front of the Empress Hotel), and before the end of October, the tracks attained Outer Wharf terminus. And then the four beautiful single-truck street cars arrived — numbers 1 and 4 on November 8, and 2 and 3 on November 13 — with their gleaming interiors of ash, furnishings of cherry, and trimmings of solid brass. Passenger seats ran lengthwise, in the fashion of the time; the motormen faced the weather, although their platforms were later to be enclosed.

Wednesday, February 19, 1890, was the very first day of street cars. The seven-block stretch of Store Street between the car barn and Johnson Street saw car number 3 several times as it trundled back and forth, getting the feel of the track in the cool winter air, with superintendent J. S. Winslow as motorman and J. Sparks the conductor. Victoria was the third city in Canada with street cars. (St. Catharines had already come in second, behind Windsor.) On the following day — abundant confidence already acquired — number 3 covered, with only the occasional mishap, much of the trackage of the two street car lines.

On Saturday, February 22, 1890, Victoria celebrated as the National Electric Tramway and Lighting Company Limited began operating all four cars over the five-mile system, albeit ceremonially. The Sunday edition of the *Colonist* newspaper tells it best:

"Pursuant to invitations issued, about two hundred prominent gentlemen gathered at the Power House, Rock Bay bridge at 1:30 p.m. yesterday where they were cordially received by the president of the street railway, Mr. D. W. Higgins and other officers of the road who escorted their guests through the engine and car rooms, etc. and explained the, in some respects, mysterious workings of the system.

Champagne was next opened, and all present drank to the success of the road so auspiciously inaugurated. Then Mr. Edward Allen, M.P.P. for Lillooet suggested that it would certainly be in order to sing 'God Save the Queen', and the suggestion with smiles and laughter was carried out with a vim, the member for Lillooet leading the choir.

At about 2 o'clock cars nos. 1, 2, 3, 4 which were waiting on the bridge were boarded by the company, and all prepared themselves for the excursion over the line. His Honour, the Lieutenant-Governor [Hugh Nelson], accompanied by his private secretary, Mr. Herbert Stanton, Premier [John] Robson, Mayor Grant

NATIONAL ELECTRIC TRAMWAY & LIGHTING CO. LTD.
FEBRUARY 22, 1890
MILES
D & J REUSS

and the City Council, members of the Provincial Cabinet and Legislature, the Bench of B. C. and many of Victoria's business and professional men composed the party and when all were seated, His Honour advanced to the front platform of car no. 1 and bowing to the citizens who thronged the roadways and sidewalks, he said:

'Mr. President, ladies and gentlemen. It is with great pleasure that I have accepted the invitation to start this car and formally declare this line open. The completion of this road, in my mind, marks a new era in the progress of Victoria, and, judging by the rapid strides with which the city has advanced of late, it is safe to anticipate that the undertaking will be financially successful to the promoters. I sincerely hope that our best anticipations will be fully realized.'

President Higgins, on behalf of the Company, briefly thanked His Honour for his kindly expressed wishes and assured him that nothing would be left undone by the company to provide the public with a safe and satisfactory service and the Lieutenant-Governor then called for three cheers for the road which were given with a will. He then turned the motor level and the wheels of car No. 1 began to revolve faster and faster as it passed down Store street followed by its three companions at a speed of about ten miles per hour.

The run to Outer Wharf was made in eleven minutes. Cars were changed and seventeen minutes later the cars were at the fountain at the junction of Government and Douglas streets, the full speed being shown on the Douglas street grade. From the Fountain at Douglas and Hillside, to the Jubilee Hospital, the terminus of the Fort Street route at Richmond Road, took about 20 minutes and the excursionists then returned to the power house where they dispersed after wishing the road long-continued prosperity. During the remainder of the day the cars made regular trips being crowded with passengers, and the conductors had their hands full of business. In the evening they were brilliantly illuminated, and, filled with passengers, dashed through the streets in busy metropolitan style: the admiration of all lovers of enterprise, convenience and progress."

The first day of operation began at 9 a.m. Sunday. The fare was five cents and business exceeded expectations: the car barn would have to be enlarged, the generating equipment needed to be supplemented, more cars had to be acquired, and new lines had to be built — immediately. Five more street cars were in.

operation by the end of the year. On October 12, service began on the newly completed "interurban" line to the village of Esquimalt — the main British Columbia location of the Royal Navy — 3.2 miles east from its connection with the terminus of the already existing street car line at Store Street, by the carn barn. The Esquimalt branch had been quickly built, three months in all, and what a line it was. It crossed over Rock Bay, just before spanning a narrowing of the harbour across five-year-old Point Ellice bridge, and then toonervilled its little single rails precariously along the north side of rutted, often muddy, Esquimalt Road, a twenty-five-minute adventure over little trestles and questionable road bed, with one passing siding en route. The obligatory trip for local dignitaries and company officials had occurred on October 9; a few minor mishaps had not in any way discouraged them or the line's potential patrons. After all they had sought civilized transportation to Victoria for over thirty years!

Because it quickly became evident that the Rock Bay bridge could not cope with the weight of the street cars, it was closed on October 24 for rebuilding, reopening on November 14. For this duration, patrons of the Esquimalt car tip-toed across the bridge from the end of the Fort Street car line at the south end of the bridge to their waiting street car. During this time three new street cars, numbers 7, 8, and 9, arrived, and were painted green to indicate that they were the Esquimalt vehicles. (Numbers 5 and 6 had made their debuts in August.) Cars 1 and 3 displayed an appropriate blue and white paint job for their Outer Wharf line duties, while red paint on numbers 2 and 4 proclaimed their predilection for the hospital (Fort Street) run. Victoria was proud of its neat, three-line, nine-car system, and Esquimalt was delighted that the navy's hundreds of sailors had land mobility, and could help rerail the little single truck cars when they erred. Soon, the street car even brought the mail to Esquimalt.

Victoria's car 3 pauses momentarily on some trestlework, Esquimalt-bound. This was the very first car operated by a B.C. Electric predecessor company. (E.L. Plant collection)

Vancouver

Vancouver finally got on track on Thursday, June 26, 1890, four months after Victoria. The *Vancouver Daily News-Advertiser* (the first newspaper in Canada to be printed by electricity) has left us with an extraordinarily careful description (see appendix for an account from the same report of the company's physical plant).

"Yesterday afternoon the first trial trips were made with a car on the electric street railway. The trial was as satisfactory as could be desired and the manner in which it was carried out without a hitch, while a proof of the care which has been exercised by the company, is also a testimony to the efficiency of its staff and the manner in which it has carried out the work.

In the afternoon a car was run up and down Westminster avenue [today's Main Street] several times, a number of shareholders and scores of citizens taking advantage of the opportunity to test the comfort of a mode of locomotion now possible for the first time in Vancouver. There are probably many persons in the city who have not before seen an electric railway in operation. But whether they had or not, all those who yesterday witnessed the initial trips made by the car of the Vancouver Electric Railway and Lighting company had before them a service as complete as that offered in any city on this continent.

In the evening, having satisfied themselves of the general satisfactory state of the track and machinery the officials of the company ran a car to the end of the track on Powell street and from there to the western terminus at the Granville street bridge. The return trip from the bridge to the power house on Barnard street [Union Street], a distance of 2.12 miles, was made in 27 minutes, including several stoppages. A run was then made to the end of the track on Mount Pleasant and the car returned to the car-house.

Today the cars will commence to run regularly. It is probable that the arrangements for operating the ordinary traffic will allow of the trips being commenced until towards noon, but before tomorrow it is expected that everything will be in order and service will be as complete as the most exacting can demand.

The track of the railway has been very carefully laid down on three-inch stringers supported by ties. The rails used are what are called 25-pound "T" rails, and the total length of the road is about three and one-half miles. A wire is run over the centre of the track at a height of about twelve feet from the ground by which the current is passed along the road. This is communicated to the car by a trolley at the end of the arm, which, by means of a spring, is kept up against the wire. The return current passes through the rails to a wire which is connected with them at short intervals, and runs along the track underneath the planks.

The company has at present four motor cars — all of which were tested yesterday, and found to work satisfactorily — and two trail cars, to be attached to the motor cars in case of very heavy traffic. They are all built by the John Stevenson [Stephenson] Car company of New York, who have the highest reputation in that line. The motor cars are fitted with Stevenson [sic] trucks, on each of which are two 10-horse power motors, made by the Thomson-Houston Electric company. These are operated by levers at either end of the cars.

The Vancouver Electric Railway and Light Company, Limited, formed by the consolidation of the Vancouver Street Railway[s] and the Vancouver Electric Illuminating company, has a capital stock of $500,000. The following are the officers of the company: President, H. E. McKee; vice-president, Thos. Dunn; secretary-treasurer, H. T. Ceperley; board of directors, Geo. Turner, J. W. Horne, C. D. Rand.

F. V. Nicholls will be superintendent for the company, and there will be about twenty employees when the works are in full operation.

Alderman J. F. Garden was the engineer who had charge of the laying of the track, and the manner in which the car swung around the sharp curves last evening showed that both the road and its designer are 'all right'."

In the editorial column of the same issue the editor observed the following: "The spectacle of a car moving rapidly along the track of the street railway yesterday excited no little enthusiasm. The smoothness with which it moved, and the entire freedom from any accidents and difficulties which marked the trial trip of the car, were a source of much satisfaction. Now that the company has completed its work; built a road which traverses the most important street in the city, and equipped it with as excellent a system and as fine an outfit as can be found anywhere on the coast, the people generally are more than reconciled to the long period which has elapsed since the city council granted permission to the company to lay its lines on the streets. Anyone who witnessed the trial yesterday, and saw the ease with which the speed of six miles an hour (the maximum allowed by the charter) was obtained, the promptitude with which the car was stopped, and the smoothness with which it traversed the sharp curves and steep grades, must have realized that the action of the company, in deciding to substitute electricity for horses as the motive power was an ample justification, by the satisfactory results obtained, for the delay which the new arrangements necessarily caused. With the excellence of its plant, the liberal terms which it has been granted by the city, and the favorable prospects of the growth in the population and business of Vancouver, there is but little doubt that the company will obtain that measure of prosperity to which its enterprise entitles it." Vancouver had Canada's fourth street car line!

Elsewhere in the *News-Advertiser* of that day was also this item: "Teamsters and all people having horses should, now that the street cars have commenced running, take great care not to

Vancouver's street car lines begin to take shape, here on Main Street — looking north across Burrard Inlet — at Powell Street in the early summer of 1889. (Vancouver City Archives)

leave horses standing on the street without being securely tied. With a little care many accidents will be prevented."

The same newspaper's Saturday edition happily advised that: "The street cars were running all day yesterday, but did not carry passengers until after six o'clock, and from that time two cars were running until ten o'clock, and were all the time as full as it was possible for them to be. No accident occurred, not even a runaway, the horses surprising people by the way they took to them!"

And on Sunday, the 29th, the *News-Advertiser* reported that: "The street cars already run much smoother. Very few sparks are seen coming from the wheels now. The conductors have not yet managed to keep a scheduled time, and in consequence last evening two cars met on Cambie street [between Cordova and Hastings], and one car had to back up to the switch."

Despite this innocuous incident, Vancouver, like Victoria, possessed a tidy little street car system, rather well befitting the upwardly-mobile, poised-for-great-growth character of its 11,000 residents.

However, the fact that the laying of the street car tracks had actually been completed more than ten months before the beginning of street car operation indicates pointedly that there is more of a story than the one reported in the *News-Advertiser*. But then Vancouverites hardly needed a reminder of their own unique experiences of the previous two years — and hadn't Victorians competitively feared losing the street car race to

Vancouver?

In fact, Vancouver's was to have been a horse car operation. First steps toward building a street railway had taken place early in 1888. On November 26, 1888 (the *Victoria Standard* had been on its toes), Vancouver city council passed a by-law which authorized George Turner, chairman of a syndicate, to build a street railway, and H. P. McCraney, a contractor, to construct a street car system, and to operate it by cable, electricity, gas, or horse. The next step was incorporation: the Vancouver Street Railways Company was incorporated by an Act of Legislature on April 6, 1889, with an initial authorized capital of $250,000; three weeks later, McCraney, an experienced railway construction man who had handled some of the big jobs on the C. P. R. right of way through the mountains, was awarded the contract for building the lines required by the by-law. The roadbed was to be completed and rails ready for operation by August 15, and so they were, at a cost of $27,716.03 for the 3.35 miles of single track. (Vancouver boasted eighteen miles of streets.)

Track laying began on Granville Street, just north of Pacific Street, at the point where the slope from False Creek levels off, and proceeded north, with the first passing siding between Robson and Georgia, the second on Powell Street, the third on Main Street, and the fourth on the Powell Street extension between Princess and Heatley streets.

But the matter of propulsion needed to be settled. It seemed clear that it had to be horse because of the perceived states of development and flux in the only other method considered, electric. Horses were purchased, and an attractive, steepled stable was constructed at the southwest corner of First Avenue and Main Street. (Since the waters of False Creek virtually lapped the edges of First Avenue, then Front Street, the floor of this imposing, 75-foot-long building was elevated some three or four feet above soggy ground.)

Meanwhile, pressures from three sources were being applied to the company's directors: electrical equipment manufacturers, public opinion, and city council. All favoured electric operation, and when city council agreed to an extension of time for the beginning of service, the directors decided for electrification. The decision was confirmed by the company on August 9, 1889, just six days before the completion of all the track work!

The change-over meant a delay — one of over ten months. The horses were sold at cost, many of them to the Guerney Cab Company, which appropriately took over the stable (still later occupied by Garvin Ice & Fuel), a Vancouver landmark until the late 1930s.

Then on May 14, 1890 the *Weekly News-Advertiser* excited almost everyone with the news that: "The citizens of Vancouver may expect to see the electric street cars running in a very short space of time now. All the cars have arrived, the last two reaching here Monday. There are six in all; two tow cars, known as the 'Mexico' type, mounted upon super-springs and running gear, and the class known as 'New York', with steel brake and plow guards." The numbering of these cars, which cost about $2,000 each, began with 10, rather than with 1, as in Victoria. Although there was a seat running the length of each side, the front and rear platforms were open, and passengers — smokers particularly — were allowed to ride on them. Cars 11 and 13 were the

"Mexico" ones; cars 10, 12, 14, and 16 were equipped with two motors, and required a motorman and a conductor.

Now there was just one more step, an eminently practical and reasonable one: on May 21, 1890, the Vancouver Electric Railway & Light Company Limited was formed — out of the Vancouver Street Railways Company — to consolidate that company with Vancouver's lighting company, the Vancouver Electric Illuminating Company Limited.

When regular service began late on June 27 with car number 14 (the same one that had made the first trial run on the previous day) it was with motorman Aubrey Elliot and conductor Dugald Carmichael. Carmichael kept the first fare, a five-cent piece (which he replaced with a coin of his own). Gloriously — it was a Friday — all children were gifted with a holiday from school.

Regular service was inaugurated, with all six cars in use during rush hour, and normal service operated by four. Two lines were instituted, neatly overlapping to double the headway through the business district. The Powell Street line terminated at Campbell Avenue and Powell Street at the Barnard Castle Hotel, operating west on Powell (crossing the C.P.R.'s branch to English Bay) to Granville and Pender streets, via Carrall, Cordova, Cambie, Hastings, and Granville streets. The Westminster Avenue line, which set out from just north of Second Avenue (then Dufferin Street) and Main, proceeded north on Main to Powell Street, en route passing the stable on the west, crossing False Creek on a new 742-foot-long bridge flush against the west side of the older road bridge, and passing the car barn at Union Street. (Located west of Main on the north side, its four tracks accommodated eight cars. Adjoining it to the west was the power house.) From Powell Street the line duplicated the "Powell Street" route westward — Powell, Carrall, Cordova, Cambie, Hastings, to Granville — but continued almost an additional mile farther south to the point at which rails had first been laid, on Granville, just north of Pacific Street.

On July 3, merely a matter of days after the beginning of street car service, the V. E. Ry. & L. Co., Ltd. unveiled its first arc lights in Vancouver; thus some seven weeks after this company's formation, Vancouver possessed state-of-the-art street car and street lighting systems. And yet the future was not really that bright, despite an infusion of $80,000 from J. W. Horne, a member of the Provincial Legislature. The company could pay off its most pressing debts, but the street car system was not making money: the city was very compact — people could still easily walk to most of their destinations — and surely a six-mile-an-hour speed limit was no help.

Nonetheless, the Vancouver Electric Railway & Light Company Limited enlarged the steam power

Dominion Day, 1890, just days after the opening of Vancouver's street car operation. The parade is coming along Cordova Street toward Carrall Street. (Vancouver Public Library)

Vancouver's car 14 scurries north across Main Street trestle on July 1, 1890. To the right is the imposing stable, built to shelter the horses which never pulled Vancouver's street cars, and passing it, Main Street (still Westminster Avenue then) climbs the hill to an already well-settled Mount Pleasant. Thornton Park and the VIA depot occupy the area in the foreground, long since rid of the waters of False Creek. (B.C. Transit)

plant, ordered a new motor generator to boost the power supply, purchased four more street cars, and let contracts for the construction of new lines required by the terms of the by-law. Thus, on October 11, work was begun extending the street car line on Main Street to the little community of Mount Pleasant, at Broadway (Ninth Avenue), almost half a mile south, rising steeply from the current terminus at Second Avenue.

New Westminster

Just over two months later, on December 17, 1890, grading for the Westminster Street Railway Company and for the Westminster and Vancouver Tramway Company commenced. Donald McGillivray, builder of most of the C.P.R.'s snowsheds in the Rockies, and also the C.P.R. bridge across the Fraser River at Mission, had been awarded the contract for construction of the line, from New Westminster, right into Vancouver, over fourteen miles. All at once, New Westminster was to have a street car operation and was to be connected to Vancouver by what would easily be the longest electric interurban railway line in Canada.

Travelling by road between the two cities was a trauma to be avoided. However, the C.P.R. did operate a twice-a-day, daily except Sunday service between New Westminster and Vancouver, via Coquitlam, a run of 24.9 miles taking about an hour and a quarter; the single fare was a steep $1.00. Each of the trains usually consisted of three cars, and some days as many as 300 round-trip passengers were carried. But a railway running directly between New Westminster and Vancouver would supply the hypotenuse for this railway triangle. It would cut the distance — and time and fare — virtually in half, excellent reason indeed for Vancouver's mayor, David Oppenheimer, to become involved in New Westminster city street

Car 11, not yet motorized, is being towed by car 18 in today's downtown Vancouver. (B.C. Hydro)

car and New Westminster to Vancouver interurban line projects. The other principals were Henry V. Edmonds, probably the wealthiest man on the British Columbia mainland; John A. Webster, an affluent retired merchant who actively promoted the interurban idea; and Benjamin Douglas, a New Westminster citizen and a director of the New Westminster Southern Railway (controlled by Great Northern Railway interests), then building from the Washington border at Blaine to the Fraser River across from New Westminster.

Two railway charters, whose bills were passed on April 26, 1890, were obtained from the Provincial Legislature. The capital of the Westminster Street Railway Company, concerned with New Westminster itself and districts adjacent

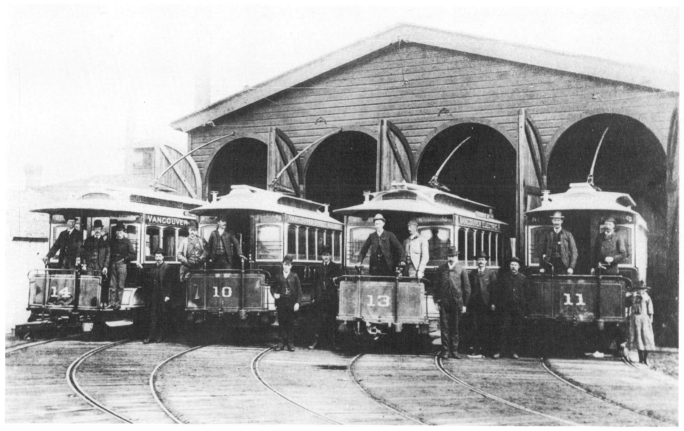

It's 1890, and two "Westminster Ave." cars, 13 and 14, sandwich car 10, its lettering not yet modified to Vancouver Electric Railway. This was Vancouver's first car barn, on the north side of Barnard (Union) Street, a half-block west of Westminster (Main) Street. (Bordertown Publishing)

up to five miles beyond the municipal limits, was fixed at $250,000, with authority to the directors to borrow by issue of bonds or debentures an amount not exceeding 50 percent of the subscribed capital stock. This company was authorized to construct street railway and lighting systems. (No authority of this kind was asked by or granted to the interurban railway.) The company, which was given the right to lease to or amalgamate with any other company operating in New Westminster or the adjoining district, had already obtained on March 13 a by-law from the city council of New Westminster giving it full power to construct, maintain, equip, and operate lines of electric railway within the city. Six miles per hour — though horse cars were never even considered for New Westminster — was again settled upon as the maximum speed. The proposed interurban line to Vancouver, the Westminster and Vancouver Tramway Company, was capitalized at $500,000 and authorized to increase this amount to such figure as a majority in value of the stockholders might from time to time approve.

Samuel F. MacIntosh, close friend of Douglas and a real estate dealer in New Westminster, was secretary of both companies; since the promoters of both were identical, it is reasonable to expect that the two companies might amalgamate, which they did, under the title of the interurban company, Westminster and Vancouver Tramway

Company, on April 20, 1891.

C. L. McCammon, who had laid out the line of the New Westminster Southern Railway, was appointed chief engineer on June 8, 1890. The logical decision was made that the initial line in New Westminster, as well as providing a convenient street car service for that city, should serve as the entrance into the city for the interurban. And so work began on what in a very few years would be the B. C. Electric Railway's flagship run, the Central Park line, an operation which people from across Canada and the United States would come to watch, photograph, and ride.

The first depot was fixed in the Douglas & Elliot Building, at the southwest corner of Columbia and 6th streets, where a two-car siding would be located on the line's south side. There was very little uncertainty regarding the direction the line had to take, no matter that a grade of 11% would be encountered: New Westminster's most thickly populated residential area had to be served, as did Queen's Park, home of the annual exhibition and venue for lacrosse, cricket, football, and baseball matches. Fortunately, people and park were closely twined.

The line, meticulously planned, proceeded eastward on Columbia Street, up the daunting grade of Leopold Place, doubling back westward on Royal Avenue to a picturesque horseshoe loop which carried the line — always up — onto aptly-

named Park Row and First Street, the principal entrance to Queen's Park. From there, most of the climbing done, the tracks ran west again, on Third Avenue, north through the Clarkson Orchard (later Pine Street), west on Fourth Avenue to Sixth Street (Mary Street then), and north along Sixth. The greatest concern then was which of four proposed routes to follow from New Westminster's city limits to Vancouver.

The directors were after land grants, and a line as dead-straight as possible to minimize the principal costs of rails and wire; the route finally chosen (approximately the proposed one called "line no. 3") was horrendous from both construction and operating points of view. Heavy grades and trestles bridging deep ravines and hollows for the nearly three miles from Central Park to Cedar Cottage — the point at which the line would become part of Vancouver's street grid — all contributed to a roller coaster profile, a costly upkeep nightmare.

The four proposed routes had been planned to provide for as much financial support as possible. (Edmonds and Webster themselves owned somewhere between one and two thousand acres between the two cities, land they had acquired years before Vancouver was even thought of as the C. P. R.'s terminal.) Landowners along these proposed routes had been encouraged to donate whatever they could of their land holdings, obviously to lure the line's final configuration in their direction; and when all the results were

tallied, a route through Central Park (a New York association, chosen by Oppenheimer) had been indicated. British Columbia's government had offered to donate a matching grant of land of up to 10 percent, and it is a tribute to Oppenheimer's persuasiveness that it did donate the full 10, despite the fact that the owners along the route donated an average of only 7.475 percent. (This donated government land, called Collingwood, 196 acres in all, extended from Earles Road to Park Avenue stations, north of the interurban route.)

The Tramway's route from New Westminster to Cedar Cottage, Commercial Drive (Park Drive then) and Eighteenth Avenue, three and a half miles short of its Vancouver destination, was now decided, if very far from settled, in another sense: from New Westminster it continued its generally northward course on Sixth Street, turning west onto Edmonds Street, which was surveyed but would not be open to use (or named) for years to come. Henry V. Edmonds owned all the land on either side of the street between Douglas Road, today's Canada Way, and Vancouver Road, today's Kingsway. From this intersection the Tramway's line bored through the tall trees and Central Park on its direct, difficult, 100-foot-wide right of way for another six-plus miles to Cedar Cottage.

On August 17, 1891, Vancouver's city council passed a by-law giving the W. & V. Tramway Company authority to construct into Vancouver from Cedar Cottage. The route would follow Commercial Drive, Venables Street (straddling an

Before the official opening of what would become known as the Central Park line, W. & V. Tramway car 2 (later 7) and one of the interurban coaches are about to cross what is today Kingsway, at Central Park, on their way to New Westminster. Notice the distinctive trolley wire hangers. (Vancouver Public Library)

arm of False Creek on a trestle between Raymur and Campbell avenues), Campbell Avenue, and along Hastings Street west to Carrall Street, crossing one of Vancouver's street car lines two blocks earlier at Main Street. Since the Tramway had no interest in offering a city service along these Vancouver city streets, and because it desired no conflict whatsoever with Vancouver's street car company, it proposed to the Vancouver Electric Railway and Light Company Limited that it build the line from Cedar Cottage to Carrall Street, which the V. E. R. & L. Co. Ltd. quickly agreed to do. The street car company could operate a city service over this section, but the Tramway's interurban cars would have precedence in running rights.

From New Westminster, a run had already been made by one of the newly-received cars as early as June 1, and two days later, twice-a-day service commenced from New Westminster to the end of track, still short of Cedar Cottage. The first trip from New Westminster to Cedar Cottage was accomplished on September 2 by Tramway street car number 8.

New Westminster's newspaper, the *British Columbian,* mirrored the city's disappointment with the Tramway on the final day of New Westminster's annual exhibition, September 25, 1891: "The Royal City [named, as it was, by Queen Victoria] has done itself proud in the great Fair and Carnival which comes to a close tonight. There were a few disappointments, of course, such as the failure of the Street Railway and the Westminster-Vancouver Electric Railway services to get into full operation."

On Thursday, October 1, the *Vancouver Daily News-Advertiser* was able to report that the line "is now completed to the City boundary [16th Avenue], and today one car will be making regular trips as far as the track is in condition. The construction of the line and its equipment has been delayed through the non-arrival of the trolley wire, but by Saturday week the cars will be running as far as the corner of Carrall and Hastings."

The same issue of the *News-Advertiser* also carried an advertisement by Rand Bros., Real Estate Agents (C.D. Rand was an officer of the Vancouver Electric Railway and Light Company), announcing acre blocks for sale, some of them fronting on the Tramway's route; that there would be the unbelievable number of seventeen trains each way daily between New Westminster and Vancouver was displayed as rather more than a footnote.

The *British Columbian* noted in its Saturday, October 3, edition that the "tram cars are now making daily trips to Vancouver, leaving this city at 8:30 a.m. and 4:30 p.m., and returning, leave Vancouver at 10 a.m., and 6 p.m. The single fare is 50 cents, and the round trip 75 cents." And the

same day's *News-Advertiser* signalled the start of a further intensified competitive spirit between the two cities: "The public will be able to come over here tomorrow on the tram cars to witness the lacrosse match as they are now making two trips each way daily. The fares are 50¢ and 75¢ for the round trip."

On Tuesday, October 6, the *News-Advertiser* had hopeful news: "Superintendent Noble of the New [sic] Westminster and Vancouver Tramway told a representative of the *News-Advertiser* last evening that he expects two cars down to Carrall street by Wednesday evening. The workmen are now stretching the trolley wire within the City limits."

Wednesday's issue of the *News-Advertiser* made first mention of the city service in New Westminster which operated the two miles from the terminus at Columbia and Sixth, up its taxing line past Queen's Park to a point on Sixth Street between Fifth and Sixth avenues, the top of the hill, in fact: "The street cars in the City portion of the Tramway Company's road are being very liberally patronised, and a service is being rendered to the entire satisfaction of the public. The conductors and motineers are courteous and obliging, and the officials seem to study the comfort and convenience of their patrons." The service was hourly on week days, two-hourly on Sundays.

Regarding the interurban line, the same day's *News-Advertiser* brought it almost to completion: "Regular passengers were carried yesterday by the Westminster and Vancouver Tramway line from New Westminster to the end of False Creek. From there the passengers walked to the Barnard Castle Hotel, and took the Vancouver street cars to the centre of the City. There were upwards of 20 persons on the car including a number of officials of the company, who came to Vancouver to attend a meeting of shareholders. The cars will be brought to the corner of Carrall and Hastings streets today and a regular service between the two cities established. The trip is expected to take less than 50 minutes, and a two-hour service will be given and in a short time a car each way every hour will be run."

Sunday's issue noted that there "were 56 passengers on the car of the Westminster and Vancouver Tramway line arriving last evening at 6 o'clock," and the issue of Friday, October 16, registered the fact that community awareness of the Tramway was in a reasonably advanced state: "A special car arrived at the depot at 4:25 last evening with a party of vocalists from Vancouver to take part in the choral services at Holy Trinity Church. The regular through tram cars are packed on every trip both ways to and from Vancouver."

Canada's longest interurban line — almost fourteen and a quarter miles in length — was an accomplished fact. From an elevation of 12 feet above sea level at the New Westminster end, and 17 feet at Vancouver's Carrall Street, the line climbed to a height of 434 feet at the Dow Road crossing, the route's midpoint. Forty-pound T-rail stamped "Blaenavon Steel, 1890" (from South Wales) was used for the single track line and its six switches or sidings. The line plunged through several miles of virgin forests, following natural grades, but at four of the most difficult locations utilizing trestles, the largest of which was 86 feet high and 120 feet long. In addition to the steep grade on Leopold Place, there were grades of 5, 6, 7, and 9 percent.

The development of electric street railway and interurban systems was so new that electrical engineers deemed it necessary to provide a complete circuit for the electrical current. What this meant for all three British Columbia trolley systems was the laying between the rails of a copper return wire, fastened with cross wires to the rails on both sides. For the Westminster and Vancouver Tramway, this first, early way of operating with electricity meant more than 17,000

pounds of trolley, feeder, and return wire. Within four years, it was discovered that the awkward return wire method could be abolished simply by soldering a short length of copper wire from one rail to the next.

The Tramway's power house, faced with corrugated iron painted red, was a rather impressive structure, built at a cost of $20,000, situated on the south side of the line — almost five miles from New Westminster and over nine miles from Vancouver — where today's Beresford Street lies, halfway between Mission and Griffiths avenues. It contained a boiler room (at first cordwood, later coal, was used to raise steam), engine room, four-stall car barn, machine shop, store room, and superintendent's office. The boiler room contained three tubular boilers of 100 horsepower each, while the engine room held two 150 h.p. high speed Leonard Ball engines belted to two 100-kilowatt, 500-volt Edison generators. (During a six-day water drought in Vancouver within a year of the Tramway's inauguration, this power house was able to supply

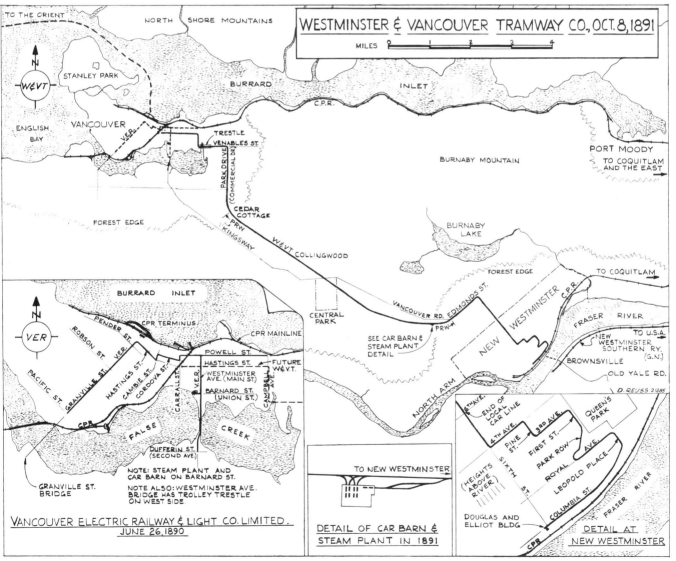

Vancouver's relatively distant street railway with power.)

Nearby the power house, a large boarding house — with accommodation for about thirty — was built for engineers, trainmen, car repairers, and section men who were obliged to live close to the plant. This neat, little "village" was completed by the construction of several cottages for the married men and their families.

Car number 12 had been the first of the Tramway's four interurbans in regular scheduled through service to the end of track in Vancouver, the middle of Hastings Street on the east side of Carrall Street. As in the Vancouver system, the Tramway's interurban cars were numbered beginning with 10 (10, 12, 13, 14), and they were impressive vehicles, highly visible in their yellow Tramway Company livery. Each of these first four 35-foot, vestibuled Brill products were equipped with two "maximum traction" trucks; exceptionally wide and roomy for their time, they had two upholstered longitudinal seats and were quite capable of carrying a splendid load of passengers, thirty of them seated. In addition, three sixteen-foot, single truck street cars had been acquired — as was the case with Victoria'a first four cars — from Patterson & Corbin. These "St. Catharines" cars, for a brief time numbered 1, 2, and 3, but soon 6, 7, and 8, were used in New Westminster city service, number 6 being the first car to operate that schedule. An eighth motorized vehicle was a 23-foot, double truck freight car. Each of the cars featured a remarkable refinement, a telephone whereby it was possible to contact the power house and the terminus offices from any point along the Tramway's line.

The freight car, number 3, had the appearance of a small, open-at-the-sides box car, with one trolley pole which could be swung to either end of the car. Ideal for quick on-and-off loading, it became known almost immediately as the "flying Dutchman" because of the heavy canvas curtains on either side of the car which flapped ominously as the car sped along if they hadn't been fastened at the bottom, or rolled up, wondow-blind fashion.

Between New Westminster and Vancouver, stops were made only at the power house, at Central Park (soon the site of a substantial station), and on Venables Street at Glen Drive. This stop, known as Largen's Corner because of Largen's blacksmith shop, was the site of a switch (or one ended siding). However, passengers other than local ones used the Tramway since it had made an agreement with the Great Northern Railway to transport its passengers and baggage between New Westminster and Vancouver. The G. N., as the New Westminster Southern, had arrived at Brownsville, a ferry ride across the Fraser River from New Westminster, on February 14, 1891.

Vancouver

On October 22, less than two weeks after the inauguration of New Westminster-Vancouver service by the Tramway, Vancouver's street car company operated its first street car on the Fairview line, thereby almost doubling its track miles at one stroke. (The land sloping from the south to False Creek had been named "Fairview" by a C.P.R. land surveyor.) This new, single-tracked line — Don McGillivary contractor — extended south from the company's original terminus on the north side of False Creek on Granville Street, crossing False Creek, ascending Granville Street (Centre Street then) to Broadway (Ninth Avenue), and then struggling its way on Broadway eastward to Main Street across seven streams on seven wooden bridges, some of them up to 150 feet in length. Costing $150,000, the Fairview line, with so few residences along its length, had swallowed up five times its original estimated cost. The new line connected at Main with the recently-completed Mount Pleasant extension from Second Avenue.

For the street car service, modifications were made to the bridge over False Creek at Granville Street (the bridge had been built at a cost of $16,000, opening on January 4, 1889). A railway trestle was attached to it in somewhat the same fashion that the street cars' crossing of False Creek at Main Street had been solved, with one difference. Since the trestle could not parallel the bridge's swing span, the track angled sharply both onto the swing span, and off it again. These two kinks were so tight that only single truck cars were able to make the journey, an annoyance not eliminated until a replacement Granville Street bridge was built in 1909.

Real estate speculation was the sole reason for the Fairview line's construction. The C.P.R. promised the street railway company 68 lots in exchange for street car service, and the C.P.R. began to create a major residential subdivision. As it auctioned off lots, land values doubled and even tripled.

The November 2, 1891 issue of the *News-Advertiser* reported that street car passengers would be taken "up Mount Pleasant hill without extra charge," and that a ten-minute service would be given on the new city-encircling Fairview line, formally opened on November 3. It was not initially operated as a belt line, as it would be so successfully in just a few years. Main and Broadway was the terminus, and street cars returned, in both directions, after reaching this point. To facilitate successful operation, a passing siding was installed on the west side of Cambie Street between Hastings and Cordova.

Electric railway history was made in the construction of the Fairview line. Horses and tackle normally hauled trolley wire into place, but 34-year-old lineman Angus MacDonald contended that the wire should be installed by electrical power, fully charged! An idea which seemed near to the height of folly proved to be successful and, in the field of street car and interurban technology, revolutionary: a street car was coupled to a tower car and a flat car, on which was fixed a large spool of trolley wire. Since the tower car had obviously the correct height for the lineman to attach the trolley wire to the positioned guy wires, the trolley wire was simply fed up over the insulated platform of the tower car and attached to the spanning guy wires as the street car pushed the two cars along under the fully charged trolley wire. (In 1893-94 MacDonald used this successful method again when the New Westminster-Vancouver interurban line's "kite-string" trolley wire was replaced, entirely without schedule disruption.)

For a time, special monthly tickets were sold for the Mount Pleasant extension, but service was shut down relatively early in the evenings all across the Vancouver system, except when there was a special show at the theatre. Special late cars were then provided. For use on Mount Pleasant, and Powell Street, the two "dinky" trailer cars, 11 and 13, were each fitted up with one motor (later two), and one operator. What a sight it must have been to see one of them grinding and sparking its way up Main Street's daunting grade!

However, a world-wide financial depression was gathering storm in 1891, and there was trouble ahead — so soon — for all three systems, and for the Vancouver Electric Street Railway & Lighting Company Limited at the very point of its greatest effort, the over-extension of itself with the Fairview line. During the summer the company had purchased four new street cars, ordered a 200 h. p. steam engine to provide needed additional power, and enlarged the power house on Union Street for this new machinery. By November, the company was at an almost impossible financial impasse, with not enough revenue from either the street cars or lighting to meet its bond interest payments, already seriously in arrears. A public stock-selling campaign was tried and was a complete failure; both directors and public were fearful.

On December 20 the company's directors asked an unenthusiastic Vancouver city council to purchase their shares, valued at $162,000, assume the bonded liability of $300,000, and take over the entire assets of the company, whose actual capital expenditure to date had been $477,822.50. The company assured the city that a potential lessee was waiting in the wings, ready to lease the street car lines for ten years. City council readied a by-law for Vancouver's voters.

Victoria

Over on Vancouver Island during 1891, Victoria's National Electric Tramway and Lighting

Victoria's car 5, vestibules already partly enclosed, rises above the muck of Store Street near the power house and barn. (B.C. Hydro)

Company Limited had acquired six more street cars, two of them double-trucked. And as early as January 17, new generating facilities — the power house now had room for 4,000 horsepower, if necessary — were opened, with the hope that they could generate enough energy to operate twenty street cars on a ten-minute headway.

Sure enough, within two months the Esquimalt line increased service to half-hourly during most of the day; and a new line was constructed from Oak Bay junction, the corner of Fort Street and Oak Bay Avenue (less than half a mile west of the Fort Street line's eastern terminus, Jubilee Hospital), due east to Oak Bay beach. (At Oak Bay junction part of a rocky outcropping had had to be blasted away for the new route.) This 1.3-mile line was inaugurated on July 1 as a shuttle service (a pattern which sufficed for this little line for some years) with half-hourly service on weekdays, hourly on Sunday. This was the National's first thrust into the municipality of Oak Bay, and the second was not long in coming, speeded by the Victoria area's great exhibition park to come, the Willows (then in its initial stage known as the Driving Park), which lay somewhat over half a mile east of the hospital. On September 26, almost precisely a month after surveying had begun, the Driving Park extension was opened, from the hospital at Richmond Road east along Fort Street to the park.

In Victoria itself a completely new line, the Pandora Avenue extension, was opened for service on December 23; it, like the two Oak Bay extensions, manifested an eastward push, leaving Douglas Street two blocks north of Yates at Pandora, proceeding east to Cook Street, then along Cook, Caledonia Avenue, a brief jog on Chambers Street, and Gladstone Street (then Chatham) to Fernwood Road, Spring Ridge, 1.13 miles in all.

For the National Electric Tramway, 1891 had

Government Street in Victoria, looking north from Fort Street (notice the track dividing) in 1892. One of National Electric Tramway's two double trucked street cars, 12 or 13, makes its way south past hitching posts to the left and horse-drawn cabs half a block in the distance. (B.C. Hydro)

Car 6, "Beacon Hill Park" emblazoned on its body, rounds onto Douglas Street from Yates Street, not really in pursuit of car 13. Victoria's city hall is to the left. (E.L. Plant photo)

been an eventful and successful year; a one day crew members' strike had flared briefly, but the most exciting moment surely had come during the spring when Mrs. Olive Dunsmuir, widow of Robert Dunsmuir — the king of British Columbia's coal mines — had lent the company $100,000. It was a year which could show for the National Electric Tramway a net profit of well over $18,000! In another way also Victoria was still the champ: the 1891 official Dominion of Canada census figures showed Victoria's population to be 16,841, Vancouver's 13,709, and New Westminster's 6,678.

The construction of new lines in Victoria continued at a fairly heady pace into 1892, the first one being a northward extension of Douglas Street from Hillside to Tolmie Avenue, a little

short of three-quarters of a mile. Shuttle service commenced on March 12, but on May 14, the quality of service was significantly improved as the extension became part of the Douglas-Outer Wharf line's operation.

On June 30, the new line to Beacon Hill Park offered its first day of street car service. Here was a line, unlike the others, not quickly announced, laid, and put into service; its construction had long been mooted. Its proposed route along Simcoe Street made very few of that street's residents happy, city council seemed to be dragging its feet, a loop around the park's bandstand was out of the question, and Tramway President David W. Higgins was rather more than annoyed. But the line got built, and immediately became the southern protrusion of a Pandora-Beacon Hill line. This new route forsook the Outer Wharf's run at Superior and Menzies streets, heading south on Menzies, then east on Niagara Street to Douglas Street (Beacon Hill Park), just under three-quarters of a mile from Superior Street. It would be eleven years before another street car line would be built in Victoria.

Starting earlier in June and continuing until about July 19, a shuttle service had again been forced — twice — onto the Esquimalt line, this time not because of any difficulty with the Rock Bay bridge, but because the Point Ellice bridge had sunk several feet due to the wood-rotting action of salt water-thriving teredo worms. One street car only, number 16, was acquired in 1892; ironically, this very car and the Point Ellice bridge would collaborate terribly in just four years' time.

In midsummer 1892, Victoria's optimism seemed at its peak, when the cry of "fire" went up in the early hours of August 7, a Sunday. Within a couple of hours, the company's power house and repair room lay in ruins, destroyed by a virulent blaze which had begun in the repair room, the first small carbarn. Luckily the street cars in the adjoining carbarn survived unscathed. Work on a new $16,300 power house was begun immediately and street car service was able to resume on September 24 with the aid of two Edison generators borrowed from the mainland's Westminster and Vancouver Tramway through the auspices of its president, David Oppenheimer. With a new Edison generator installed, full street car service was restored on December 6. (For three days in September, the company had allowed the Jockey Club to use the company's trailer cars, numbers 10 and 11, as horse-drawn cars bringing its patrons to the races from Fort and Government streets.)

Vancouver

For the Vancouver Electric Railway, 1892 began as 1891 had ended — troubled. Widespread opposition to the very idea of purchasing the company convinced city council to do nothing, certainly not submit a by-law to the voters. When in July the company held a general meeting, the shareholders unanimously passed a resolution authorizing the sale of $138,000 unissued capital stock and to raise by sale of new bonds the sum of $500,000, a sum certainly to be used in part to fulfil its street railway line construction commitments with the city. The company was able neither to sell a single share nor to find anyone to float the desired bond issue. Before the end of the year, the company's combined street railway and light deficit was approaching $1,300 per month.

New Westminster

For the Westminster and Vancouver Tramway, 1892 was a year of at least three-fold increase: three more gorgeous Brill interurban cars, numbered 15, 16, and 17, were acquired at a cost of $6,500 each; at the power house four 125 h. p. John Doty tubular boilers, and two 250 h. p. "Ideal" high speed engines belted to two 200-kilowatt, 500-volt Edison generators were installed; and a complete machine and repair shop and an armature room were erected and equipped.

And there were great doings on Tramway property on October 8. The municipality of Burnaby, embracing all land between New Westminster and Boundary Road (the west side of Central Park), and between Burrard Inlet and the Fraser River, came into existence with the election by acclamation of a reeve and councillors at a meeting in the power house, which of course lay within the new municipality. (Half a year earlier,

on April 13, all the land south of Vancouver to the Fraser River, and to the east to Boundary Road, had been incorporated as the municipality of South Vancouver.)

In New Westminster, the market, a lower mainland tradition, was founded. For years unorganized marketlike buying and selling had flourished along the river at Lytton Square, which soon had become known as Market Square, the foot of Church Street, between Front and Columbia Streets. In 1892 the haphazard trading was organized by the city into a market, opened November 4, situated in a big shed just west of Market Square. Now it was able more efficiently and conveniently to serve the scores of fishermen, Indians, loggers, miners, and settlers who coursed into New Westminster on and along the Fraser River.

The July 19, 1892 issue of the Canadian Pacific Railway's annotated timetable described New Westminster as "one of the foremost towns in the province. At New Westminster are the Provincial Penitentiary and Insane Asylum. The town has many handsome buildings, and is the headquarters of the salmon canning industry, which is represented by a dozen or more extensive establishments. It has also large saw-mills, the

Car 15, its maximum traction trucks splendidly displayed, rests on a flat car, almost ready for the long journey to New Westminster from Philadelphia, its place of building. (Bob Webster collection)

In an extremely rare photo, Westminster & Vancouver Tramway cars 12, 14, and the "flying Dutchman" (far left) meet at Central Park station in 1892. Number 14's entraining passengers seem oblivious to the photographers; not so car 12's crew and kids, headed for New Westminster. (Burnaby Village Museum)

Car 13 will be leaving in a moment for New Westminster from its Vancouver terminus, the middle of Hastings Street at the east side of Carrall Street. It's late afternoon in October 1892, a time of going home for well-dressed businessmen. (B.C. Hydro)

product of which is shipped largely to China and Australia. Steamers ply regularly to Victoria."

Having said that, it indicated in a further reference to steamship service that New Westminster had lost a round to Vancouver: "From Vancouver steamers ply daily to Victoria (excepting Monday), on which day Victoria is reached via New Westminster."

Victoria

For the National Electric Tramway, 1893 was a year of searching for more money, both for current commitments and future planning. It seemed that the city of Victoria might purchase the company, going as far as having a firm of auditors place a value on it, $576,686.75. A veritable deluge of snow — six feet on some of the street car lines — in early February offered a brief distraction from the more pressing issue of funding. Late in the year Messrs. Sperling and Company, from London, England, offered £100,000 at terms which moved the company's directors to confirm the acceptance of the offer on November 2.

During the summer Victorians had rejoiced. Just when the population and influence contest — it had really been no contest after the C.P.R.'s arrival in Vancouver — with Vancouver had forever been lost, a magnificent new Parliament Building for the province of British Columbia was having its foundation anchored on the same attractive tract of land, bounded on two sides by a

street car line, which presently held the original legislative buildings. The two mainland cities, especially New Westminster with its strong prior claim to capital status, as well as the mainland generally, were deeply perturbed and thoroughly chagrined about the further entrenchment of Victoria as political capital of B.C.

On December 4 at a directors' meeting of the National Electric Tramway and Lighting Company Limited, a cable from R. M. Horne-Payne of the Sperling company was read, which advised changing the name of the company to the Victoria Electric Railway and Lighting Company Limited. Apparently, "tramway" had connotations of horse car to British investors.

Vancouver

In January 1893 the company asked the city of Vancouver to guarantee an issue of $400,000 of five percent bonds. Naturally, these would be used to build more street car lines, but more importantly would redeem the $300,000 in company bonds outstanding and liquidate other debts. The company proposed that the city would take over the company, in the event the company should default, for the bonded debt of $400,000, in which case the shareholders would lose their investments completely. The by-law, finally submitted on April 27, was not endorsed by Vancouver's ratepayers.

In February at the annual meeting, the following directors had been appointed: Isaac

Oppenheimer (president), William Farrell, Thomas Dunn, C. D. Rand, and H. T. Ceperley (secretary-treasurer). But exactly two weeks after the defeat of the by-law, the company went into liquidation. The Vancouver Loan, Trust, Savings and Guarantee Company Limited, H. T. Ceperley, manager, took possession of the company for the bondholders. When this trustee company advertised the sale of the company, no satisfactory bids were received, and negotiations were initiated by Vancouver's city council!

The trustee company acted with vigour in another direction as well. Service on the lonely 1.7-mile, virtually uninhabited Broadway section of the Fairview line was axed on May 14, as was all service east of Main Street on Powell Street; Mount Pleasant service was reduced from hourly all day to two-hourly in the mornings and evenings. Residents affected by these abandonments and cutbacks were furious, but, as hoped by the trustees, the much-reduced street car system began to show a slight profit; and in July the trustees even got necessary permission from the Supreme Court to borrow money to help pay for a project which had been in progress when liquidation had overtaken the company, the double tracking of the street car line from Main and Powell streets to Hastings and Granville.

New Westminster

For the Westminster and Vancouver Tramway — obviously a completely different type of operation — 1893 was its peak year. Its capital expenditure in 1892 had been $164,377.08 (over $50,000 more than the Vancouver company's), and its 1893 expenditure would be $87,883.57.

On February 21 the Tramway actively began considering building a line to Queensborough, a project which would only be brought to fruition twenty years later by a Tramway successor company.

For New Westminster's fifth annual exhibition, operated every September by the Royal Agricultural and Industrial Society, the Tramway introduced some new ideas: from Vancouver, the return fare on the interurban was identical, whether one alighted at Queen's Park or farther on at the terminus on Columbia Street (New Westminster's merchants were indeed pleased); and together with fifteen-minute street car service from Columbia Street to Queen's Park, the Tramway had fitted up a waiting room in a vacant

The power house and barn of the Westminster and Vancouver Tramway on the south side of the line in Burnaby. Its position today would be off Beresford Street, between Mission and Griffiths avenues. The line's little caboose languishes in the background, far right. (B.C. Hydro)

store next to its office on Columbia Street. Nonetheless, the *British Columbian* expressed some displeasure with the Tramway's exhibition service, specifying that it had not handled it too well and wondering why the C.P.R. had not run a fuller Vancouver-New Westminster service.

Just one month later,† the Tramway put into service a new, more direct line into New Westminster from its point of crossing the Vancouver Road (Edmonds, today), down Twelfth Street and along to the terminus, decidedly speeding up the inter-city interurban service and eschewing the quite personable but rather bizarre original line into New Westminster.

Car 14 heads south on Granville Street toward Georgia in this view, from the C.P.R.'s hotel, northeastward along Burrard Inlet, North Vancouver on the far left shore, Hastings Street receding into the distance at far right. (Vancouver Public Library)

Having reached 1893, the Vancouver Electric Railway and Light Company Limited could look back on the 1892 performance of its street car lines, for each of which profit and loss was separately kept.

	Powell Street line	Mount Pleasant and Fairview line
January, 1892	$165.23	$351.74
February	156.38	338.39
March	167.41	419.89
April	166.15	368.45
May	163.25	472.51
June	169.13	509.62
July	202.38	454.23
August	196.55	348.80
	$1,386.48	$3,263.63

Unfortunately, for the same time period the Powell Street line showed expenses of $4,030.46, the Mount Pleasant and Fairview line $10,558.43. In addition, McGillivray had been paid $17,718.88 for his Fairview line work, while $12,200 had gone for those rails. McGillivray had received a further $1,378.77 as the contractor for the two blocks of Westminster and Vancouver Tramway-operated rails on Hastings Street, Main to Carrall streets; and McCraney, the contractor for the original street car layout, had only just been given his payment, $20,270.75, during 1892.

† *The B.C. Electric Employees' Magazine, April 1918, p. 2.*

However, the awesome steepness of Twelfth Street for the half-mile before it arrived, flat, at Carnarvon Street clearly mitigated against its future use for heavier interurban and freight operations, but for the time being, what an improvement the new 2.4-mile cut-off was! The lightly curving, largely uninhabited stretch between Edmonds, known then simply as "the junction" (the equivalent of Twentieth Avenue), and City Limits station at New Westminster's boundary, Tenth Avenue, was soon to have a station called Wise Road at the point where Fourteenth Avenue crosses today, and from the beginning had a passing siding at Twelfth.

When this line was first proposed, New Westminster's city council had been unhappy about the idea of the Tramway's proposed running on Columbia Street from Twelfth, which meant not only that the new line would have a level crossing with the C.P.R., which ran on Carnarvon Street (today's Columbia Street!), but also — and more significantly for the city — that its two streets feeding west from the downtown area would both be clogged with rails. (It would be some forty years later that the streets and tracks in this area would be realigned, causing the disappearance of the original Columbia Street at this point, and the rechristening of Carnarvon Street as Columbia.) This stumbling block was hurdled with ease when Sir William Van Horne himself arrived on the scene and granted the Tramway running rights over the C.P.R.'s tracks. It seemed no problem at all that new bonded rail had to be laid and trolley wire installed.

But what of the Tramway's original route from New Westminster to Edmonds, now that the interurbans no longer used it on a regular basis, and the street cars ran only as far as Sixth Street and Tenth Avenue (the city limits) from the company's New Westminster office? Not surprisingly, the section on Sixth Street to Edmonds was left intact; cars from Vancouver were routed that way when events, particularly lacrosse games, were held at Queen's Park, and it must be stressed that Vancouver possessed nothing to equal Queen's Park, its sporting events and its exhibition.

Throughout 1893, the Great Northern Railway's daily advertisement in the *British Columbian* carried a bold reminder for travellers: "Tickets sold and Baggage checked between Vancouver and all stations in connection with Westminster and Vancouver Tramway Co." It still meant a ferry crossing of the Fraser from New Westminster to Brownsville — a bridge was then still more than ten years in the future — whence the daily train left at 9:20 a.m., arriving in Seattle at 5:15 p.m. (Its Brownsville-bound twin left Seattle daily at 9 a.m., arriving in Brownsville at 4:50 p.m.)

On December 18 a new Tramway schedule from traffic manager G. F. Gibson's office went

Looking west along a still single tracked Columbia Street. The "flying Dutchman" is making its way uphill and to Vancouver, while one of the tramway interurbans recedes in the distance. (author's collection)

into effect, one which employed two interurban cars and one street car. Fourteen trips were run each way between New Westminster and Vancouver, hourly from 8 a.m. to 9 p.m.; on Sunday only, one interurban car sufficed for six trips from New Westminster, at 9 and 11 a.m., and 1, 3:30, 6, and 8:15 p.m., and seven from Vancouver, at 8 and 10 a.m., and 12, 2:30, 5, 7, and 9 p.m. The city street car service operated hourly, from the city limits between 7:30 a.m. and 8:30 p.m., and from the company's office on Columbia Street between 7:55 a.m. and 8:55 p.m., with a late car at 10 p.m. The Tramway ordered six more Brill interurban cars — to add to its seven — which, alas, never needed to be delivered.

Victoria

Lack of money remained the issue during 1894 in Victoria. In accepting the terms of Sperling and Company, the directors of the National Electric Tramway were bound to change the name of the company. This change occurred by special act of the provincial legislature on April 6, when the National Electric Tramway was reborn as the Victoria Electric Railway and Lighting Company Limited.

Earlier in the year the company had instituted a construction program in which vestibules were added to the street cars, thereby finally affording rain, snow, and wind protection to the exposed motorneers, as the company called them. In 1894 the company also began designating specific stopping places for the street cars, a definite departure from the former spontaneity, but by this time already a desirable sophistication. Three more street cars arrived — Victoria now had nineteen — and two further passing sidings were installed at Yates and at Richmond Road on Fort Street, which was developing into a veritable trunk line with its double-pronged servicing of Oak Bay.

Despite the promised cash flow from Sperling and Company, the company was anxious to be sold; the city made overtures, as did other groups, but nothing of note transpired. The company waited anxiously for an arrangement it had initiated with Sperling and Company during the summer as part of its ongoing effort to right itself, but by year's end new company president, Major Dupont, had to report that the company was $31,087 more in debt than it had been the year previous.

The schedule of the W. & V. Tramway in late 1893, as placed in the New Westminster British Columbian *newspaper. Mary Street is today's Sixth Street.*

Westminster & Vancouver Tramway Co.
(LIMITED.)

COMMENCING MONDAY, DEC. 18, the following service will go into effect.

INTERURBAN SERVICE.

The W. and V. Tramway was indeed at its physical peak: it had 16.464 miles of track (17.023 including the C.P.R.'s contribution), and its physical plant included:

350 linear feet of trestling,
45,000 cedar ties (25¢ each),
1,070 tons of rail,
97,000 pounds of spikes,

15 switch stands,
6 miles of fences and cattle guards,
800 poles, and
700 trolley brackets (between, not in, the two cities).

On the Central Park line just east of Cedar Cottage, looking toward New Westminster, in 1894. Disaster has overtaken Tramway car 15; fortunately, there were no casualties. Notice the return copper wire for the electric current lying between the rails in the technological fashion of the time. (Vancouver City Archives)

Vancouver

In January 1894 the trustees offered to sell the whole Vancouver street railway and lighting system to the city of Vancouver for $380,000. Though the trustees had sensed a moderate enthusiasm about the idea among ratepayers, when the day for voting, May 30, came the public once more turned down the purchase proposal.

Meanwhile on April 11, a new company, the Consolidated Railway and Light Company, with an authorized capital of $1,000,000, had been formed, of mixed local and English investors. The general manager was 38-year-old, Toronto-born Victoria businessman and member of parliament, Frank S. Barnard, son of Francis J. Barnard, founder of the Barnard Express of Cariboo Road fame. The Consolidated company had been created for the precise purpose of acquiring the Vancouver company from the trustees, which it quickly accomplished for the bargain sum of $290,000. Fairview and Powell Street soon regained their street cars, and the Mount Pleasant line returned to its former brand of service; furthermore, the double tracking of the key east-west section of the downtown Vancouver line — Main to Granville streets — was completed by summer at a cost of $11,636.52, and work was immediately begun double tracking Granville from Hastings to Robson streets, in preparation for a new line which would soon be heading westward on Robson toward Stanley Park.

New Westminster

The Westminster and Vancouver Tramway had lived somewhat of a charmed two years, though such an existence had been accomplished largely through the company's propensity for turning a blind eye to realities. For the W. & V., 1894 was a melancholy year of reckoning. The international depression, accelerated by the previous year's American banking panic, would not relax its grip for another two years. The Tramway's brief fling at high living was forever in the past. Though experts from all parts of the world had lauded it as the most perfect and best equipped system on the continent, too little paid up capital and a lack of population, particularly between the two cities, spelled big trouble.

Even the city service in New Westminster had become unprofitable, but the Tramway still talked of building to Queensborough and announced its intention of running a new line northeast to Sapperton. When car 15 on its way from New Westminster to Vancouver left the tracks and rolled onto its side to the north of the line, just east of Cedar Cottage, the Tramway's difficulties seemed only accentuated. When a bolt of lightning struck the power house, burning out its dynamos, the end was imminent. The Tramway had overspent massively; money for repairs was simply not available.

Widespread flooding of the Fraser River in May brought despair and misery to Fraser Valley residents and heavily involved the citizens of New Westminster in the rescue and alleviation of this unprecedented disaster. In June the Bank of British Columbia hit the Tramway with the threat that it would not pay the interest on the company's bonds, which would fall due the following month; all through 1893, notes had fallen due, but the Tramway had been unable to pay them. Secretary-treasurer P. N. Smith tried frantically to get help, but on August 10, the Tramway went into receivership, Smith acting as trustee.

Victoria

There was joy on February 9, 1895 when it was announced that the Victoria company had received $109,055 from Sperling and Company. By the end of April, it had completed the laying out and construction of five-acre Oak Bay Park at the end of the Oak Bay extension, and a new passing siding was put into service on the line in order to facilitate better street car service to this beautiful company park project. But by the end of May the company was $84,375 in debt, and on June 4, the Victoria Electric Railway and Lighting

Provincial government appraisers evaluated the Westminster and Vancouver Tramway Company during the year, and by July 31, their figures were ready:

Track and bridges	*$187,998.40*
Cars	*69,200.00*
Buildings	*25,950.00*
Electric Machinery	*16,700.00*
Steam Plant Machinery	*31,400.00*
Distribution	*30,206.00*
	$361,454.40

Company went into receivership. Company secretary John McKilligan became one of the interim receivers, and he tried everything in his powers to save as much of the situation as possible, even travelling to England to meet with Sperling and Company officials, who were not particularly encouraging. But McKilligan kept pressure on the Sperling group, urging them to take over Victoria's street railway on behalf of the bondholders.

Vancouver

In Vancouver the double tracking of Granville from Hastings Street to Robson was completed in 1895, and before the year was out Granville was double tracked to Davie Street. But 1895 was a year of new street car lines as well. The Tramway line from New Westminster which came down Hastings to Carrall Street made no connection with the Vancouver city line at its only opportunity, Main Street; furthermore, Hastings Street had still not been opened up between Carrall and Cambie streets, and the C.P.R.'s right of way between the waterfront and False Creek which crossed Hastings just west of Carrall was still fenced in. All this changed in 1895 as a double tracked street car line was laid on the two blocks of Hastings Street between Carrall and Cambie streets. At the same time, the Tramway's line on Hastings between Carrall and Main had been double tracked, and excursions could then be run

directly from New Westminster to Stanley Park and English Bay. It was now a priority to get the waiting New Westminster bound interurbans off Hastings Street by building an off-street depot. Fairview cars made Hastings between Main and Granville their route, while the Mount Pleasant line used the original downtown route, connecting with the new 1.23-mile Robson line — Granville to Denman Street, Denman to Alberni Street, Alberni to Chilco Street, and Chilco to Georgia Street — completed also in 1895 on a five-year lease, which simply meant that the city had an option to purchase the line after five years. (For some time before the line was ready, street cars had been running as far as Bute Street.)

New Westminster

The assets of the Westminster and Vancouver Tramway Company were auctioned at sheriff's auction, Trapp's Auction Room, New Westminster, on April 13, 1895, their purchaser, Frank S. Barnard, acting for the Consolidated Railway and Light Company. The price: $280,000. (The Westminster and Vancouver Land Bonus Act, finally granting the Tramway its promised 196 acres of Collingwood, had been passed by the provincial legislature on the same day that the Consolidated company had been incorporated, April 11, 1894.) Both New Westminster and Vancouver systems, whose major creditors had been the Bank of British Columbia and the

In 1896 Victoria's system took stock of the extent of its street car lines, revealing the following details:

Line Description	Rail	Feet
Fort Street, Government to Harrison	56 lb. T-rail	5,860
Fort Street, Harrison to terminal	38 lb. Girder & T-rail	4,719
Oak Bay Avenue, Fort to terminal	40 lb. T-rail	7,897
Esquimalt Road, Rock Bay to terminal	40 lb. T-rail	17,202
Spring Ridge, Douglas to terminal	38 lb. Girder rail	5,989
Beacon Hill, Courtney to terminal	38 lb. Girder rail	6,527
Outer Wharf, Menzies to terminal	38 lb. Girder rail	3,626
Douglas Street, Yates to terminal	38 lb. Girder rail	8,748
Johnson & Store Streets, Government to Rock Bay	38 lb. Girder rail	2,417
Government Street, Courtney to Johnson	38 lb. Girder rail	2,897
Pembroke Street, Store to car barn	38 lb. Girder rail	1,127
Yates Street, Government to Douglas	38 lb. Girder rail	580
	(12.80 miles)	67,589

All twelve Victoria sidings and turn outs were laid with 38-pound girder rail.

	Feet		
Fort Street, at Vancouver	205	Superior Street	180
Fort Street, at School	207	Pembroke Street	200
Fort Street, at Dunsmuir	207	Esquimalt Road	209
Oak Bay, at Foul Bay	240	Caledonia Avenue	286
Oak Bay turnout at terminal	154		2,529
Jubilee Hospital turnout	181		
Douglas Street, at fountain	230		
Douglas Street, at city hall	230		

Sidings and main lines together totalled 13.27 miles.

Looking up New Westminster's Columbia Street on May Day, 1896. Though the two interurban coaches are still in Westminster and Vancouver tramway paint, Consolidated Railway and Light Company is now the operator, its shingle visible in an alcove of the Douglas & Elliott Building to the right, the depot (at Sixth Street) of the interurban run to Vancouver. (B.C. Hydro)

Yorkshire Corporation, had now been brought together under the same ownership, which had in fact been created by these two creditors. Although strictly local ownership was obviously in eclipse, British capital as well as beginning recovery from the international depression brought to everyone involved in both cities a sense of imminent hope and stability and a renewed confidence in the growth that everyone knew, even instinctively, was the birthright of British Columbia.

On November 22, 1895, a cable was received in Vancouver announcing that a London syndicate headed by Robert M. Horne-Payne had purchased and taken over control of the properties and assets of the Consolidated Railway and Light Company. Horne-Payne already at the age of 24 had been a partner in Sperling and Company, and Barnard had met him in Nelson, B.C. early in 1894 when Horne-Payne had accompanied Van Horne on a C.P.R. inspection tour. Barnard had urged Horne-Payne to take a look at the street railway situation in Vancouver and New Westminster, which he did, and he was so impressed that upon

his return to England he raised enough capital to take over the Consolidated company by recommending purchase to his principals and forming the Railway Amalgamation Syndicate, with a capitalization of £200,000 which guaranteed Consolidated enough money to pay its debts.

Sperling and Company took possession of the Victoria Electric Railway and Lighting Company Limited on January 8, 1896, appointing McKilligan receiver and manager, and on April 11 Frank S. Barnard, again for the Consolidated Railway and Light Company, purchased the company at auction for $340,000, outlasting two other bidders. Less than one week later, on April 17, the Consolidated company, by special act of the provincial legislature, shortened its name to the Consolidated Railway Company, and increased its capitalization to $1,500,000.

A month later, a new open street car, number 20, arrived, too wide for most of the lines. In addition to its twenty street cars, the Victoria system had a construction car and a snow plow: however, its most prized piece of rolling stock was street car number 16, valued at $4,082.20, a curious vehicle with six wheels on three well-spaced axles.

On Tuesday, May 26, the third day of festivities celebrating the birthday of Queen Victoria, schools were closed and buildings were decorated; the day was warm and inviting. Empire was at its height, and Victorians were making their way en masse across 640-foot-long Point Ellice bridge on their way to Esquimalt to revel in the feature event of the day: military and naval exercises, as well as sports, and even a mock battle, with Her Majesty's soldiers and sailors providing the heroics, aided by the local militia.

Car 16, on its way to Esquimalt, halted briefly at the power house on Store Street to change crew and seemingly to challenge a few more passengers to jam aboard. With 142 souls, number 16, the "big car," rolled across Rock Bay bridge. Motorneer George Farr (Harry Talbot was the conductor) slowed somewhat to distance his street car from number 6 as he came to the first of the two 150-foot, Pratt truss centre spans of Point Ellice bridge. Car 6 was just leaving the bridge's west approach. At 1:50 p.m. car 16 was about one quarter of the distance across the first span, when, in a survivor's words, reported in the *Colonist*, "something snapped and the car dropped about 18 inches, then ran on for about 15 feet. There came another cracking sound and the whole thing went down, the car canting to the right. [The street car tracks lay on the north side of the bridge's roadway.] The motorman leaned over to see what was the matter. He never looked up again, for the whole roadbed gave way and, in the fall, he was struck on the head by timbers and irons from the truss." The conductor of car 6 testified that the bridge had swayed more than usual when his car had negotiated the bridge. Moments later the entire span and street car 16 had plunged directly into the water. Those on the right side of the car had virtually no opportunity to escape since the car did not sink to the bottom but hung, half-submerged, fouled by the wreckage of the bridge. Those who had ridden the outside platforms had the best chance for survival, but 55 passengers, including the motorneer and conductor, died, largely because of the carelessness of the city of Victoria, with whom the responsibility for the upkeep of the bridge lay. It was easily established that rotted timbers in the floor structure caused the collapse; just as certain was the fact that car 16 had been criminally overloaded.†

Hundreds of people crowded the water's edge, those with small boats working feverishly to rescue survivors, while divers worked through the day and night in their quest to recover those who hadn't survived, many of them children; of the survivors, 27 were seriously injured. On May 30, a crane hoisted ill-fated car 16 out of the harbour. Even today, Canada's most catastrophic street railway accident is not forgotten in Victoria.

Esquimalt — the end of the line. The track, which originally used the trestle to the left, has already been relocated and soon a small shelter will be constructed next to the car stop. (B.C. Hydro)

Other local bridges now faced scrutiny, and by July 30, the two wooden trestles on the Esquimalt line were removed and the tracks relaid on the adjoining road. Meanwhile a ferry at the Point Ellice bridge had gone into service, though it was not operated by Consolidated; for inspection purposes the Rock Bay bridge was closed for a time as was Government Street's James Bay bridge.

The Esquimalt street car service had been in operation all this time, but obviously only as far as the west end of Point Ellice bridge; through street car service from downtown to Esquimalt recommenced only on December 4 when a temporary, eighteen-foot-wide pile bridge, just south of the ruined bridge, was opened to street car traffic. (It had already been receiving pedestrian and vehicle traffic by November 7.)

Crossing any of the three bridges, street cars were now limited by the city to thirty passengers. The company dealt with this order in the case of James Bay bridge by transferring passengers from the west, north, and east of the corner of Fort and Government streets to its smaller street cars, which then ran the two southward routes across this bridge to Beacon Hill and Outer Wharf.

Barnard had spent rather too freely, utilizing operating revenue for capital cost; this and the potential claims for damages as a result of the Point Ellice bridge disaster sowed fear in the heart of even the most swashbuckling investor. In August the Railway Amalgamation Syndicate backed away, refusing any more assistance to Consolidated, and on October 13 the Consolidated Railway Company was taken over by receiver William Farrell of the Yorkshire Corporation who offered it for sale at public auction in Vancouver on November 17. No one

† R.M. Binns, "The Point Ellice Bridge Disaster," *Canadian Rail*, April 1969, pp. 98-107.

Car 16, "Fort Street & Esquimalt," after the collapse of Point Ellice bridge on May 26, 1896, a catastrophe which snuffed out the lives of 55 riders. (B.C. Hydro)

was interested. However, within a month the Consolidated company was sold to an eastern Canadian group, the Colonial Railway and Investment Company, which in turn sold it for £462,000 to a new entity, the British Columbia Electric Railway Company Limited which was incorporated on April 3, 1897, under English laws, with head office at London, England, in Threadneedle House. The Canadian headquarters was logically located in Vancouver, initially on the first floor of the steam plant on Union Street, but shortly at 163 West Cordova Street.

Thus, somewhat more than seven daring, exciting years had elapsed since street car service had first appeared on Canada's Pacific coast. This precarious time of dreaming and desperation by local investors was forever gone. Undismayed by the terrible loss and ruin of Point Ellice and the collapse of Consolidated, Horne-Payne was still supremely optimistic regarding the future of

British Columbia and the possibilities that the development of the electric utility business offered. Upon his return to London from Victoria, he had immediately set himself to raising fresh capital to take over the Consolidated company, which he did, the transfer to the B. C. Electric taking place on April 15, 1897.

II

1897-1903:
Consolidation and B.C. Electric

The directors of the new company (several of whom had been part of the Railway Amalgamation Syndicate) were Robert M. Horne-Payne, chairman (a post he was to retain until 1928); Frank S. Barnard, managing director of the company in British Columbia; J. Horne-Payne; A. C. Mitchell-Innes; R. N. Laurie; G. P. Norton; and R. K. Sperling. They immediately appointed Copenhagen-born Vancouver resident Johannes Buntzen as general manager, and R. Henry Sperling (of the same family as one of the directors) general superintendent.

Victoria

Locally, day to day perspectives had that compelling quality which tended to obliterate the larger corporate goings on. How better to illustrate that fact than by reference to a letter written on April 13 by the Victoria system's superintendent M. C. Cheney to "J. B. McKilligan, Esq., Manager, Victoria Branch, Consolidated Railway Company."

> *"Re the convenient carrying capacity of our cars, I think the 16 foot cars can conveniently carry seventy-five persons, the 24 foot cars one hundred, the large open cars one hundred and twenty and the small open cars ninety each. The maximum that can be carried is at least twenty per cent more. The cars are strong enough to carry all that can be possibly gotten into them."*

Victoria in regular service was at this time operating four cars on Fort Street, two on Esquimalt, two on Oak Bay, three on Beacon Hill, and three on Outer Wharf.

Vancouver

During 1897 Vancouver was able to add another 1.23-mile street car line to its slowly growing track map, a route which quickly became

In 1897 population estimates revealed the following:	
New Westminster	*6,550*
Vancouver	*22,800*
Victoria	*19,300*
All British Columbia	*146,000*

known as "the Stanley Park line." It headed west from Granville Street on Pender Street, angling eventually into Georgia Street, which it followed the remaining four blocks to Chilco Street, where it connected with the Robson line. (A wye had also been laid south on Denman, connecting with the Robson line at Alberni Street.) Street car service had been run on this line before construction all the way to Chilco had been completed. All along Pender Street, the north side fell away to the harbour, while the south side already held numerous residences; apparently the line was built on this curious street because it led more directly to the new post office, and a number of influential people living along Pender wanted to pick up their mail as they came to their offices.

Former W. & V. Tramway number 8 has retained its number while working Vancouver's Powell Street line. Being photographed at Campbell Avenue, the end of the line, are conductor J.C. Barton, centre, and G. Lenfesty, to be first president of Local 101 of the Street Railwaymen's Union. (B.C. Hydro)

New Westminster

To celebrate the sixtieth year of Queen Victoria's reign, the new station (only a platform), installed in 1897 on the New Westminster to Vancouver interurban line (now styled "Westminster branch" by the B. C. Electric) where Imperial Street crosses the line in Burnaby, was named Jubilee. So important an inaugural event was this for the small community growing up east of Central Park that a special police force — one man — was hired by Burnaby's municipal council to keep order. Farther west along the line, just as Cedar Cottage had acquired its name through the simple expedient of an early settler building himself a cottage of cedar (some distance away, actually), so Grant Street, two blocks north of First Avenue on Commercial Drive, was named after a settler who, to be certain the interurban would drop his freight off for him, nailed a "Grant" sign to a stump. As the forest was cleared along Commercial Drive, its descriptive name of Park Drive disappeared and as Buffalo Park station lost its park, and then its buffalo, it became simply the stop at Fourteenth Avenue, on Commercial.

Though the ownership was new, special trains from Carrall Street to the lacrosse games at Queen's Park were a still-growing, continuing connection with the old Tramway image; these lacrosse specials usually consisted of a number of flat cars, fitted up with rows of benches and safety railings, towed by a freight motor. Picnic specials from Burnaby and New Westminster to Stanley Park were already common, and soon shoppers' specials would also be run in to the big department stores in Vancouver (not, alas for the New Westminster merchants, to the Royal City). In the years to come, the operation of New Westminster's little street car service would be extended north on Sixth Street, following the original interurban route, through a tiny community in Burnaby, up the hill from New Westminster city limits (known locally for its remoteness as "little Siberia") and all the way to Edmonds. In the meantime, the consolidation on the mainland of the New Westminster and Vancouver systems meant that street cars would be exchanged between the two, a gain in flexibility for the future.

Victoria

The rush to the Klondike gold fields, begun in 1897, continued on in 1898 until the fall. Though New Westminster and Vancouver felt its effects, Victoria played an even larger role. But on February 10, 1898, Victoria was inundated by non-gold-rush visitors who had been among the thousands invited to attend the opening of the new ornate Parliament Building. Its effusive grandeur trumpeted the arrival of great times, greater prosperity, and surely even the mystery and thrill of a new century, just lying in wait.

Victoria's passenger receipts for the year ending March 31, the first year of B. C. Electric operation, totalled $73,538.26. And by July, Victoria's street car system finally went "big city" — it had its first double trackage, 1.364 feet of it on Government Street.

Vancouver

During 1898 in Vancouver a line was projected on Bidwell Street to English Bay from the Robson line; however, when a line was built to English Bay, it found its route one block east on Denman Street instead. An innovation of much help to travellers in a hurry in a quickly-growing city came on June 8 with the introduction of a street car light system for identification: Pender Street cars used a green light, Fairview white, and "main line" cars red.

New Westminster

In New Westminster, the unthinkable happened: a catastrophic fire destroyed the entire business district and a large section of the residential area in the few hours between 11 p.m. on Saturday, September 10, and early Sunday. No one knows how it started, but the flames surged furiously, aided by a wind, from the hundreds of tons of hay stored at the Brackman-Ker Milling Company adjacent to Front Street near Lytton

Car 26, with motorman R.W. Nunn, loiters for a moment at its Oak Bay terminus. (B.C. Hydro)

Square. Market, canneries, opera house, C.P.R. station, churches, business blocks, warehouses, mills — everything west to Tenth Street and north to Royal Avenue was destroyed. Incredibly, the only brick buildings left standing were the Burr Block and the Queen's Hotel, neighbouring four- and three-storey structures on the north side of Columbia, at Fourth Street.

The September 17 issue of the *British Columbian* included the following description:

"The whole heavens seemed afire, clouds of sparks and large pieces of flaming shingle being carried by the wind to alight on the clustering dwellings to leeward, added to the terrors of the inhabitants of that section.

By the time the flames were finally got under control, the wind had greatly subsided, and, in the sickly light of Sunday's dawn, thousands of citizens (the whole town having been early aroused and on the streets) looked down on the smoking remains of what, six hours before, had been as beautiful, well-built and well kept a city as there was on this coast."

The Burr Block (later called the King Edward Block) had been functioning as the terminus, a logical mid-town location, near the market, for somewhat over a year. A temporary terminus was set up some distance west at the edge of the fire's impact, the foot of Tenth Street. This depot was in fact a former Tramway caboose (boldly lettered "W.V.T. Co."), four-wheeled, without a cupola, and blocked fore and aft with two timbers to keep it stationary.

Before the year was out, a single spur had been laid south on Begbie Street against the east sidewalk, from Columbia, with trolley wire hung from Tramway trolley brackets of the type used on the interurban line between the city boundaries of New Westminster and Vancouver. The B. C. Electric built its first New Westminster depot (later it became the Bank of Nova Scotia Block) on that southeast corner, but it lasted just over a year as the limited capability of the one spur track turning westward onto Columbia Street tied up traffic more than was tolerable and the city also did not care to have freight handled from the sidewalk.

Despite the fire, the tenth annual exhibition of the Royal Agricultural and Industrial Society was held on schedule that September; and until a new market was built, again at the foot of Church Street, temporary quarters were found for it in an old building on Library Square.

After one year of activity, the British Columbia Electric Railway Company Limited announced that its 50 street cars and interurbans, on 40 miles of single track, had carried 3,654,300 passengers; that it had 28,068 lamps in service; and that its gross income for the year had been $318,724. During 1898 the company put into operation the first hydro-electric plant in British Columbia — the very first of many the B.C.E.R. would construct

— on the Goldstream River, about fifteen miles from Victoria.

Victoria resident Frank S. Barnard resigned from his position as managing director of the B.C.E.R. in British Columbia on April 14, to be replaced by former general manager, Johannes Buntzen. He did, however, remain a member of the company's directorate. And the B. C. Electric had its new much-needed head office building and at the same time a presentable Vancouver terminus for the line of the Westminster & Vancouver Tramway, all in one $24,000 building on the company's property at the southwest corner of Carrall and Hastings streets. This two-storey brick building, designed by Francis Rattenbury, architect of the Parliament Building in Victoria, was officially opened on September 2, 1898. At this time the company effected a link at

After the disastrous New Westminster fire of September 10 and 11, 1898, the former Tramway caboose found perhaps its most gainful employment, functioning at Tenth Street and Columbia as the temporary depot for the interurban run to Vancouver. (B.C. Hydro)

Victoria's ladies take eagerly to the somewhat spartan furnishings of car 11, Outer Wharf-bound.

B.C. Electric's new head office and Vancouver interurban depot, 1898, at the southwest corner of Hastings and Carrall streets. It would be replaced within just a few years by a new building on the same site.(B.C. Hydro)

Carrall Street with C.P.R.'s adjacent English Bay Branch, from the harbour to Kitsilano Beach (Greer's Beach then), and it began developing a freight yard behind, south of the new depot-head office.

Victoria

For most Victorians, one of the great occasions of 1899 was the inauguration of the grandiose, octagonal-towered exhibition building, as well as what was said to be the finest race track on the west coast, both located on the Willows fairground, old Driving Park. The street car extension of eight years ago to the Park was poised to pay off.

In November, small, metal fareboxes were introduced to Victorians. The fare was 5¢ cash, 6 for 25¢, 8 for 25¢ in rush hours during weekdays, and 8 for 25¢ for students riding between 8 a.m. and 5 p.m., excluding weekends; a trip to Esquimalt cost 10¢.

Vancouver

In Vancouver, the B. C. Electric unveiled plans in late February for a new car barn on Main Street, one block south of the present one; and on the first day of July, the B. C. Electric commenced a program of closing in the vestibules of its open cars, a long overdue venture which would take nine months to carry out. One street car line was completed during the year, the six-block, double tracked line on Denman Street reaching English Bay at Davie Street from Robson. Vancouver passenger receipts for the year ending March 31, 1899 had amounted to $75,166.40, $22,378.16 in excess of the previous year's!

New Westminster

The former Westminster and Vancouver Tramway system for the year ending March 31, 1899 showed passenger receipts totalling $62,080.70 (up $9,248.10 from the previous year's) and baggage receipts of $528.10 (up $172.25). Express earnings, $11,614.89, were recorded separately for the first time. Maintenance of equipment costs were down $522.35 to $3,987.50, but maintenance of way costs were up $598.56 to $3,413.53, largely accounted for by a program of regrading and filling in trestles on the interurban line which had begun during the year. However, the big news for travellers on the interurban line was the arrival on September 12 of two large new interurban cars, appropriately named "Vancouver" and "Westminster." These 38-foot-long Ottawa Car Company products, costing $5,500 each, instantly gave the New Westminster-Vancouver operation a standard of quality unrivalled anywhere at that time; furthermore, they were the first of the company's rolling stock to have four motors, rather than the conventional two, and to have two trolley poles, rather than a single one which was swung from one end to the other. Appropriately, the B. C. Electric designated them "first class cars."

The B. C. Electric was spending money: its capital expenditure during 1899 on the mainland had been $160,651.26 (up from 1898's $49,848.55), and on Vancouver Island $88,677.53

Car 14 and crew create conditions for an end-of-the-line study at Esquimalt. Note the sailing ship at far right.(B.C. Hydro)

($79,729.55 in 1898). But an appropriately prophetic way to usher out the nineteenth century, simultaneously proclaiming the twentieth, is to point with severely mixed emotions at the twenty-sixth day of September, 1899, the day the very first automobile invaded the streets of Vancouver.

When the twentieth century appeared on Canada's west coast there were few fears about the future. The world's recent depressed past was well out of the way; an unbridled optimism on every front and lunging forward toward the future characterized the spirit of the Canadian far west. Within the second decade of British Columbia's street railway services, Vancouver's population alone would surge to 100,000.

Victoria

The three cities were, however, still relatively cozily contained in 1900. They became quite thoroughly rural after a street car ride of ten minutes from the downtown core of each. Victoria may have had a population of 20,219, but it was still nothing unusual to see the Oak Bay shuttle street car loaded with firewood as it clanged away from its outer terminus. Motorman and conductor would simply have walked the short distance to the beach and cut up the driftwood for fuel,

especially if they lived along the line and could throw off their respective loads in front of their homes.

During January in Victoria, a better ticket deal than ever in the system's ten-year history was introduced, 25 tickets for one dollar; furthermore, special navy and army tickets were introduced. During July the last visible remains of the tragic Point Ellice bridge were dynamited into oblivion, overseen by the three and a half-year-old "temporary" crossing.

By April 1 Buntzen had completed his valuation of the company's Victoria operation:

Electrical Machinery	*$97,590.50*
Steam & Water Plant, Machinery and Tools	
	29,718.30
Rolling stock	*43,500.00*
Track	*108,666,67*
Lines & Poles	*50,418.48*
Buildings, Stone & Brick	*13,100.00*
Buildings, Frame	*3,100.00*
Real Estate	*24,800.00*
Office Furniture, Fixtures & Sundries	*878.00*
	$371,771.95

Vancouver

In Vancouver during 1900, the laying of street car tracks became a feverish activity throughout the city. On April 23, work began on improving the Powell Street line and double tracking and extending the track on Main Street. Track work was being rushed on three other fronts: the building of a new double tracked line on Davie Street from Granville to Denman streets; the double tracking of Robson Street; and the replacing of the original track on Granville Street. So many men were at work that the company had decided as early as February to deliver wage packets directly to their crews by means of a street car, which they called a pay car.

The company's two False Creek crossings, on Granville and Main streets, received assessments of $5,000 each; the trestle on Georgia Street at the approach to Stanley Park was valued at $1,000, while the two trestles on Broadway — much regrading and filling had gone into eliminating the five smaller trestles — between Cambie (Bridge Street, then) and Ash streets and between Heather and Willow streets were worth $400 each to the company.

Normal Vancouver city service in 1900 regularly employed thirteen of the company's double-ended cars, four to English Bay on the Robson line from Broadway and Main (along Main), four to English Bay on the Davie line from Broadway and Main (again along Main), three on the Fairview line from Broadway and Main (east along Broadway) to Hastings and Cambie, and two on the Stanley Park-Powell Street line.

New Westminster

New Westminster began 1900 with a vigorously twentieth century stroke: on January 19 the company's transit employees in that city formed Local 134 of the Amalgamated Association of Street Railway Employees of America (founded

Buntzen's assessment of the Vancouver system during the year set forth its track situation in the following detail.

Miles	Line	Value
1.30	Robson St., 1st track to park	$15,529.51
1.23	Pender St., 1st track to park	12,749.92
0.78	Granville St., double track Hastings to Robson	10,944.22
1.33	Hastings St., Cambie to Main, & Main, Hastings to Georgia (Harris, then), double track	30,141.33
1.00	Denman St., double track	17,563.40
2.00	Davie St., double track	27,869.97
0.84	Granville St., double track Robson to Davie	11,164.53
1.00	Robson St., 2nd track	12,802.90
2.84	Fairview line, Broadway to Davie	29,820.00
0.67	Powell St., Main to Campbell	8,040.00
3.71	Main line, Broadway to Georgia; Hastings to Granville via Main, Powell, Carrall, Cordova, Cambie, & Hastings	42,665.00
16.70		$219,290.78

Among Vancouver's 26 street cars listed below can be found the five former Westminster & Vancouver Tramway interurbans which the company had recently incorporated into the Vancouver system, renumbering them 30, 32, 34, 36, and 38, finally stripping them of their original Tramway paint scheme.

2	13-bench open cars	$ 7,000.00
4	10-bench open cars	10,800.00
5	26-foot bodies, closed cars	15,000.00
10	small closed cars	20,000.00
2	new closed cars @ 3,600	7,200.00
2	trailers	1,000.00
1	convertible car	3,600.00
1	construction car	500.00
2	flat cars	500.00
4	dump cars	1,000.00
1	hand trolley	150.00
		$66,750.00

The one "convertible car" listed above (number 28) was unique: it had been specially created and furnished by its builder, the J. G. Brill Company, for an exhibition in St. Louis, Missouri, in 1899. Deemed the very latest and best in street car design, it was purchased immediately after the exhibition by the B. C. Electric and put to work on Powell Street. Number 28 had fourteen transverse rattan seats and two long seats at each end, but what made the car convertible was the fact that its windows could be pushed up and into the ceiling, and its sides removed by catches, for summer use.

September 15, 1892), more commonly known as the Street Railwaymen's Union, the S.R.U. The first signer of the Local 134 charter was Sid Gregory, who retired in 1946 as general agent, transportation division, New Westminster, having joined the company on May 1, 1894. At the time of the local's formation, motormen and conductors worked a 10¼-hour day, seven days a week, at 20 cents an hour. Paid vacation time was an unheard-of concept. Soon after the advent of Local 134, a new contract was negotiated and a wage increase of two cents an hour was won.

Finally, the interurban line had a terminus at New Westminster comparable in quality to the one in Vancouver; costing almost $10,000, it was opened for business on March 26. This "Tramway Block" was an entirely successful undertaking, in contradistinction to the ill-conceived stone and brick depot constructed only a little more than a year earlier at Columbia and Begbie streets.

The new depot was located on the south side of Columbia, in the block between Eighth Street and Begbie, a block containing four equal-sized lots, the B. C. Electric acquiring the second from Eighth for the depot. The new building was a solid, one storey stone and brick structure, the east half containing offices and waiting room, the west half a two-track covered bay for the interurbans and "City" street cars.

On April 11, the *British Columbian* newspaper let it be known that the B. C. Electric's plans for the interurban line included a name for each of its cars, rather than a number. The new "Vancouver" and "Westminster" had been thoroughly successful, and at least to match them in some respects the two Tramway interurban cars which had not been sent to a life of street car work in Vancouver earned a reprieve of a few years; number 17 was named "Burnaby," number 13,

"Richmond," and both had their two motors doubled to four. (Although the B. C. Electric ran, as yet, no service to Richmond, perhaps the naming of car 13 was the company's in-house acknowledgement of the fact that grading for the right of way of the still-unrelated Vancouver and Lulu Island Railway was vigorously under way at this time.)

In addition to the four interurban cars, two street cars for the flagging "City" service remained, a service which had begun with fascination but had drooped after the honeymoon to the point where in 1900 its average monthly receipts totalled $420. It occurred to the company (which really means Johannes Buntzen) that it might try stimulating the situation by building a new line along Columbia Street beyond Leopold Place to Sapperton. On May 9 the B. C. Electric informed city council that it was ready ($12,000 was needed) to build the 1.2-mile "Sapperton Extension." Work began on July 24 and was

Freight car 7, here with J. Sullivan, Bill Cook, and D.H. Miller in 1900 on the Central Park line, would finish out its life as express car 1801. (Geoff Meugens collection)

Buntzen's evaluation of the New Westminster operation totalled $338,524.18, comprising the following components:

Right of way: 6⅕ miles between New Westminster and Vancouver (75 acres)	$ 7,500.00
Electrical machinery	17,000.00
Steam plant, machinery and tools	14,200.00
Bridges	12,000.00
Track	162,000.00
Poles (1156) with arms, pins, insulators	5,780.00
Transmission line poles	450.00
Copper wire	24,877.08
Old terminus	5,418.44
New terminus	9,717.64
Power house and carbarn	5,000.00
Way stations	1,000.00
Boarding house	2,000.00
Fencing of track	2,566.02
Real estate (District lots 36 and 51 in South Vancouver) — 188 acres @ $100	18,800.00
Other real estate in New Westminster, Burnaby, and South Vancouver	16,565.00
Rolling stock	33,650.00

In addition to the six passenger cars, "rolling stock" included two motorized freight cars (3 and 4), a wood car, flat car, handcar, speeder, and four push cars.

Number 6 (formerly W. & V. Tramway 1, then 6), smartly rebuilt, running the Sapperton line, with the Royal Columbian Hospital forming a logical backdrop. Conductor D.H. Miller and motorman J. Sullivan are clearly in charge. (Peggy Webb collection)

† Anthony A. Barrett and Rhodri Windsor Liscombe, *Frances Rattenbury and British Columbia: Architecture and Challenge in the Imperial Age* (Vancouver, B.C.: University of British Columbia Press, 1983), p. 114.

quickly completed, with a passing siding just north of Cumberland Street, to the Royal Columbian Hospital, which had been waiting eleven patient years for the street car.

The British Empire and the world were dumbfounded by the announcement of the death of Queen Victoria on January 22, 1901. She had reigned for 63 years, seven months and two days, defining an entire era, one in which imperial expansion and power had raised the Empire to a position of world dominance completely without precedent. The very name "British Columbia" reflected the strength of the dynamic entity over which the Queen had presided, even at its most remote. The city of Victoria celebrated her name in its own, and New Westminster would forever bask in the knowledge that the Queen had been asked in 1859 to supply a name for the new city on the Fraser River, and she had replied "that Her Majesty has been graciously pleased to decide that the capital of British Columbia shall be called New Westminster."

Victoria

Small wonder then that when the Queen's grandson — who would become King George V in 1911 — and his wife, the Duke and Duchess of Cornwall and York, visited British Columbia on September 30-October 3, an intense excitement of a quality never before experienced on Canada's Pacific coast swept Vancouver and Victoria. Both cities were resplendently decorated, Victoria's Parliament Building outlined for the first time for the celebration by architect Francis Rattenbury with long strings of hundreds of light bulbs.†

Rattenbury had been called upon earlier in the year to design a new car barn on the south side of Pembroke Street, at Store Street, the projected cost of which had expanded from $15,000 to a final $19,000. New Westminster brick entrepreneur John Coughlan functioned as contractor.

But then there had been the disappointment over the "Palace Cars." The success of the two Ottawa Car Company-built interurbans on the Westminster branch had induced the B. C. Electric to lay out $18,000 for three more slightly smaller, but even more luxurious, cars from the same builder during the previous September. No

Car 22, soon after its arrival in Victoria in 1901, facing west on Fort Street at Richmond Avenue. Conductor Albert Collis and motorman Vic Grounds seem more than pleased with their fancily painted charge. (Bill Walker photo)

An undecided dog is not about to deter cars 16 and 12 from passing in front of what is today the Cordova Street facade of Army & Navy Department Store. Men dominate this early 1900s scene, the heart of Vancouver's business district; double track came quickly here. (Vancouver Public Library)

equipment order to this time had been accompanied by such detailed press coverage, photos (interior and exterior), punditry, and the like. Of course these four-motored vehicles were headed for the Esquimalt line, the street car operation with the most interurban character, and length.

When they arrived in March, the delights of these cars, numbered 21, 22, and 23, were immediately apparent: larger than any cars on the Victoria system and better proportioned than the two New Westminster interurbans, each had a separate smoking compartment, pushbuttons for signalling the conductor, upholstered seats, and newly-invented safety fenders ("cowcatchers") at each end.

And the disappointment? It had two aspects: since the city had done nothing about the inadequacy of the bridge at Rock Bay (the city was doing something about Point Ellice), the cars were too heavy for it and were unable to serve Esquimalt, being wasted on the "Fort Street and Oak Bay Beach" run when they went into service on May 3. Secondly, the company really needed another car for the New Westminster to Vancouver interurban line, and at least one of these three cars would fill the bill nicely. Victoria lost car 21, which arrived in New Westminster to be named "Gladstone," after the great British statesman, orator, and author who had died in 1898.

Vancouver

In Vancouver during 1901, only one new line was built, single track on Main Street south from Broadway (Ninth Avenue) to Sixteenth Avenue, Vancouver's boundary with the municipality of South Vancouver. The double tracking of Main between Georgia Street and Broadway had concurrently been accomplished. By late June, however, Fairview line track had been almost completely relaid, and the C.P.R. was encouraging the company to build a new line into the Kitsilano area, a venture the company refused to embark on unless the C.P.R. laid the track and strung the trolley wire, something the C.P.R. was not about to do.

During 1901 the company induced Vancouver's city council to agree to a consolidation of franchises. The fact that leases for each of the various street car lines expired at different times created an encumbrance for the company in that each line — and each new line — had to be negotiated separately. This consolidation of these short-term franchises obviously also enabled the company more readily to interest new capital in Vancouver. Dated October 14, the agreement with the city made the company's Vancouver operations subject to purchase on February 11, 1919,

and every five years thereafter. For consolidation there was a price to pay, and the company agreed to it: increased percentage of its earnings in payments to the city; extensions to street car lines, farther south on Main Street (already accomplished) and east on Powell; and city regulations in regard to maximum fare, minimum service, and speed limit (8 to 10 miles per hour). The company even extended free passes to city officials.

New Westminster

New Westminster began 1901 with a snowfall that not only shut down the interurban run to Vancouver, necessitating travel between the two cities via the C.P.R., but also brought down the car barn on January 10 with the weight of the snow.

The fare to Central Park was 20 cents — 10 cents for settlers; car 21 — "Gladstone" — was an integral part of interurban service by midyear; and on November 14, there was first notice in the press of a pending development that would revolutionize the B. C. Electric's very existence: the company's intention to lease property from the city of New Westminster to build car shops on the west side of the foot of Twelfth Street.

On the labour front across all three systems, the company had 400 regular employees — the best paid men in Canada, it claimed — none of whom was compelled to work on Sunday. All together, they worked to transport 5,336,310 passengers during 1901.

Dominion census figures for 1901 showed Vancouver with a population of 27,010, Victoria with 20,919, and New Westminster with 6,499; together British Columbia's three largest cities totalled 30% of B. C.'s 178,657 inhabitants. Oak Bay district had 360 residents, 1,331 lived along the Esquimalt line, and at Esquimalt itself, there was a count of 5,200 military and naval men. Nothing quite reveals the newness, the pioneering character of the province quite so well as the fact that only a third of its residents were British Columbia-born.

Victoria

For Victoria 1902 meant the promise of its first new street car lines in years. One — to be called the Gorge loop — would branch off the Esquimalt line, head for the Gorge bridge, and return to downtown via Gorge Road to Douglas Street; the second would run out to the cemetery at Foul Bay.†

During the first three months of the year the new, brick, twin-gabled, eight-track car barn (the press called it "sheds") on Pembroke Street had been inaugurated, and work had begun on a masonry embankment to replace James Bay Bridge. The car barn could house forty cars, measured 160 feet (on Pembroke) by 240 (along Store Street), and boasted a fireproof roof. As well, plans for a handsome stone and steel bridge at

† "The B.C. Street Railway and Lighting Company," *Victoria Daily Colonist*, 13 April 1902, p. 12.

Mount Pleasant car 30 (formerly W. & V. Tramway 10) and Fairview car 44 seem about ready to go their separate ways from Denman and Davie streets in Vancouver. Number 30 still sports its original trucks, but it is fetchingly repainted in a more flamboyant B.C. Electric paint scheme. (Bob Webster collection)

Sprinkler 188 (later 550, then S.50) keeps the dust under control at Stanley Park. Grouse Mountain can be seen in the background at far left. (author's collection)

Point Ellice had been adopted and tenders called for, a project for which the company expected to contribute about $20,000.

By 1902 the B. C. Electric had replaced all the ties throughout the Victoria system, and had added to the double track on Government Street by doubletracking Yates Street, and Douglas Street north to Pandora; thus the system was double tracked from the city hall south to the Parliament Building. But there was more work to be done. The company felt strongly that almost half the system (6⅛ miles) needed new track immediately; the original, outmoded 38-pound girder rail was still there, probably worn down to thirty pounds by 1902.

During the year the company learned it could lose the western 400 yards of the Esquimalt line through expropriation; His Majesty's government's proposal entailed taking over the land between Esquimalt village and the end of the track running to the top of the hill above the Naval cricket ground.

Vancouver

February was the month of snow for Vancouver. Incredibly, in 1902, no street cars operated for six weeks! In fact the cars had been left on the streets where they had been snowed in, and when they were finally dug out, they slunk between banks of snow as through railway cuts.

By mid-May a large B. C. Electric gang was at work laying new street car rails on the C.P.R.'s unused right of way between False Creek and Kitsilano Beach, anticipating a formal agreement with the C.P.R. still two years into the future. The one new line completed during the year, however, was the 5,096-foot extension on Powell Street east to Cedar Cove (Victoria Drive), then one block farther east on Dundas Street to Semlin Drive.

New Westminster

In New Westminster undoubtedly the big story of 1902 was the commencement of construction in April by the province's Department of Public Works of a bridge across the Fraser River. The Great Northern Railway had been waiting over a decade to get into New Westminster and Vancouver, and very soon the B. C. Electric would begin casting active, eager eyes across its forming shape to the forested richness and population potential of the Fraser Valley south of the river.

During 1902, improvement of the interurban line's right of way, begun in 1899, was brought closer to completion, but there was bigger news. On September 4, the company announced that the construction of its car building shops at the foot of Twelfth Street hill was almost completed, and that its first task would be the building of twelve new street cars, six open, and six closed, for winter traffic, modelled on the company's "large Fairview cars," numbers 46 and 48, Ottawa Car Company products of 1900. How wonderfully clear-sighted the company really was! They were right — this corner of Canada would experience during the next decade such an explosive expansion that not having a car-building plant would be completely unrealistic and irresponsible.

A B. C. Electric subsidiary of 1898, the Vancouver Power Company Limited, began its practical life in 1902 when it started work on a hydro-electric development to serve the New Westminster and Vancouver areas. The site selected was, like Victoria's Goldstream, about fifteen miles distant, northeast of Vancouver, using 2,300-acre Coquitlam Lake water flowing through a 12,750-foot-long tunnel westward, with a 32-foot drop in elevation, into 460-acre Lake Beautiful (to be dammed and renamed "Buntzen"), and thence in penstocks down to a power plant (it soon became two) on Indian Arm, an extension of Burrard Inlet. The first project tackled was the most demanding one, the drilling of the tunnel between the two lakes.

One other event which would have an enormous impact on the B. C. Electric's very style of operation in the near future was the first journey on June 30 of a passenger train on the just-completed Vancouver & Lulu Island Railway, a steam railway operating from Vancouver to Steveston, 16.9 rail miles to the south, on the Fraser River. (The C.P.R. had leased this company for a period of 999 years from August 31, 1901.)

The Canadian Pacific Railway made certain of something else as well — on May 23, 1903 it insured for itself virtually complete control of all passenger service between the Lower Mainland and Vancouver Island by placing the seal on its purchase of the unrelated, but similarly named, Canadian Pacific Navigation Company Limited and its fourteen vessels. Within a couple of months, Captain James W. Troup, soon to be named general superintendent of the C.P.R.'s new British Columbia Coast Service, would be talking about a future fleet of C.P.R. coastal steamers, each named for a "Princess," as the C.P.R.'s trans-Pacific liners were each named "Empress." At the time of the purchase, the C.P.N. had been offering, in addition to its sailings to northern B. C. and Alaska, daily return trips between Vancouver and Victoria, and sailings between New Westminster and Victoria two or three times weekly. Understandably, Victorians, inevitably faced with a sea trip to reach the mainland, were more than pleased by the involvement of the transportation colossus in their concerns. With possible equal interest, they took notice as well of their first automobile, which appeared on Victoria's streets during the year.

Victoria

Not to be outdone in 1903, the B. C. Electric in Victoria began following through on its announced track building plans, starting work on a new line toward the cemetery, south from Fort Street on Cook Street. Concurrently, the outer 0.354 mile of the Pandora extension, Cook and Caledonia streets to the community of Spring Ridge (at Fernwood Road), and the outer 0.663 mile of the Esquimalt line, Constance Avenue to the end of track, had their original rails removed and new ones laid. (In January, the Victoria & Sidney Railway had moved its depot into the centre of town, necessitating the construction of its new line across the street car tracks on Douglas Street at Fisgard Street.)

Vancouver

August 1903 found the B. C. Electric involved in a number of downtown Vancouver issues. City council was receiving considerable citizen pressure for an extension of the street car line from the entrance of Stanley Park, at Georgia and Chilco streets, to Brockton Point, about three-quarters of a mile, including a new 800-foot bridge. (The causeway did not exist at that time.) Although the company had already made a rough survey for such a route, Buntzen squelched the idea permanently in late October by his vigorous opposition to it.

The company announced on August 8 that "main line" street cars would soon be using Hastings Street exclusively between Main and Granville, rather than the original routing along Powell, Carrall, Cordova, Cambie, and Hastings. To this end, the B.C.E.R. centred its entire track-building program for 1903 on the intersection of Main and Hastings: this crossing acquired the company's only "grand union" set-up, ever; in other words, from each one of the double track lines on Main and Hastings streets, a street car could make both left and right turns, or cross straight through, a rarity on any system! Integrated with this comprehensive junction system was the double tracking of Hastings one block east to Gore Avenue.

Within a week's time, the company was able to

Cordova Street, looking east from Cambie Street in 1903, with a Robson-bound street car approaching. (Vancouver City Archives)

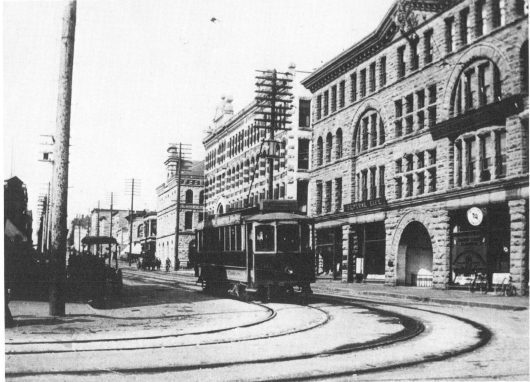

Vancouver's Granville Street in 1903, car 36 (formerly W. & V. Tramway 16) having just made the turn off Hastings Street. Left-hand drive would remain in effect for almost two decades more. The track continuing to the right along Hastings was never used and never formed a wye. (B.C. Hydro)

increase service on the Fairview line by virtue of a new passing siding on Granville Street between Fourth and Fifth avenues, and on the Powell-Pender (Stanley Park) line with another newly-installed siding on Powell Street between Dunlevy Street and Jackson Avenue.

Dense fog was certainly not unknown in Vancouver during its early years, and even the almost complete absence of traffic as we know it today was not a factor in forestalling accidents, as the crews and passengers of cars 34 and 38 realized on December 6. Two men were badly injured in a collision between these two street cars on the south end of the Main Street bridge, at noon.

New Westminster

B. C. Electric's car shops began building in February 1903, and by the end of March two interurban cars named "Delta" (later 1203) and "Surrey" (later 1204), patterned after the two "first class cars," were taking shape while awaiting the arrival of seats from eastern Canada. The company's plan was to have the two ready for the exhibition in September. A month later the shops began to make preparations to build their own seats. A batch of four-wheel street cars was by then under construction, cars 24 and 25 for Victoria (in service in April and October, respectively), and

50, 52, 54, 56, and 58 for Vancouver. In addition, two freight motors (locomotives) were being built.

On the interurban line, all the bridges had been filled in by April, and work was progressing on fencing in the right of way, with the exception of a mile or two through dense forest where a fence really didn't seem necessary.

Passenger business on the interurban line was growing unbelievably. Hourly service was maintained throughout the day, with an added car for each of the 5, 6, and 7 p.m. trips from Vancouver; though these three trips were called "double headers," the two cars were not coupled, but ran independently, a dangerous practice at best. In addition, there was a 5:30 p.m. trip from Vancouver to Central Park only. Travelling the line in 1903, one would have seen clusters of farms and homes almost all along the way, with many new homes under construction.

The two interurban cars were ready for New Westminster's annual exhibition, "Delta" being outshopped on September 21, "Surrey," exactly one week later. Both were officially entered in the exhibition, and the judges awarded a diploma (the highest award for manufacturers) in each case. *The British Columbian* has left a satisfying description:

It's 1903 in New Westminster as a "City Car" ventures up Columbia Street for the climb past Queen's Park to the top of Sixth Street (depot to the right). (New Westminster Public Library)

"In the handsome passenger cars, the frame is built of Douglas fir, cedar and maple — all native woods except the maple. The use of British Columbia woods for car finishing was never tried before, and the expedient was considered risky by experts. But after making some experiments, Superintendent Driscoll felt quite safe in proceeding, which he did with most satisfactory results, and in "Delta" and "Surrey" it is generally admitted that the company has two of the handsomest and best equipped electric cars in America." †

At the exhibition the cars "attracted a great deal of attention, and were somewhat of a surprise to Eastern people, who could hardly believe anything so handsome could be produced from so-called soft woods."

The British Columbian emphasized New Westminster's indebtedness to the B. C. Electric, culminating its essay in a paragraph about the car shops:

> *"A large and constantly increasing staff of skilled mechanics is employed at the carshops, to whom the highest current wages are paid. The establishment of this institution has added a couple of score of families to New Westminster's population, and from present indications it will mean much more in the near future."*

Two beautiful, full size railroad style interurban coaches (significant departures from the company's past), and two locomotives abuilding: here at virtually one stroke were the harbingers of the B. C. Electric's future, the business of moving both people and freight on a grand scale!

Earlier in the year the company had constructed its first purely freight line (although it soon found other uses for part of it), the track to the brickyard of John Coughlan, contractor for Victoria's recently-built car barn. This line, three-fifths of a mile long, proceeded east from the corner of Fourth Avenue and Pine (the switch had been installed in 1902) along Fourth Avenue, downhill directly through Queen's Park, across McBride Boulevard, and down into the brickyard — an awesome grade so steep that never was more than one flat car of bricks handled at a time by a locomotive. These bricks — often two car lots a day — were usually hauled into Vancouver via Sixth Street to the north, Edmonds, and in on the interurban line, altogether a particularly dangerous operation in those days of primitive link-and-pin couplers. At year's end, the B. C. Electric even made public for the first time the quantity of freight it had moved during the year, 6,158 tons. A small "office building" (really a kind of dispatcher's shelter) had been erected in 1903

† "Electric Tramline to Chilliwack," *The Daily Province*, 19 January 1905, p. 7.

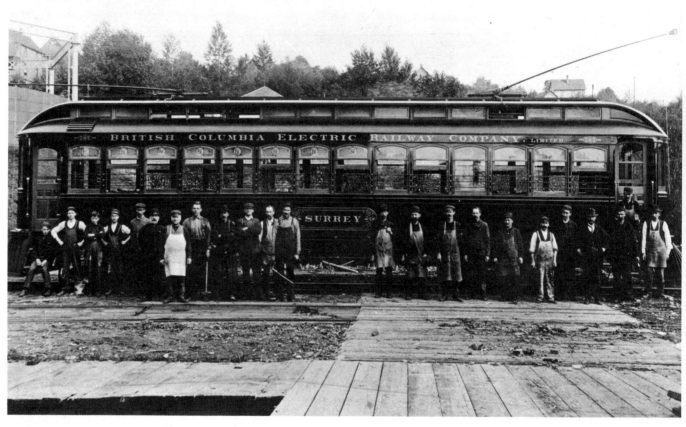

"Surrey," the second of the company-built name cars, poses with its artisans and craftsmen in front of the shops on Twelfth Street in New Westminster. (B.C. Hydro)

at Queen's Park to expedite street car, special events, and freight operations.

The original 2,000-horsepower steam plant on Union Street in Vancouver had been the city's electric source all these years, but on December 17 the first power was delivered from Lake Buntzen, allowing the steam plant a soon-to-come respite. (Four years later it was temporarily put into service to offer some help during an unusually cold winter.) In a few months another 20,000-volt, two-circuit transmission line from Lake Buntzen to a new substation adjoining the old Westminster & Vancouver Tramway steam plant would bring greatly stepped-up electric power to New Westminster and Burnaby.

May 1903, compared with the previous year's May, illustrates the B. C. Electric's health, as well as some growth patterns.

	May 1902	May 1903
Gross Earnings		
Vancouver street cars	$11,514	$13,522
Victoria street cars	9,854	10,459
New Westminster street cars and interurbans	8,795	10,902
Lighting	15,511	20,782
	45,674	55,665
Working Expenses	29,409	32,642
Net Earnings	$16,265	$23,023

Locomotive 503 hauls a load of bricks from the brick yard just east of Queen's Park. (B.C. Hydro)

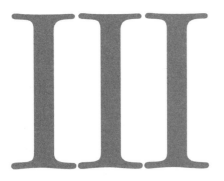

III

1904-1913:

The Great Decade

Victoria

Victoria's 1904 was a "good news-bad news" year. The bad was manifested in a vicious conflagration which burned out most of the industrial section of Victoria, that area immediately to the south of the Pembroke Street car barn. The barn was fortunately spared. The good news was the new bridge, finally, at Point Ellice — double tracked, but later single — opened on April 18. The four-span, through truss bridge, erected at the old location by Victoria Machinery Depot, would do for 53 years. (Originally double-tracked it was later single.) The B. C. Electric had also undertaken to double track the Esquimalt line west from the bridge to Constance Avenue, deep into Esquimalt. The bridge was a superb piece of workmanship, the new trackwork to Esquimalt a well-built boon to riders and crews, but as long as the bridge at Rock Bay was inadequate, the same little single-truck street cars had to pussy-foot their way out to Esquimalt, leaving cars 22 and 23 — and others to come — in the city, too weighty to dare Rock Bay. The B. C. Electric immediately began looking for ways of circumventing this impediment. The new line from Fort Street south on Cook Street to Pakington Street was also ready for business in 1904, as was the new double track on Government Street on its new roadbed between Humboldt and Belleville streets, superseding the

James Bay bridge.

Twenty-two street cars were operating the company's Victoria branch in 1904, three open cars (numbers 10, 11, and 20), the rest closed (2 - 9, 12 - 15, 17, 18, and 22 - 26). All were double enders, and only four had two sets of trucks, 12, 13, 22, and 23. Seven other pieces of rolling stock made occasional appearances: one construction car, two center dump cars, two side dump cars, one flat car, and one "snow broom."

Vancouver

During February of 1904 B. C. Electric had opened its new Vancouver car barn, built in stages, at the northwest corner of Main and Prior streets, one block south of the old car barn. The Prior Street facility had the distinction of being the largest car barn in Canada west of Toronto, as well as the largest in any Pacific coast city. Its Main Street frontage was 264 feet, Prior, 120 feet, making it the largest one-storey structure in the city. Nine parallel tracks gave it a 45-car capacity; the barn's modernity was clearly indicated by its electric hoisting apparatus, four full-length repair pits, and two long, eighteen-foot-wide skylights.

When the company announced, in August 1903, its intention to change its main line from Powell, Carrall, Cordova, Cambie and Hastings, to Hastings only, it met with well-focused opposition, principally from merchants on Cordova Street, who claimed that property and rents would be materially damaged by such a change. A suit against the B. C. Electric was threatened in February; the agreement of 1901 between the city and the company had been specific: "The company is bound to run its cars on what is called the main line, that is, from the corner of Ninth avenue [Broadway] along Westminster avenue [Main Street], Powell, Carrall, Cordova, Cambie, Hastings, Granville, Robson, Denman and Davie Streets, each day except Sundays between the hours of 7 a.m. and 11 p.m., at intervals not exceeding ten minutes."

The B. C. Electric's wish to give Hastings Street a greater share of its downtown traffic was soundly-based. Since the opening up of Hastings Street in 1895 and the completion of the interurban depot on Hastings three years later, the

It's been a long time since Victoria's Cook Street looked like this at Pendergast Street. (Victoria City Archives)

street had begun to acquire a commercial upper hand over Cordova Street, Vancouver's quintessential downtown street from the beginning. Furthermore, in November, Woodward's had opened a new department store, the city's largest, on Hastings at Abbott Street.

Since city council was not insensitive to this new reality, it agreed in June to adopt Buntzen's proposal of "alternate cars;" street cars would soon alternate between Cordova and Hastings, the Hastings Street cars operating south on Main to 16th Avenue, the Cordova Street cars on Main to Broadway.

In the same month, on June 4, Vancouver street cars operated for the first time on electricity generated by water-power from Lake Buntzen, which had been renamed from Lake Beautiful in March.

Toward the end of June the company let it be known that it would venture out of Vancouver into the municipality of South Vancouver by means of a new street car line to the cemetery at Thirty-third Avenue (Bodwell Road then), extending its line on Main Street south from the boundary at Sixteenth Avenue. It is thoroughly understandable that the citizens of Vancouver had been clamoring — as those of Victoria had — for some form of everyday transport to the cemetery.

The first cemetery line car made its run for members of the Street Railwaymen's Union to attend a funeral on August 20. Only reballasting of the line remained to be done, and to that end Buntzen had made a land arrangement with the C.P.R. for the B. C. Electric to run a line west from Main Street on Thirty-third Avenue for about a thousand feet to a new gravel pit at Little Mountain. On Friday, September 16 — the same day the downtown "alternate cars" plan went into effect — the 1.59-mile cemetery line, south on Main to Thirty-third, and east to Fraser Street, began its every-twenty-minutes regular schedule. No one seemed surprised when the company announced exactly one week later that a new three-storey "terminal station" would be built at Hastings and Carrall to supplant the six-year-old depot-head office.

During the summer, the business of running street cars out to Kitsilano had finally been formalized between the B. C. Electric Railway and the Canadian Pacific Railway:

"Whereas by an Agreement made the ninth day of July, A. D. 1904, between the Electric Company of the first part, the Pacific company of the second part, and the Right Honourable Lord Strathcona and Mount Royal and Richard B. Angus, both of the City of Montreal, therein called "the Trustees", of the third part, it was agreed amongst other things that the Electric Company should forthwith electrically bond the track of the Pacific Company ..., running from Granville Street, north of False Creek, to a point called

Greer's Beach, or Kitsilano, and operate continuously a good, proper and efficient electric street car service over the said track; that the Trustees should convey certain lands to the Electric company, and that the Agreement should remain in force until the 11th day of February, 1919, with a conditional provision for renewal."

The "certain lands" was a gift of twelve acres immediately adjacent — on the southwest side — to the junction of the Kitsilano line and the Steveston-bound, C.P.R.-leased Vancouver and Lulu Island Railway, the future site of the B. C. Electric's Kitsilano barn and shops. (In January residents of Ladner, almost five miles southeast of Steveston across the widest mouth of the Fraser River, had begun agitating for an interurban line, a B. C. Electric one.)

By year's end the company had built a double tracked street car line connection from Granville at Pacific to the C.P.R.'s English Bay branch a block and a half south, which would soon become, westward, the company's Kitsilano line. At the same time the two blocks between Pacific and Davie on Granville Street had been double tracked, as had the three blocks of Pender Street between Granville and Burrard.

The opening of Vancouver's Prior barn in 1904, one block south of the obsolete barn on Barnard Street. This view is to the northwest across Main Street. (E.L. Plant collection)

Not many riders, but entry and exit was quickly gained on convertible cars such as number 35. (V.L. Sharman collection)

"Delta" (later 1203), left, and
"Westminster" (later 1200, then
1601) pause for a photo stop at
Central Park station's passing
siding. (Ted Clark collection)

New Westminster

The company's passenger tariff of March 20,
1904 for its interurban line displayed the
following array of station information:

Miles	
0	Westminster
2	Westminster City Limits
3	Power House
3.5	Highland Park
4	Royal Oak
6	Central Park
7	Collingwood
8	Earle's Road [sic]
9	Gladstone
10	Vancouver city limits
12.19	Vancouver

A one-way ticket cost 35¢, and a return was 60¢;
through returns could be purchased on board the

In 1904 the Vancouver branch of the B. C. Electric was operating two line cars (L1 and L2),
two snow plows, two dump cars, one flat car, and 35 single truck, double ended street cars
of both types, convertible and closed.

The Convertible Street Cars	The Closed Street Cars	
21	8	38
23	10	42
25	12	44
28	14	46
29	16	48
31	18	50
33	20	51
35	22	52
60	30	54
61	32	56
62	34	57
63	36	58

interurban cars, whereas returns to intermediate points could be purchased only at terminals. The fare for riding between any two neighbouring stations was five cents, and fifty pounds of baggage was allowed as accompaniment on all tickets.

Obsolescence stared into the face of the steam plant of the old Westminster and Vancouver Tramway's power plant on April 1. (The conjunction of April Fool's Day and thirteen years of reliable service does not make for a fitting enough epitaph.) On that day, Lake Buntzen electricity began its work for the Westminster branch, both interurban and city services.

The event that all of British Columbia's lower mainland had so long awaited finally happened on July 23 — the official opening of the double decked bridge across the Fraser River at New Westminster. Vancouver and New Westminster were now easily accessible to the Fraser Valley's farmers and producers, and this valley — which would quickly become one of Canada's richest growing and dairying areas — now was open to settlement and development of such scope as could not have been foreseen by a bridge-less, even isolated, populace. New Westminster was ecstatic, of course, and Vancouver, though farther distant, was not unaware of what the bridge could mean to its future. The Great Northern Railway's entry into New Westminster, and its terminating in Vancouver, gave travel generally, and travel between Canada and the United States particularly, a whole new dimension.

British Columbia's Lieutenant-Governor, Sir Henri Joly de Lotbiniere, officially opened this remarkable steel bridge, accompanied by Premier Richard McBride and every dignitary

imaginable. Toll-paying highway traffic would use the 2,850-foot upper deck, while the railway would use the lower level, which has a basic length of 2,492 feet, excluding the railway approaches at either end. The bridge, costing a numbing (at the time) one million dollars, rests on eleven piers, six pedestals, and three abutments; its swing span measures 361 feet in length.

The Vancouver, Westminster and Yukon Railway, financed by the GNR, had begun construction of the fourteen-mile Vancouver to New Westminster connection in February 1903, and with the opening of the bridge, only one short segment of its line was unfinished, that stretch along the Fraser River below the penitentiary in New Westminster. On August 10 the B. C. Electric got to work on its adjacent 1,350 feet of track on

Already developing a larger station repertoire, the former Tramway line had still a few years to reach its many-stationed, double tracked, Central Park line status. (author's collection)

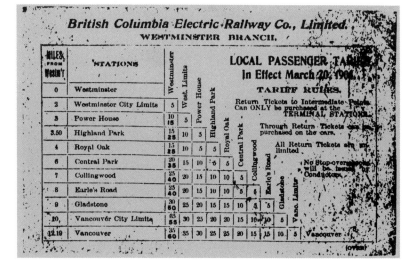

Car "Westminster" (ultimately 1601, and the prototype for B.C. Electric's interurban coaches to come) rolls out of New Westminster's depot in early 1904. Located on Columbia Street between Begbie and Eighth streets, it would in a very few years be replaced by a larger depot. Car 26, "City and Sapperton," had just arrived with Vancouver-bound passengers. (B.C. Hydro)

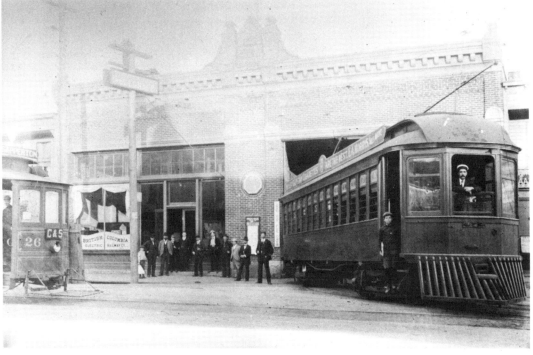

Columbia Street, graded with a purpose, and relocated its line in order to allow the G. N. room to run between it and the river. Great Northern rail operations into Vancouver were able to commence only thirteen days later, making a level crossing with the street car line on Main Street just north of Second Avenue.

During the same month of August, the B. C. Electric's car-building shops in New Westminster were destroyed by fire. Incredibly, before the year was out, new car shops on an even larger scale were built up on the burnt-out site. The destroyed shops had been able to construct eight passenger vehicles in 1904: closed street car 26 for Victoria; closed street car 51 and convertible street cars 60, 61, 62 and 63 for Vancouver; and two more of the big double-ended, non-multiple unit interurban cars, "Langley" (later 1202), outshopped on June 18, and "Vancouver" — named for the original "Vancouver" which itself had been gutted by fire earlier in the year at the Carrall Street depot. This new "Vancouver," which would in a few years become number 1201, had been delivered, ready for operation, on June 6.

During 1904, New Westminster street car service was operated by four single truck street cars, numbers 6, 24, 26, and 27. The two routes, "City" and "Sapperton," were indicated to waiting riders by a roof sign with the appropriate destination at each end of the car, as well as by a smaller sign above the street car's headlight, indicating "C," "S," or "C & S."

The interurban line meanwhile operated eight passenger cars: two of the original cars, "Burnaby" and "Richmond;" "Westminster," the one remaining of the prototypical pair from the Ottawa Car Company; "Gladstone," Victoria's former number 21; and the four new B. C. Electric products, "Delta," "Langley," "Surrey," and "Vancouver." In addition, there was number 3 (the "Flying Dutchman"); number 4, an open freight car; and 5 and 7, closed freight cars (the last three were built by the B. C. Electric, number 3 lengthened and modernized by the company). These four, as well as the interurban cars, each had four motors in their double trucks, the most powerful of the twelve cars being 5 and 7 with four 50 horsepower motors each, as opposed to the 35 horsepower motors in the other ten cars. Thirteen non-motorized pieces of rolling stock complete the 1904 roster picture for the Westminster branch: two dump cars, eight small dump cars, two flat cars, and one snow plow, all built by the company.

At the New Westminster depot two necessary refinements were added during the year, a motormen's and conductors' room, and gates for the two-track loading bay, should a car or two have to be secured inside for any length of time. In addition the company had spent over $3,000 on its Twelfth Street track, regrading and

raising it at the city limits.

A large non-transportation action by the B.C. Electric was the incorporation on April 29 of a subsidiary, Gas Investment Company Limited, which less than three months later acquired control of Vancouver Gas Company Limited. And in December of 1904, to counter the competition of gas companies in the field of home lighting, and to entice homeowners to start using electricity, the B. C. Electric proclaimed its willingness to pay half the cost for wiring homes.

If 1904 had seemed to the B. C. Electric a year of extraordinary expansion, it can be viewed today in retrospect as merely the first of ten successive years of phenomenal growth, growth which the company had cannily foreseen to a large extent. But who would have believed at year's end that 1904's figure of 6,065 tons of freight hauled by the company woud lead to 448,750 tons hauled in 1913? That 69 street cars and interurbans in 1904 would become 357 in 1913? Or that 1904's 8,869,486 passengers carried would be multiplied by nine in 1913?

Victoria

The year 1905 was even headier than 1904. In Victoria the company planned a new local head office building, designed by Rattenbury in the Edwardian classical style, a handsome, two-storey brick building at 1016 Langley Street, the southwest corner with Fort. The old offices at 25 Yates Street had been straining for replacement for some time.

This was also the year of Gorge Park. The new $25,000 street car line to the park did not form a circle, as the company had originally planned; nonetheless it was successful from the very beginning, terminating (as was the case with the Oak Bay line) at a company-developed park, one of the Victoria area's most idyllic beauty spots. The new 1.61-mile line left the Esquimalt line at Henry Street for its journey through west Victoria and north Esquimalt to the Gorge, a picturesque narrowing of the far upper reaches of Victoria's harbour waters. The first block on Henry to Catherine Street was single tracked, but the four blocks on Catherine to Skinner Street were double tracked, as were the 3,320 feet of track on Craigflower Road between Russell and Arcadia streets — and wonder of wonders, the terminus was a loop, the B. C. Electric's first!

The Gorge Park line had begun operating already early in 1905 when track was in place as far as Tillicum Road, over one-third of a mile short of the abuilding loop, but when the line commenced full service in May, it ran fifteen-minute service and carried up to 4,000 passengers a day. The long-awaited opening of Gorge park on July 26 was reported with

(author's collection)

delightful period fervor in the next day's issue of the *Daily Colonist*.

"WONDERFUL TRANSFORMATION IS WROUGHT BY STREET RAILWAY COMPANY: The opening of the B. C. Electric Railway Company's new park at the Gorge took place last evening with great eclat. The occasion will long be remembered in the history of Victoria as a celebration, as it were marking the parting of the ways between the old regime and the new.

"The successful completion of the first of the series of new departures which are to transform the somewhat stagnant summer evening life of the city complained of by tourists into a thing of movement and beauty. Of the ultimate success of this new venture on the part of the company everyone felt or said they felt assured, but no one ventured to predict the astounding alacrity with which the Victorian public responded to the call of progress and flocked in their thousands to see the new park.

"Last night the capacity of the company's rolling stock was taxed to the uttermost and car after car was filled to overflowing. Car after car succeeded in its place, nor did the strain relax until a happy crowd of about three and a half to four thousand persons were landed safely in a fairyland of sylvan beauty lit by countless electric lamps and enlivened by the strains of a good military band. Around the centre of attraction, the band stand, which itself bristled with points of electric light, the scene was difficult to briefly describe. The effect of the electric lights cleverly arranged amongst the interlacing trees was one, the stagic excellence of which it would be hard to exaggerate, producing as it did a conception of depth and distance that was really and wonderfully artistic. The ubiquitous reporter wandering amongst the groups overhead the conversation of two evident old-timers: 'It's beautiful,' said one after a long silence. 'Beautiful,' replied his friend, 'I call it wonderful. I feel as if it were all a dream.' Such indeed seemed the feeling of all, admiration mixed with wonder at what had been achieved in the space of three short weeks.

"The scene, viewed from across the placid waters of the Arm, was most striking and beautiful. Almost every small boat, launch and canoe in town, and they could be counted by the score with their human freight, were in evidence dotting the entire expanse of the water, while on the green sward immediately beyond the boats thousands of people passed to and fro under the innumerable electric lights. And as a background for all towered the sombre masses of the grove of pines."

It was indeed an opportune time for the B.C. Electric in Victoria to begin running one of its open street cars as an observation car, an operation simplified at the scenic Oak Bay end by double tracking 3,420 feet of Oak Bay Avenue from the junction at Fort Street to the Victoria-Oak Bay boundary at Foul Bay Road.

On July 27 the B. C. Electric's gas company acquired control of Victoria Gas Company Limited, and the company's announcement in September that the Rock Bay steam plant would soon acquire a further generating unit was hardly unexpected, in view of heightened electric power demands during the previous year and in 1905.

Vancouver

On the lower mainland, 1905 came in with a shock for the B. C. Electric when on January 19 a J. Burtt Morgan, general manager of the Chilliwack Light & Power Company, presented detailed plans to New Westminster and Vancouver city councils and boards of trade for a fifty-mile New Westminster to Chilliwack interurban line. He had cost estimates ($15,000 per mile), government bonuses, power source and transmission, and more, seemingly worked out to a nicety, altogether a decided prod to the B. C. Electric to get moving on a project it would not wish to concede to anyone else.† (The fact that Morgan's plans were more than a passing fancy, and worthy of the B. C. Electric's concerns, is confirmed by a vote of confidence and support which New Westminster businessmen gave Morgan, even eight months later.)

On the following day, at noon, the B. C. Electric made one of the most significant announcements in its history: it would lease from the C.P.R. the Vancouver and Lulu Island Railway. The B. C. Electric would begin immediately stringing trolley wire for electric operation, build a large substation at Marpole (Eburne then), use the same type of interurban car being used on the Westminster branch, and construct new electric locomotives for freight hauling.

Part of the company's acquisition was the 2.3-mile industrial "south shore" line, currently under construction. It ran from Lulu Island Junction (the point at which the new Kitsilano street car line — the C.P.R.'s old English Bay branch — and the Vancouver & Lulu Island Railway parted company at the west end of Kitsilano trestle, the False Creek Crossing) along the southern edge of False Creek west almost to Main Street. Further, the B. C. Electric would shunt freight between the Carrall Street depot and the V. & L. I.'s (now B. C. Electric's) Granville station, under, and just west of, the north end of Granville Street bridge.

On April 3 the $108,000 job of electrifying the V. & L. I. began, the workmen housed in a cannery just across the Fraser River's north arm at Marpole; and on the nineteenth day of the same month, the formal agreement for the leasing of the V. & L. I. by the B. C. Electric from the C. P. R. was signed. It called for a high calibre of operation and maintenance by the B. C. Electric, and contained a number of interesting directives: freight cars were to be run over the line at least three times daily; both companies would perform all necessary freight switching functions for each other;

† *The British Columbian*, Supplement, December 1904, p. 161.

electrification and other responsibilities in regard to a new Marpole to New Westminster line would be handled in the same fashion that the company would be dealing with currently existing V. & L. I. matters; and the C. P. R. itself would finance and construct any new industrial spurs in the False Creek area (on the south shore line). The B. C. Electric was required under its agreement with the C. P. R. to pay $25,000 per year for the first ten years of the lease and $30,000 for each of the next eleven.

The V. & L. I. had been incorporated as long ago as 1891. The C. P. R. had encouraged the B. C. Electric's involvement with it, even before it itself had leased it, even before right of way clearing for the line had begun in mid-February 1900 between Sixteenth Avenue and Marpole, and even before it had been decided whether the V. & L. I. would cross Sea Island to Lulu Island, or veer east in time to avoid Sea Island (both islands together comprising the municipality of Richmond). The company remained fairly aloof until the upturn in the economy and the arrival of Lake Buntzen power.

Eburne (Marpole), 8.9 rail miles from the C. P. R.'s Vancouver depot on Burrard Inlet at the north end of Granville Street, is located on the north side of the Fraser River's north arm, the southernmost tip of today's Vancouver. In 1905 it was a major sawmilling centre. Between it and Vancouver was land largely uninhabited, but owned by the C. P. R. The rich delta land of the eight-mile journey (whose rails had been laid in

22 days by 30 men) from Eburne farther south to Steveston was already at that time well dotted with dairy and produce farms. Steveston itself was a major fishing and canning centre (at its peak it had 29 canneries) with a population of close to 3,000.

Small wonder that the C. P. R.'s twice-daily steam passenger train over the V. & L. I. had quickly been dubbed the "Sockeye Limited." This "limited," usually consisting of an engine, baggage car, and day coach, left the C. P. R. depot in Vancouver, running backwards on C. P. R. main line almost to Main Street; it then switched onto the English Bay branch, ran forward across B. C. Electric street car lines on Powell and Hastings streets, passing the Carrall Street depot, the C.P.R.'s shops and roundhouse, the V. & L. I.'s Granville Street junction station after running under Granville Street bridge, before crossing False Creek on the Kitsilano trestle. Immediately, there was Lulu Island Junction, where the V. & L. I.'s own 56-pound rail began, the operation having used original C. P. R. trackage for its first 2.7 miles from Vancouver.

Magee (at Forty-ninth Avenue) and Eburne were the only stations in today's Vancouver. The North Arm Bridge across to Lulu Island was composed of: one 345-foot trestle, north end; four Howe truss spans, 80 feet each; one Howe truss span, 100 feet; one steel draw span, 134 feet, on a masonry pivot pier; and one 876-foot trestle, south end. Three stations followed, Cambie, Brighouse, and Lulu, before the arrival — an hour having elapsed since leaving Vancouver — of the

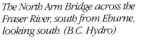

The North Arm Bridge across the Fraser River, south from Eburne, looking south. (B.C. Hydro)

"limited" in Steveston, whose substantial two-storey, 23- by 46-foot station, on the west side of the line just north of Moncton Street, contained a ticket and telegraph office, baggage room, general waiting room, kitchen, one living room, and two bedrooms. A 198-foot platform, and an adjacent 510-foot siding and 30- by 60-foot freight shed were added to this substantial station. Each of the six intermediate stations featured 9- by 25-foot open shelters on 135-foot platforms, as well as — with the exception of Granville — a siding.

The first passenger train had run out to Steveston on June 30, 1902, in preparation for the official opening day run from Steveston back to Vancouver on the following day, Dominion Day. Fortunate indeed that this event of such significance was covered by the Steveston correspondent of the *Daily Colonist*, which published his report in its edition of Sunday, July 6:

"The official opening of the line took place under somewhat inauspicious climatic conditions but the more important feature of the start, successful running and a well patronized train were all that could be desired. At the Steveston terminal, nearly five hundred passengers, gathered from the nearby river landing, boarded the train, and at 9 o'clock sharp to the accompaniment of a cheer and shouts of good wishes from the whole Steveston population, the engineer turned on steam, and the train made up of five first class coaches and an observation car, moved slowly out. The first stop was made at the contractor's camp to take up a number of the men who have been working on the line, and who, at the expense of their employer, all enjoyed a well deserved holiday. The journey from this point is not at all interesting, in a scenic sense. The country is flat in the immediate vicinity, and never can offer any great inducement to the sight-seeing tourist. But that, however, is the last thing thought of in the line laying. The opening up of one of the most fertile tracts of farming land in the province being the recognized necessity that compelled the construction of the Lulu Island railway. That this line was needed, there can be no doubt, thousands of acres of farming land hitherto dependent on stage coach and wagon connection with Vancouver, are now tapped in their very richest parts, and what is more important than all to the dairy farmer, the markets can now be reached in about half an hour as against some three hours in the old way. A second stop was made at No. 2 Road, and at this point some four miles from Steveston, where a station is to be erected, and at No. 3 Siding, where some more passengers came aboard, a second depot will go up. The line up to this point is not yet ballasted, and locomotion over it necessarily slow, but from this on to Vancouver the line is entirely completed with the exception of station houses. For some few miles from this point on, the track is over an uncleared peat prairie, which up to this time has scarcely been touched by settlers owing to the difficulty experienced in getting to it, but now that a way has been opened through it, considerable development will likely progress. The first stop at a completed station is at Inglewood township, and immediately beyond it the train comes over the Arm on a high trestle bridge, and half a mile beyond, Eburne station is reached. Past it a cut is made through a more elevated country, and dense bush. Magee road is soon passed, and although no stop was made here, at this point a station will be placed in the near future. From this on to Vancouver a few more stopping places are passed, and in Vancouver itself, several stops are made at convenient points before the general terminus is reached. The whole journey was made in one and a quarter hours, which, considering the fact that the track has only been finished for a few days, should be reckoned pretty good time."

The electrification of the V. & L. I. Railway having taken less than three months, June 26, 1905 was set as the trial date for electric locomotion, and the new "Eburne" (later 1206) was chosen as the vehicle to take the official party on a slow-running inspection tour over the whole of the line on that date. The "Eburne" and her equally new sisters, "Steveston" (later 1207) and "Richmond" (later 1205) were completed by the New Westminster shop crews just barely in time for the beginning of service on the new line. They were identical to the five name interurbans running on the Westminster branch, except that the fourteen windows on each side were now being grouped into pairs by seven upper windows of coloured glass, and that the non-smoking and smoking sections seated 32 and 24, respectively, rather than 36 and 20. The "Eburne," in her resplendent B. C. Electric coat of jade green, with gold trim and black undercarriage, attracted much attention on her first run, and although the substation was not yet ready, power was supplied from Vancouver.

By early fall, an eighth interurban car, "Burnaby" (later 1208), was ready; the old "Burnaby" and "Richmond" were assigned to less rigorous service and renumbered 39 and 37, respectively.

On July 3, final connections were made for power transmission by the new substation, across the river on Lulu Island, and thus powered, one of the new cars, filled with B. C. Electric and C.P.R. officials, made a last inspection tour, leaving Granville station at 11 a.m. The C.P.R.'s "Sockeye Limited," with two passenger coaches and one baggage car drawn by a steam locomotive, made its last run from Steveston into Vancouver on the same day.

Regular interurban service by the B. C. Electric began on the following day at 7 a.m. when the first car left its "temporary" station at the foot of Granville Street on the north shore of False Creek, running hourly service until 10 p.m. The Granville station, on the north side of the line, became a transfer point for street car and interurban riders on the same day, as the Kitsilano street car line also commenced service, operating from the corner of Granville and Robson streets south on Granville to Granville station on the interurban line, and then west across False Creek on the same former V. & L. I. trestle the new interurban line used, and on farther west to Vine Street, where a station similar to those on the interurban line had been built on the north side of the line. (The old C.P.R. trackage which had continued three blocks more to Trafalgar Street had already been removed.) The wire for the electrification of the Kitsilano line had cost $5,000, $45,000 for the 128 tons of copper wire for the V. & L. I., and all of it strung in the same extraordinary fashion Angus MacDonald had devised for the Fairview line fourteen years earlier. In the bonding of rails sixteen tons of copper costing $8,000 had been used, while 10,500 glass insulators secured the trolley wire.

The first day of interurban operation to Steveston proved wildly successful, if one ignores a freight car derailment in the late afternoon near Magee. Newspapers extolled the "new electric rolling palaces" and noted the standing-room-only crowds. A reporter for the *Vancouver Daily Province* on one of the first day's trips has left us an enthusiastic, lyrical account.

"After crossing False Creek, the line climbs the heights of Fairview around what is known as the Horseshoe, so named from the double curve which the line takes to get up the grade. Heavy forest with occasional farms is passed until Eburne is reached, and the wide expanse of the North Arm of the Fraser River, dotted with the numerous islands, is spread out to view. From Vancouver to Eburne the trolley line is carried on a single pole and bracket construction. Crossing the North Arm of the Fraser on the splendid swing bridge, a change is noticeable in the overhead construction of the line. A double pole line is used with a cross-arm, strongly braced. This precaution is taken owing to the soft nature of the ground during the winter and spring rains. Running along through that double row of poles gives the line the appearance of going through a long tunnel of timber.

As soon as Eburne is passed, the fields, rich, level and luxuriant, at once claim attention. Even were it pitch dark these fields would stimulate the curiosity and engage the attention of a passenger. Acres upon acres of beautiful white and red clover are passed. The exquisite perfume from the myriad of blossoms is something that defies description. All the perfumes of Arabia would not rival the almost intoxicating odors that float through the open car windows as mile after mile of this rich clover is passed.

It is an interesting study to watch the facial expression of some of the passengers in the Steveston car as this district is being passed. The man who for months, perhaps years, has been accustomed to the smell of the city's smoke,

cinders and asphalt, leans back in his seat, throws out his chest, and fills his lungs full of scented ozone.

It is no ordinary growth of clover that is harvested on Lulu Island. On several fields big, husky teams were toiling to drag a mower through the luxuriant mass, while in one particularly heavy growth two teams were hitched to the mower. Think of it, ye agriculturists from the effete East! Two teams on one mower and both pulling hard at that.

Then the oats are worth going miles to see. Fields of them stretching as far as the eye can see — the stems growing so thick and close together that one wonders how they all managed to grow up out of the fertile soil. Nearing Steveston the land seems to improve, and some particularly fine fields of oats are seen. It was on one of these fields that the record yield of 115 bushels of oats to the acre was obtained last year. Meditate on that for a while and compare it with what is considered a heavy yield in the East when 65 bushels are obtained — and then marvel not that the fertile delta is called the Garden of British Columbia.

Looking strangely out of place amid its background of miniature haystacks, the substation at Eburne, where the high-potential current is "stepped down" to the commercial voltage, is passed shortly after leaving Eburne. Here is where the big rotary transformer gets in its work. The substation is a very massive concrete structure with walls two feet thick and is as nearly fireproof as human ingenuity can make it. This is the point at which the high-potential current will also be reduced before being transmitted to the canneries, where in a short time the coy cohoe and sockeye will go from the water to the breakfast table entirely manipulated by electric machinery. The Steveston electric lighting system, now approaching completion, will also be supplied with current through the Eburne substation.

Everyone had heard of chasing deer with dogs, but who ever heard of a deer chase in which the pursuer used an electric train? That was the unique experience which Mr. Harry Manley, one of the motormen on the Steveston line, had yesterday. It happened during one of his first trips in the morning. The car was southbound, and was approaching Magee Station when two pretty fawns came out on the track about a quarter of a mile ahead of the car, and gazed in surprise at the approaching tram. They appeared hypnotized by the strange sight, and it was not until the car was within a hundred feet of them that they turned and ran up the track ahead of the car. Conductor Manley sounded the pneumatic whistle several times and chased the animals for several hundred yards along the track, until they finally turned and dashed into the forest.

Game appears to be thick all along the line. Pheasants and grouse are a common sight, according to the motormen on the new line, and their statements seem not to lack verification, for a hen and brood of young pheasants were sighted by a Province reporter."

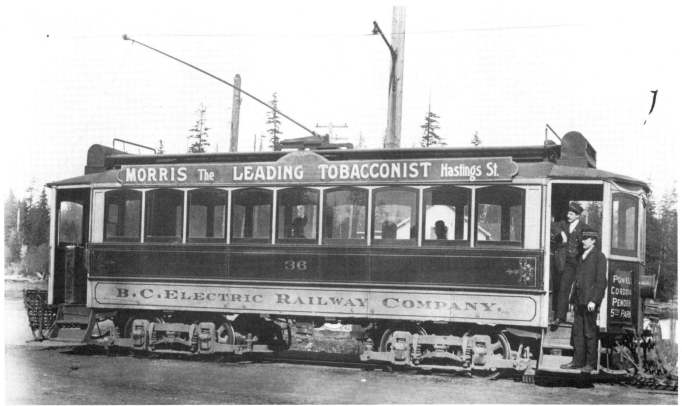

Car 36 (formerly W. & V. Tramway 16) waits at Vancouver's Stanley Park with two passengers, its original trucks replaced. (Vancouver Public Library)

Return fare from Vancouver to Eburne was 40¢, and to Steveston and back, 85¢. Riders on Sunday and holidays needed 30¢ and 75¢, while commercial travellers paid 60¢ for the Vancouver-Steveston return jaunt, clergymen, half fare. During rush hours, half-hourly service was run between Vancouver and Eburne.

Operations were handled by the local agents at Granville Street (where manager Harry Hemlow had his headquarters), Eburne, and Steveston. A car bound for Eburne or Steveston would receive a clearance form simply stating that an interurban car was to be met (and at which siding) or that, for example, the car was "clear to Eburne." (For a time, a staff-passing system was tried but not with any satisfying success.) Freight engines did not receive any clearances; their crews merely reported to the agent that they were headed for Eburne, Steveston, or some intermediate point, and they would wait for the first car to come along and send a brakeman out as a flagman.

In addition to the presence of a telephone at every station, each car carried a portable telephone which could be used along the line, every tenth pole having been equipped with the capability of handling a telephone connection. As one would expect, the Kitsilano trestle across often fog-bound False Creek had signal lights installed at each end, more than a necessity with interurbans, street cars, and "freight" cars (the early electric locomotives) on the move.

The first of two freight cars New Westminster-built for the Steveston line was number 102 (later

1802), looking little different from a passenger car, save that it had no windows. Equipped with standard freight couplers and airbrakes, the forty-foot-long 102 went into service on July 7, its 200-horsepower low-geared motors enabling it to pull two railway flat cars in addition to its own load of freight. It must be said that despite assurances from Buntzen many merchants on Hastings and Granville streets were unhappy about the prospect of these freight cars and their loads occupying those downtown streets between the B. C. Electric's two Vancouver depots.

As preparations for the new Steveston and Kitsilano lines had been at their height, Buntzen had left for London to become chairman of the board of directors of the B. C. Electric, turning the role of general manager over to Rochfort Henry Sperling, effective July 1. And on June 10 the Coquitlam tunnel between Lakes Buntzen and Coquitlam had been opened for water; it had been christened on May 6, the miniature electric locomotive used for the construction of the tunnel pulling three cars "decorated with flowers and bunting, and brightly illuminated with incandescent lights" through the nine by nine-foot tunnel from west to east, the guests having reached the tunnel's entrance via Indian Arm and boat across Lake Buntzen.

The only street car line activity during 1905 in the Vancouver system, outside of the Kitsilano line addition, was the double tracking of Hastings from Gore to Jackson Avenue. Grandview district, that area bisected by the New Westminster interurban's passage on Commercial Drive, was beginning to be attractive to home builders and real estate speculators. Agitation for a street car service from downtown Vancouver through Grandview and out to Cedar Cottage on the interurban line's track had already begun in earnest.

Twenty-six street cars (including the first three, 72, 74, and 75, of a new series of large, double trucked street cars being built at New Westminster) furnished regular service on the Vancouver system in 1905, six on Robson, going as far as Broadway and Main; six on Davie, running south to Sixteenth and Main; six on Fairview, from Cambie and Cordova along Granville and east on Broadway to Main; five on Powell Street-Stanley Park; two of the smallest on Kitsilano; and one from Sixteenth and Main to Thirty-third and Fraser, surmounting the top of a considerable bank (later cut level) within a block of reaching Fraser Street. This, the car to the cemetery, called at houses, an obvious expediency since hardly any streets were open in this still remote suburb-to-be.

New Westminster

New Westminster celebrated 1905 by erecting imposing new exhibition buildings at Queen's Park, and the B. C. Electric continued in the throes of its $25,000 program of replacing original track, a five-year effort to be brought to completion in 1907.

North Vancouver

The municipality of North Vancouver had lain tilted up and against steeply rising mountains, almost two miles across Burrard Inlet from Vancouver, since its incorporation in 1891. Moodyville and its sawmill, situated at the foot of Moody Avenue in North Vancouver, had in fact been in 1862 the very first settlement and the first industry on Burrard Inlet. To it had operated the first cross-inlet ferry in 1866 from Gastown on the south shore, the precursor of Vancouver. By 1905,

Lonsdale Avenue, an imposing, precipitous, messy main street somewhat over half a mile west of Moodyville, had firmly established itself not only at inlet's edge as the ferry terminus, but also as the commercial centre and forest-penetrating north-south life line of a municipality still languishing, with a population of about 1,500.

On August 16, the B. C. Electric officially completed negotiations with the municipality for a franchise to operate a five-mile street car system as well as electric lighting and power. Scarcely three months earlier Buntzen had written North Vancouver's municipal council to express interest in doing just that, and Sperling, his successor, had quickly completed all arrangements with the council by August 9. Power would be brought across the inlet at its tightest point, Second Narrows — almost three miles east of Lonsdale — on giant masts, 215 feet high, hewn from North Vancouver's forests.

Within a few weeks, company surveyor Jorgensen and his party of men were hard at work defining the route of the street car line from the ferry wharf up Lonsdale to Twenty-first Street. Here the five-acre park of the local horticultural society (today's lawn bowling green) was also being surveyed, as the B. C. Electric had agreed to clear and fence the park in preparation for the society's next annual exhibition.

On December 12, the *Vancouver Daily Province* reported comprehensively on the progress of the new North Vancouver system.

"The facilities for getting about in North Vancouver will be greatly increased by the electric cars which will be running early in the coming summer, not only furnishing intercity means of transit but acting as a feeder to the ferry.

The plans submitted by Mr. R. H. Sperling, general manager of the British Columbia Electric Railway Company, to the Municipal Council last night show the proposed route, the main line being straight up Lonsdale avenue to Twenty-first street, the site of the proposed recreation park and for the present the terminus of the line. A branch from this main line westward will pass along Third street, crossing the reserve if the necessary permission can be secured. That obtained, the Keith road would be taken and its course followed to Capilano Canyon.

The eastward branch, with Moodyville as the general objective point, will traverse Third street to St. David's road, St. David's road to Fourth street, and along Fourth street to Queensberry [sic] avenue. Originally five miles was the distance contracted for, terminating at the Bauer estate.

The Queensberry avenue speedway project had caused the people of the city to ask for an extension as far as Fifteenth street, making a little more than six miles of rails. After discussing the matter, Twelfth street was suggested by Mr.

These four rare early passes show the Lulu Island branch in its first B.C. Electric year, as well as the shuffle in the general manager's chair from Buntzen to Sperling. (Norman W. Williams collection)

Sperling as the extent of the line on Queensberry avenue making about the six miles mentioned. This suggestion will be dealt with at the next regular meeting of the Council. The change is the only one from the original plan, and may lead to the speedway being shortened to reach Twelfth street instead of Fifteenth, as originally planned.

According to the terms of the agreement between the British Columbia Electric Railway Company and the North Vancouver municipality, the company is to maintain a half-hourly schedule both on the Lonsdale avenue and the Capilano Canyon-Moodyville lines in the summer and hourly during the winter months. When the cars start running about next June they will be run on the half-hourly schedule, although it is confidently expected that in a short time a fifteen or twenty minute schedule will have to be adopted on the Capilano line during the summer months to accommodate the heavy tourist travel which will undoubtedly patronize that line. The many splendid scenic advantages possessed by the Capilano Canyon, together with the popularity of that stream as an angler's resort will make the new line extremely popular.

In the easterly direction the general opinion among the Councillors was that the extension in that direction was the best possible, as it would afford rapid communication with the ferry and Vancouver city to the residents of Moodyville.

Regarding street lights, Mr. Sperling asked the Municipal Council to submit a list of the lights desired, and their location. Work is to be commenced as early as possible in the spring both on the tramway and the construction of the light and power lines.

The visitor from week to week cannot help being struck with the evidence of improvement; new buildings, sidewalks, roads, etc. being seen on every hand.

For the B. C. Electric in Victoria, 1906 meant the opening of the company's new head office building on July 26; four months of work (tenders had been called as recently as early March) and $15,000 had produced the attractive and spacious structure the company had so long desired.

In March, two of the newly-built, double trucked "70" series street cars, 70 and 71, arrived in Victoria from the company's New Westminster shops, with six more for Victoria under construction. Former Vancouver cars 33 and 34 entered service in December. Starting in 1906 a regular feature of the street car scene in Victoria was the sight of gravel cars being hauled from the pits at Spring Ridge to fill in James Bay for the construction of the Rattenbury-designed C.P.R. Empress Hotel. In the same year the regions west and north, Oak Bay and Saanich, were incorporated as municipalities, recognition that current growth was a portent of even greater expansion to come.

On British Columbia's lower mainland, 1906 opened with arguments in North Vancouver about the proposed street car routing, particularly

Car 59 in New Westminster on Sixth Street at Cliff's Can Factory. (B.C. Hydro)

that of the Capilano line. Many favoured a belt line which would run west from Lonsdale to Forbes Avenue, north to Fifteenth Street, and east to the Lonsdale line. Many felt strongly that the east-running Lynn Valley line should also be belted, and also come back, west to Lonsdale along Fifteenth.

The east-west route for the lines branching off Lonsdale in either direction was equally contentious. The company initially favoured Third Street, but over two hundred property owners petitioned for First Street, because it was then a significant business street and was closer to the wharves. Throughout all the debates in council meetings, in the press, and in the barber shops, Sperling was the soul of patience and tolerance.

On January 11 grading began on Lonsdale and east on First Street, as well as at the car barn and substation site. Concurrently, a decision was made to distribute the 400 tons of rail along the route rather than storing them at the wharf a block east of Lonsdale.

The giant lumber mill having opened at Fraser Mills (Millside then), east along the Fraser River from New Westminster, there was much agitation for the C.P.R. to electrify its line at least as far as the mill. Understandably New Westminster's mayor Keary was in the forefront of these urgings.

The B. C. Electric's car building shops announced their program for the year, which included 18 to 20 new cars, of which eight would be double-truck modified Narragansett type, semi-convertible street cars, open in summer, closed in winter, and handsomely finished in rosewood, ash, and maple. Two more large interurbans were planned (only "Coquitlam" — later 1209, 1500, and 1312 — was completed during the year), as were four twenty-foot single truck street cars, as well as the cars planned for Victoria, and a work car and several dump cars for North Vancouver. In addition, former Westminster & Vancouver Tramway cars 37 (originally 13, then "Richmond") and 39 (17, then "Burnaby") were to be partially rebuilt to bring them into better conformity with Vancouver's city street cars: cross seats would replace the two long side seats, and new, larger vestibules would be created.

If there was agitation for transit to Millside, an even greater commotion was set up all through January and February by residents of Port Moody who demanded the B. C. Electric build a street car line north from the end of its Sapperton Extension on North Road to Port Moody, a distance of some five miles. The residents of North Road were every bit as anxious for street cars as Port Moody's citizens, who had a petition circulating before the end of January.

Optimism was rife, times were good, everything seemed possible, and promoters with brain-popping schemes were abroad. (For example, a Vancouver businessman, J. A. Moore, announced in February that an electric railway would be constructed between Vancouver and Portland, Oregon via Bellingham, Everett, and Seattle — close to 350 miles!)

Prosperity brought with it more movement of people and more traffic, and in February C.P.R. general superintendent Richard Marpole (in just a few years to be geographically enshrined in place of Eburne) ordered protection gates for the C.P.R.'s level crossing of Hastings Street, just west of the company head office. Heavier traffic invariably breeds regulations, and the provincial legislature provoked the anger of the company by its proposed legislation to prohibit open street cars. Sperling retorted that ninety percent of the citizens would oppose such a move, and that open cars handled crowds with greater simplicity and dispatch; in addition, if safety was an issue, the company felt it had been taking good care of that by giving all its new street cars centre aisles and attendant cross seats.

By early March a new, four-block-long Vancouver street car line to Recreation Park was virtually complete, running from Robson and Granville, east on Robson to Homer Street, and south to Smithe Street, where a long siding was being installed opposite the entrance of the park. Before the month was out the company announced its intention to build a new street car barn on Main Street at Thirteenth Avenue, more than a mile north of its present overloaded barn at Prior Street. To that end, the company purchased sixteen adjacent lots in April for $9,750.

In New Westminster the company's abortive postfire depot at Columbia and Begbie streets was finally sold, and in March its car shops announced that special street cars similar to the "60" series, but with more powerful motors and better brakes for coping with the eight percent grade on Lonsdale, were being built for the North Vancouver system.

On June 26 an event transpired which would henceforth dictate and define the development of the whole lower mainland (that splendid Fraser River delta region of the province between the Pacific Ocean at Vancouver and Steveston, and the narrowing of the mountains a hundred miles to the east): the incorporation of the B. C. Electric-controlled Vancouver, Fraser Valley, and Southern Railway Company. Its Dominion of Canada charter empowered it, among other

Running orders despatched in Steveston in 1906 communicate simply and directly to the crew of car "Eburne" (later 1206). Ten months previously "Eburne" had been the first interurban coach out to Steveston. (Bob Webster collection)

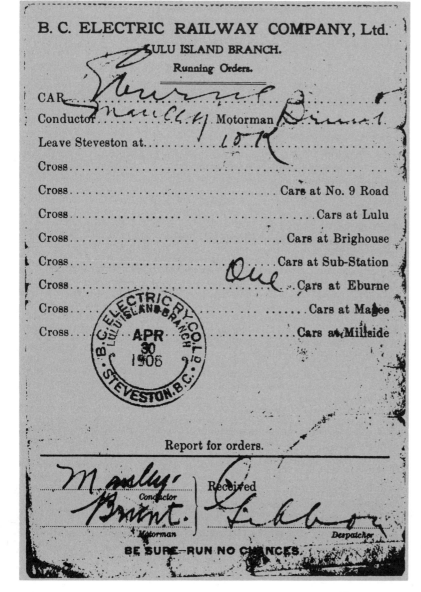

things, to build a railway line to Chilliwack, an imperative especially now that the Great Northern Railway (in the guise of the Vancouver, Victoria and Eastern Railway) was driving through its new 29-mile line. Operational in 1908, from Cloverdale it would extend eastward through Aldergrove and Abbotsford to Huntingdon at the U. S. Border; the V. V. and E. was very definite about a new line eastward from Abbotsford to Chilliwack and beyond. Within three weeks of incorporation came the word from the B. C. Electric that preliminary surveys for the new interurban line to Chilliwack would begin shortly.

On August 15 electric lights lit up North Vancouver for the very first time, and Saturday, September 1, was street car day. For the beginning of service, cars 14, 16, 24, 25, 26, 60 and locomotive 915 (later S. 62) were floated by scow across the inlet — although not all of them had arrived by Saturday — and unloaded just east of the foot of Lonsdale at Wallace Shipyards, connected by a spur line to the street car line at Esplanade. (This spur served as a storage place for the street cars until the car barn at Third and St. David's Avenue was ready.) At the northeast corner of Lonsdale and Esplanade (the road east to Moodyville) the company's first modest, wood-frame office already stood.

Only the Lonsdale line was ready, and only about three-quarters of a mile of it up the hill to Twelfth Street, but service commenced on this short run. At 6 a.m. on Saturday morning motorman Bert Giffen, with conductor W. D. Jones, wheeled out number 14, the first car in Vancouver sixteen years earlier, and proceeded up the big hill for the first time, picking up the first paying rider in North Vancouver, Charles Musson. Coming back down the hill, the car when it

reached Sixth Street exceeded the clause in the franchise agreement which stated: "The speed of cars shall not exceed ten miles an hour." Since another street car had been set at the foot of the line, it acted as a shock absorber, saving number 14 from a dunking in Burrard Inlet. The resultant damage was covered up by a large Union Jack, and the service continued without interruption until evening, when another derailment took place, due to the car overrunning some ties placed at the ferry wharf end of the line. The first day's trips had attracted 408 riders.

Two days later was Labour Day, September 3, a fitting day for a more festive beginning, and all the cars had arrived by then. Car 25 was the first car up, and on its way down it emulated car 14, as a *Province* reporter related. "The car coming down the hill struck a place where the rails were slippery from the morning dews, and skidded along although the wheels were tightly locked by the brakes. Sand had been applied to the rails at the point, but as the rails are elevated had fallen to the side. The runaway was going at two miles per hour, but bumped into a sister car standing at the foot of the hill with sufficient force to put the vestibule out of business." Once the seemingly obligatory first trip pile-up was out of the way, everything worked smoothly, 2,047 riders enjoying a new kind of Labour Day.

On Friday, a night shift was added, and on the Monday following, September 10, the westbound line, which later grew to become the Capilano line, began operating from the foot of Lonsdale to First Street, west to Mahon Avenue, north to Keith Road, and west almost to Fell Avenue, 1.45 miles in all. Motorman Walter Haig and conductor Dick Fawcett guided the first car. This track had actually been in use for some time, but only by gravel cars

Convertible street car 25, its entire right side opened for easy rider access, prepares for an opening day run up — and down — North Vancouver's precipitous Lonsdale Avenue. The crew appears to be awaiting a few more riders from a docking ferry. The background reveals B.C. Electric's first North Vancouver office (with the "Pedro" ad), a street car on the temporary spur to the barge landing, and the planked Esplanade to Moodyville. (B.C. Hydro)

Broadway and Main Street, the heart of Mount Pleasant, in 1907, car 51 swinging westward onto Broadway and car 86 about to turn onto Broadway East. The downhill to downtown on Main is evident in the right background. (Vancouver Public Library)

By 1907, "Resident Director" was no longer a feature of company passes. (Norman W. Williams collection)

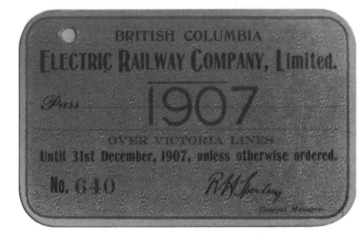

being hauled with ballast from Keith Road hill to other areas of the new system.

By the end of October the line on Lonsdale Avenue was in operation to Twenty-first Street (1.41 miles), and the eastbound line which eventually would run into Lynn Valley was operating from the ferry wharf to First Street, east to St. David's Street, north to Fourth Street, east to Queensbury Avenue, and north to Nineteenth Street, the top of Grand Boulevard, a run of 2.45 miles. Before year's end the car barn along this line was ready to shelter North Vancouver's curious collection of street cars.

In mid-October the electors of Chilliwack turned out to give their verdict to the B. C. Electric's interurban intentions, and returning officers announced 260 voters in favour, and 39 against, the minority apparently expressing its opposition to the operating of interurbans on Sundays.

Before the year was out, it was clear that the interurban line from Vancouver to Steveston (which in 1906 claimed a population of 10,000, and boasted of eight-foot-wide boardwalks, a big, colourful Chinatown, and an opera house) would acquire a logical connecting line between Eburne and New Westminster. As part of the V. & L. I. agreement, the C.P.R. would build it, and the B. C. Electric would operate it, and to that end C.P.R. surveyors commenced taking levels for the new line on the morning of December 13.

By the end of the year, the Vancouver street car system had placed two new services into operation, one on a completely new 1.62-mile line which ran east from Main and Georgia Street (Harris then) to Vernon Drive, north to Frances Street, and east to Victoria Drive; one car gave twenty-minute service. Double tracking of the interurban line from Hastings at Jackson Avenue right through to Cedar Cottage was completed during the year, and a street car service to this growing Grandview district was inaugurated, running from Hastings and Main to First Avenue and Commercial Drive. Double tracking had in

What a line-up! From left at the north end of Kitsilano trestle one street car, three name interurban coaches, freight car 102 (later 1802, Stave Falls line), and freight motor (locomotive) 101. (B.C. Hydro)

fact proceeded beyond Cedar Cottage as the company made it clear that this key interurban operation, to keep pace with settlement, needed two tracks. In Vancouver, Main Street from Broadway to Sixteenth Avenue had also been double tracked, and nine of the "70" series street cars had appeared on Vancouver's street car lines during 1906.

For Victorians 1907 brought a raging fire on the third of July, which destroyed the block bounded by Store, Herald, Government, and Chatham streets (a block from the car barn), ruining the homes of 250 families. Two visible improvements characterized the company's 1907 year in Victoria: an $8,000, Rattenbury-designed, 60-by-120-foot car barn addition containing paint shops, storage tanks, etc.; and the double-tracking of two blocks of Douglas Street, from Pandora Avenue to Fisgard Street. Former Vancouver street cars, 35 and 36, had gone into service in April, the larger 73 in May. The year ended with another spectacular fire, this one destroying the resplendent exhibition buildings at the Willows on December 27.

On the lower mainland, 1907 began on an exhilarating note as the company signed an agreement with the provincial government on January 10 for running rights on the Fraser River bridge at New Westminster. The B. C. Electric was given permission to connect its tracks to those

already on the bridge, bond the rails, "and to erect on the bridge and its approaches overhead trolley wires, telephones and telegraph wires and all other light and power wires, or cables, necessary for the operation of its system on the South side of the Fraser River."

In North Vancouver, the street car system was still growing: the municipal council gave permission to the company on February 18 to extend its westward line one-third of a mile farther along Marine Drive from Fell to Mackay Avenue, which it did, simultaneously installing a passing siding at Bewicke Avenue.

In New Westminster the Sapperton Extension was continued three blocks north from the Royal Columbian Hospital to Braid Street (Distillery Road then) after a spate of wrangling between the company and city council in March. The council was dissatisfied with what it felt was poor service and poor street cars; the company said it would put in the new track as soon as the city improved the quality of the street, and would indeed willingly supply a twenty-minute service throughout the city. That solved, the company's Junction station at the confluence of the Vancouver road (Kingsway-Twelfth Street) and Edmonds Street was happily dignified by an appropriate name change to Edmonds.

In March location surveys were completed for the new nine and a half-mile Eburne-New

The ferry landing at the foot of Lonsdale Avenue, North Vancouver, with a view to Vancouver across Burrard Inlet. (North Shore Archives)

Alex Turner poses by Sapperton car "Gladstone" (the name is faintly visible on the side of the car), briefly number 21 in Victoria and destroyed in a 1908 wreck. (Geoff Meugens collection)

Westminster interurban line, and in April the company got into the wharf business in New Westminster, a superb idea at the time in view of its burgeoning freight aspirations, fueled by the prospect of the new lines to Eburne and Chilliwack. The B. C. Electric purchased from Gilley Bros. the lessee's rights to the lease of four adjacent water lots at the foot of Eighth Street, together with the wharves and buildings already constructed, for $35,000, plus an annual rental fee of $600 for the first five years, subsequent rentals to be arranged.

Two of the big interurban cars were outshop-ped in New Westminster in 1907, "Chilliwack" (later 1210, then 1602) and "Sumas" (later 1216, 1501, and 1216 again). The same year two "steeple-cab" locomotives — not "freight cars", but recognizable locomotives — numbered 900 and 901 were ready for action.

On June 1 the most heavily populated area of North Vancouver municipality, the townsite clustered around Lonsdale and the ferry wharf, broke away from the municipality and became the city of North Vancouver, a move contemplated for some time. Its new council met for the first time on the tenth of the month.

On July 16 the C.P.R. awarded the contract for constructing the Eburne-New Westminster line to J. B. Bright, and on August 1 grading operations commenced along the north arm of the Fraser River near Boundary Road. (December completion was unrealistically mooted.)

Later that same month, on August 26, B. C. Electric general manager Sperling, with accompanying officials, turned the first sod for the Chilliwack line at Scott Road, two miles east of the New Westminster depot. Sperling had stated three weeks earlier that the company had completed all its agreements, including the right to use roads where desired or convenient, with the six municipalities through which the line would pass — Surrey, Delta, Langley, Matsqui, Sumas, Chilliwhack — and that as soon as the directors in London gave their approval, tenders for grading

S S CAMP

the line would be called. The B. C. Electric estimated that the "New Westminster-Chilliwack Railway" would cost $2,500,000 and would take two years to build. On November 21, the B. C. Electric purchased, for $1,500, the shares of the Vancouver, Fraser Valley and Southern Railway Company. When the *Province* announced two days later that the B. C. Electric was thinking of building an interurban line to the U. S. border at Blaine, Washington, it seemed merely to be acknowledging that the charter of the V., F. V., & S. also empowered it to build "to United States Boundary at or near Douglas," the Canadian side at Blaine.

In North Vancouver number 915, somewhat of a smaller prototype for the new 900 and 901, was finding enough to do, functioning as work car, wrecking car, snow plow, and especially as locomotive when the occasion arose for it to haul logs from the Capilano line up to the new Diplock-Wright Western Corporation sawmill at Seventeenth Street and Sutherland Avenue, just a block east of Grand Boulevard. It was in fact involved in the first accident of the dunking-in-Burrard Inlet variety when it attempted to haul from the wharf a flat car loaded with motors destined for the mill; near Second Street it was evident that wheel slippage exceeded forward

motion, with the result that flat car and motors fully engaged the waters of the inlet, number 915 barely escaping, hanging precariously onto land.

As one may well expect, the B. C. Electric, appreciating that the cable car steepness of Lonsdale was to be its primary operating worry in North Vancouver, soon installed a heavily sand-covered safety switch between Second and Third Streets which was always open (to the west) for every downhill bound Lonsdale street car to enter. To avoid running onto the car-stopping safety switch, a street car had to stop dead at Third for the conductor to throw the spring switch to allow the car to proceed to the ferry wharf. (Not surprisingly then, the Lonsdale line street cars remained two-man vehicles right to the end despite the fact that Capilano and Lynn Valley eventually became one man street car lines.)

With an eye to the impending extension of the westward line to the Capilano River, and to make provision for recreation at the new terminus, the B. C. Electric purchased 160 acres of Capilano Canyon between the first and second canyons (today's suspension bridge and Cleveland Dam) for purposes of park development.

In Vancouver the year's new line involved Broadway, double tracked 2,810 feet east from Main to Fraser Street (Scott then). The Robson

Four street cars press up Lonsdale Avenue, away from the ferry wharf, the car at far left already making the turn onto the Lynn Valley line. (North Shore Archives)

Locomotive 915 has just lost its load to Burrard Inlet at the foot of Lonsdale Avenue in North Vancouver. (North Shore Archives)

A transfer ticket from September 1908. (Bob Webster collection)

creating a two-barn system, which could give substantially better service to its street cars, its employees, and its customers. After all, only 175 automobiles were registered in all of British Columbia in 1907!

Nonetheless there was bound to be an encounter between a street car and an automobile. It happened, for the first time, in Victoria, at the corner of Douglas and Yates in January 1908; the Outer Wharf street car involved survived, as happily did the passengers in both vehicles.

Street car ridership would show a year-long increase in 1908 over that of 1907: in January 326,200 fares were collected, in contrast to 271,866 in the same month a year previous. In the peak month of July, 89,224 more passengers used the street car service than did in July 1907! On January 20 the inner harbour area of Victoria took a major step closer to acquiring the delightfully harmonious aspect so well known today, particularly by ocean-arriving travellers and tourists, with the opening of the C. P. R.'s magnificent Empress Hotel, designed by Rattenbury, on the now-filled backwater formerly known as James Bay.

Though the city of Victoria had appeared to interest itself during 1908 in becoming the B. C. Electric's competitor in the development of electric power, nothing came of the idea as the company agreed to spend $35,000 in extending its Cook Street line east to the cemetery. It also went

line began operating from this new point, arriving at English Bay via Robson Street and returning along Davie; the Davie line from Main and Sixteenth Avenue ran its English Bay route in the reverse direction, almost creating a mini-belt line.

By 1907 the Vancouver system had more street cars than the Prior Street facilities could house, including more of the "70" series during the year, with the result that cars which could not be packed in were parked overnight on Main Street itself. That year the new twin-gabled, wooden, Mount Pleasant barn was opened at the southwest corner of Main Street and Thirteenth Avenue,

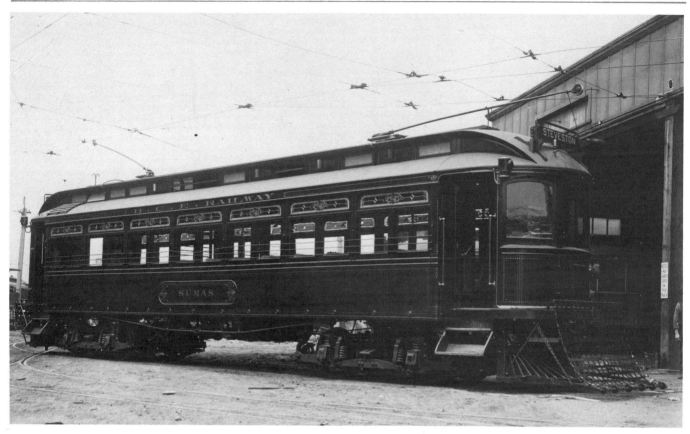

B.C. Electric car building at its finest, "Sumas" (later 1501 and 1216), dark green and near new, displays a wealth of exquisite detail, including electric marker lamps. (B.C. Hydro)

ahead with plans for building a 1,683-foot line from Fort Street north to Mayfair Drive, to the gravel pits of the Lineham-Scott Sand and Gravel Company at Mount Tolmie. When city council insisted that the company was legally prevented from operating freight movements over city streets, it needed only a perusal of the original charter of November 1888 for everyone to realize that the company indeed had the right to haul freight, and that the B. C. Electric probably hadn't needed to threaten the city with non-construction of the cemetery line if the company didn't have its way with its desired Mount Tolmie gravel pit extension.

By the end of the year both lines were under construction and the spending of $50,000 on new street cars was announced. (Cars 75 and 107 did arrive during the year.) The fare was five cents (6 for 25¢, and 25 for $1); tickets for use during non-rush times on weekdays were 8 for 25¢, and weekday-only tickets for students were 10 for 25¢. The special tickets for the long run out to — or in from — Esquimalt sold at 5 for 25¢, or ten cents each.

In the lower mainland 1908 was marked on January 1 by the creation of the municipality of Point Grey, the area south and west of Vancouver from the boundary at Sixteenth Avenue south along Cambie to 59th Avenue, west to Ash Street, and south to the Fraaser River. The municipality of South Vancouver lost more than half of its area through this massive break-away action,

stimulated by many of those now resident in the new municipality and by the Canadian Pacific Railway. Anxious to develop a high-lying portion of its land holdings there into a new elite area — to be named Shaughnessy Heights after Lord Shaughnessy, president of the C.P.R. — it wished to do so in a climate and setting over which it had more control potential. Vancouver's west end, effectively served by the B. C. Electric's Davie and Robson street car lines, was about to lose its status as the residential area of the rich and powerful. Land clearing began immediately, following Richard Marpole's blueprints for this luxury subdivision which would lie between Fifteenth · and Forty-first avenues, and Arbutus and Oak streets.

At this time Vancouver's struggling suburb, Fairview, was finally coming into its own. Vancouver General Hospital, a block north of Broadway at Heather Street, had recently been opened; Fairview's streets had been greatly improved, and more and more houses were filling every available lot and corner; and the B. C. Electric had just completed the double-tracking of Broadway from Granville to Main streets, as well as Granville from the bridge at False Creek to Broadway.

The completion of this track program set the stage for a new type of operation for the Fairview line. The pattern of running street cars in both directions from a terminus, Broadway and Main, was jettisoned in mid-January in favour of "belt" running, cars operating continuously — without switching ends — on each belt, along Main, Hastings, Granville, and Broadway, delivering twenty-minute regular service, and ten-minute rush hour service when four cars were employed on each of the inner and outer belts.

The middle of January meant the end of the "cemetery" street car, but only in the sense of a name change. A petition generated by one Reverend Ebenezer Robson indicated resident unhappiness with riding a street car labelled "cemetery." Renaming the car "Mountain View" (the name of the cemetery) seemed successfully to eradicate reflections about man's inevitable end.

Hastings Street moved even more aggressively forward as Vancouver's leading shopping street with the opening at Richards Street of the nine-storey department store of David Spencer (later Eaton's, today Sears). Competition with Woodward's, just three blocks east, was high, and a Spencer's advertisement appeared on January 16 in local newspapers announcing a special interurban car from New Westminster to bring shoppers to its "white-wear" sale. It was during the same month that the B. C. Electric began making serious noises about double tracking the New Westminster-Vancouver interurban line in its entirety.

In early April the company let it be known for the first time that it could become interested in extending its eastern line in North Vancouver beyond Nineteenth and Grand Boulevard into Lynn Valley, but as a logging railway, not a passenger line, at least for the time being. During the same month, Chilliwackers, anxious for the coming interurban line, but really quite as desirous of better quality electric lighting, elicited through the leadership of Mayor Cawley and his council the promise from the B. C. Electric of a temporary, wood-fired steam plant. For Chilliwack, 1908, its year of incorporation, meant an acceleration in dreams as never before.

As can be imagined, the company's frustrations in regard to the antiquated Granville Street

The original freight shed and depot at Steveston. The softness of the land required bracing between the power poles that supported the trolley wires. (B.C. Hydro)

crossing of False Creek, especially in view of the extraordinary growth of Fairview and its new belt line operation, were reaching rather dire proportions. This was alleviated to a great degree on May 18 when acting general manager F. R. Glover signed an agreement with the city of Vancouver for operating privileges over a new steel high level bridge immediately to the east of the old one. It would be double tracked, rental would be $4,000 per year, and freight was not to be countenanced on it. The company would be allowed to operate its interurban cars to Eburne and Steveston over the new bridge only with special, specific permission from the city, something the B. C. Electric might well become interested in requesting, especially since the grading of the new Eburne-New Westminster line was proceeding well, and track-laying had already begun.

May was the month of beginning for the Chilliwack line as tenders were called for construction of the first 13.5-mile section between New Westminster and the Great Northern town of Cloverdale. A chartered freighter was soon steaming from Liverpool, England across the Atlantic and around the toe of South America with seventy-pound rail from Dick-Kerr and Company Limited, the same organization that would build the B. C. Electric's first three heavy, railway-type, electric locomotives. In neighbouring Washington state, the Nooksack Valley Traction Company was organized with the aim of constructing interurban lines from Bellingham north to Canada at Blaine and Sumas, connecting with the Chilliwack line. Unlike the B. C. Electric's, these plans failed.

Though the final route of the Chilliwack line had been chosen with an eye to achieving grades as favourable as possible, offers of free land, municipal bonuses of land, and locations — current and potential — for passengers and freight were considerations the company never let slip from view. By 1908 there still remained a devilishly difficult unsolved problem — the route to employ between Abbotsford and Chilliwack, a distance of some eighteen miles by crow. A shallow 30,000-acre lake between two 3,000-foot high mountains — with the Great Northern already committed to the nearer, northern lake-edge route hugging Sumas Mountain — lay in the new line's path. There had been forty years' talk of draining the lake, and during the year the B. C. Electric purchased the three-year-old Sumas Development Company which had been created for the express purpose of doing just that. In a flurry of excitement, advertisements were placed in some dailies in England in an attempt to lure settlers to farm the reclaimed lake bed, a superb idea — until the company figured out the reclamation costs. The B. C. Electric forgot about lake draining and decided in the late spring of

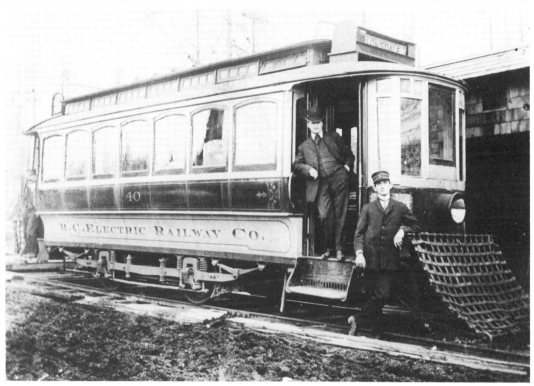

1909 to build south from Abbotsford to the United States border at Huntingdon, then eastward, just staying shy of the lake's lapping waters by clinging to Vedder Mountain and spending much money, time, and effort, and upkeep, on fill for this problematic section of right of way. (Huntingdon had been served by a C.P.R. line from Mission City through Abbotsford since 1891, the same year the adjacent U. S. town of Sumas had been reached by the Seattle, Lake Shore & Eastern and the Bellingham Bay & British Columbia, later Northern Pacific and Milwaukee Road, respectively.)

In June 1908 the company announced its intention to double track the Vancouver (Granville station) to Eburne interurban line, and on the Chilliwack line, the contract for the second section of grading, the twenty-six miles from Cloverdale to Abbotsford, was awarded to contractors Ironsides, Rannie, and Campbell, with completion on June 1, 1909 as the target. Robert Howes was the superintendent of construction for both sections.

Before October was out the New Westminster car shops had completed four more of the big interurban cars, three of them with names one would expect an owner building a Fraser Valley line to Chilliwack to bestow, "Cloverdale" (later 1211), "Abbotsford" (later 1212), and "Sardis" (later 1214, then 1600). The fourth, "Ladner" (later 1603, then 1322), is a reminder of a projected idea, unfulfilled.

A B. C. Electric transmission line crossing the wide mouth of the Fraser River between the Steveston side and Ladner had been completed late in 1906, spanning the river on what were reputed to be the highest transmission line towers in the world (wooden ones at that), two of them over 320 feet high, one 280 feet, and the other 260 feet, with a span between each of 2,000 feet, carrying the cables 165 feet at the lowest point above high water. The company already had purchased four acres of property in Ladner for an interurban railway line terminus and had planned a bridge across the Fraser, but a line was never built, the town being left to the Great Northern Railway. However, the company did announce at this time that plans were under way for a new terminus in Vancouver, a central passenger station and office building on the site of the current structure of the same description, Hastings at Carrall Street.

October 15 was a day of significance for the Chilliwack line, but not just as the deadline for tenders for supplying fir ties for the more than fifty miles of track beyond Cloverdale to Chilliwack. Two thousand tons of rail for the New Westminster to Cloverdale section (ties had already been distributed along the grade) arrived in New Westminster on that day. A crane had been rigged on the B. C. Electric's wharf to unload the rails from the large ocean-going scow and the several smaller scows which had been floated by two tugs from Vancouver, where the steel had arrived earlier in the month by Blue Funnel Line freighter. With grading to Cloverdale ready from the Fraser River bridge, the laying of rail awaited only the completion of the long, wooden trestle approach to the east end of the Fraser's crossing.

Shortly before midnight on Saturday, Novem-

Rebuilding and double tracking of the Tramway line is well underway in this 1908 photo, as one of the name interurban coaches, "Central Park & Way Points," stays deftly out of trouble. (B.C. Transit)

ber 7, tragedy came forcefully to the New Westminster-Vancouver interurban line just west of Beaconsfield station. The fast-moving, two-months-old "Ladner" westbound, utterly demolished the smaller, New Westminster-bound "Gladstone" in dense fog, the result of the Cedar Cottage switchman's error. Motormen Murdoch Macdonald and Ralph A. Jamieson, of "Ladner" and "Gladstone," respectively, died in the wreck. Seventeen passengers were hospitalized and several more suffered minor injuries.

Not much grading work had been accomplished during the year on the new Eburne-New Westminster interurban line, but efforts were renewed more intensively in mid-November, even a start to track-laying from New Westminster.

On December 1 rails were delivered on the south side of the Fraser River at New Westminster and at Cloverdale, allowing two track gangs to be at work on the Chilliwack line. By this time surveys were already complete for the line's entry into New Westminster from the bridge along river-hugging Front Street, one block below Columbia Street.

A. G. Perry, arriving in North Vancouver on December 2 to become the manager of that little operation, reminisced some years later about that day, on which he found "a street railway 'system'

with five miles of track, three wee, dinky cars operating a half-hour service, and to celebrate my coming we carried 706 passengers that day." During the year the Lonsdale line had been extended a quarter mile to Twenty-fifth Street, and a passing track had been set in place on Lonsdale between Fifteenth and Sixteenth streets.

On December 16, the company made a franchise agreement with the provincial government for constructing and operating lines in two of the five adjacent "Vancouver" areas not yet part of Vancouver: Burnaby; Point Grey; South Vancouver; 2,950-acre Hastings Townsite, lying between the harbour and Twenty-ninth Avenue (the northern edge of Collingwood), and Nanaimo Street and Boundary Road; and the little, 350-acre rectangle of District Lot 301, bordered by Main Street, Sixteenth Avenue, Prince Edward Street, Knight Road, and Twenty-fifth Avenue. Both Fraser Street and Kingsway, prime candidates for next year's new street car lines, passed through D. L. 301.

No new street car lines were laid in Vancouver during 1908, although double tracking was accomplished on Georgia Street between Main and Vernon, and on Pender Street between Burrard and Georgia Street to the west; furthermore, the track layout at Stanley Park was rebuilt and refined. In addition to new, company-built street cars added during the year, a splendid set of ten, 150-159, had arrived from Brill.

Vancouver in 1908 had 228 miles of city streets, twelve miles of which were paved with wood blocks!

In New Westminster a new siding had been installed alongside Queen's Park on First Street, and the Royal City's street car system had been modernized at a stroke with the placing in service of ten large new street cars during the year, 100 to 106 and 108 to 110.

The pressure for more electric power had led the company to begin enlarging the Coquitlam tunnel and adding to its hydro-creating facilities at Coquitlam Lake. It now owned 138 street cars and interurbans and had transported 22,908,170 passengers and 37,859 tons of freight during the year. This was also the same year the provincial government had begun constructing a system of trunk roads suitable for automobile traffic.

In Vancouver in 1908, 48 street cars provided regular service on eight lines.

Fairview — inner belt	*7 cars on 6-minute headway*
Fairview — outer belt	*7 cars on 6-minute headway*
Main, 16th to English Bay via Davie	*8 cars on 8 minute headway*
Scott Street (Fraser) to English Bay via Robson	*8 cars on 8-minute headway*
Cedar Cottage to Robson Street	*4 cars on 15-minute headway*
Specials	*2 cars*
Stanley Park-Cedar Cove (Victoria Dr.)	*4 cars on 10-minute headway*
Kitsilano, Clark & Harris (Georgia St.)	*6 cars on 12-minute headway*
Mountain View	*2 cars on 10-minute headway*

TRY DUKE'S SMOKING MIXTURE — THE BEST TOBACCO IN THE MARKET.

It was a phenomenal decade of growth, the years from 1904 to 1913, and for Victoria 1909 was the beginning of the greatest real estate boom in its history. The B. C. Electric completed its new Mount Tolmie line as well as the desired gravel pit spur. In addition it opened the new two-mile extension west through the Fairfield district and past the cemetery at Ross Bay, running five blocks south on Cook Street from Pakington to May Street, and then on May and Fairfield Road to a loop at Foul Bay Road (107 was the first car). As well, a new double tracked line on Government Street running north from Johnson Street six blocks to the car barn had been laid, the single track on the one block of Government south to Yates double tracked in the process. The Oak Bay line was treated to double tracking from the city limits, Foul Bay Road, to Oak Bay's municipal hall at Hampshire Road, and a loop had been constructed at the Willows, spaciously utilizing Eastdowne Road (Willows Road then) and Fair

and Epworth streets.

In May new single trolleyed, single end street cars appeared on Victoria streets for the first time, ready to be employed on lines which ended in loops. Air brakes, an innovation as well, were installed on these new cars at the Pembroke barn, and what with their "Detroit" platforms — six and a half feet long and extraordinarily roomy, rattan seats, and gates (the increase in vehicular traffic was doing away with the time-honoured procedure of jumping on and off moving street cars), Victorians began travelling in a brand of style and comfort that cars 22 and 23 had only hinted at. The new cars, 50 and 117 to 123, necessitated changes in layout of downtown trackage to allow for one way running, adjustments which would be accomplished during the two years to come. Indeed, motormen were to have a respite; no more would passengers be allowed to ride in the front vestibule with them. An excellent public relations gambit was the

Car 20, comfortably stocked with golf clubs, looks very attractive at Oak Bay. Standing at far left is Frank Barnard, a company pioneer, with conductor R.A.C. Dewar. Motoneer Arthur Pugsley is surrounded by the company's Victoria manager, A.T. Goward, seated, and, standing, traffic superintendent H. Gibson. (B.C. Hydro)

Sightseeing car 123 enjoyed only a brief stay in Victoria. This photo captures 123 in 1909 at Government and Yates streets. (Victoria City Archives)

The Observation Car

Is the best and most satisfactory way of seeing this beautiful city

Esquimalt   The Gorge   Oak Bay

Making Two Trips Daily
Leaving the Cor. of Yates and Government Sts. at
9.15 a.m. and 2.15 p.m.

FARE 50 CENTS

British Columbia Electric Railway Company, Ltd.

Observation street car 123 went to work in 1909 for Victorians and their tourists, offering a graciously lingering approach to sightseeing the area. (B.C. Hydro)

elimination of the ten-cent fare to Esquimalt — five cents would now do the job.

In summer the New Westminster shops completed two superb observation cars, frankly patterned after those in use in Montreal, with seats so arranged that each was slightly elevated over the one in front, much on the same principle as seats are arranged in a theatre. Both were, of course, single end cars. Number 123 arrived in Victoria in time still to partake of the summer's tourist season (number 124 went to work in Vancouver), and immediately adopted a pattern of two three-hour trips daily. It ran at 9:40 a.m. and 2:40 p.m., from the corner of Government and Yates streets, first out to Esquimalt for a fifteen-minute visit, then to The Gorge for a twenty-minute stop (and walk), and finally all the way east to Oak Bay, with a ten-minute respite there. Who could possibly resist such a trip, especially for the fifty-cent fare!

The mouth of the Jordan River, 37 miles west of Victoria, was the scene during summer 1909 of feverish engineering activity which would culminate in Vancouver Island's largest electric power site, the B. C. Electric's Jordan River hydro-electric development. This project would require two very different — each unique — railway lines for construction and later maintenance purposes.

On the lower mainland 1909 was, as in Victoria, a year of massive activity and energetic accomplishments. On the Chilliwack line the town of Cloverdale became even more dependent on

the B. C. Electric with the opening of the Great Northern's new sea level line on January 27 between the south end of New Westminster bridge and the United States border; the historic eighteen-year-old main line through Cloverdale was obsolete, now only lightly used. Gone were the twice daily passenger trains between Vancouver and Seattle through Cloverdale. (Between Vancouver and Cloverdale, 29 miles, the southbound express took 66 minutes.)

In May Vancouver cars 40 and 42 had been barged across the inlet to North Vancouver for use there; and the laying of a new track had begun, from the Vancouver-Eburne interurban line eastward steeply up the middle of King Edward Avenue (Twenty-fifth) to Granville Street. Its purpose had nothing to do with transit; it was the supply route for the hauling of materials for the opening up of splendid Shaughnessy Heights subdivision. One of its major tasks entailed bringing gravel from the loading dock on the south shore line to the holding bunker at Granville and King Edward, a dangerous operation which resulted in frequent injuries, and even one loss of life. Gravel was loaded in small, four-wheeled cars, with link-and-pin couplers, which were shunted by locomotive 900 one at a time up to the bunker, at which point they were unloaded by placing a timber under a corner of each car body to cause it to tip its load.

It was at this time as well that rail renewal work was in full swing between Vancouver and Eburne.

Except on curves, 56-pound rail was being used. In addition, the old-fashioned stub switches were being removed all along the line (except on the south shore branch), and new spurs were installed westward to the brewery at Twelfth Avenue, and to the new race track on Lulu Island.

A new double-tracked line was opened for operation on May 13, laid on Cordova Street, west four blocks from Cambie Street to Granville Street (directly in front of the C.P.R. depot), and north one block to Hastings. The Powell Street (Cedar Cove)-Stanley Park line immediately laid claim to it (Powell having been double tracked its length east from Main Street to Victoria Road) and was followed on June 2 by the Davie Street operation.

On June 10, the company made a franchise agreement with the municipality of South Vancouver, giving the municipality the option of purchasing its street car lines at the end of forty years, and every ten years thereafter.

July saw the appearance of the sixteenth, and last, of the named interurban cars, "Matsqui," built as a motorless trailer and equipped with special drawbars similar to those of "Eburne" and "Steveston" for the purpose of being operated with them to form a three-car unit, B. C. Electric's first multiple-car train. The drawbars proving unsuccessful, a time-consuming annoyance, "Matsqui" was motorized and would become car 1215.

Since 1909 was to be the year of the P.A.Y.E. — pay-as-you-enter — street car in Vancouver, it came as no surprise when the company announced on July 18 that fourteen new P.A.Y.E. street cars had been ordered for the Fairview belt line.

North Vancouver's system suffered one of those foot-of-Lonsdale accidents on August 12 despite the fact that the end of track was actually a couple of hundred feet from wharf's edge. Lonsdale car 62, with conductor Jones and motorman John Kelly, ran away when its brakes failed. Kelly suffered a broken leg as he and two passengers jumped off the car, but Jones sustained no injury as he rode the car into Burrard Inlet.

On August 21 Richmond municipality celebrated the opening of Minoru Park (later known as Brighouse Park) race track, and what a money-maker (with its loop for the special interurban runs) it would be for the Lulu Island branch over the years! Named after King Edward's Epsom Derby winning horse, the track lured 7,000 people to it on this first day. Thereafter, interurban cars, as well as street cars, crammed to the sills, operated directly to the Lulu Island track from Granville station. The B. C. Electric was seeing only too clearly that its prize interurban cars would have to be rebuilt to allow for their use as components in two-, three-, or even four-car trains in multiple unit fashion. Meanwhile, the company also ran trains of benched — and fenced — flat cars pulled by electric locomotives, even the imposing, new Dick-Kerr motive power arriving for Chilliwack line work. Off-duty, cupola-topped, C.P.R. observation coaches made pilgrimages to Minoru behind Dick-Kerr power.

Vancouver's first P.A.Y.E. street cars went into service on August 29, the same month that the city officially renamed Ninth Avenue as the already widely accepted Broadway. But the big news was made on Labour Day, a sunny September 6, when

The July 27 timetable for the Vancouver-Eburne-Steveston interurban line, the Lulu Island branch, displayed the following stations and time frames.

Minutes from Steveston		Minutes from Vancouver
47	Vancouver	0
42	Millside	5
37	9th Avenue	10
32	Kerrisdale	16
30	Magee	18
25	Eburne	25
20	Tucks	28
18	Sub Station	31
16	Rifle Range	33
13	Brighouse	36
10	Lulu	38
7	No. 8 Road	40
4	No. 9 Road	43
0	Steveston	45

Half-hourly service was run on the Vancouver-Eburne section, hourly over the whole distance between Vancouver and Steveston. Since the company's interurban cars were not equipped to be coupled together, Vancouver-bound cars were double-headed on weekdays from Eburne at 7:55 and 8:55 a.m. and at 3:55, 5:55, and 6:55 p.m., and on Saturday and Sunday hourly from 7:55 p.m. to 11:55 p.m. (and on the half hour from Vancouver). On Sunday, thirteen trips were double headed from Steveston into Vancouver, twelve in the southbound direction.

Observation car 124 leads a parade of street cars in the opening ceremonies of Vancouver's new Granville Street Bridge. Earl Grey, Canada's governor general, stands tall behind the headlight, Lady Grey, and Vancouver's Major Douglas to his left. At far left is the head of the contracting firm that built the bridge, W. Armstrong. (B.C. Hydro)

the new half-million-dollar Granville Bridge was officially opened with much fanfare, and great relief. The first vehicle across, and back to the Hotel Vancouver, was observation car 124, beautifully decorated, filled with dignitaries, chiefly Mayor C. S. Douglas and Canada's Governor General, His Excellency Earl Grey, and Lady Grey, and piloted by motorman R. Piper and conductor J. McSavaney. Fairview cars obviously used the new swing span with relish, and developers and settlers had better reason than ever now to begin opening up the west side of Vancouver and Point Grey. New street car lines were on the way. Later in the same month, a new, steel, double-tracked, single-leaf bascule bridge was in place over the shallower, shorter crossing of False Creek at Main Street.

On August 24, the company announced that it had secured a terminal site at Huntingdon on its Chilliwack line. Less than two weeks later some settlers near Chilliwack chased B. C. Electric officials off the new railway right of way at gunpoint because of their alleged failure to pay the settlers for their land. By the end of September, track laying was complete from the Fraser River bridge to Cloverdale, and electrification of that

section immediately began, as well as track laying east from Cloverdale. On October 1 the first train, drawn by the company's 525, a Baldwin 2-6-0 steam locomotive purchased in May, operated from New Westminster with a load of lumber and construction materials. On October 30, electrification was sufficiently advanced on the Fraser River bridge to allow an electric locomotive over it and into Surrey municipality to help with construction work. (Two of the three steel locomotives ordered from Dick-Kerr in England had already arrived, a special wharf having been fashioned safely to unload them.)

New Westminster city gave the company permission on November 3 to construct a temporary track connection with the Chilliwack line, and to construct a temporary shed for use as a station at such time when the company would tear down the present station and commence building a new one. On the following day it was announced that six towers nearly 200 feet in height would be erected on the Fraser River bridge to carry the wires for electric power out with the Chilliwack line and to the Fraser Valley. Further, a contract was let to T. R. Nickson & Company for the construction of five reinforced

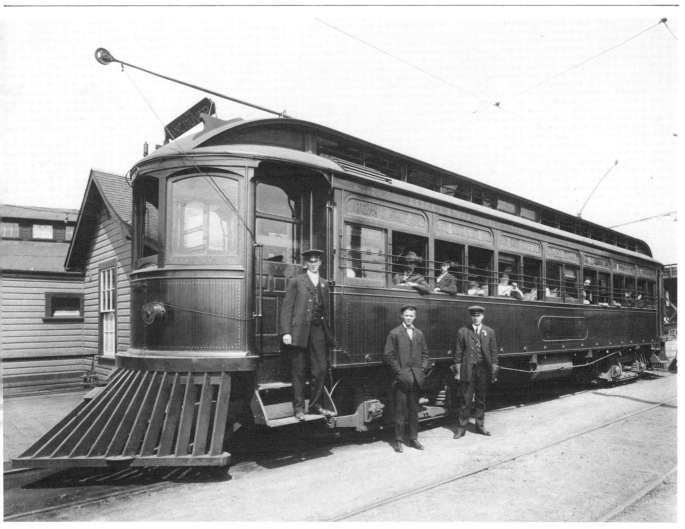

concrete substations, at a cost of over $25,000 each, at Cloverdale, Coghlan, Clayburn, Vedder Mountain, and Chilliwack. They would be linked together by two 34,600-volt, three-phase power circuits drawing power from Plant No. 1 at Lake Buntzen. On the main and second floors would be high-ceilinged switching rooms, with storage rooms in the basement and a self-contained suite on each side of the taller centre section.

On December 7 work was begun on track at Eighth Street in New Westminster for switching cars between the New Westminster-Vancouver line and the Chilliwack line. By the twentieth of the month, electrification of the line was complete to Cloverdale.

The new Eburne-New Westminster line had been ready on September 15, and exactly two months later, having been turned over to the B. C. Electric by the C.P.R. (since the new line was, of course, a part of the Vancouver & Lulu Island Railway), it began interurban and freight service under the aegis of the B. C. Electric Railway. The company had on October 26 negotiated a further agreement with the C.P.R. for a twenty-one-year term, renewable for a further twenty-one years, in respect to the Vancouver & Lulu Island Railway as

well as the Kitsilano line. In November a key railway connection was made between the south shore line of the Lulu Island branch and the Great Northern Railway's main line into Vancouver at a point just north of First Avenue and Quebec Street: this was the B. C. Electric's first flirtation with any railway other than with paternal Canadian Pacific.

The Eburne-New Westminster line unavoidably crossed through Burnaby on boggy, difficult-to-maintain land. Population, though initially almost nonexistent between the terminals, would be drawn over the years toward this "southern" line, and within a year an hourly passenger service, a milk train originating daily in Langley municipality, and a three-times-weekly freight service would use this level, fast-running connector. With the completion of the Chilliwack line, and the various steam railroad connections it would gather to itself, the New Westminster-Eburne-Vancouver route would afford the B. C. Electric important connections in Vancouver with national and international railways, something the old Tramway interurban line between New Westminster and Vancouver could never hope to do with its prohibitive grades and miles of street

At Granville (Street) station (the north end of Granville Street Bridge is visible at far right) in October 1909, car "Richmond" (later 1205) poses with (from left) conductor Frank Dumaresque, Jim Findlay, and begloved motorman George Boston prior to a journey to Steveston. (author's collection)

running.

And now there was to be yet another interurban line, also connecting Vancouver with New Westminster, but utilizing a route through central Burnaby, north of the original Tramway line. It would be built, as was the Chilliwack line, under the title of the Vancouver, Fraser Valley & Southern Railway, and would soon become known as the Burnaby Lake line, concurrently with the original New Westminster-Vancouver interurban line's designation as the Central Park line. With the promise of bonus land worth well over $100,000 to build the Burnaby Lake line, the company had little difficulty in perceiving this venture as real estate promotion.

By September 24 the B. C. Electric had located the new line through the western part of Burnaby, and on November 1 a gang of men got to work clearing land through Hastings Township for the line. (Burnaby's municipal council at this time discussed the possibility of a line north of Burnaby Lake to Port Moody, where the residents were still thoroughly unhappy with their transit lot.)

The B. C. Electric's worst accident ever occurred during the early morning of November 10, very near the spot where car 15 had overturned fifteen years earlier on the New Westminster-Vancouver interurban line. Car "Sumas" had left the depot at Hastings and Carrall at 5:50 a.m., bound for New Westminster with 23 men aboard. It had just left the city streets at Cedar Cottage and was approaching Lakeview when it was hit by a runaway flat car loaded with 12-inch by 12-inch timbers, which shot ahead off the flat car, virtually demolishing the interurban car. Fourteen men were killed in what is today known as "the Lakeview disaster."

The flat car load was being delivered to a new iron foundry over a mile east of Lakeview at the southeast corner of the line and Nanaimo Road when the couplers between it and a box car let go, allowing the car to get away. With its heavy load, and a loss of 58 feet of elevation between the two stations, the speed of the flat car was considerable at its contact with the moving "Sumas."

The brakeman had stayed for a time with the flat car, fully applying the brakes to no avail, before he had jumped; the motorman of locomotive 503 had followed the flat car down the track, blowing the whistle frantically, trying to warn oncoming traffic. The crew was exonerated, and criminal charges brought against them were dropped; the B. C. Electric voluntarily contributed $135,000 to the families of the dead men and to those who had been injured.

For Vancouver the last three months of 1909 brought an extraordinary array of new street car lines. Driven into uninhabited areas, they were designed to bring people in for settlement.

On October 23, a new double tracked line on Fourth Avenue between Granville and Alma streets, over two miles, was opened, with the street car service originating at Granville and Smithe streets. (For a brief, initial period, Vine Street was the western terminus.)

On November 6, the line on Hastings Street was extended two and three-quarter miles east from Campbell Avenue, through Hastings Townsite, to Boundary Road, with only the section east to Vernon Drive double tracked. Two street cars operated half-hourly service from Hastings and Carrall. Nanaimo Street defined Vancouver's eastern boundary, necessitating a further fare for riders going east, but since the company was aware of the sweetness of few impediments and the luring of the potential settler, within three days it offered settlers tickets at ten for fifty cents!

Acquiescing to a request by Vancouver's city council, the B. C. Electric agreed on November 17 to install fenders on all street cars operating within the city's limits. That out of the way, a three-fifths of a mile extension of the Powell Street line went into operation on December 18, on Dundas Street, east from Semlin Drive to Templeton Drive, then Eton Street, and Nanaimo Street to McGill Street. Three days later, the Hastings East run acquired another street car and twice as frequent service.

Before the year ended, the B. C. Electric had a new two-pronged street car line through D. L. 301 deep into South Vancouver: on Kingsway, double tracked from Broadway to Knight Road, and single tracked from there to Victoria Road, and south to Forty-first Avenue (Wilson Road then), almost precisely three miles; and a more than two-mile-long line on Fraser Street (North Arm Road) double tracked from Kingsway to Twenty-fifth Avenue, single tracked to Forth-ninth Avenue (Ferris Road). The Fraser line was in service on December 23.

By year's end, Vancouver had its first sky-scraper, the Dominion Bank Building at the northwest corner of Hastings and Cambie streets, for many years known, at least locally, as the tallest building in the British Empire. The city also had a population of 85,387, including D. L. 301, Hastings Townsite, Point Grey, and South Vancouver, a figure which would swell to 120,068 by the end of 1910!

In November 1909 in North Vancouver, the Patterson Lumber Company, which had secured the contract for extending the eastward line into Lynn Valley, started work on the extension. Patterson would do the grading and track laying, and the B. C. Electric would string the trolley wire, for this heavily timbered route.

On December 30, Sperling wrote a letter of revealing significance to the company's London secretary, George Kidd (Kidd had joined the company's office in London in 1907, and would come out to Vancouver as comptroller in 1911, succeeding Sperling as general manager in 1914). "About 37½ acres of land, including right-of-way, has been purchased at a cost of $22,500 on the south side of the Fraser River adjoining the Company's Chilliwack line, which will be used as freight yards and engine sheds, etc., for the Fraser Valley Branch. The property has almost 330 feet of water frontage on the Fraser River. The Great Northern tracks which cross the property on a 30-foot high trestle should not interfere with laying out of tracks underneath. It was necessary for the Company to secure some water frontage on the Fraser River, as our Local Manager, Mr. Purvis, states that he can close up $45,000 log-hauling contracts, providing the Company can unload the logs into the Fraser River."

Across the complete transportation system of the B. C. Electric, 29,649,715 passengers had been carried to their destinations in 1909.

For the B. C. Electric on Vancouver Island, 1910 meant continuing work on the large scale power project at Jordan River, and beginnings of the Victoria to Saanich interurban line. Extending some seventeen miles north from Victoria's city limits, and often as narrow as two miles, this northward projecting thumb of land called Saanich Peninsula occupied for Victorians much the same niche as the Fraser Valley did for New Westminster. The Great Northern Railway's Victoria & Sidney Railway had operated steam trains between Victoria and upper peninsula Sidney since 1894, but many residents of Saanich — and Victoria — felt keenly that faster, more modern, and more efficient service was not only possible, but also necessary. The B. C. Electric certainly perceived growth potential and real estate speculation possibilities.

Though the company had first talked about a Saanich interurban line as long ago as 1906, it was only in May of 1910 that it finally approved the construction of a line from Victoria to Deep Bay (Deep Cove), more than twenty miles distant, near the northwest tip of the peninsula. The cost would be about half a million dollars. In the following month two survey parties, one near Mount Douglas, the other at Royal Oak, began their search for a route. In November the precise line was chosen from three which had been mapped out: it would leave Victoria by swinging west off Douglas Street and out on Burnside Avenue.

For the construction of a new two-track car barn and yard just east of Douglas on Cloverdale Avenue, the street car line was extended three blocks beyond the city limits on Douglas Street from Tolmie Avenue. As well during 1910, Cook Street was double tracked from Fort Street to May Street, as was the one block of Henry Street on the Gorge line and the two blocks of Douglas between Yates and Fort streets.

The corner of Yates and Douglas received a large clock, actually intended to supply company personnel with the correct time, and in June, the Victoria system followed Vancouver's lead, placing its first pay-as-you-enter street cars in service. During the year, new street cars 125, 183, and 184 had arrived from the shops in New Westminster, and during the last month of the year, the annoyance of the Victoria & Sidney Railway's trains clattering over the street car line on Douglas Street ended with the opening of the new V. & S. depot at Blanchard and Fisgard Streets.

On the lower mainland, track laying was complete to Abbotsford by early January 1910, grading was continuing east, and a contract had been awarded for the building of the new Great Northern line from Abbotsford east to Chilliwack and Hope,† a matter of pressing concern for the B. C. Electric. By the seventeenth of the month the company had purchased 560 feet of water frontage on the south side of the Fraser River across from New Westminster at $40 per foot; there was certainty in the company that a city centre would develop at that location.

On the eighteenth, the Board of Railway Commissioners for Canada ordered the Great Northern Railway to continue offering passenger service on its New Westminster Southern Railway between Cloverdale and New Westminster. Though it would be summer before the B. C. Electric could institute a passenger service between the two cities, Great Northern was anxious to rid itself of this line, and had already agreed to sell the ten-mile section between Port Kells and New Westminster bridge to the new transcontinental Canadian Northern Pacific Railway, later part of the Canadian National Railway.

Manager T. Driscoll of the company's car shops in New Westminster announced on February 6 that his staff of 95 experienced men was gearing up for work on a $450,000 order for forty street cars, six interurban cars, two locomotives, and one hundred freight cars. Furthermore, the addition to the shops was almost finished.

On the twenty-second of the month, Sperling apprised Kidd further in regard to the Chilliwack line:

> "Our Fraser Valley Branch line has been built through the most fertile valley on the south side of the Fraser River, with a view to obtaining as much of the local trade as possible.
>
> "The roadbed, exclusive of the overhead construction, will cost in the neighbourhood of $10,000 per mile, whereas the Great Northern Line from Sumas to New Westminster cost, I believe, in the neighbourhood of $50,000 per mile. The G. N. Ry. Co. went to this heavy expense as they desired to obtain a grade which would be less than 1%.
>
> "As I have already reported to you our Line has grades not exceeding 2½%, and to reduce this

† Vancouver Daily Province, 13 January 1910, p. 3.

grade to any appreciable extent would entail relocating many miles of line."

Later in the month Superintendent Allan Purvis clarified to Sperling the situation with bridges on the line. There were five:

1. *approach to south end of Fraser River bridge*
2. *300-foot pile trestle 75 feet high - "Dry Gulch Bridge" — two miles east of New Westminster*
3. *"Salmon River Bridge" — 750 feet long, 25 feet high*
4. *at mileage 32.5 — 300 feet long, 40 feet high*
5. *Howe truss span across the Vedder River* †

By the end of February surveys for the Burnaby Lake line were completed, and there was much talk of a line to Fraser Mills, as well as the assured one — now that plans were being prepared — from New Westminster to Queensborough to service the numerous industries springing up there. Work was also just beginning on a new cut-off line at the New Westminster end of the old Tramway interurban line. What with the enticing prospects of B. C. Electric's growing freight business and interurban trains (rather than single-running cars), this most heavily travelled interurban line needed to rid itself of the daunting, dangerous ten percent grade on the Twelfth Street plummet down to the car shops and Columbia Street.

In February also, Vancouver's recently built Victoria Road line commenced a twenty-minute service from Kingsway and Broadway to Forty-First and Victoria, and the company responded to the city's request by beginning to install safety lifeguard-fenders, of the Watson type, on each street car.

The Lulu Island branch enjoyed a welcome, unseasonable rush to Minoru Park on March 25 when it brought most of the 3,500 on-lookers there — using eight extra cars — to witness Californian Charles K. Hamilton flying his Curtiss-type pusher biplane, the first airplane flight in western Canada. Some believed he had flown as briskly as 55 miles per hour.

But March meant even more to the company

than running admittedly lucrative extras. The first two of eight interurban cars had arrived for the Chilliwack line. Six passengers cars of opulent magnificence — and two baggage-express cars — had been ordered, four from the American Car Company, four from Ottawa, and they were even larger than the company's sixteen home-built "name" interurbans. Rudimentary head rests were incorporated into the rattan seats, two toilets and a water cooler were new civilized features, and the cars were faster, more powerful, and could be run in multiple unit trains. The first arrivals, from American Car, were passenger car number 400 (later 1300) and combine (designed for both passengers and express) 401 (later 1400). Among their most fascinated oglers were the staff and officials of the car shops, which almost immediately set to work planning and building their own copies of the new interurbans!

By March-end ballasting was the major activity of the New Westminster-Cloverdale section and rail was in place all the way to Abbotsford. Gravel was obtained at Sullivan, where the company was building a spur for deeper penetration into this gravel pit, one which the B. C. Electric would use for the life of its electric operation. Between Abbotsford and Chilliwack, grading was close to completion.

April began with the company at work building a new car barn at the foot of Twelfth Street in New Westminster. A major concern was to get the street cars off Columbia Street, where many of them had to be left overnight because of the lack of storage space. However, the new building would also contain sophisticated facilities for repairing the street cars and interurbans in use on the company's lower mainland systems. Sperling let a cat out of the bag when he wrote Kidd of the B. C. Electric's intention "to establish our yards, repair shops, stores, etc., on the land recently purchased on the south side of the River, and we intend by degrees to move our terminals to the south side of the Fraser River." ‡

For the impending opening of the Lynn Valley line, North Vancouver acquired four more street cars from Vancouver in April: 28, a marvel on her arrival in Vancouver a decade earlier, and three of the Westminster & Vancouver Tramway cars, 32, 34, and 36. And on the Chilliwack line, even before the month was out, rail laying crews headed east out of Abbotsford, Chilliwack-bound.

On May 4, milk train service, as well as the shipping of small freight articles, commenced between New Westminster and intermediate points on the way to Cloverdale and Langley, then seven-tenths of a mile northeast of Milner. (Today's Langley was named Berry.) The train left Langley at 7 a.m., Vancouver, at 6 p.m. The line was not in sufficient state yet to allow for passenger service; furthermore, the line was intensely preoccupied with transporting large quantities of construction materials.

† Purvis to Sperling, 26 February 1910, B.C.E.R. collection, University of British Columbia, Box 87.

‡ Sperling to Kidd, 15 April 1910, B.C.E.R. collection University of British Columbia, Box 87.

At far left the original Eburne (Marpole) station. Taken in 1910, the view is to the east from Hudson Street. (B.C. Hydro)

Looking east across the siding on First Street to some of Queen's Park's exhibition buildings, 1910. (New Westminster Public Library)

May 13 signalled the opening of the 2.24-mile Lynn Valley extension from Grand Boulevard and Nineteenth Street, north to Twentieth, east to Sutherland Avenue, and then along the north side of Lynn Valley Road across some boggy patches and occasional trestle work to Dempsey Road. The seemingly official inaugural team of motorman Giffen and conductor Jones was in charge of the dignitary-filled first street car which left lower Lonsdale at 3:40 p.m. The trip went well, Friday the thirteenth or not, even to the point of a delightful interruption by students of Lynn Valley School along the way for a short ceremony and welcome.

Public service commenced on the fourteenth, a new passing siding on Queensbury having been installed. Less than a week later, the *North Shore Express* related its good feelings about the new line's setting:

"The line after leaving the old terminus at the corner of 19th Street and Queensbury Avenue [Grand Boulevard today] first traverses a short piece of thickly wooded territory, delightful to the eye in its primeval beauty. The line then follows the Lynn Valley pipe line road to the terminus located at a point 1200 feet north of the junction of Hoskins road. This portion is mainly through the cultivated and opened parts of the district, with the picturesque Lynn Valley Creek and Canyon to the east and the long range of snow capped mountains piercing the horizon to the north and west."

On the fourteenth of May, Vancouver area residents witnessed the inauguration of two more street car lines, the Hastings Park line, double tracked from Nanaimo and McGill streets, east five blocks to Renfrew, and single tracked around the block of Renfrew, Eton, and Kaslo streets (a shuttle car connected with the Powell Street line, whose track had just been double tracked to Nanaimo and McGill from Victoria Road); and the Main Street South line, over a mile south from Thirty-Third Avenue to Fiftieth, single tracked. Since the double tracking of Main Street was now ready south to Twenty-fifth and a wye had been installed there, the Davie-Main cars made that their terminus, rather than Sixteenth, and a shuttle car operated to Fiftieth from Twenty-fifth, as did the Mountain View shuttle, always a small four-wheel street car.

On May 12 the company announced that its location plans for the Burnaby Lake interurban line between the end of New Westminster's Sapperton street car line and Commercial Drive in Vancouver had received government approval, and that the contract for the clearing and grading of the new line had been awarded to Vancouver's M. P. Cotton. The line's traversal of Hastings Townsite was limited to a franchise agreement of

Car 60 languishes momentarily at the end of Lynn Valley Road. (North Shore Archives)

twenty-one years from December 16, 1908, the date of the original agreement.

The six remaining Chilliwack interurban cars had arrived by May 20: the baggage-express cars from the American Car Company, 300 and 301 (later 1700 and 1701), and the four cars from the Ottawa Car Company, two passenger cars, 402 and 404 (later 1301 and 1302), and two combines, 403 and 405 (later 1401 and 1402). Cars 404 and 405 arrived as non-motored trailers, though identical in design to 402 and 403. All eight Chilliwack cars were put to work on the company's Lulu Island and Westminster branches.

Four days later, the tragic "Sumas" rolled out of the car shops, rebuilt, capable of being coupled to other cars and run in multiple units, and with a number, 1216. Gone were the massive wooden pilots at each end; begun was the rebuilding of the sixteen "name" interurban cars.

With the swing span of the Fraser River bridge open and the B. C. Electric's power lines at the height of 165 feet above the water at the time, the four-masted sailing ship "Mariechen" found, late in May, that her 178-foot high masts did not allow her to proceed upriver, a dilemma which only added to the company's concerns at a time of energy expenditure and expansion. In North Vancouver, surveys began on June 4 for the extension of the westward line into the Capilano district, up Fell Avenue from Marine Drive.

On the fourteenth of June began the demolition of the company's New Westminster depot to make room for its new $80,000 one, and on the following day, steel reached Huntingdon. Wire-stringing was nearing Abbotsford, and crews were already erecting poles and hanging trolley wire between Vedder Mountain and Chilliwack. But the unusual activity was occurring between Whatcom Road and Vedder Mountain where three dredges were struggling with the waters of Sumas Lake to construct a three-mile-long, seventeen-foot-high grade which would prove

resistant to the lake's activities.

Sperling reported on June 23 to Kidd that the company now had 890 feet of water frontage and 43.074 acres along the south shore of the Fraser, all amassed at a total cost of $51,298.75. He added that "the milk business offering at the present time will require the running of eight big box cars every morning. From the present it appears that the two Dick-Kerr locomotives [911 and 912] and the two steam locomotives [525 and a borrowed one] will be insufficient to handle the business, and we shall probably require two more locomotives to be delivered in the Spring of 1911 [Dick-Kerr 913 and steam locomotive 940]."

Despite the B. C. Electric's activities across the bridge, the company had just purchased ten lots close to its New Westminster shops and barn, near the junction of the interurban lines to Vancouver and Eburne, for the purposes of developing a much needed freight yard.

On June 30, surveys completed, contracts were awarded for North Vancouver's 1.67-mile Capilano extension. Its route would proceed north on Fell Avenue, west on Twentieth Street to a 450-foot-long, 98-foot-high trestle crossing of McKay Creek, then along Twenty-Second and through to School Street (obliterated today, but the precise location of the freeway) and Bowser Avenue.

On July 1 the first passenger train, cars 301 and 405, made its inaugural journey between New Westminster and Langley (soon to be renamed Jardine), therewith incorporating the milk service. (Over one hundred cans a day were already being brought into Vancouver.) Fraser Valley Branch Time Table No. 1 had the second class mixed train leaving Langley at 7:30 a.m., arriving in New Westminster at 8:50 a.m.; the return run left there at 5 p.m., arriving in Langley at 6:15 p.m. A five-minute halt was obligatory at Cloverdale. Small yards were in place there and at Milner, ten-car sidings at Shops, Kennedy, Hyland,

The new line to Renfrew Street from Powell Street brought citizens directly to the opening of Vancouver's first exhibition in 1910. (Vancouver Public Archives)

Meridian, and Shannon (later Hall's Prairie).

In Lynn Valley, a raging bush fire, which had started near Rice Lake, destroyed a quarter of the new street car line, including poles and overhead, on July 10. The company had been admitting that its sparsely-populated North Vancouver system was running at a heavy loss, yet anything but rebuilding the Lynn Valley line was certainly out of the question.

With track in Vancouver recently in place on Alma Street from Fourth to Tenth Avenue (with a wye at Fourth), the B. C. Electric awarded a grading contract for slightly over a mile of new single track on Tenth to Sasamat Street at 62 cents per cubic yard; it was estimated that about 14,000 cubic yards of earth would be handled in excavating and filling. Before the end of the year track would be laid as well on Sasamat north to Fourth Avenue.

Rails in Stanley Park were a lure to many despite Buntzen's squelching of any B. C. Electric participation years earlier. This is evidenced in the application of a G. J. Ashworth, and his to-be-chartered "Electric Railway Construction Company," to Vancouver's park board on August 10 for permission to construct a half million-dollar electric railway around the park. Though many board members favoured the scheme — rather intricate and innovative — nothing ever came of it.

On August 15 Vancouver finally caught up with New Westminster in one regard with the grand opening of the first exhibition of the Vancouver Exhibition Association. Canada's Prime Minister, Sir Wilfrid Laurier, attended, as well as 5,000 participants, most brought to the Hastings Park site by rows of street cars over the Powell Street line and its near-new extension to the park. The exhibition's showpiece was surely the quadruple-towered, barrel-roofed Industrial Building (torn down in 1936), immediately to the south of today's Pacific Coliseum. The six days of the fair drew a total of 68,000 people, many of whom saw for the first time that eastern Vancouver and Hastings Townsite offered attractive residential possibilities.

The remoteness of much of Point Grey, so much a part of older, settled Vancouver today, is evinced in this excerpt from a report written by G. H. Franklin, the local manager of the Lulu Island branch, on that same August 15: "The roadbed of Section No. 1 from Vancouver to Magee, is in fair condition. The section men have been surfacing track, cutting weeds, and making general track repairs. We have had considerable trouble with bush fires around Magee station and were obliged to keep a watchman in the neighbourhood for several nights." Seven days later the Vancouver street car system carried 122,455 passengers, a single day's record.

During the month of August, the B. C. Electric's only competitor of note throughout its history, the Western Canada Power Company Limited, was building a railway from the C.P.R. main line at Ruskin, thirty-five miles east of Vancouver on the north bank of the Fraser River, some six miles

The first train to Chilliwack in New Westminster at 10 a.m., boarding the special guests who had arrived on another interurban coach from Vancouver. (New Westminster Public Library)

Time Table

Leave Vancouver (Granville St. Station)	9:00 a.m.
" New Westminster	10:00 "
Arrive Cloverdale	10:40 "
Leave Cloverdale	10:50 "
" Milner	11:00 "
" Mount Lehman	11:34 "
" Clayburn	11:45 "
" Abbotsford	11:55 "
" Huntingdon	12:05 "
" Sardis	12:55 "
Arrive Chilliwack	1:00 p.m.
Leave Chilliwack	3:00 "
Arrive New Westminster	6:00 "
" Vancouver	7:00 "

1:00 p.m.—Opening Ceremonies

Driving of the last spike and declaring the road open for traffic by the Honorable Richard McBride, Prime Minister.

1:15 p.m.—Luncheon

CHAIRMAN—Mr. R. H. Sperling, General Manager.

Toast List

The King.

The Lieutenant-Governor of British Columbia.

The Dominion of Canada.

The Province of British Columbia.

"The Three Cities" (Vancouver, New Westminster, Chilliwack).

The Fraser Valley.

Transportation.

The Press.

(B.C. Hydro)

At Chilliwack, B.C.'s premier Richard McBride has just driven the last spike. (B.C. Hydro)

north to its power dam project on Stave Lake. The railway would be in service by early October; the W.C.P. Company would not be in the B. C. Electric's controlling hands for another ten years.

By September it was decided that the Burnaby Lake line would definitely connect with the Vancouver city street car system at Commercial Drive, and that cutting to a permanent grade would be left for the future, a future, in fact, which never arrived. Street running in Vancouver would necessitate operating freight cars by special permission only, a limiting factor in the line's success.

An improvement was made in the Fraser Street service on September 14 when its runs were extended into downtown Vancouver, to Powell and Main streets, rather than returning to south Fraser from Broadway and Kingsway.

Monday, October 3, was set as the day of the formal opening of the 63.8-mile Chilliwack line,

the longest interurban railway line ever to be built in Canada. The Fraser Valley branch, as the company wished to designate the line upon its completion, passed through five municipalities (as well as touching a sixth, Delta, for two-thirds of a mile) with a total population of fewer than 18,000 (and Chilliwack's itself was a mere 1,500!). The line had been built for $3,500,000, entirely without government assistance, and the company had, in fact, purchased much of its own right of way. What the B. C. Electric had manifested from the very inception of the great project was a faith that the Fraser Valley would grow, and that the line itself would stimulate growth.

The interurban cars to be used for the line's inaugurations had to be decorated, but when? Cars 301 and 405 were unavailable; together they had been a three-month fixture on the run to Langley, and the other six were vigorously engaged delighting passengers, particularly on the Lulu Island branch. On Saturday morning, October 1, baggage-express car 300, combine 403, and passenger car 402 were coupled together, in that order, and taken for a trial trip over the new line. Late that night the three cars were rolled into the shops at New Westminster and a scene of great activity commenced: each was thoroughly cleaned; hardwood floor matting was laid in the two passenger cars; benches and tables were made for, and installed in, the baggage-express car; and elaborate bunting and decorations were attached to all three. How unfortunate that ill health prevented Johannes Buntzen from participating in line opening celebrations.

October 3 began for general manager Sperling and his assistant, F. R. Glover, at 8 a.m. when they met British Columbia's Lieutenant-Governor Thomas Paterson and Premier Richard McBride — each with his assistant — who had sailed from Victoria on the C.P.R.'s overnight steamer. From the C.P.R. dock in Vancouver Sperling took the party by automobile to the Vancouver Club for a quick breakfast, then on to Granville station to board a special interurban car which left at 9 a.m. for New Westminster, via Eburne, filled with B. C. Electric, city, municipal, and board of trade officers and officials. Upon its arrival just before 10 a.m., everyone alighted and, together with the New Westminster delegation, boarded the waiting special three-car train which left promptly at 10, in charge of conductor A. B. Clark, motorman Arthur Brooks, and brakeman Bruce Walker.

From this point the enthusiastic report in the *Chilliwack Progress* continues the first day's story:

"Monday the 3rd of October will rank as the greatest day in the history of Chilliwack, marking as it does the commencement of rail communication with the outside world, by the inauguration of the British Columbia Electric Railway service.

For the occasion the company had invited a large party representative of the cities of New Westminster and Vancouver and the rural municipalities between Chilliwack and the Coast, and headed by Lieut.-Governor Paterson and Premier McBride with Hon. Price Ellison, minister of lands. Mr. Ralph Smith, M.P., of Nanaimo also was in the list of guests, and of course the local representatives for the federal and provincial houses, Mr. J. D. Taylor, M.P., and Mr. S. A. Cawley, M.P.P., were in attendance, together with Mr. Thos. Gifford, M.P.P., for New Westminster and Mr. F. J. MacKenzie, M.P.P., for Delta. Mayor Lee and the aldermen of New Westminster, acting Mayor Ramsay and the aldermen of Vancouver; President Lusby of the New Westminster Board of Trade and Vice-President McLennan, of the Vancouver board were with the party, together with the publicity commissioners for the two cities. The special excursion train left New Westminster at 10 o'clock in the morning, the Vancouver guests having come by regular tram [sic] via the Eburne line.

This special train consisted of three gaily decorated coaches; two passenger and one baggage. Stops were made at Cloverdale, where the company's sub-station was inspected, and at Milner, the Langley Prairie station, Mt. Lehman, Clayburn, Abbotsford and other points. Good time was made along that portion of the road, the track being down for considerable time and well ballasted. From a short distance east of Abbotsford the road was not so good owing to the heavy rains of the past week and slower time was made, while at Sumas Mountain it was found that a pole had fallen across the track owing to the storm of the night before, thus destroying the electric communication for the last stage, so that the train was pulled in by one of the company's steam engines, arriving shortly

before 3 p.m. At Sardis a stop was made to enable the councils of the city and township of Chilliwack to come aboard and experience the pleasure and honor of being among the first passengers to enter the city on the new line. All along the line as the train passed the residents turned out to cheer and welcome it. Chilliwack turned out en masse and with a brass band, handkerchief waving and steam whistles shrieking showed their appreciation of being able at last to get out of the woods.

Little time was lost in detraining and within a few minutes Premier McBride stood bareheaded with sledge hammer and spike and well and truly drove to the head the last spike that connected the Garden City of Chilliwack to the commercial cities of New Westminster and Vancouver. Upon the completion of this task Mayor Munro, on behalf of the councils of Chilliwack and the Board of Trade of the City of Chilliwack, presented General Manager R. H. Sperling with an address of appreciation and welcome, which was suitably replied to by that gentleman and the invited guests repaired to the hall of St. Thomas' church and partook of a bountiful spread tastefully set out by host McLennan of the Empress hotel. The choir was occupied by R. H. Sperling, Lieut.-Gov. Paterson and Premier McBride being seated on either side of him, and the guests to the number of 150 taxing the capacity of the hall.

The repast being done justice to the chairman proposed the toast to the King, which was received with musical honors, the Chilliwack orchestra, which was present for the occasion, leading. The next toast, proposed by Mr. Sperling, was that of the Lieut.-Governor of the Province of British Columbia. In introducing this toast, the chairman expressed his regret of the absence of Director Buntzen, who was unable to be present owing to illness. It was due in a large measure to Mr. Buntzen and Mr. Horne-Payne that the Chilliwack line had been built. The company had confidence in the undertaking and the future of the province, else they would not have spent the sum of $20,000,000 in it. He hinted at plans of the company with regard to the service and stated that chair cars in addition to the regular passenger cars would be used on the road in time. The Chilliwack line was but a beginning of the work the company would undertake in the Fraser Valley.

After the Lieut.-Governor had been toasted that gentleman in returning thanks, referred to the good work accomplished by the B.C.E.R. He thought they had made no mistake in building through the Fraser Valley to Chilliwack. Transportation was one of the greatest needs of the province and the solving of it was one step towards knitting closer together the districts of the province.

F. R. Glover proposed the toast to the province of British Columbia, and in response Premier McBride acknowledged the great compliment paid him by the B.C.E.R. by asking him to drive the last spike in the Chilliwack tram line. In looking into the future he could see that everything augured well for the success of the Fraser Valley line. He spoke briefly of the transportation problems of the valley. A great development had already taken place and with the aid of electric power a very great deal more could be expected. T. J. Trapp in proposing the toast of the Dominion of Canada, coupled with it the names of Ralph Smith, M.P., of Nanaimo, and J. D. Taylor, of New Westminster. Both gentlemen replied in brief stirring addresses, loud in the praises of the B.C.E.R. and their firm faith of the future of the province. L. B. Lusby, president of the New Westminster Board of Trade, proposed the toast of the three cities, Chilliwack, New Westminster and Vancouver. This was responded to by Major Lee, of New Westminster, Acting Mayor Ramsay, of Vancouver, and Mayor Munro, of Chilliwack. All three thanked the B.C.E.R. officials for the honor extended to them and complimented them on the enterprise of the company and the despatch with which the road had been built and equipped. Mayor Munro stated the valley had been waiting twenty years for this event and building hopes for better transportation facilities. They were often disappointed, but at last the hopes of the residents had been realized. Thos. Gifford, M.P.P. for New Westminster, proposed the toast to the Fraser Valley. S. A. Cawley, M.P.P. for Chilliwack; F. J. MacKenzie, M.P.P. for Delta; Reeve Hutcherson, of Delta; Reeve Poppy, of Langley; Reeve Merryfield, of Matsqui; Reeve Campbell of Sumas, and Reeve Wilson, of Chilliwack, replied and voiced the sentiments of their municipalities in brief speeches. The toast of the press followed; and then an impromptu toast by Premier McBride to the B.C. Electric Railway Company, coupled with the names of General Manager Mr. R. H. Sperling, his assistant Mr. F. R. Glover, and the manager of the Chilliwack line Mr. Allan Purvis." †

Sperling's diary finishes this wonderful day with the following entry: "Left Chilliwack about 5 p.m., under electric power, used steam locomotive [number 525] from Vedder Bridge to Mile Post 49 [Vedder Mountain station], and ran from Mile Post 49 to Westminster under electric power, thence by special car, arriving Vancouver 10.30." ‡

Glover's diary corrects the arrival time to 10:13 p.m., and notes that "Manager of Interurban Lines Purvis, Chief Dispatcher Sterling and Train Master Elson, handled the movement of the train, everything being carried through without a hitch," despite the fact that only the Cloverdale, Clayburn, and Chilliwack substations were operational. ∗

Sperling in his diary explains the problem at Vedder Mountain more precisely than the *Progress* was able to: "Owing to an accident to a lineman, due to one of the poles falling over and pulling down overhead work, the journey could not be made under electric power."+ Sperling had received an illuminated copy of the mayor of Chilliwack's address, and Sperling sent Premier McBride the spike maul McBride had used in driving the last spike.

The spirit of the thorough report of the opening day's activities by the *Vancouver Daily Province* pervades these four excerpts:

"No official, however, would have enjoyed as fully the triumphs of the hour as Mr. J. Buntzen, the active head of the concern during the period when the company was building up from the small things of the past so as to be able to undertake the great undertaking marked by the day's ceremonies, who was unable to be present.

"When the line was planned in 1907 and the investment approved by the London board three survey parties were at once sent out to run trial lines. To Mr. F. N. Sinclair, C. E. was allotted the field covering the route finally selected and officials of the road today admitted that when Mr. Sinclair was sent out there was but little thought that the extension would be constructed according to his surveys. His report, however, showed such grades and promising territory tapped that it received far greater consideration than was anticipated and was finally approved as covering the selected route.

"The field surveys were then handed to a board of experts who considered the conditions noted and presented an estimate of the probable cost of the line. This sum was considerably less than the amount noted above as the cost, the excess arising because as the management of the road studied the situation, it became apparent that at the very outset the line should be constructed in a strictly up-to-date manner as regards grades, electrical equipment, terminal yards, etc., on account of the enormous traffic which would develop along the line through the certain development of the district in the near future.

"It was at Huntingdon that members of the party learned that the tram company has a terminal site covering a large area, this leading to the immediate conclusion that the concern was well located at the international boundary to link up with some electric traction company operating in Washington, thus forming the Seattle-Vancouver tram system such as is judged to be one of the certain developments of the near future.

"Interviews with the municipal councillors

† "Electric Line Opened This Week," *Chilliwack Progress*, 5 October 1910, p. 1.

‡ Mr. Sperling's diary, B.C.E.R. collection, University of British Columbia, Box 28.

∗ Mr. Glover's diary, B.C.E.R. collection, University of British Columbia, Box 28.

+ Loc. cit.

A power pole having fallen across the track because of a storm during the previous night, the festive, three-car, first interurban train to Chilliwack had to be towed the final few miles by B.C. Electric steam locomotive 525. (Bob Webster collection)

from the various districts on the train showed the large area of rich country which will be opened by the new tramline the acreage being as follows: Surrey, 75,000; Langley, 77,000; Matsqui, 55,000; Sumas, 20,000; Chilliwack, 70,000. The districts are improved to a varying degree, but it was stated that in no case has the improvement reached the standard which will immediately result on account of the transportation facilities afforded by the operation of the new line. The land was said to be admirably fitted to form the base of food supplies for the hundreds of thousands who will certainly live in Vancouver and New Westminster in the near future. In the words of one rural representative, 'you need us and we need you and this line is going to be the connecting link which will bring us together for our mutual advantage.'

"Not only is the territory tapped by the line one which will be a valuable source of food supplies but in many parts it is covered with valuable timber areas which have heretofore been untouched because of lack of transportation facilities. Members of the party commented on this fact while on the trip of the day and the officials of the tram company promptly replied that in ordering the rolling stock for freight purposes over the extension consists of 100 flat cars, 50 box cars and ten stock cars." †

Regular service began on the following day with two passenger trains and one milk train in each direction daily, and one daily passenger run in each direction between New Westminster and Jardine. The first Chilliwack-bound train from Vancouver on October 4 carried 72 passengers, but the westward runs were more crowded, due in part to the fact that New Westminster's exhibition had opened on the same day. Return fare from Vancouver to Chilliwack was $3.00, $1.85 for the three-hour one-way journey; past New Westminster, forty-two stations were in place.

The two steamboats calling at points along the south side of the Fraser between New Westminster and Chilliwack would hang on for a while, but soon would be gone. The C.P.R.'s *Beaver* steamed upstream to Chilliwack Landing on Mondays, Wednesdays, and Fridays, returning the following days, while the Royal City Navigation Company Limited's *Paystreak* left New Westminster on Tuesdays, Thursdays, and Saturdays, also returning the following days. Both used the Brackman-Ker wharf in New Westminster for their 8 a.m. departures; Chilliwack departures were at 7 a.m.

Much work needed yet to be done. The old track of the C.P.R. in New Westminster from its yards to the station was turned over to the B. C. Electric for the use of the Fraser Valley branch and

† "Last Spike Driven on Chilliwack Tramline," *Vancouver Daily Province,* 3 October 1910, p. 19-20.

British Columbia Electric Railway Company

District 3

TIME **2** TABLE

TAKING EFFECT AT 24.01 O'CLOCK

Tuesday, Oct. 4, 1910

(GOVERNED BY PACIFIC TIME)

For the Government and Information of Employees only

R. H. SPERLING,	**F. R. GLOVER,**	**ALLAN PURVIS,**
General Manager	Asst. General Manager	Manager Interurban Lines

---

Rules Governing Fraser River Bridge Interlocked

Approaching the north end of the bridge on the B. C. Electric Railway, and 1200 feet from the home signal, is a distant signal; at the end of the bridge is a home signal; on the Great Northern Railway at the end of the bridge is a home signal. The clear indication of either home signal will permit a train to pass across the draw to the south end of the bridge to a two-arm home signal, the top arm of which leads to the G. N. Main Line towards Seattle and the lower arm to the B. C. Electric Railway. The dwarf signal at the same location permits a train to pass to the Guichon branch of the Great Northern Railway.

Approaching the bridge from the south end and 1200 ft. from the home signal on the B. C. Electric Railway, and 1800 feet from the home signal on the line of the G. N. Railway, is a distant signal.

The home signal on the B. C. Electric Railway, on the main line of the G. N. Railway and on the Guichon branch, permits a train to move to a signal 870 ft. from the draw. This signal being clear permits a train to pass to the north end of the bridge to a two-arm home signal, top arm leading to G. N. Railway track and the lower arm to the B. C. Electric Railway.

All distant signals are three positions at 45 degrees, which indicates that the section of the track between it and the home signal is clear; and at 90 degrees indicates that the home signal ahead is at 90 degrees, or the clear position.

All Distant and Home Signals go to the stop position the instant a train passes them.

All trains accepting a home signal at either approach on the bridge must move by the home signal governing in the opposite direction before a route can be changed.

The call for signals is four short blasts of whistle, and trains must not pass home signals until clear indication is given, which must be acknowledged by two short blasts of whistle.

Trains must not exceed speed of six miles per hour over Fraser River Bridge—or three minutes.

(author's collection)

was being repositioned. The roadbed, particularly along Vedder Mountain, needed more ballasting. And on the eleventh, the company announced its intention to spend $100,000 to build yards, car barns, and repair shops, devoted exclusively to the Fraser Valley branch, on the south side of the Fraser River; the track space would accommodate 250 cars, the car barn 20 cars and locomotives. Small wonder that the Fraser Valley branch's first station over the bridge was named "Shops."

In Vancouver on October 11, the Cedar Cottage street car line was connected with the Fourth Avenue line, using the newly built double track on Richards Street for the four blocks between Hastings and Robson streets and the newly double tracked section of Robson between Richards and Granville; five-minute service was instituted. Though still without regular service, Robson had been double tracked between Richards and Homer streets and a new double tracked line had been laid two blocks farther to Cambie Street and four blocks north to Hastings Street.

In North Vancouver plans were going ahead for extending street car barn facilities, and all-night street lighting was introduced.

While the New Westminster-Vancouver interurban line was instituting half-hourly service on October 20 with two cars throughout the day until 9 p.m., the question of double tracking the Vancouver-Eburne line was under vigorous discussion by the B. C. Electric. On the Westminster branch, the company planned to run double headers until its double tracking was completed. On the Burnaby Lake line, 300 men were working day and night through a lengthy spell of particularly bad weather on clearing and grading. Headquarters camp had been set up at Deer Lake, with two subsidiary camps on either side; muskeg, immense boulders, sink holes, and dense forests made this relatively short new project one of the most difficult yet undertaken.

The evening interurban from Chilliwack on October 24 was delayed by a mud and rock slide at Vedder Mountain which buried the track to a depth of five feet for fifty feet. Several hundred men, hastily gathered from construction and

section camps, rushed to the scene and had the line cleared in two hours. This most difficult stretch had posed challenges for construction crews whose task it had been to carve its winding route into the mountainside and keep it away from Sumas Lake, and since the rails had still not been properly ballasted and bonded, speeds of six or seven miles an hour were the limit. Not surprisingly, and considering that not all five substations were yet in operation, a new schedule went into effect on November 1 with schedule time for the journey increased to three and a half hours. (The new schedule also instituted a Friday market special between New Westminster and Evan-Thomas.) Stations at the following locations were inaugurated with this schedule: Bergstrom (mile 7.8), Harmsworth, County Line, Yarrow, Woodroofe, and South Sumas.

In New Westminster on November 15, a contract was let to Messrs. Broley and Martin for the construction of the new interurban depot, two storeys high (but constructed to facilitate the addition of further storeys) and 132 feet square, at the southeast corner of Columbia and Eighth streets. Street car service at this time on both City and Sapperton lines was every twenty minutes, half-hourly on Sunday; freight service to Vancouver left New Westminster daily at 7:20 and 11:20 a.m. and 3:20 p.m., and departed Vancouver at 9:20 a.m. and 1:20 and 5:20 p.m.

Over two weeks earlier general manager Sperling had outlined the company's car building programme for the ensuing year, an unprecedented half-million-dollar commitment for 122 new cars, including fifty for Vancouver alone, just five for New Westminster, and two luxury chair cars, three combines, three passenger cars, two locomotives, and twenty-five box cars for the Fraser Valley branch. Sperling stressed that the need for new, and more, equipment was so great that the New Westminster shops, running to full capacity, could not keep up; consequently he had placed a number of car orders with other builders as well.

On November 2, just four days after Sperling's announcement, the *Chilliwack Progress* switched from touting trams to acknowledging automobiles:

"H. Hooper of Vancouver, who has been in the valley the past week or 10 days demonstrating to prospective buyers the splendid qualities of the Hupmobile, made a record trip from this city to Abbotsford yesterday. With S. Pugh they made the trip in two hours 10 minutes. The time is authentic, being telephoned back to Chilliwack upon their arrival at Abbotsford.

The trip is the most remarkable one considering the state of the road and it is a practical tribute to the qualities of the Hupmobile as a utility car. Across the Sumas Prairie the axle of the car dragged through the mud and water. Dr. Swift of Abbotsford came back with Mr. Hooper

A pass from the first year of operation of the interurban line to Chilliwack. (Norman W. Williams collection)

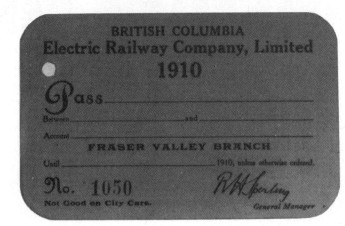

BRITISH COLUMBIA
Electric Railway Company, Limited
1910
Pass
Between _____ and _____
Account _____
FRASER VALLEY BRANCH
Until _____ 1910, unless otherwise ordered.
No. 1050
Not Good on City Cars.   General Manager

today and the same good time that was made yesterday was repeated today."

Nonetheless, Chilliwack's residents were anxious to begin receiving their mail via the B. C. Electric rather than by steamboat.

Two accidents bedevilled the Fraser Valley branch on November 18, both in the vicinity of Vedder Mountain. In one the steam locomotive left the rails and capsized into a ditch, severely scalding the conductor; in the other, a drunken construction worker who had lain down across the track was decapitated by an interurban car.

Just three days later the B. C. Electric called for tenders for its new Vancouver depot, and on the same day, the Western Canada Power Company applied to the Dominion government for a charter to build a street car line between Vancouver and New Westminster, via Port Moody.

As the year wound down in Vancouver, a new double tracked street car line had been laid the 1.2 miles on Broadway to Trafalgar Street from Granville although initial service, begun on December 2 with one car, ran only to Maple Street. In addition during 1910, Broadway had been single tracked somewhat over three-quarters of a mile to Commercial Drive from Fraser Street, and double track had been extended north from Broadway on Granville to Sixteenth Avenue. Furthermore, the Great Northern had built for the B. C. Electric a new steel bridge on Commercial Drive between Eighth Avenue and Broadway across its new, deeply cut entrance into Vancouver. Many street cars had been added during the year, including five (160-164) from John Stephenson Company and five (165-169) from Ottawa. With more lines and more street cars had come again the need for more street car storage space. In Vancouver, the answer had been fairly easy: lay tracks in the open south half of the block occupied by the Mount Pleasant barn, a task accomplished during the year.

Early in December the company had laid off two hundred men from its Fraser Valley branch construction camps, leaving 150 men in five camps ballasting the Vedder Mountain-Chilliwack section for another couple of weeks. By the end of the year, this section was felt to be as satisfactory as any other part of the line, although a washout near Cloverdale on the afternoon of December 23 was more than a little unsettling. Baldwin steam locomotives 536 and 537, helpful in the construction of the Chilliwack line, had been sold late in the year.

Two days before Christmas, graders made a connection at the end of the Sapperton line with the Burnaby Lake line, a matter of much relief after so much effort. With growth permeating all aspects of the company's operations, every new project seemed imbued with a rush to finish the job. But speed was an issue in industry and rush

was everywhere, commerce as well, necessitating a new, fast package express service four times a day each way between New Westminster and Vancouver.

During 1910 the complete B. C. Electric transportation system had carried 39,727,014 riders — up ten million over the previous year — on 200 street cars and interurbans; 41,142 tons of freight had been hauled. Three more — but only three — stupendous years were waiting in the wings.

Government regulation is the inevitable concomitant to expansion, and so it was that a railway department came into existence in 1911 in British Columbia, instituting strict supervision over the B. C. Electric's street car and interurban lines. Interurban line operations were to be brought under standards rules provided by the government (already adhered to on the Fraser Valley branch), and double headers were now illegal; the "name" interurbans would all have to be rebuilt and rewired for multiple unit operation, a project the company had already undertaken out of necessity for its Westminster branch.

In the Victoria area preliminary work had commenced in April on the Saanich line, two camps with 200 men between Victoria and Stelly's crossing, twelve miles out, having been set up to clear the right of way. A contract was then let on September 13 to Messrs. Moore and Pethick for the first eighteen miles of this new interurban line from Victoria to Deep Bay.

On the tenth of September, a 3,200-kilowatt generator was set in motion at the Jordan River hydro-electric development, delivering its power (via a 45-mile transmission line) to the city of Victoria for the first time. Incredibly, three very different types of railway lines had been created

Car 123 poses at Gorge Park, motoneer poised to swing his excursionists through Victoria to Oak Bay. (B.C. Hydro)

for the construction and maintenance of the development.

Initially, all materials were brought by tug and scow to the Jordan River wharf, where a steam derrick hoist (later electric) transferred the materials to cable car flats. These flats were then drawn by horses the less than half-mile to the power house, where they were run onto the second railway, an inclined one almost two miles in length, powered initially by a steam donkey engine at each end. This 36-inch gauge cable line rose 1,150 feet, with a maximum grade of 48%, to Forebay Reservoir (from which four penstocks rushed water down to the power house).

At Forebay, derricks transferred the loads to the flat cars of another railway line, not this time a cable car operation, but a 5.3-mile, 36-inch gauge line with twenty-pound rail on wooden ties, gravel ballast, special work, bridges and trestles, ending at Diversion Dam. Here was a virtually unknown operation of splendid importance, one which would not be shut down until 1971 when a Jordan River redevelopment project would be brought to fruition.

Initially seven horses, then an eleven-ton Davenport tank steam locomotive, and later a succession of gas locomotives and gas cars provided motive power. During the life of its operation, the line's main job ultimately was to provide a means of inspecting, maintaining, and rebuilding the 31,600-foot, fir wood, box-type flume which brought the water for the power house down to the reservoir. The flume itself was eight feet wide, six feet high, and supported for almost its entire length on trestle work. It had a gradient identical to that of its accompanying railway, $\frac{1}{10}$ of 1% (a one foot rise every thousand feet), allowing the water to flow through it at approximately four miles per hour.

This little railway also hauled all the sacks of cement, reinforcing steel, lumber, supplies, and men (at the height of activity, 1,100 men had been at work on the Jordan River project) for Diversion Dam, the largest dam in Canada when completed in 1912, as well as for Bear Creek Dam, four miles to the east. It had two, small, attractive stations, Diversion and Forebay, the location of the maintenance camp, barn for locomotives, gas cars, and rolling stock, bunkhouses, cookhouse, and housing for personnel. The B. C. Electric had even built during the construction period a sawmill at Forebay which supplied all the project's lumber requirements. Though both the railway from the wharf to the power house and the inclined railway would be superseded by roads (the inclined railway not in its entirety), the Forebay-Diversion line, with its beautifully scenic loop momentarily away from the flume at Alligator Creek, was an integral part of the Jordan River development for sixty years.

Although no new lines were constructed in Victoria in 1911, Fort Street was double tracked from Douglas to Cook, and between Harrison and St. Charles streets; and Richmond was double tracked between Fort and Pembroke streets.

By the end of the year eight and a quarter million Victoria and vicinity riders had been transported by the company's street cars (numbers 185, 186, 231, and 232 had been added to the fleet), over 100,000 electric lights were in service, and on Christmas Day local residents had been delighted by the opening of Canada's first artificial ice arena, a $110,000, 4,200-seat building at the northeast corner of Cadboro Bay Road and Epworth Street in Oak Bay.

On the lower mainland in 1911 the B. C. Electric's activity reached extraordinary new heights. On January 11, mail service to Chilliwack, but not to intermediate points, was given to the Fraser Valley branch, despite the fact that the line was in the middle of a one week closure due to snow storms and felled power poles and lines, particularly at Vedder Mountain. The dredge *King Edward* had meanwhile begun a three-month project, at a cost of $150 per day, of filling in the company's South Westminster proposed shop area.

The winter of 1911 brought heavy snowfall to the Vancouver area. On January 11 four interurban cars were snow bound on the Westminster

The Victoria branch (H. Gibson, traffic superintendent; A. T. Goward, local manager) was divided into nine street car lines, each identified by a coloured-lights-and-signs system displayed by every street car:

Beacon Hill-Spring Ridge (Fernwood)	*- one green light, and green signs*
Cloverdale - Outer Wharf	*- one white light, and white signs*
Esquimalt	*- one red light, and red signs*
Foul Bay	*- green and white lights, and green and white signs*
Gorge	*- two green lights, and green signs*
Oak Bay	*- red and white lights, and red and white signs*
Willows	*- two red lights, and red signs*

A "university school car" ran partly up the Mount Tolmie gravel pit line from Government Street three times weekly, twice on Saturdays. As an occasional car, it did not use lights or signs.

Large sheet metal signs were mounted on each side of a street car's headlight, diagonally marked with the appropriate colour and lettered with its destination. At night, the coloured lights, placed at each end of the street car's roof, identified the route.

branch, one even off the rails, necessitating the use of teams and sleighs for the removal and dispersal of passengers. But the snow did not stop the beginning of track laying on the Burnaby Lake line one week later, moving from the Sapperton end with a gang of 150 men.

In Vancouver January 13 saw the start of a one car shuttle service on Broadway between Fraser and Commercial, followed by the opening for service of the new line from Fourth Avenue and Alma Street to Fourth and Sasamat Street, via Tenth Avenue, on February 25.

On February 9 in New Westminster, the most recent of a series of washouts caused by melting snow at the north end of the Fraser River Bridge delayed the morning interurban from Chilliwack. Four days later company gangs, which had just completed double tracking the line from the car shops to the depot, crossed the bridge to Lulu Island and turned the first sod for the new Queensborough line.

On the same day, the company, having received a new mail contract, began delivering mail to intermediate points on the Fraser Valley branch. A mail clerk was added to the train's staff for the one trip each way daily except Sunday. Post offices were already in place along the line at Cloverdale, Milner, Mount Lehman, Clayburn, Abbotsford,

Locomotive 904 on the Chilliwack line, westbound with ballast on the approach to the bridge over the Fraser River at New Westminster. (Bob Webster collection)

Numerous stations on the Burnaby Lake line were named after company officials and prominent residents:

	Miles from Vancouver
Commercial Drive & 5th Avenue	2.5
Hastings Townsite (Boundary Road)	4.9
Horne Payne	5.1
Hastings Road (Douglas Road)	6.9
Sprott	7.7
Burnaby Lake (half a mile southeast of Great Northern's Burnaby Station)	8.3
Raeside	8.8
Vorce	9.2
Laursen	9.5
Hill Siding	9.8
Cumberland Road	10.3
Stormont Road	10.7
Cariboo Road	11.1
Craig Street	11.9
Sapperton	12.3

Huntingdon, Sardis, and Chilliwack — although Cloverdale could only be served by the Great Northern, Abbotsford by the C.P.R. — and before the year was out post offices would be opened at Langley Prairie, Coghlan, and Rand.

February in New Westminster also meant permission to construct a passing siding on Pine Street on the city line, but more importantly the revelation of plans to build a new street car line up Eighth Street from Columbia, east on Carnarvon, and up Sixth Street to join the city line at Fourth Avenue, before swinging west on Sixth Avenue to Twelfth Street. (This last Sixth Avenue segment, never built, would have created a belt line. City council had actually suggested further, to no avail, that a new line be built from the entrance of Queens Park north to Sixth Street, thus scrapping the zig-zaggy portion of the city line.)

At noon on February 27, the last spike of the Burnaby Lake line was driven, at a point in Hastings Townsite. On Wednesday, March 1, car "Westminster," crowded from vestibule to vestibule with officials and guests, left the Carrall Street depot at 11:30 a.m. sharp for New Westminster over the new line which swung sharply east from Commercial Drive at Sixth Avenue. Arriving at New Westminster at 12:45 p.m., it rested for fifteen minutes before setting out along the Sapperton line for the return run. The length of the line was 14.7 miles, although only 9.8 miles constituted the new line, the remaining distance being street car track run at both New Westminster and Vancouver ends. Although levelling and ballasting were still to come in some places, the company had been careful to run this return trip on the precise day to which it was bound by a contract with Burnaby municipality. Regular service was not an immediate concern.

By March 14, the interurban depot at Carrall Street was in the hands of a demolition company, and a shack on Carrall, with newly laid adjacent tracks, formerly occupied by the Vancouver Gas Company, was serving as a temporary station during the building of the new one. Office staff and officials had moved half a block east on Hastings to temporary quarters in the Holden Building. On the same day, the new sixty-pound rail, single track street car line on Fraser Street south from Forty-ninth Avenue to Fifty-Ninth (Page Road) was in operation for the first time. The complete cost of constructing its 2,700 feet was $10,815.70.

Chilliwack's splendid cement and wood depot was ever nearer to completion, now that its waiting rooms and offices were finished; in addition, 65,000 yards of gravel were set to be used to raise the height of the yard up to four feet to allow track to be laid in to the depot.

The Fraser Valley branch was an astonishing phenomenon, sometimes bringing in as many as 9,000 gallons of milk a day. Since the introduction of the interurban line, the two Chilliwack creameries had turned from making butter and cheese to the more lucrative business of selling milk and cream to the residents of New Westminster and Vancouver. Before the interurban, Chilliwack had exported no fresh milk; after the interurban, Chilliwack imported the butter it needed!

Before the interurban, residents of the Chilliwack area had made their way to New Westminster in one of three fashions, all of them time consuming, none of them spiritually uplifting: on Yale Road, a boggy slit through the trees; by steamer from Chilliwack Landing, after a stage trip from Chilliwack; and by stage, again to Chilliwack Landing, by the small, wood burning ferry *Minto* to Harrison Mills on the north side of the river, thence by C.P.R. (The steamers and ferries, with one exception, would be gone by 1920.) Large stations, each with an agent, were in place at Cloverdale, Milner, Abbotsford, Huntingdon, and Chilliwack. Langley Prairie, Clayburn, and Sardis would soon join them. Meanwhile, the Great Northern had gotten lost in its quest for Chilliwack, only about half of its line having been graded from Abbotsford to Chilliwack.

The Friday farmers' train was as big a success as the company had foreseen. The March 3 trip, for example, arriving at New Westminster at 9:50 a.m., brought 110 passengers and a baggage-express car loaded with produce and over 1,600 gallons of milk.

March in New Westminster proved to be a productive month in a number of ways: the company decided to re-lay the street car line from Edmonds to Queen's Park with sixty-pound rail (work began in May); seventeen cars were under construction at the car shops, including three new Fraser Valley interurbans, 1303 - 1305, patterned on 1300 - 1302 (baggage-express 1704 had just been delivered); its new wharf, with a 200- by 60-foot warehouse, all completed on April 12, was under construction at the foot of Eighth Street; the new depot was acquiring walls; rails on the new Queensborough line had been laid half way to the city limits at Ewen; and grading work at the north end of the Fraser River bridge had solved the problem there.

At the end of the month the company, in Vancouver, took steps to fill in the unsightly hole west of Vine to beyond Yew Street at the end of the Kitsilano line. It would also fill in the trestle and extend the platform, all in the interest of customer safety.

On April 1 residents at Byrne Road along the Eburne-New Westminster line received their desired shelter, and two days later, the company declared the Burnaby Lake line ready for business, awaiting only the formal sanction of the Dominion inspector. On the following day, a new passing siding was laid at Highland Park, allowing for fifteen-minute interurban service on the Westminster branch. Double tracking of the line was making good headway, and work had begun on the new, circuitous cutoff that would eliminate running the terrors of Twelfth Street hill. On the Fraser Valley branch, electric locomotives 952 and 953, as well as steam locomotive 525 (needing some alterations to bring it up to B. C. inspection standards) were hard at work. New stations had been added at Newton (mile 8.0 originally) and Evans, Bergstrom had been renamed Hazlitt, and Marshall Creek had been eliminated.

Was there a boom in Chilliwack? F. J. Hart & Co. Ltd., auctioneers, had chartered a four-car interurban train from Vancouver to Chilliwack for Saturday, April 22 ($2.25 return — $2 from New Westminster, lunch included). Two hundred people came aboard, the train arrived at 12:30 p.m., meals and refreshments were served at the opera house, and a whole subdivision of 114 lots, at one quarter cash, balance six, twelve, or eighteen months at six percent interest, was disposed of for $50,000. (The property handled is bounded by Young, Railway, Williams, and Third Avenue.)

In Langley, B.C. Securities was offering land from $250 an acre, and Kennedy Bros., Ltd. was offering lots near Kennedy station in Surrey at $300 to $500 an acre. At Cloverdale some of the larger tracts of land had been surveyed and cut up to be sold in parcels of three to ten acres. Company crews were in fact at work near Cloverdale in late April constructing a dyke to prevent the inundation of large areas of land at high tide. Very soon, lots would go on sale in Huntingdon priced between $200 and $1,000.

In Vancouver "owl" cars, offering service after midnight until as late as 3:20 a.m. with the payment of a double fare, were the innovation of the year when they began service on April 17. Two cars operated Fairview, four on Grandview-Fourth Avenue, two on Hastings Park-Stanley Park, two on Kitsilano-Harris (Georgia East), one on Main-Davie, and one on Robson-Broadway East.

The Fraser Valley branch made more news in May: milk was now being brought in bottles to New Westminster from Huntingdon; stations on the line were equipped with heaters, which could be switched on or off, as the weather demanded; work had begun on the two covered tracks, each holding three cars, at the Chilliwack depot; tenders were called for a car barn in Chilliwack (the 150-foot long freight shed was already in place); and in Abbotsford, the C.P.R., despite having arrived from main line Mission through Clayburn and to the border at Huntingdon as long ago as 1891, was taking the B. C. Electric seriously, building a new depot across the tracks from the

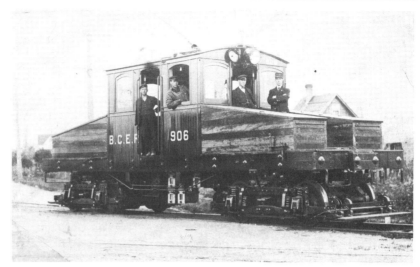

B. C. Electric's and constructing a new yard. At the same time, the Great Northern was driving piles over Montrose Street on its entry from the west to its new depot in Abbotsford, and erecting — at the insistence of New Westminster's Board of Trade — a 30- by 10-foot station building at Otter Road, somewhat more than three miles south of the B. C. Electric's line, where Warwhoop station would be erected within six months.

The beautiful weather and the first lacrosse game of the season had combined to make New Westminster's Empire Day (May 24) celebrations the most successful in years. (Fortunately, since New Westminster's traditional May Day had been a muddy washout.) The great bulk of the travel into and out of the city, most of it to Queen's Park, was of course handled by the B. C. Electric; approximately 12,000 people were carried. To handle this volume of traffic, 32 cars were used — nine large interurbans; seven of the large, newer, double truck street cars (briefly termed "suburbans"); eight city cars; and eight flat cars — in addition to the usual schedule. Despite the complexity of vehicle movements involved, only fifteen minutes were lost on the entire day's schedule on the interurban line from Vancouver,

Rarely-photographed locomotive 906 before its sojourn on Vancouver Island. (Peggy Webb collection)

An ad from the may 16, 1911 edition of New Westminster's newspaper.

Typical company newspaper advertisement in spring of 1911.

Car 158 moves south on Granville across Dunsmuir Street in 1911, C.P.R.'s Vancouver depot rising massively at the foot of the street. (Vancouver Public Library)

Lacrosse was king on the Pacific coast of Canada in 1911, and the B.C. Electric routes to the games were indispensable, as this newspaper ad confirms.

while the Eburne-New Westminster line fell behind twenty-five minutes. The Fraser Valley branch operated four-car trains rather than the usual three. For Vancouver, May was its peak month ever, as its street cars carried 3,384,228 riders.

There were rumors aplenty about new B. C. Electric interurban lines, obviously sparked by the Fraser Valley branch's success. One rumour had a line being run into Aldergrove from the main line;

another had the company purchasing the lonely Great Northern line from Cloverdale to the border; and yet another suggested the desirability of extending the line sixty miles beyond Chilliwack to the Steamboat Mountains. It was, however, a fact that the B. C. Electric had entertained the notion of extending the line thirty miles along the Fraser River to the town of Hope. Since traffic was still swelling, Sunday, June 4, saw the beginning of a new schedule of four passenger trains each way daily, as well as a daily milk, fruit, and vegetable express.

On June 13 in Vancouver, the Broadway West and Hastings East lines were connected, running from Broadway and Trafalgar to Hastings and Boundary Road, and one day earlier had finally seen the beginning of regular service, hourly, on the Burnaby Lake line. Interurban cars 1005 and 1008 had been assigned to the new run, with express car 507 (once numbered 7 and 107, and in the future, 1801) making two daily way freight journeys.

In the same month the company took delivery of three non-motored (they soon had motors installed) interurban cars, 1306 - 1308, from the G. C. Kuhlman Car Company in Cleveland. They were perhaps the company's most beautiful cars, even forty years later, with their distinctively

rounded vestibule windows, two-leaf vestibule doors hinged to fold against the car body, and full Empire-style ceilings, tinted and decorated to harmonize with the arch-top windows and ventilators and the rich African mahogany finish.

By July the double tracking of the Central Park line, the Westminster branch, had progressed to the point where an autumn end to the project was too optimistically mooted. There was much congestion on the line, particularly at Cedar Cottage where a street car loop utilizing Fifteenth Avenue and Findlay Street was being prepared for October operation. On July 27 the company announced its plans to build the much-clamoured-for Millside (Fraser Mills) interurban line from New Westminster, and on the 30th, the long-awaited Baldwin electric locomotives, 980 and 981, arrived for use on the Fraser Valley branch. They were designed to handle twenty freight cars on a 2% grade. Nonetheless, management felt that the line still needed a better steam locomotive, and Purvis recommended buying one for $17,000.

In Vancouver, another new street car line, the Shaughnessy Heights line, had begun operating by offering a one car shuttle service, starting on July 17 on Granville between Broadway and Sixteenth Avenue.

All during August the 115 men of the car shops worked in a frenzy to finish 25 steel frame, single end street cars for Vancouver, and to finish converting the older interurban cars to multiple unit operation. The shops had recently delivered six double ended P.A.Y.E. street cars to Vancouver. By the last day of August the Burnaby Lake line (the company took pains to style it as the Burnaby branch) had earned $10,045.61 in its short life.

On September 11, the company celebrated the opening of its splendid new two-storey interur-

ban depot in New Westminster. The three tracks running diagonally under and through the building, on to the track leading to Chilliwack along Front Street, were apportioned in the following fashion: the interurbans from Vancouver and Eburne entered on the north track (the one nearest the waiting room) and departed on the centre track, while the Fraser Valley branch had the south track entirely to itself. (The company's freight shed lay a mere couple hundred feet south, at the edge of the Fraser River.) The *British Columbian* reported on not a few of the $80,000 depot's unique features:

> "On the ground floor is a large public waiting room as commodious as any west of the splendid C.P.R. waiting room at Winnipeg. A ladies' waiting room and various ticket and engineering offices are also situated on the ground floor and a special constable named Robinson has been appointed to maintain order in the waiting rooms and platform, and to announce the trains. On the first floor there are twenty-one offices, eleven occupied by various officials of the

Granville Bridge serves as a backdrop for this eastward view of car 1203 (formerly "Delta"), about to leave the Steveston line's original depot in Vancouver, Granville station, crossing Kitsilano trestle almost immediately, Syd Kerr in charge. (B.C. Hydro)

Locomotive 902 hauls a ballast train in Vancouver southward on Oak Street at Twenty-second Avenue in 1911. (B.C. Hydro)

company, including the local manager, the manager of interurban lines, the general traffic manager, trainmaster, general roadmaster and car accountant. There are also four bedrooms for emergency crews on this floor as well as a class room for instructing motormen and conductors in which the trainmaster gives regular classes. A room has also been set apart for testing the sight and hearing of motormen and conductors. The ten remaining offices will be rented meanwhile, but with the growth of the business of the company the whole premises will be requestioned." †

With the inception of a new Fraser Valley line time table on October 8, more stations were in place, at Norris, Warwhoop, Bradner, Brentwood (to be renamed St. Nicholas), and Knight Road; two weeks later, passenger service to Chilliwack was reduced from four to three daily return trips, with another train daily only as far east as Huntingdon.

September in Vancouver had seen the extension of another new single track street car line, Main Street, from Fiftieth Avenue south to Sixty-third (Rosenberg Road then); at the same time, the double tracking of Main was completed between Twenty-fifth and Thirty-third avenues. On October 7, the 4,643-foot-long single tracked Earles Road line commenced operating, employing a single shuttle car between Victoria Road and Earles on Kingsway. The new street car loop at Cedar Cottage around Findlay Street and Fifteenth Avenue also went into service at this time. Three days later, the Shaughnessy Heights line was extended to Twenty-fifth Avenue (King Edward), the one car shuttle service still terminating at Broadway.

As November opened, the tracks west on Thirty-third Avenue to the quarry from Main Street were being shifted from the south side of the street to the centre and double tracked, in preparation for a large lumber and building supplies outfit to be built at the southwest corner of Thirty-third and Ontario Street. On the second of November the provincial government announced its million-dollar scheme for draining Sumas Lake.

Just before 7 a.m. on November 4, the shriek of wheels grinding on rails could be heard for blocks as a freight train rushed down New Westminster's Twelfth Street hill to its doom. The big hill claimed the life of conductor Fred Cooper, badly injured the motorman and trolley tender, and did thousands of dollars worth of damage. Frost, dew, and ordinary dirt had combined to make the rail too greasy for locomotive 906, its four box cars, and one flat car to negotiate the curve turning into Columbia Street. Air and electric brakes had been powerless to hold the train; all six pieces of equipment — locomotive included — were demolished, parts of the wreckage being thrown up to thirty feet from the

† "New Electric Tramline Depot," *British Columbian*, 21 September 1911, p. 1.

track. Such a calamity had always been feared. What with larger, longer passenger and freight movements no longer just in the future, the wisdom behind the building of a new cut-off line was readily apparent.

In North Vancouver the Lynn Valley line was disrupted once more as the heavy rains of November 19 caused the collapse of the wooden supports of the flumes of Hastings Mill near the street car line's terminus, causing the washout of 500 feet of track.

On November 23 the B. C. Electric made the decision to construct an unusually difficult line from Royal Oak on the Central Park line north to the proposed prison farm (Oakalla). Its sole purpose would be to ship construction materials to the building site. Before the month was out, the Kitsilano line had been double tracked west from its trestle.

Purvis' coveted 2-6-2 Baldwin steam locomotive — actually costing $17,500 — having arrived, arrangements were being made to secure water for its operation at New Westminster, Jardine, Vedder Mountain, and Chilliwack, while coal platforms were to be installed at Cloverdale and Abbotsford. Numbered 940 (older 525 became 941), it made its successful trial trip on December 9 as far as Cloverdale, and immediately became active hauling a work train.

Incredibly, two street car lines ceased operating on December 15, the line from Fourth and Alma to Fourth and Sasamat, and the line on Granville from Sixteenth to Twenty-Fifth. The cause for this action was really quite basic, a disagreement over franchise terms between the B. C. Electric and the municipality of Point Grey.

The morning of December 16 could have brought the company another tragedy, but everything conspired to allow for a happy ending to a harrowing ride. Interurban car 1201 had left Vancouver at 6 a.m. for Eburne and New Westminster, well-filled with passengers, most of whom had alighted by the time Kerrisdale (Forty-first Avenue) had been reached. Near Royal station (Fifty-first Avenue), already on the fairly steady down-grade to Eburne, the car's trolley came off the wire and the motorman found the car's brakes to be inoperative. With two miles of fast running still to Eburne, the car gained speed enormously, screamed through Eburne, somehow negotiated the perilous right hand curve onto the bridge to Lulu Island (the switch was always open to Steveston, rather than to New Westminster), crossed it, eventually slowing to a very quiet halt a mile and a half south of the bridge. Conductor Batten fortunately retained his presence of mind to the extent that he persuaded some persistent passengers to forget the idea of jumping.

North Vancouver saw its delightful "mountain railway," the Capilano street car line, brought into

service during the year; and operations on the Lynn Valley line were aided by the installation of a passing siding on Fourth Street.

In New Westminster, the double tracking of Columbia Street, together with pavement and airy, ornamental, between-the-tracks trolley wire hangers, had indeed changed the character of its imposing commercial thoroughfare east to Leopold Place. Four city cars were in service on the City line, which now ran well past the city limits, right through "little Siberia" to Edmonds and Kingsway; for the more efficient operation of the lengthened service, a three-car siding, used for meets, had been installed during the year at Cliff's Cannery, Sixth Street at Twelfth Avenue. The incoming interurbans obviously offered service down Twelfth Street to the depot, six cars regularly being employed between New Westminster and Vancouver. The depot-to-Sapperton run operated three street cars.

Because of the preponderance of single track, "operators" were on duty at the junction at Edmonds and Kingsway, and at the siding at

Edmonds and Eighth Street (Canada Way), Pine Street, and Queen's Park. A lunch room was even maintained on Fourth Avenue near Queen's Park for street car crew members who were unable to get home for meals; coffee, tea, and sandwiches were served.

In Vancouver, only one single truck street car was still regularly active, that on the lightly travelled Mountain View line. In November, an eight-block street car connection had been built, double tracked, on Commercial Drive between Venables and Powell streets, crossing Hastings on the way, and serviced by one shuttle car. During the year, Broadway had been double tracked between Fraser and Commercial; West Georgia, Pender to Chilco; Vernon Drive, Georgia to Frances; and Granville, Sixteenth to Twenty-fifth, had been similarly treated. And the province's Minister of Railways published the ruling, regarding the operation of street cars, that "on business streets of a City, speed must not exceed twelve (12) miles per hour, and on other streets eighteen (18) miles per hour."

Columbia Street, attractively double tracked and finished, was now the sophisticated business street New Westminster had always wished for.
(New Westminster Public Library)

Vancouver had swallowed up District Lot 301 and Hastings Townsite during the year. The Dominion government's census of 1911 revealed the following population figures:

Chilliwack	*1,657*
New Westminster	*13,199*
North Vancouver	*8,196*
Point Grey	*4,320*
South Vancouver	*16,126*
Vancouver	*108,597*
Victoria	*31,660*

In 1911 the B. C. Electric's 267 street cars and interurbans had carried 55,046,581 riders; Victoria Day alone, in Victoria, had seen 45,000 people ride street cars. Freight tonnage hauled almost doubled from 1910's total to 77,598; though altogether the company had 647 pieces of rolling stock, it was still not enough. The greatest headache for the company was acquiring enough vehicles for its burgeoning passenger and freight traffic. After all, in British Columbia there was only one automobile for every 116 persons.

In Victoria 1912 was a peak year for track laying and for real estate speculation. Approximately eighteen miles of the Saanich line had been cleared by February, and the B. C. Electric decided in March that it would operate a street car service on Burnside Road, the route out of Victoria for the Saanich line, from Douglas to the city limits at Washington Avenue; the street cars on this run would display a white sign with a red diagonal band. Another street car line was being readied for its thrust beyond the Willows and north to a fabulous, new Oak Bay residential development, "Uplands," for which advertisements for lots selling from $3,000 to $55,000 began to appear in May. By the following month, another new line on Hillside Avenue, east from Douglas, was double tracked to Cook Street, across the Victoria & Sidney Railway's main line on Rose Street.

At the end of June, the following street cars were in Victoria service, of which sixteen were pay-as-you-enter cars, six of them single enders: 1-6, 8, 9, 11-13, 20, 22, 23, 25-27, 30, 50, 69-71, 73, 107, 117-123, 183-187, 231-234, and 250-255, the last eight new arrivals since the beginning of the year.

Service on the Mount Tolmie line came closer to being a reality in July with an experimental rush hour run from downtown on weekends; the residents had looked with some envy at even the limited service being run for students, though others too could ride. It was in this month as well that clearing of the Saanich line's right of way was finished. Grading was close to completion, and track laying was soon to begin.

Esquimalt incorporated as a municipality, and in September the company geared up for bringing electricity to Saanich and a street lighting system to Oak Bay. September was the peak month for riders on the Victoria branch; 967,186, almost 200,000 more than the previous year's total, were carried.

In November, the first unit of the company's standby steam plant at Brentwood Bay, on the Saanich line, was placed in operation; its purpose was to supplement, and be auxiliary to, the power arriving from Jordan River. On November 29, the first street car travelled the full length of the double tracked Hillside line, 5,720 feet from

Recently arrived 236 at work on the double tracked Hillside line. (Victoria City Archives)

In August a 36-point edict came from the province's attorney-general, under authority of the Tramway Inspection Act, prescribing "the equipment and appliances for the operation of tramways and street railways in British Columbia." It included the following directives:

1. *no standees are allowed on interurban coaches;*
2. *a separate compartment for baggage and mail must exist on interurban coaches carrying such;*
3. *street cars must be equipped with doors or gates, automatic projecting fenders and automatic wheel guards, wire mesh window screens, destination signs visible by day and night, and rail sanding devices;*
4. *the speed limit on city streets is ten miles per hour, eight on business streets;*
5. *a "car full" sign must be displayed when that fact is the case;*
6. *a notice of each car's passenger capacity must be displayed;*
7. *cars must be standardized: all plans for new cars must be submitted to the tramway inspector for approval;*
8. *no riding on bumpers or steps;*
9. *the height of the bottom step of each car must not be more than sixteen inches above the ground; and*
10. *all operating employees must pass a rules examination and an eye and ear test.*

The company was given until the end of the year to accomplish these adjustments and demands.

Douglas to Cedar Hill Road, altogether a showpiece run with its freshly paved street and sidewalks. The new line offered service right into downtown, the new Hillside destination being signified by red and green diagonal signs. The Hillside line would transport 45,667 riders by the end of the year.

All of B. C. Electric's single track street car operations employed the commonly used "staff system." In Victoria a box, in which a baton-like stick was kept, had been nailed to a telephone pole at each passing siding. The motorman of the first car to reach the siding removed the stick. He handed it through the window to the motorman of the other car when it arrived, who then returned the stick to its box. Very simple the system was, and safe.

During 1912, Victorians were finally done with Rock Bay bridge: by laying a new double tracked line on Government from the car barn north to Douglas, and another new double tracked line on Bay Street from Douglas west to the point on Esquimalt Road where the line from the old bridge swung on to it, the run to Esquimalt now safely avoided Rock Bay altogether. In fact the street car line on Johnson and Store streets was rendered meaningless, the Johnson stretch being abandoned, the Store Street section south of Chatham Street taken over by the Esquimalt & Nanaimo Railway (which itself was leased in 1912 by the C.P.R.).

The Burnside line was also completed during the year, double tracked the 3,260 feet from Douglas to Washington Avenue. A spur was laid from the Spring Ridge line on Cook Street to Royal Athletic Park, and a major adjustment was made on the Outer Wharf route during its double tracking from Government Street through to St. Lawrence and Erie Streets. The original track on the one block of Erie between St. Lawrence and Dallas Road was ripped up and relaid on Ontario Street, a block south, its new passage of entry to the outer wharf.

Further double tracking in 1912 was accomplished on the following routes: May Street, Cook to Joseph streets; Menzies Street, Superior to Niagara streets; Cook Street, Pandora to Caledonia avenues; Government Street, Belleville to Superior streets; and Douglas Street, Fisgard Street to Burnside Road. In addition, company office space having become extremely limited, even in its relatively new Victoria building, a third floor was added to the head office, as well as an extension on its west end. During 1912 the B. C. Electric's Victoria branch carried almost eleven million riders, three million more than in 1911.

For the B. C. Electric on the lower mainland as well, 1912 was a year to remember. On January 12 the Broadway East-Robson service was extended east along Broadway to Commercial Drive. By the following week, company crews in New

Eight street cars jam a crowded Government Street in this 1912 Victoria view north from Yates Street. (B.C. Hydro)

Westminster had finished laying double track from Columbia and Eighth Street up the hill to Carnarvon Street, east to Sixth Street, and up the hill, again, to a connection with the city line at Fourth Avenue; only the two curves and the connection at Columbia had yet to be built. By this time also, the massive job of double tracking the Central Park line had been completed west from Cedar Cottage to Highland Park, 1.2 miles west of Edmonds.

On the Fraser Valley branch, the company put a steam shovel to work at its Sullivan gravel pit, ten miles from New Westminster, on February 27. The gravel had three principal destinations: the many new spurs on the branch itself, the Queensborough line, and the new double track to come between Eburne and Vancouver. On March 2 a box car ran away for a mile and a half, before it ditched, on the hill at Mount Lehman, fracturing the brakeman's ribs, tearing up track, and tying up the line for six hours.

Stringing of trolley wire on the 2.1-mile interurban line from New Westminster to Queensborough was accomplished on March 6, and on the following day, the B. C. Electric announced that work would now begin in earnest on the 3.6 mile cut-off line for the Central Park line into New Westminster from Highland Park station. This was also the day of the incorporation of West

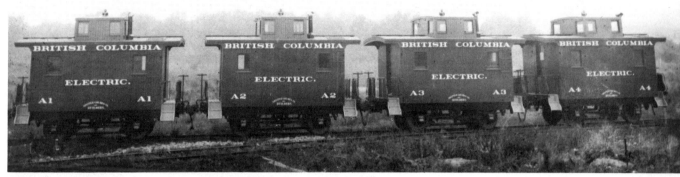

The company's first cabooses, purchased from Seattle Car Manufacturing Company. (Gerry Stevenson collection)

Vancouver, the large municipality across the Capilano River, west of North Vancouver, and though there would be talk over the years regarding a street car service there, such a thing never happened.

The first electric track switch in the complete B. C. Electric system was installed on March 18 at Broadway and Granville for the northwest corner, southbound. (Traffic still operated on the left side of the road, and would continue to do so until the last day of 1921.) Its success prompted the installation of another on March 27 at Pacific and Granville, southbound. What a relief it must have been for conductors to see that their future might not include continually jumping out of their street cars to switch tracks manually!

Also on March 27, the B. C. Electric announced its awarding of a $250,000 contract for the largest interurban car order it would ever make, to the St. Louis Car Company for twenty-two passenger cars and two baggage-express cars. (This would later grow to twenty-eight and four, when the company would accept six cars ordered and then cancelled by Pacific Northwest Traction, for its line between Bellingham, Mt. Vernon, and Sedro Woolley in neighbouring Washington State.) The terms of the contract demanded that the car builders start shipments within 85 days of the receipt of the order. The roof of each car was to be of the arch type — new research had been claiming that such a design afforded better ventilation — similar to that of the new 300-series street cars, and slat seats used in these new street cars would also be adopted for the ordered interurbans, it being clear to the company that rattan seats were unsanitary. (Thankfully, this was but a passing notion.) Niles Car and Manufacturing Company of Niles, Ohio would supply the baggage-express cars.

Afternoon rush hour in Vancouver had become hectic to the point that 140 street cars were in the street at that time on weekdays. By April 12, twenty-five new cars from Brill, 300-324, had been integrated into Vancouver's system. In North Vancouver the double heading of street cars was deemed absolutely necessary because of the fact that, like it or not, the ferry system across Burrard Inlet dictated the regularity and quantity of passenger traffic. And yet it was a headache of special intensity, as illustrated on April 6 when car 16 rear-ended car 34 at Phillip and Twenty-Second as they were double heading the Capilano line.

One of the most unusual projects ever undertaken by the company came to fruition on May 1 with the opening of the 6,456-foot prison farm spur from Royal Oak on the Central Park line to the abuilding Oakalla prison farm buildings. Work on the $11,295.25 B. C. government-owned spur had begun a month earlier, the line running down the east side of Royal Oak Avenue, six feet from the road's centre line, with a passing siding along the way. Despite the fact that the spur's northern half descended at an 8% grade, and its last 620 feet were 9% with a very sharp eastward curve at the steepest point, the company was able to deliver 115 cars of construction materials over the next five months, each car taken down singly by its locomotive! In wet weather there were no deliveries. In October a drum-and-cable system to be installed at the top of the incline to let cars down the grade was approved by the company, but never effected. (Though the provincial government informed the company on May 31, 1915 that the spur was no longer required, it lay largely unused for a number of years before its removal.)

On May 3 the car shops were given the go-ahead for multiple unit rewiring and rebuilding of the last three interurban cars to require this treatment, "Westminster" (1200), "Chilliwack" (1210), and "Ladner" (1213), all three in bad shape and needing a paint job. Approval was given at the same time to reconstruct three other 1200s into passenger-mail cars; thus "Coquitlam" (1209), "Sardis" (1214), and "Sumas" (1216) were to be renumbered 1500, 1501, and 1502, respectively. (In the event, 1209 did become 1500, but 1214 became passenger trailer 1600, and 1216 became 1501.)

The ten smaller interurban cars (1000-1009) that the company had purchased from Ontario's Preston Car & Coach Company in 1910 had arrived, as ordered, without multiple unit equipment. (As street cars, they were originally to have been numbered 400-409.) During 1911 the car shops had rectified this situation, and had also

fitted them up with end-door vestibules of the same design with which the "name" interurbans had been refashioned and raised their bodies to allow for better coupler alignment. Furthermore, street cars 82 and 83 had been rebuilt with interurban motors and controls, multiple unit equipment, heavier trucks, and interurban style vestibules, emerging as interurban cars 1011 and 1012. Thus, aside from the larger 1300s, 1400s, and 1700s in use on the Fraser Valley branch, the company would possess, when the last three 1200s were rebuilt, 29 multiple unit interurban cars for use on its Westminster, Burnaby, and Lulu Island branches.

The very first segment of what would become Vancouver's most loved street car line, the Oak Street operation, went into service on May 20, Oak Street between Broadway and Sixteenth Avenue, double tracked. On May 3 the short diagonal of Kingsway between Main Street and Broadway had been laid, double tracked, allowing through running out Kingsway (still called Westminster Road) without the annoyance of contending with the Broadway and Main intersection.

Monday, June 10, was the day Millside (Fraser Mills) had so long desired. Its gigantic Canadian

The inauguration of passenger service to Millside (Fraser Mills) by 1001 and 1002 on June 10, 1912 attracted a wide cross-section of New Westminster's businessmen and company officals.
(B.C. Hydro)

Times, stations, and mileages for the Fraser Mills line had the following aspect:

Minutes	Miles		Miles	Minutes
0	.0	Fraser Mills	3.7	25
4	.7	Riverton	3.0	21
6	1.0	Abbatoir	2.7	20
—	1.1	G.N. Crossing	2.6	—
7	1.2	Braids	2.5	19
8	1.7	Keary Street	2.0	17
9	1.8	Brewery	1.9	16
10	2.0	Brunette	1.7	15
—	2.8	Leopold	.9	—
25	3.5	New Westminster	.0	0

(The greater length for the return trip is due to the looping around the block at the New Westminster depot which would be instituted in 1913 on February 1.)

Track being laid in the new Carrall Street station. Hastings Street in the background welcomes their exit. (B.C. Hydro)

Western Lumber Company mill, arguably the most important lumber mill in Canada, employed over 700 men, and for them and their families, travelling anywhere meant walking to the Sapperton line. But now it was ready, a two-mile line branching east off the Sapperton line onto Brunette Street, then mounting its own 0.8 mile private right of way, donated as an incentive to the company by the mill, as had been the ties and poles. After a trial trip on that day, hourly service was immediately instituted. Only passenger service was operated for the time being, but freight service would begin very shortly, as soon as the track was completed south from the terminus directly into the mill buildings themselves, competition indeed for Canadian Pacific and Great Northern.

In Vancouver, June 6 had seen the Main Street line extended three blocks south from Sixty-third Avenue to Marine Drive (River Road then). Four days later, double tracking of a new eight-block line from Robson via Richards and Pacific streets to Granville was finished, allowing traffic to use it while the five blocks of Granville between Robson and Drake were being freshly double tracked in a record twenty-two days. June 1912 for the Edmonds area meant the circulation of a petition asking for a bigger, more capacious station for this very busy junction point, both for passengers and for freight. On the Lulu Island branch it meant the opening of the summer horse racing season (there were even four harness races) on the 29th at Minoru Park (a twenty-mile round trip from

Vancouver). As the ad said, "Trams leave Granville station at 12:30 p.m., 1 o'clock and 1:30, and a special of three cars will be held in readiness to run at 2 p.m. Admission (Including Round Trip Tram Tickets) $1.25." Later in the summer, car racer, Barney Oldfield, would appear at Minoru Park as a special feature on a racing card.

In North Vancouver, by the end of June eight of the large Vancouver street cars which had begun arriving by cross-inlet barge in May 1911 were then in regular service. In addition to these vehicles, 150 - 157, the older 24, 28, 32, 34, 36, 40, 42, and 60 were still there, most often spending their time in the small storage area opened during the year adjacent to the car barn. Old 14 and 16, as well as S.62 (formerly 915), had been scrapped in North Vancouver in April, while track had been laid six blocks farther on Lonsdale to Windsor Street.

Though its waiting room still wanted finishing touches, on August 6 the first interurbans nosed into the superb new B. C. Electric head office building and interurban depot, at the same old location, Hastings and Carrall streets. The one track off Hastings Street split into two in the depot, while another track from Hastings, essentially for freight movements, found room between the west side of the new structure and the C.P.R. line. South behind the depot, these tracks combined to cross Pender Street singly on the way to the company's ever-growing Carrall Street yard.

The building was magnificent. Designed by architects Somervell and Putnam, the handsome, five-storey edifice was erected at a cost of $420,000 and authoritatively proclaimed the power and comprehensiveness of the B. C. Electric. It measured 190 feet on Carrall and 71 feet on Hastings, and its covering of brick exterior walls over concrete foundations and frame was attractively highlighted by terra cotta trim. Three hundred officials and office workers moved in with alacrity and pleasure.

The city also had had enough of temporary measures around the head office site, and issued instructions, via the board of works, to the company on August 20 to remove its temporary tracks on Hastings into the frame building on Carrall which had been serving as the interurban station. The city was also not amused that the company had laid new track across Pender Street, but on C.P.R. right of way, ostensibly to avoid seeking permission from the city to cross the street.

Another lonely, area-opening, one car shuttle line (though a siding was in place between Third and Fourth avenues) commenced operating in Vancouver on August 25 when the 1.3-mile, single tracked Nanaimo Street line, Hastings to Broadway, first offered its twenty-minute service. September 7 was the first day of double tracking work on the Vancouver-Eburne interurban line; in a very brief time the section from Twenty-fifth Avenue to Eburne was ready, and the rest was in place before the year was out. On September 9 — a new, detailed agreement to be signed by Point Grey municipality and the B. C. Electric on the following day — Point Grey got back the street car services it had been without for the previous nine months. On the same day, Point Grey gained a new single tracked line whose opening had been delayed by the dispute — the section, somewhat over a mile in length, on Oak Street from Sixteenth to King Edward, then west to Granville Street.

The company was also in the process of rebuilding its older lines with rather well-timed ferocity. During the two midsummer months, Hastings between Main and Cambie streets, Broadway between Ontario and Bridge (Cambie) streets (over 2,300 feet, accomplished in twenty days), and Frances between Vernon Drive and Victoria Road (2,880 feet in just twenty-one days!) acquired modern, sophisticated roadbed and

A sun kink has developed in the freshly laid track on King Edward Avenue, west to Granville Street. (B.C. Hydro)

trackage. The double track on Frances replaced the street's original single track.

The Canadian Northern Pacific Railway having arrived in Chilliwack, after braving the construction horrors of the Fraser Canyon, the B. C. Electric and the C.N.P. set an interlocker in place on September 12 at the southern edge of Chilliwack where the two lines crossed. On September 16 B. C. Electric commenced passenger service from New Westminster to Jardine Street on the 2.1-mile, side-of-the-road Queensborough line, built, unlike the Fraser Mills line, without incentives or concessions from the numerous industries ready to benefit from its operation. It used a new track, rather than the Central Park line's, between New Westminster's depot and the hundred-foot bridge across to Queensborough. On the day following, a five-cent settlers' rate was introduced on the Vancouver-Eburne interurban line, as well as on the street car lines in Point Grey; two days later, Point Grey received more street car service when a single car offering fifteen-minute service began its labours on remote Wilson Road (today's Forty-first Avenue) from a connection with the interurban line at Kerrisdale to Dunbar Street, 6,958 feet to the west.

How the B. C. Electric prepared for royalty! For the visit of their Royal Highnesses, the Duke and Duchess of Connaught and their daughter, Princess Patricia (the Duke was then Canada's Governor-General), the company decorated its head office building with a blaze of lights and

These passes particularize their restricted areas of use. The Burnaby Branch was to become better known as the Burnaby Lake line. (Norman W. Williams collection)

Car 1304, "Connaught," with Canada's governor general, the Duke of Connaught, on board, stops at Edmonds and Kingsway on September 21, 1912 before proceeding down Twelfth Street to New Westminster. (Ted Clark collection)

Specially decorated for the Duke of Connaught, car 1304 was temporarily titled "Connaught." Note 1304 over the doorway. (B.C. Hydro)

royal motifs. (This was their second visit. What changes they must have observed since their first trip in 1890.) But the company outdid even itself. Selecting one of its New Westminster-built Fraser Valley branch interurban cars, the fifteen-month old 1304, the company sent it back into the car shops for an extraordinary transformation, and when it reappeared, it had been freshly painted; it also bore the royal coat of arms, twice on each side, the name "Connaught" and the company's name in full, both delicately, but boldly, lettered in gold on each side.

Its interior, with seats and partitions removed, resembled a well-appointed living room, with carpet, curtains, and upholstered chairs, mostly in cream and green. The orange glass of the upper arches of the windows was masked by the curtains, and red light bulbs were strategically installed elsewhere to resemble an open fire in a grate.

The Duke and his party (the Duchess stayed in Vancouver) boarded "Connaught" at the Hastings and Carrall depot at 10:45 a.m. on September 21 for a trip to New Westminster over the Central Park interurban line. All traffic on the line had been halted at 10:30 a.m., all spurs and sidings had been spiked, and a pilot car with police officials ran five minutes ahead. Thousands of people gathered along the route to catch a glimpse and wave. From Edmonds, the party proceeded via the Twelfth Street routing into New Westminster, where an honour guard of one hundred members of the 104th Regiment and its band welcomed the royal party. Continuing their tour by automobile, the Duke and his entourage visited, among other sights, the huge mill at Fraser Mills. The return trip to Vancouver, with motorman Freure and conductor Grimmer still on duty, was taken on the Lulu Island branch via Eburne.

The royal visit is remembered in the name of the bridge, in place until 1984, on Cambie Street in Vancouver. The Connaught Bridge, which

Their Royal Highnesses officially opened on September 20, replaced an obsolete one built in 1892. The area through which the Central Park interurban cars would pass upon completion of the Highland Park cutoff is still today called Connaught Heights. Car 1304 soon reverted to normal life and service, its transformation having been quite magical and certainly short-lived. (It is the only Fraser Valley interurban still in existence today, at Glenwood, Oregon.)

October 14 was the first day of street car operation over the Connaught Bridge; two-car, ten-minute service ran on the double track from Hastings, south on Cambie Street to Robson, east one block on new track to the bridge, and over it south to Cambie and Broadway. On the same day street cars began service on the new, double tracked, 1.2-mile Sixteenth Avenue line between Oak and Main streets. (The Oak-Cambie section had actually been ready in July.) The last new street car line of 1912 for Vancouver was the extension in Point Grey on November 14 of the Sasamat line west on Fourth Avenue to Drummond Drive, 2,497 uphill feet of single track. The new wyes at Broadway and Trafalgar and at Hastings and Boundary allowed the company's thrust away from double ended street cars on busy lines to gather more momentum, specifically in the matter of the Broadway West-Hastings East Line which became a single end street car operation on November 28, running on Hastings, Richards, Robson, and Granville streets through downtown.

Late in November the B. C. Electric announced a scheme to do away with the always unsatisfactory terminus of the Lulu Island branch interurban cars, the Granville (or Granville Street) station. Passengers arriving there on the Lulu Island branch and desiring to reach Vancouver by street car lines other than the overlapping Kitsilano-Harris were obliged either to walk a couple of blocks up and along Granville Street or to climb the winding stairs on Granville Bridge. Furthermore, the Granville station, really only a typical interurban line shelter, gave little protection from the weather, had inadequate washroom facilities, lacked a waiting room, and had a platform both too short and too narrow.

The company proposed a gracious, chateau-style terminus attached to the west side of Granville Bridge, approximately one block north of its south end, and resting on twenty-five-foot pilings thrust into the bed of False Creek. On the

On Ewen Avenue with the Queensborough line shortly after its opening for service on September 16, 1912. New Westminster rises in the background. (New Westminster Public Library)

A new box car, acquired in 1912 from Seattle Car and Foundry Company. (Gerry Stevenson collection)

While new special work is being installed off Broadway, north on Cambie Street to Connaught Bridge, a temporary single track on the south side of Broadway keeps the street cars moving. (B.C. Hydro)

† "Contract for Cars Runs to $500,000," *Vancouver Daily Province*, 26 November 1912, p. 26.

bridge in front of the proposed depot passed the Broadway West-Hastings East, Fairview, and Grandview-Fourth Avenue street cars; at the rear of this depot would be located the tracks for accommodating the Lulu Island branch interurban cars. (Initially, it was planned to have the interurban cars approach the depot on Granville Bridge, coming from a Fourth Avenue connection with the interurban line, and swing west off the bridge, before reaching the depot, onto the platform of the depot. On December 10, the approach, to avoid congestion on Fourth, was redesigned to one over a short bridge on Third Avenue.) Such a terminal would assure rapid, convenient interchanges of riders between the interurban line and the street car lines. The depot would consist of two wings, each about 40 by 23 feet, with a connected, covered passageway, 25 feet in width, between the interurban tracks and the street car line.

On November 26, the company placed a $500,000, sixty-five-street car order (subsequently reduced to forty) with the Preston Car & Coach Company. An official of B. C. Electric clarified the company's concerns in the following manner:

> *"The placing of this large order with an eastern firm at this time does not by any means mean that the B. C. Electric Railway Company has abandoned its policy of car building at its New Westminster shops. At the present time our traffic requirements are such as require large additions of rolling stock in the shortest possible time and we must meet these conditions in the best possible manner. With the large amount of repair work incident to the greatly increased amount of rolling stock we now carry, it is not practicable to turn out from the New Westminster shops cars at the rate demanded by the growth of the company's business, hence the order noted has been given to an eastern car building concern. I may say, however, that at present the needs of the company on all branches of its*

system for new rolling stock during 1913 are being drawn up and the orders for the work will shortly be arranged. When these allotments are made it will be found that ample work to keep the New Westminster car shops constantly busy, has been apportioned to that plant." †

On Monday, December 2, a longer, safer, completely double tracked Central Park line went into service between New Westminster and Vancouver, using the just-completed 3.6-mile Highland Park cut-off, thereby eliminating the always worrying hill on Twelfth Street. This new section swung away toward the south from Highland Park station to describe a wide, sweeping arc in its run back to the former mainline at Twelfth Street Junction, a little over half a mile short of the depot. Though the cutoff had cost over $183,000, it was really a marvellous solution to the vexing difficulty of getting to New Westminster from Vancouver without resorting solely to river bank travel, and at no point did the new grade exceed 3 per cent.

The substation at Earles Road along the line in Vancouver had been inaugurated earlier in the year, and in the double tracking of the route through Vancouver and Burnaby, the grade had been smoothed out, new street crossings and stations built, and former station names such as Epworth (Lakeview), Ferguson (Beaconsfield), Boundary Road (Park Avenue), and Keefer (McKay) finally obliterated.

The cutoff actually reduced terminus-to-terminus running time by ten minutes, despite the fact that the cutoff had lengthened the line. No more were there delays at Highland Park, the end of double track (where there had been an operator to assist movement). And since the remaining 3.6 miles from Highland Park to the New Westminster depot were single tracked, this section had been operated on the staff system — the passing siding was at the orphanage on Twelfth at Dublin Street — with its attendant potential for delays. (Although the interurban cars had made passenger stops on Twelfth Street, none were ever made south of Fifth Avenue, this being the beginning of the steepest part of the notorious hill.)

The opening of the cutoff meant the end of dispatching interurban movements, both to Carrall Street and to Eburne, from Twelfth Street Junction. All dispatching would now emanate from the depot in New Westminster. The Highland Park cut-off also meant access to a valuable gravel pit on Connaught Hill.

What it signified for the city of New Westminster was the complete restructuring of its street car system, something the company carefully planned: new rails had been laid the entire distance of the original line from Edmonds via Queen's Park to Leopold Place, and a new siding on Edmonds Street at Sixth Street replaced the one at Eighth Street; Columbia Street had been double tracked from the foot of Twelfth Street to east of Leopold Place; a new, more direct, double tracked line had been laid between Sixth Street and the depot; track had been laid on Begbie Street to afford a loop around the city block containing the depot; and an unusual passing siding-turnout system had been installed on Twelfth Street at Sixth Avenue.

New street car lines began service on December 2: the Edmonds-Sapperton (No. 1) line operated from Edmonds, down Twelfth to Columbia Street, and out to Sapperton; the old city line run was extended to Highland Park (to connect with the Central Park line), becoming the Highland Park-Sixth Street (No. 2) line; and the new Eighth-Carnarvon-Sixth Street connector would soon be combined with the lower end of the city line to offer a belt service. Interurban cars operated the Fraser Mills line, while the Queensborough line employed a single street car between the depot and Jardine Street. (At this time, only the No. 1 line and the Burnaby Lake line used the loop around the depot block at Begbie Street.) Twelve two-man double ended street cars were responsible for the service: 92 and 97, newly transferred to New Westminster, and 100-106 and 108-110.

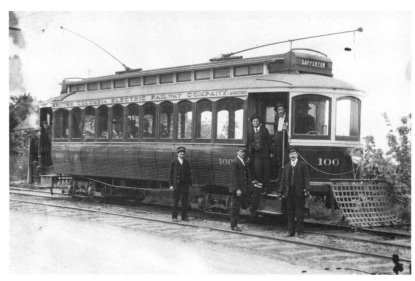

As part of its preparations for December 2, the company had been in the process of installing derail switches (similar to the one on Lonsdale Avenue in North Vancouver) on the steepest part of the hill on the new line on Sixth Street between Fourth Avenue and Carnarvon Street, but by December 4, only the first one, just below Queen's Avenue, had been installed. Around 11:25 p.m. in the evening, street car 103

Car 100 features a particularly dashing paint style. (B.C. Hydro)

Interurban coach 1011 existed for a scant fifteen years, posing here in 1912 at Cumberland siding on Columbia Street, Brunette branching off at left background to Fraser Mills. (George A. Culbert photo)

proceeded gingerly past the derail, but then began skidding because of the frozen mud and water on the rail; brakes and applications of sand did not affect its accumulating flight in any way. Skidding across Royal Avenue, and plunging four more blocks, the car's momentum was halted only by the sharp turn to the right of the tracks onto Carnarvon, a course the car disdained in favour of derailing, almost cutting itself in two on impact with a light pole, and missing a Dr. Hall's residence by inches. Miraculously, motorman, conductor, and two passengers escaped with their lives. Within days, derail switches were installed at Royal Avenue and at Agnes Street. Now that freights and interurbans no longer used Twelfth Street, Sixth and Carnarvon became the system's most notorious danger spot.

In Vancouver, company officials were excited about what they saw as a new trend in street car design. It was the "nearside" car, number 501, tested on Robson Street on December 19. One of the company's cars had been rebuilt for the experiment. It had no rear platform, and passengers entered and left at the front, where the front platform had been enlarged to accommodate both the motorman and the conductor. The motorman controlled both entrance and exit doors. At the rear of the car was a circular seat, as well as an emergency door controlled by the conductor. "Nearside" referred to the custom of stopping for passengers before crossing a street, already an established rule in Vancouver on paved streets.

During the year the Kitsilano trestle, used by both Kitsilano-Harris street cars and Lulu Island branch interurban and freight cars, had been double tracked (though not the span itself), the south track being the rail added. The city market, at the curve on the west side of Main Street north of First Avenue, had had a new double tracked spur run into its facilities, and a new double tracked line had been laid in the two blocks of Davie Street between Granville and Richards.

Fraser Street had been double tracked between Twenty-fifth and Fifty-third avenues, Hastings Street between Vernon Drive and Victoria Road.

With the dizzying proliferation of street car lines threading their respective ways throughout the city, the time had come for a type of destination sign more visible than the aesthetically pleasing one mounted on the roof over the motorman's window. Now large metal signs were hung below the motorman's window, not unlike those in Victoria: Grandview was a rectangle divided diagonally by red and white, Hastings East was a red ball on white, Stanley Park had green and white diagonal areas, the Fairview belt line was solidly white, and so on.

In the Fraser Valley, timber and lumber had meant little in 1910. However, the interurban line to Chilliwack changed all that. Modern transportation to the valley, together with the desires of settlers to build homes and farm their land, opened the area to the lumber industry. By spring of 1912, close to a dozen and a half saw mills, shingle mills, and lumber camps had attached themselves to B. C. Electric spur tracks. Logs were shipped to South Westminster, where they were dumped into the Fraser River from a 3,971-foot spur running south from the main line. Though the company was ecstatic about the business, it was unhappy with damage done to its flat cars during the dumping operation. A cable operated by a donkey engine was hooked to the arch bar of one of the flat car's trucks. The cable was then passed under and over one end of the load, and the donkey engine wound in the cable, tipping the car and spilling the load. The company's worries seem well founded!

Along the Fraser Valley branch, five more post offices had opened up during the year: Bellerose (later Belrose), Bradner, Dennison, Gifford, and Sperling. Cloverdale, Abbotsford, and Huntingdon were receiving passenger train service from the Great Northern Railway, but its operations offered little threat to the B. C. Electric:

At the end of 1912, the B. C. Electric's street car and interurban system could be displayed in the following way:	
City and Suburban	Miles of Single Track
New Westminster	7.55
North Vancouver	10.63
Vancouver (including Point Grey and South Vancouver)	77.43
Victoria (including Esquimalt, Oak Bay, and Saanich)	28.95
	124.56
Interurban	
Central Park Line	18.52
Burnaby Lake Line	10.06
Fraser Valley Branch	72.42
Lulu Island Branch	33.21
	134.21
Total	258.77

one mixed train daily except Sunday from Cloverdale to New Westminster and return, in addition to a mixed train three times a week to and from Vancouver. A daily-except-Sunday mixed train connected Cloverdale with Abbotsford and Huntingdon, the trip lasting an hour and forty minutes westbound, three hours eastbound!

What must Ladner — hungry for an interurban line — have thought of the organization in the state of Washington during the year of the International Railway and Development Company, its aim to construct an electric railroad from Seattle to Ladner! Not surprisingly, this extraordinary idea never became reality.

Thirteen more street cars, 241-249 and 275-278, had arrived from Brill, and over ten million more riders had used B. C. Electric's street cars and interurbans in 1912 than in 1911, a record 65,581,267 on 281 vehicles. Freight tonnage hauled had more than trebled, to 256,083 tons. And for the first time, B. C. Electric management had discussed the use of motor buses.

The greatest twelve-month period in Victoria's history was 1913, the year the city's famous ornamental cluster light standards were installed. Real estate was the excitement of the day, and new subdivisions were springing up all over the Victoria area. The Empress Hotel had just opened an extension; new buildings were popping up everywhere, such as the ten-storey B. C. Permanent Loan Building at the corner of Douglas and Johnson streets, which remained Victoria's tallest structure for almost half a century; and while Victoria's older houses began to be torn down, its first apartment block was being erected. And delighting everyone with their beauty and

New trackwork on Pandora Street, leading east off Douglas, with three tracks into the new interurban depot to the left. (Provincial Archives of B.C.)

Inaugural Trip
ON THE
Saanich Interurban Railway

FROM
Victoria to Deep Bay
June 18, 1913

(B.C. Hydro)

The crew of line car L.5 stringing trolley wire in preparation for the opening of the Victoria-Deep Bay interurban line. (B.C. Hydro)

size, the C.P.R.'s new liner *Empress of Russia* and the new Canadian Australian liner *Niagara* arrived on their maiden voyages (as they did also in Vancouver).

In January the B. C. Electric purchased the conveniently located Pythian Castle Hall on Douglas Street between Cormorant Street and Pandora Avenue for conversion into the interurban depot for the Saanich line. Work began shortly on special track work for the three depot tracks.

By the end of February, some significant steps had been taken in regard to Victoria's street car roster: 20, 25, and 50 had been scrapped; and 188, 193-194, and 237-239 had been added. Only one open car remained, number 11. Of the 49 street cars, twelve — numbers 117-122 and 250-255 — were single enders.

Oak Bay received its street lighting in April with the installation of 225 lamps, the delay having been due to postponed arrival of equipment. With the opening of the Japanese Tea Gardens at Gorge Park on April 27, it is small wonder that all street car travel records were shattered on the May 24 holiday by people travelling to Gorge Park, especially since a scenic railway had also been added to the park's blandishments.

Even three years ago, in 1910, B. C. Electric's directors had not been thoroughly convinced that a Saanich interurban line could be a success, but they did know the company had $250,000 to spend somewhere on the Victoria branch. This money represented the provincial government's order to the company to do a work of significance, in exchange for the company's having received a street railway and electric light monopoly in the Victoria area. Since a Saanich interurban seemed a fit project, the company had combed the peninsula for land owners who would donate land for the new line. Little came of this effort, and so the B. C. Electric incorporated a subsidiary on June 28, 1911, Columbia Estate Company Limited, created for the purpose of buying and holding

real estate. Believing that land values would simply keep skyrocketing, the company staked the success of the Saanich line on real estate speculation, shaky ground, indeed, in 1913.

By spring, six new interurban cars of the St. Louis Car Company order, 1239-1244 (the very ones first ordered by P.N.T.); one new baggage-express car from Niles, 1706; and locomotives 953 and 981 were in place, ready to go. They had arrived by sea at Sidney, and had been brought by the Victoria & Sidney Railway to Saanichton, where they had been switched over to the adjoining Saanich line and brought in to Victoria. (Car 1707, a twin to 1706, and locomotive 952 would spend a few of the summer months on the Saanich line before being sent to the lower mainland's interurban lines.)

The new line, constructed and equipped at a cost of $910,563, was a masterful piece of work, cleanly graded, embodying extensive rock cuts and fills, but requiring only three trestles: from Victoria, the first was at Interurban Road (the line's former right of way today) where it meets Charlton Road; the second, near the intersection of Interurban and Alan roads; and the third, at the point where Interurban Road and Viaduct intersect. The line had been well ballasted, north and south from Butler's gravel pit where the company had employed two Marion steam shovels.

The line measured precisely 22.96 miles from the Victoria depot to the shore of Deep Bay, running its first two and a half miles in Victoria, on Douglas Street and Burnside Avenue. Twenty-one stations, excluding Victoria's depot — shelters similar to some of those found on the company's Chilliwack line — had been judiciously spaced along the line. A lengthy gravel pit spur snaked away at a point just south of Stellys (13.6 miles out); an interchange with the Victoria & Sidney Railway had been temporarily in place at Saanichton (mile 14.9); and a spur four-tenths of a mile long had been laid from Patricia Junction (mile 20) west to a passenger platform at Patricia Bay. (A spur line was later run to Tod Inlet.) Unfortunately, the line had not been able to run into Sidney, the peninsula's largest community, because the franchise of the V. & S. Railway disallowed any other railway from coming within a mile of it.

On June 18, the "Saanich Division" was officially opened, and as on the Fraser Valley branch, Lieutenant-Governor Paterson, who had once been manager of the Victoria & Sidney, and the now Honourable Sir Richard McBride, K.C.M.G., Prime Minister of British Columbia, were aboard, giving the inaugural journey its special distinction. The interurban train, beflagged and beribboned, left its Victoria depot at 11:25 a.m. with about one hundred guests; baggage-express car 1706 led the way, followed by 1240 and 1242. After a leisurely,

Baldwin-built 981 at work on the Saanich line. (Collection of Peter Daniell)

non-stop run on a brilliantly sunny day, the party arrived at Deep Bay at 12:30 p.m. and undoubtedly found its attention drawn to the beautiful view across Saanich inlet to the Malahat. Upon alighting, the guests gathered around Premier McBride who hammered in a silver spike, steadied in position by Victoria branch manager Goward, and encouraged by general superintendent G. M. Tripp, superintendent of interurban lines F. D. Picken, and other company, provincial, civic, and municipal officials. On the return trip, a visit was made to the company's Brentwood steam plant near mile 11.6.

Regular service commenced on the following day with six runs from Deep Bay to Victoria, seven in the reverse direction, two each way only to Saanichton, and seven short runs each way to Eberts, 5.4 miles from Victoria. The Sunday service was a considerably reduced one. The one way fare from Victoria to Deep Bay was seventy cents — return was simply double. Weekdays only, two freight runs were made in each direction. (The Great Northern's Victoria & Sidney Railway was at the same time operating three passenger trains in each direction.)

From Victoria's depot (the company called it Cormorant yard), the interurban trains swung onto Douglas Street from the Cormorant Street exit, passing to the west in two and a half blocks the new Saanich Division freight depot (termed Douglas Discovery yard); a further yard spur bent north from the line at Burnside Avenue and Harriet Road.

Residents along the Mount Tolmie line finally got street car service in July, although the blue-signed cars came along only on an hourly basis. On July 2, P.A.Y.E. street cars became the rule on the Foul Bay, Oak Bay, Willows, and Uplands line, the latter, with its brilliant destination sign — an orange circle enclosed by red background, having just come into operation. The line's 7,570-foot length was entirely single tracked on unpaved road — Cadboro Bay Road (beyond Willows), Dalhousie and Dunlevý streets, the latter becoming Midland Road upon its entry into the prestigious Uplands subdivision — ending in a loop at Midland Circle, which was paved. Only the last half mile of the line was actually inside Uplands, but that section had been blessed with graceful ornamental trolley poles. In preparation for the line's opening, the single track on Cadboro Bay Road from Foul Bay Road west to the start of the new line had been double tracked, as had Fort Street (Cadboro Bay Road) west from Foul Bay Road to St. Charles Street, 6,630 feet in all.

On August 22, pay-as-you-enter street cars were introduced on all remaining Victoria lines. By the end of the month Douglas Street had been double tracked from Burnside Avenue (also newly double tracked between Washington Avenue and Carrol Street) to Tolmie Avenue, 2,380 feet, and

the new eighteen-car capacity Cloverdale car barn, two blocks beyond, and east, was opened on September 5. It was a wood frame building, 384 by 38 feet, covered by galvanized iron.

B.C. Electric officials celebrate the inauguration of the interurban line to Deep Bay, June 18, 1913. (Victoria City Archives)

BRITISH COLUMBIA ELECTRIC RAILWAY COMPANY LIMITED

B.C.E.R. No. 3   SAANICH DIVISION   D.R.B.C. No. 3

SPECIAL PASSENGER TARIFF
SHOWING
SINGLE FARES BETWEEN ALL STATIONS

ISSUED JUNE 12TH, 1913   EFFECTIVE JUNE 26TH, 1913

(B.C. Hydro)

British Columbia Electric Railway Company

SAANICH DIVISION

**TIME TABLE
No. 2**

TAKING EFFECT AT 24.01 O'CLOCK

Sunday, Nov. 2nd, 1913

(GOVERNED BY PACIFIC TIME)

For the Information and Government of Employees only

R. H. SPERLING   A. T. GOWARD   F. D. PICKEN

(Provincial Archives of B.C.)

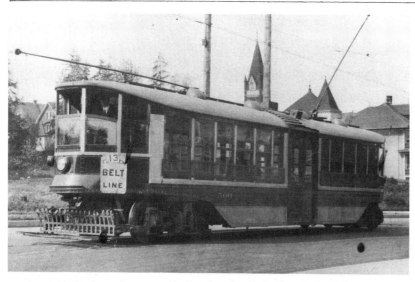

Hobble skirt car 500 eastbound on Broadway between Ontario and Quebec streets in 1913. This one-of-a-kind B.C. Electric vehicle was not a success: possibly the motorman even complained about lack of head room. (Barry Sanford collection)

In October the B. C. Electric joined in a venture with West Coast Development Company to offer a combined interurban - ferry service to the Gulf Islands via Deep Bay, $1.25 being the total fare to any of the islands. Because there was too little passenger business, and the vessel was not large enough for freight, the experiment capsized after

about a month.

During October as well, street cars were being equipped with doors at both ends, although passengers, under the P.A.Y.E. regimen, were entering and departing the vehicles at the front door only. After four months of operation, the Saanich interurban line seemed to be in need of increased service frequency; in the following month students using the Saanich line were able to make a return trip for a one way fare.

On the lower mainland January 2, 1913, marked the introduction of multiple unit interurban service on the Central Park line, with seven-and-a-half-minute frequency between Carrall Street and Central Park from 3 p.m. to 6 p.m. Rush hour service on the Vancouver-Eburne line, its newly-completed double track initiated on January 3, graduated to an every-fifteen-minutes level; the Vancouver-Eburne journey took 23 minutes, the Eburne-Steveston, 22, and the Eburne-New Westminster, 24.

During 1913, the Queensborough line was designated as the initial section west from New Westminster of the Canadian Northern Pacific's new line, currently under construction, from New

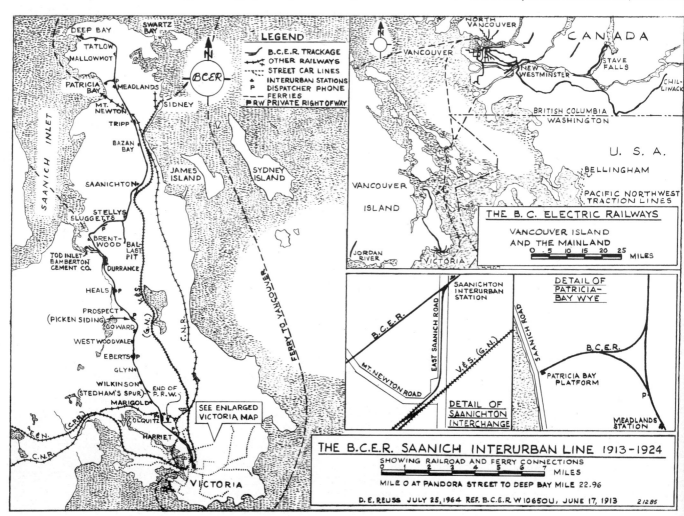

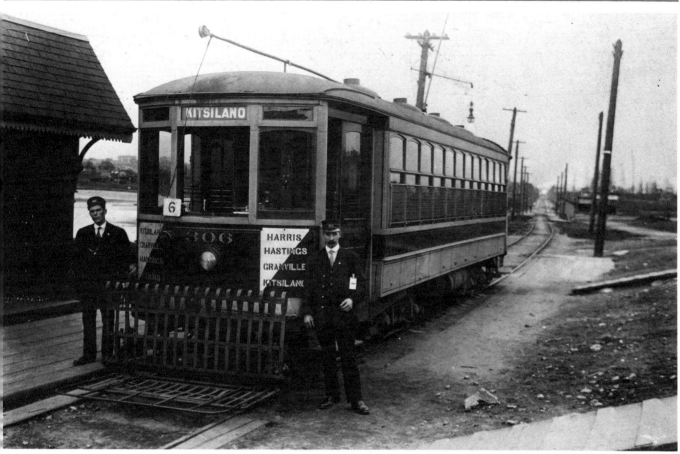

Westminster to Steveston (connecting there with the B. C. Electric) along the southern edge of Lulu Island.

On January 19, the new single tracked line on Oak Street from King Edward Avenue south to Marine Drive, then west to Eburne station, was inaugurated, two cars giving half-hourly service. The passing siding on this almost 3.4-mile stretch had been installed at Forty-fifth Avenue.

In Vancouver, March 18 was the trial date for the company's new, "stepless", or hobble skirt, car, number 500, designed by the New York Railways to make it possible for women of current fashion actually to board a street car. This steel, centre-doored, Brill product had a floor merely seven inches above the rails. Operated for a few months, most visibly on the Fairview line, 500's idiosyncrasies soon submerged its few delights, and it quickly hobbled into storage.

The Burnaby Lake line began offering half-hourly service on April 15, and on the following day, the company announced plans to build a car barn, completed within a few months, at the junction of the Kitsilano line and the Lulu Island branch. Before the month was gone, the building of Horne-Payne substation on the Burnaby Lake line, just across Boundary Road into Burnaby, was begun, as were plans for extensive car shops there, to which end the company had purchased in March the north half of Burnaby District Lot 118

from Columbia Estate Company for $80,062.50. It was the company's intention that the Horne-Payne shops be the main repair and car building venue, and that the new Kitsilano, Prior Street, Mount Pleasant, and New Westminster barn and shops be subsidiary to it.

Service on the Oak Street line commenced running directly from Eburne to Hastings and Cambie on May 10 with four street cars on a twenty-minute headway; in rush hour extra cars operated as far south as King Edward Avenue. On May 11, New Westminster's 3.1-mile belt line was put into operation, running on Columbia,

Car 306 has just arrived at Kitsilano Beach, its western terminus. This line would soon be double tracked and given a loop turn-around. (Jack Lobban collection)

The waters of Vancouver's False Creek course eastward under Main Street's bascule bridge, 1913. (E.L. Plant collection)

Leopold Place, Royal Avenue, Park Row, First Street, Third Avenue, Pine Street, Fourth Avenue, Sixth Street, Carnarvon Street, and Eighth Avenue.

During May the company had packed steam locomotive 940 off to the Baldwin Locomotive Works in Philadelphia for its transformation from coal-burner to oil-burner. Meanwhile the last of the company's order to Baldwin, five of the finest electric locomotives of their day, arrived in the same month; they would be the last motive power purchased by the company for the next thirty-three years. Numbered 970 to 974, these reliable locomotives, costing $26,500 each, quite outclassed the three Dick-Kerr locomotives, giving the B. C. Electric precisely the kind of motive power it needed in its relatively recent role of freight hauler.

Two new lines opened for service on June 2: 2.4 miles of single track with one street car half-hourly joined Tenth and Forty-first avenues by running on Crown Street, Sixteenth Avenue, and Dunbar Street; the other was a thirteen-block single track extension on Victoria Road from Forty-first to Fifty-fourth Avenue, whence street car service now operated to Powell and Main, rather than just to Seventh and Main. A double tracked wye north from Kingsway at Victoria Drive was also set in place. Eight days later single track on Fraser Street was opened, seven blocks from Fifty-ninth Avenue to Marine Drive. Fraser Street cars began operating through downtown to Oak Street and King Edward rather than turning back at Granville and Robson.

In June the company laid a temporary track to the waterfront east of Lonsdale (the same location chosen in 1906 for the first delivery of streetcars to North Vancouver) to facilitate delivery of the last street cars ever to reach North Vancouver, numbers 158 to 162.

During the summer of 1913, the Vancouver system offered a three trips daily, two-hour sightseeing jaunt by observation car. It ran from Granville and Robson streets, along Granville, Hastings, Campbell, Venables, Commercial (often as far south as Broadway before returning north), Powell, Main, Broadway, Oak, Twenty-fifth,

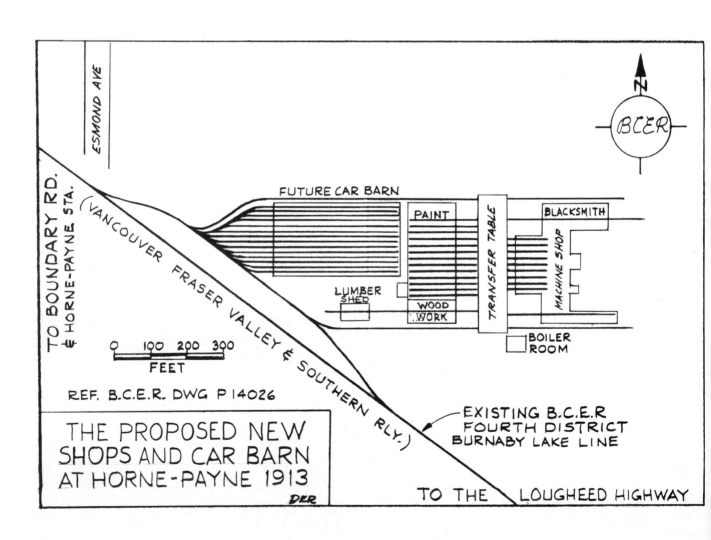

THE PROPOSED NEW SHOPS AND CAR BARN AT HORNE-PAYNE 1913

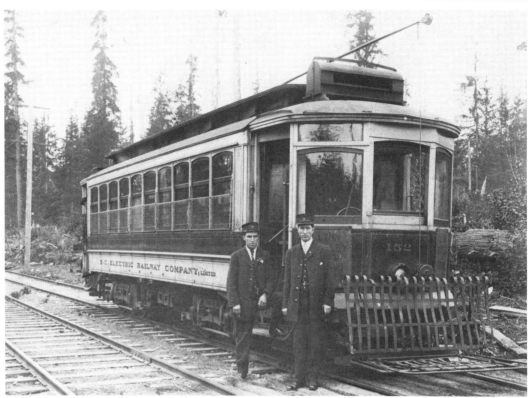

Nicely-finished 152 returned to Vancouver after spending many years in North Vancouver, here on the Lynn Valley line. (B.C. Hydro)

Granville, Davie (ten minute stop at English Bay), Denman (to Stanley Park), and Robson, back to Granville.

On June 11, two masked men held up an interurban car on its Eburne-to-New Westminster run at 9:30 p.m. They boarded the car at McRae Road Station, each brandishing a gun, and robbed the thirteen passengers, motorman, and conductor of $50 and a gold watch. One of the two actually gave the command, "Stand and deliver!" Having accomplished their mission, they kept everyone covered, backing away to the opposite ends of the car. The company offered a reward of $250 for information but the two had disappeared into the underbrush without a trace. Motorman Barnes is said to have covered the distance to New Westminster in record time to give the alarm.

All summer long, gangs were vigorously engaged in constructing a nine-mile steam railway line — the company called it the "Port Moody-Coquitlam Railway" — from a point at the very eastern extremity of Burrard Inlet to the dam project at the foot of Coquitlam Lake on which the B. C. Electric had been labouring since 1908. Connecting with the C.P.R.'s three-year-old Port Moody-Ioco branch, the new railway ran east for two miles before turning north to follow the Coquitlam River to the dam, crossing the river twice, $4\frac{1}{4}$ and $6\frac{3}{4}$ miles from Burrard Inlet, each time over a bridge comprising three Howe truss spans.

Robert McNair, of Robert McNair Shingle Company, and the B. C. Electric had collaborated on this railway project, even in its planning. The company had wished to haul supplies and materials up to the dam; McNair had been anxious

The Canadian Society of Civil Engineers, Vancouver branch, takes a trip on B.C. Electric's little-known Port Moody — Coquitlam Railway to visit the company's dam on May 10, 1913. (B.C. Hydro)

(Above left)
New Westminster barn with Twelfth Street in the background toward the right, leading to the depot and centre of town. (B.C. Hydro)

(Above right)
New Westminster barn, with a rare view of mail car 1500, once name car "Coquitlam," and ultimately 1312. (B.C. Hydro)

One of the three new Dick-Kerr locomotives with lacrosse fans bound for New Westminster. (Ted Clark collection)

to haul timber down to his mill. The company made him an offer which he accepted: the B. C. Electric would build a railway using forty-pound rail on a superb 66-foot right of way; in a twenty-five-year deal, McNair would have the right to operate the line upon his promise to pay $50,000 toward construction costs, and $50,000 per annum for ten years. The B. C. Electric-McNair agreement had been signed on October 1, 1912. Steam had been preferred over electric power because the B. C. Electric estimated steam costs to be $50,000, and electric (with proper equipment) to be $140,000. The company was convinced there would not be sufficient return to meet its capital investment if it went electric.

On July 3, Coquitlam and New Westminster councils endorsed the idea of approaching the B. C. Electric about extending its Fraser Mills line to Port Coquitlam. (Fraser Mills itself had been incorporated some three months earlier.) The idea was rejected by the company, as the route would merely have parallelled the C. P. R.'s through the same area. Furthermore, the company pointed out that it had an agreement with the C.P.R. to electrify the C.P.R.'s line, if and when required by the C.P.R.

Cloverdale bustled more than ever after the opening of a good quality gravel road on July 12 from the Fraser River bridge to the U.S. border,

via Cloverdale's main street. In a province of 7,000 automobiles, this model thoroughfare was called the Pacific Highway.

Point Grey was collecting many B. C. Electric street car lines, and in late summer, Point Grey's council came up with a unique idea for a new street car line that was never built, but could have provided a useful service. Council even got to the point of starting to secure a right of way for it; the route would have connected Eburne with Forty-first and Dunbar, running along the Fraser River's uninhabited foreshore.

At this time another new Point Grey street car line, on Forty-first between Kerrisdale and Granville, was being rushed to completion. Half of the rails were already down, and a steam shovel was preparing the line at Granville Street. This line was being laid under an agreement with the C.P.R. (the line ran, of course, through C.P.R. land) according to which a certain number of miles of track were to be laid within a given time. When Granville had been reached, rails would be pushed through all the way to Main Street.

Just before noon on Sunday, September 8, a two-car train of express cars, taking produce and exhibits from Lulu Island to the exhibition in Chilliwack, collided about half a mile east of Abbotsford with New Westminster-bound locomotive 972 and caboose A.4. John Plewes, motorman of the leading special train car, 1700, died shortly after reaching Sumas Hospital, and one of the conductors and four brakemen were badly injured. Both trains had been moving at a good speed and, as misfortune would have it, they met on a sharp curve with little chance for the motormen to brake effectively, try though they had. Motorman Plewes' train had been regularly-scheduled No. 500; the engineer of 972 had overlooked its existence. (Car 1700 would languish, out of service, five years before repairs were done.)

Vancouver's revised street car schedule of Thursday, September 18, sounded an ominous chord: it showed not only a decrease in service frequency (ridership was down from the same month of the previous year), but also a hike in fares. Unemployment in British Columbia had begun to climb, and the world scene, particularly the situation in the Balkans, was causing fears and widespread losses of confidence in what had been a roaring economy with a mania for building.

Nevertheless on September 18, South Vancouver went ahead with plans for a new street car line on Forty-first Avenue between Cambie and Main streets, and discussed plans to continue the line eastward in 1914 to Victoria Road. The approved 3,410-foot section would be built, but would never have street car service.

The B. C. Electric was still, however, planning for the future. On September 27 it published designs for a new $300,000 car barn on the southern half of the lot currently occupied by the Mount Pleasant barn. This new, concrete structure would be double decked, capable of holding 120 street cars. (The existing car barn on the north half of the block stored sixty.) The upper deck facility would require access track to be laid west up the hill on Thirteenth Avenue from Main Street, then south for one block on Quebec Street. The designs were extraordinarily felicitous, particularly the ornamental, residence-facing facade along Quebec Street.

And there were two Vancouver street car lines for which plans were firm. One was an extension on Kingsway from Joyce Road to Central Park, now that the 3,368-foot single track on Kingsway east to Joyce from Earles Road had been opened for service on September 29. The other was a line the company had been anxious to build in 1913, but had not accomplished — a connection north on Victoria Road from Kingsway to Cedar Cottage, a route the company had wished its Joyce Road street cars to use. Neither of these lines was built.

Furthermore there was corporate planning, and worry. On the tenth of October, the B. C. Electric announced that it might seriously consider selling its Vancouver system to the city. Its profit of $342,671 for the year ending June 30,

1913 compared unfavourably with its 1908 profit of $339,217, despite having done three million dollars more business in 1913. Whereas its capital investment in 1908 had been $12,000,000, it was $43,500,000 in 1913.

Signs of other kinds of adjustments were plentiful for Vancouverites. Reclamation of the one mile by half-mile area of False Creek tidewater east of Main Street was underway. For the purpose of building a freight yard and a new depot, the Great Northern Railway was carrying out this massive project, using fill from the deep cut it had carved through Grandview to make its

In one of the Fraser Valley lines few accidents, the motorman of Chilliwack-bound baggage-express car 1700 was killed in this collision with locomotive 972 on September 8, 1913, just east of Abbotsford near the Great Northern overpass for its line east to Kilgard and Cannor. (Bill Boston collection)

The south lot of Vancouver's Mount Pleasant barn before its double decking. (B.C. Hydro)

Car 75 moves along Kingsway between Knight and Earles, the subgrade for the double track to come now ready for its six-inch concrete slab. (B.C. Hydro)

An early view of Sixteenth Street yard in New Westminster, replete with B.C. Electric box cars. (Ted Clark collection)

entry into Vancouver a more level approach. (Fill had also been brought from the G. N.'s Sapperton gravel pit, as well as from the cut it had made at North Road to eliminate the level crossing there.) Then on October 21, Westminster Avenue from Alexander Street on the waterfront to Sixteenth Avenue officially became Main Street, and Westminster Road, from its commencement at Main and Seventh Avenue east toward New Westminster, officially became Kingsway.

On the Burnaby Lake line, Hastings Townsite station was renamed Horne-Payne on November 16, coinciding with the already-named new substation at that point. Work had just begun on the new Vancouver depot of the Lulu Island branch; its platform off Granville Bridge would be 118 by 140 feet, supported by a network of pilings driven deeply into False Creek. This platform and its attractive, well-equipped station would be approached from the west over a short, double tracked trestle. Ladner had so badly wanted the Lulu Island interurban to link it with Vancouver and New Westminster, but since such a development seemed less likely year by year, considerable joy gripped Ladner when a ferry from Woodward's Landing, four miles east of Steveston, began operating on November 20 to a landing on the south side of the Fraser's big south arm, merely 1.7 miles north of Ladner itself. This was certainly an improvement over the previous prospect of being able to reach Vancouver only three times a week on a Great Northern mixed train taking almost four and a half hours!

The Lulu Island branch would soon be affected by an unusual development in False Creek under Granville Bridge: a man-made island was created with silt dredged from the channel. When completed, it would become the site of factories and industries, to be served by the south shore line of the Lulu Island branch.

In New Westminster, the Fraser Mills line became part of the street car system on December 7, having been operated as a branch of the Burnaby Lake line to that date. As a result the Fraser Mills line was connected (in passenger operation) with the Queensborough line, using the 1000-class interurban cars; the new line was designated No. 3. In the same month two large projects had been brought to completion: the

The market at New Westminster in 1913, Columbia Street above it. (New Westminster Public Library)

building of the urgently-needed, 300-car capacity freight yard, nicely nestled in the curve of the hillside west of the car shops; and an eight-track car barn, 240 by 104 feet, between the existing barn and the car shops for both street and interurban cars. A brief section of new track, connecting the Eburne-New Westminster and Central Park lines at Sixteenth Street, facilitated the efficient operation of freight through the new yard.

The impending opening of the Panama Canal had held New Westminster in an excited state through much of the year. Its increasingly busy wharves had been placed under the control of the newly-created New Westminster Harbour Board, and all was optimism, and more, in regard to what the canal would do for the Royal City.

On December 22, the 10,000-foot-long Hastings Extension line opened, the only street car line ever poked into Burnaby from Vancouver. The entire line lay along Hastings Street, from Boundary Road east to Ellesmere Avenue, bringing it neatly onto the southern fringe of the Capitol Hill district. One street car easily provided a half-hourly service on this nine-minute run. The company's franchise agreement with Burnaby apropos this extension, signed eight months earlier, on April 28, had given the municipality the right to purchase the line at the end of thirty-six years and six months, and every ten years thereafter.

In Vancouver, a new double tracked connection on Fir Street between the Lulu Island branch at Fir and the Fourth Avenue street car line — as well as the short new double tracked connection on Third Avenue west to the new depot — had been laid. In addition, Kingsway had been double tracked from the west all the way to Earles Road, the added track being the north one, and the new line on Forty-first between Main and Cambie was in place, as was the quickly-built, longer, 5,596-foot section from Cambie to Granville. Vancouver (Point Grey and South Vancouver, at the time) had a 3.8-mile crosstown line on Forty-first Avenue, most of it through a remote, completely unsettled area — it was a line no passenger would ever ride. The last street cars from Brill, 279-299 and 325, and two from Preston, 326 and 327, had been placed in service during 1913.

Out in the Fraser Valley, what would become the Fraser Valley Milk Producers' Association had been formed on June 18, and on the first of the month, Sullivan Station had acquired its post office. The C.P.R. had discontinued its thrice weekly steamer operation with the *Beaver* between New Westminster and Chilliwack Landing at the end of September, but the *Paystreak* would struggle on a few months more. The first eight Fraser Valley branch interurban cars had lost their original numbering scheme, and all of the line's interurban cars had had their General Electric motors and controls replaced by heavier duty, more powerful Westinghouse equipment, the trailers 1306 - 1308 being so equipped as well.

IV

1914-1929:

Trouble, Innovation, and Recovery

Logging on the Saanich line with locomotive 981. (B.C. Transit)

With two of the 970-type locomotives fitted up with snow plows at both ends, the Fraser Valley branch was ready for 1914's ice and snow. The heavy snows of January 1913 had surprised everyone, but it would be different in the new year: Victoria and New Westminster had each received a new snow plow, Vancouver one, to add to its three; locomotives 952, for the lower mainland interurban lines, and 953, on the Saanich line, had also been equipped with snow plows.

But in the areas that ultimately really mattered, 1914 would be a year of going backwards, and a time to recognize that the golden years of 1909 to 1912 were phenomena, things of the past in more than a chronological sense, and that the world, indeed, would never be the same. Who would have thought that Fairview-type car 274 would be the last street car ever built by the car shops when it poked its vestibule out into the sunshine of June 14, 1913?

By the end of the new year, the number of passengers carried would slide from 69,639,764 in 1913 to 56,350,788, freight tonnage hauled

from 448,750 to 357,013.

On May 6, 1914, Sperling would become a director of the B. C. Electric, and George Kidd would become general manager; there would be happiness and satisfaction when Frank Stillman Barnard (later Sir), one of the B. C. Electric's founding fathers, would be appointed the province's Lieutenant-Governor. Vast excitement and enthusiasm would accompany the opening to commerce of the Panama Canal on August 15; but much of the world would be dumbfounded and horror-stricken by the Great War, begun on August 4, with Canada loyally at Britain's side.

In Victoria, the Uplands and Burnside lines had been united as one service in April. In the following month, the B. C. Electric made plans to erect a structure, The Chalet, at Deep Bay, as a draw, and a venue, for outings and picnics on the Saanich line. The company added to it over the years to create a most attractive and inviting facility.

Passenger business on the Saanich line was definitely not booming, and on May 23 the company put into effect reduced return fare rates,

122

the first of many attempts to stimulate ridership. The Marigold district, recently settled by many young families — who had petitioned in July for lower fares — was hit particularly hard when many men went to war. It was increasingly obvious to the B. C. Electric that the pretty Saanich interurban line already was an economic misadventure, and that the line would be almost impossible to save.

"Jitneys" ("jalopies") began to appear on Victoria's streets toward the end of November — automobiles whose drivers cruised the streets offering transportation for a five-cent payment. (The small five-cent coin was called a jitney.) They gave quick service, offered destination flexibility, and quite likely introduced many people to riding in automobiles. The jitney idea, born in Los Angeles, was undoubtedly exciting, and best of all, for jitney owners, no government regulations, rules, and edicts played hob with their efforts in the field of transit. The B. C. Electric, as most other Canadian and U. S. transportation companies, was justifiably in a state of near-panic.

During 1914 double tracking work had been accomplished on two fronts, the almost half mile of Fort Street between Cook and Harrison streets, and slightly over half a mile of Pandora between Douglas and Cook streets. By year's end at Jordan River, the two-year-old power house had had already its third generator installed, doubling its output capacity, and all work had been completed on the huge diversion and storage dam.

The first day of 1914 on the lower mainland was one of considerable excitement at North Vancouver's foot-of-Lonsdale street car terminus as a new railway operation began, from a station just a few yards west. The Pacific Great Eastern Railway's first trip left at 10 a.m. with a train of two steel gasoline combination coaches — 150 passengers aboard — bound for Dundarave, sixteen minutes west across Capilano River into West Vancouver. In Vancouver, car barn space was at such a premium that even some of the 181 street cars used in afternoon rush hours were being stored at Carrall Street yards.

The Port Moody-Coquitlam Railway's first seven miles from Burrard Inlet was certified complete on March 7 — speed limit was ten miles per hour. The B. C. Electric had constructed a small wharf at the terminus to which logs would be brought from Coquitlam Lake. Since McNair owned the waterfront property, by agreement the wharf would become his in a few years. Steam locomotive 940, sent to the line in the previous year, would stay most of 1914.

There had been much talk all through the early months of 1914 about the now almost-legendary idea of extending a line north from Sapperton to Port Moody, as well as about the plans the company had prepared for a cutoff into New Westminster for the Burnaby Lake line.

Since there had come to be so much confusion within the company itself in regard to the designations of its interurban operations, the B. C. Electric made official a system-wide simplification, one which lasted the life of the lines:

District 1 - *the original Tramway line, variously called the New Westminster-Vancouver line, the Westminster branch, and the Central Park line*

District 2 - *the Lulu Island branch, variously known as the V. & L. I., as well as the Vancouver-Eburne, Eburne-New Westminster, and Steveston lines (Eburne soon would be renamed Marpole.)*

District 3 - *the Fraser Valley branch, or Chilliwack line*

District 4 - *the Burnaby branch, Burnaby Division, or Burnaby Lake line*

District 5 - *the Saanich branch, or line*

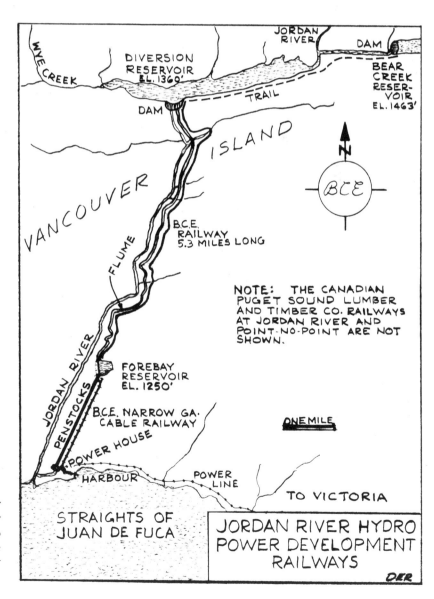

May 1 marked the cessation of the magnificent craftsmanship and artistry of the New Westminster car shops. On that day, the last of its three final masterpieces, interurban cars 1309-1311 — popularly known as the "Connaught cars" — had been turned out as fit for service; 1309 had already appeared on February 17, 1310 on March 14. (Influenced by their St. Louis-built interurbans,

the company had designed these three with an arch roof, rather than with the typical railroad-style monitor roof.) Of the 296 full size, double truck street cars — numbered 69 - 355 and 381 - 390 — placed into operation since 1905, 147 had been built in New Westminster; of the company's 83 interurban cars (1003 had been destroyed by fire on January 13 in the New Westminster car barn), 30 had been built there. During its ten years the car shops had also constructed locomotives, single truck street cars, freight cars, and work equipment of all descriptions. The B. C. Electric's roster of interurban cars was now firm — its very last interurban car had arrived, and no more street cars would augment the current list until 1922.

On May 10 the new depot for District 2 interurban passenger trains, the "Eburne Car Terminal, Granville St. Bridge," as the company designated it, was opened for traffic, and what a delight it was for riders to make an interurban-street car transfer merely by passing through the centre arch of the depot. New Westminster and Steveston trains used track number 1, and Eburne trains track 2. A police officer was always on traffic duty (the city charged the company $1200 per annum for him).

The very next day had seen a passenger interurban car added to the consist of District 3's milk trains 500 and 501. Farther into May the B. C. Electric let a contract for the construction of a connecting track at Huntingdon with the Milwaukee Road across the border at Sumas. This connection would allow through billing of freight in the originally loaded car from all U. S. points into New Westminster and Vancouver. By the end of May preliminary work on this connection east of Huntingdon had begun. On April 1 a post office had opened at Newton; on New Year's Day Yarrow's post office had changed its name, from Majuba Hill.

On July 1 street car operations on the Sixteenth Avenue line were extended to Oak and Broadway. On July 23, superintendent W. H. Elson issued a bulletin to trainmen of Districts 1 and 4, and to the New Westminster city operation, which limited freight trains to four empty or three loaded cars coming up the steep "asylum" grade, westbound

B. C. E. PORT MOODY - COQUITLAM RAILWAY

During the month of March five of Vancouver's newest street car lines acquitted themselves in the following ways:

	Earnings	Earnings per car mile (cents)
Dunbar Street	$ 467.28	8.91
Hastings Street Extension	545.25	8.91
Oak Street	4,583.99	17.74
Sasamat Street	1,761.88	17.87
Wilson Road (41st, Kerrisdale to Dunbar)	1,025.21	18.42

The Wilson Road line's seemingly inflated per car mile figure is due to its being a connection with the Lulu Island branch, to which 74% of the earnings should actually be credited.

on Columbia Street to Leopold Place; he added to this directive later in the year by stipulating that the locomotive always be on the down grade end of the train.

By the end of August, the Dick-Kerr locomotives had had their original unsatisfactory controls replaced by Westinghouse equipment and their numbers, 911-913, altered to 990-992. (The three were really not as suited to freight hauling as they would have been to hauling passenger trains.)

In August, the double tracking of Main Street between Thirty-third and Fiftieth avenues had been accomplished, and by October, new track work was in place on Thirty-third Avenue between Main and Fraser streets, the annoying grade at the Fraser end leveled by a cut. During

New Westminster, east along Columbia Street on May Day, 1914; the decade-old railway-highway bridge across the Fraser River dominates the background. (New Westminster Public Library)

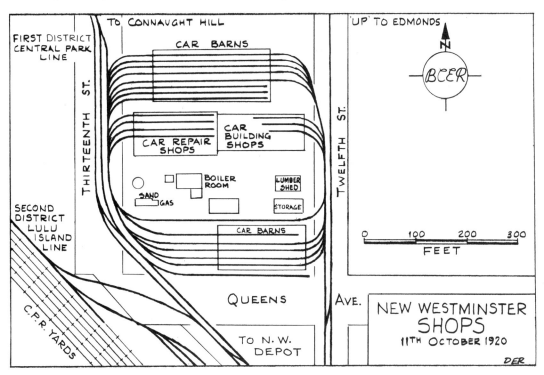

125

The west, three tracked platform of the Granville Bridge station, built entirely on piles driven into the bed of False Creek. (B.C. Hydro)

(Right)
A central Park line transfer ticket of 1914 vintage. (Bob Webster collection)

The wonderful canopy, in place during the early years, over both loop tracks at the Chilliwack depot. (Peggy Webb collection)

the year track on Broadway had been extended eastward from Commercial Drive over the new 305-foot Great Northern viaduct toward Victoria Road; it would be a dozen years before this double track would be extended to make a connection at Nanaimo Street. As well in 1914, Hastings Street had been double tracked from Victoria Road to Renfrew Street.

December 7 was a day of additions and adjustments. With a wye installed at Fiftieth Avenue and Main Street, and the track at the south end of Main connected with the Eburne-New Westminster interurban line, the Main Street South shuttle began operating, between Fiftieth and the intereurban line. Alternate Main-Davie street cars travelled as far south as Fiftieth, the others still turning back at Twenty-fifth Avenue. The Mountain View operation thus ceased, the section on Thirty-third retaining only rush hour service. Two weak lines were twinned, Harris

Street and Stanley Park, and the Kitsilano line was mated with the Hastings Park (Powell Street) line. It was a great relief when the large car barn addition at Mount Pleasant was opened (without the decorative touches originally announced).

In 1914 on the Central Park line, Earles Road trestle had been filled in. In New Westminster, a south-pointing, five-car wye had been installed at Arbutus Street on the "Fourth Avenue Extension," the line through Queen's Park to the brick yard. Car 166 had suffered a derailment, fortunately without any injuries, when its forward truck was forced off the track on Sixth Street at Eleventh Avenue because of an accumulation of ice; though the car had tipped precariously ditchward, it happily failed to embarrass itself. In mid-November, the Edmonds-Sapperton street car line's service was improved to a twenty-minute headway, and the city had wisely completed the widening of Front Street.

During 1914 had flickered the final attempt at establishing an interurban line between the Chilliwack line at Huntingdon (Sumas) and

Bellingham, via Lynden, with the organization in the state of Washington of the Blaine-Lynden Electric Railway, but it was too late now.

By the end of December, the B. C. Electric's government-stimulated program of installing steel mesh gates on all street cars, begun in 1913, was well along, with 96 so equipped and 38 others fitted with doors.

But it was not the new gates that kept passenger business in the doldrums; at the beginning of 1915 more than sixty jitneys in Victoria and upwards of two hundred in Vancouver were

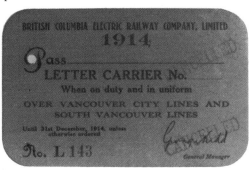

seducing riders away from the street cars and sapping the patience and resources of the B. C. Electric. Some jitneys even displayed destination signs identical to those used by the street car lines. A jitney driver in many cases was a family man who had been thrown out of work by the prevailing difficult times and realized his automobile could be his source of bread. Often he was a returned serviceman. Open touring automobiles, fitted up with benches — sometimes even with handle bars, could carry up to nine people, and rush hour often found jitney operators running fast, non-stop jaunts to relatively distant points. Initially, company and city legal advisers were at a loss to counter the argument that anyone had a perfect right to give a lift to properly appreciative friends.

In an effort to deal with the jitneys, the company slashed street car fares in Victoria on May 10 to eight tickets for 25¢, a step which brought jitney operators to city hall in protest. At the same time, the company revamped its street car schedules to serve Victorians more conveniently than ever: seven and a half-minute service on Oak Bay; ten-

It's a warm July 1, 1914 morning, and the three recently completed "Connaught" cars — here in order: 1311, 1310, 1309 — the last interurban coaches built by B.C. Electric, have just pulled through New Westminster depot, the brick building behind the last two cars. Messrs. (left to right) Elson, Sterling, Webb, and Spring, top company interurban officials, will undoubtedly climb aboard for the trip to Chilliwack. (B.C. Hydro)

(Left)
This letter carrier's pass of 1914 highlights the B.C. Electric's penetration of the municipality of South Vanouver as well as the new general manager, George Kidd. (Norman W. Williams collection)

Georgia Viaduct west from Main Street in 1926, its tracks neatly in place, never to be connected at either end, let alone used. (Vancouver Public Library)

minute on Burnside-Hillside; twelve-minute on Outer Wharf-Cloverdale, Beacon Hill-Spring Ridge, Gorge, and Esquimalt; and fifteen-minute on Uplands.

In 1915 the Victoria system was operating the following street cars: 1-9, 11-13, 23, 27, 30, 69, 70, 123, 125, 126, 128, 183, 194, 231-240, 250-259, and 381-390. In addition its roster also included sprinkler car S.52, sweeper S.58, motorized flat car S.60, freight car S.61 (formerly Westminster & Vancouver Tramways number 3), dump car S.102, and line car L.5. Locomotives 905 and the rebuilt 906 were shared with the Saanich line, which had the following rolling stock available: interurban cars 1239-1244, passenger-mail car 1501 (added during the year), baggage express car 1706, and locomotives 953 and 981.

The company continued to persevere with the Saanich line, introducing in September a market produce special in the form of a freight car which would be attached at Saanichton on Friday to the interurban train leaving there at 6:25 a.m.; it would gather up produce at the various stations on its journey into Victoria. Since there turned out to be very little to collect, this new idea was abandoned after a trial period of several weeks.

In Vancouver, the B. C. Electric rerouted lines through the downtown area, moved their termini closer to its heart, and speeded up running times

on all main lines, the better to cope with the intensity of jitney competition. The closing of Connaught Bridge, badly damaged by a fire on April 29, had done nothing to help matters, nor had the wrecking of street car 165 by a runaway box car on Main Street hill in February.

On the Fraser Valley branch more and more spurs were shooting in all directions off the main line, many of them extended on more than one occasion. (An example in April was the 250-foot extension of the Mount Lehman Timber & Trading Company's Cooke's Spur at mile 31 at a cost, including rental, of $156.75, overhead wire not included.) On May 1, Rand post office was altered to County Line; on May 19, King's Mill Spur (later just Kings) became a flag stop for all trains; and on June 15, Mufford Crossing (Topham Road today) became a flag stop for trains 450, 451, 8, and the Friday market special.

May in Vancouver meant fares at eight for 25¢, as in Victoria, and a change in city by-laws permitting a higher speed limit for street cars. Only 152 street cars were needed for rush hour service, and by late June, the cars operated only out of Mount Pleasant and Prior Street barns, the Kitsilano barn not being necessary for storing cars in regular service.

On July 1 the half-mile, half-million-dollar Georgia-Harris Viaduct was opened, a venture by the city of Vancouver to connect Main Street at Harris Street (Harris was renamed Georgia within three months), three blocks south of Hastings, with Georgia Street, over top of the company's Carrall Street yards and C.P.R. tracks. The idea was an excellent one, and the bridge had opened with the company's double tracked rails as part of its paved surface; the B. C. Electric had signed an agreement with the city on September 19 of the previous year for a rental payment of $3,600 per annum. But street cars never ran on the bridge; routing them over it would have meant by-passing Vancouver's chief commercial area, as well as laying new connecting track from its western end. Had the B. C. Electric wished to operate over it, the company would ultimately have found it perhaps not sturdy enough to endure the pounding of metal wheels on steel rails. The structure was compounded of four different designs; the mixture of the viaduct's concrete covering was too lean and crumbly; and the rollers on which its supporting columns were designed to move at their bases soon had rusted solid, causing the viaduct to deflect in a number of directions. Unfortunate that this route which offered interesting options for transit movements could not have been developed for street car operation; incredible that the Georgia Viaduct actually stood until its demolition in summer 1971.

By July the final mile and a half to the dam on the Port Moody-Coquitlam Railway was not in use, as it was generally in bad shape and in need of ballasting. In actual fact McNair was vigorously pursuing logging operations along the rest of the line with a 35-ton, six-wheel, oil-burning saddle tank locomotive from the Canadian Locomotive Company of Kingston, Ontario. As rolling stock he had six of his own forty-one-foot, 60,000-ton flat cars, numbered 1, 3, 5, 7, 9, and 11, and two, 4009 and 3001, leased from the B. C. Electric; then there were thirteen Seattle Car Company-built logging cars — lettered with the B. C. Electric's name — numbered 8501, 8503, 8505, 8507, 8509, 8511, 8513, 8515, 8517, 8519, 8521, 8523, and 8527, of which the "11", "13", and "15" were leased from the company.

July on the Fraser Valley branch witnessed the destruction by fire of the station at Newton and the damaging of its adjacent freight building. In two letters to president Kidd, general superintendent of the company's railway department, W. G. Murrin (he had in the previous spring been appointed to this role of overseer in charge of Vancouver city and suburban transportation departments, as well as the mechanical department) related some of the wide-reaching types of concerns Canada's longest interurban line had in 1915:

July 22, 1915.
"I enclose herewith, for your approval, appropriation requesting the expenditure of

$30.40 to cover the cost of moving the milk stand at Sardis to the regulation distance from the rail, and also the erection of a milk stand at Knight Road. At the present time milk shipments from Knight Road are quite heavy and it is very heavy work to lift these ten gallon cans from the Station Platform into the baggage car."

November 8, 1915.
"I enclose herewith, for your approval, application for the expenditure of $750.73 to cover the cost of building a road crossing at Kennedy Road where it intersects our Fraser Valley Branch near Kennedy Station.
In this connection the Municipality of Surrey has requested that a road be constructed at the above mentioned point and as the road was gazetted previous to our building the Fraser Valley Branch we have to carry out their request."

Eleven street cars, 97, 102, 106, 108, 164, 166, and 319-323, were delivering service in New Westminster, with thirteen street cars, 150-162, and line car (former street car) 28 taking care of North Vancouver. The only single truck street cars still available for service anywhere on the B. C. Electric were Vancouver's 53, 57, and 59, the latter two, in fact, already slated for retirement.

The Commercial Drive line with its one car shuttle operation between Powell and Venables streets succumbed on November 1 to any transit line's terminal malady, lack of patronage. This was Vancouver's first service shutdown. On the last day of November street car number 100 surprised and delighted its riders — they could see the motorman, and they could actually look out the front of the car and enjoy their journey more, just as on the jitneys. The black paint had been removed from the bulkhead between the motorman's vestibule and the passenger section, a procedure followed in short order with the rest of the street cars. (When darkness fell, the motorman could draw a newly-installed curtain across his side of the bulkhead.)

The Canadian Northern Pacific finally went into full-fledged operation with tri-weekly service

This brochure from 1915 uses the script-form "B.C. Electric" which became familiar throughout the company's territory. (Vancouver City Archives)

The Ohmer fare register of limited repute hangs above the head of the centre gentleman in one of the B.C. Electric-built "1200" interurban coaches. (Bill Boston photo)

eastward out of Vancouver in November, employing the Great Northern's line to New Westminster, as well as its depot on Pender Street in Vancouver. The route along the south bank of the Fraser was sixteen miles shorter between Vancouver and Chilliwack than the B. C. Electric's, but well removed from most Fraser Valley centres of activity.

What the local interurban lines had needed for some time was a fare collection routine which coped with their relatively fast schedules, large number of stations, and continually embarking and exiting riders. Thus it was that on Districts 1, 2, and 4, and the Saanich line, the Ohmer fare register system went into operation on December 6. This highly visible mechanical device extended the length of the interurban car at a height of about six feet. The register itself, activated at the beginning of a conductor's nine-hour shift by his personal identification key, and by a further "impression" key, was installed at the bulkhead separating the main seating area of the car from the smoking section. A cord was looped along a rod which ran the length of the car, and as the conductor collected each fare, his specific task was to turn the rod to that particular fare quantity collected, and pull the cord — bell dinging — to register the amount. Although instructions to conductors were explicit, and capitalized — "REGISTER EACH FARE SEPARATELY AS COLLECTED — NEVER BUNCH THEM," this command, in the event, was almost impossible to carry out in busy times especially, and the ringing up and pocketing of fares became haphazard. Despite the incentive of a merit system devised by superintendent Elson, the Ohmer register was ultimately unsuccessful, but well remembered.

The last day of 1915 was also the last day of 8 for 25¢ fares in Vancouver and Victoria. They seemed to have made little impact; the jitneys were still rolling. The B. C. Electric was searching for relief measures: its ridership in 1915 had been down almost fourteen million to 40,599,623. Even freight haulage had plummeted almost 100,000 tons — surely not the fault of the jitneys — to 258,029 tons.

As 1916 began with its continued concerns about the war and the absence of any mitigating trend in the lagging, stumbling economy, Vancouver Island and the lower mainland were crippled by a snowfall to end all snowfalls. The snow had begun to fall in January, but the bulk of it arrived in February, 36.5 inches alone in Vancouver, for a total depth of 65.9 inches in the mainland city. Victoria, with four feet of snow, drifting to a height of ten feet whipped up by a relentless wind, was paralyzed by "the big snow" on February 3. Though the Saanich line with its snow plow-equipped locomotive had managed to keep rolling, street cars, stranded all over the system, found operation impossible. It was February 11 before regular service could be said to be the norm. During the eight days of deserted and impassable streets, the B. C. Electric had employed a locomotive and flat cars to deliver the necessities of life to the area's extremities, Esquimalt and Oak Bay. When Victoria was back to normal, the soldiers who had worked so vigorously to clear the street car lines of snow were given one month of free trips on the street cars.

In June on both Vancouver Island and lower mainland operations, the B. C. Electric began publication of a weekly fold-over leaflet, called *The Buzzer* (Volume 1, Number 1 still had no name) which was dispensed from mounted holders on every street car and interurban car. This little informational journal, begun as another attempt to influence riders in regard to the jitney situation, is still being published today by the B. C. Electric's successor. Schedule information, brief articles, notices of current events, accolades, and company news were always features of *The Buzzer*. Although the masthead was changed occasionally through the years, the jokes were always a part of it. The very first one in the first lower mainland issue deserves quotation:

> *"The car I use today I've been using steadily for six years. It has taken me to my office in town and back and it hasn't cost me one halfpenny for repairs yet."*
> *"Great Scott, what a record! What car is it?"*
> *"The tramcar."*

The Saanich line's return fare to Victoria for soldiers stationed in Sidney was set at a low fifty-cent rate in June. The competing Victoria & Sidney Railway, running directly into Sidney, was able to retain most of the soldiers' business by following suit with an identically-lowered fare. In December, the B. C. Electric enlarged the facilities of The Chalet at Deep Bay, in an attempt to lure more customers to the Saanich line.

On the lower mainland, the B. C. Electric divested itself of its superfluous steam locomotive 940, selling it on March 6 to Wanecicin Iron and Metal Company; the B. C. Electric had already disposed of 941, ex 525. The need for steam on

Deep Bay itself and the Chalet from the northern terminus of the Saanich line, Deep Bay. (B.C. Hydro)

the long electric line to Chilliwack was in the past.

Speeded-up running times, more frequent headway, penetration of shuttle lines into downtown Vancouver, more rush hour extras, more running on Granville Street rather than Richards to draw the theatre crowds — all these gambits were tried by the company in Vancouver in its attempts to stem the jitney tide and stimulate patronage. On March 15 the Connaught Bridge was reopened and the Oak Street line was connected to the Georgia Street East line; on the same day Thirty-third Avenue between Main and Fraser saw its last street car in regular service. This short stretch would henceforth serve as a convenient training track for new motormen, as a useful emergency connector, and as part of the route followed by school specials between Mount Pleasant barn and Fraser and Forty-first Avenue.

Although the term "Eburne" lingers even today in and around its old home, particularly on the south side of the river, it officially became "Marpole" on June 1. The combination of relatively new interurban lines and similarly new major league freight movements occasionally precipitated a problem in need of a quick solution. Thus, superintendent Elson's edict of August 23 to freight crews operating the Burnaby Lake and Fraser Mills lines not to allow their trains to pass on Columbia Street at the curve at Leopold Place and at the curve near Brunette siding at the intersection of Cumberland Street, for fear of scraping sides. Before long, necessity would dictate the double tracking of this section of

Columbia Street between the province's penitentiary and the Fraser River.

Very soon after *The Buzzer* came an equally useful informational and public relations stroke, the first issuance on October 12 of publicly-available timetables. The jitney menace was continuing to batter the company's very existence, but it is clear today that the B. C. Electric in its efforts to cope with the jitney was growing more conscious of its public, creating a better brand of service, and laying the groundwork for quicker and better-focussed recovery from the economic doldrums of the time. It had even created a second, though more conventional, open air observation car for Vancouver from redundant street car 29.

Train 501, the milk train, consisting here of cars 1709, 1708, and 1707, at Meridian on March 18, 1916, bound for Vancouver. (B.C. Hydro)

One of the more comprehensive passes, allowing access to the Central Park, Lulu Island, and Burnaby Lake interurban lines as well as the North Vancouver and Vancouver city lines. (Norman W. Williams collection)

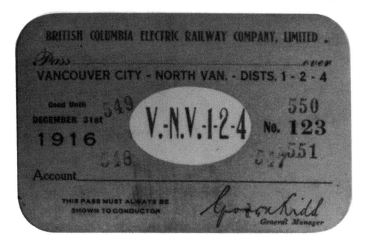

In this 1916 photo Vancouver-bound 1310 and 1309 slip past Cloverdale substation and into its depot before crossing the Great Northern's line (in foreground) to Hazelmere and Blaine. (B.C. Hydro)

In Vancouver, Stanley Park street cars on October 24 began looping around the Horse Show building at Georgia, Chilco, Alberni, and Denman streets, rather than wyeing to the north at the park's entrance. Just over a week later, an attempt to alleviate the afternoon rush hour crush at the intersection of Main and Hastings streets was instituted by positioning an extra conductor at the front door of each street car to accept riders' fares, permitting riders to enter the car at the front. This helpful innovation would spread to other overloaded locations, and continue as a feature of the company's operations.

The Fraser Valley really paid little attention to the much-delayed start of service over the Great Northern's Abbotsford-Chilliwack line in late September with its thrice-weekly mixed train between Vancouver and Hope. (The last five and a half miles into Chilliwack from the west were run on the Canadian Northern Pacific.) This kind of operation, as well as making little impact along its own line, affected the Fraser Valley branch not one whit. The six-year-old line had had a busy time of it: the Chilliwack station grounds had been filled and landscaped; a roadway had been constructed alongside Huntingdon wye for use in connection with loading spruce bolts; and an accident on Mount Lehman hill had resulted in extensive damage to three B. C. Electric box cars, 4070, 6036, and 6254, the latter burnt in the clearing of the wreckage.

As the year was drawing to a close for the line to Chilliwack, improvements had been initiated on at least three fronts. Firstly, a double line of wooden stringers was being installed on each of its twenty-nine wooden bridges to strengthen them. Secondly, 33,700 fir ties were set to replace the old ones in the line's 1917 tie renewal program, $12,132 for the ties, $12,221 for labour. Thirdly, $770 was to be spent for a little No. 34 Fairbanks-Morse "motor car" to replace the line's one worn-out gasoline speeder.

The Chilliwack line had grown up very quickly. By the end of the year, it met five major railroads at five locations: the C.P.R., C.N.P., and G.N.R. at New Westminster; the G.N.R. at Cloverdale; the C.P.R. at Abbotsford; the Milwaukee Road and Northern Pacific at Huntingdon; and the C.N.P. and G.N.R. at Chilliwack. Incredibly, it now had 74,108 feet of interchanges, spurs, sidings, and wyes.

Elsewhere on the interurban system, the New Westminster barn area had about 9,000 feet of track, the nearby freight yard 3,400 feet, and the Kitsilano yard 9,000 feet, while the Canadian Pacific-Great Northern connecting, freight only, south shore line of the Lulu Island branch had spawned twenty-three spurs into the industrial maelstrom of the False Creek area. Being street run at both ends, the Burnaby Lake line would never operate freight traffic of any consequence, evidenced in its total of less than a mile of sidings

and spurs.

On the Vancouver street car system, excluding the 4,017-foot quarry and gravel pit spur west on Thirty-third Avenue from Main Street, the five, short Pacific Coast Lumber Company spurs off Thirty-third and Ontario Street, and the trackage into the city market, twelve sidings were operational, the one at Oak Street and Forty-first Avenue actually only a spur:

Location	Length (feet)	Car Capacity
Dunbar St. at 35th Ave.	271	3
41st Ave. at Oak St.	355	6
Fraser St. at 58th Ave.	312	3
Hastings St. at Rupert St.	267	2
Hastings St. at Willingdon Ave.	279	3
Main St. at 54th Ave.	464	7
Main St. at 58th Ave.	218	2
Oak St. at 22nd Ave.	233	2
Oak St. at 41st Ave.	153	1
Oak St. at 49th Ave.	276	3
10th Ave. at Discovery St.	380	5
Victoria Dr. at 42nd Ave.	420	6

On the North Vancouver system, aside from the twenty-one-car capacity, 1,390 feet of car barn and yard facility between Third and Fourth streets at St. David's Avenue, seven passing sidings were in place:

Location	Length (feet)	Car Capacity
Fell Ave. at 16th St.	452	7
4th St. at Moody Ave.	400	6
Grand Boulevard at 15th St.	346	5
Keith Rd. at Bewicke Ave.	315	4
Keith Rd. at 13th St.	222	2
Lonsdale Ave. at 15th St.	462	7
Lynn Valley Rd. at Fromme Rd.	400	6

The following list of the New Westminster system's eleven passing sidings excludes a number of industrial spurs as well as the interurban-freight operated Fraser Mills and Queensborough lines:

Location	Length (feet)	Car Capacity
Columbia St. at Cumberland St.	350	3
Columbia St. at Braid St.	324	2
Edmonds spur	833	14
Edmonds St. at 6th St.	542	8
1st St. at Queens Park	281	3
Pine Street	509	6
Power House (0.3 mile west of Edmonds)	563	7
6th St. at 12th Ave. (Cliff Can Factory) -spur	256	3
6th St. at 13th Ave.	407	6
12th St. at 6th Ave.	658	12
12th St. at 12th Ave.	407	6

Strathcona station (Thirty-seventh Avenue), looking east, the highest point of elevation, at 241 feet above sea level, on the Vancouver-Marpole interurban line. Point Grey Secondary School today occupies the land just across the tracks. (B.C. Hydro)

British Columbia Electric Railway Company, Limited

1917

Pass   No. 50

Between   and

Account

SAANICH BRANCH

Until   1917, unless otherwise ordered.

COUNTERSIGNED BY

GEORGE KIDD.

LOCAL MANAGER   GENERAL MANAGER

NOT GOOD ON CITY CARS

*(Left)
A Saanich line pass, a rarity indeed. (B.C. Hydro)*

Vancouver-bound train from Chilliwack, 1402 and 1302, leaves behind Vedder Mountain, its station and its substation, one of five similar installations along the line. (B.C. Hydro)

The good news at the end of 1916 was the slight increase in the number of passengers carried, 42,905,020; the bad news was definitely the plummeting of freight tonnage farther still to the lowest figure since 1911, 218,065.

The B. C. Electric began 1917 with a resolve to remove jitneys from all city streets. A Victoria company spokesman claimed that the B. C. Electric was losing over $350,000 a year because of the jitneys, a fact not to be ignored by Victoria, or Vancouver, each of which received a percentage of the company's earnings.

On the lower mainland in 1917, January began with North Vancouver's city council planning to join the B. C. Electric at the ferry wharf with the Pacific Great Eastern Railway, a simple connection. The B. C. Electric would be the distributing agent. A more difficult problem was that of moving the P.G.E.'s heavy cars on the city's steep grades. (That this plan was not brought to fruition goes without saying.)

In New Westminster, procedures for the effective use of the company's depot and its loop line around the depot, using Begbie Street, took a further step. On February 13, two-car passenger interurban trains began using the loop, rather than changing ends. Twenty-minute service on the Central Park line and hourly on the Burnaby Lake line were the norms. Three days later, just across the river, the Fraser Valley Milk Producers' Association began operating in earnest; with its unique policy of open membership to milk producers, it was to become very successful in its co-operative measures to control the marketing of dairy produce.

On March 1, the Canadian Northern Pacific opened its new line to Steveston which had been precariously laid on elaborate piling and trestle work along the south shore of Lulu Island for over twelve miles from the end of the B. C. Electric's Queensborough line. That the company, in the face of its close, sometimes mysterious relationship with the C.P.R., was able to grant permission to the C.N.P. to operate over its tracks is remarkable; that the C.N.P.'s Steveston line existed for a brief sixteen months is not quite so remarkable, since smoldering, simmering peat fires gradually undermined the route, eventually destroying a 4,000-foot trestle. (A later line, built from New Westminster rather than through Queensborough, again effected a Steveston connection with the B. C. Electric, in addition to a connection near Tucks.)

Spring 1917 had been a particularly active season for the Chilliwack line. A five hundred-foot guard rail had been installed on the difficult curve where the previous year's accident had occurred. Slides along Vedder Mountain — first due to frost, then to heavy rains — and rain-caused mud slides in the cut east of Dennison and the cuts east of Abbotsford had consumed an unusual amount of time and effort in February and March. Tie renewal was a major project not only all along the line generally, but also on four specific spurs: Sullivan Pit (mile 9), Salmon River (mile 23), Bissel (mile 29), and Hygienic Dairy Company (mile 35); all four newly underpinned spurs were needed as passing tracks for freight trains, the current sidings being too short.

New spurs had been built (as an example, the 713-foot Chilliwack Evaporating and Packing Company's spur had been completed in two weeks at a cost of $1,882.12), but a number of spurs had also been removed, as had (prophetically — vis-à-vis logging along the line) the diamond crossing near Sullivan of the Surrey Shingle Company, which had finished its logging operations there. The work of repairing approximately five hundred broken or defective rail bonds between County Line and Chilliwack carried right on into the summer, as did smaller jobs such as roofing over milk stands and building cattle chutes at Abbotsford and Huntingdon.

May had seen the closing down of the Great Northern's old main line to the U.S. border through Cloverdale from Port Kells. (The Blaine-Hazelmere section would be abandoned in the following year, the line through Cloverdale in 1919.) It had also been the month of selling off a dozen of the outfit cars (eleven of them thirty-three-foot flat cars) the company had purchased, with one exception, in November 1908 for use in building the line to Chilliwack: 1045, 27642, X-2, X-3, X-4, X-5, X-6, X-7 (forty-foot, bought in September, 1909), X-10, X-11, X-13, and X-35. Most had gone to the International Timber Company for one hundred dollars apiece.

The fast-fading Saanich line had just seven years of life remaining, the nearby Victoria & Sidney Railway would capitulate in but two years, and along came the Canadian Northern Pacific to open a third Saanich peninsula route, this one terminating at Patricia Bay whence passenger and freight could be shipped across Georgia Strait and up the Fraser River to Port Mann, five miles east of New Westminster on the Canadian Northern Pacific. (B. C. Electric had previously rejected the C.N.P.'s request to operate trains over the Saanich line, which after all had a spur to Patricia Bay.) The new sixteen-mile line, based on one of the B. C. Electric's Saanich line surveys, commenced regular service with two runs of its gas-electric motor car, daily except Sunday, on April 30. (This line's grade had actually been ready more than two years previously, but the unavailability of rail had stalled completion.) B. C. Electric's Saanich line interchanged with C.N.P.'s Patricia Bay line at Tripp. Jitney operations actually would benefit both lines since the faltering of the Victoria & Sidney Railway would instigate a jitney run between Sidney and Tripp in a year's time.

On June 13, all conductors, motormen, and

Tod Inlet on the Saanich line featured not only a refreshments kiosk, but also a sign to the right advertising ice cream. (Geoff Meugens collection)

barn staff — members of the S.R.U. — went on strike for higher wages. Only the Fraser Valley and Lulu Island branches were in operation. When the provincial government appointed economist Dr. Adam Shortt of the federal Civil Service Commission to study the issues of fares and jitneys, and arrive at recommendations, the way was clear for general manager Kidd and the union to resume wage negotiations, and the men went back to work on June 21. Shortt's commission began public sessions in mid-July.

Long-time Victoria resident, Fred Hall, a model-builder, historian, and writer, was a passenger on the B. C. Electric's Saanich line on Monday, June 4, 1917; here is his splendid, valuable account, written almost sixty years later:

"At the Interurban Depot, located at 1505-1517 Douglas Street, between Pandora and Cormorant, stand two sleek modern cars numbered 1243 and 1244. They were built in St. Louis, Mo., only four years previously, have an overall length of 54 feet and a seating capacity for 62 passengers. Each car weighs more than 34 tons.

Painted a glistening dark green with brown trim, they have gold lettering and numbers to match. A gold decorative line runs the length of the car and over the front windows is a highly-polished brass whistle. They are capable of speeds up to 60 or 70 miles an hour, or more.

It is a pleasant day, and the clock on the City Hall says 25 minutes past one. In the B. C. Electric office adjoining the tracks, last minute passengers are busy purchasing their tickets for the 1:30 train. We join them, buy our tickets and board the car.

The interior is comfortable and roomy. It is finished in gleaming hardwood and smells slightly of varnish and disinfectant. There is a wide aisle between the two rows of rattan seats, with a division roughly two-thirds of the way down beyond which is a smoking section with wooden seats.

The City Hall clock strikes the half hour (it used to strike then), there is the conductor's "All aboooooooard", and with a hiss of releasing air brakes and a soft, almost imperceptible jerk, we are on our way.

But very slowly. It is an extremely sharp curve from the depot onto Cormorant Street, and another equally sharp from Cormorant to Douglas. The big cars squeak and groan protestingly as they ease themselves cautiously around both corners. The rule of the road hadn't been changed in 1917, and the two-car train moves over onto the left hand track, utilizing a cross-over switch located about in front of where Miss Frith's store is now located.

We are now at Fisgard Street. The Hudson's Bay store is there, but empty and unoccupied. All the street level windows are boarded up and painted green. This store wasn't opened until a few years later and in the meantime was used on several occasions for a Home Products Fair. Although we are unable to see them from our car window, there are several large two-storey homes immediately behind the Hudson's Bay building. On the opposite side of Douglas Street is the Masonic Hall and a large vacant lot with billboards.

The cars pick up speed as they proceed down Douglas Street towards Pembroke. On the left, between Chatham and Discovery, is the Interurban Freight Depot, with facilities for the handling of various types of merchandise destined for the fast-growing communities of the Saanich Peninsula. Two high-speed express and baggage cars, numbers 1706 and 1707, provide fast and frequent service.

After crossing Queens Avenue, we see on our right the new Bay Street Armory, completed just two years previously in 1915, and a little further on, the much older North Ward School. There is a brief stop at Hillside Avenue to pick up a man with a suitcase — doubtless a travelling salesman bound for some country store.

When passengers pay a cash fare, the conductor reaches up and turns a long rod running the entire length of the car. At the end is a dial showing figures and a pointer which can be turned to show the amount paid. The conductor pulls a cord, a bell rings and the transaction is recorded. A sort of remote control cash register.

With gradually increasing speed, the cars continue on Douglas Street, make the turn onto Burnside and in a few minutes, with a squeaking of brakes, stop at the first station, Harriet Road. Here is a small spur track, sometimes occupied by a freight locomotive or line car. There are piles of poles, ties and other railroad paraphernalia.

More passengers board the car, there is a 'ding-ding' of the bell and we set off down the long down grade to the next station, Tillicum. At this point, the interurban cars leave the public roads and enter their own private right-of-way, now named Interurban road.

Now we really move! We streak past rock cuttings on one side and catch a glimpse of Colquitz Creek on the other. There is a hollow

sound as we cross a small trestle bridge, the tracks make a slight turn to the left and we arrive at Marigold Road.

There are many new homes going up in the district and across the railway tracks are two country grocery stores, one owned by a George Benner and the other by Mr. Jones. After Marigold comes Wilkinson Road followed by Glynn, Eberts, Westwoodvale, Goward, Picken, Prospect Lake, Heals, Durrance Road and Brentwood.

Here the track makes a sharp right turn and proceeds down what is now Wallace Drive. With frequent 'toot-toots' the big cars attain high speed on the straight level track and in a few minutes arrive at Saanichton.

Some of the passengers get off here and walk down the road to the Prairie Tavern, which is still standing at Mount Newton Cross Road. The next stations are Bazan Bay, Tripp and Sidneway which, owing to a 30-year franchise held by the

V. & S., is the closest any competing railway can come to Sidney.

After Sidneway comes Meadlands, Patricia Junction (with a seldom-used spur track going down to the bay), Mallowmot, Tatlow and finally Deep Bay.

This is truly the end of the interurban line. A short section of double track, a platform and a little red shelter with a white sign bearing the two words DEEP BAY.

We are 23 miles from Victoria and our trip has taken exactly one hour and 10 minutes. This may seem slow by today's standards, but one must take into consideration the somewhat circuitous route and frequent stops. The train crew reverses the trolley poles in preparation for the return trip to Victoria while we walk down the grassy slope towards The Chalet." †

Much road surfacing and paving was being carried out all through Saanich in 1917, encouraging automobile use and the easier

Interurban coach 1242 at Deep Bay, the northern terminus of the Saanich line. The motorman wears engineer's coveralls, a not unusual habit on the Chilliwack line as well. (Ted Clark collection)

† Fred Hall, "Railways to Saanich," *The Daily Colonist*, 9 May 1976, pp. 14-15.

Granville Bridge, to the north, from its south end, during the time of the Great War. To the left is the convenient Vancouver terminus of the Lulu Island branch. An interurban coach is visible past the railing. The second automobile is a jitney. (B.C. Transit)

Oak Bay car 187, heading for town on Fort Street, leaves a few riders at the Cook Street intersection in this photo from the time of the Great War. (Fred Hall photo)

movement of freight by trucks. To shippers, the procedure of shipping freight on the Saanich line seemed more bothersome than ever, what with delivering the goods first to the interurban freight depot on Douglas Street, then dealing with tariffs and possibly complicated way-bills, and finally having the good set off at unattended stations, still needing to be brought to their ultimate destinations.

During the month of June, North Vancouver's city council and police commission began dealing with a problem that had almost come to a head: the quantity of automobile traffic, street cars, ferries, and pedestrians at the Lonsdale street car terminus-ferry wharf. In September follow-up plans were being discussed for the repositioning of the street car tracks along the east side of the ferry wharf.

B. C.'s Minister of Railways, the Honourable John Oliver, was quoted on the matter of converting traffic from operating on the left side of the road to the right, causing general manager Kidd to dispatch a strongly-worded letter to him on October 16. It indicated his displeasure with the very idea, let alone its cost to the company of almost half a million dollars ($30,000 alone to rebuild the special work at Columbia and Begbie streets).

Six days later, Murrin and Department of Railways inspector William Rae left for Seattle, Spokane, and Calgary to study the operation of one man street cars. This fact-finding mission motivated a delegation of company employees to meet with Premier Brewster to argue against one man street cars. Murrin had already enthused that one man street cars would be an appropriate innovation for a system such as Victoria's.

Sighs of relief and gratitude were breathed throughout B. C. Electric officialdom in November when Dr. Shortt's report was made public. Among its recommendations were two which were particularly pleasing: jitneys were not to compete with street cars — they interfered with the effectiveness of a quality street car service, and street cars manned by only one operator would be a useful and relevant departure for the company.

In Victoria, the Outer Wharf street car line's very name had gained added meaning during the year with the completion of a four-year project, the $2,260,000 Ogden Point docks, at the line's terminus. Capable of docking the largest ocean-going liners and vessels of all types, they remain to this day Victoria's major harbour facility.

By the end of the year, the Port Moody-Coquitlam Railway had been relaid with 56-pound rail; McNair was still operating the one steam locomotive, and now used twelve flat cars and twelve logging cars. Great Northern's new depot in Vancouver on the reclaimed flats of False Creek had opened, to be shared initially by the Canadian Northern Pacific; and the B. C. Electric's Georgia East line, running three blocks to the north, had taken its last step before oblivion: on December 3, it had been disconnected from linkage with any other line, being left its quiet shuttle between Main Street and Victoria Road. It had been a year of new issues, and there had been more than a few gains: the number of passengers carried, though still well back of 1913's peak, had climbed to 46,618,234, and freight tonnage hauled had come back nicely to 324,280.

As 1918 opened, the upper Fraser Valley was crippled by weather conditions and their aftermaths. A three-day ice storm beginning December 27 piled ice to a depth of three to four inches on wires. Damage to wires and 550 poles that crashed to the ground, and from track washouts from streams swollen with the "silver thaw" on New Year's Day totalled $150,000. Indeed, a completely new water course had been created just east of Huntingdon, which now

required bridging. The Vedder River had overflowed its banks, washing out track to a depth of four feet in places for three-quarters of a mile; somehow the line's bridge at the river had survived. Chilliwack was without light and power for many weeks, many of its own lighting and telephone poles strewn about the streets. Railway operations and restorations east of Huntingdon were run well into February by three steam locomotives the company had borrowed from the C.P.R., Timberland Lumber Company, and Shearwater Lumber Company. It was not until a week or two after the beginning of the storm that the section from Huntingdon west to Coghlan could be operated by electricity.

In Vancouver January 15 marked the permanent closing to shipping of the bridge on Main Street at diminishing False Creek; for ease of street car operation, the break in the trolley wire at the bridge's span was eliminated. The still woeful business conditions and the still unmitigated jitney competition may certainly have been causes for the operation of a mere 117 street cars in afternoon rush hours, farther down yet from 1917's 161. Nonetheless, for a hockey game in March at the 10,500-seat arena near Stanley Park, 53 special street cars had crammed the tracks in the area waiting to spirit the fans away to their homes.

Late in April the news came: the city of Vancouver had been given the go-ahead by the provincial legislature to clear the jitneys from its streets. Gradually they left, last of all from their bumpy "interurban" journeys between Vancouver and New Westminster; Victoria was still three months away from similar legislation.

In 1918 Steveston was still without fire engines, a daring, disastrous shortcoming. When a shack

behind the Star Cannery flamed to life on May 4, the result within a few hours was 600 homeless Chinese and Japanese families and losses amounting to half a million dollars. Some of the boardwalks, the post office, a bakery, three canneries, a drug store, and three hotels between the Fraser's dike and Moncton Street were destroyed. Although the town would rebuild, it had forever lost a long-cumulating colour and character. Fortunately, for the company, its station had not been affected and all freight cars had been pulled east away from town.

At the same time on the Lulu Island branch, the construction of a new substation in Point Grey at King Edward Avenue had begun, a reinforced concrete building measuring 100 by 60 feet, surrounding the old 80 by 60 feet substation. (The first one was demolished when the new substation's concrete roof was in place.) As preparation for the increase in power, a new high-tension line had recently been erected from the Central Park line's Earles Road substation.

Street car conductors in Vancouver had begun selling a B. C. Electric-produced map and street guide on June 3, an early public relations gesture. At the same time motormen and barn workers threatened strike action increasingly throughout the month of June. Wages were again the issue, and on July 2, the men went on strike all across the company's system, with only the railroad Chilliwack and Lulu Island lines bristling with business.

By July 11 the strike was settled, and on the following day regular service was resumed. One week later, extra fares on "owl" cars were cancelled and, more importantly, a six-cent fare went into effect. In Victoria, city council banned the jitneys from its streets, but despite this ruling,

Looking north through Main Street's bascule bridge, soon to be dismantled because of the partial reclamation of False Creek. The new Great Northern depot (Union Station) is already in place to the right. (Ted Clark collection)

successful removal would elude city and company there for another two and a half years. On August 12, street railway men across the system achieved an eight-hour workday, a civilized development which allowed as well for the hiring of many new men.

The termination of the Great War on November 11 was the signal for celebrations of a kind never previously witnessed, or felt. There was great joy and myriad prophecies were made; for some the expectation was to revert to the peacetime normalcy of 1912-1913. For others, perhaps more far-seeing, the future held further changes.

With the end of the war, attention could be paid to the more mundane issues of living. For the B.C. Electric, the C.P.R. crossing of Hastings near Carrall Street was downtown Vancouver's biggest traffic problem (and would remain so until a tunnel was built). To illustrate, Grandview street car 114 was delayed by this C.P.R. crossing on November 21 going west at 1:20 p.m. for seven minutes, going east at 3:53 p.m. for seven minutes, and going east again at 5:41 p.m. for two minutes.

The B. C. Electric also had difficulties with fog. On December 24, as an example, nineteen Vancouver street cars — about 180 were in service during the period the fog was at its most dense — were involved in collisions, all of them damaged, three of them heavily. The company's inspectors at key intersections had performed the virtually impossible task of trying to maintain some semblance of a schedule.

Some problem solving had already begun during the year with the company's expenditure of $229.02 for surveys for a private right of way for the Central Park line into Vancouver; everyone had really had enough of the three and a half miles of street running from Cedar Cottage to Carrall Street, especially since the New Westminster end had so neatly been solved by the Highland Park cut-off. The Saanich line seemed not to allow for solution, although the company would continue to over-extend itself on the line's behalf. When the Dominion Observatory had been opened during the year — its telescope was the world's largest — the company had altered the name of Picken station (mile 7.4) to Observatory siding, and had run special trips on Saturday evenings to take visitors to the talks and demonstrations at the observatory.

Gratifyingly, passenger numbers over the whole system were up in 1918, to 53,718,182, and freight tonnage hauled had climbed to 365,830.

By 1919 any talk of building barns, repair shops, or yards across the Fraser River bridge from New Westminster and at Horne-Payne had long evaporated. Only the presence of Shops and Horne-Payne interurban stations were reminders of the pre-Great War dreams. New Westminster was the hub of the B. C. Electric's railway operations and would remain so. Some three hundred interurban passenger trains pulled out of its depot daily, all under standard train rules. With the exception of District 2's obvious allegiance to the Kitsilano barn, all interurban cars and locomotives, as well as New Westminster street cars, were cleaned and repaired at the New Westminster barn under the direction of general foreman T. Tokely. The repair and inspection of B. C. Electric's freight cars — 192 box cars, 198 flat cars, 55 dump and construction cars, 34 service cars of an exotic variety, as well as eleven cabooses (four, A.1 - A.4, were beautiful, little four-wheelers) — was handled at New Westminster's Sixteenth Street freight yard. (During the war the former car building shops had been used for the manufacture of shells.)

All dispatching of passenger and freight trains was done by telephone at New Westminster under the direction of chief dispatcher William Maxwell, with three "tricks" or shifts during the 24 hours. The maintenance of the interurban lines came under the direction of engineer of way E. L. Tait, headquartered in Vancouver, while roadmaster William Stormont and bridge and building master J. M. Archibald worked out of New Westminster. On the Fraser Valley line, six section gangs — each usually consisted of four men and a foreman — looked after the line's maintenance. Four gangs were allocated to District 2, with one each to Districts 1, 4, and the city lines of New Westminster. W. D. Power, at Vancouver, was the general freight and passenger agent, while freight agent John Donald at New Westminster was the overseer of the company's freight operations. Thirteen locomotives were available on the lower mainland system, 904, 950, 951, and 952, and the more powerful steel equipment, 970-974, 980, and 990-992. (901 and 902 were in use almost exclusively on Vancouver's street car lines.)

Freight train operations on the line to Chilliwack had the following configuration in 1919: a way freight left New Westminster daily at 7 a.m. for Abbotsford, and return; a through freight left New Westminster daily at 9:45 a.m. for Abbotsford, returning the following night; and another freight left Abbotsford for Chilliwack every morning, returning in the afternoon. Two freights were operated in the following manner on the Lulu Island branch: one crew was in charge of the south shore line, as well as the main line to King Edward Avenue; the other operated daily at 7 a.m. from the company's interchange with the C.P.R. (just east of old Granville station) for Steveston, returning to Vancouver after having run the leg from Marpole to New Westminster and return. A yard locomotive operated on the Central Park line every day, another every night; freight sheds were situated at Highland Park, Edmonds, Royal Oak, Central Park, Collingwood East, and Cedar Cottage. The B. C. Electric at this time was interchanging an average of 800 freight cars per month with its connecting steam railroads. Meanwhile, a daily average of 475 cans of milk was being brought in by the three-car milk train that left Chilliwack at 8 a.m. (Who had time to notice, or even care, that service between Abbotsford and Chilliwack on the Great Northern had been abandoned, after a mere two and a half years, on February 23?)

The Fraser Valley survived the scare of another ice storm on March 1 when a mixture of sleet and rain fell in the Langley Prairie and Matsqui areas. Although trolley wires were covered by an icy coating, service continued.

The B. C. Electric Employees Magazine was begun in the previous year. A piece entitled "The Unknown Valley" by the operator of the New Westminster substation, B. S. Harton, in the April, 1919 issue, shows a valley in transition, and gives an interesting account of the Chilliwack line.

"Now we have climbed the ascent on the south side of the river and obtain an almost bird's-eye view of the picturesque Royal City. Each mile brings some new object of interest, until about thirteen miles from Westminster we reach Cloverdale, and pass the first of the five massively built substations which handle the demand for transportation, light and power along the valley.

At Hall's Prairie we get an uninterrupted view of majestic Mount Baker. On a clear evening the magic of the sunset throws a rose-tinted robe over the towering snow-clad battlements and graduates the shadows of the adorning foothills to the deepest imperial purple, making a picture of impressive beauty.

Langley Prairie is another link in the chain of prosperous communities along our route, and shows recent development in the way of new stores adjacent to the station.

Two and one-half miles farther on we arrive at Milner, another of the practical demonstrations of successful settlement. The next station, Jardine, about three-quarters of a mile farther on, is privileged to be the eastern terminus of the early morning trains to and from Vancouver. The Saturday "Owl" special leaves Vancouver at 11:25 and reaches Jardine at 1 a.m.

Four and three-quarter miles brings us to Coghlan, where the second substation, twelve miles from Cloverdale, is situated. In this district we find logging and lumbering active. The mill at Beaver River covers quite a large area, and adds considerably to the size of the freight trains by its shipments.

We are now descending the eastern slope of Mount Lehman, and after passing the station of that name we obtain a comprehensive view of Matsqui Prairie, with Mount Hatzic forming a background across the river. Passing Gifford and Glover, we now reach Clayburn. The Matsqui substation stands to the south of the track, flanked by a grove of shady maples under whose wide-spreading branches the dog-tooth violet and trillium fill the air with their sweet perfume in the spring.

Clayburn has a well-deserved reputation for the quality of its bricks turned out from local clay, whence its name is derived. The creamery close to the station also makes large shipments of high-class butter.

St. Nicholas adds one more to our list of industries. This time it is honey of exhibition quality, gathered from the abundance of clover growing in the vicinity. Closely allied by this fragrant link to the dairy, it helps to fulfil the scriptural ideal of the Promised Land: "A land flowing with milk and honey."

The peaceful rotundity of the word "abbot" lends its characteristics to Abbotsford, our next stopping place. Sheltered and with an air of stability, it thrives in a hollow of the hilly range separating Matsqui and Sumas prairies. Passing Delair and Vye, we reach Huntingdon, a place of some importance on the boundary line between Canada and the United States. The B. C. Electric Railway (representing John Bull) has struck the southern trail to shake hands with Uncle Sam. Long may the respective flags of these two nations wave a stately welcome to each other across the narrow dividing, and also uniting, street, and their customs officers ally their forces against the unpatriotic smuggler.

A straight run of six and one-half miles across a corner of Sumas Prairie brings us to Sumas substation, situated at the foot of Vedder Mountain. Our track now follows the winding south-east shore line of Sumas Lake, a large body of water that periodically turns a vast tract of what should be valuable land into a derelict waste of waters. On account of this, it was necessary to cut a way in the solid rock of the hillside to construct the line, adding considerable expense to the project. The beauty of the mountain sides and the play of light and shade on the surface of the lake lay undisputed claim to our attention, until we find ourselves crossing the Vedder River, the Mecca of all good followers of old Izaak Walton. On more than one occasion this river has left a record of destruction along its banks in its impetuous haste to reach a far-off objective, illustrating Tennyson's lines: "Raw Haste, half-sister to Delay." Unfortunately this is typical of many things in the province.

Still speeding on we come in touch once again with man's industry and notice particularly the Borden milk evaporating factory at South Sumas. The hop gardens at Sardis make a charming picture in their season, reminiscent of cool drinks in bygone summers. Vegetable and fruit evaporating has also been added to the company's products. Close to Sardis station is Coqualeetza Institute, a fine building dedicated to the training of Indian boys and girls.

The track now turns northward, between cultivated fields drained by an efficient dyking system. Amputated orchards and trees, with huge limbs snapped off by the ice storm which made the closing days of 1917 memorable, stand silent witnesses to the havoc wrought by a meddlesome chinook. We are all well acquainted with the evil effects of "hot air" in public life; some maintain it is used largely in Vancouver to dry up the wet.

As we slacken speed for our final stop at Chilliwack we see the fifth and last substation on our right. Chilliwack and its wide extent of prairie land is encircled by mountains, the most noticeable being Mount Cheam. After doing justice to an excellent lunch at an hotel, we fill in the remainder of the time at our disposal before the train returns by exploring the locality, and discover among other items of interest an evaporating plant, a cheese factory, lumber mills, and imposing high school, municipal hall, city hall, court house, a spacious post office, a movie theatre, a drill hall, extensive exhibition grounds, local telephone and water supply companies, four churches, and, last but not least, four banks — unimpeachable witnesses that the Fraser Valley proposition has dollars at the end of it."

The Saanich line lost its two railroad competitors during the year, the Victoria & Sidney Railway, with its last passenger run on April 30, and the Canadian Northern Pacific even earlier in the year. (The V. & S. suffered immediate abandonment while the C.N.P. line would struggle on with sixteen more years of little freight.) Some in Sidney had hoped that the B. C. Electric would take over the V. & S. segment into Sidney for interurban operation, but that never happened, the C.N.P. in fact requisitioning the brief Sidney end of the V. & S. On the first of May, the Saanich line acquired Sidney's mail business,

a further annoyance to Sidney (because of the necessary earlier closing of the post office and the line's distance from town) which had already lost its quarter century's link with Victoria. There was, however, always some kind of jitney run into Victoria — jitneys were on the streets of Victoria again, city council's orders having been rescinded on technical grounds — and in five months, a former B. C. Electric employee would begin a bus service between the two centres! In July the Saanich line would have its large locomotive, 981, removed and sent back to New Westminster.

In Vancouver sightseeing by street car was the thing to do. Observation car 123 had been languishing in Victoria, actually disused for a few years, and had been brought to Vancouver in mid-April to join car 124 and the older, more conventional 29, used usually as a backup, or occasionally to transport an accompanying band or musical group.

The jitney by-law was also repealed in Vancouver, but only for the twenty-five-day duration of the system-wide strike once again by conductors, motormen, and barn workers which had begun on June 5 in support of the general strike in Winnipeg. During the strike, the company had fitted up truck bodies in buslike fashion to transport its employees to and from their homes. "Jits" courted little good will, charging up to ten cents a lift, and that without

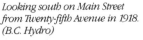

Looking south on Main Street from Twenty-fifth Avenue in 1918. (B.C. Hydro)

Observation cars 124, 29, and 123 on Vancouver's Dunbar Street, with sightseeing guide extraordinaire, Teddy Lyons, standing, second from the right. (B.C. Transit)

transfer privileges.

Further evidence of the efficacy of travel by means other than rail was hammered home, during the last days of the strike, when two aviators attempted a flight over the Rocky Mountains from Lulu Island to Calgary. On their first lap they flew the sixty-five miles from Minoru Park to Chilliwack in fifty-five minutes. They were guests of honour in Chilliwack at a banquet and ball, much as the B. C. Electric's opening day entourage had been, fewer than nine years ear-lier.

During July the temporary substation at Kennedy, virtually the top of the tough 2.6% grade of the Fraser Valley line east from the Fraser River bridge, had been replaced by a more permanent one of corrugated iron; this more powerful installation had been a priority for some time. In the following month, a $25,000 project of track renewal was begun on the rather run-down Marpole-Steveston line.

Once again, a visit by royalty — this time none

The ferry has just arrived at North Vancouver from Vancouver in 1919. As motor vehicles roll off, and others inch on, most ferry patrons head for one of the three street cars. At the intersection in the photo, the Capilano car will break to the right, the Lynn Valley to the left, and the Lonsdale will keep coming up — and up. (Ted Clark collection)

At Bellerose on the Chilliwack line, looking northeastward over Sumas Lake, not too many years before its draining. (B.C. Hydro)

other than the successor to the throne, the Prince of Wales — threw Vancouverites into a tizzy and brought almost every available street car out onto the streets for the great day, September 22.

Out in the Fraser Valley, farmers were producing enough surplus milk that the Fraser Valley Milk Producers' Association had begun retailing milk (in May), necessitating the creation of a milk evaporating plant at Delair and a utility plant at Sardis (both on the B. C. Electric's Chilliwack line). Nonetheless, the 30,000-acre expanse of Sumas Lake was more than ever a tantalizing vision of dairying land, and its reclamation took a vital step toward realization when property owners met at Huntingdon on November 24 to vote in favour of the lake's draining.

Several winters of heavy snowfall had helped towards organization of snow-coping equipment. By 1919 a pattern had been established; traffic superintendent W. H. Dinsmore was in command, while master mechanic G. A. Dickie saw to the readiness of men and equipment at the Prior Street barn. Locomotive 904, fitted up with snow clearing "wings," would set out around 1 a.m. to clear an eight-foot swath on either side of the tracks. The cane department had about five tons of rattan on hand for the rotary brooms of the four sweepers, each with specific routes: S.53 on Fairview, Oak, and Sixteenth Avenue; S.54 on Powell Street, Hastings East, Georgia East, and up Commercial to Cedar Cottage; S.56 to Stanley Park, and on all of the Point Grey lines; and S.57 on Broadway East, Kingsway, Fraser Street, and Victoria Drive.

Late in the year, the B. C. Electric's "own" Sir Frank Stillman Barnard — knighthood had come in 1918 — stepped down from his post as British Columbia's Lieutenant-Governor. By year's end it was clear that the first year without war had seen

some gains — ridership had been up to 60,692,700, although freight tonnage was back somewhat to 331,794. Overall, business conditions could still not be termed more than fair, but expectations were inordinately high for 1920.

At the beginning of the year, motormen were having problems with someone mischievously inclined tampering with the reverse handles on the interurban cars at Granville Street station. More importantly, by March 1920, 198 street cars were moving rush hour traffic in Vancouver, and New Westminster's interurban depot had been remodelled, including now a news stand, cigar store, and soda fountain. On April 17 a freight derailment spilled lumber all over the tracks at Mount Lehman, near where Gifford fill was replacing a trestle, necessitating the transfer of the passenger trains throughout the day.

April 16, however, was one of those great days once again in Point Grey; one and three-quarter miles of new single track street car line was opened from King Edward Avenue, south on Granville to Forty-first, then west to the interurban line, Kerrisdale. (The section on Forty-first had actually been laid before the war.) This event spelled the end of the Wilson Road shuttle between there and Dunbar Street, since every second street car proceeding from the Fraser line south on Granville Street from downtown now ran past King Edward to Forty-first, and right through to Dunbar, giving a twenty-minute service, as well as a new alternate route to the interurbans for Kerrisdale residents heading downtown. Not only did the street car with its frequent stopping places take considerable business from the interurban — after all, one did not even have to transfer to a street car at Granville Street station — both interurban freight and passenger trains suffered the ignominy of forever after having to stop dead before crossing the street car line's diamond at Forty-first. Sightseeing runs, soon to resume for the summer, would henceforth include this new line in their lengthened circuit. During 1920, the tracks on Forty-first between Granville and Oak streets were removed, and those beyond to Main Street were ultimately paved over; it was still as it had been when the tracks had been laid before the war — no settlers along the whole abandoned stretch.

Even the south end of Main Street was still only slightly settled. Those who did live there were accustomed to locomotive 902 having a twice-weekly sortie with the horrendous grade of the street car line north from Marine Drive, as it hauled wood up Main Street to the mill off Thirty-third Avenue. Two city conductors and two city motormen were in charge of this operation, which required bringing each freight car one by one up the hill.

May in New Westminster means May Day, and in 1920 it meant a record 17,121 passengers transported to Queen's Park by nine cars. (Four were always used in regular service on the Queen's Park line.) May in North Vancouver meant that city council was more than ever exercised by the dangerous congestion at the foot of Lonsdale Avenue, what with street cars, ferries, automobiles waiting to get on ferries, the P.G.E. terminal, and the ubiquitous, unpredictable pedestrians.

The Saanich line in May was running five trips each way daily between Victoria and Deep Bay, with short run trips to and from Eberts, Saanichton, and Meadlands. Sadly, this same May its interurban cars received their last coat of paint on track eight of the Pembroke Street barn.

May in the Fraser Valley brought this astute analysis from a lengthier statement by a B. C. Electric official:

> *"The transformation of the Fraser Valley from a timber camp to a farming district is going on rapidly and this transformation is affecting the company's business. At present a large part of our revenue comes from the sale of electric power for mills and from the hauling of lumber over the railway line. To some extent this business will continue for several years, but the camps are being compelled to go farther back from our lines.*
>
> *The day will come when the revenue from the lumber industry will be negligible and then we shall have to depend upon the development of the valley as a farming community. Our railway, freight and passenger revenue will have to come from chicken, dairy or fruit farms. Our light and power revenue will have to come from the supplying of these farms with our service."* †

It was on May 18 that a large trestle replacement project on the Chilliwack line began. Number Two trestle at Dry Gulch, about two and a half miles east of the Fraser River bridge, was due for rebuilding at the very least, but surveys earlier in the year had determined that a completely new line was not only possible, but also, in the long run, preferable. A narrow gauge railway line, complete with a Davenport locomotive, six dump cars, and a steam shovel, was set in place for transporting the necessary fill material, 85,000 tons of it. Before the year was out, a graceful 350-foot long fill, 65 feet high at the point where a massive new culvert was in place to accept the seasonal waters of the stream, and with a roadbed eighteen feet in width, was ready for traffic; the little narrow gauge line had supplied all 55,000 cubic yards of it. Together, the filling of Dry Gulch and the building of the Gifford fill at Mount Lehman would cost $18,929.65.

The difficulties encountered throughout the previous ten years of dealing with the crowds flocking to Vancouver's exhibition were solved on June 26, when a new, $6,000 street car track was opened on Renfrew Street for the five blocks

A Saanich line train, 1240 and 1241, pauses in Victoria near line car L.5. (Geoff Meugens collection)

between Hastings and the end of the Powell East extension at Oxford Street. Now a looping of street cars using both Powell and Hastings lines was possible, eliminating the previous traffic-blocking pattern of wying cars at Renfrew and Hastings. Concurrently, the company had double tracked its line on Hastings between Renfrew and Boundary Road, and what with the city's widening and paving of Hastings, the exhibition's new main entrance at Hastings and Renfrew was inaugurated, supplanting its previous entrance at the park's northwest point. Everything was ready for opening day, September 11.

The Chilliwack line was always the operation that attracted special runs, and with good reason. July 12 offers a particularly fascinating instance, the local Orange lodges having decided to go travelling. The B. C. Electric ran two sections of No. 2 from New Westminster, and two extra trains from Vancouver, each consisting of five cars. These four trains ran from New Westminster in sections twenty minutes apart, returning from Chilliwack in the same fashion, with a total of 1,375 passengers.

In July on the Central Park line, two or three special trains were run virtually every day, most of them for Sunday School picnics to Stanley Park. (Small wonder that the company had recently elaborated its special track work at the park.) Regular service on the Central Park line was being run by six two-car trains, increased by six more two-car trains and one single car during rush hours. Cars in use on the line, as well as on the Burnaby Lake line, were 1000-1002, 1004-1009 (1011 and 1012 were out of service), 1217-1225, and 1227-1238. (Of the 1200s, the last to be transferred from the Central Park to the Lulu Island line had been 1201-1204 and 1208, to join with 1205-1207, 1211, 1212, 1215, 1226, 1702, 1703, and 1802 there.)

Yet, despite heavy rush hour traffic on the Central Park line, passenger earnings were down 25% from 1912. The line's traffic in 1920 came more from commuters than it did in 1912; and in

† "Fraser Valley Developing as Power Market," *The B.C. Electric Employees' Magazine*, June 1920, pp. 2-4.

WESTMINSTER CITY LINES			
28		CHILD	ADULT
FROM	TO	SINGLE FARE	
West'r.	Royal Oak	5	5
	Park Avenue	10	15
	Lakeview	10	20
	Vancouver	15	25
West'r. Limits	Patterson		10
	Coll. East	5	15
	Cedar Cottage	10	20
	Vancouver	15	25
Edmonds	Royal Oak	5	5
	Park Avenue	5	10
	Beaconsfield	10	15
	Cedar Cottage	10	20
	Vancouver	15	25
Power House	West Burnaby	5	5
	Coll. West	5	10
	Nanaimo Road	10	15
	Vancouver	10	20
Gilley	Patterson	5	5
	Beaconsfield	5	10
	Cedar Cottage	10	15
	Vancouver	10	20
HONORED			
West'r.	Vancouver	CHILD	ADULT
When punched for return conductor at Highland Park or rath St. Junction will exchange this duplex for regular round trip ticket.	RETURN	25	25

A duplex fare receipt, used by passengers transferring from New Westminster city street cars to the Central Park line. (Ted Clark collection)

In Victoria, street car service had already become more engagingly explicit with the painting of a route number on each line's signs, thus:

1 — Oak Bay
2 — Outer Wharf-
   Cloverdale
3 — Beacon Hill-
   Fernwood
4 — Esquimalt
5 — Gorge
6 — Foul Bay
7 — Hillside
8 — Burnside
9 — Uplands
10 — Mount Tolmie
11 — Willows

spite of a return fare of thirty-five cents, fifteen cents less than in 1912, the automobile had cut into the line's "regular" traffic, leaving it with the low-fare, rush hour commutation business. In North Vancouver, the Pacific Great Eastern Railway's boast of having carried five thousand people on an August weekend was easily bested by the 18,668 carried by the three street car lines on the same Saturday and Sunday.

Summer was winding down, and on the last day of August, work finally began on the long-awaited, two million-dollar project of draining Sumas Lake. And Labour Day, a few days later, offered a convenient comparison of passengers carried on the four lower mainland interurban lines: District 1 - 12,916; District 2 - 4,790; District 3 - 3,437; and District 4 - 1,534. In the month following, a new depot, complete with commodious waiting room, candy store, and even electric fittings showroom, was opened at Marpole to serve passengers of District 2 interurban trains, as well as those using the lengthy Oak street car line.

In Victoria a new traffic by-law was passed on December 1 prohibiting the operation of jitneys along routes already served by street car lines. The legislation also forced jitney operators to comply with rules and regulations in regard to franchises, safety, and the like. Not surprisingly the demise of jitneys was complete.

The B. C. Electric's only competitor on the lower mainland in the field of electric power, the Western Power Company of Canada Limited (until 1916, the Western Canada Power Company Limited), was acquired by the company on December 20. At this time the W. P. Co. boasted a hydro-electric generating station at Stave Falls, some five miles northeast of Ruskin; 82 circuit miles of 60,000-volt lines; 140 circuit miles of 13,000-volt lines; a large receiving station at Ardley in Burnaby near the Burnaby Lake line; fourteen substations of various capacities; a distribution system supplying an area on the north side of the Fraser River extending from Vancouver to Nicomen, and on the south side, the municipalities of Matsqui and Sumas; and a 5.85-mile steam railway (still recovering from a rain-induced washout in October) running along the west side of Stave River between Ruskin and Stave Falls. A gradual abandonment of some duplicate electrical facilities took place after the B.C. Electric took control.

The railway in its eight years of operation had been instrumental in the building of the power plant, had performed a passenger service for Western Power Company employees and settlers, and since 1916 had been used for logging by the Abernethy & Lougheed Logging Company. Its difficult route had necessitated twelve trestles and twelve trestle-work supported fills, and the building of the dam at the northern end of the line had required a saddle-tank locomotive with attendant dump cars.

At the time of its take-over, the railway's equipment roster comprised two shay locomotives (numbers 1 and 7) and a passenger-baggage coach once owned by the C.P.R. The line's fifty-pound rail connected with the mainline of the C.P.R. just west of Ruskin station, where the Western Power Company Railway had its own station and freight shed a few hundred feet north of the junction. Stave Falls itself — "Austins" would be its official railway designation — had become a considerable community, and encompassed the railway's station, freight shed, round-house, and yard facilities, where logs from Stave Lake were loaded onto flat cars for the trip down to the big mills along the lower river at Ruskin.

The routine of the daily passenger train was well established by this time: leave Stave Falls with passengers and mail, and lumber cars, at 8 a.m., picking up passengers, some milk, and carloads of lumber and shingles along the way, struggling gingerly over the steep canyon section between Wilson's and Siwash — other stations were Hall's, Yeo's, Anderson, and, nearer Ruskin, Stoltze, and Heaps — before settling onto the C.P.R.'s siding at Ruskin; wait there for two eastbound trains, the Agassiz (later Mission) local and No. 2, the transcontinental, which arrived at 9:41 a.m. and 10:20 a.m., respectively; and return to Stave Falls as soon as all formalities had been looked after. A one way fare cost twenty-five cents (return was double), purchased from the station agent at Stave Falls or from the conductor on board. Lesser fares were required of those embarking at the intermediate stations. The freight rate was two cents per hundred pounds. The line possessed its own freight rate structure and bills of lading, and its employees enjoyed the same privileges accorded those of the largest steam railroads.

The B. C. Electric's first action upon taking over the line was to bring one of its men from New Westminster, R. V. Mills, to Stave Falls to be the line's roadmaster. Another action was to submit one of its G.M.C. trucks to the ministrations of the mechanical department at Prior Street barn. What emerged was a truck on flanged wheels with a complete coupler assembly at the front for shunting cars around and an inside-mounted capstan for loading and incidental hauling. The G.M.C. would go into service in June 1922, saving the expense of the steam locomotives, handling passenger and small freight hauls, and operating as a switcher in the yard at Stave Falls. A small hand-operated turntable would even be built at Ruskin to turn it around.

During 1920 the only old-time stub switches still remaining on company lines, those on District 2's south shore line, were replaced by the modern, safer variety still in use today. This line had been busier than ever during the year, now

146

Hastings Street, photographed to the east from Carrall Street station in 1921, displays much street railway traffic (two interurbans are passing in the foreground) and only moderate automobile traffic, as yet. (B.C. Hydro)

that four-year-old, reclaimed Granville Island (Industrial Island then) contained twenty-five varied industries, all serviced by B. C. Electric's freight operations via a bridge branching off to the island between Second and Third avenues. (Within three years, any remaining industrial sites on the island would be claimed.)

The McNair-run Port Moody-Coquitlam Railway had come under some specific company scrutiny during the year, revealing that the cost of constructing the railway — track, bridges, etc. — had been $168,396.82, and the cost of the right of way, $37,647.88. It was apparent that the rental from McNair did not begin to pay the interest and depreciation on the B. C. Electric's investment. Originally it had been estimated that the line would cost $75,000 and that about $100,000 would be realized from the sale of logs obtained from clearing Coquitlam Lake. However, the railway had cost almost three times its estimate, and the salvage from logs was a mere $39,000.19. Thus, after McNair's lease payments would cease in 1923, the company would have the full charge of almost $20,000 per annum in interest and depreciation to bear.

Passengers carried in 1920, 69,137,995, approached 1913's record, as did the freight tonnage of 430,931. The next year would see the B. C. Electric turn all its operations sideways in readiness for the change in the rule of the road at midnight, December 31, 1921.

As 1921 began, the efficient, safe running of the Sixth Street and Queen's Park operation in New Westminster was the ongoing cause for concern it had always been. The street car, eastbound on Columbia Street, had to make a connection with the car from Sapperton at Leopold Place before heading up the hill and past Queen's Park to its terminus at Fourth Avenue and Sixth Street. Before it could leave on its return trip, it had to meet both north and southbound street cars travelling on Sixth Street. The Highland Park bound street car itself had another meet at the siding on Edmonds Street, and was given a scant four minutes to travel from it to Highland Park to connect with the Vancouver bound interurban train. Even if it arrived precisely on time, its schedule allowed the crew only a two-minute layover before setting out on the journey back into New Westminster. The only solution for the Highland Park bound street car, and its crew, was to pass Fourth Avenue, whether or not the Queen's Park car had arrived. Beginning July 4, on evenings and Sundays, the Sixth Street cars would make a westerly circuit of the Queen's Park belt line.

On the Vancouver system, "skip stop" street car service was begun on February 1 on the Kerrisdale route. This entailed stopping at every other stop only, and the success of speeded-up service encouraged the company to adopt it on its other heavily-travelled Vancouver lines as well. Kerrisdale residents received a further boon with the introduction of "limited" service on the fourteenth of the month; this meant that street cars on their way out from downtown picked up only passengers whose destinations lay south of Broadway.

In early February the company let it be known that it was interested in building new cutoff routes for both Central Park and Burnaby Lake lines from Commercial Drive, eastward to False Creek's

In spring of 1921, the big St. Louis interurban cars were still maintaining a fairly healthy service up and down the Saanich line despite the steady decline in patronage. (B.C. Hydro)

TIME TABLE

BRITISH COLUMBIA ELECTRIC RAILWAY CO., LTD.

SAANICH INTERURBAN DIVISION

ISSUED MARCH 26TH. 1921

READ DOWN

Train Number	35	33	31	29	27	25	23	21	19	17	15	13	11	9	7	5	3	1	Miles from Victoria
STATIONS	Daily Except Sunday	Sunday Only	Daily Except Sunday	Daily Except Sunday	Sunday Only	Daily Except Sunday	Daily Except Sunday	Daily	Daily Except Sunday	Daily	Daily Except Sunday	Sunday Only	Daily Except Sunday	Daily Except Sunday	Daily Except Sunday	Sunday Only	Daily Except Sunday	Daily Except Sunday	
	P.M.	P.M.	P.M.	P.M.	P.M.	P.M.	P.M.	P.M.	P.M.	P.M.	A.M.	A.M.	A.M.	A.M.	A.M.	A.M.	A.M.	A.M.	
Lv. ... VICTORIA ... Ar.	11.30	10.20	9.20	8.30	7.30	7.30	5.30	4.30	3.30	1.30	11.00	10.30	10.00	9.00	8.00	7.30	7.00	6.37	.0
..... HARRIET	11.41	10.30	9.30	8.41	7.41	7.41	5.41	4.41	3.41	1.41	11.11	10.41	10.01	9.10	8.11	7.41	7.11	6.47	1.9
..... TILLICUM	11.43	10.32	9.32	8.43	7.43	7.43	5.43	4.43	3.43	1.43	11.13	10.43	10.13	9.12	8.13	7.43	7.13	6.49	2.6
..... MARIGOLD	11.46	10.34	9.34	8.46	7.46	7.46	5.46	4.46	3.46	1.46	11.16	10.46	10.16	9.14	8.16	7.46	7.16	6.51	3.4
. BLACKWOOD ROAD .	11.47	10.35	9.35	8.47	7.47	7.47	5.47	4.47	3.47	1.47	11.17	10.47	10.17	9.15	8.17	7.47	7.17	6.52	3.8
.... WILKINSON	11.48	10.36	9.37	8.49	7.49	7.49	5.49	4.49	3.49	1.49	11.19	10.49	10.19	9.17	8.19	7.49	7.19	6.54	4.3
.... GLYN	11.49	10.37	9.38	8.51	7.51	7.51	5.51	4.51	3.51	1.51	11.21	10.51	10.21	9.18	8.21	7.51	7.21	6.55	4.8
...... EBERTS	11.51	10.39	9.40	8.53	7.53	7.53	5.53	4.53	3.53	1.53	11.23	10.53	10.23	9.20	8.23	7.53	7.23	6.57	5.4
.. WESTWOODVALE ..	11.52	10.40	—	8.54	7.54	7.54	5.54	4.54	3.54	1.54	11.24	10.54	10.24	—	8.24	7.54	7.24	—	6.2
..... GOWARD	11.53	10.41		8.55	7.55	7.55	5.55	4.55	3.55	1.55	11.25	10.55	10.25		8.25	7.55	7.25		6.7
... OBSERVATORY ...	11.55	10.43		8.57	7.57	7.57	5.57	4.57	3.57	1.57	11.27	10.57	10.27		8.27	7.57	7.27		7.4
..... PROSPECT	11.56	10.44		8.58	7.58	7.58	5.58	4.58	3.58	1.58	11.28	10.58	10.28		8.28	7.58	7.28		7.9
.... HEALS	11.58	10.46		9.01	8.01	8.01	6.01	5.01	4.01	2.01	11.31	11.01	10.31		8.31	8.01	7.31		8.9
.... RIFLE RANGE	12.00	10.48		9.04	8.04	8.04	6.04	5.04	4.04	2.04	11.34	11.04	10.34		8.34	8.04	7.34		9.7
.... DURRANCE	12.01	10.49		9.05	8.05	8.05	6.05	5.05	4.05	2.05	11.35	11.05	10.35		8.35	8.05	7.35		10.2
.... TODD INLET	12.03	10.51		9.08	8.08	8.08	6.08	5.08	4.08	2.08	11.38	11.08	10.38		8.38	8.08	7.38		11.2
.... BRENTWOOD	12.04	10.52		9.09	8.09	8.09	6.09	5.09	4.09	2.09	11.39	11.09	10.39		8.39	8.09	7.39		11.6
.. MARCHANT ROAD ..	12.08	10.54		9.12	8.12	8.12	6.12	5.12	4.12	2.12	11.42	11.12	10.42		8.42	8.12	7.42		12.2
.... SLUGGETTS	12.10	10.55		9.13	8.13	8.13	6.13	5.13	4.13	2.13	11.43	11.13	10.43		8.43	8.13	7.45		12.5
..... STELLYS	12.14	10.58		9.17	8.17	8.17	6.17	5.17	4.17	2.17	11.47	11.17	10.47		8.47	8.17	7.47		13.6
.... SAANICHTON	12.17	11.00		9.20	8.20	8.20	6.20	5.20	4.20	2.20	11.50	11.20	10.50		8.50	8.20	7.50		14.9
EXPERIMENTAL FARM	12.23	11.06		9.26	8.26	—	—	5.26	—	2.26	11.55	11.26	—		8.55	8.26	—		16.8
.... BAZAN BAY	12.25	11.08		9.28	8.28			5.28		2.28	11.57	11.28			8.57	8.28			17.4
.... TRIPP	12.26	11.09		9.29	8.29			5.29		2.29	11.58	11.29			8.58	8.29			17.8
.... SIDNEWAY	12.28	11.12		9.32	8.32			5.32		2.32	12.02	11.32			9.01	8.32			
.... MEADLANDS	12.30	11.15		9.34	8.34			5.34		2.34	12.04	11.34			9.03	8.34			18.8
.... MALLOWMOT	—	—		9.39	8.39			5.39		2.39	12.09	11.39			9.08	8.39			19.4
...... TATLOW				9.43	8.43			5.43		2.43	12.13	11.43			9.12	8.43			20.9
Ar.... DEEP BAY ... Lv.				9.45	8.45			5.45		2.45	12.15	11.45			9.15	8.45			22.3
	P.M.	P.M.	P.M.	P.M.	P.M.	P.M.	P.M.	P.M.	P.M.	P.M.	P.M.	A.M.	A.M.	A.M.	A.M.	A.M.	A.M.	A.M.	23.0

READ UP

Train Number	2	4	6	8	10	12	14	16	18	20	22	24	26	28	30	32	34
STATIONS	Daily Except Sunday	Daily Except Sunday	Daily Except Sunday	Sunday Only	Daily Except Sunday	Daily Except Sunday	Sunday Only	Daily Except Sunday	Daily	Daily Except Sunday	Daily	Daily Except Sunday	Daily Except Sunday	Sunday Only	Daily Except Sunday	Sunday Only	Daily Except Sunday
	A.M.	A.M.	A.M.	A.M.	A.M.	A.M.	P.M.	P.M.	P.M.	P.M.	P.M.	P.M.	P.M.	P.M.	P.M.	A.M.	A.M.
Lv. ... VICTORIA ... Ar.	7.20	8.45	9.45	10.15	10.45	11.45	1.15	1.30	4.15	5.15	7.15	9.15	10.05	10.15	11.15	12.15	1.30
..... HARRIET	7.10	8.36	9.36	10.05	10.36	11.36	1.05	1.20	4.05	5.05	7.05	9.05	9.55	10.05	11.05	12.05	1.20
..... TILLICUM	7.08	8.33	9.33	10.02	10.33	11.33	1.02	1.17	4.02	5.02	7.02	9.02	9.53	10.02	11.02	12.03	1.18
..... MARIGOLD	7.06	8.30	9.30	9.59	10.30	11.30	12.59	1.14	3.59	4.59	6.59	8.59	9.51	9.59	10.59	12.01	1.16
. BLACKWOOD ROAD .	7.05	8.28	9.28	9.58	10.28	11.28	12.58	1.12	3.58	4.58	6.58	8.58	9.50	9.58	10.58	12.00	1.15
.... WILKINSON	7.03	8.26	9.26	9.56	10.26	11.26	12.56	1.10	3.56	4.56	6.56	8.56	9.48	9.56	10.56	11.59	1.14
.... GLYN	7.02	8.25	9.25	9.55	10.25	11.25	12.55	1.09	3.55	4.55	6.55	8.55	9.47	9.55	10.55	11.58	1.13
...... EBERTS	7.00	8.23	9.23	9.53	10.23	11.23	12.53	1.07	3.53	4.53	6.53	8.53	9.45	9.53	10.53	11.56	1.11
.. WESTWOODVALE ..	—	8.21	—	9.51	10.21	11.21	12.51	1.06	3.51	4.51	6.51	8.51	—	9.51	10.51	11.55	1.10
..... GOWARD		8.20		9.50	10.20	11.20	12.50	1.05	3.50	4.50	6.50	8.50		9.50	10.50	11.54	1.09
... OBSERVATORY ...		8.18		9.48	10.18	11.18	12.48	1.03	3.48	4.48	6.48	8.48		9.48	10.48	11.52	1.07
..... PROSPECT		8.15		9.45	10.15	11.15	12.45	1.00	3.45	4.45	6.45	8.45		9.45	10.45	11.50	1.05
.... HEALS		8.12		9.42	10.12	11.12	12.42	12.58	3.42	4.42	6.42	8.42		9.42	10.42	11.47	1.02
.... RIFLE RANGE		8.10		9.40	10.10	11.10	12.40	12.56	3.40	4.40	6.40	8.40		9.40	10.40	11.45	1.00
.... DURRANCE		8.09		9.39	10.09	11.09	12.39	12.55	3.39	4.39	6.39	8.39		9.39	10.39	11.44	12.59
.... TODD INLET		8.07		9.37	10.07	11.07	12.37	12.53	3.37	4.37	6.37	8.37		9.37	10.37	11.42	12.57
.... BRENTWOOD		8.06		9.36	10.06	11.06	12.36	12.52	3.36	4.36	6.36	8.36		9.36	10.36	11.41	12.56
.. MARCHANT ROAD ..		8.03		9.33	10.03	11.03	12.33	12.49	3.33	4.33	6.33	8.33		9.33	10.33	11.38	12.53
.... SLUGGETTS		8.02		9.32	10.02	11.02	12.32	12.48	3.32	4.32	6.32	8.32		9.32	10.32	11.37	12.52
..... STELLYS		7.57		9.27	9.57	10.57	12.27	12.45	3.27	4.27	6.27	8.27		9.27	10.27	11.32	12.47
.... SAANICHTON		7.55		9.25	9.55	10.55	12.25	12.43	3.25	4.25	6.25	8.25		9.25	10.25	11.30	12.45
EXPERIMENTAL FARM		—		9.19	9.49	—	12.19	12.37	3.19	—	6.19	—		9.19	10.19	11.27	12.42
.... BAZAN BAY				9.17	9.47		12.17	12.35	3.17		6.17			9.17	10.17	11.25	12.40
.... TRIPP				9.15	9.45		12.15	12.34	3.15		6.15			9.15	10.15	11.24	12.39
.... SIDNEWAY				9.11	9.41		12.11	12.30	3.11		6.11			9.11	10.11	11.21	12.36
.... MEADLANDS				9.10	9.40		12.10	12.29	3.10		6.10			9.10	10.10	11.20	12.35
.... MALLOWMOT				9.05	9.35		12.05	12.25	3.05		6.05			9.05	10.05	—	—
...... TATLOW				9.02	9.32		12.02	12.22	3.02		6.02			9.02	10.02		
Ar.... DEEP BAY ... Lv.				9.00	9.30		12.00	12.20	3.00		6.00			9.00	10.00		
	A.M.	A.M.	A.M.	A.M.	A.M.	A.M.	Noon	P.M.	P.M.	P.M.	P.M.	P.M.	P.M.	P.M.	P.M.	P.M.	A.M.

PASSENGER DEPOT, 1503 DOUGLAS STREET. PHONE 1969

drained flats, and along their southern edge to Carrall Street depot. With times becoming somewhat brighter, it seems obvious that the B. C. Electric would have wished to do something useful with the almost $75,000 worth of property it had assembled for the Burnaby Lake line's right of way along the north side of Sixth Avenue from Commercial Drive, veering through onto Fifth to Clark Drive. The Central Park line's cutoff would slant northwest off Commercial Driver near Cedar Cottage, and usurp the bed of China Creek to the south side of Sixth Avenue and St. Catherine Street, where it would enter St. Catherine Tunnel, disgorging from it just east of Fifth Avenue and Fraser Street. Continuing west along the northern edge of Fifth Avenue, the proposed right of way swung to the north side of the lane between First and Second Avenues, crossed Main Street, and curved to cross False Creek slightly west of the Great Northern's bridge.

In March, the company began the centring of a work train at the St. Nicholas gravel pit just north of Abbotsford. In April it graciously courted potential visitors to the observatory along the Saanich line with an article in *The Buzzer* from which the following is excerpted:

> "On alighting at Observatory Station, the visitor will find a sign post pointing the way along a short footpath leading from the station to the broad roadway, which makes an easy ascent to the Observatory at the summit.
>
> The visitor, as he follows the course of this winding road, finds an ever-changing view of surrounding country unfolded before him at every turn. The view from the summit is easily one of the finest and most comprehensive to be found anywhere. On a clear day — and it usually is clear — there is an almost limitless vista of sea and distant mountains.

> The journey from Victoria to Observatory station takes about 25 minutes. When coming back from the Observatory, you can make a variation in the journey down the mountain by taking the trail instead of the road. Look for the sign post on the road, just below the Observatory. By coming down this trail, you can leave the Observatory and be at the station in ten minutes or less." †

By April the company knew it was time to start converting its system to right hand operation, but it wasn't sure where to begin. The changeover would cost the B. C. Electric $933,397.67, of which the provincial government would pay $350,000. Confronted by a myriad necessary preparatory tasks, the company was aware that track and wire would need to be the very last elements to be reworked, so the mechanical department at Prior Street, under master mechanic Dickie's direction, was instructed to begin experimenting with street car rebuilding procedures. The one man cars were the obvious first priority.

Thus on May 1 car 279 was brought into Prior Street barn, the great concern being to find the best method of creating new door openings in front and rear right hand sides, and new door openings between the motorman's vestibules and the car's passenger area. Method established, including the affixing of new steps, work proceeded rapidly in Victoria at Pembroke Street barn and in Vancouver, where some fifteen cars at a time were removed from service for the conversion work to be done. All these changes had then to be boarded up and rendered inoperable until the arrival of the new year.

To help relieve the congestion at Prior Street, eight rush hour street cars were stored at Carrall Street yards, and on June 27, the new roof trackage

Left-hand drive is still the order of the day in this colourful view east on Columbia Street from Eighth Street. An interurban coach recedes in the distance, bound for Fraser Mills or Vancouver via Burnaby Lake, while a Brill street car on the number one line heads for Sapperton, retaining its Edmonds sign for the return. (Bob Webster collection)

† "Have You Visited the Observatory?" *The Buzzer* (Victoria edition), 25 April 1921, pp. 1-3.

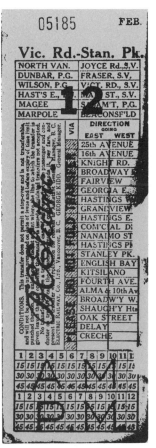

A Vancouver street car transfer from the early 1920s. P.G. is Point Grey, S.V., South Vancouver. (Ted Clark collection)

at Mount Pleasant barn was ready for occupancy, capable alone of storing 63 street cars. So meticulously were the electrical, maintenance-of-way, mechanical, and traffic departments organized, and such was the quality of their staffs, that the whole program proceeded hitch-free, and the street car systems met all maximum demands for service throughout the preparatory period. New destination signs showing a different number for each route were added to the front of the roof of each car during its reconstruction.

Though the railway-style interurban cars did not require alterations, their stations needed to be shifted so as still to be on the near side of level crossings. Since the stations on either side of the line on the Highland Park cutoff had been built in expectation of right-hand operation, they were ready for the new order. Other necessary work on District 1 and 2 interurban lines was the adjustment in elevation of tracks on curves for opposite operation on double tracks. At the depot in New Westminster, the interurban trains would, after the changeover, loop from Columbia Street onto Begbie and Front streets, thus entering the depot from the back, rather than from the front.

The B. C. Electric in 1921 was interested in building three new sections of street car line in Vancouver: on Cambie Street between Broadway and Sixteenth Avenue; on Victoria Road between the Central Park line and Kingsway; and on Forty-first Avenue between Main Street and Victoria Road. None of the three would ever be built. A new stretch of track did, in fact, begin giving service during July with the inauguration of the roadway on Main Street replacing the now-dismantled bridge at False Creek. (During the construction of the new street, street car service had been maintained over a shoo-fly to the east side of the roadway.)

On Vancouver street cars, the Cleveland fare box went into service on July 17 (December 14 in Victoria), replacing the original, portable, Coleman jug-type boxes. Since the fare increase to six cents two years previously, the old jugs had simply been too small to hold all the pennies and nickels. The new thirty-one-inch high, twenty-nine-pound boxes remained on B. C. Electric's street cars to the very end of their operation.

By mid-July in Vancouver, 102 street cars had been converted for right-hand operation. All the later Brill cars (200s and 275s) and most of the company's own 260s had already been rebuilt, twenty-six of them in one record week. The concern now was with the four different styles of the 38 "Narraganset" street cars and the various odd ones, each one requiring special treatment.

July in Victoria was a month of rerouting street cars in the downtown area with the repaving of Government Street and the relaying of new track in concrete. In New Westminster, service on the Highland Park-Sixth Street line had been cut

down to three street cars after 7 p.m. during the week and all day Sunday, a fourth car being operated only on Saturday night. On the Burnaby Lake line, a new station, Queen's Avenue (four hundred feet west of the diamond crossing with the Great Northern Railway), went into service on August 22. In North Vancouver, the Pacific Great Eastern's run to Whytecliff took its first step into oblivion in September by curtailing service.

It was, however, in the Victoria area that a furor was created on September 21 with the company's announcement that two-man street car service would be replaced by one man cars in the interests of economy. Not all councilmen agreed, and Esquimalt's council went on record as being opposed to such a change.

Nonetheless, the B. C. Electric in the next month ordered ten steel, single truck, one man, lightweight (eight tons, as opposed to the typical street car's twenty-five) "safety cars," known by the name of their designer, Charles O. Birney, the engineer in charge of street car design and construction for U. S. transit operator, the Stone & Webster Corporation.

The Birney cars had been a response to the threat of jitneys and private automobiles. Because of their lightness (and length — just 28 feet) their operating costs were low, and because of the safety feature of a "dead man" control which immediately halted the car if the motorman released the controller, their success had been extraordinary, over 4,000 of them having been built in the first four years since they had begun service in 1916. Though they were relatively rough riding and underpowered, the Birneys, with their low operating costs, could provide more frequent service and an attendant increase in business; and their "dead man" feature was a remarkable safety advance, combining in one control handle the brake, sander, door opening device, and emergency valve. Though Victoria's Birneys were not due to arrive until the new year, the company began operating one man "safety cars" — 381 had been the first — on the Gorge and Mount Tolmie lines on November 11. Though not, of course, Birneys, they had had similar control equipment installed. In Vancouver, the first "safety car," number 167, had gone into service on December 9 on the Dunbar line.

The first and second days of January 1922 turned out to be friendly days for a one-time adventure such as changing the rule of the road. The first was a Sunday, the second the official observance of New Year's Day; on neither day were possibly tentative street car movements to be submitted to the rigours of the week day rushes.

Massive quantities of track work accompanied the change from left to right: cross-overs had to be reversed, many even to be relocated or removed; wyes had to be reversed; branch-offs (as at Cedar Cottage) had to be altered; automatic electric switches (seventeen in Vancouver alone) had to be moved; the derails on Sixth Street in New Westminster had to be moved to the opposite track; and the hand operated derails and signals where Vancouver's street car lines crossed the Great Northern Railway had to be moved to the opposite tracks. Obviously, the corresponding trolley wire suspensions and frog positions would all require adjustments. This work, as well as that of once again reconstructing the street cars to remove their redundant doors and steps, would keep gangs and crews occupied for many months.

Soon after midnight on January 1, work gangs all across the B. C. Electric's system reversed cross-overs, trolley wire, and switches. In the car barns, crews removed the barriers from the new street car entrances and barricaded the old ones. The day, long-awaited, and by many, long-feared, arrived and the first streetcars crept out of their protective barns at 6 a.m. Everyone was cautious, but just as the preparatory period had been free of incident, so was the inception period. The fact that interurban and street car passengers now had to cross the tracks at Highland Park and, worse still, at Granville Bridge station, in the teeth of heavy traffic, posed new questions requiring fairly rapid answers. Hockey fans leaving Denman Arena by the thousands were delighted, however, not to be required to loop around Chilco and Alberni streets to travel eastward. In New Westminster, riders were inconvenienced by a new rule of no stops for street cars and interurban cars between Twelfth Street Junction and the depot; with the change to the right, the space between the inbound line and the neighbouring C.P.R.'s was dangerously narrow.

The world had been slowly rising from its post-war slump, and 1921 had been a year of almost struggling free. B. C. Electric's ridership had attained a record high, 70,920,420, and freight tonnage hauled had slid only slightly to 412,534.

Some of the metal destination signs discarded when destination rollers were installed. (Bob Webster collection)

Though the jitneys were gone, automobiles were everywhere, crowding the street cars and swarming over their tracks, especially in downtown New Westminster, Vancouver and Victoria. There was one car for every sixteen British Columbians.

If 1921 had been the year of preparation for right-hand operation, 1922 was indubitably the year of one man operation. The old metal signs — yellow for Davie, white for Fairview, red for Robson, etc. — had already been junked by the one man cars and replaced by illuminated signs and large block numbers. (These changes would come yet to the two-man cars.) Adjustments were still being made to accommodate better right hand service. The ten Birneys had arrived in Vancouver from Preston Car & Coach Company for assembling at Kitsilano shops and would begin operating on Victoria's No. 2-Cloverdale-Outer Wharf line in March. (They would occasionally operate rush hour service on the number 6 line as far as May and Joseph streets — the number 7 run, and sporadically on the number 3 line.) On March 1, the six blocks of Victoria's newly rebuilt line on Cook Street between Rockland Avenue and Pakington Street were inaugurated. This section had been built ahead of schedule at the urging of city council to help relieve the unemployment situation.

One man street car service went into effect on the various routes in Victoria in the following sequence:	
February 13	— Mount Tolmie - Burnside (2 cars)
February 27	— Beacon Hill - Fernwood (3 cars, 1 extra)
	— Outer Wharf - Cloverdale (3 cars, 1 extra)
March 9	— Oak Bay (5 cars)
	— Uplands (3 cars)
	— Willows (2 cars)
April 1	— Foul Bay - Hillside (5 cars, 4 extras)
April 16	— Esquimalt (4 cars)
	— Gorge (3 cars)

Thirty one man cars, with six extras, were giving Victoria its complete street car service. In a letter to inspector of railways, William Rae, H. Gibson, the company's traffic superintendent in Victoria, summed up the new operation and its hopes in the following way: "In fact, outside of anything happening out of the usual, I do not think that we can do much better. The only thing that is wanted now is more people to carry."

Some route number reorganization had occurred together with the inauguration of one man operation. Burnside (No. 8) and Mount Tolmie (No. 10) runs had been combined as No. 10, forever eliminating a No. 8 run. Foul Bay (No. 6) and Hillside (No. 7) were similarly through-run as No. 6; and No. 7 was relegated to use on the

Canada's official census of 1921 revealed these population figures:	
Burnaby	12,883
Chilliwack	1,767
Chilliwhack (municipality)	3,161
Esquimalt	3,458
Fraser Mills	600
Langley	4,881
Matsqui	3,763
New Westminster	14,495
North Vancouver (city)	7,652
Oak Bay	4,159
Richmond	4,825
Saanich	10,534
Sumas	2,299
Vancouver (including Point Grey and South Vancouver)	163,220
Victoria	38,727

(Above left)
Stave Falls station, July 1922.
(Gerry Stevenson collection)

(Above right)
Locomotive number 1 trails part of its train into the engine house at Stave Falls, 1922. (Gerry Stevenson collection)

short run on Foul Bay to Joseph Street. (Foul Bay in later years became Gonzales.)

Eight one man operations went into effect in Vancouver: on February 1, Dunbar (Tenth Avenue and Crown Street to Forty-first) and Sasamat (Fourth Avenue and Alma Street to Fourth and Drummond Street); on April 1, Oak Street and Hastings East Extension; and on June 1, Main Street South, Georgia East, Nanaimo Street, and Sixteenth Avenue. These lightly travelled routes operated each with one street car, except for the Sasamat line which employed two and the Hastings Extension which acquired a rush hour

extra on May 1.

Out in the Fraser Valley, both the Sumas Lake and Stave Falls areas were scenes of great activity. The first preparatory phase for draining the lake had been completed on April 7 with the creation of Vedder Canal, which both diverted the Vedder River and formed a drainage passage for the waters of the lake. From Stave Falls the company had already electrified the railway some three miles south to Wilson's, and would complete this work to Ruskin by year's end. Four hundred men were working at Stave Falls on new dam, power house, and spillway installations, and Wilson's (or

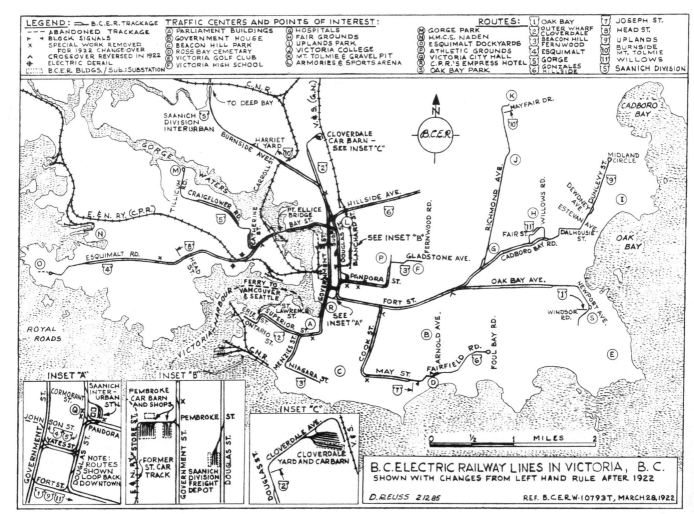

B.C. ELECTRIC RAILWAY LINES IN VICTORIA, B.C.
SHOWN WITH CHANGES FROM LEFT HAND RULE AFTER 1922

D. REUSS 2.12.85   REF. B.C.E.R.W.-10793T, MARCH 28, 1922

Red Bridge) would be the site of a second dam which would submerge the whole of Stave valley.

One man street cars went into operation throughout the New Westminster system on Sunday, May 14, well clear of the traditional tumult of May Day, the fifth of the month. (The new large fare boxes, already in use in Vancouver and Victoria, had made their helpful appearance on April 27.) Electric switches had been installed at Twelfth Street Junction and at Columbia Street and Leopold Place, a real boon to the solo operators. In addition, new connections had been constructed at Columbia and Begbie streets to allow Burnaby Lake and Central Park interurban trains to leave the depot by Front Street. No. 1 — Edmonds-Sapperton street cars operated thrice hourly, a trip in either direction consuming thirty-three minutes. No. 2 — Highland Park-Sixth Street also appeared every twenty minutes, taking forty-

one minutes for the complete run from Highland Park, down Sixth Street to the depot, up Columbia Street, and past Queen's Park to Fourth Avenue and Sixth Street; the return trip, again via Queen's Park, took an extra minute.

As well in May, a baggage car for hauling fruit through to Vancouver had begun augmenting the consist of the night train from Chilliwack, an improvement which brought fruit fresh to the market in the morning. During a seven-week period of the summer, forty carloads (twelve tons each) of fruit were brought in from the Valley.

July 18 was the day of completion for a fascinating, creatively-handled, three-month project on the Chilliwack line, the setting into place of the new five hundred-ton, 175-foot and 125-foot steel spans across the Vedder River. The $75,000 bridge had been constructed on temporary piers thirty-six feet away from the old

As Birneys so often did, 409 is destined only for Joseph Street on the Foul Bay (Gonzales) line, and will continue south on Douglas Street, disdaining a right turn here onto Yates. (B.C. Hydro)

(Below left)
G.M.C. truck, equipped for railway duties by the B.C. Electric, is set to leave Stave Falls station for the run down to Ruskin. (Gerry Stevenson collection)

Below right)
Former C.P.R. coach in Western Power Company lettering adjacent to the engine house at Stave Falls, 1922. (Gerry Stevenson collection)

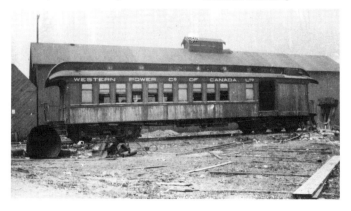

The Central Park line, New Westminster-bound train is about to cross Kingsway in this late 1922 photo. A platform on the left and a substantial shelter for Vancouver-bound riders have replaced the original depot which stood in the empty space to the left. (B.C. Hydro)

† David C. Jones, "The Strategy of Railway Abandonment: The Great Northern in Washington and British Columbia, 1917-1935, *The Western Historical Quarterly*, April 1980, p. 149.

wooden bridge. In typical B. C. Electrical fashion, not one passenger or freight movement disruption occurred, even during the final placing of the spans.

Otherwise in the territory of the Fraser Valley branch, the Great Northern continued to persist, however weakly. Its mixed train from Ladner, daily except Sunday, operated the forty-six miles to Huntingdon through Cloverdale and Abbotsford, the Cloverdale-Huntingdon segment consuming approximately two and a half hours of running time. On Tuesdays and Fridays another mixed train covered the five-mile Abbotsford-Kilgard run in twenty minutes. (The G.N.R.'s track east from Kilgard to the connection with the renamed Canadian National at Cannor was torn up by the end of the year. †) During the month of July, out of a total of 783 freight cars the company's interurban lines had interchanged with steam railroads, 629 had contained forest products.

The Saanich line experienced some badly needed positive excitement during the summer months: on July 27 a three-car interurban special brought some two hundred company employees to Deep Bay for a picnic; and on August 15 the Liberal party's picnic, also at Deep Bay, had required the chartering of four special trains, a

final extra leaving Deep Bay at 11:30 p.m. During this period Saanich council was attempting to impose some controls on jitney operators in its municipality, but without any success; the arguments for both sides would continue.

At Stave Falls, locomotive 980 arrived on September 14 from New Westminster to do the log hauling and larger jobs. Express car 1802 upon its arrival on November 14 would see much work in passenger and mail service, giving the G.M.C. the opportunity of doing some of the lighter yard work at Stave Falls and functioning as the spare vehicle for the line.

September 1 had marked the opening of Vancouver's newly built, $75,000, double tracked street car line on Broadway between Trafalgar Street and Alma Street, eleven blocks to the west; 87-pound rail had been used. This line would relieve the frequent congestion at the terminus of the Fourth Avenue line, where Dunbar and Sasamat street cars left with all the downtown-bound riders.

In New Westminster, four one man street cars were in use on the Edmonds-Sapperton line (No. 1), five on the Highland Park-Sixth Street (No. 2), which was now operating northward via Queen's Park. Between 4 and 6 p.m., one extra car was in service on each line. The Fraser Mills-

Queensborough line employed two interurban cars.

At exhibition time, two extra street cars operated between the depot and Queen's Park, and from Vancouver, two special two-car interurban trains operated directly to the park via Edmonds and Sixth Street. The two extra exhibition bound street cars used both a conductor and motorman with a fare box at each end of the car; and operators would be stationed at both Leopold Place and Queen's Park to aid with the movements of the street cars. In addition, extra conductors would be on duty at Queen's Park and at the corner of Sixth Street and Fourth Avenue to help with fare-collecting and to assist generally.

On Sunday, September 24, hourly service recommenced on the Burnaby Lake line, a return to pre-war ways before the inception of service only every two hours. The Saanich line, however, presented a darker picture. Freight revenue on the line had decreased to such an extent (only a little milk and four carloads of wood per week) that, practically speaking, this aspect of its operation had been dispensed with by October, and on the twenty-sixth of the month, the B. C. Electric submitted to the Department of Railways blueprints and specifications of five one man cars it wished to operate on the Saanich line.

On October 2, the creator and instigator of the formidable B. C. Electric concept, Johannes Buntzen, died in Copenhagen, Denmark. That his name is still remembered today, largely by virtue of Lake Beautiful having been renamed Buntzen, is just as it should be, for he was in fact one of the builders of British Columbia itself. Buntzen was an extraordinary man, magnificently at the right place, and at the necessary time.

Street car number 136 was scrapped by the company after it had suffered irreparable damage in a collision with a Great Northern locomotive and freight on December 27. In fact, only one of its two trucks was capable of further use, the other necessitating junking.

During the year, Oak Bay had acquired Oak Bay Park (Windsor, today) from the B. C. Electric, on condition it be used as a playground; North Vancouver's former showpiece street car, 28, had been fitted up as a snow plow-flanger-line car; and a jitney service, mostly for Ladner residents, had begun between Woodward's Landing and Vancouver. The number of passengers carried in 1922 was down somewhat to 67,553,023, and freight tonnage hauled had dipped sharply to 321,081. Salaries for conductors and motormen started at 48½ cents per hour, and rose to 58½ after two years' service; operators of one man cars received 64½ cents per hour.

If 1922 lay claim to characterization as the year of the one man car, surely 1923 displayed the evidence for being termed the year of the bus. The jitney had shown that a motor vehicle, installed with some kind of improvised body, could directly challenge the street car's quarter-century

At the end of 1922, the street railway and interurban system's trackage situation was as follows, the Jordan River and Port Moody-Coquitlam lines not included as they did not provide scheduled passenger service.

MILES OF RAIL

DIVISION	MAIN TRACKS Single	Double	Total	Other Tracks	Total Mileage
Vancouver City and Suburbs	25.54	40.47	106.48	5.98	112.46
North Vancouver	9.72	.10	9.92	.67	10.59
New Westminster	11.74	3.30	18.34	4.72	23.06
	47.00	43.87	134.74	11.37	146.11
Interurban Division —					
1 — Main Line Intercity	....	8.41	16.82	5.32	22.14
2 — Lulu Island Lines	19.38	6.56	32.50	13.08	45.58
3 — Fraser Valley	63.73	....	63.73	12.94	76.67
4 — Burnaby Lake Line	11.71	....	11.71	.82	12.53
	94.82	14.97	124.76	32.16	156.92
Stave Lake Railway	5.85	....	5.85	2.30	8.15
Total on Mainland	147.67	58.84	265.35	45.83	311.18
Victoria Division	8.92	14.86	38.64	2.32	40.96
Saanich Interurban	21.36	....	21.36	3.08	24.44
Total on Vancouver Island	30.28	14.86	60.00	5.40	65.40
Total for System	177.95	73.70	325.35	51.23	376.58

Total First Main Track, or route mileage, 251.65
Under "Other Tracks" are included all sidings, passing tracks, industrial and other spurs, and tracks in terminal yards and shops.

supremacy in urban transit. The B. C. Electric would hand credibility to the upstart pretender within the year. Nonetheless, the company too would wage a brave battle on behalf of the beleaguered Saanich line.

In Vancouver, 1923 began with a somewhat ominous order that all Central Park trains and Grandview street cars would in future flag across the Great Northern's Burrard Inlet-False Creek railway line where it crossed Venables Street near Glen Drive. In Victoria, figures released at the end of the month revealed that the Saanich line had attracted only 17,830 riders in January. (There had been 27,504 in January 1921, and still 24,421 in January 1922.) By contrast, in the current January, the Central Park line had carried 295,649, the Lulu Island line 149,559, the Burnaby Lake line 41,080, and the Chilliwack line 28,434.

February featured a snow storm and blizzard which, at least for a few days, February 13 to 15, brought back the memories, and fears, of 1916. The snow plow cleared the Saanich line neatly, and for a couple of days it had many of its passengers and milk and freight patrons aboard again, what with buses and trucks completely helpless. In Vancouver the four rotary sweepers had operated almost continuously for thirty-six hours, work gangs sometimes even using picks to open up tracks that were iced to a depth of three inches. Vancouver's flanger was again helpful to

all road traffic in that it cleared the street well on either side of the track, effectively creating a clean roadway for traffic, thereby keeping it off the sweeper-cleared tracks. A rapid thaw brought everything back to normal very quickly.

It was in March that the company sold Shay locomotive number 7 from its Stave Falls operation to Vancouver Machinery Depot for $4,500. During the same month work had begun on rebuilding the Central Park line's wooden, ten-year-old, 978-foot long (ten to thirty feet high) Gladstone trestle, lying between Gladstone and Nanaimo Road stations. This $30,000 project was designed to allow one open track over the trestle at all times during its reconstruction.

The problem of traffic congestion at the Lulu Island line's station on Granville Bridge created by the changed pedestrian movements to opposite sides of the bridge (since the switch to right-hand operation) began to be dealt with in March by the company and the city. The best idea seemed to be to run the interurban cars over the bridge, looping them around Davie, Richards, and Pacific streets. Another proposal had suggested operating street cars on the line as far as Marpole.

In November 1922, the B. C. Electric and the city had come to a new franchise agreement, which contained a motor bus clause binding the company to operate buses where there was reasonably good roadway. It would bear half the deficit on operation up to $5,000, the city to pay the remainder out of the percentage of gross fares paid to it by the company.

The area southeast of Broadway and Commercial offered a nigh-perfect opportunity for a first bus line: the residents wanted a street car service, which the company felt was not justified; the city owned numerous lots in the area which it was interested in selling; and the roads were quite adequate for buses. They were even further improved for the beginning of service of the Grandview Highway bus line on Monday, March 19. Its route stretched somewhat more than two miles from its terminus at Broadway and Commercial, to Rupert Street and Twenty-second Avenue, via Grandview Highway and Renfrew Street. Two two-ton Model 20 truck chassis had been ordered from the White Motor Company, and the two bus bodies, seating twenty-one, had been manufactured in Vancouver by G. W. Ribchester. Though service had begun with one bus providing half-hourly service, the second bus was added for afternoon rush hours on April 9, and for morning rush hours on April 16.

Cars 22 and 23, late of the Willows line, had been the first choices as candidates for one man cars on the Saanich line, and number 22 made the official-laden trial run on April 11. Freshly painted, it presented itself handsomely. The crew members at Pembroke Street barn had outdone themselves in creating a virtually new vehicle: the

---

By the beginning of 1923, all Vancouver street cars were equipped with new signs boldly displaying a number, as well as new fore and aft lettered destination signs, all of them roller-mounted as well as illuminated. (The Vancouver cars had not displayed the night time route-defining lights that Victoria's had.)

1 — Fairview
2 — Davie - Main to 25th
3 — Main to 52nd (52nd later renumbered 50th)
4 — Grandview - Fourth Avenue
5 — Robson - Broadway East
6 — Fraser (51st Avenue) - Shaughnessy (51st later renumbered 49th)
7 — Fraser (Marine Drive) - Kerrisdale
8 — Hastings East - Broadway West
10 — Victoria Road - Stanley Park
11 — Joyce Road
12 — Kitsilano - Hastings Park
15 — Nanaimo Road
15 — Hastings Extension
16 — Sixteenth Avenue
17 — Oak - Marpole
18 — Sasamat
18 — Dunbar

Adjustments during 1923 would give number 8 to both Nanaimo Road and Hastings Extension lines, 9 to Victoria Road (to Forty-fourth Avenue), 13 to Hastings East-Broadway West, 14 to Dunbar, and 15 to Sasamat, the use of number 18 being eliminated.

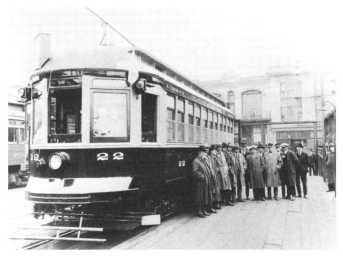

interior was attractive and bright, and new "safety car" controls and special motors and trucks had been installed. Stops were made at every station, doors opened and closed, and riding qualities were found to be excellent.

The company had gone to a great deal of work in preparing for April 11: 34 new platforms had to be built, since stations would be needed on both sides of the line for one man service (the original stations had been built on the west side of the line); four stations needed to be moved to the required near side of an intersection; spring switches had to be installed so that the operator would not have to leave the vehicle; platforms for milk cans needed their heights adjusted; and new stations were ordered installed, as well as flag stops initiated, between Harriet and Tillicum Road stations. (The company had designated nine flag stops between the Victoria depot and Marigold, abandoning Tillicum station in the process.) These adjustments, as well as numerous others, including a different system of fares, were required of the company by the Department of Railways. Provincial inspector of railways, William Rae, rode the trial trip.

The B. C. Electric's lease agreement with Robert McNair having expired, the company agreed on April 14 to sell the Port Moody-Coquitlam Railway to Messrs. Thurston-Flavelle Limited, a lumber concern which marketed "Beaver Brand" and "Western Red Cedar." The sale included the railway itself and the lands which it occupied, and thus a little-known railway passed out of the hands of the B. C. Electric, ultimately to be a victim of the depression to come.

In New Westminster, beginning on April 20, Marpole bound interurban trains were ordered to wait at Twelfth Street Junction for the inbound street cars from Edmonds to afford a certain transfer connection for riders. On April 30, the Stave Falls line received another locomotive, this time old steeple-cab number 950. (It would be back in New Westminster in fall for a lengthy period of repairs after being involved in an

accident, but would return to Stave Falls in February to stay the length of the line's life.)

An inbound six-car interurban train from Chilliwack on Sunday, May 13, carried 363 passengers, a figure generally accepted as the record to that time. The Lulu Island line's new-depot problems had been largely solved by the end of May, Vancouver's Board of Works having approved the routing into downtown over Granville Bridge, and the Board of Railway Commissioners having authorized a rail connection at Fourth Avenue just west of Granville between the interurban line and the street car line on Fourth Avenue to allow the interurban passenger trains access to city streets. The new depot would be a remodelled wooden, two-storey, false-fronted store on Davie Street at the southeast corner with Seymour Street. A partition would be built to separate the waiting room and news stand from the ticket office and crew area.

The operation of one man, pay-as-you-enter cars on the Saanich line began on Sunday, May 27, and everything went well despite the fact that a very few shelters and platforms still required altering. The station's ticket office had been permanently closed on Saturday, as all fare and ticket arrangements were henceforth to be conducted by the car's operator. Five Victoria-Deep Bay and a variety of shorter destination runs were still made on the new schedule, but round-trip, commutation, and settlers' tickets had been abolished.

With the new system, the operator used a Cleveland fare box; next to it he had a cabinet containing a supply of "hat check" tickets in compartments, one for each of the eleven zones into which the thirty-one stations were grouped. As the new public timetable directed:

> "On boarding the car, tell the operator the name of the station to which you wish to go.
> The operator will tell you the amount of fare.
> If you have the EXACT fare, place it in the fare box.

(Above left)
On April 11, 1923, the first of the two cars converted for one man operation made a trial trip to Deep Bay and back. Waiting to board is a company of fourteen officials, reading from left to right: H. Gibson, T.R. Myers, C.A. Cornwall, S.J. Halls, E.N. Horsey, A. Inglis, G.M. Tripp, L. Palmer (operator), A.T. Goward, W.H. Armstrong, W. Rae (provincial inspector of railways), C. Watkins, G.C. Clarke, S.G. Peele. Mail car 1501 (formerly "Sumas," ultimately 1216) waits to the left in the Victoria depot compound. Pandora Street forms the background. (David Reuss collection)

(Above right)
Rebuilt for one man operation on the Saanich line, cars 22 and 23 display newly sparkling interiors. (David Reuss collection)

(John Oastler collection)

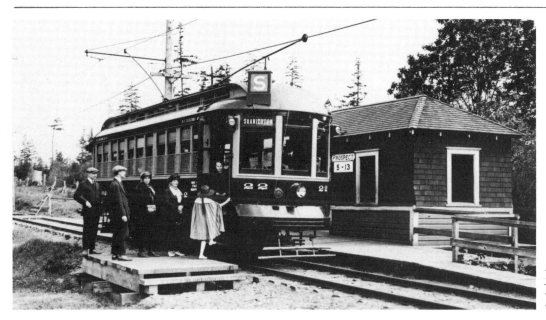

During the Saanich line's last year of service, car 22 and its surroundings seem to be in harmony for success. (B.C. Hydro)

The third, and final, Vancouver depot of the Lulu Island branch, Davie Street station. (B.C. Hydro)

(B.C. Hydro)'

If you HAVE NOT the exact fare, hand your money to the operator and he will give you the necessary change to enable you to place the exact fare in the fare box.
The operator will then give you a hat-check or zone ticket.
Retain this ticket as evidence of fare paid.
On leaving the car at your destination, first exhibit the hat-check to the operator and then place it in the fare box as you pass out."

Sheets of eighty five-cent tickets were sold for $3, a reasonable substitute for the lost commutation rate.

In New Westminster on Sunday, June 9, the company initiated a schedule adjustment which was welcome news to many: street cars would henceforth meet the Great Northern Railway's morning train to Crescent Beach and White Rock. On the same Sunday westbound Central Park trains began making their last passenger drop-off point before Carrall Street station the near side of

Carrall (giving time for the depot crossover track to be thrown), rather than Columbia Street, one block earlier. Out in the Fraser Valley, the second post office within a year, Dennison, was closed, on June 15. (Remote Bellerose had closed on the last day of the previous September.) And in Vancouver, street car 270 was the last vehicle to be rebuilt for right hand operation. On June 20, George Kidd's title was changed from general manager to that of president; William G. Murrin rose to the vice-presidency on the same day.

By the end of June, the six passenger interurban cars, as well as baggage-express car 1706, had arrived on the lower mainland after a brief decade on the Saanich line. Car 1706, with heavier duty Westinghouse motors and controls installed, quickly became a bellwether of the Chilliwack line, and 1239-1244 were immediately able to relieve the overworked 1300s from Central Park line work, help with travel to the races at Minoru (Brighouse) set to begin on June 30, and handle the numerous picnic specials to parks and beaches.

Often at high water, the heavily filled approach of the Chilliwack line to Vedder Mountain from the west was flooded on both sides, a sight few remember today. It became a part of history with the pumping out of Sumas Lake starting on July 4.

On August 25, the double tracking in Vancouver of Victoria Road between Kingsway and Forty-fourth Avenue and the installation of an east-pointing wye at Forty-fourth to turn rush hour extras were ready for operation. In preparation for the new Davie Street station, $15,000 was spent installing new curves at Davie and Richards streets, at Pacific and Richards streets, and at Fourth Avenue where the interurban line crossed.

In connection with the New Westminster Exhibition from September 10 to 15, half-hourly service was run directly to Queen's Park on the

The double loop at Chilliwack, looking north from Chilliwack's substation in June 1923. The station canopy now covers only one track. (B.C. Hydro)

Looking directly east to Vedder Mountain (and station), which the line must hug to avoid Sumas Lake, on its way to Chilliwack. (B.C. Hydro)

Road Number	Station Number	Miles from Victoria	TIME TABLE No. 11 Taking Effect 24.01 o'clock SAANICH DIVISION STATIONS
1	1	.0	Cormorant and Douglas Streets **VICTORIA** Double Track to Carrol Street
	2	1.9	P............HARRIET............Yard
	3		Burnside Road Way Points ......
2	4	2.6	............TILLICUM............
	5	3.4	............Marigold............
3	6	3.8	............Blackwood Road............
	7	4.3	............Wilkinson............
	8	4.8	............Glyn............
	9	5.4	P............EBERTS............
4	10	6.2	............Westwoodvale............
	11	6.7	............Goward............
	12	7.4	P............OBSERVATORY SDG............
5	13	7.9	............Prospect............Spur
	14	8.9	P............HEALS............
6	15	9.7	............Rifle Range............Spur
	16	10.2	............Durrance............Spur
7	17	11.2	............Todd Inlet............
	18	11.6	............Brentwood............
	19	12.2	............Marchant Road............
	20	12.5	P............Sluggetts............Spur
8		13.1	P............Pit Jct............
	21	13.6	............Stellys............Sour
	22		............Prosser Ave............
	22	14.9	P............SAANICHTON............
9	23	16.8	............Experimental Farm............
	24	17.4	............Bazan Bay............
	25	17.8	............Tripp............Spur Interchange C. N. Ry.
	26	18.8	............Sidneway............
10	27	19.4	P............Meadlands............
	28	19.6	............Patricia Jct............Sour
	28	19.8	............Gibson's Crossing............
11	29	20.9	............Mallowmot............Spur
	30	22.3	............Tatlow............
	31	23.0	P............DEEP BAY............

Pay-as-you-enter service with one man cars 22 and 23 commenced on the Saanich line on May 27, 1923. (B.C. Hydro)

Central Park line from 12:30 p.m. to 9 p.m., with a last departure at 10 p.m.; stops were at Broadway and Commercial, Cedar Cottage, Collingwood East (where an experimental illuminated station sign had been installed earlier in the year), and Central Park only. Trains left Queen's Park half-hourly between 1:30 p.m. and 9 p.m. (The cross-overs at Cedar Cottage, Beaconsfield, Collingwood East, and Central Park had still not been turned about for right hand operation, and the one at Cedar Cottage was, in fact, out of service.

What a day October 1 must have been in Victoria! To celebrate its golden jubilee, the department store firm of David Spencer acquired the complete Victoria street car system and the Saanich interurban line for the day. Everyone rode free, guests of Spencer's. The system carried record numbers of passengers, and how

Mount Pleasant barn, with Main Street flowing North to the right. The tall spire of St. Giles United Church, later Evangelistic Tabernacle, pierces the sky at far right. (B.C. Hydro)

delightful it must have been to see the Saanich cars crowded with picnickers, as well as with riders who never used the service otherwise. The carnival spirit reached its zenith when schools were out and students overwhelmed the street

cars.

At Cloverdale, a long overdue adjustment was made. On October 6, the moribund north-south Great Northern line was finally to lose its priority at the interlocking plant; the signals would now

Combine 1400 glowers impressively in front of the barn at New Westminster on Twelfth Street, the beginning of the notorious hill in the left background. (Geoff Meugens collection)

show line clear for the B. C. Electric, and when it was necessary for a G. N. train to cross the Chilliwack line, a G. N. employee would operate the signals. † The Vancouver-Marpole interurban line gained another station on October 24 when Twenty-ninth Avenue became a stop; over the years it became particularly well known as the station at the entrance to Quilchena Golf Club.

North Vancouver's city council had been discussing the issue of one man street cars for some time. In May, general manager Kidd had met with North Vancouver city and municipal officials to discuss the safety and viability of the cars on the north shore. It was in November that the city council of North Vancouver took a stand — against one man street cars.

In Vancouver November 3 marked the day that the B. C. Electric was able to do what it had initially wished — run street cars from Alma and Tenth Avenue directly to Dunbar and Sixteenth. The awkwardness of the "detour" around Crown Street and Sixteenth was eliminated (the rails were removed) with the laying of track on the newly-created connector street, Dunbar Diversion. Three days later, Hastings East-Broadway West street cars began operating straight through to Dunbar and Forty-first Avenue, as well as to Fourth Avenue and Drummond. (One man cars disappeared from Dunbar on the previous day.) Other adjustments included the employment of the skip-stop arrangement on Dunbar, and the elimination of street car service on Alma Street between Fourth and Broadway.

December 1 was the last day the Marpole, Steveston, and New Westminster interurban trains operated out of their unique station at the south end of Granville Bridge. Beginning on December 2, they turned east onto the street car line at Fourth Avenue (rather than a block later at Third, to head for the old depot) for half a block, and then ran over Granville Bridge and along Granville Street itself to Davie Street, with a right turn for one more block to the far side of Seymour Street, there to wait in the middle of the street in front of the new depot for their departure signal.

During 1923 the long desired ideal of a private right of way from Commercial Drive to Carrall Street had received enthusiastic endorsation from the B. C. Electric's directors. With such a route into the heart of Vancouver, the company could have escaped the C.P.R.'s hip pocket and become able, with considerable independence, to make its own hauling and switching arrangements. But when the Dominion Railway Commission demanded a half million-dollar, high-level bridge over Main Street, enthusiasm fled. Since the C.P.R. was unwilling to risk its profitable arrangements with the B. C. Electric, it conceded to the company, in renegotiating their V. & L. I. agreement, permission to haul Northern Pacific cars in from Huntingdon; to gain long hauls by bringing cars

in from the interchange at Abbotsford, rather than merely locally in the New Westminster-Vancouver area; and to publish through rates for points in the United States, as well as in Canada east of Winnipeg. (These new freedoms for the company would not take effect until early 1925.)

Residents of Cloverdale had been wooed during the year by the paving of the Pacific Highway through to the international boundary; it was ironic that the Chilliwack line had conscientiously conveyed the necessary materials. The Great Northern Railway's daily-except-Sunday mixed train between Port Guichon and Huntingdon-Sumas was struggling.

West Vancouver had long been interested in transit; they would never get it from the B. C. Electric, but what they had received from the company during 1923 was electric light, a not inconsiderable boon, and a rather tardy one at

McKay Avenue station on the Central Park line. (Bob Webster collection)

† W.H. Elson, Superintendent, "Bulletin No. 152," 6 October 1923.

The three Fraser valley line Niles cars nicely in line, B.C. Electric's ad of 1923 emphasizes the importance of dairying to the B.C. Electric. (B.C. Hydro)

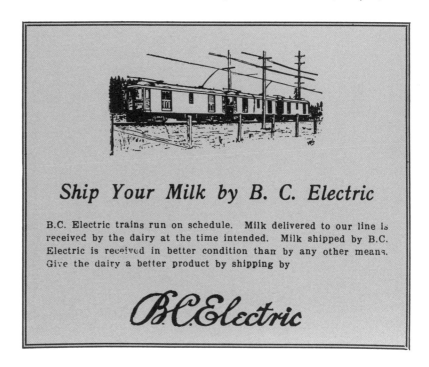

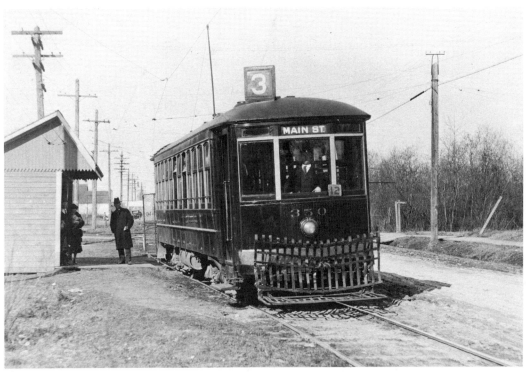

Car 350 at Fiftieth and Main in 1923, about to back onto the wye in preparation for its metamorphosis to a Davie car. (B.C. Hydro)

that, considering the municipality's proximity to everyone else who already had it. Somehow, the company had conspired to transport virtually the same number of riders in 1923 as it had in 1922 — 67,441,665 — but freight tonnage hauled was up to 378,136.

The Ohmer fare registers had finally almost outlived their borderline usefulness, at least on the heavily-travelled Central Park line, where a coupon book approach to fares supplanted the Ohmer system early in 1924. Ohmer use on the Burnaby Lake and Lulu Island lines was soon terminated.

The big news early in the year, however, was the completion on January 31 of the dam and its accompanying 47,400 horsepower power plant at Stave Falls, from where three newly-strung transmission lines brought electric power to Horne-Payne receiving station on the Burnaby Lake line. But the company, not content that the potential of Stave Lake and River had been challenged, would start work on yet another power installation there during the year. In addition to the new power plant, the B. C. Electric's largest, the company's other six were producing a further 110,700 horsepower: Lake Buntzen, No. 2, 35,800 h.p.; Lake Buntzen, No. 1, 28,200 h.p.; Jordan River, 21,500 h.p.; Vancouver steam plant, 16,800 h.p.; Brentwood Bay, 5,400 h.p.; and Goldstream, 3,000 h.p.

Immediately, the B. C. Electric launched a different power project, one again involving Stave Lake and, more particularly, neighbouring Alouette Lake over the mountains to the west. Its attractiveness to the company lay in its height of 140 feet above Stave Lake, and in its capability of

being connected to Stave Lake by a 3,485-foot tunnel, thus massively augmenting the power potential of the Stave system. In addition the company would build a dam at the southern outlet of Alouette Lake to raise the lake further, permitting even greater development of power in the future on the Stave.

To get men and equipment to the lake, the B. C. Electric on March 22 began the construction of a four-mile railway line along the eastern bank of the Alouette River between the headquarters camp of the Abernethy & Lougheed Logging Company and the southern rim of Alouette Lake. From the camp (the site of Allco Park today in Maple Ridge), it was but four miles farther southwest on the logging company's own railway line to a connection with the main line of the C.P.R. one mile east of Haney. Since Ruskin was a mere eight miles east of this junction, and Vancouver was twenty-seven miles to the west, transportation would be easy. Alouette Lake would soon be extremely accessible, an eight-mile haul by one of the seven Abernethy & Lougheed steam locomotives from the C.P.R. line.

The contract for the company's four-mile line would be carried out by Messrs. Stewart & Barber, who established four camps of 225 men along the line, and built a sled road adjacent to the right of way for the entire distance to maintain temporary transportation. It was a difficult railway line to build, requiring many culverts, heavy cuttings and embankments, and a 600-foot trestle.

The company had reconsidered its ticket-and-fare philosophy for the Saanich line, and put a weekly pass system into effect on Monday, March 31. The passes, valid from the first car Monday to

Carrall Street station and head office in 1924. C.P.R.'s line from Burrard Inlet to its interchange with the B.C. Electric, east of Granville Bridge, runs past the depot at far right, next to B.C. Electric's own utility track. (B.C. Hydro)

the last car Sunday, were an incredible bargain. Ranging in cost between fifty cents for a Victoria-to-Harriet Road pass to $4.30 for one all the way to Deep Bay, the passes were good for an unlimited number of rides, and were transferrable to any member of the pass purchaser's family. The company even had made arrangements with the Capitol, Dominion, and Royal Victoria theatres to give Saanich line pass-holding patrons free admission on specific days. During the first month, the company sponsored an essay contest for pass-holders; three prizes would be presented for the letters or essays best describing the ways in which "the weekly pass had been found useful, economical, pleasurable." The first week saw 77 passes in use, the second, 90. One-way fare from Victoria to Deep Bay was still a low sixty-five cents.

In April, the press reported that the B. C. Electric was planning to build its cutoff line from Cedar Cottage to Carrall Street, using the tunnel projected three years earlier and the old Great Northern main line along the southern edge of drained False Creek and across False Creek west of Main Street. However, by the end of September

the company had given up its dream of excellence for the Central Park line.

There was, indeed, a new dream. The Grandview Highway bus run had succeeded to the extent that the company, encouraged, had incorporated a subsidiary, British Columbia Rapid

Form No. T.S. 2604

BRITISH COLUMBIA ELECTRIC RAILWAY CO. LTD.
INTERURBAN DIVISION
EMPLOYEES' WATCH RATING CARD

Mr. _L. Palmer_ Occupation _Operator_

No. of Movem't _13376.5.5_

Maker _Hamilton_

Grade _14J_

Date Last Cleaned _May 27th 1924_

Name and Address of Cleaner _M & D_

W & D old Inspector _Victoria_

Address

INSTRUCTIONS. This card is to be preserved and carried by employees at all times when on duty, and presented to Inspector, together with his watch, during the first and third weeks of each month, oftener if possible.

Week No.

_____

This Pass is good between VICTORIA
and

Station No.

7

WILKINSON
and intermediate points

Expires

_____

Rate $ .90 cents No. 1093
Renew Your Pass in Good Time

"USE A PASS AND SAVE THE DIFFERENCE"

*An example of the new type of
pass tried on the Saanich line.
(author's collection)*

Transit Company Limited, on February 12 to purchase bus and truck lines that were competing with the B. C. Electric's interurban passenger and freight operations between Vancouver, New Westminster, and Chilliwack. Five Fageol buses and one White bus (with bodies by Tupper and Steele) — each seating twenty-two — were ordered, a nine-foot-wide canopy was added to the Columbia Street side of the New Westminster depot, and both it and the Carrall Street depot were fitted up with premises for the new motor coach subsidiary. When service began between Vancouver and New Westminster, with trips every twenty minutes, on May 1, riders were amazed by the luxury of these low slung "safety coaches" with their velour upholstery and mahogany woodwork. Here was competition for the Central Park and Burnaby Lake lines, especially depot to depot. Street car operators and interurban car motormen were asked to give the buses the right of way around the New Westminster depot because "they cannot stop and start with the same facility as in the case of an electric car."

Beginning on Monday, May 5, an early morning interurban passenger run, daily except Sunday, was added to the Chilliwack line's schedule, leaving New Westminster for Cloverdale at 5:30 a.m., and departing Cloverdale on the return journey at 6:05 a.m.

For the Saanich line, a streamlined, cut-down schedule went into effect on May 11. It emphasized Tod Inlet, the line's station for the then already famous Butchart Gardens, and offered fifteen trips in either direction daily: five over the whole of the line, seven to and from Saanichton, two to and from Brentwood, and one to and from Prospect. Travel time between termini now took eighty to eighty-five minutes. The B. C. Electric was still advertising accommodation at The Chalet in early May, but by later in the month it had sold it and five acres of land to a Mr. S. Jones for $10,000. On June 22, the weekly passes were abandoned; they had simply not been able to attract a significant quantity of new riders.

There was rejoicing in the Fraser Valley when, on June 26, the last of the water of Sumas Lake had been pumped out, and 6,000 of its acres had been seeded to timothy. A lush dairying and farming kingdom with excellent soil and a sophisticated drainage grid would soon appear in an area previously best known for its virile mosquitoes and its propensity for flooding itself into a massive, muddy, shallow waterscape. (In the same month, the F.V.M.P.A.'s butter, casein, and cheese plant at Sardis had gone into production.) The interurban trains could now curl around Vedder Mountain without fear of the sometimes lapping water. The total cost of eliminating this nuisance was close to four million dollars.

During the same month, a golden eagle with a wing span of six feet, ten and a half inches, attacked an interurban train as it felt its way around Vedder Mountain. Motorman Bert Johnson stopped his train, alighted, and stood face to face with a bird ready to fight on. He managed to knock the eagle dizzy with a switch iron, and threw it into the baggage-express car, whereupon it revived and attacked the baggage man, who killed it.

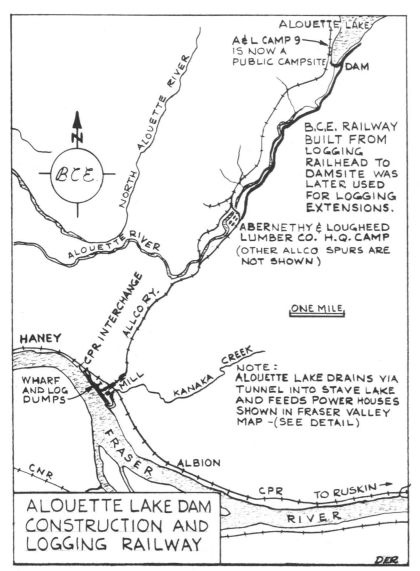

Freight traffic became a great factor in the B.C. Electric's success. Here locomotive 973 hauls a complete train of shingles on June 23, 1924. (B.C. Hydro)

June meant the horse racing season was near, and for Richmond in 1924, it meant the opening of its second race track, Lansdowne, situated about half way between Marpole and Minoru Park. Both tracks would be used on an alternating basis with four seven-day sessions. Rather than constructing a loop, as the B. C. Electric had done at Minoru, it ran in a lengthy spur to the west of the interurban line from a point one hundred feet north of Rifle Range (later Lansdowne) station.

Vancouver's street car system experienced some of its greatest days between June 25 and July 5, when the British naval fleet visited the city. During this same time period Vancouver also celebrated the Potlatch, Dominion Day, and the Fourth of July. Sailors received free rides, a parade delighted everyone and disrupted everything, beaches were crowded, the fireworks at the Potlatch were the best ever, Hastings Park attracted thousands, horse racing at the tracks out in Richmond was in full gallop, and the warships put on a thrilling searchlight display. And the street cars? They carried 192,119 riders on Saturday, June 28; 189,564 on June 30; and 173,675 on Dominion Day, July 1, all the while, battling for downtown street space with thousands of automobiles.

Throughout the summer track work continued. Main Street was completely overhauled with new track and pavement between Second Avenue and Kingsway; and on the Marpole-New Westminster interurban line, a mile-long siding — the longest on the B. C. Electric system — was laid eastward from its junction with the line to Steveston. This was another visible manifestation of the prominent role freight was playing in the company's success, as well as the beginning of a yard which would grow at its eastern end.

On July 10, the "Alouette branch railway," including sidings, spurs, and the landing dock with track running onto it at Alouette Lake, was completed, ready for use. (Scows and towboats were already on the lake.) In the railway's construction, twenty-four acres had been cleared and 97,000 cubic yards excavated; ballasting had amounted to 6,000 cubic yards, and 441,000 board feet of timber had gone into trestles and culverts. When the B. C. Electric's need for the track had passed, it would become part of the Abernethy & Lougheed logging operation, abandoned in 1931.

The following table dryly displays the facts underpinning the reason for the Saanich line's disappearance. Years are twelve-month periods from July 1 to June 30; the loss figures do not include any interest on the investment, but are the straight losses in operation.

Year	Passengers Carried	Loss in Operation
1914	280,436	$ 10,848.56
1915	272,565	19,906.10
1916	223,014	28,359.33
1917	243,156	29,860.57
1918	236,725	30,267.84
1919	263,527	28,394.62
1920	348,470	21,308.14
1921	369,813	27,345.12
1922	338,989	22,093.20
1923	271,236	24,795.55
1924	248,610	19,120.07

Car 72 powerfully hangs on to Quebec Street, seemingly reluctant to test the roof tracks of Mt. Pleasant barn. (Ted Clark collection)

Operator Rhodes at Deep Bay with one man car 23 poses in the late evening sun before placing the trolley wheel to the wire for the return to Victoria, one of the Saanich line's last runs. (author's collection)

For the adjacent Stave Falls line, a small unnumbered locomotive had been fashioned on the former single truck of street car 48. With its uncanny resemblance to Fontaine Fox's cartoon trolley car, small wonder that company employees — even official documents — referred to the little shunter as "Toonerville." Able to motivate not much more than two flat cars at a time, its support, until its scrapping in 1937, was nonetheless valuable.

It was inevitable that the buses would make inroads into interurban business. A new operating pattern, initiated on the Central Park line, seemed to confirm that. On July 14 all Central Park line trains leaving Carrall Street for New Westminster between 8:10 a.m. and 2:50 p.m. would uncouple the second car before crossing Kingsway at Central Park, leaving it to be picked up by the next westbound train.

The company placed two more Fageol buses

into service on its intercity run on August 28. These seated thirty-five, the absence of running boards on either side providing room for thirteen more seats than the earlier buses. During New Westminster's exhibition time, the buses advertised a twenty-five-cent one way fare to Queen's Park, while the interurban cars replied with a fifty-cent return tab, including entrance to the park.

In North Vancouver, the B. C. Electric turned over, as a gift to the city of Vancouver, its 145 acres of Capilano Canyon, a short walk north of the outer terminus of the Capilano street car line. The gift was presented to the Vancouver Board of Trade on behalf of the company by President George Kidd, to be held in trust by the board for the use of the public.

On the Vancouver-Steveston interurban line, Monday, October 6, was the last day one of the baggage-express cars, 1702 or 1703, handled the Monday-Wednesday-Friday way freight. This type of business would henceforth be handled within the operation procedures of the regular freight trains. Consequently, only on Chilliwack line trains, including their brief passage over the Central Park line into Vancouver, would the 1700s be regularly in evidence. Ten of them were more than the system now required.

B. C. Electric vice-president in Victoria, A. T. Goward, wrote a reasoned letter on August 25 to the Minister of Railways proposing the discontinuation of service on the Saanich line at the end of October, "thus giving two (2) months notice before doing so." He furthermore listed and described the operations of the many bus and stage lines working Saanich peninsula, and that they "in every instance serve much the same territory as that served by the interurban."

The September 22 issue of the Victoria edition of *The Buzzer* led off with an explanation entitled "Why the Interurban is to Suspend Service." By this date, the company had already announced the line's imminent demise in the newspapers. As Goward had stated in his letter: "..... the Management has come to the conclusion that our service is not a necessity and is not needed by the community." Cars 22 and 23 whistled up and down the beautiful Saanich line for the last time

(B.C. Hydro)

On the Stave Falls line in 1924, the little, single truck, unnumbered locomotive has just begun its thirteen years of toil. (B.C. Hydro)

on October 31, the final trip out of Victoria at 11:30 p.m., and back in from Saanichton at 1:15 a.m., November 1.

Victoria and Saanich residents were most unhappy about a loss they really had not believed could happen. The Saanich line had done much to settle the district around Wilkinson, Glynn, and Eberts, and it had been the most convenient way to reach the Dominion Observatory and the Experimental Station at Bazan Bay. "The passing of an institution ....." began the report of the *Victoria Daily Times.*†

For a while schemes for retaining this or that section of the line cropped up, but nothing ever came of any of them. Saanich council even struck a committee to consult with the company in an effort to save some part of the line. One idea which came the closest to succeeding was the suggestion that buses with flanged wheels operate a service between Eberts and the Burnside street car line terminus at Harriet Road. Cars 22 and 23 did return to their street car ways, but how peculiar that their run should be Mount Tolmie-Burnside; the terminus of the Burnside run — the Saanich line's access route — was now cut back three blocks to Carroll Street. Locomotive 953

went for scrap.

In Vancouver the Grandview Highway bus line had been extended three blocks to Twenty-fifth Avenue and Rupert Street on October 27. In November all Vancouver street cars began being equipped with rear end route number signs. Business had accelerated on the Dunbar run to the extent that ten-minute rush hour service had begun on November 17, with a helpful, newly installed passing siding at Thirty-third Avenue. Two days later, the Connaught Bridge, closed since August 15 for repairs, reopened, with Oak street cars returning from their detour time on Granville Bridge.

Out in the Fraser Valley branch, milk pick-ups began at Patterson Road, approximately nine hundred feet west of Rand, on November 23. And finally people had begun to notice the efforts that Fraser Valley substation operators, resident with their families in the five reinforced concrete, castlelike structures, were making to create colour and life about them. During the coming years, the substation at Vedder Mountain would even have special interurban trips for horticulturists run to it. An article in a current edition of the *Chilliwack Progress* gave recognition to the

† "Saanich Line to Cease To-night," *Victoria Daily Times,* 31 October 1924, p. 7.

Car 313 moves east on Cordova Street, from Granville, past Vancouver's C.P.R. station on its 8 — Powell Street run. (Bob Webster collection)

efforts being made in its city.

"The B. C. Electric substation, city, has been improved in appearance through the painting of all exterior woodwork and the laying of new sidewalk. The grounds, through the efforts of G. A. Smith, engineer in charge, and Mr. Langbridge, have been made very attractive also. Neatly kept lawns and flowering plants in beds, across the front and on each side, set off the big power station. The trees planted in the spring, on the triangular piece of property approaching the city depot, have grown very nicely. The city is preparing to lay cement sidewalk down Young road, on the B. C. Electric side of the street, which will greatly improve the thoroughfare and the appearance of this section of town."†

One could almost forget that the real work of the substation was to convert alternating current to direct current, used by the motors of the rolling stock, and to be distribution facilities for serving light and power customers all along the Fraser Valley line. The power supply required for the interurban cars and the freight trains was still supplied by two 34,600 volt, three-phase circuits erected on the railway's right of way, and connected to the power system at Burnaby substation.

In late December, the Fraser Valley line was plagued by numerous instances of its track being heaved by frost, the worst problems having been encountered between Harmsworth and Bradner. And in Cloverdale at year's end, the Great Northern Railway was still operating 2.61 miles of the otherwise abandoned New Westminster Southern Railway.

† "Beautify Grounds About B.C. Electric," *The B.C. Electric Employees' Magazine,* November 1924, p. 31.

As 1924 closed, it became apparent that the hoped for positive growth trends in ridership and freight tonnage had not materialized; the former was up slightly to 69,585,740, the latter down to 351,308. Victoria's street cars and the two Saanich cars had combined to carry 8,494,095 riders during 1924.

In early 1925 on weekdays, the Oak Bay line was providing mostly seven and a half-minute service, as was the Willows line with its overlapping Uplands cars. Outer Wharf-Cloverdale, Fernwood-Beacon Hill, Gorge, and Hillside-Foul Bay were providing twelve-minute service, the last named six-minute on the Foul Bay end to Joseph Street. Esquimalt and Uplands cars ran every fifteen minutes, Mount Tolmie-Burnside, every half hour.

On the lower mainland, extra interurban trains were frequently run to augment regular movements, especially on the Marpole-New Westminster line, abounding in mills and factories. The B. C. Electric was usually able to adjust the operations of these extras to the working hours of the men, a case in point being the withdrawal from service on May 2 of the 3:05 p.m. train from Marpole to New Westminster, as well as the 4 p.m. return. This extra run was no longer required because a number of the mills had changed their working hours.

For Fraser Mills, one extra interurban train even left on work days from Twelfth Street and Tenth Avenue in New Westminster for Fraser Mills, where, as all employees' extras, it turned south at the end of its private right of way (the regular end-of-line shelter and platform at the east side of King Edward Avenue), and ran another half mile directly into the mill works themselves. (The men would also be picked up for their return at this mill site.) Here was service indeed.

The Fraser Mills line always seemed to be busy. Two-car St. Louis-built interurban trains were the rule, and on Saturday night especially, they were packed with people coming into New Westminster. One mile west of the Fraser Mills station was Abbatoir station, better known to all habitues of the line as "Packing House." (Its long platform, invariably covered with people, had acquired a new station building during the previous year.) Since the fare from Fraser Mills to Packing House was six cents, and from there to New Westminster another six cents, conductors (it was not a run for rookie conductors) were driven almost to distraction by the fact that those who had boarded at Fraser Mills tended to claim they had boarded at Packing House. This chaos led further to the fare-saving riders fleeing the train with utmost speed upon its arrival in New Westminster.

The side-of-the-road Queensborough leg was relatively quiet; although there were many industries at the ends of the line's long spurs, riders were fewer, and station shelters were nonexistent. Freight was run during the day on the Queensborough line, but gradually came to be run only at night on the Fraser Mills end. (After all, the 2.7 miles between Packing House and New Westminster depot were street run, and competing with the street car lines and the Burnaby Lake interurban, let alone automobile traffic, was daunting and dangerous.)

Two refinements to the system were made in 1925: time-recording punch clocks were installed at the ends of the Kitsilano and Stanley Park lines on April 21, and automatic signals, to replace the staff system, were installed on Tenth Avenue on the Sasamat line on July 3. But the big news came on July 16, when six new two-car, multiple unit street cars went into rush hour service, four on Fraser-Kerrisdale and two on Grandview-Fourth Avenue.

These twelve new steel street cars were a sensation. (Who can ever forget the curved seat at the curved end of each trailer!) "Motor cars" (700, 702, 704, 706, 708, 710) and "trailer cars" (701, 703, 705, 707, 709, 711) together seated 103 passengers, and there was spacious standing room, with a neat wooden rail for standees to hang on to rather than straps. Though both types of cars were similarly-motored and identical in length, the trailer had no large number destination sign on the front of the roof. The motor car's wide loading doors were at the back, the trailer's at the front; together they swallowed rush hour passengers with ease, especially as both conductor's enclosures were set well back from the roomy vestibules.

The company had opted for these Montreal-built, Canadian Car and Foundry Company products, rather than Toronto's front-loading "Peter Witt" street cars. The six three-man sets had cost $250,000, and four more sets were on the way. A significant feature of the new cars was the motorman's multiple unit control, the first of its kind in scheduled service in Canada, the main controller being under the car. The motorman's small controller had only three positions — starting, half, and full speed — and in an ordinary start, all a motorman had to do was throw his handle to full speed, and the camshaft, controlled by a current-limiting relay, would do the rest.

In place of the now decidedly outmoded, projecting, Watson front end fender each car was equipped by the company with H. & B., Liverpool type life-guards, similar to those already installed on the one man safety cars, and soon to be in position on every street car. The new (the company had actually tested them as long ago as 1915) "cow catcher" consisted of a swinging gate hanging from the bumper, with a "cradle" located

A.B.C. Electric newspaper ad of 1925. (author's collection)

about four feet back under the car. If an object struck the gate, a connecting rod tripped the "cradle," dropping it to the rails to pick up and protect the object.

Inside, the new street cars had a wood finish of birch, mahogany-tinted, with cream enamel ceilings. But it was their strikingly attractive exteriors, carmine red with cream trim, that motivated company officials in a flash to abolish the familiar jade (Pullman, some thought) green-with-gold-trim paint scheme and embrace the new gorgeous red for all their rolling stock!

By July the Saanich line was already in tatters beyond Harriet Road. Of the 2,200 tons of rail being lifted, 2,000 would be sent to the lower mainland, as passenger-mail interurban car 1501 already had. Saanich municipality had made arrangements with the company to obtain fourteen miles of the line's right of way for modification into street and road use. (Its old right of way between Tillicum and West Saanich Road is even today known as Interurban Road.)

In Vancouver, Forty-first Avenue's double track between Granville Street and East Boulevard had been laid by August 21. As with all new track work during the last two years (and in the future), the company had used 93-pound rail (seven inches in height and in sixty-two-foot lengths), laid on fir ties two feet apart with centres encased in concrete, eight inches of stone block pavement against the rails. All this rested on an eight-inch concrete slab foundation. As in all projects of this type, the B. C. Electric carried out the work, and the city or municipality contributed payment in compensation.

At the depot area in New Westminster, safety zones at the tracks on Columbia Street had been defined with the purpose of allowing riders safely to transfer between street cars and interurbans on the street itself. Since the 1300-type Chilliwack interurban cars were the only passenger rolling stock without window guards, now so necessary on city streets and double track, crews on the cars always kept the windows on the devil strip side (facing the on-coming track) closed on the Central Park line segment of their movements. The Central Park line was additionally the one operation which employed the safety feature of fog lanterns.

Exactly at 12:30 p.m. on Saturday, September 19, the Honourable John Oliver, premier of British Columbia, turned a gold key which started in motion the fifth unit of the completed Stave Falls power plant, increasing its capacity to 79,000 horsepower. The water surging through the Alouette Lake-Stave Lake tunnel had made this advance possible. The party of dignitaries and company and municipal officials had left Vancouver by special train at 9 a.m., transferring onto two of the B. C. Electric's St. Louis-built interurban cars at Ruskin for the scenic six-mile

trip north to Stave Falls. (The two cars stayed on the Stave Falls line for a number of weeks bringing a variety of parties, including one of over one hundred journalists, to the massive power project the B. C. Electric had wrought.)

With the opening of the University of British Columbia on its new site on Point Grey in the fall of 1925, the B. C. Electric inaugurated a bus service from Tenth Avenue and Sasamat (a small bus garage had been constructed on the southeast side of Trimble Street) using six new Leyland-engined, Tupper & Steele-coached vehicles. Elsewhere on the Vancouver system, on September 16, new passing sidings were initiated on the east side of Granville Street between Thirty-fourth and Thirty-fifth avenues and on Forty-first at McDonald Street, and a one man shuttle street car went into service on King Edward Avenue between Granville and Oak streets, running downtown to Robson and Richards streets in rush hours beginning November 16.

At Burrard Inlet's Second Narrows, the point at which the company's transmission line crossed from Vancouver to North Vancouver municipality, a combined road-railway bridge costing $1,800,000 was opened for traffic on November 7. Though the bridge was a sturdy steel structure, its relative lack of height above the water would make it a hazard for shipping, especially during the inevitable fogs. Nonetheless, the north shore and Vancouver sides of the inlet had a connection of enormous potential; 3,000 automobiles alone crossed it on the first day.

Vancouver's Prior Street barn had been suffering from severe overload for a dozen years, and by the last day of November, the company had accomplished a move to the new Kitsilano car repair shops, adjacent to the barn there. The blacksmith shop, carpenter shop, machine shop, and the controller, welding, wheel and axle, and winding departments had been installed there, as well as the new facilities of paint shop and erecting shop, each with a six-car capacity. Neither of the latter shops had had facilities to call their own before this move and the previous seven shops and departments had together increased their square footage of space from 11,506 to 12,896. Prior Street barn found itself better capable of functioning as the barn it really was, and traffic of all kinds on Main Street in the Prior area regained a modicum of freedom.

The incorporation on December 4 of B. C. Motor Transportation, Limited, organized by, and a subsidiary of, the B. C. Electric, brought the company heavily into the field of bus and truck transport, a step with enormous implications for the future. This new creation acquired all property of British Columbia Rapid Transit (it obtained complete control in 1932), in addition to twelve bus and truck lines, including Pacific Stages, Gray Line, Yellow Cab, and Fraser Valley

Freight. The new subsidiary had, of course, been created for the specific purpose of removing these carriers from competition with the B. C. Electric's transportation system. (Within a year, Ladner would finally have a B. C. Electric transit link with Vancouver after B. C. Motor Transportation acquired White Star Motor Line and its buses.)

A week before the close of 1925, the Burnaby Lake line, still traversing territory largely uninhabited, added a new station to its schedule, Douglas, at the line's intersection with Royal Oak Avenue in Burnaby, fourteen hundred feet west of Hastings Road Station.

New Westminster was operating twelve one man, double end street cars on its system (this identical dozen would remain until the end of street car service), 98, 163, 164, 166, 167, 184, 186, and 319-323, as well as snow sweeper S.55. Not in use, stored at New Westminster barn, were interurban passenger cars 1011 and 1012, interurban express car 1800, and forlorn hobble skirt car 500. Still on the active list in Vancouver were sprinklers S.50 and S.51, but older, double truck street cars 31, 33, and 35 were in storage at the Carrall Street yard — they would be scrapped in April 1926. Single trucked 53 and 57 were there too, the former a salt car, the latter a lamp car. The only other single truck street cars in operation were Victoria's ten Birneys.

The company's intercity buses were carrying small parcels and light express, and in New Westminster making connections at the depot with bus runs to Essondale, Coquitlam, Port Moody, Port Hammond, and Port Haney. At the same time that New Westminster added a bus orientation, it lost in 1925 a sixty-seven-year-old tradition when the Fraser River sternwheeler, *Skeena,* tied up in New Westminster for the last time.

For the year 1925, twenty-two of Canada's sixty-two electric railways had shown increases in passenger traffic, and the B. C. Electric was one of them, with a modest increase to 71,796,794 riders, third highest in Canada after Montreal and Toronto. In the matter of freight, B. C. Electric led all electric lines, carrying 396,474 tons (by comparison, the London and Port Stanley Railway carried 361,899 tons, Montreal Tramways 351,055 tons, and Niagara, St. Catharines & Toronto 294,497 tons). And in route miles, the B. C. Electric was the largest of all sixty-two electric lines, with 346.52 miles (Montreal Tramways, 292.68; Toronto Transportation Commission 227.40; Winnipeg Electric company 117.38).

The start of 1926 was noteworthy not only for the replacement of the old carbon filament globes with new tungsten lamps on the street cars and interurban cars but also for the company's announcement that 1926 would be the greatest track building year in Vancovuer since the last of

the sensational years, 1913.

In North Vancouver, plans were underway by the Harbour Board to build a connecting railway line between the Second Narrows Bridge and the terminus of the Pacific Great Eastern Railway at the foot of Lonsdale; 147 men were at work building a highway to the top of Grouse Mountain; and the company had proposed to city council the operating of one man cars on the Capilano and Lynn Valley lines. In February the council relayed its opposition, on safety grounds, to the patient B.C. Electric.

The Vancouver system's new single tracked, six-block line from east of Commercial Drive to Nanaimo Street was opened on February 8, becoming part of the Nanaimo street car's regular run from Hastings and Nanaimo streets. Just five days later, the Georgia East line, which had struggled so long, suffered complete abandonment. It was not unexpected, since its route, from Main Street to Victoria Drive, lay only two to three blocks from frequent street car service on

This newspaper advertisement well defines the B.C. Electric's concerns in 1926. (author's collection)

Hastings Street. On the fifteenth, the Kitsilano-Hastings East line was broken into its two sections; since the combined run endured so many bridge opening and railway crossing delays, it was felt better to run two shorter services and consequently keep both better on schedule.

On the interurban system, since Douglas station on the Burnaby Lake line had been causing some confusion because of the existence in Burnaby of venerable Douglas Road, the station's name was changed on February 15 to Murrin. On the line to Chilliwack, yet another post office, Evanthomas, was opened on March 1 at Evan-Thomas station. (Mails at that time left New Westminster on passenger train No. 2, and departed Chilliwack on No. 7, daily except Sunday.) By April 26, Sexsmith station on the Steveston line was relocated eight hundred feet north to Patterson Road from its previous location. A new stop for the Chilliwack line's trains was inaugurated on May 4 at the point where passengers to and from the newly established hop fields on Sumas prairie's reclaimed area would alight and board. This stop was located a mile and a half east of Vedder Mountain, where the highway between New Westminster and Chilliwack, today's Yale Road at this point, came close to the right of way.

The Fraser Valley interurban line had been more affected by the automobile, especially since the advent of paved roads, than any other of the interurban lines; passenger business was no longer what it once was. And thus it was that the B. C. Electric on May 1, under the aegis of B. C. Motor Transportation (the Rapid Transit Company had in preparation been transferred to it on March 10), commenced a bus service to Chilliwack, leaving New Westminster daily at 8 a.m., 11 a.m., 4 p.m., and 9 p.m. Two Fageols handled the business, in addition to express parcels, in a one way journey of two hours and fifty-seven minutes. The interurban trains took two hours and forty minutes. At the same time, the company had inaugurated a freight truck operation to Chilliwack, using the new road recently opened across the old lake bed between Abbotsford and Chilliwack. To run this service, the company had assiduously bought up the major existing truck lines, and, in order to compete with the farmers' own trucks and those of wholesalers and delivery outfits, had established a system of commodity rates and classifications, just as railroads had long ago.

In North Vancouver, the four-month rebuilding of imposing three-deck, single track, frame bent McKay Creek trestle on the Capilano line had begun on May 24. B. C. Motor Transportation was already running eleven daily return trips to and from Vancouver over the Second Narrows Bridge, which saw the first locomotive over it in June. (In the same month, a delegation to city council displayed plans for another bridge, this one at First Narrows, the site of today's Lions Gate Bridge.)

Across the B. C. Electric's system, particularly in the Vancouver area, new substations were being built and old ones were being updated and enlarged, as service to the company's customers, as well as for its own transportation system, made ever greater demands. New power projects reflected such demands, as did the additions over the years to existing power systems. In 1926 the B.C.

July 1926 on the Jordan River line at Diversion station. (J.M. Elliott photo)

Pembroke Street barn in Victoria displays six faces, three of them in the new red and cream, three in the discarded green. (B.C. Hydro)

Electric's operations could be said to embrace a population of 375,000 in a territory of 1,500 square miles, all served by 3,240 employees.

Because residents east of Huntingdon objected to the name Evan-Thomas, both station and post office were changed to the area's historic designation, Upper Sumas, on June 16. On the following day, superintendent Elson issued a notice to Central Park line conductors, motormen, and trainmen and New Westminster operators:

> *"There has just been a case of an Interurban westbound train pulling away from Highland Park, after waiting the arrival of connecting City Car, and leaving passengers behind, through a misunderstanding of signals as between the Car Operator and the crew of the Interurban train, the car operator giving a signal with the gong that he had passengers to transfer, but the crew of the Interurban understood the signal to indicate that he had none.*
>
> *To avoid the possibility of a recurrence of anything so regrettable and absurd, no signals are to be given by the City Car to a waiting Interurban train at Highland Park, unless in the day time, in clear weather, when an unmistakable and clear hand signal can be given, if the City car has no passengers to transfer."*

Elsewhere on the New Westminster system, the gradual building up of housing along the company's street car line on Edmonds and Sixth streets began to be reflected in the installation of new street car stops. On June 23 the first new stop was added at Britton Street, just east of Twelfth Street.

In Vancouver, Wednesday, July 14, marked the arrival of eight new two-man, single end street cars (356-363), identical in appearance to the motor cars of the 700-series, but lacking their necessary remote control equipment. These Canadian Car & Foundry products went into service within twenty-four hours on Dunbar and Hastings East. Four more of the 700-series two-car, multiple unit sets were on the way to Vancouver, and would arrive shortly to give the company twenty of these street cars, numbered 700-719.

Earlier in the summer, the company had experimented with a bus service beyond Chilliwack as far as Hope; and on the Burnaby Lake line, the filling in of the long trestle at Burnaby Lake was occupying the energies of a large crew. On July 16 on the Burnaby Lake line, a new station, Windermere Street, went into service, and on August 1, a new post office,

Stillbridge, was opened at Hastings Road Station. (Its mail would be picked up by the line's regular New Westminster-bound mail train, No. 412.) On District 2, new semaphores, equipped with lights only — red and green — were being installed at the Kitsilano trestle and the drawbridge at Marpole. September 18 was the date on which Abbotsford's post office began to be served exclusively by the B. C. Electric, as the C.P.R. was anxious to jettison mail delivery on its Huntingdon branch.

The Provincial Exhibition in New Westminster set attendance records during its 1926 run. On Labour Day alone, the interurban lines carried 37,300 (despite the fact that twelve interurban cars had had to be transferred on the same day to District 2 to run race track specials), and on the last Saturday of the fair, New Westminster's street car system carried 27,400, about eight thousand more than on a regular Saturday. As always, extra operators were stationed at the corner of Columbia Street and Leopold Place (where two street car and two interurban lines came together), at Queen's Park, and at the corner of Sixth Street and Fourth Avenue.

September was the month of completion for the company's sophisticated double tracking project in Point Grey, again using 93-pound track. Alma, Dunbar Diversion, Sixteenth, and Dunbar Street to Forty-first Avenue (from Tenth Avenue) were ready on the twelfth; Tenth, from Alma to Sasamat streets, was completed exactly two weeks later.

In North Vancouver the completion of the rebuilding of McKay Creek trestle had meant the resumption of through street car service and the opening of the park at its terminus. The three-line system was operating thirteen two-man, double end street cars (150-162), with number 28 along as an all-purpose work car.

Each of Vancouver's 262 street cars had its specific home. Seventy-eight of them were domiciled at the Prior Street barn: 29, 123, 124, 130-135, 137-149, 170-182, 222-229, 311-317, 700-719, and 356-363; and the other 184 at Mount Pleasant barn: 69-97, 99-122, 127, 129, 168, 169, 183, 185, 187, 190, 191, 193, 195-221, 230, 241-249, 260-310, 318, and 324-355. Among the street cars at Mount Pleasant were Vancouver's fifteen one man cars — 73, 78-80, 82, 83, 88-92, 99, 107, 168, and 169. (Cars 82 and 83 had been completely rebuilt during the year from interurbans 1011 and 1012, respectively.) In addition, Vancouver's roster included snow sweepers S.53, S.54, S.56, S.57, S.63, and S.64; snow plows 901 and 904; wrecking car F.4; locomotive 952; sand car 53; and stock (supplies) car 1801. Line cars L.2, L.3, L.4, and L.6 patrolled the whole lower mainland system, while 500, S.50, and S.51 were in storage at New Westminster.

Interurban cars assigned to the Central Park, Burnaby Lake, and Fraser Mills-Queensborough lines were 1000-1002, 1004-1009, 1217-1238, and 1240-1243. Locomotive 951 served all three routes. The Lulu Island line's interurban cars, the only interurban cars housed at Kitsilano barn, were 1201-1208, 1211, 1212, 1215, 1239, 1244, 1501, 1702, and 1703; its locomotives were 974, 990, and 992. The Chilliwack line's allotment included interurbans 1300-1311, 1400-1402, 1500, 1600-1603, 1700, 1701, and 1704-1709, and locomotives 970-973, 981, and 991. Particularly to aid riders in distinguishing among the various interurban lines, especially at New Westminster's depot, the Central Park line cars carried white signs; the Burnaby Lake, green; Marpole-New Westminster, red; and Steveston, blue.

On November 1, another new stopping place for New Westminster's Sixth Street cars was initiated, Curragh Avenue, which was then just being opened up, approximately half way between Gilley Avenue and the Highland Park terminus to the west. On December 1, the company's truck line to Chilliwack, Fraser Valley Freight Line, moved its base of operations in Vancouver from the Carrall Street yard to 82 Water Street, and in New Westminster to the

At Broadway and Commercial in October 1927, looking east. The Nanaimo shuttle street car at far right is still painted green; downtown-bound 280 sports the new red and cream livery, as does the company's very first bus, ready to service the pioneering Grandview Highway route. (B.C. Transit)

facilities of Chapman Motor Cartage. After all, Frank Chapman was superintendent of the company's motor freight service.

The year ended with a series of snowfalls. Bus aficionados and drivers learned that lurching into a ditch (as the company's bus between Chilliwack and Hope did on the seventeenth) and having dinner at a welcoming farm house was about the best they could do under such weather conditions in 1926. The first really thick, heavy snow came on the twenty-third, but the street car and interurban systems experienced no untoward difficulties.

During the year, New Westminster had opened its new, capacious market at the foot of Church Street, hemmed in by interurbans on the Front and Columbia street sides, and by street cars on the latter, of course. The new Lougheed Highway had opened on the north side of the Fraser River all the way to Agassiz, and nearby Harrison Hot Springs had bubbled with excitement at the opening of its large, new hotel on May 24, almost six years after the original had been destroyed by fire. The economy was on an upswing, and the B.C. Electric, with its expansions, could benefit from it. Both passengers carried and freight tons hauled were nicely up — to 72,944,517 and 409,313, respectively.

January 1927 began with more snow; all the sweepers and even snow plow 952 saw frantic action from the afternoon of the twelfth through the night into the morning of the following day. Special late interurban trains were a regular feature of Christmas eve and New Year's eve operations, but in 1927 a train left Carrall Street depot at 2:30 a.m. on New Year's Day headed for the Fraser Valley.

Long-time, well-known B. C. Electric employee (and author and poet), Edmund Pugsley, penned the following description in January of some aspects of the company's freight operations:

"Packed carefully in iced refrigerator cars, the long train of oranges, bananas, watermelon, grapefruit — with lettuce, rhubarb, cantaloupe and berries and other seasonal fruits and vegetables in the off-season periods — arrives at the boundary town of Sumas, Washington, in the evening, daily except Saturday, where an engine operated by "white coal" calmly awaits its job of transporting the precious cargo on its last lap.

In order that this may be accomplished expeditiously, a train crew is held at Huntingdon, where they sleep — when they're not fighting off mosquitoes and flies — through the heat of the day, and are called by the station agent when he hears the long warning whistle of the arriving Northern Pacific train.

The ceremony of exchanging way-bills, custom papers, and seal records, of customs inspection, car inspection, switching and air-brake testing is accomplished with a rhythmic motion born of long practice and a knowledge of the necessity for haste by all concerned. In a

remarkably short space of time, the fruit train moves on into Canada, operated by Canadians, with luscious southern fruit for Canadian consumption.

The night draws in, but the train moves steadily onward.

For men must work and fruit we must eat,
Be it lemons sour or oranges sweet.

The Fraser Valley farmer sees the glare of the electric headlight, hears the steady roar of the heavy train over the rails, and catches a glimpse of the green markers at the rear of the caboose as it speeds on up hill and down, across prairie, through timber, meeting the east freight at Kennedy, and finally, after a steady grinding of brakes, a long whistle signals the towerman on the Fraser bridge for a clear board.

A brief halt at New Westminster depot to register, and perhaps obtain fresh orders from the night despatcher, and again 'Archie' throws a high-ball to the motorman, and the sleeping town is left behind.

At Marpole all but perishable or rush freight is cut out to avoid doubling the heavy grade and to assure the arrival on time in Vancouver, and soon residents of Kerrisdale, Strathcona, Talton place and a portion of Kitsilano may sleepily turn over in bed with the knowledge that they have yet several hours to enjoy their sleep before it is necessary for them to get down to business, which may, or may not, involve in some way the fast fruit train that passes in the night.

At the northern end of Kitsilano bridge the final stop is made, and there the cars are sorted out, all Water street fruit turned over to the waiting C.P.R. yard engine for placing at the various warehouses for morning unloading, which, by the way, completes a delivery that is 24 hours earlier than former schedules.

'Archie' and his train crew then retire to their bunks in the caboose, there to await the night and time to start east again with a heavy train of lumber for eastern Canada and States, and empty refrigerator cars for the south." †

Fraser Valley Motor Freight had been acquiring more truck lines, and by early 1927 their sixteen trucks and two trailers serviced Crescent Beach and White Rock, Hammond and Haney (the "Port" had been dropped with the final victory of road over river), and Ladner, as well as stops on the south side of the Fraser Valley. As the interurban system was steadily, aggressively involving itself with larger national and international freight movements, the truck system had corralled most of the L.C.L. (less-than-carload) local freight business.

When the C.P.R.'s Mission-Huntingdon branch quit carrying mail at the end of January, Chilliwack line trains 2, 3, and 7 took over this service. During the first few months of 1927, several new stations were built on lower mainland lines. On February 11, Shaughnessy station on the Marpole-New Westminster line was inaugurated. Located one block east of Oak Street, it became the first stop

† Edmund Pugsley, "Fruit Juice on Our Freight Line," *The B.C. Electric Employees' Magazine*. January 1927, pp. 10-11.

Cars 123 and 124 definitely dominated Vancouver's sightseeing travel until 1950. (John Oastler collection)

east of Marpole, conveniently serving the entrance to an abattoir and a McNair mill. On the Chilliwack line, 6.3 miles east of New Westminster, a new station, Hunt Road, was put into service on April 1. Precisely two weeks later, the Steveston line acquired a new station, Ferndale Road, some three-tenths of a mile south of Lansdowne.

The B. C. Electric's new cross-over interchange track with the Canadian National Railway at the north end of the Fraser River bridge was placed in service on June 4, with trolley wire extending for a distance of fifteen car lengths east from Front Street. In the same month, New Westminster's street car operators had been cautioned again not to exceed series speed northbound on Sixth Street between Agnes Street and Royal Avenue, and over the derailer at that point. Very early on June 12, one of the company's buses, bearing the sign "Fraser Canyon" over the top of its windshield, travelled past Chilliwack and Hope, all the way up the canyon for the first time, to

Chapman's, 130 miles from Vancouver. The road was almost fit enough for the company to consider regular service.

In Vancouver, new, better quality track on Hastings Street between Renfrew Street and Boundary Road was opened on June 16, and on August 22, similarly newly relaid double track was inaugurated on Broadway between Granville and Trafalgar streets.

The company renamed 24th Avenue station on the Marpole line 22nd Avenue as of August 15, acceding to the requests of residents as well as Point Grey municipality. Eight days later on the Chilliwack line, De Graw Crossing — new hop fields had just been begun at that point — one-quarter of a mile east of Kidd, became a flag stop for all passenger trains; and on October 11, Vanderhoof, eight-tenths of a mile east of Huntingdon, also became a stop for passenger trains. The company had meanwhile been authorized by the Board of Railway Commission-

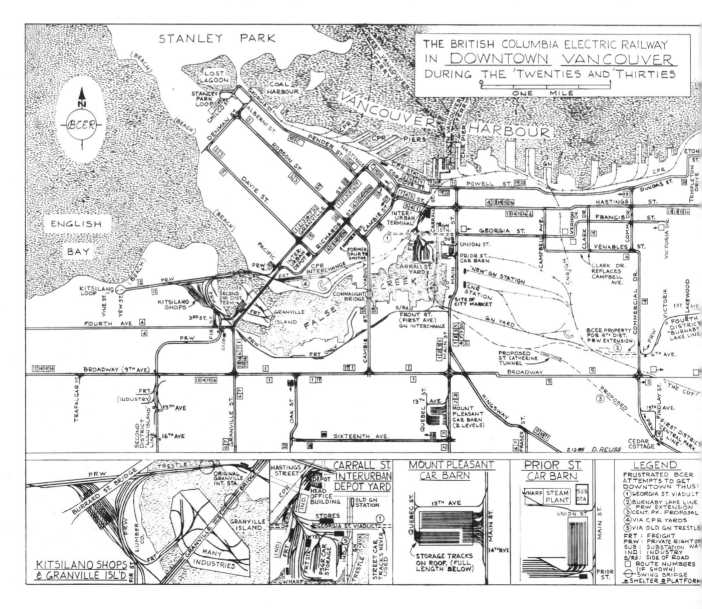

The laying of track on Clark Drive in August of 1927 to circumvent the dangerous crossing with the Great Northern on Venables Street. (B.C. Hydro)

ers to construct a new interchange track to the C.P.R.'s line in Abbotsford. The nine hundred-foot-long connection would be laid across Pine Street from the B.C. Electric depot at Hazel Street to the C.P.R., just beyond the intersection of Maple and West Railway streets.

In Vancouver, the big news in autumn was the first Montreal-Vancouver flight in September, a thirty-six-hour journey piloted by Earl Godfrey. But for the B. C. Electric, it was without doubt the scrapping of nine blocks of street car line, intersected by a steam railway, where a death had occurred when a street car and train had collided in fog. Campbell Avenue from Hastings to Venables streets, and Venables, east to Clark Drive, part of the original Westminster &

Vancouver Tramway route, were struck from company track rolls in the early hours of October 20, and when regular service got going at dawn, a new double tracked line on five blocks of Clark Drive supplanted the thirty-six-year-old route for the Grandview-Fourth Avenue street cars and the Central Park, Chilliwack, and Burnaby Lake line interurbans. The new stops along Clark were indicated by a band of white paint on appropriate telephone poles.

Along the Chilliwack line, a post office (the last one to the opened on the line) was opened at Hall's Prairie on October 31. Near five o'clock on the afternoon of Friday, November 11, began one of the Fraser Valley's infamous snow-hail-sleet storms, this one ending on the Tuesday following

On Hastings Street, east from Columbia Street to Main Street, homeward-bound street cars and interurban coaches go, still dressed in green. Only the Robson car shines in red and cream. (B.C. Hydro)

in a "silver thaw." The entire countryside had been transformed into an ice palace, beautifully hung with gigantic crystals and cloaked in gorgeous, glittering ice. The high-tension line between Abbotsford and Huntingdon had broken in four places; poles and wires were down at Sardis; and interurban operations on Tuesday were in disarray: the broken overhead wire between Delair and Vye had largely been the cause of the milk train's arrival in Chilliwack at 10 p.m., despite having pulled out of New Westminster's depot at 3:05 p.m. (The afternoon train from Chilliwack had not arrived at New Westminster until 11:30 p.m.)

November for New Westminster's system meant a street car shuttle service between the Sixth Street line at Fourth Avenue and the foot of Park Row, via Queen's Park, during the regrading and repaving of Royal Avenue. In New Westminster, North Vancouver, and Vancouver, November 24 was the date by which company workmen had completed the installation of Canadian General Electric heating units under the seats of its street cars. It was on this same day that Oak Street car number 89 went into service with another innovation, an automatic, treadle, door-opening exit step.

On the Marpole line, three changes of station names went into effect on Sunday the twenty-seventh: Angus, Magee, and Royal became 45th Avenue, 49th Avenue, and 51st Avenue. Hjorth Road, its shelter completed after some delays, assumed its position as a new station on the Chilliwack line 2.6 miles east of New Westminster on Sunday, December 11.

On this same Sunday, the worst snow storm in more than a decade hit the lower mainland. (Victoria was just brushed by it.) The snow had begun falling early Saturday evening, and by Sunday morning the continuous fall, together with the unusual cold, had rendered the maintenance of street car and interurban service, let alone light, gas, and power services, almost impossible. The six sweepers used over four tons of Java swamp cane in the first five stormy days alone, and three tons of salt a day were dumped onto the rails by car 53. On Sunday, 24 Vancouver street cars had been compelled to return to car barns with frozen air and allied maladies. Although the wing plows were employed with great success, the worst source of trouble had still been, as usual, the use of the cleared street car lines by automobile and trucks. The bus and truck services had been cancelled outright, but the interurban trains went right through to Chilliwack, preceded by a snow plow when necessary.

While Sunday had been the lightest day for traffic in years on the interurban lines, a record for volume was set on Monday when automobiles were eschewed in favour of the friendly confines of the on-track interurban cars. Fighting the first ten heaviest days of the snowstorm was estimated by the company to have cost $18,000.

During 1927 in North Vancouver, a committee had been formed to study the idea of a bridge at First Narrows, and work was well underway on a tunnel under Lonsdale Avenue to connect the Harbours Board railway from Second Narrows Bridge with the Pacific Great Eastern Railway. The new bridge had begun to make an impact on the north shore: 1927's 1,944,227 fares paid were down 34,799 from 1926; riders travelling on transfers issued in Vancouver were down 3,541 to 189,249. Nonetheless, greatly increased numbers of hikers had been carried on Sundays and holidays. Across the whole of the B. C. Electric system, 1927 had been a year of further gains, 75,113,022 riders being carried. The business of freight hauling had set records in 1927: 481,690 tons (exceeding 1913's high!) brought in a revenue of $898,478.

By early 1928 it was apparent that New Westminster's viability as a deep-sea port was assured. During the first two months of the year, thirty-two freighters, ten more than during the corresponding period of 1927, had docked in the wharf area of New Westminster, some of these using the B. C. Electric dock. This business did, of course, boost the company's freight business, which was going better than ever, three freight crews having been added in the first two months of 1928. On the New Westminster street car system, the Highland Park-Sixth Street line now required five rather than four cars, and the Edmonds-Sapperton line had been speeded up by seven minutes. Even the Burnaby Lake line was busier, two-car trains operating frequently

Victoria's street cars assumed this revised schedule on October 24, 1927. (Victoria Archives)

REVISED STREET CAR SCHEDULES
(Subject to Change Without Notice)

WEEK DAYS

Route and Route Number	First Car from City A.M.	Last Car from City P.M.	First Car from Terminus A.M.	Last Car from Terminus P.M.	Frequency of Service
OAK BAY (1)	6.00	11.40	6.20	12.00	See Footnote A.
OUTER WHARF (2)	6.10	11.46	6.19	11.55	12-Minute Service all day.
CLOVERDALE (2)	6.16	11.40	6.25	11.49	12-Minute Service all day.
FERNWOOD (3)	6.10	11.46	6.19	11.55	See Footnote B.
BEACON HILL (3)	6.16	11.40	6.25	11.49	
ESQUIMALT (4)	6.00	11.45	6.22	12.07	15-Minute Service all day.
GORGE (5)	5.54	11.42	6.12	12.00	12-Minute Service all day.
HILLSIDE (6)	5.52	11.40	6.04	11.52	See Footnote C.
FOUL BAY (6)	5.52	11.40	6.10	11.58	
JOSEPH STREET (7)	Terminate at Joseph Street on above route.				
UPLANDS (9)	5.56	11.41	6.18	12.03	15-Minute Service all day. See also Footnote D.
MT. TOLMIE (10)	6.15	11.15	6.35	11.35	30-Minute Service all day.
BURNSIDE (10)	5.55	11.25	6.05	11.35	30-Minute Service all day.
	P.M.	P.M.	P.M.	P.M.	
WILLOWS (11)	12.03	8.03	12.18	8.18	See Footnote D.

SUNDAYS

	A.M.	P.M.	A.M.	P.M.	
OAK BAY (1)	7.50	10.50	8.10	11.10	See Footnote E.
OUTER WHARF (2)	7.50	10.50	8.00	11.00	See Footnote F.
CLOVERDALE (2)	8.10	10.50	8.20	11.00	See Footnote G.
FERNWOOD (3)	9.05	10.45	9.15	10.55	20-Minute Service all day.
BEACON HILL (3)	9.05	10.45	9.15	10.55	20-Minute Service all day.
ESQUIMALT (4)	9.00	10.45	9.22	11.07	15-Minute Service all day.
GORGE (5)	9.05	10.45	9.25	11.05	20-Minute Service all day.
HILLSIDE (6)	8.50	10.50	9.02	11.02	15-Minute Service all day.
FOUL BAY (6)	8.45	10.45	9.02	11.02	15-Minute Service all day.
UPLANDS (9)	8.56	10.41	9.18	11.03	15-Minute Service all day.
MT. TOLMIE (10)	9.15	10.15	9.35	10.35	30-Minute Service all day.
BURNSIDE (10)	8.55	10.25	9.05	10.35	30-Minute Service all day.
WILLOWS (11)					See Footnote H.

— A —
6.00 a.m. to 7.00 a.m., 20-minute service. 7.00 a.m. to 12 noon, 10-minute service. 12 noon to 8.00 p.m. 7½-minute service. 8.00 p.m. to 11.00 p.m., 10-minute service. 11.00 p.m. to 11.40 p.m., 20-minute service.

— B —
6.10 a.m. to 12.05 p.m., 12-minute service. 12.05 p.m. to 8.05 p.m., 10-minute service. 8.05 p.m. to 11.55 p.m., 12-minute service.

— C —
12-minute service between the Hillside and Foul Bay termini throughout the day.

— D —
6-minute service between the Hillside terminus and Joseph Street between 8 and 9 a.m., and from 11 noon to 8 p.m.

— G —
A 15-minute service during this period, which in conjunction with the Uplands cars (9), gives a 7½-minute service during the same period to the Willows. First car from the Willows (Special), 6.11 a.m.

— E —
7.50 a.m. to 8.30 a.m., 40-minute service (Special). 8.30 a.m. to 10.50 p.m., 20-minute service.

— F —
7.50 a.m. to 9.10 a.m., 40-minute service (Special). 9.10 a.m. to 10.50 p.m., 20-minute service.

— G —
8.10 a.m. to 9.10 a.m., 40-minute service (Special). 9.10 a.m. to 10.50 p.m., 20-minute service.

— H —
This route will be served by the Uplands cars (9) all day on Sundays.

For details of early cars on Sunday mornings, see next page.

A 1927 view of the entrance to Stanley Park. Street cars still looped around Alberni and Denman streets. The loop still used today by buses was yet to come. (Vancouver Public Library)

between Carrall Street and Hastings Road, and additional locals also finding a place for themselves.

The Fraser Valley line depot at Milner was closed as an agency and train order station and its order signal set at "clear" on April 1. (Nearby Langley Prairie station had sapped most of its necessity.) Thus, the number of full-fledged operating railway stations on the line had been reduced to seven: Cloverdale, Langley Prairie, Clayburn, Abbotsford, Huntingdon, Sardis, and Chilliwack. (The Milner station was soon demolished, replaced by a more typical shelter station.) The Lulu Island line acquired another passenger interurban car on April 25 with the reconstructing of Saanich line passenger-mail car 1501 back to its former passenger-only shape and number, 1216.

An analysis of Vancouver's system reveals the following patterns for 1927:

	Name of Line	Length in Miles	Car Mileage	%	Revenue Passengers	%
1	— Fairview (inner and outer)	5.7	896,674	9.3	6,545,877	11.6
2-3	— Davie-Main	6.4	942,969	9.8	6,904,499	12.2
4	— Grandview-Fourth Avenue	7.6	1,382,964	14.4	8,950,096	15.8
5	— Robson-Broadway East	5.2	803,711	8.4	5,781,454	10.1
6-7	— Fraser-Kerrisdale	12.1	1,271,686	13.3	7,015,085	12.4
8	— Hastings Park (Powell Street)	3.7	303,968	3.3	1,571,946	2.8
9-10	— Victoria Road-Stanley Park	7.4	682,014	7.1	3,550,016	6.3
11	— Joyce Road-Stanley Park	7.1	402,535	4.2	1,943,449	3.5
12	— Kitsilano	2.5	182,926	1.9	945,812	1.7
13-14	— Hastings East-Dunbar	10.3				
13-15	— Hastings East-West Point Grey	11.1	1,884,285	19.9	10,227,053	10.0
13-16	— Hastings East-Sasamat & 10th	9.3				
17	— Oak-Marpole	6.3	244,025	2.6	1,072,029	1.9
18	— Sixteenth Avenue	1.6	87,033	0.9	346,866	.6
	Main Street South	1.2	75,844	0.8	142,498	.3
	Nanaimo Street	1.9	106,738	1.1	328,523	.6
	Hastings East Extension	1.9	110,189	1.1	362,044	.7
	Grandview bus		82,565	.9	284,375	.5
	University bus		85,243	.9	465,892	.9
	Chartered		1,899		8,877	
	Observation		9,389		16,467	
	Race buses		5,367		6,266	
			9,562,024		56,470,124	

The table above includes the statistics for the King Edward street car line in those of the 6-7 line. The Oak-Marpole, Sixteenth Avenue, Main Street South, Nanaimo Street, and Hastings East Extension runs were handled by one man street cars.

No. 2 went north on Main Street only to Twenty-fifth Avenue; No. 6 went north on Fraser Street only to Forty-ninth Avenue and west on Forty-first only to East Boulevard; and No. 9 operated only between Forty-fourth Avenue and the post office.†

† Harland Bartholomew et al, *A Plan for the City of Vancouver British Columbia Including Point Grey and South Vancouver and a General Plan of the Region 1929* (Vancouver, B.C.: Vancouver Town Planning Commission, 1929), p. 136.

This late-twenties photo shows car 389 moving north on Government Street and leaving the provincial government's Parliament Buildings behind for the federal government's navy yards at Esquimalt. (B.C. Hydro)

The success of the B. C. Electric having caught the aggressive attentions of eastern Canadian investors, it became, with much negotiating, a Canadian company on May 19, after thirty-one years as a British one, with the incorporation of the B. C. Power Corporation Limited on that date. It had purchased the preferred and deferred ordinary shares of the B. C. Electric; thus Robert Horne-Payne and his colleagues had been succeeded by Herbert Holt and A. J. Nesbitt as the company's principal directors, but the B. C. Electric name remained intact, as did Kidd and the managerial corps.

A fire that had ignited in the kitchen of the Langley Hotel on May 21 quickly spread through the building and out onto the B. C. Electric's adjacent Langley Prairie station and freight shed, destroying them both, as well as much of the centre of the town. The two-hour conflagration had cost the B. C. Electric alone $30,000, but by the beginning of July, the company had completed a new, larger station and a new freight shed. It had also been in May that the construction of the dam at the outlet of Alouette Lake was completed. Inter-lake tunnel, generating plant on the west shore of Stave Lake, 10.6 miles of transmission line between the Alouette and Stave Falls plants: the Alouette aspect of the B. C. Electric's power system was complete.

In North Vancouver, the Capilano line had long transported holidayers and tourists to the Capilano suspension bridge, hung precariously across the Capilano River somewhat over a half mile north of the street car line's terminus. A second bridge was added on July 2 about a mile farther upstream (where Cleveland Dam is today). This remarkable $10,000 structure was 250 feet long and swung 425 over the second canyon of the river.

New Westminster had been experiencing a new boom — building permits for the month of July would reach a record high — and the commencement on July 16 of the building of what would be its greatest dockside facility, Pacific Coast Terminals, added authentication to the city's importance as an ocean shipping port. The spade used for the ground-breaking ceremonies was the same one used for a similar ceremony almost twenty-one years earlier to inaugurate the interurban line to Chilliwack.

An institution was mourned on August 2 with the death of Carrall Street station's popular depo

The interurban system in 1928 was inter-changing freight in the following fashion:

Connecting Railway	Station
Canadian Pacific	*New Westminster*
Canadian Pacific	*Carrall Street*
Canadian Pacific	*Granville Street*
Canadian Pacific	*Abbotsford*
Canadian Pacific	*Huntingdon*
Canadian National	*New Westminster*
Canadian National	
(via G.N.)	*Granville Street*
Canadian National	*Chilliwack*
Pacific Great Eastern	
(via C.P.)	*Granville Street*
Vancouver Harbour	
Terminal (via C.P.)	*Granville Street*
Great Northern	*New Westminster*
Great Northern	*Granville Street*
Great Northern	*Cloverdale*
Milwaukee Road	*Huntingdon*
Northern Pacific	*Huntingdon*

The Granville Street connection (where a B. C. Electric office was situated) was located just east of Granville Bridge and the original station of the Lulu Island branch; the C.P.R. called this same connection Drake Street interchange. The Great Northern connection in Vancouver was, of course, at the east end of the south shore line, Granville Street the nearest B. C. Electric office.

master, George W. Ross. Upon his arrival in Vancouver in 1910, the Boer War veteran had joined the C.P.R.'s police force prior to becoming the B. C. Electric's depot master at New Westminster. When the new station opened in 1912 at Carrall Street, Ross was there with his huge, friendly voice, aiding customers and employees alike.

Summer on the Chilliwack line had seen the construction of a 2,000-foot spur from near where Reclaim station would be opened on September 23, over half a mile west of Kidd, down onto reclaimed Sumas prairie to serve the crop producers of the area. Then on August 21, special interurban trains transported about a thousand people from Vancouver and New Westminster to gather in the hop harvest. On the Burnaby Lake line, Hastings Road station had been renamed Douglas Road at the request of Burnaby municipality to conform with its renaming of this old thoroughfare.

In New Westminster, the steepest section of Twelfth Street, between Fifth Avenue and the bottom of the hill, had received full-width, curb-to-curb pavement and the company's track, new 93-pound rail, all completed on November 7. This short, difficult stretch had been as treacherous for motorists, with its patchy pavement only on the east side of the street, as it had been for interurban operations before the Highland Park cutoff. Remarkably, street car service over this stretch

The second Langley Prairie station, today the site of a parking lot. (E.L. Plant photo)

had been shut down only between August 21 and 23, buses shuttling between Fifth and Queens Avenue on Thirteenth Street. On September 14, Graham Avenue at Sixth Street became a stopping point for street cars, and two weeks later Seventeenth Avenue (just two blocks north) did likewise.

In Vancouver, a new wye and passenger loading area had opened on September 11 on Boundary Road, north, at Hastings, a veritable wedge having been deftly carved out of the hillside in the midst of Boundary. At this time, 250 street cars were in service during the maximum rigours of afternoon rush.

September was also the month of farewell for Robert Horne-Payne, the action-oriented dreamer and motivator who had done so much to make the success of the B. C. Electric possible, a success that had brought about his retirement through take-over four months earlier. Though he had suffered a stroke which kept him an invalid at Brentwood, near London, he had remained the leader, a strong and able bulwark who personified the vigour and vision of the B. C. Electric. Chairman of the B. C. Electric throughout its entire life until

Well-beloved Carrall Street station master George W. Ross stands at far right in this congregation in and around car 53. (Mrs. D. Corson photo)

The new wye at Boundary Road off Hastings Street. (B.C. Hydro)

its acquisition by B. C. Power, he had personally raised and sent out millions of dollars of British capital for the development of British Columbia. Horne-Payne would die within the space of a few months, on January 30, 1929.

Sapperton disappeared on October 8. Approved by residents of that district and New Westminster's city council, it was henceforth to be known as North Westminster. At the end of the month, the company revealed that a record had been set for interchanging freight cars over a one month period, 1570: with the C.P.R., 801; N.P.R., 407; G.N.R., 202; C.N.R., 122; Milwaukee Road, 30; and P.G.E., 8. L.C.L. business was really irrelevant now; the big freight revenue stemmed from whole car loads!

The busiest intersection for street cars, interurbans, and automobile traffic alike, Vancouver's Main and Hastings streets, began an experiment on October 18 with the introduction of automatic traffic signals. But when streets were not busy other problems were wont to arise. Street car operators in New Westminster received a dash of advice from superintendent W. H. Elson on November 8:

"Some Car Operators on the last trip for the night, when taking their cars to the barn, are running at excessive rate of speed, which must be discontinued, immediately. There is no necessity for this — schedule speed must not be exceeded, and, any Operator detected in this will be severely dealt with."

Another active intersection in Vancouver, Main Street and Broadway, had found helpful simplification its lot, starting on December 14, when a newly-laid curve and cross-over tracks enabled street cars from Broadway East to head north to the Mount Pleasant barn without running a traffic-stalling wye operation at the intersection.

In North Vancouver, street car and ferry patrons at the foot of Lonsdale found their westward travel pattern altered on November 29, the day the Pacific Great Eastern Railway terminated its money-losing service to Whytecliff. Out on Lulu Island, the race track at Lansdowne had become Vancouver's airport in 1928, used by the Aero Club of B. C., B. C. Flying Club, and military and commercial aircraft.

During the year, the Fraser Valley line had seen its Chilliwack substation doubled in capacity. By

Interurban
AND
Motor Coach
Trips
FROM
VANCOUVER

British Columbia Electric Railway Co.
B.C. Rapid Transit Company

(Geoff Meugens)

this time there was a substantial settlement of Mennonites, largely from Saskatchewan, Manitoba, and Mexico, in the Yarrow area. They created a village patterned after their old Russian villages, and brought in lumber for their first houses and buildings on the interurban line. Such business certainly contributed to the B. C. Electric's record-shattering 487,896 tons of freight hauled in 1928. Ridership during the year was up even farther, to 77,063,656.

On the last day of 1928, George Kidd retired as president of the B. C. Electric, to be replaced on New Year's Day by W. G. Murrin. The same day the municipalities of Point Grey and South Vancouver became part of Vancouver, the city thereby attaining its completed geographical size. For riders this amalgamation soon meant the end of paying a second fare at Vancouver's former city limits.

Special operations of interurban trains were always a feature of the lower mainland system, imposing sights whenever they roamed out of the regular territory and onto the street car lines. One example in the early part of the year was a daily special train, run in the morning from Hospital Street on the Sapperton line. It brought 350 pupils, from Richard McBride school, which had been destroyed by fire, into New Westminster, to Technical and Central schools.

Ordered by the Board of Railway Commissioners to give half-hourly service on the Burnaby Lake line until December 31, 1929, the B. C. Electric began delivering it on February 11, from New Westminster at 5:30 a.m. and from Vancouver at 6 a.m. until the last trip at midnight. On Sunday, service from New Westminster began at 7 a.m., 8:30 a.m. from Vancouver.

The contract for the construction of the B. C.

Car 240, resplendently red painted, swings off Douglas Street onto Fort Street for its journey to Foul Bay, soon to be laundered to Gonzales. (Fred Hall collection)

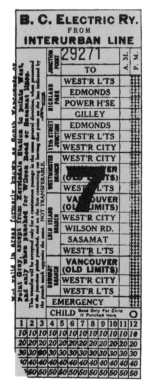

An interurban transfer from 1929, immediately following the amalgamation of the municipalities of Point Grey and South Vancouver with the city of Vancouver. (Ken Hodgson collection)

Forebay station on the remote Jordan River line in 1929. The parties of Canada's governor general and B.C.'s lieutenant-governor make up the excursion group. (J.M. Elliott photo)

Electric's new dam two miles above Ruskin was awarded on February 21 to Stuart Cameron & Company Limited. The first task was the temporary relocation onto an immense wooden flume of Stave River to enable the dam to be constructed. Three power shovels, overhead cableways, and narrow gauge steam trains were used for this work, which would not be completed until November. The second task was the relocation of 3.47 miles of the Stave Falls railway, beginning 1.82 miles north of Ruskin, and finishing 0.56 miles from Stave Falls. The total length of the Ruskin-Stave Falls line would become 6.21 miles.

The contract for this work had been awarded to Vancouver's Ellis Cotton Company, whose bid of $134,736 had been the lowest of nine. The completion of the new line by mid-September was imperative for its transporting of materials for the later stages in construction and the building of the power plant. The original line would become submerged by the lake (to be named Hayward on March 1, 1932, after R. F. Hayward, head of the old Western Power Company of Canada) which the new dam would create. The new railway line, to lie neatly above the projected level of the lake, required the movement of about 170,000 yards of earth, hard pan, and rock. Nine trestles (three thousand lineal feet of trestle work), 1,800 feet of culverts, and forty acres of clearing were necessary, with two hundred men providing the effort. All the while, the lower end of the line was hauling materials and men up to the new dam site from Ruskin.

On the Fraser Valley line a portable substation had been added at Kennedy to boost the ability of the locomotives to haul heavier loads up the long hill from the east end of Fraser River Bridge. A test run with two 970-type locomotives pulling 650 tons showed that they could maintain a speed similar to that they formerly attained with less than half that load. Freight business over the line was such that another crew had had to be created for it, as another one also had been for the Lulu Island branch. Effective March 15, the Fraser Valley line's Craigs station had been moved half a mile west to the Worrall Road crossing.

By March in North Vancouver, concern had been widely expressed over the large number of automobile accidents and run-aways on Lonsdale Avenue, a growing problem for the community during the last three years. In April, the B. C. Electric requested permission to operate one man street cars in North Vancouver, but was, at least for the moment, rebuffed, this time by the street car crews who insisted that such equipment was unsuitable for the special conditions of North Vancouver. On April 24, the Harbour Board's tunnel under Lonsdale (constructed at the insistence of North Vancouver's city council), linking its railway from Second Narrows Bridge with the P.G.E., was opened with the running of a special seven-car train. It was pulled from Vancouver's C.P.R. depot by a Harbour Board locomotive over the bridge and through the tunnel, Governor-General and Viscountess Willingdon adding lustre to the celebration. (They had recently visited the power development at Jordan River, enjoying a ride on the little railway there as well.)

In Vancouver, a new fare of seven cents (four for twenty-five cents) for the entire amalgamated area of the city came into effect on April 15. (In August, fares at ten trips for seventy cents would come into effect in Point Grey only.) On the same day, New Westminster's Sixth Street car line acquired yet another stopping place, Fourteenth Avenue.

An impasse of almost two years' duration for the Great Northern Railway came to an end on May 1 with the cooperation of the B. C. Electric Railway. The G. N. had been anxious to abandon its Abbotsford-Kilgard segment, but found that the lively presence of the Clayburn Brick Company at Kilgard made it impossible to obtain permission to do so from the Board of Railway Commissioners. To withdraw, the G. N. was forced to lease the line at a low rate to the brick company, and provide rails for the B. C. Electric to build a spur to it from its line eight-tenths of a mile east of Abbotsford at mile 40.08.† "Kilgard Spur" curved gradually eastward at an upward grade of one and a half percent, joining the "Kilgard Brick Yard Railway" one mile east of the Great Northern's trestle over the B. C. Electric and C.P.R. lines to Huntingdon. Each of the two transfer (or interchange) tracks at the Abbotsford end of the spur had already been equipped with derails. (The C.P.R. played a major role in hauling the brick company's trains, often employing a 4-6-0 steam locomotive such as number 527.) On October 4, Kilgard would officially be designated a B. C. Electric station, number 357. (G.N. had abandoned it on April 30.)

Steveston station was closed permanently on May 20 as a freight station and train order office, although trains continued to register there. Freight billing and car reporting would be handled from Marpole. Tickets, rather than being sold at the Steveston station, would now be sold at the store of Tom Leslie, who also began attending to the company's light and power business. Elsewhere on District 2, Dominion Mills station on the Marpole-New Westminster line was moved nine hundred feet westward to Doman Road, effective on May 23. Two days earlier, a new Westinghouse motored and controlled interurban car, 1312, had made its appearance. (Its heavy trucks and powerful motors, combined with a car body lighter than that of the original 1300s, would make it a speedy favourite of motormen, although the absence of a toilet would normally keep it off the Chilliwack run.) This car had been languishing as passenger-mail car 1500, after earlier incarnations as "Coquitlam" and 1209.

With the arrival of June came the annual $8,000 weed-spraying attack on the tracks of the interurban lines. The equipment consisted of four flat cars and a locomotive pushing; the leading car contained the sprinkler system, the second a 10,000-gallon water tank, and the third and fourth the concentrated German-made, weed-killing chemical; a system of pipes connected the tanks. As the train puttered along at ten miles an hour, the water and chemical would be mixed in the tank of the front car in a ratio of eight to one; 12,000 gallons of chemical were usually spent in a summer's work.

June was also a month of picnics. One of the largest annual picnics occurred on the fourteenth in 1929, when the school children of Surrey municipality took the long, exciting trip to Stanley Park on spacious, comfortable Chilliwack line interurban cars.

The twelve-month period ending on June 30 showed the B. C. Electric to have carried 78,500,381 passengers on 15,619,612 passenger car miles, and to have paid wages totalling $5,995,183 to over four thousand employees. It had 105,908 light and power customers, and 45,044 gas customers. The bus fleet had grown to twenty-three, the trucks and trailers to twenty-one, but the interurban rail freight system had 456 express, freight, and service cars of its own.

The B. C. Electric and the province's Department of Railways had laboured manfully over a new Chilliwack line schedule, and on July 1 it went into effect. The company with good reason had argued for a service reduction: in 1921 the Chilliwack line had carried 451,793 passengers, but in all of 1928, only 264,739 had used the service. In the new schedule, daily locals to Jardine and Friday morning trains to Mount Lehman were absent; a Friday morning special, not on the timetable either, would run as a passenger extra under train orders to Jardine. The three daily eastbound trains left Vancouver at 8:20 a.m. (No. 2), 1:25 p.m. (No. 4), and 6:20 p.m. (No. 8), arriving at Chilliwack at 11:40 a.m., 4:50 p.m., and 9:35 p.m.; westbound, they departed Chilliwack at 8:05 a.m. (No. 3), 1:40 p.m. (No. 5), and 6:20 p.m. (No. 7), arriving at Vancouver at 11:15 a.m., 4:55 p.m., and 9:35 p.m. The milk train (No. 500) left Vancouver at 2:05 p.m., arriving at Chilliwack at 6:15; every morning it (No. 501) left Chilliwack at 8:10 a.m., getting to Carrall Street at 12:55 p.m.

The summer brought a significant flourish to Steveston's repertoire (and to the B. C. Electric's interurban business) with the inauguration of steamer service by the C.P.R. from its new dock at the foot of Seventh Avenue, the extreme west end of the town. The six-year old, 165-foot *Motor Princess* would give a number of years of effective automobile ferry service between Steveston and the Vancouver Island town of Sidney. (It ended its runs for the first summer on September 8.)

In view of the successful mushroom business built up over the years, and the role that the B. C. Electric could play in its success, the entrepreneur's name appears almost apologetically at the end of this order of July 6 to Burnaby Lake line crews:

"The 8.30 District 4. Train from New Westminster will pick up a box of mushrooms at Cariboo Road for Vancouver, and deliver to Carrall Street baggage room, where it will be billed up. The shipper is Mr. Money."

For New Westminster there could scarcely have been a more melancholy year than 1929, the final year of its renowned Provincial Exhibition. The glorious Septembers ended on July 14 with a conflagration that destroyed a number of the exhibition buildings at Queen's Park. True, a last

† W.H. Elson, Superintendent, "Bulletin to Train Crews, Agents, and All Concerned," 1 May 1929.

fair would be held in September under massive tents — Britain's Right Honourable Winston Churchill would open it — but it would be the last one of a unique, tradition-rich series. The exhibition's demise prefigured that of the B. C. Electric's New Westminster street car system, almost as if the annual excitement pumped renewing life into the street car operation.

By July 16 in Vancouver, new double track had been laid on Oak Street between Broadway and Sixteenth Avenue, as it had been earlier on the four blocks of Hastings Street between Main and Princess streets, where the devil strip between the two tracks had been so narrow that passing street cars and interurbans had actually scraped. In New Westminster, the double track on Columbia Street at the curve at the foot of the hill east of Leopold

Place still gave street cars, interurban, and freight trains the same sort of difficulty. For this location, there were standing orders for there to be no passing whatsoever.

If the hard working, well-equipped Chilliwack line had been experiencing difficulties luring passengers, the Great Northern, by contrast, was destitute. It finally admitted defeat by discontinuing all operations on its line to Huntingdon from Cloverdale on August 1,† shutting down the six stations: Lincoln, Otter, Aldergrove, Sarel, Abbotsford, and Huntingdon. (The G. N. segment from Cloverdale west to Ladner had still time to contemplate its impending doom.)

In New Westminster, the massive Pacific Coast Terminals, with its newly developed refrigeration plant served by the B. C. Electric, opened officially

† G. Fern Treleaven, *The Surrey Story*, (Cloverdale, B.C.: Surrey Museum and Historical Society, 1970), II, p. 59.

on September 2, bringing to New Westminster wharf-railway-storage facilities that almost alone made the city a world-class port. During August and into September, four of the former Saanich line interurban cars, 1240-1243, had their 1200-type, General Electric motors and controls removed, as well as their trucks. With the substitution of heavier trucks and the more powerful Westinghouse motors and controls (identical to the equipment on the Chilliwack line interurban cars), they were renumbered 1314 to 1317, respectively.

It had taken only eighteen days, and on September 27, new double track was ready for use on Granville Bridge. During the tearing up and laying down, street cars and interurban trains had been diverted, one track at a time, over Kitsilano trestle and past the shops. Three days later, a new passenger stopping point was initiated on the Fraser Mills line at Paradis Road, about 1,400 feet west of King Edward Avenue, on the north side of the line, but connected to the stopping point by a trail. On October 1 came one of the first cutbacks of mail service; both Elsona and Fraser Arm ceased on that date to be served by the Central Park line.

November and December were unusual months for the company on the lower mainland. A serious water shortage in all the lakes had brought with it severe power shortages, causing street car operations to be reduced, and those on Powell Street, Nanaimo, Main Street South, and Hastings Extension to be supplemented by buses. On November 16, six one man cars began

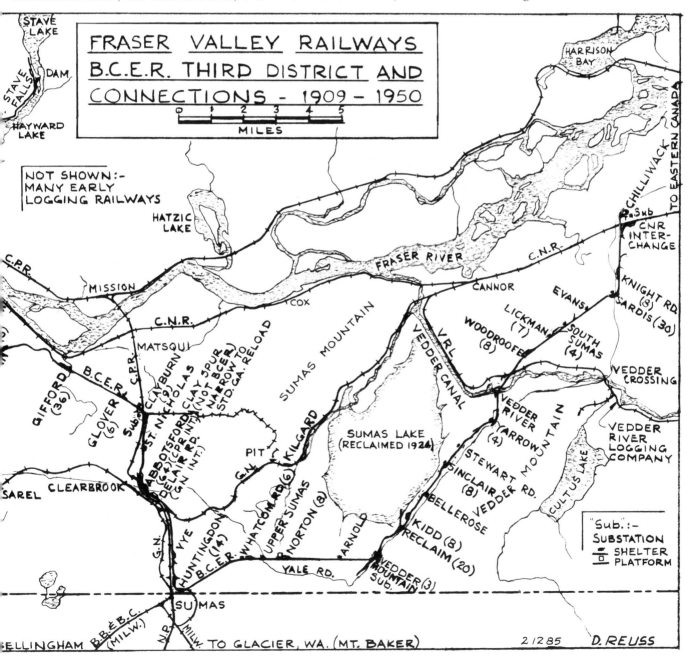

operating on the Powell Street line.

During November, fifteen new steel frame cars, numbered 364 to 378, had been delivered to the company by Canadian Car & Foundry. These front entrance cars, with centre and rear exits, were all at work on the Victoria Road and Robson lines by December 3. Attractively furnished (the most comfortable seats yet seen on B. C. Electric street cars) and equipped with all the latest safety features, these "steel lightweights" could be operated as two-man cars — the conductor's booth was to the right of the centre exit — or one man cars. The latter mode is the one the B. C. Electric really had in mind with this street car order; all fifteen had indeed been painted with the large cream cross over the front exterior below the motorman's window to denote their one man character and each came equipped with an air whistle, at the rear under the platform, to be used as a back-up signal when the car was being operated as a one man vehicle.

In Victoria, B. C. Electric bus service had begun in December, the Haultain Street line, with three U-type Yellow Cab buses, each capable of carrying twenty-three passengers. Fifteen-minute service was run on weekdays, half-hourly on Sunday. Another of the former Saanich interurban cars had been reworked in December, its number becoming 1318, from 1244; it was the only one of the former Saanich passenger cars to retain its original wooden pilots. Two losses during the year had been baggage-express car 1702 and line car L.3, both scrapped because the company had more of each type of vehicle than it required.

A further gain in prestige and credibility for the B. C. Electric's interurban freight program came in 1929. The Board of Railway Commissioners had held in the case of "Canadian Pacific and British Columbia Electric Ry. Cos. v. Canadian National Rys. et. al." (36 CRC 263) that the B. C. Electric was subject to Dominion jurisdiction by nature of its operations, and upheld a previous order requiring the establishment of through rates with the Canadian National Railway.

In Vancouver during 1929, 68,000 more street car miles had been operated than in 1928. One could stand on weekdays for the hour between 4:30 and 5:30 p.m. at the corner of Hastings and Main streets and watch 324 street cars make their way through this intersection. Then there were the interurban trains which did likewise; the Central Park line had twelve two-car trains in operation at this time, the Burnaby Lake line fewer, fifty percent of its passengers riding no farther than Horne-Payne. Special street cars were much in evidence: a special car always waited at 5 p.m. at Richards and Drake streets to take men from the C.P.R. shops directly through the city and out to Victoria Drive; and special cars were always in place at about the same time for the men coming from the engineering works and mills in the vicinity of Connaught Bridge. With all the construction of new homes in Kerrisdale, it was that line which carried full loads in both directions in rush hours, downtown workers riding one way, building trades workers the other. What one saw only with difficulty was the staff of seventy-five men on duty, day and night, in the car barns, keeping the street cars fit for operation.

The street cars and their interurban kin carried 77,694,731 passengers during 1929. Freight revenue had soared $100,000 above that of the previous year, approximately one million dollars of the company's annual freight revenue now deriving from interconnections with the big steam railways. Each year was one of new records; 533,391 tons of freight hauled was yet another!

V
1930-1938:
Adjustments and New Directions

Frost heaves in the track of the Chilliwack line in January 1930 were probably the most severe ever, particularly at various points around Vedder Mountain, and just east of Mount Lehman station. In addition, ice, caused by running water, lay across the track at many places, necessitating cautious running.

March saw the inauguration of the Bay Street substation on the southeast corner at Government Street in Victoria, and, on the fifteenth, the completion of the bridges over Stave River to the new power house site, enabling the shipping of machinery and fittings by rail directly to the building. (Concrete pouring for the 195-foot high,

420-foot wide dam began on April 26.)

March 15 was also the day all fifteen of the new street cars went into regular service on the Victoria Road (Victoria Drive today) line exclusively; on the following day a pattern emerged which had them deployed as one man cars during regular hours, two-man cars in rush hours. On the same day, Fourth Avenue street cars began making the turn onto the new double track on Alma Street (completed on January 30), terminating their runs, alternately, at Broadway.

On the Fraser Mills line, interurban cars continued to stop in front of the packing house despite the fact that a new station had been

B.C. Electric acquired fifteen of these street cars, 364 - 378, from Canadian Car & Foundry in 1929. Though ultimately destined for one man use, here, at Stanley Park on February 19, 1930, 366 works as a two-man car. (B.C. Hydro)

inaugurated in May nearby at the east side of the Brunette River. In North Vancouver, May was the month of yet another attempt by the B. C. Electric to establish one man cars, but both city and district councils were adamant in their opposition. For the Chilliwack line, competition with its sister buses was by now a fact of life; although the interurban and bus operations covered different in-between territory, they did meet each other in the larger centres, where the buses used the interurban stations as their stations. The timetables of both services had felicitously been arranged so that interurban and bus departures alternated. Although the fare for travelling by bus was higher than by interurban, a special combination Chilliwack return ticket allowed the holder to travel either by interurban or bus.

In Vancouver, two new passing sidings on the Oak Street line, at Thirty-seventh and Fifty-seventh avenues, were placed in service on May 16, allowing a fifteen-minute rush hour service to be run. (The spur on the south side of Forty-first was eliminated.) Morning rush hour service in May required 238 street cars in Vancouver, exactly one hundred more than in 1919; afternoon rush hours needed 265 cars, up ninety-two from 1919. On May 23, the company initiated a new bus service from Fourth and Alma to the beach at Spanish Banks.

Summer brought out the *Motor Princess* to ply again her thirty-five miles of seascape between Steveston and Sidney, twice each day. Though she was due to dock at Steveston at 11:45 a.m. and 6:45 p.m., her purser would telephone Mr. Leslie if a late arrival was expected, and Mr. Leslie would notify the conductors of interurban trains No. 255 and No. 309 to hold their trains for as long as ten minutes to embark passengers from *Motor Princess*. By the end of July, the Lulu Island line's interurban roster consisted entirely of twelve formerly-named cars, 1201-1208, 1211, 1212,

1215, and 1216. The Fraser Valley line was still the proud possessor of 1300 to 1311, the 1400s, 1600s, and 1700s, while Central Park-Burnaby Lake shared the 1300s, in addition to the 1000s, 1217-1238, and 1312-1318. (Later in the year, 1239 would receive the same reworking her Saanich mates had earlier acquired, becoming 1313, but baggage-express car 1703 would be scrapped.)

In Victoria, line car L.5, snow sweepers S.58 and S.59, auxiliary service car S.61, and locomotives 905 and 906 were in support of its fleet of forty-nine street cars, 22, 23, 125, 126, 128, 188, 189, 192, 194, 231-240, 250-259, 381-390, and 400-409.

Vancouver's Joyce Road street cars had begun operating over double tracked rails on July 16 between Earles Road and Joyce on Kingsway. (For the five weeks of track work, buses had given service over this section.) During the summer, the special loading platform for company employees on Hastings Street directly opposite the head office had been removed. As everyone else, they now boarded street cars at the corner of Carrall Street, thereby eliminating the surge of employees at crucial times through the loading concourse of the interurban trains.

On the north side of the Fraser River, closely hugging the main line of the C.P.R., the first bus on a once daily, round trip basis began a service all the way to Agassiz and Harrison Hot Springs on August 1. In Vancouver, August 15 marked the first day of one man street car service on the Kitsilano line, albeit only on Sundays.

September was the month of relocating tracks on Front Street in New Westminster, but it was also the time for the Chilliwack line to disentangle itself from the Great Northern Railway at Cloverdale. By September 26, the G. N. had removed its portion of the interchange with the B. C. Electric; the Chilliwack line's portion, beginning west of the Pacific Highway and curving north, remained intact to be used as a team track and for storage.

When an out of control freighter knocked one of the spans of the Second Narrows Bridge into Burrard Inlet on September 19, business surged for the street car-ferry combine, but no one could have predicted that more than three years would elapse before its reconstruction.

In Vancouver, the company set two new bus lines in motion on October 6: McDonald Street (between Broadway and Forty-first Avenue) and Granville Street South (between Forty-first and Marpole). With this act, the B. C. Electric indicated with certainty that the building of street car lines was a phenomenon of the past. Here were two lines which were logical candidates for street car operation: they were relatively lengthy; they did not jut probingly into new areas, as did the Grandview, U.B.C., and Spanish Banks lines; and they made street car connections at either end.

In New Westminster, the hill on Sixth Street

Car 164 at rest after skidding backwards down Sixth Street hill to the sharp turn at Carnarvon Street, October 21, 1930. No serious injuries resulted, and the car was rebuilt for further New Westminster service. (New Westminster Public Library)

Three of the Chilliwack inter-urban coaches, brought to Ruskin over the C.P.R., wend their way on November 18, 1930, filled with dignitaries, to the official opening of the new Ruskin power plant. (B.C. Hydro)

worked its black magic once again on October 21. Street car 164, proceeding uphill at 9:30 p.m., had just stoppped near Cunningham Street when the accumulation of leaves with moisture on the rails caused it to begin sliding backwards. By the time its downward flight had reached the sharp turn at Carnarvon Street, two blocks below, its speed was too great for a successful negotiation of the curve, which it jumped, coming to rest half on its side, having crashed into a light and trolley pole. Although 164's windows had had to be broken to rescue its twelve passengers, fortunately none of them, or operator Archie Bomstead, had been seriously injured. It was obvious that more derails were necessary on Sixth Street than those already in place.

Although its new generator had turned over for the first time on October 14, the Ruskin power plant was officially dedicated on November 18 by B. C.'s Lieutenant-Governor R. Randolph Bruce. Bruce, together with Premier S. F. Tolmie, senators, civic and municipal officials, businessmen, company president Murrin, Kidd, and Sir Frank S. Barnard travelled to Ruskin by special train, and to the new power installation on a three-car interurban train of wood 1300s especially brought over for the occasion. The Lieutenant-Governor, by passing his hand over a silver ball, set the huge generator (the largest then in physical dimensions in Canada) into operation, sending out 47,000 new horsepower of electric energy. The new plant used the fall of 130 feet

which takes place in the water from the time it leaves the Stave Falls installation, three and a half miles upstream, until it is spent just north of Ruskin. The completion of the Ruskin plant also meant more power for the railway line, whose electric supply was always weaker as it travelled south from the existing plant at Stave Falls. Now a separate installation had equalized the railway's supply.

Just ten days later, the 18,000 horsepower fourth unit at Jordan River was inaugurated, the culmination of five years of activity. At both Jordan River and Ruskin, the B. C. Electric's railway

Summer 1931 at Kitsilano Beach, where the new loop at the foot of Yew Street is traversed now by one man street cars. Stanley Park lies to the left across English Bay, whose beach is dominated by the Sylvia Hotel. (Vancouver Public Library)

West on Hastings Street from Richards Street in 1931. Car 298 is doing the short run on Main Street, as No. 2, to Twenty-fifth Avenue only. Spencer's on the right became Eaton's and, latterly, Sears. (Vancouver Public Library)

Soon to begin their fifth decade of service, New Westminster's street cars followed these patterns. North Westminster would soon revert to Sapperton. (Bob Webster collection)

operations had worked magnificently to make these power projects even possible. With construction out of the way, the two railways resumed their unassuming, normal routines, the Jordan River line tending the precious flume and looking after all the company's needs, and the Stave Falls line servicing its area, be it company business, a little local traffic, or hauling logs — and always lured to Ruskin to meet the big C.P.R. trains and view the majesty of Mount Baker to the east, mystically capping the Fraser River.

The line to Chilliwack was feeling some of that same pressure that had dragged the Saanich line into oblivion, but, of course, the B. C. Electric had been able superbly to nurture its freight hauling capabilities, offsetting, at least for the company, the knowledge that 1921's figure of 451,793 passengers carried on the line had dropped to 211,012 for 1930. The effects of the depression were already making their impact, but it was a fact that each of the previous eight years had seen a drop in patronage on the Fraser Valley line. For the first time since 1923, total B.C.E.R. ridership fell, though slightly, to 76,113,550, still the third highest total in the company's history. Because of the freight operation's close ties with the steam railways, it too felt their struggles, tonnage hauled falling back to 454,111, not aided in the least by the temporary lack of business being experienced by the lower mainland's lumber mills.

One man street cars went into service on Vancouver's Joyce Road line with the completion of a new loop east off Joyce Road just south of Kingsway on January 16, 1931. What with the increase of road traffic everywhere, New Westminster's busy Columbia Street too had begun to react to the years-old activities of the Burnaby Lake and Fraser Mills interurban trains. Their speed was felt to be excessive though their maximum was legally twenty miles per hour, and motormen had instructions to make free use of the foot gong as they approached each intersection. It became mandatory on March 25 for all inbound street cars, interurban cars, and freight trains to come to a full stop at the east end of Albert Crescent (the intersection of Columbia with the approach to the bridge), interurbans emitting two blasts from their whistles, and street cars gonging.

On February 17, the Burnaby Lake line's Crown Avenue station was eliminated and a new one inaugurated, Gilmore Avenue. Here was another minor adjustment for a line whose Burnaby length had still not attracted enough settlers and residents to make operation through this lushly sylvan area worthwhile.

Vancouver's Kitsilano line became an all-week one man street car operation (rather than on Sundays only) with the completion on March 16 of a new loop at the foot of Yew Street, thereby cutting the line back one block from Vine Street. On the same day, the Victoria Road line also went completely one man, even eschewing the added conductor who had performed during rush hours on the newest series of street cars.

During March, two of the St. Louis interurban cars, 1237 and 1238, had thrown off their lighter

1200-style motors and trucks to join the earlier-converted Saanich interurban cars as heavy duty 1320 and 1319, respectively, all eight of them known as "converteds" to their crews. The heavily travelled, finely-scheduled Central Park line thus had access to twenty-one powerful interurban cars, 1300-1320, with which it could maintain a fast, effective service. As well in March, street cars 128, 192, and 251, deemed surplus in Victoria, had arrived in Vancouver, following the already transferred 125, 126, and 194.

Regular street car service ceased over the new track on Alma Street between Fourth Avenue and Broadway on May 23, giving way to the Spanish Banks bus which now had as its new eastern terminus Broadway and Alma; the lack of patronage on this five-block stretch had not warranted the sophistication of street car service. Fourth Avenue street cars again terminated their run at Fourth and Alma, as they had for so many years.

Chilliwack's substation began supplying electricity to the Agassiz-Harrison area on May 11, a result of the company's purchase fifteen months previous of the interests of the Chilliwack Electric Company. The company at this time was receiving $5.20 for each load of sack mail hauled by train No. 2 to Chilliwack in the forward compartment of one of the three 1400s; other trains received $3.20 for hauling mail. Meanwhile, the B. C. Electric had inaugurated on May 3 a summer bus service on Sundays only between Vancouver and Hope at a $3.00 return tab; and three days a week the company operated its two eight-passenger Studebaker sedans from the front door of Chilliwack's Empress Hotel all the way to Kamloops.

The Fraser Mills line added another station to its repertoire on June 15, Blue Mountain Road. This newly opened road approached the track from the north, touching it at a point about one thousand feet east of the Laminated Materials crossing. The bridge over Brunette River, inevitably a spot of some concern for the company, was improved during the year with the superimposition of considerable quantities of fill.

In Vancouver, July 1 had been the appropriate day for the inauguration of the summer-only Kitsilano Beach bus line between the Kitsilano line's loop and Broadway and McDonald Street. Two days later, the B. C. Electric took great pride when the first baseball game in Canada was played under artificial night lighting: 8:30 p.m. was the time; Athletic Park (later Capilano Stadium), at Fifth Avenue and Hemlock Street, was the venue. It was July 19 when Joyce Road street cars began their summer-only service (it would actually carry on until November 22) to Stanley Park on Sundays, and on July 22, Vancouver Airport opened on Sea Island, a stone's throw from Marpole, with a three-day air pageant seen by

thousands, many of them travelling across the bridge from Marpole by bus. Lansdowne track could get back to horse racing exclusively, although cabins were beginning to be built by the track as a form of hedge against the encompassing depression. A vigorous July ended, for the company at any rate, with the initiation on the twenty-ninth of the new street car loop at Victoria Road and 54th Avenue.

Commencing August 13, track relaying on Sixth Street hill in New Westminster necessitated special operating modes, sometimes with merely one way operation, but during most of the day a fairly regular kind of service. The presence of the old Tramway route east off Sixth and past Queen's Park to Columbia Street allowed for some ingratiating variations. During the day, a staff (to be passed from operator to operator) was left in the telephone booth at Sixth Street and Fourth Avenue. Inbound cars from Highland Park did best by not running too fast from Cliffs south to Fourth, thus avoiding a long lay-over at Fourth, waiting for the up-hill street car to labour its way to the meeting point.

For Vancouver's exhibition, August 22 to 29, the company had installed bus service between Kingsway and Slocan Street and Hastings and Renfrew streets. In North Vancouver, improvements had been made to the Lynn Valley line's track on Grand Boulevard between Keith Road and Nineteenth Street, and to the special trackwork from First Street south at the ferry terminal. The North Road area north of Sapperton (and toward Port Moody) was still anxious for a street car or interurban service at this time. Burnaby's council had gone so far as to request neighbouring Coquitlam municipality to ask for tenders for a bridge over the Brunette River at North Road (the boundary between the municipalities) in the hope that the B. C. Electric would be encouraged to lay tracks across it, and even farther.

Within a month of each other, three stations on the Chilliwack line were shut down as agency stations and train order offices. Since the Clayburn Brick Company's heavier involvement during the previous two years with its operation at Kilgard, its 1904-established Clayburn plant, somewhat over a mile east of Clayburn station, had been closed down. For the B. C. Electric this closure meant a falling off of receipts at its Clayburn agency from $2,298.36 in September 1929 to $137.64 in September 1931; passenger ticket sales and milk and baggage revenue had remained much the same, the losses being sustained in freight interchange with the brick company's own railway line from the brickworks which had connected with the Fraser Valley line in a southward-turning wye just south of the station. (At its peak, the six-mile railway's roster had consisted of two locomotive, six hopper cars,

B.C. Electric's Clayburn station to the left leads on to Vancouver in this north-looking photo. Both stations have been gone for more than half a century. (B.C. Hydro)

twenty dump or construction cars, ranging from three to five yards capacity, and six flat cars, all engaged in working in the clay and shale deposits east of Clayburn.) Clayburn station closed on October 31, soon to be replaced by a more conventional shelter-type station.

On November 30, the Cloverdale station also lost its status as an agency and train order office, its work load being added to that of agent R. F. Powell at Langley Prairie. Fortunately, the Cloverdale station was not demolished at the time, nor was the Sardis station — shut down on the same day — which was moved and became a dwelling. (Nine days earlier, the Great Northern had closed its Cloverdale station and its line west to Colebrook, on the Vancouver-Seattle main line.)

Although the B. C. Electric had carried 3,445,072 fewer passengers in the year ending June 30 than it had for the same period two years earlier, it had actually operated 772,101 more miles of street car, interurban, and bus services. During the year ending June 30, the Vancouver system had run 10,661,204 miles of service, the Victoria system 1,875,642, the combined New Westminster and interurban systems 2,803,605, and the North Vancouver system 397,909. Tallies for the month of October, compared with October of 1929, showed 544,139 fewer riders in Vancouver (only the Hastings Extension and Oak Street lines showed gains), 52,220 fewer in Victoria, 24,365 fewer in New Westminster, and 7,537 fewer in North Vancouver. In a comparison of the same months in regard to the interurban lines, only Burnaby Lake was up, by 4,049 riders; the Central Park line was down 37,414, the Lulu Island line 36,252, the Fraser Mills-Queensborough line 16,507, and the Chilliwack line 8,166.

In Vancouver, newly double tracked Granville Street between King Edward and Forty-first avenues was opened for service on November 8. The downward trend of the depressed time had continued during 1931 with only 343,320 tons of freight hauled and 74,249,659 passengers carried.

Ridership would dip even lower in 1932, and "depression schedules" would come into effect around the whole system. The Lulu Island line's Sunday and holiday service was reduced from every fifteen minutes to half-hourly; on the Burnaby Lake line, base service was hourly, with Vancouver-Horne-Payne service half-hourly on Sunday between 8:30 a.m. and noon. Although the municipality of Burnaby had passed a by-law for a bridge over the Brunette River, and the B. C. Electric's franchise provided for a line to be built on North Road from the connection with the Burnaby lake line at North Westminster (Sapperton), could it really have been believed that the times themselves would allow this oft-mooted extension to materialize?

In New Westminster, a new stop for Highland Park-Sixth Street cars on Pine Street at Third Avenue went into effect on March 15. Beginning May 27, the Sixth Street-Fourth Avenue-Queens Park belt operation began running only the clockwise direction after 7 p.m. and on holidays, its counter-clockwise circuit being maintained by outbound Highland Park-Sixth Street cars. Queensborough interurban line's few stops were increased by one on June 1 with the institution of a stop some six hundred feet before the terminus, immediately in front of the new Italian Community Hall.

In Vancouver, nine of the 700-series leading units had begun working the Grandview-Fourth Avenue line on March 16, but on Sundays only. Two days later, "Sasamat" disappeared as a destination for street cars, replaced at the request of residents by "West Point Grey." On May 16, the street car service which had been running south on Granville Street to King Edward Avenue and east to Oak Street began operating through to East

By year's end, British Columbia sported one automobile per 6.2 persons, and the new Dominion census revealed the following population statistics:

Vancouver	246,593
Victoria	39,082
Burnaby	25,564
New Westminster	17,524
Saanich	12,968
North Vancouver (city)	8,510
Surrey	8,388
Richmond	8,182
Oak Bay	5,892
Chilliwhack (municipality)	5,802
Langley	5,537
North Vancouver (municipality)	4,788
Matsqui	3,835
Esquimalt	3,274
Chilliwack (city)	2,461
Sumas	1,812
Fraser Mills	616
Abbotsford	510

Boulevard instead. It used double ended street cars until July 16 when the new Kerrisdale loop was opened on the south side of Forty-first Avenue just east of East Boulevard, allowing single ended cars to take over. One double ended, one man street car shuttled on beautiful King Edward between Granville and Oak. It was also on May 16 that four of the two-car 700-series "trains" went into morning service on Dunbar-Hastings East to cope with increased patronage in the Dunbar area.

Langley substation at Cloverdale had already become one of the garden spots of the town, but it was Sumas substation at Vedder Mountain, with operators E. Rippon and F. Marshall, which had over the years grown to be the best known and most visited. The May 25 issue of the *Abbotsford, Sumas, and Matsqui News* describes the results of their work:

"Over 170 different varieties of high-grade roses — including several specimens imported direct from Ireland, and said to be the first of their kind to bloom in B.C. — are to be found in the garden which has not involved great expenditure, for practically every specimen growing so wonderfully is the result of a clever graft of a bud upon the briar of a wild rose carefully transplanted from a nearby hillside. While Mr. Rippon is specializing in roses, he has not overlooked the beauty of humbler flowers and carnations and gladiolas are generously represented in orderly borders around the building.

Colleague of Mr. Rippon in operating the substation plant is Mr. Marshall, formerly of Burnaby. In three years he has become so smitten with flower-love that his rock garden, set around a small mountain stream flowing past the north side of the building, also makes a bid for the

admiration of visitors. Not only has Mr. Marshall utilized what was formerly a barren, rocky plot, which very few would visualize as having floral possibilities, but he is also terracing the mountain side with rockery and Alpine plants. Fronting the power station, even an abandoned piece of rock-strewn trackage has been beautified with a miniature fishpond and grotto.

Granted these men have the leisure with little distraction of city bustle to disturb their effort. But to find in that out-of-the-way spot such unostentatious love of floral beauty, expressed in painstaking labor, is surely a most heartening aspect of human character!"

The new timetable for the Fraser Valley line went into effect on June 12. It speeded up the running times of all three passenger trains and retained the milk train, and the Friday market day and Saturday "owl" specials. Though train no. 2 left Vancouver at 8:25 a.m., its 1700-type baggage-express car had already left at 8:10 a.m. for New Westminster to be loaded there and joined with the passenger section upon its arrival at New Westminster for the run to Chilliwack.

The Chilliwack line's freight trains were run at night, one in each direction, six days a week, each with a five-man crew. Leaving Kitsilano (10 p.m. was the usual time), often with locomotive 972 or 974, a District 2 crew until the previous year took the freight right to Huntingdon. With the inception in the previous year of District 3 crews only on District 3, pro-rating was no longer necessary as a compensating process.

Substantial yards were located at Cloverdale, Langley Prairie, Abbotsford, Sardis, and Chilliwack. The nineteen spur tracks on the line were handled by a flying switch: one man would tend the switch, and another would ride the car behind the locomotive, cut it off when sufficient speed was attained, and then climb to the top of the car to set the hand brake when the car was clear of the spur. Since nine of these blind sidings (only one entrance switch) were without "yard limit" board protection, trains had to be protected in accordance with standard rules at these locations. From nine to twelve of the line's spurs would regularly be switched on each trip, each way.

At the point where the line crossed the C.P.R. at Clayburn, the Chilliwack line was governed by an interlocking plant which could only be operated when one of the crew entered the shed containing the control over the diamond crossing. He would be locked in until his train had passed over the block, and should anything have happened to the train while on the block, this crew member would be unable to leave the building until the crossing was clear.

Because of several heavy grades in each direction, freight trains were frequently required to "double," leaving a portion of the train behind with one crew member; in such instances, the conductor would ride the front portion alone and

DETAIL OF CHILLIWACK YARD
0 100 200 300 FEET
BCER

DEPOT ORIGINALLY HAD GLASS CANOPY OVER TRACKS.
BCER DEPOT
N
YALE ROAD
HOPE AVE.
FREIGHT SHED
SUB STATION
CAR BARN
SAND HOUSE
1st
2nd
NOTE: A SINGLE TRACK BARN REPLACED THAT SHOWN IN 1937.
CHEAM AVE.
YOUNG ROAD
3rd
CHILLIWACK EVAP. & CANNING COMPANY
4th
CHESTERFIELD AVE.
5th
TO VANCOUVER
BCER

Fronted by a nonexistent number 1334, this early thirties brochure covers the precise bounds of Sumas Lake with hop fields, a handy solution. (Geoff Meugens collection)

BCElectric INTERURBAN TRIPS
1334

set it out at the top of the grade. Occasionally, one of the 970s with two crew members aboard would join an eastbound freight as a pusher for the 2.6 percent hill to Kennedy, frequently even staying with the train and pushing, on its return westward, up the 2.7 percent grade of Mount Lehman hill from Gifford. Eastbound freights were sometimes split at Harmsworth; the first load would be put into the siding at Sperling, and then the second load would be retrieved. The same procedure would be repeated, using Bradner, yet farther east, as the point of connection. This Harmsworth-Sperling-Bradner "long double" coped with eastbound grades of 1.6, 2.2, and 2.3 percent. Westbound, the worrisome grade, in addition to the Mount Lehman climb, was the one from Sullivan (officially, Bear Creek hill) with a long 2.5 percent, finally mitigating to 2 percent before reaching Kennedy. Peculiarly-situated Abbotsford required a short, grueling 2.5 percent climb from the west, 1.5 percent from the east. It was during this year that the Chilliwack line's locomotives had been equipped with Kahlenberg Bros. model S.2 twenty-inch air horns.

July 16 saw the beginning of massive cuts in street car schedule frequency. Twenty fewer motormen and conductors in Vancouver alone were required, and only the Dunbar and West Point Grey lines escaped cutbacks. As incentive to riders, a $1.25 weekly street car pass (transferable!) went into effect on October 3. Victoria's was only $1.00. At the same time, the lead cars of the 700s worked solo during the day, attaching their trailer units only if absolutely necessary. (The 700s had recently been fitted with coupling devices superior to the original equipment.)

July 17 was a banner day for all downtown traffic in Vancouver, particularly for street car movements on Hastings and Powell streets. This was the day upon which C.P.R. trains on the old English Bay branch began using the new tunnel under downtown which connected the C.P.R.'s waterfront terminal facilities with its yards, shops, and roundhouse along False Creek. A forty-two years' headache had been almost miraculously lifted, eliminating from both crews and passengers the chief among downtown Vancouver travel tensions. July 1 had already seen the opening of a new bridge across False Creek, east of Kitsilano trestle, connecting downtown's Burrard Street with Kitsilano's Cedar and Cornwall streets. This splendid four-lane structure, called Burrard Bridge, had been built with the capability of carrying street car tracks on a second, lower level — alas, never needed.

None of this, however, prevented July from being one of the worst months in years for accidents to rolling stock. The three costliest — fortunately, there were no injuries to passengers — occurred on the sixth of the month in New Westminster when 164 tail-ended 323 just west of

Edmonds; on July 16 in Vancouver when 1315-1307 tail-ended 1314 at Main and Hastings streets; and on the following day in Vancouver when an empty 1204 clipped 972 on the way to Kitsilano barn. The company deemed these three major accidents to be entirely due to the negligence of the trainmen concerned. Superintendent Elson charged them with a lack of vigilance, stressing that "luck is a fallacy and will fail you every time. A man makes his own luck and you will never find a careful man in trouble caused through his own neglect." †

The Chilliwack line had its yard limit boards removed on November 9 at Sullivan, Cloverdale, Milner, Sperling, and Bradner; and on the thirteenth, a further revised timetable went into effect. No. 500, the milk train, left Vancouver at 4 a.m., arriving at New Westminster at 4:45 a.m. and at Chilliwack at 7:20 a.m. On the return, it departed at 8:10 a.m., arriving at New Westminster and Vancouver at 10:56 a.m. and 11:35 a.m., respectively. The major change was in the Saturday "owl" which had been leaving New Westminster at 4:05 p.m. for Mount Lehman; it now became a truer owl, sneaking east out of New Westminster at 12:15 midnight, arriving at Mount Lehman at 1:30 a.m., and finding its way back to New Westminster by 2:40 a.m.

The one man street car concept finally achieved reality on cold, wet December 1 in North Vancouver with the conversion of the No. 3-Capilano line, giving twenty-minute service (as before) with two street cars. Preparations for this much-debated move had been thorough: motormen had been brought over to Vancouver to practice becoming one man car operators on Renfrew Street, a line used otherwise only for special events; seven of North Vancouver's street cars were being revamped as one man cars at the North Vancouver barn, 150, 151, 154, 157, and 160-162; and car 160 in late November had made a special trip over the Capilano line piloted in turn by three employees who were already trained as operators. Aboard with them were, among others, company transportation assistant E. W. Arnott, traffic superintendent W. H. Dinsmore, and government inspector William Rae.

The North Vancouver public too had been very much part of the preparations as company inspector George Sharman had carried on demonstrations aboard regularly scheduled street cars. On one such, the ferry-wharf-bound Capilano car he was riding had been just rounding the corner from Twentieth Street onto Fell Avenue when he announced:

"'Ladies and gentlemen. You are riding in a one man street car. Some of you are sceptical as to the safety of this car under one man operation. I am going to speed up the car going down this hill, and we will conclude that the operator faints. Please keep your seats because there is not the slightest danger.'

A few dubious people became uneasy, but they retained their seats. The car speeded up. 'Give it full power,' said George. Then, as the car attained its highest speed, 'Now faint!'

The motorman fainted (apparently), releasing all the controls. Without any human assistance the car came to a fully-controlled stop, and at least a number of North Vancouver passengers were convinced of the safety of one man cars."†

All across the B. C. Electric's system, street cars were being equipped with chrome safety stanchions, for standees particularly, and the rear of each car was being fitted with a red tail light. In the company's light and power sales department, an agricultural division had been created for the purpose of studying and promoting the uses of electricity in agriculture. As a service to farmers in the Fraser Valley and on Vancouver Island, the company also had become involved in the sponsorship of a series of fifteen-minute radio (station CNRV) addresses on agricultural problems by University of British Columbia faculty members. These welcome safety and public relations measures did not obscure the fact that the number of passengers carried during 1932 had slid virtually to the 1920 level with 69,862,419 riders, and that freight tonnage of 249,285 had dipped lower than 1912's figure.

From February 5, 1933, interurban train dispatchers received a respite with the withdrawal of the necessity of Central Park line and Davie Street-Marpole local interurbans to acquire terminal clearances, in either direction. Conductors on the Marpole run, however, would continue to report to the train dispatcher at Marpole.

The snows of January had finally brought out old North Vancouver street car number 28 on the last day of the month to help clear the tracks and supply tools to the workers, who could not help noticing some of the car's former brilliance in the presence still of a few of its original plush seats.

The No. 2-Lynn Valley line commenced one man street service on March 1 with the same frequency as before, every twenty minutes, and three cars. Two weeks later, a new siding at William Avenue on Lynn Valley Road went into use, replacing the existing one at Fromme Road which was then dismantled; this new switch would allow for an easier maintenance of the line's schedule. On the No. 1-Lonsdale run, which would remain a two-man operation to the end, near side stops, replacing the far side ones, were put into effect on April 10, permitting street cars to make safer and better hillside starts and stops, especially with the proliferation of cross-street road traffic.

Cutbacks and unemployment swirled about the B. C. Electric in 1933, mirroring the times. In mid-January, twenty laid-off Vancouver motormen and conductors had been taken back into service, and

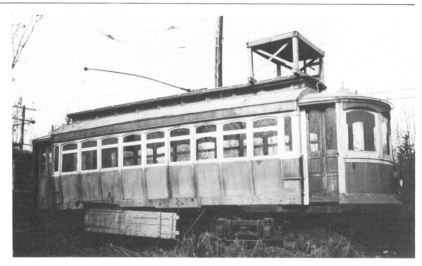

Once-proud street car number 28 finished its labours in North Vancouver as a line car. (V.L. Sharman photo)

as the year progressed the regular crew members took one day off in six to provide work for the men on the extra list. The B. C. government even moved the annual date for relicensing automobiles from the first of January to April 1.

On March 31, Langley Prairie and Huntingdon stations were closed as agency and train order offices, functioning as prepaid stations for freight and flag stations in all respects, but they continued to be stops for all timetable trains shown due to stop there. Langley Prairie's dispatch telephone remained in the waiting room, Huntingdon's in the baggage room. Beginning April 9, Abbotsford's station was closed on Sundays, the conductor of No. 7 locking the waiting room door on Sundays, and the conductor of No. 500 unlocking it. (Before long, Abbotsford station was also terminally reduced in status.) The conductors of these same trains began the identical procedure, but on a daily basis, with the Langley Prairie station on August 6.

In New Westminster, the coordination of interurban and street car movements, fine tuned to a nicety through the years, was invariably a source of wonder to newcomers. The Marpole-bound interurban train, as an example, would

† "Safe Control," *The B.C. Electric Employees Magazine*, May 1933, p. 1.

A commutation ticket for the Lulu Island line, with only a minimum number of stations conductor-punchable. (Bob Webster collection)

LULU ISLAND BRANCH 10 Ride Commutation Ticket	Marpole	Cambie	Rifle Range	Garden City	Brig-house	Blundell	Brass-comb	CITY LINES PUNCH HERE			
								25	13	1	JAN.
								26	14	2	FEB.
British Columbia Electric Railway Co., Limited								27	15	3	MAR.
Good for one continuous trip between								28	16	4	APR.
VANCOUVER and Station punched in margin.								29	17	5	MAY
Subject to conditions of contract								30	18	6	JUNE
FORM C. 3 *Void if detached*								31	19	7	JULY
49350 NO STOP-OVER ALLOWED *D.E. Buverin PRES.*									20	8	AUG.
									21	9	SEP.
									22	10	OCT.
	Steves-ton	Fraser Street	Argyle	Glen Lyon	20th St. West. Lr.	H' FARE PUNCH HERE			23	11	NOV.
									24	12	DEC.

always wait at Twelfth Street Junction for the street car coming down Twelfth Street hill from Edmonds; even if the car was late, but in sight below Sixth Avenue, the crew would wait for the operator to cozy his street car alongside their 1200.

On April 10 New Westminster's street cars and interurban cars ceased their stopping point at the main entrance to B. C. Penitentiary opposite the cairn. Three days earlier, planning had commenced for the elimination of the level crossing Twelfth Street made over the rails of the B. C. Electric and the C.P.R. on its way to Columbia Street, one block south, on which only the single track of the Queensborough line lay between McNeely Street and the Queensborough bridge. The one C.P.R. and the two B. C. Electric tracks together lay on what was then called Carnarvon Street. With completion of this massive project, in eighteen months' time, a brand new Columbia Street would lie adjacent to, and north of, these tracks. It would eliminate the level crossing, although there would be a continuing tussle at the east end, before reaching Eighth Street, where for a couple of blocks the two B. C. Electric tracks had to unite themselves with Columbia Street in preparation for their entry into the depot. Nonetheless, the gains were a boon to both rail and road traffic. At the same time, the Queensborough line's track was removed from old Columbia Street and relaid as the fourth track, farther south, on this impressively renewed rail and road entry into downtown New Westminster.

The inauguration of a morning newspaper on April 24, the *Vancouver News Herald* (replacing the *News*), meant the organization of interurban transportation to convey the news to all parts of the lower mainland, and with dispatch. Only the Burnaby Lake line was superfluous in this endeavour, the Central Park line taking the newspapers on its 5 a.m. trip out of Carrall Street, the Steveston car at 5 a.m. from Davie Street, the New Westminster (via Marpole) car at 5:30 a.m. from Davie, and the Chilliwack line earliest of all with the eastbound milk train from Carrall.

On June 1 the Marpole-New Westminster line gained a station with the induction of Sussex Avenue, four blocks east of Glen Lyon. The use of white flags as day classification signals on interurban trains operating on the double track lines, Central Park and Davie Street-Marpole, was discontinued on June 19; only "extras" on the single track lines would in future use white flags.

During the summer, Mount Lehman became an active shipper of prairie-bound loganberries, their crates carried by the Fraser Valley line to Chilliwack for transfer to the C.N.R. Summer was also the time of effecting a connection at Sardis between the morning interurban train to Chilliwack and the Cultus Lake-bound bus from Chilliwack, though ten minutes was the maximum

wait.

By mid-September, baggage-express interurban cars 1704 and 1705 had been forever separated from their unique milk train past. Their motors and controls had been removed more than two years previously for further work in 1319 and 1320, respectively, and now their radial bars were blocked for main line use only (no tight curves on city streets) and their body features coarsened; 1704 and 1705 had thus been newly prepared for almost two decades of service as crews' boarding cars. In New Westminster, Simpson Street, just south of the Royal Columbian Hospital, became a stop for both Burnaby Lake interurban trains and street cars on September 15.

In Victoria a couple of weeks later Spencer's did it again! To celebrate its diamond jubilee, the David Spencer department store leased the entire B. C. Electric system in Victoria and placed it at the disposal of the citizens of Victoria and district, free of charge. The peak of the free travel occurred between 4 and 6 p.m., when released school students joyrode from Outer Wharf to Mount Tolmie, Uplands to Esquimalt, and all other points possible. Some 70,000 guests were carried during this frenetic October 2, and each operator received a $2.50 scrip, negotiable at Spencer's store.

In October repairs were made to four of the

(Right and next page) Two advertisements from 1933 demonstrate the company's hydro thrust in the rural areas of the lower mainland. (B.C. Hydro)

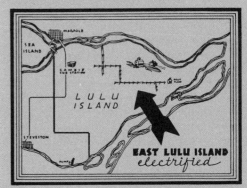

7 MILES OF NEW POWER LINES TO SERVE THE FARMERS OF EAST LULU ISLAND

EAST LULU ISLAND *electrified*

HAVE POWER EXTENDED TO YOUR FARM!

F 17-33

BRITISH COLUMBIA ELECTRIC RAILWAY CO.

SYMBOLS of PROGRESS

THERE goes the mail plane... Involuntarily we stop to look and wonder... The aeroplane is one of the most spectacular symbols of modern progress.

Less spectacular, but no less striking, is the progress being made in farm electrification. Many are taking advantage of the guarantee revenue basis for power line extensions offered by the B.C. Electric.

Ask your local B.C. Electric Light and Power representative how, simply by guaranteeing a relatively small monthly payment, a great many Fraser Valley farmers have had power extended to their farms.

★**Have Power Extended to Your Farm**

F 16-33

BRITISH COLUMBIA ELECTRIC RAILWAY CO.

Chilliwack line's bridges on Sumas prairie, those crossing Yale Road at Upper Sumas; McGregor crossing, half a mile east of Norton; Arnold's Slough; and the road just west of Vedder Mountain. By the end of the month, heaters had been installed (for the first time) in the vestibules of all the interurban cars, and attention was then turned to similarly equipping New Westminster's street cars.

Effective November 4, Canada's Board of Railway Commissioners gave Great Northern Railway's Vancouver, Victoria & Eastern Railway and Navigation Company permission to abandon its unused, decaying line of track between Colebrook and Huntingdon-Sumas. There were conditions, and G. N. readily complied with them.

A yet neater tightening of the New Westminster system occurred on November 18 when operators of No. 2 street cars, eastbound on Columbia Street for Sixth Street and Highland Park, began making a calculated connection at Leopold Place with New Westminster-bound Burnaby Lake interurbans. And on December 11, a new stop at Mission Avenue, just west of Burnaby substation, on the street car run to Highland Park was installed. On the Fraser Mills line, much needed crossing signs had been set up at Blue Mountain Road and at Fraser Mills. In Vancouver,

heavily used Hastings Street had had its double track renewed between Princess Street and Campbell Avenue by November 10.

On Monday afternoon, December 11, sleet, freezing as it fell, came driving out of the northeast, coating everything with a heavy wrap of ice, inches thick. The area between Abbotsford and Chilliwack was most affected, but the storm centred on the Fraser Valley line between Delair and Vye, where both high-tension circuits were practically destroyed and eighty sections of line were broken. Huntingdon to the south was the scene of extraordinary destruction. Company linemen worked through to Wednesday, when another storm struck, undoing most of the repairs already done. By the following day, power was restored to Chilliwack, as well as to the Sumas pumping station, the instrument largely responsible for keeping Sumas prairie from returning to Sumas Lake. On the following Tuesday, interurban car 1211 suffered considerable damage to two of its motors because of storm-related flooding on the Marpole-New Westminster line, which had its ballast washed out from under the track west of Glen Lyon.

The number of route miles run on the Vancouver system in 1933 was down 444,687 miles to 10,168,640; the Victoria system reached a further low of 6,117,329 passengers carried, 579,422 down from 1932; and freight hauled amounted to an incredibly low 218,776 tons. Only 63,190,419 passengers had been carried on the whole system, fewer than in 1912!

In Vancouver, 1934 began with the altering of the bottom rear step of street cars 329-355 to provide a wider tread and easier, safer rider access between each car's platform and the ground. On the Chilliwack line, the use of the train register at Jardine was abolished on January 27, and the telephone was immediately removed; this meant that Friday's westbound market train would have to report to the dispatcher from Milner, or at the first phone available. Effective February 3, Western Red Cedar Mills, between Rowlings and Kerr Road, became a station on the Marpole-New Westminster line (or as the company was beginning to call it, "Westminster-Marpole Sub-division").

By early February, the field change-over switch (shunt) equipment — which allowed for higher speeds — on the 1300s, 1400s, and 1700s had

(B.C. Hydro)

FARM SERVICE NEWS

A Magazine of Service published every month by the British Columbia Electric Railway Company for the rural residents of the Lower Mainland

B.C. Electric's weekly street car and bus passes were colourful productions, worthy of collecting. This Vancouver city example from 1934 was "not good on interurban cars east of Cedar Cottage or south of 22nd Ave.", (Norman W. Williams collection)

passing to the "cut field" positions (6 and 11 on the master controller) before the interurban train had reached its top speed in series position 5, or a speed of at least eighteen miles per hour at position 10 in parallel. This field shunt equipment was hardly relevant to the operation of these big cars on the Central Park line; the added zest would, however, be missed on their Chilliwack line adventures.

On February 8, the Chilliwack line initiated a new station, Vedder River, six hundred feet west of the bridge over the river. On the same day, the company took steps to replace five hundred feet of trolley wire, stolen from its installed position on the wye at Huntingdon! Later in the month, the reinforcing of the concrete floors of each of the line's five substations began; the floors had cracked and opened at the beams, sagging an inch or more between them. In early March, the company began constructing an electric power service line to supply electric light to sixty-seven

been eliminated by placing a blind gasket in the air line where it went into the switch. For almost two years, there had been an officially-expressed concern about the continuing occurrence of motor flash-overs, caused by some motormen

The routes taken by Vancouver's street cars through the downtown area followed this pattern in the summer of 1934:

1	— Fairview	— Main, Hastings, Granville
2,3	— Davie-Main	— Main, Hastings, Granville
4	— Grandview-Fourth Avenue	— Granville, Robson, Richards, Hastings
5	— Robson-Broadway East	— Main, Hastings, Granville
6,7	— Fraser-Kerrisdale	— Main, Powell, Carrall, Cordova, Granville
8,10	— Hastings Park-Stanley Park	— Powell, Carrall, Cordova, Granville
9,10	— Victoria Road-Post Office	— Main, Powell, Carrall, Cordova, Cambie, Hastings, Granville, Cordova, Carrall, Powell, Main
	(10 denoted summer only Stanley Park destination)	
11	— Joyce Road	— Main, Powell, Carrall, Cordova, Cambie, Hastings, Granville, Cordova, Carrall, Powell, Main
12	— Kitsilano	— Granville, Robson, Richards, Hastings, Granville
13	— Hastings East	— Granville, Pacific, Richards, Hastings
14	— Dunbar	— Hastings, Richards, Pacific, Granville
15	— West Point Grey	— Hastings, Richards, Pacific, Granville
16	— Sasamat & 10th	— Hastings, Richards, Pacific, Granville
17	— Oak-Marpole	— from Cambie and Hastings streets, via Cambie, Robson, and Connaught Bridge

This was the first summer that the interurban system's weed killing rig made its forbidding appearance on Vancouver city streets, annihilating the weeds on the Main Street South, Sixteenth Avenue, Kitsilano, and Oak Street lines.

Victoria's street cars used the following routes through downtown:

1	— Oak Bay	— Fort, Douglas, Yates, Government, Fort
2	— Cloverdale-Outer Wharf	— Government, in both directions
3	— Beacon Hill-Fernwood	— Douglas, Yates, Government
4	— Esquimalt	— Douglas, Yates, Government
5	— Gorge	— Douglas, Yates, Government
6	— Hillside-Gonzales (Foul Bay)	— Douglas, Fort
7	— Hillside-Joseph Street	— Douglas, Fort
9	— Uplands	— Fort, Douglas, Yates, Government, Fort
10	— Burnside-Mount Tolmie	— Fort, Douglas
11	— Willows	— Fort, Douglas, Yates, Government, Fort

houses located in the Mennonite settlement adjacent to Yarrow station.

February and March were months of track improvement work in Vancouver. So many passengers had complained about the rough-riding track on Forty-first Avenue between Balsam and Dunbar streets that 1,200 yards of new ballast was put in and the grade raised two inches. Fraser Street between Twenty-fifth and Thirty-third avenues received similar treatment, its first overhaul since the track had been laid. On Victoria Road, the rough track between Forty-fifth and Fifty-fourth avenues — street cars were even being damaged by its poor condition — acquired a gravel base for the first time. Even downtown's Main Street track would be relaid by August 8 between Powell and Hastings streets.

Superintendent E. Sterling began a crack-down late in March on interurban motormen who substituted their own private whistles for the two regulation ones already in place on each car. In April the iron telephone wire installed in 1910 on the Chilliwack line, now in very poor shape, began to be replaced by new copper wire, signalling improving communication.

Sapperton made its inevitable comeback on May 23, New Westminster's city council rescinding its resolution of almost six years earlier whereby the old, historic designation of "Sapperton" had been changed to mundane "North Westminster." Few in the interim had thought of the region as anything but Sapperton.

The Steveston interurban line's bridge over the

One corner of the exquisite garden of Clayburn substation is overseen by the substation's operator, Mr. McCullough, in this 1934 view. (B.C. Hydro)

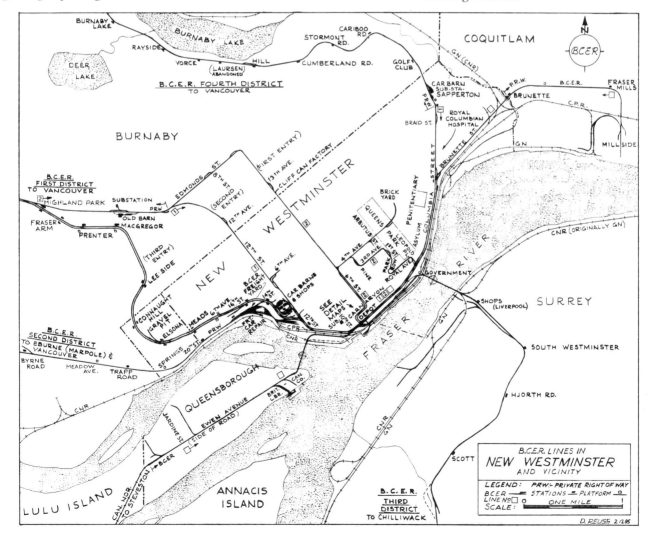

Completed in fall of 1934, the new four track right of way along the southern edge of Columbia Street gave the two tracks nearest the street to the B.C. Electric, the third one to the steam railroads, the outside one — here occupied by car 1232 — again to the B.C. Electric, its line to Queensborough, whence this interurban coach is headed. (Geoff Meugens photo)

north arm of the Fraser River was closed down from Sunday evening, June 3, until 2:30 p.m. on Monday, June 11, while almost one-quarter of the bridge was reconstructed at a cost of $10,000, in readiness for another racing season. Passengers had been shuttled to the Steveston line at Sexsmith from Marpole by bus. On June 30, over 1,500 horse racing fans were transported by the interurban cars to Lansdowne Park, 1,700 on July 2. The C.P.R.'s annual summer auto ferry service between Steveston and Sidney had gone into effect on June 16, leaving Steveston daily at 12:30 noon, and 7:15 p.m. daily except Sunday, arriving at Steveston daily at 11:45 a.m., and 6:45 p.m. daily except Sunday. Interurban crews again had been instructed to wait up to five minutes to help passengers make connections.

The reopening of Second Narrows Bridge — it had been out of commission since its damage by an out of control ship — on June 18 had necessitated an adjustment to street car schedules, now that buses were once again able to cross Burrard Inlet. A two-year tie renewal program — 3,000 ties would be needed — was begun in North Vancouver in June, as it was in New Westminster and on the four interurban lines.

New Westminster would require 3,500 ties; the Central Park line, 6,500; the Lulu Island line, 12,500; the Chilliwack line, 19,000; and the Burnaby Lake line, 4,500 — all at $1.00 apiece, except for the 6 x 8 x 8-inch ties used on the two city systems which cost $1.75 apiece. Vancouver, not to be entirely outdone, got around to installing heaters in the vestibules of its street cars, replacing its time-honoured, and worn, portable ones; and the interurban cars would have iron hand-holds installed to help riders negotiate their steep step wells.

Vedder Mountain station's decaying, ant-infested section house was replaced by a new one, and on July 1, despite the depressed times, Chilliwack's Dominion Day Cherry Carnival had much of the flavour of former times, especially with interurban train no. 7 impressively consisting of five interurban cars. Work was meanwhile continuing throughout the summer on the renewal of the substructure and deck of the Central Park line's Gladstone trestle. On the Marpole-New Westminster line, the station at Main Street (shared with the street cars of the Main Street South line) was rebuilt, the open portion of its shelter being cut away and the remaining section remodelled to make an enclosed shelter.

The B. C. Electric reached out in a different way in Vancouver on Sunday afternoon, July 8, with the inaugural concert at Stanley Park's new Malkin Bowl, attended by more than fifteen thousand people, given by the Vancouver Symphony Orchestra, sponsored by the B. C. Electric. Three more B. C. Electric symphony concerts would be presented during the summer at the same beautiful venue, and on September 24, the orchestra, again under company sponsorship, would inaugurate a weekly series of radio

Excluding the company's special railway operations at Jordan River and Stave Falls, the year ending December 31, 1934 revealed these figures:

	Passengers Carried	Track Route Miles	Track Miles Computed as Single Tracks
Vancouver	49,445,841 (including 17 buses)	64.15	119.77
Victoria	6,439,454 (including 3 buses)	23.39	40.55
New Westminster	1,767,931	15.08	21.00
North Vancouver	1,386,985	9.82	10.58
interurban lines	4,861,358		
Central Park line		8.59	23.40
Lulu Island line		25.69	45.83
Fraser Valley line		63.83	76.92
Burnaby Lake line		9.69	10.45
Total	63,901,569	220.24	348.50

Interurban line mileages exclude joint city track.

broadcasts.

In New Westminster, the costly realignment of the Columbia Street system west of the depot was brought to completion in the fall. On October 12, a new diamond was installed at Twelfth Street Junction, the meeting of the street car line from Edmonds with the interurban system. Three days later, McNeely Street, McInnis Street, Tenth Street, Carnarvon Street, Eleventh Street, and Royal Avenue were all instituted as stops for both Edmonds-bound street cars and Vancouver and Marpole-bound interurbans between the depot and the junction. Since eastbound vehicles would have had to deal awkwardly and dangerously with the presence of the adjacent C.P.R. track, they made only one stop, just before the depot at McNeely, when the C.P.R. line had veered off to its own station. By the end of the month, a small shelter station ($75 for labour and materials) was in place at Twelfth Street Junction.

At Sardis, the 1912-built freight shed and platforms had burned to the ground in October, and the company saw no need for rebuilding. On the Steveston line, Francis Road, between Blundell and Woodwards, began life as a station on December 6; and the breaking of one of 1709's axles near Bradner on the same day led to the finding that it, one of the baggage-express car's original axles, had travelled 784,170 miles. Eight other of the Chilliwack cars, 1301-1303, 1306-1308, 1401, and 1402, were creating difficulties at the two Clark Drive corners, at Hastings and Venables streets, since their bulky step wells did not clear at these curves; the only solution consisted in motormen taking care not to allow these interurban cars to pass each other on these two curves.

During 1934, a few more route miles had been run in Vancouver than in the previous year, but Main Street South street cars were running on dark evenings only to Marine Drive, unless there was an interurban connection to be made, to avoid an epidemic of armed robberies at street car terminals, and Victoria had plummeted to its lowest point, having carried only 6,053,441 riders on its street cars.

Eighteen substations were providing electric power for the street car and interurban operations, eight in Vancouver (Bodwell Automatic-Thirty-third Avenue, Dunbar Automatic, Earles Road, Fir Street, Haro Street, Horne-Payne, Main Street, and Point Grey); Bay Street in Victoria; and those in Burnaby, Chilliwack, Surrey (Cloverdale), Langley (Coghlan), Lulu Island (Cambie), Matsqui (Clayburn), New Westminster, North Vancouver, and Sumas (Vedder Mountain). The lower mainland's Lake Buntzen, Alouette, Ruskin, and Stave Falls power plants and the Vancouver steam plant were together producing 225,500 horsepower, while the Jordan River and Goldstream power plants and the Brentwood

steam plant on Vancouver Island were producing 44,075.

In addition to street car and interurban equipment, the company's freight-oriented rolling stock encompassed seven cabooses, twenty-seven service cars, and 343 freight cars of various types. Fares were still six cents (6 for 35 cents) everywhere except in Vancouver where seven cents (4 for 25 cents) was the going rate, 9 for 50 cents during slack times, Sundays, and holidays. Commutation tickets at 10 for 70 cents were available between North Vancouver and Vancouver, passengers transferring by the North Vancouver ferries.

Freight tonnage hauled plunged to 198,618 tons, the lowest figure since 1911. With regulations and restrictions introduced by the United States, the production of manufactured timber products by British Columbia mills and factories for marketing in the U. S. had been considerably curtailed. In addition, the adverse conditions rampant in Canada's prairie provinces had drastically cut back their need for lumber, farther decreasing the B. C. Electric's freight activities.

That the depression was a troubled time had not deterred long-needed repairs to rolling stock, right of way, and trackside installations. On the Chilliwack line many of its original shelters, platforms, telephone booths, tool houses, and freight sheds were rebuilt or refurbished for the first time during 1935. Warwhoop and Vye were two stations which had their deteriorated open portions cut away and the rest renewed.

Surely the worst time of snow and ice in the

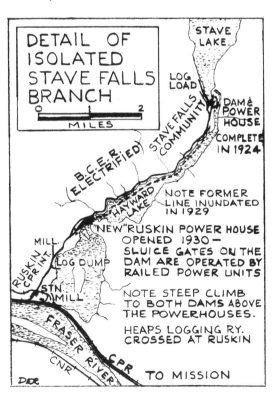

DETAIL OF ISOLATED STAVE FALLS BRANCH

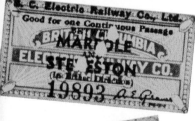

The silver thaw of early 1935 near Huntingdon. Two line car crews try to make sense of the massive confusion wrought by the ice. (B.C. Hydro)

A cornucopia of tickets through the years. (Ted Clark collection)

lower mainland's history began on Saturday, January 19, 1935, a colder day than any on that date in twenty-six years. On Sunday, a raging blizzard howled into action out of the east just after noon, smothering Vancouver with up to two feet of snow by early Monday; Surrey received up to four feet of snow on its already frozen ground on Sunday evening, and farther east at Gifford, the New Westminster-bound interurban train wisely left one of its two cars at the base of Mount Lehman hill, but still worried through swirling snow, toppling trees, and dangling wires for thirteen hours before reaching its destination. Drifts eight feet deep were already plentiful. Coated with ice, the trolley wire's arcing lit up the Fraser Valley with a dazzling light show. By Monday morning, rain was heavy in Vancouver, where street car operations were in limbo, except for Fairview inner. No trains whatsoever were able to operate. Throughout the Fraser Valley, swollen streams were washing out bridges and curdling roadbed into formless ridges of earth and gravel. Flooding throughout the valley caused loss of human life and the drowning of livestock.

On Monday the silver thaw began once more as rain turned to sleet in the Fraser Valley, freezing on power lines to a thickness of ten inches; by the afternoon, the crashing lines had isolated Chilliwack, silent and dark, even with its twenty-nine inches of snow. Neither C.N.R. nor C.P.R. were able to move, and would not for nine days.

By Tuesday the Serpentine flats around Cloverdale were flooded, and even the B. C. Electric's rails almost went under. On the Marpole-New Westminster line, a washout near Kerr Road brought that line to a halt, but by 11 p.m. the last street car line to achieve operation again in Vancouver, Dunbar, got going.

On Wednesday, there was no service on the Chilliwack line, although a train had started out for Coghlan, only to turn back at Sullivan when confronted with water to a height of two feet over the track as far as the eye could see. By Thursday, flooding had assumed yet larger

The Chilliwack line near Huntingdon during the record snows of January 1935. (B.C. Hydro)

proportions in the Fraser Valley, where so much snow already had lain on the ground before the rains had come, and by Friday, evacuation was the only solution for thousands as the reclaimed bed of Sumas Lake filled to a height of ten feet, even fifteen in places. Powerfully swollen Bear Creek demolished the Chilliwack line's bridge at that point but records were broken in rebuilding it by Monday, the twenty-eighth. Breaks were developing in the dykes along the north side of the newly paved Abbotsford-to-Rosedale highway across Sumas prairie on Friday, and at 10 p.m., a wash-out destroyed one of the company's new transmission lines, throwing the crucial, water-clearing Sumas pumping station out of operation.

On Saturday morning the rain abated somewhat, 12.96 inches having fallen in Vancouver since Monday. Tremendous snow slides had occurred at the eastern end of Vedder Mountain as well as at Mount Lehman and Kilgard. One snow cut was a mile long and seven feet tall along one side of the track. On Monday telephone service was restored to Chilliwack, and on Tuesday, the twenty-ninth, the first interurban train ventured east as far as Mount Lehman. On Wednesday, service was extended to Abbotsford, with freights only working to Huntingdon to pick up long-stalled goods at the border connection with the Milwaukee Road and Northern Pacific. Steam derrick B.3 was out, working ahead of augmented line crews who

were untangling wires, straightening poles, and dealing mile by mile with the devastation. Whole sections of track had been washed out and miles of trolley wire were down.

Summer 1935 is humming in this view from Glover east toward Clayburn. Only the bicycle suggests an intruder. (B.C. Transit)

The first bus to reach Chilliwack since January 21 arrived there — via Agassiz, however — on February 5. On the following day, power was restored as far east as Vedder Mountain substation, and on February 8, the high tension line to Chilliwack was back in service. The first interurban trip to Chilliwack since the beginning of the storm left New Westminster on February 11, and on the following day full passenger service resumed. It would be weeks before normal

B.C. Electric's last snow sweepers, S.65 and S.66, pose adjacent to Kitsilano shops — their place of building — in 1935. (B.C. Hydro)

A completed trainmen's wage ticket from 1935, crediting the crew of the milk train. (Ken Hodgson collection)

This form was used during the 1930s by the company for reporting its delivery of freight cars to other railways, in this case its own, leased Lulu Island line, the Vancouver & Lulu Island Railway. (B.C. Hydro)

electric service would once more be in place throughout the valley. More than fifty-two inches of snow would fall during the winter of 1934-35, all except fourteen of them in January during the period known even today as "the big storm."

A minor refinement, though not unnoticed, on February 1 in Vancouver was the introduction of "tear-off" transfers, replacing the "punched" variety in use for so many years. Also during February, ten further single end Vancouver city street cars had their Watson fenders (installed 1908-1912) replaced by H. & B. Life Guard fenders. Fog was still the generator of accidents on the B. C. Electric's system, a resounding example occurring on February 9 when interurban 1303 crashed into the rear end of street car 501 on Hastings Street at Vernon. The wyeing of street cars at Main Street and Fiftieth Avenue became a significantly happier occasion with the erection of a lavatory for motormen and conductors at that point on February 19; the rented one (five dollars per month) at Twenty-fifth Avenue could now be dispensed with!

Plummeting freight tonnage had prompted the company to sell some of its box and flat cars to

Timber Preservers Limited during the month, but adjustments to interurban passenger stops were often made. The inauguration of a new station on the Chilliwack line at Liverpool Road (six poles east of Shops), eliminated the stop at Shops, on February 23, whose station was moved to the new location. The Langley substation at Coghlan now became the final one of the five Fraser Valley line substations to be rehabilitated, at a cost of less than four thousand dollars; new switching equipment, better overload protection, and rewiring were the main concerns. By March 23, the 1,234-foot connection east of Huntingdon with the Milwaukee Road had been entirely removed in favour of more convenient operation right in Huntingdon-Sumas.

The storm of too-immediate memory had inspired the company to order the building of two new snow sweepers, S.65 and S.66, at a combined cost of $9,500, for the Vancouver system, and they were ready to go by fall, superbly crafted by the Kitsilano shop. To comply with a request by Vancouver's city council to reduce drafts and cold inside street cars, the company began in late April a program of replacing the open gates of the cars with new rear doors, also manually operated; street cars 241-249, 275-299, and 325 were to be the first so equipped, at a cost of $450 per car.

The month of May brought an extensive effort of repairs to track and paving of permanent track in New Westminster, ninety percent of this work on Columbia Street. It also signalled the demotion of baggage-express car 1701, a milk train stalwart, to camp outfit car, demotorized, for use by extra or bridge gangs on the interurban lines. The Burnaby Lake line's original platforms at Golf Links, Cariboo Road, Stormont, Cumberland, Hill, Rayside, Burnaby Lake, Vorce, and Murrin, by now dangerously decayed, were rebuilt during the month; and all along the District 2 interurban lines, broken fencing was replaced, particularly on Lulu Island. At fourteen places on the Chilliwack line, fifteen-year-old rail was being replaced.

On May 19 in Vancouver, Joyce Road and Victoria Road street cars began their annual Sunday-only runs to Stanley Park, rather than terminating at the post office at Hastings and Granville streets; and on June 15, the C.P.R.'s *Motor Princess* commenced its usual summer series of sailings between Steveston and Sidney. On June 11, a program of renewing 432 piles with timber posts (one hundred had been removed in 1934) on twelve-year-old Gladstone trestle on the Central Park line had gotten under way, preparing the trestle for another eight to ten years of good service. On the day following, the rebuilding of twelve of the line's more decrepit platforms was begun.

Though Vancouver had its Dominion Day parade on July 1, much of the action was elsewhere: ten interurban coaches, loaded to capacity, had run to the Chilliwack Cherry Festival, a great success attended by record crowds; and all interurban cars available were in use on the Lulu Island branch carrying record numbers to the races at Lansdowne. It too was cause for celebration that the company's freight business was improving, especially in the shipping of shingles to eastern Canada; a night freight was even operated on District 2.

In New Westminster, the stop on Columbia Street at Lorne, so close to Begbie and the depot, was wisely abolished on July 7 for both street cars and interurban in either direction. Later in the summer, the company offered the single fare as a return fare to Chilliwack line riders coming in to Vancouver for the exhibition. Intersecting the Burnaby Lake and Central Park lines, a bus service was inaugurated on August 28 along Renfrew and Slocan streets between Eton and Kingsway in Vancouver; and on September 22, the Joyce Road

and Victoria Road street cars returned once more to their post-summer post office ways on Sundays.

On the Fraser Mills line, an original length of track, the "Brunette spur" opposite the old Brunette Mill, was removed on November 14; and on December 17, Plywoods, a new station between Dominion Mills and Boundary Road on the Marpole-New Westminster line, was instituted. In New Westminster itself, the belt line around past Queen's Park and down Sixth Street continued to be operated in a counter-clockwise fashion by two street cars. Best of all, the recovery already perceived earlier in the year had continued to year's end, producing up-beat statistics, slight but encouraging: 64,455,164 riders had been carried in 1935, and 215,119 tons of freight had been hauled.

The *B. C. Electric Employees Magazine,* February 1936 issue, bestowed its tongue-in-cheek Order of the Woodpecker rather fittingly for an event that occurred on February 4.

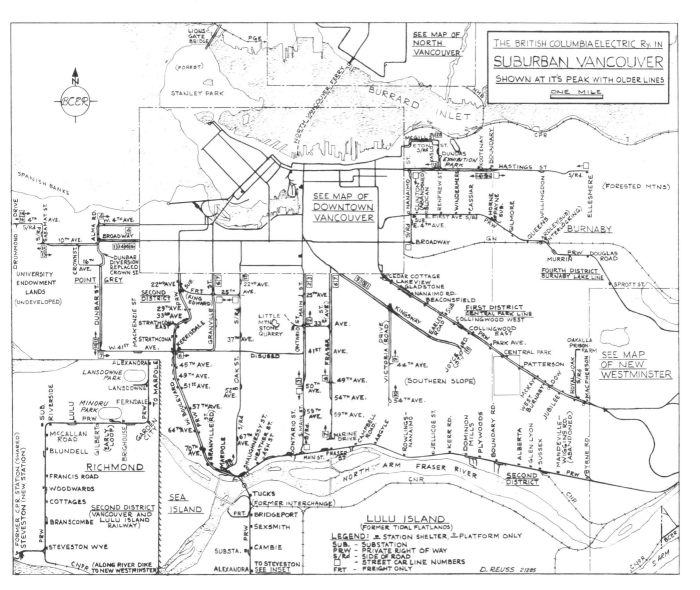

All is quiet at the end of the Capilano line as car 159 pauses before its run to the ferry wharf. (North Shore Archives)

(Whenever Granville Bridge was open, blocked, or out of commission, street cars using it were re-routed via Kitsilano trestle, Fir Street, and Fourth Avenue.) The citation read:

"On this occasion, the enemy attacked in formation of a broken axle on Granville street bridge and traffic was diverted over the Kitsilano trestle. In the darkness, the motorman carefully avoided the direct route back to Fourth Avenue, but led his passengers and those in succeeding cars an enjoyable trip around by the Kitsilano Beach loop, viewing the Kitsilano shops on the way back, and thus to Fourth Avenue. In the meantime Granville street bridge had been cleared, but the passengers were charged no more for the extra half hour spent in the cars."

An event of a completely different kind was the death on April 11 of Sir Frank Barnard, K.C.M.G., at his family home, "Clovelly," in Esquimalt. He had been an enormous force for British Columbia, not only furnishing the life for its street car systems in the late 1800s, but also serving as its distinguished lieutenant-governor, and even working with Sir Richard McBride to purchase two Chilean submarines for the protection of the province's coastline during World War I!

Mail was very much a business of the interurban lines, transported, in 1936, by the following trains:
District One
— 12, 4, 128, and 2's baggage car
— 3, 91, 7
District Two
— 230, 278
— 237, 285
District Three
— 2, 4, 8
— 3, 7
District Four
— 420
— 409

In Vancouver, some major street car line adjustments were actualized on April 16. The Hastings Park (Powell Street) No. 8 street car began operating to the post office only, and was renumbered 20; the Victoria Road cars took over the Stanley Park service, with the Joyce Road cars joining them daily after 9 a.m. The latter two lines were now drawing riders from such a large and well-settled base that the new connection seemed thoroughly inevitable, the Powell Street operation lapsing steadily into a run reasonably well patronized only during rush hours. At this time, a maximum of 248 street cars was in service on week days during rush hours on the Vancouver system.

New Westminster's May Day celebrations, its sixty-sixth, necessitated, as always, special operations by the company. The parade led down Eighth Street from the Russell Hotel to Columbia, along Columbia to Leopold Place, and thence to Queen's Park. Special late interurban cars left the park for Vancouver after the May Day Ball at the auditorium, and one late street car left via Sixth Street, Edmonds, and down Twelfth to the barn, while another headed down to Leopold Place and out to Sapperton before returning to the barn.

North Vancouver street cars 152 and 158, surplus there, were returned to Vancouver on May 27, and rebuilt into single end cars for Vancouver service. Saturday, June 13, once more brought the return of summer auto ferry service between Steveston and Sidney, one day after the Kitsilano loop was reopened on the east side of Yew Street, rather than on the west, providing for the desired increase in park space.

Members of the Employees' Amateur Gardeners Association, with their wives and families numbering about eighty, travelled by special interurban train on June 24 from Carrall Street (which now held a freight yard area of over twenty-four acres) to Vedder Mountain. The purpose of the expedition was to gather twenty-five sacks of moss and two tons of rock and shale for the rockery display, the crowning feature of the association's annual flower show in the B. C. Electric's store at Granville and Dunsmuir streets. Good food served at the substation by the Marshalls and Rippons and singing on the trips out and back helped create a day the participants long remembered.

Dominion Day in Vancouver signalled the beginning of two months of celebrations commemorating the city's golden jubilee. Following the parade, over 100,000 people thronged into Stanley Park, while thousands flocked to the beaches, particularly Kitsilano and English Bay. Horse racing at Lansdowne drew such crowds that a special ticket office was set up in Marpole station to sell only tickets for the race track. The newly unveiled Jubilee Fountain on Stanley Park's Lost Lagoon attracted more thousands, the peak time around 9 p.m. when as many as ten thousand onlookers surrounded the lagoon to be pleasured by the fountain's display of coloured lights. On July 2, the cornerstone of Vancouver's extraordinary new city hall at the corner of Cambie Street and Twelfth Avenue was laid by former Canadian Prime Minister R. B. Bennett. The ceremony was especially relished by Mayor Gerry McGeer, the dynamo who sparked the city hall concept, a brilliant refutation of the depression's power.

Effective Friday, July 17, a new station between Highland Park and Royal Oak, McPherson Avenue, on the Central Park line was initiated as a two-month experiment, loading and unloading to be done for this period from the middle of the street. If successful (it was), stations would be built (they were). At the end of the month, preliminary work having begun on the New Westminster side for the new high level bridge for road traffic only across the Fraser River, all street cars and interurbans on Columbia Street eastbound from the east end of Albert Crescent to the Great Northern shelter were restricted to a speed of four miles per hour.

In Vancouver, the first day of August was the last day of street car service on King Edward Avenue between Oak and Granville streets, its work replaced by an extension of the Cambie Street bus line. Jubilee celebrations hit a high with the arrival of the Lord Mayor of London, England, Sir Percy Vincent, on August 18, and a disastrous low with the destruction by fire of the city's 10,500-seat ice arena, once the world's largest, at the north foot of Denman Street on August 20.

To allow for grading to be done in connection with the new bridge at New Westminster, a newly-laid single track line was put into operation at Columbia and Leopold Place on Wednesday, November 4. This necessitated the operation of a shuttle service from Sixth Street and Fourth

Avenue via Queen's Park to Leopold Place, with the Highland Park street cars running east on Columbia Street only to Dufferin Street, whence it was but a short walk to the shuttle car. It also meant that Sunday Highland Park cars avoided their usual outbound routing via Queen's Park, proceeding instead directly via Eighth, Carnarvon, and Sixth streets. In addition, Sapperton passengers were transferred from No. 2 to No. 1 street cars at the depot only. At Leopold Place, a flagman was on duty to govern movements. At

A 1936 Victoria weekly pass, signed by Vancouver Island company vice-president Goward. (Bob Webster collection)

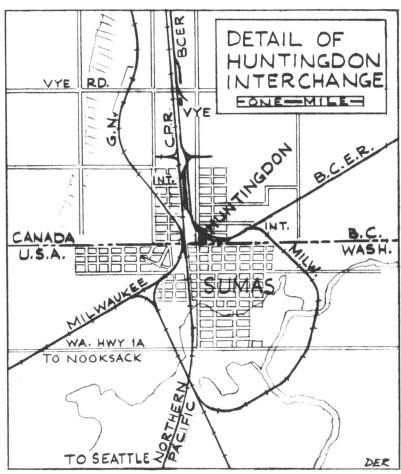

Chilliwack's original car barn burns to the ground on January 6, 1937. Fortunately, the operation of the substation to the left was unaffected. (B.C. Hydro)

Highland Park, a practice instituted only on January 31 continued, that of opening the door of the rear car of a two-car train as well as the door of the lead car, quickly to load Vancouver-bound riders from the connecting street car. (On the trip to Vancouver, the lead car would be filled first before access to the trailing car could be gained.)

As if not enough trouble had been created for New Westminster's street cars by the bridge project, B. C. Electric's new "8th Avenue (Cross-Town)" bus service went into operation on December 14, running from Twentieth Street along Eighth Avenue to Sixth Street, beside the street car line to Sixth Avenue, and then east to Sapperton via Cumberland Street, Richmond Street, and Eighth Avenue. The twenty-minute service by two twenty-one-passenger Ford buses met a real need, but the buses did introduce a single different strand of transit to a small system in a neat, well-contained city — which might well find it advantageous to deal with only one form of transit, especially since the new bridge would bring so much additional road traffic swirling about its street cars. The successful infiltration of this bus line in fact foretold the end of New Westminster's street car and interurban car operation.

The Fraser Valley had recovered well from the winter destruction of the previous year. In the Chilliwack area, dairy production and marketing was, of course, the major activity. The Fraser Valley Milk Producers' Association's twelve-year-old utility plant at Sardis, the largest and best equipped of its kind in Canada, was the centre through which three-quarters of the milk produced in the district passed. During 1936 the plant handled 140 tons of milk daily, of which twelve tons was shipped to Vancouver for the fluid market. The fifty-six-person plant, working around the clock, had manufactured 2,500,000 pounds of butter in 1936, a similar amount of powdered milk, 500,000 pounds of casein, and 400,000 pounds of cheese.

Hop-growing had developed to the point that three companies near Sardis had seven hundred

acres of hops under cultivation and two companies on reclaimed Sumas prairie had another five hundred, the total value of the crop in 1936 equalling three-quarters of a million dollars. Lumber, logged by the Vedder Logging Company — its railway line crossed the Chilliwack line half a mile east of the Vedder River, and hugged the eastern flank of Vedder Canal — would still be an active economic contributor to the area for a few more years; this company boomed its logs in Vedder Canal, towing them out to the Fraser River and westward to tidewater. During the year, the Mennonite raspberry farmers of Yarrow had formed the Yarrow Growers' Association (which would develop into a formidable force in the community), and even 120,000 pounds of tobacco had been grown on Sumas prairie.

Gratifying to the B. C. Electric were the even greater increases that 1936 brought over those of 1935: 67,381,477 passengers had been carried during the year and 298,225 tons of freight had been hauled.

The burning of the car barn in Chilliwack to the ground in less than an hour on January 6 got B. C. Electric's 1937 off to a less than positive start. It was fortunate that the east wind encouraging the blaze kept it from contacting the substation, distanced only by thirty feet, and that the alertness of employee "Buck" Miller allowed a locomotive, two cars, and a caboose to leave the burning building in time. The company set about replacing it almost immediately, building a wood frame and corrugated iron structure, 134 x 20 x 20 feet, to house two cars, and with living quarters for train crews.

Snow was the real troublemaker of early 1937, starting with distinction on December 28 of 1936. On the evening of January 16, a Saturday, Vancouver climaxed three weeks of snow with a silver thaw, repeated in somewhat milder form five days later. Ice conditions, never worse, necessitated driving street cars with the front window down for the sake of visibility, and motormen coming off shift were visions of ghostly iciness. Vancouver's hills were almost impossible, and beginning January 12, seven sweepers — they always went to work when snow reached a depth of an inch and a quarter — were out, and occasionally all eight were in use. S.55, in North Vancouver since October 1934, was a phenomenon of industry there. In Vancouver, two salt cars were working the bridges and hills, and three flangers were available for the worst situations. B.5 and 901 had been rigged up to scrape the ice from rails and their attendant grooves. The maintenance-of-way department had a force varying between one hundred and one hundred and fifty men out nightly, and by the end of 1937's snow session, around February 20, when twelve inches of snow hit Chilliwack, approximately one

hundred tons of salt had been spread on Vancouver streets and the sweepers had worn out nine tons of broom cane at a cost of sixty dollars per sweeper per night.

In New Westminster, the snow sweeper had kept all lines open, concentrating especially on the Sixth and Twelfth Street hills, and the Central Park and Chilliwack lines had each employed, as usual, a locomotive fitted up with a plow. The new Eighth Avenue bus line had barely kept its service going, and only with the greatest of difficulty since the city of New Westminster owned no snow clearing equipment. Victoria received its massive snowfall mostly during the first week of February; six feet of snow was not uncommon in outlying districts. Frozen ice to a diameter of four inches on the wires had even brought down the transmission line from Jordan River. The street cars of New Westminster, North Vancouver (snow had accumulated there to depths of five and six feet with no loss of street car service), Vancouver, and Victoria once again had demonstrated their value as the most dependable means of transportation, smoothly and efficiently cruising where buses and automobiles were left to flounder.

In Victoria, the expiry of the B. C. Electric's transportation franchise in 1938 was giving rise to speculation, mostly of the variety that street cars would be discarded in favour of buses, maybe even trolley buses. Although a number of bus companies were highly interested in becoming more involved in the Victoria and district picture, the B. C. Electric indicated it might agree to a bus service to Esquimalt on an experimental basis.

By the end of February in Vancouver, 118 street cars had had their rear gates removed and folding doors installed, leaving only 55 cars still to be rebuilt in this manner.

Adjustments to the milk train's schedule occurred on two occasions. Its 8:30 a.m. leaving time from Chilliwack was set back on March 15 to 7:50 a.m. This allowed it to run to the Sardis utility plant as an extra ahead of No. 3 to carry out any loading to be done there, and — picking up its schedule leaving time from Sardis at 8:39 a.m. — still enabled it to arrive in Vancouver on time. Secondly, with its withdrawal from Sunday service because of lack of business, its last Sunday return trip was on March 28.

The visit of Japan's royal prince and princess on March 30 to Vancouver required special operations by the interurban system. Two special two-car interurban trains filled with Japanese-Canadian children were run from Steveston directly to Powell Street Grounds (Oppenheimer Park) to the procession, and return; and extra interurban trains on the Fraser Mills-Queensborough line brought people to New

Two scuttling Birneys in a Victoria view in which the Empress Hotel, Parliament Building, and Washington's Olympic Mountains dominate. (Gus Mawes photo)

On upper Columbia Street in May 1937, street car 167, No. 2 — Sixth Street, will turn north at Leopold Place and make its journey over the 1891 Tramway route past Queen's Park to Highland Park. (Norm Gidney photo)

Westminster's Great Northern depot (shared by Canadian National trains) to pay their homage to royalty as they passed through on their way east.

In April, on the south side of the Burnaby Lake line at Kamloops Street, the company began clearing the ground for a large, new, $385,000 substation. The surrounding area, once served by Main Street substation, was being additionally supplied by two temporary substations, one on Powell Street near the sugar refinery, the other on Commercial Drive at Sixth Avenue. The new Grandview substation would replace both of these and be richly equipped to supply the necessary loads to the industrial needs of Burrard Inlet's south shore.

Vancouver's nine-for-fifty-cents tickets were in use at this time all day on Sundays and statutory holidays, and on all other days between the hours of 9 a.m. and 4:30 p.m. On the Fraser Valley line, a

one way fare plus one-third served as the return fare from Friday to Monday, and coming into effect for Sundays and holidays in June, July, August, and September was an excursion of a one way fare for a return trip from New Westminster to any point on the line. Vancouver to New Westminster cost thirty-five cents. The B. C. Electric made available to the public an attractive brochure entitled "Interurban Trips" which contained many suggestions for interesting jaunts on the system.

Beginning April 1, Vancouver's street car motormen were allowed to break in as bus operators; those doing so would have service seniority on any new lines, but would rank below bus operators on established bus routes. Four days later, a one week's holiday scheme for motormen, conductors, and operators went into effect. It was only a few weeks before the two observation cars reinstituted their two-hour, fifty-cent trips at 10 a.m., 2 p.m., 4 p.m., and 7 p.m. daily.

One day after the company's usual summer schedules had gone into effect, the first tangible indicator of the impending discontinuation of New Westminster's mixed street car-interurban operation came with the removal on May 15 of the Fraser Mills line's diamond crossing of the C.P.R. south of its main Port Coquitlam-New Westminster line. As of Monday, June 7, commencing at 8 a.m., special employee interurban trains ceased running into the mill area itself.

The city of New Westminster had cooperated closely with the company during the past few months in the matter of replacing street cars with buses, and by mid-July enough new buses — four Macks and ten Kenworths (seven more buses would soon arrive from Ottawa Car) — were on hand to make a changeover possible. The lower mainland edition of *The Buzzer* of July 23 had something to say to Vancouver riders about buses:

"Just in case some persons might say that Vancouver is next in line for bus transportation downtown, may we point out that transportation in a city of 20,000 and in one of 250,000 is entirely dissimilar. In small cities there is a trend towards rubber-tired service, either by internal combustion vehicles or trolley buses, but in large cities with congested traffic, large capacity vehicles with low cost electric power are still a necessity."

Vancouver, after all, had only twenty-five buses, and employed a maximum of nineteen on its eight lines: Cambie-King Edward, Grandview Highway, Granville South, Kitsilano Beach, McDonald Street, Renfrew Street, Spanish Banks, and University. Victoria continued to have three buses available for its three-mile Haultain line.

On July 20 a party of old timers rode the last street car to Sapperton and return, the car carrying on to the Twelfth Street barn where the car's operator checked in, and left for home with an emotional shake of his head. It was the last day of

DETAIL OF NEW WESTMINSTER DEPOT TRACKAGE

N

(B.C.E.R.)

8 ST.

"PRW" – PRIVATE RIGHT OF WAY

5 FORMER C.N.R. TO QUEENSBORO
6 COLUMBIA ST.
7 CARNARVON ST.
8 L. TO R.: CNR, FRONT ST., BCER, CPR, GN
9 TO SAPPERTON
10 GN DEPOT
11 FRASER RIVER BRIDGE, NOTE ROAD ON TOP
12 FRONT ST. & CPR, GN
13 2 BCER TRACKS 1 CPR " (+ CNR) 1 BCER " TO QUEENSBORO

1 BCER DEPOT
2 BCER FREIGHT SHED
3 BEGBIE ST. LOOP
4 CPR DEPOT

DER

street cars on the No. 1 Edmonds-Sapperton line and on the Queen's Park line from Sixth Street and Fourth Avenue to Leopold Place and Columbia Street.

At Sapperton, the Burnaby Lake line's eastern terminus-to-be, a new three-track, 200 x 43 x 24 feet, wood frame and corrugated iron interurban barn had been built, one in which all regular maintenance and repairs could be carried out (it had two car pits), and which even had a night mechanic on shift from Monday to Friday. As well, a new substation had been erected at Sapperton. At Twelfth Street, part of the barn had been reconstructed for bus occupancy and maintenance, and at the depot in New Westminster, $7,000 had been spent on interior improvements, including new wicket arrangements, modern lighting, and revamping of waiting room, barber shop, and restroom facilities, as well as a public address system to replace the depot master.

What particularly excited the city was the imminent removal from Columbia Street of the tracks and the still attractive poles supporting the trolley wire — after all, the new highway bridge across the Fraser would be pouring automobiles in great quantities onto this bustling commercial thoroughfare within four months.

On Wednesday, July 21, the Fraser Mills-Queensborough and Highland Park-Sixth Street lines were still operating, the latter shorn of its historic, lovely Queen's Park route, and forced to stop not only (as always) at the Edmonds station on the west side of Twelfth Street, but also on the east side at the drug store to transfer its passengers to the waiting Twelfth Street bus. The Highland Park-Sixth Street line was able to enjoy briefly, until August 1, running up Columbia Street as far as the site of bridge approach construction at Albert Crescent. That day was also the last day for the Fraser Mills-Queensborough interurban cars. The Fraser Mills line, totally isolated, was abandoned, the rails on its private right of way east from Brunette Street removed; the Queensborough line became forthwith part of District 1 and continued its extensive freight operations. The displaced interurban cars found immediate work on the other lines and the street cars were transferred to the Vancouver system.

The company's mind in Vancouver had been on snow removal, clearly motivated by events of just a few months ago as well as the yet vivid memories of 1935. Old locomotives 901 and 904 had been fitted with front blade and wing assemblies as long ago as 1921 for operation as snow flangers on Vancouver's streets, but in July, they were completely rebuilt with wing plows provided with brake cylinder mechanisms to lift them by air pressure. New bodies patterned after those of the sweepers replaced the old ones, and new numbers, S.100 and S.101, respectively, brought the new equipment homogeneously into the snow removal family.

August 9 was the last day for the Burnaby Lake interurban cars to rumble up Columbia Street from the depot to Sapperton on their way to Vancouver, and only the first four morning trips, the interurban cars on their way out to service the line, runs 401, 403, 405, and 407, had that pleasure. No interurban cars came into the depot, all eastbound Burnaby Lake trains from that day terminating at Sapperton.

During August and September, correspondence flew between the company and the city of Vancouver, and between both and the province's Department of Railways. Under consideration was the creation of a cross town street car line on Broadway between Alma Street and Commercial Drive, necessitating a diamond crossing at Main Street; and the extension of the No. 5-Broadway East line's service east from Commercial Drive to Nanaimo Street, necessitating the double tracking of Broadway, east to Nanaimo. The company resisted both of these proposals pressed by the city, which would give no guarantees to the company regarding its expenditure on new track the city might well soon wish to replace with pavement (in the case of Broadway East).

On August 23 and 24, District 2 operated interurban train specials every fifteen minutes between Davie Street station and the race track at Brighouse (old Minoru Park), where the Chrysler Motor Company was presenting a free show, "Hell Drivers," featuring stock cars rolling over, charging through flaming walls, and flying from ramps. Thousands attended.

President W. G. Murrin of the B. C. Electric announced to Vancouver's city council on September 18 that the company would put into service a number of new "super trams" on Vancouver lines if the Canada Transport Association was successful in its efforts to obtain a special customs dispensation to import from the United States certain parts necessary in construction of the ultra-modern street cars at a reasonable price. Transportation manager E. W. Arnott explained that the price of the new type of vehicle, the Presidents' Conference Committee (P.C.C.) car, plus customs duty, was prohibitive for a Canadian corporation. The councilmen in turn complained about the stepladder-like access to the present older cars and their remarkable ability to sway passengers into a frenzy of seasickness, only to be assured by Murrin that the company had just embarked on a street car reconditioning program, partially inspired by its gates-removal program.

The city of New Westminster surprised the company with its wish immediately to pave even the short block of Columbia Street between Begbie and Eighth streets. This meant new, hasty plans, and on September 21, the Begbie Street loop was operated for the last time by the

Highland Park-Sixth street cars, as well as the interurbans, and on the following day, the tracks on Columbia were paved over! Since the street car tracks down Eighth Avenue turned only to the east onto Columbia — not to the west, in the direction of the car barn — the street cars serving the Highland Park-Sixth Street line now could reach the barn only by travelling all the way west to Highland Park, and then operating, controls reversed, on the Central Park line's Highland Park cut-off back into New Westminster to Twelfth Street. At no time were the street cars to exceed fifteen miles per hour, effectively tying up following interurban trains.

Clearly there was another decision to be made. The Highland Park-Sixth Street line was supposed to have stayed in operation until the municipality of Burnaby made the roadway on Edmonds Street and the northern reaches of Sixth Street fit for bus operation. Now it was obvious that the company, with good reason, had little interest in running a rump service that required so much added employee time, running time, and the inconvenience of stopping dead at the bottom of Eighth Street.

September 30 was quickly selected as the last day of operation of Highland Park-Sixth Street cars within New Westminster's city limits, from Columbia and Eighth streets, to Carnarvon, and on Sixth Street north to Tenth Avenue, where a shelter was constructed for riders of the two street cars which would continue to shuttle in Burnaby between Tenth Avenue and Highland Park until the roads were improved. By this date, Columbia Street was already free of poles and trolley wires, its tracks paved over (most of the original Tramway Queen's Park route was left intact, clearly visible until the late 1960s) and a centre line painted in.

The meticulous professionalism with which the B. C. Electric dealt with the movements of the street cars over interurban trackage may be seen in the following directive:

TRANSPORTATION DEPARTMENT
New Westminster, B. C.,
September 29th, 1937.

TO MOTORMEN, CONDUCTORS & ALL CONCERNED: DISTRICT 1:

EFFECTIVE FRIDAY, OCTOBER 1ST, two City cars will move over District 1 each day between Westminster Barn and Highland Park and vice versa, leaving Westminster Barn at 5.31 and 5.51 DAILY EXCEPT SUNDAYS. ON SUNDAYS at 7.31 and 7.51, leaving Highland Park for Westminster daily following the last Interurban train except Saturdays when there is an Extra train out of Carrall Street at 1.00 A.M.

These City cars will register at Highland Park and report to the dispatcher the same as any other train in both directions. A Conductor will be placed on each City car while making these moves — he will report to dispatcher before leaving Westminster Barn, also when into clear on City lines at Highland Park. On the return trip to the barn at night Conductors will report to the dispatcher before leaving Highland Park and when into clear at Westminster Barn.

Interurban trains will use caution approaching and passing Highland Park when these City cars are liable to be occupying the main line and will run with extreme caution between Westminster Barn and Highland Park and vice versa during the times shown for City car movements.

Conductors in charge of City cars will equip themselves with three fusees, one white and one red lantern, and three torpedoes.

City cars will not exceed a speed of fifteen (15) miles per hour between Highland Park and Westminster, and will reduce to ten (10) miles per hour crossing over switches at Connaught Pit.

Conductors on Eastbound District 1 trains due Highland Park after 24.00K. will in addition to registering their trains, report to the dispatcher from that point who may have instructions regarding City cars.

E. STERLING,
Superintendent.

The new four-lane highway bridge across the Fraser River at New Westminster just west of the old bridge was officially opened on November 15, with the first day toll free. Built at a cost of four million dollars — toll booths in place at its Surrey approach — the new bridge was named after British Columbia's premier, T. D. Pattullo. The roadway was removed from the top level of the old bridge, whose bottom level continued to serve the B. C. Electric, Canadian National, and Great Northern trains. The year 1937 had indeed been one of great change in the old Royal City.

The just-begun street car rebuilding program would, during the nine coming years, transform over one hundred and fifty Vancouver and Victoria cars, seven of them in 1937, car 197 the first. All iron gates continued to be systematically replaced, as were the old fenders, but it was in many of the tall Narraganset-type street cars, their high deck roofs removed and their tops rounded off sleekly to match those of the Brill-type cars, that the word "modernization" was aptly embodied. Additional exterior refinements included a new type of headlight, metal flashing over the front and rear bumpers, and roof ventilators.

Inside, the wooden slat-type seats were supplanted by tubular frame seats with leather-covered "Dunlopillo" foam cushioning, all fashioned at Kitsilano. A brown linoleum floor with non-skid metal scuff plates between the seats and in the aisle replaced the old wooden slat floor. The interior was given a coat of green paint from the floor to the window sashes, the woodwork, instead of highly-varnished walnut, became a natural light oak, and the ceiling was white. A new buzzer system was installed, two five-bank rows of heaters of 450-watt capacity per heater were provided, and the lighting was improved. Finally — all of this at a cost of seven to eight thousand dollars per street car — tubular steel stanchions and hand grip rails replaced the former leather straps provided for standing, or moving, passengers. Each rebuilt car was, in fact, new, stunningly so! Patrons clamoured to get aboard each reincarnated street car as it made its appearance back on the streets.

The year again had shown some improvements over the previous one; passengers carried in 1937 had been up to 70,875,942, 11.3 percent of Canada's transit riders. Montreal Tramways with 208,208,793 riders and Toronto Transportation Commission with 154,851,715 exceeded the B. C. Electric's total, but fourth place Winnipeg was hardly close with 41,579,017. Freight hauled was nicely up to 349,164 tons, due in part to additional tonnage handled over Canadian railways as a result of ship and dock workers' strikes in United States Pacific ports, and also because of the continued activity of the lumber and wood products business.

In Vancouver, 1938 began with the inauguration of its ninth bus line, Knight Road, between Kingsway and Forty-first Avenue, on January 10. In Victoria, 1938 would be the year (in December) of the expiry of the B. C. Electric's street railway franchise, and it was not the intention of the company to ask for another franchise. It was negotiating with the city and surrounding municipalities to replace the street railway with a bus system. The B. C. Electric's street car operation, and its Haultain bus, were already meeting with considerable competition from bus operators, Royal Blue Line Company and Vancouver Island Coach Lines Limited, the former

even operating over a common route with the B. C. Electric's Haultain bus and under a similar service headway, garnering forty-three percent of the traffic. The total annual bus mileage, 677,500, run by these two carriers, though restricted to the boarding of passengers enroute within the city limits (excepting Haultain), was serious competition to the B. C. Electric's annual street car and bus mileage of 1,750,000.

Of the 40.548 miles of single track, 30.084 were in Victoria, 4.152 in Esquimalt, 3.843 in Oak Bay, and 2.469 in Saanich; 23.408 miles were in paved streets, 15.235 in unpaved streets, and 1.905 on private right of way, in car barns, and in yards. Over twelve miles each of 56-pound and 70-pound rail was supplemented by some 60- and 87-pound rail. The total cost of maintenance of way and structures for the twelve-month period ending June 30, 1936 had been $37,178.92.

For its Victoria street car and bus operation, the company employed 139 people in the following manner:

Maintenance of Way	*19*
Mechanical	
Shops and Car Barns	*23*
Garage	*2*
Transportation	
Street car operators	*73*
Bus operators	*4*
Others	*6*
Executive and Clerical	*12*

While Victorians were pondering what seemed to be their last year of street cars, it was business as usual on the lower mainland. Trainmen on the interurban lines were reminded at the beginning of the year that a two-car passenger train required only one trolley pole in use, a train with three or four motored cars required two poles, and one of

At the beginning of 1938, forty fully automatic, one man, safety car type street cars were available for service, one less when car 384 would be sent to Vancouver in June: 22, 23, 188, 189, 231-240, 250, 252-259, 381, 383, 384, 387-90, and 400-409. (Cars 382 and 385 had been sent to Vancouver in August 1937, 386 in December 1937.) Regular street car service called for twenty-nine of them to be in use on the 30.43 miles of the eight lines.

Lines	Miles of Route	Cars	Headway
1 — Oak Bay	3.21	5	7½-12 min.
2 — Cloverdale — Outer Wharf	3.08	3	12-20 min.
3 — Beacon Hill — Fernwood	2.84	3	12-20 min.
4 — Esquimalt	3.99	4	12-15 min.
5 — Gorge	3.13	3	12-20 min.
6 — Gonzales (Foul Bay) — Hillside (includes 7 — Joseph St.)	4.76	6	10-15 min.
9 — Uplands (includes 11 — Willows)	4.14	3	15 min.
10 — Mount Tolmie — Burnside	5.28	2	30 min.
	30.43	29	

At the Pembroke car barn and shops and the Cloverdale car shed together, fifty-two street cars could be stored, forty under cover.

more than four cars required three poles. It was imperative that one pole only be in use when a train passed an electric switch. Carrall Street-bound trains had to pull down all trolley poles except the one on the leading car before reaching Main Street; and trains eastbound from Carrall were supposed to put up an extra pole immediately after passing Main Street, pulling it down again before reaching the electric switch at Clark Drive. On District 2, only the pole on the lead car was allowed up between Davie Street station and the electric switch at Granville and Fourth Avenue.

Interurban cars at this time were being equipped with "Golden Glow" headlights, not removed from the cars at the end of a run as the old ones were, but placed face down under the long seat in the smoking compartment. On District 2 interurban cars, the old type carbon lights had been fitted with "Golden Glow" reflectors.

On the Chilliwack line, a new station at Arnold's Slough, appropriately called Arnold, was initiated on February 15. On March 20 in Vancouver, the two-car multiple unit street cars began being withdrawn from Sunday service on the Grandview line in favour of operating Fraser-Kerrisdale. In March as well, Southlands substation, at Forty-first Avenue and Dunbar Street, was the third new substation — Sapperton and Sasamat were the others — placed into operation during the last few months. A fourth would shortly be under construction at Hastings Street and Templeton Drive.

The silver-plated shovel, first used when the initial sod was cut for the Chilliwack line, and again when Senator J. H. King ceremonially started New Westminster's Pacific Coast Terminals project, was presented to the archives of the city of New Westminster on March 22 by the estate of its late city clerk, W. H. Keary.

Friday, May 27, was a big day for the interurban lines as five three-car trains transported capacity loads of school children from the eastern part of Burnaby to their annual sports day. This year it

was held at new Confederation Park, north of Hastings Street off Willingdon Avenue, the street car run's passing siding at that point proving particularly fortuitous. This sports day, in fact, served as the official opening of a much-needed north Burnaby park.

In Vancouver, June 4 marked the completion of the re-laying of new street car tracks on Granville between Robson and Pacific streets, and the concurrent widening and repaving of the road itself. On Sunday, June 12, Stanley Park acquired its well-designed, spacious off-street loop, splendidly situated and still used today by trolley cars and buses. Regular street cars used the Alberni and Denman streets return route into downtown for the last time on Saturday night, and Alberni Street was thereafter consigned to the function of storage track, much needed for Stanley Park special runs and events at Denman Auditorium.

Commencing July 25, the company began making a check of the passengers handled daily on the Highland Park shuttle street car run. During this period work was getting underway on the improving and paving of Sixth Street in Burnaby and Edmonds Street, preparation for buses. It was at this time too that the shuttle cars' operators were officially enjoined not to wait, westbound, at the west end of the Power House siding for the eastbound street car, but rather to stay at the siding's east end where the platform of Griffith Avenue station was situated. Within a few months, Queen's Park would reacquire some of its lustre, and its crowds, with the opening of Queen's Park Arena.

In September, the Burnaby Lake line's large Grandview substation went into service, and out on Chilliwack line territory, the Great Northern Railway's line to tidewater at Ladner (Port Guichon) from Colebrook was finally abandoned on October 17, Ladner Lumber Limited apparently unable to fulfil its twenty-cars-per-month commitment.[†] Just north of Ruskin, the capacity of the power plant there was doubled in November with the opening of a second 47,000 horsepower unit, handsomely attended to once again by the Ruskin-Stave Falls railway line.

The date had unfortunately arrived, December 4, the last complete day of the last of New Westminster's street cars, the all-Burnaby, Highland Park shuttle. Jack Gibson, who had piloted the first one man street car to Highland Park in 1922, brought the last one, car 98, to Highland Park and down over the Highland Park cutoff to Twelfth Street barn in the early hours of December 5. The Highland Park-Edmonds section, on private right of way, would remain in place as track for industrial use, but the rails on Edmonds and Sixth streets were ripped up immediately. A new bus service commenced on the fifth, making connections with the Central

[†] "Vancouver, Victoria and Eastern Railway and Navigation Company," (St. Paul, Minnesota: Office of Comptroller, Great Northern Railway, 1949), p. 6.

Its work in New Westminster finished, street car 98, the last one in the Royal City, poses briefly at the barn on Twelfth Street before passing over to Vancouver for more years of service. (Bob Webster collection)

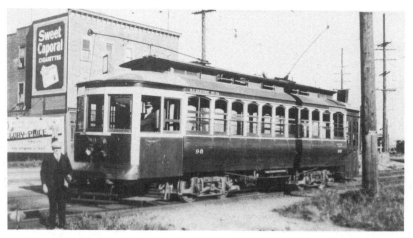

Park line's interurbans at Fraser Arm station, the next station east of Highland Park, because of its easier accessibility by road. Though the telephone was left in Highland Park booth in case train crews required it, beginning December 19, all New Westminster-bound trains registered their departure at Fraser Arm rather than at Highland Park. Over forty-seven years of street car service in New Westminster had ended simply, without fanfare, with typical B. C. Electric efficiency.

December 5 not only marked the end of street cars in New Westminster, but also the expiry of the company's street car franchise in Victoria. Yet nothing had happened. The city's franchise committee had met with B. C. Electric president Murrin, whose message had been that the company did not intend to continue street car operations indefinitely after the fifth, but that they could be continued as a matter of convenience until some other form of transit was organized. The company felt that street cars were inappropriate for a city of Victoria's size, and was adamant about not spending a penny more on the street railway system. (Only a minimum of track maintenance had occurred in the last two years.) It claimed to have lost $60,503 on its Victoria operation in the last year, after deductions for depreciation; Murrin estimated, however, that three-quarters of a million dollars would have to be spent to give Victoria an adequate bus service. As 1938 slipped away into 1939, the street cars were still forging out to the suburbs from their tight, busy downtown loop, serving over 61,000 Victoria and vicinity residents, the occasional Birney still straying from the cozy neatness of its Outer Wharf journeys onto the Gonzales (Foul Bay was now passé) line as short run No. 7 to Joseph Street in rush hour.

On the lower mainland, snow came earlier than usual, pasting Vancouver with seven inches on December 6, then retreating for a spell, only to attack again on December 26, interrupting the holiday festivities of many company employees. The Alouette power plant went out of commission on December 27 because of snow damage to the transmission line to Stave Falls, and on the twenty-eighth, Matsqui substation at Clayburn was crippled, all high tension lines serving it out of commission. During these three days, thirty inches of snow had fallen on Chilliwack, and the last interurban train from Chilliwack into Vancouver during the evening of December 27 had arrived at 3 a.m. the following morning, nearly six hours late. However, no trips on the Chilliwack line were cancelled throughout this inclement period.

Though Vancouver's city council had rejected an offer by the B. C. Electric in the fall to purchase twenty-six new streamlined P.C.C. street cars because they were one man operated, an announcement made at a meeting of the

North Vancouver's diminutive street car barn at Fourth Street off St. David's Avenue. (V.L. Sharman photo)

Vancouver section of the American Institute of Electrical Engineers that one such car would shortly arrive to perform as a demonstration car had been confirmed by the company on November 22. Ordered on May 13, it arrived on December 17, completely obliterating thoughts of snow for any who saw it, but the general public would have to wait until the new year to have its first close look.

The spectacular, new, three-lane suspension bridge at the First Narrows of Burrard Inlet, the real opening to the harbour shared by Vancouver and North Vancouver, was ready, and named Lions Gate Bridge after the extraordinary, two-headed mountain peak guarding Vancouver from the north. The bridge opened to pedestrian traffic on December 20, and a week later to road traffic; the B. C. Electric inaugurated an intercity bus run over it between North Vancouver and Vancouver. Needless to say, this toll bridge affected not only North Vancouver, but gave citizens of West Vancouver an access to Vancouver they had only dreamed of, having depended heavily on the West Vancouver ferry, and the one at North Vancouver, if they were motorists.

Mainly as a result of American regulations controlling the export of manufactured wood products, freight tonnage hauled in 1938 was down to 290,306 tons, a reduction in total traffic receipts of $35,000 from 1937. The number of passengers carried on the complex system was up again, though disturbingly slight, to 71,528,921.

Though passenger travel on the Fraser Valley line was but a shadow of what it had been, the

Passengers transported on the four interurban lines compared with 1912 in the following ways.		
	1912	*1938*
Central Park line	3,049,007	2,840,616
Lulu Island line	1,633,359	1,515,832
Burnaby Lake line	446,147	714,969
Chilliwack line	398,716	159,328
Total	5,527,329	5,230,745

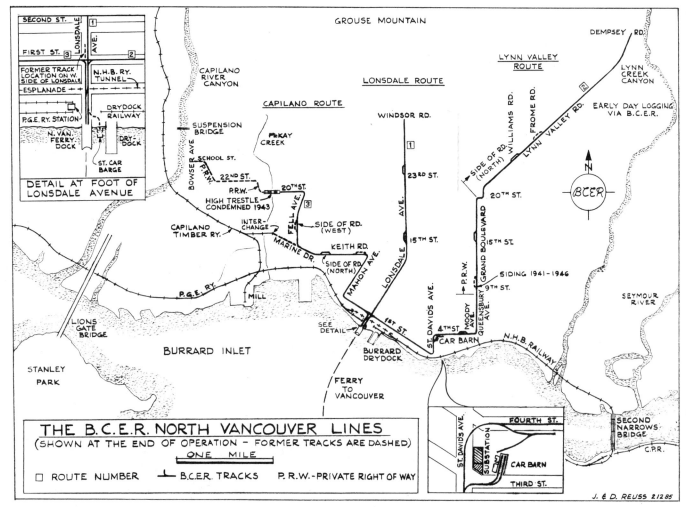

THE B.C.E.R. NORTH VANCOUVER LINES
(SHOWN AT THE END OF OPERATION – FORMER TRACKS ARE DASHED)
ONE MILE

☐ ROUTE NUMBER ⊢ B.C.E.R. TRACKS P.R.W. – PRIVATE RIGHT OF WAY

J. & D. REUSS 2.12.85

long line to Chilliwack did enable the company to place within the top ten Canadian railways in terms of mileage:

Canadian National	*23,169*
Canadian Pacific	*17,220*
Northern Alberta	*923*
Temiskaming & Northern Ontario	*515*
Quebec Central	*357*
Pacific Great Eastern	*348*
Algoma Central & Hudson Bay	*323*
Dominion Atlantic	*304*
British Columbia Electric	*220*
Esquimalt & Nanaimo	*211*

The year had been an outstanding one from the point of view of its street car rebuilding program, and a public that was soon to savour the joys of the new P.C.C.s had already in 1938 experienced the thirty-one "new" rebuilt street cars that had appeared during the year to add to the seven of the previous year. The public was thoroughly delighted by the B. C. Electric's commitment to vehicle modernization, readily appreciating that the changes were more than cosmetic.

VI

1939-1945:
Renewal and Triumph

It was January 18, 1939 before the P.C.C. street car, numbered 400 (clashing with Birney numbering, but doubtless cashing in on the then-current prestige of "the 400"), went on public view in Prior Street barn. This light-weight, comfortable, modern car, operated by foot pedals rather than by hand levers, charmed everyone — even more so when it went into service on the Stanley Park-Victoria Road run on January 27 — except the Street Railwaymen's Union, the Trades and Labour Council, and anyone else viewing with alarm the accelerating trend in transit generally away from two-man to one man operation. Partially built by the St. Louis Car Company, car 400 had been shipped to Canadian Car and Foundry Company for completion, the B. C. Electric thereby escaping the prevailing high import tariffs on vehicles built completely in the United States.

Though there had never been an accident between Thirteenth and Fourteenth Avenue on Main Street, the site of Mount Pleasant barn and the approximately two hundred street cars calling it home, concern was being expressed at this time by both the city and the province about the dangers inherent in switching these cars in and out of the barn, particularly in view of the increasingly heavy vehicular traffic on Main and the delays the street cars' movements caused. Many street cars making their way in and out of service were routed via Sixteenth Avenue to overcome congestion at Main Street and Broadway, but this did not obscure the fact that seventy-four street cars were being switched on weekdays between 6 p.m. and 7 p.m. virtually in the middle of Main Street.

Though the B. C. Electric's through freight to connect with the Northern Pacific at Huntingdon and the Canadian National at Chilliwack, leaving New Westminster daily at 4:15 p.m., was handling a good business, its milk train (often in years gone by consisting of up to five baggage-express cars, but most often three) was not. On Saturday, February 18, the milk train, reduced to one car, 1709, rolled its last load, fifteen tons of powdered milk, to Carrall Street under the care of conductor Ed Smith and motorman Jim Campbell, himself completing almost twenty-nine years of milk train operation. (Jack Stefens, then on the through

The P.C.C. operator's view, north on the Connaught bridge over False Creek. (B.C. Hydro)

freight, held the record for longest service as a conductor on the milk train, having joined the company in May 1911.)

At one time, it had been even more than a "milk train," handling a substantial eastbound traffic of groceries, merchandise, and machinery for stores up and down the valley. Despite the milk train's demise, the Chilliwack line continued to handle express freight and less-than-car lots on the baggage-express car section of the morning passenger train to Chilliwack and the noon train returning.

J. B. Mouat, assistant superintendent, interurban and New Westminster city lines at the time, was part of the milk train's crew in 1911 when they sped four-car trains filled with milk, meat, and produce to the New Westminster market — often unloading there took half an hour — and to Vancouver. His flavourful reminiscences have the ring of authenticity:

"In those days, made up in three or four-car trains, how gaily they covered the miles from Vancouver to Chilliwack, filled with empty milk

219

The interior of B.C. Electric's first P.C.C. car. (B.C. Hydro)

† J.B. Mouat, "Early Days of Freighting in Fraser Valley Recalled as Train Dropped," *The B.C. Electric Employees Magazine*, March 1939, p. 8.

cans as well as personal and household requirements for the farming community along the line. A brief stop at this station or that, or at some farmer's milk stand, and off went two, three, ten or twenty cans, and then away east again. A short stop at Chilliwack and then the return trip. This was when work really started.

Alongside a milk stand built level with the car decking, the brakeman was out before the train had really stopped. Then over with the gang plank and all the boys grabbed the cans and rolled them into the car. Another stop, this time three or four cans on the ground beside the track. 'Spot the second door, Jim,' and down went two men — each grabbed a handle — 'up she goes,' a foot on the step, a hand on grab handle, 'High Ball' and so, on and on.

By this time cans are piled two high with ropes around the top tier. In a corner of one car are a number of veal — over there, maybe two, maybe ten of those huge trunks of some travelling salesman (remember, boys), and on into Carrall street yards. Track number 10 clear, the doors of the shed wide open, Dave Swaddling's abuse: 'Where the heck have you been?' and then such a scurrying. Crew, shedmen and milk carriers

each to a can, and what a pride it was to roll a can half the length of the shed with one hand. Once in a while it would overbalance and then you got bawled out.

How glad the farmers were those days for the 'milk train'. No matter what the condition of the roads, no matter the weather — snow, sleet, rain or fog, 'To-o-o to-o-o toot toot, here she comes,' right on time.

Then the highways went through and along came the trucks. 'Easier to have the milk picked up at the farm gate,' said the farmer. 'Easier to have it delivered at the milk depot,' said the retailer. Those old cars now standing in the yards would remember how surprised they were not to stop at this stand today, and at that crossing tomorrow. No more milk, it's going in by truck now." †

Five of the original ten interurban baggage-express cars were already scrapped or in service as demotorized crew cars, 1701-1705, and three of the remaining five found themselves out of work after the milk train's disappearance. Cars 1700 and 1706 remained in active service to the very end, but 1707, 1708, and 1709 were sidetracked. Car 1708, in poorest condition of the three, was stripped of its equipment and burned at Kitsilano shops in June. Before long, 1707's motors and controls were removed as preparation for its reconditioning as an outfit car, a role it played rather well, displaying itself prominently for a number of years in the siding overseen by Vedder Mountain substation. Car 1709 would begin serving for ten years in Chilliwack as a relief vehicle, most of the time in the new car barn, nicely furnished with long side-benches for those occasional emergencies, especially along Vedder Mountain, which could isolate the eastern end of the line. At such times, 1709 could carry passengers, express, and anything else to connect with through trains beyond the break.

On the Lulu Island line, Granville bridge was becoming a worry. From March 20, cars of the 1300 and 1400 variety making their way west from Carrall Street along Hastings and Granville streets to the shops at Kitsilano were ordered to make their route only via Kitsilano trestle, never Granville Bridge. As well, three- (or four-)car interurban trains, often bound for the race track, were banned from that date. In fact, a two-car train was not to be followed by another interurban train by less than a distance of 250 feet. Beginning April 12, mail bound for Dominion Mills was carried by train number 336 from the Davie Street station at 7 a.m., and from Dominion Mills to Davie Street by the train leaving New Westminster at 3 p.m., number 343.

For the first time, a Vancouver bus line operated into the downtown core when the Cambie line started coming to Dunsmuir and Seymour streets on May 16. Its extension coincided with the removal from service of that part of the Sixteenth Avenue street car line which operated to downtown via Cambie Street from Broadway and Oak Street; this line henceforth operated with one shuttle street car between Sixteenth Avenue and Main Street and Broadway and Oak only.

The month continued with the official opening on the twenty-fifth of Vancouver's tallest building at the time, the magnificent Hotel Vancouver (the construction of this C.N.R. project had begun in December 1928), and concluded resoundingly with the visit to Vancouver, Victoria, and New Westminster on May 29 to 31 of Their Majesties King George VI and Queen Elizabeth. Of all the decorated street cars, none glided more smartly than Victoria's Birneys, and of all the celebrations, none induced such profound and nostalgic emotions as the gathering of ten thousand children at Queen's Park to welcome and celebrate the royal visitors.

At mid-year on the Stave Falls line, two tugboats, a launch and a boat, all B. C. Electric-owned, were available for use at Stave Falls, one launch at the Ruskin plant. The 6.206-mile railway's 7.803 miles

of sixty-pound single track, with its various installations, including five and a half miles of telephone circuit, were currently valued at $248,222, its two locomotives, express car, and converted truck, $26,591 together.

For the twelve-month period ending June 30, 1939, the Victoria system had operated 1,733,420 car miles, the lower mainland street car and bus systems, 12,899,568. Vancouver's 116.477 miles of single track were being operated by 304 street cars, North Vancouver's 10.535 miles by eleven street cars. New Westminster was employing twenty-one buses, Vancouver thirty-five.

On the interurban system, only three wooden locomotives remained, 950 at Stave Falls, 951 at Carrall Street, and 952 at New Westminster, fitted up with a snow plow. Six cabooses were in operation, A.5, A.7, and A.9-A.12; A.12, the most recent, was already ten years old. (A.5, the company's first double truck caboose — 1915 — was still in active service.) Twenty-eight box cars, all built between 1910 and 1913, were active, as were eighty-six flat cars, and a variety of service vehicles, twenty in all. (Thirty-six buses were in use on their own "interurban" routes.)

August 1 was the day a future B. C. Electric president, A. E. "Dal" Grauer, joined the B. C. Power Corporation as general secretary, and if he might have escaped the notice of some at the time, this talented scholar and administrator, with deep, pioneer roots in Eburne and Richmond, would quickly become the poised leader to guide the B. C. Electric through some of its most challenging days.

That the interurban system itself was equal to any challenge was a boast it made good with the arrival in New Westminster over the Great Northern Railway from Bellingham of the seventy-nine cars, in four trains, of the Ringling Brothers, Barnum and Bailey Circus. Late August 25, early Saturday morning August 26, B. C. Electric's locomotives hauled the trains west to Marpole, where the circus equipment, wagons, and livestock were unloaded and then taken by circus personnel to Sea Island, the site of the afternoon and evening performances. Thousands of people attended these shows, as others attended the races at Brighouse on the same day, a vintage day for District 2. After the evening performance by the circus, everything and everyone was reloaded onto the four trains (which made a spectacular sight of their own on yard track just east of Marpole) for the journey back to New Westminster in the early hours of Sunday morning, whence the Great Northern reclaimed them, setting out for Seattle, the next show town.

One of the very few mishaps in which passengers were injured occurred on Saturday night, September 23, on the Chilliwack line near Sardis. Two spikes had been driven into a rail joint, causing interurban car 1311 to leave the

This newspaper ad publicly announced the demise of the milk train. Car 1709 would bring in the last dairy load. (author's collection)

Snow flanger S.101 clears the track, and more, as three of Vancouver's street cars get ready to take advantage of its efforts. (E.L. Plant photo)

track and smash into a telephone pole, injuring three people. An R.C.M.P. investigation followed; the culprit, however, was never identified.

The beginning in September of what would become World War II had one immediate effect on Victoria's street car system: by mutual consent, and with a sense that a petroleum shortage might be a concomitant of these new hostilities, the street cars continued to operate at the request of the city, no further attempts being made to remake the whole operation. Because the further period of operation remained indefinite, it was decided before year's end to renovate the interior and exterior of each street car, Pembroke Street's paint shop attaining new heights of activity.

On October 22, the traffic superintendent of the Vancouver and North Vancouver lines, W. H.

The Jordan River flume and adjacent narrow gauge railway line in April 1940. (J.M. Elliott photo)

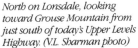

North on Lonsdale, looking toward Grouse Mountain from just south of today's Upper Levels Highway. (V.L. Sharman photo)

Dinsmore, died after a brief illness at the age of 62. He had entered the company in early 1901, rising through the ranks, first as conductor, then inspector, chief inspector, and acting traffic superintendent, city lines, to hold his ultimate post for twenty-three years of vital and intelligent direction. His replacement was W. H. Cottrell.

Almost twenty-six years of retirement, an inappropriate fate for an exciting, one-of-a-kind street car, came to a nasty close in December with the selling of hobble-skirt car 500. Purchased for $15,704, it fetched fifty dollars from a scrap dealer. Only its two controllers survived, to be installed in street cars 300 and 301. Another chapter had closed on November 9 with the withdrawing from service of the Steveston Wye, its north switch spiked and its lamp removed; the freight business was not the force it had once been in the Steveston area.

During 1939, twenty-three more street cars had been rebuilt in the company's ongoing refurbishing program, bringing to sixty-one the number of "new" old street cars brightening Vancouver's streets. The complete railway system, excluding only the track at Jordan River, now stood at 336.527 single track miles. The company had carried 72,667,204 passengers, a discouragingly small increase over the previous year for a transit company that had operated 330,000 more passenger miles on the lower mainland alone than in 1938! Freight tonnage hauled was up slightly to 306,931.

The B. C. Electric's second bus line in Victoria, a feeder to the Esquimalt naval barracks, was inaugurated on February 14, 1940, and within a few weeks, a number of newly renovated street cars glided out onto the streets of Victoria. On February 15 in North Vancouver, number 28, all-purpose work car, and one-time demonstration quality street car, was officially destroyed by burning, thieves under cover of the adjacent bush already having removed almost anything of value. S.55 had been in North Vancouver for over five years to deal with the snow, a line car would soon be shipped over from Vancouver, and the expense of reconditioning 28 was too great in view of her age.

Line car L.2 arrived in North Vancouver on March 11, shipped by truck across Lions Gate Bridge. The line car's trucks were taken over separately, the car itself supported by fifty-foot timbers on its own conveyance. Under the direction of freight superintendent J. R. Walker, six men prepared the timbers, set the line car in place on them, and transported it to North Vancouver, reassembling it there, all within the space of three days.

In Vancouver on March 16, the agreement with union representatives that bus operators would sign up on new running sheets at the same time with street car motormen, conductors, and operators went into effect. Two days later, staff operation on the section of the Oak Street line between the end of double track at Sixteenth Avenue and the first siding at Twenty-second was replaced by Nachod light signals.

Friday, April 26, was the day the gas famine began, creating greater war fears, as well as new and extra transit schedules; it also was the day on which three more P.C.C.s were ordered. On June 15, the company created a force of well-trained, disciplined guards whose duty was to protect the B. C. Electric's many properties; it would be quickly built up to the strength of a battalion company, with full military training and firearms for defence purposes in emergencies. Working closely with the Royal Canadian Mounted Police and provincial and city police, they guarded the power plants and dams, as well as transmission lines, on a twenty-four-hour basis. Guards within the cities, monitoring gates and entrances, would report hourly by telephone, and inspectors, head guards, and contact drivers were sworn in as special provincial constables. The force was 100 percent British, 92.5 percent of it consisting of ex-servicemen of every rank from private to major.

June was always the time of the race track runs, and 1940's June was no different, with twelve interurban cars set to service the 9.1-mile excursions between Davie Street and Lansdowne, June 29 to July 6, at 12:35, 12:55, 1:20, and 1:40 p.m., and 2:30 p.m. as well on Saturday. On July 1, a fifteen-minute service was operated between 12:30 and 2 p.m., and on Wednesday and Saturday a special train left New Westminster at 1:15 p.m. direct to the track. July 1 was also the day of the Fraser Valley line's much-anticipated annual special excursion train (one dollar return!) to the Cherry Festival in Chilliwack, departing Carrall Street at 7:45 a.m., New Westminster at 8:25 a.m. One had to acquire tickets early for this over one hundred and fifty-mile journey, a magnificent and thrilling bargain.

Street car and bus motormen, conductors, and operators had been granted an additional four days holiday time beginning in June, giving them a total of fourteen days. On July 1, the summer-time Kitsilano bus service went into effect, as it had now for many summers. And on September 12, a new station on the Steveston line, McCallan Road, halfway between Blundell and Riverside, was placed into service.

On the Stave Falls line, interurban express car 1802, fitted up with benches, was still performing its "passenger" runs, under the direction of conductor Bert Kemp, motorman Watt Allan, and trainman Charlie Middleton, but the bad news was that the provincial government had condemned as unsafe nine of the line's trestles. In Surrey, the new King George Highway from the main road through the south side of the Fraser Valley to the U. S. border, crossing the Chilliwack line at

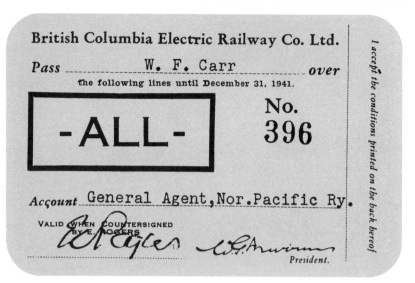

This, the most comprehensive pass of all, was a rarity. (Bob Webster collection)

Newton, had been completed during the year.

In Vancouver, nineteen more street cars had been rebuilt in 1940. The number of passengers carried was up to 76,411,790, and freight tonnage was up dramatically to 487,173, about 90,000 of these tons representing the B. C. Electric's part in the shipping of British Columbia lumber by rail to Atlantic ports for export to Britain, a further 60,000 tons of lumber and shingles consigned for military construction on the prairies and in Eastern Canada. The company reckoned that an additional 25,000 tons had been obtained in cross-Canada shipments of commodities that in peace time would have been ocean-routed through the Panama Canal.

An exciting opening to 1941 was the arrival on January 4 of three new P.C.C.s, numbered 401-403, from the shops of Canadian Car and Foundry in Montreal, where, as with 400, their bodies had been built; everything else had come from St. Louis. (This St. Louis-Montreal pattern would apply to each of the company's succeeding P.C.C. orders.) Costing $26,500 each, they embodied the latest improvements, based on the experiences other companies were having with the 1,400 such street cars currently in service. No transit vehicle could compare with the P.C.C. for safety, silence, speed and acceleration. On January 9, rolling stock inspector William Rines took a party of company officials and guests for a brief excursion on car 401 along the Fourth Avenue line, and exactly a week later, all four of the P.C.C.s went to work on the Kitsilano line, car 400 forsaking Victoria Road. What a sight they were, competing with the freights on 1,565-foot-long Kitsilano trestle! The four cars, handled by regular operators Art Butler, Joe Crookall, Joe Griffith, Archie Hambrook, Fred Johnson, Harry Knott, J. B. McKay, Doug Parkes, and C. M. Smith, provided precisely the quantity of regular service which the Kitsilano line required. Inspector George Sharman had taken especial care to train enough

Car 1402, baggage door to the rear, clatters over the Central Park line's Gladstone trestle with 1302 on a fine 1941 morning. (Kenneth S. Macdonald photo)

motormen to operate the cars as reliefs, when necessary.

Out on the Fraser Valley line, the one resident agent remaining along the length of the line from New Westminster was celebrated in the May issue of *B. C. Electric Employees Magazine*:

"Dotting the entire length of B. C. Electric's interurban line to Chilliwack through the fertile Fraser Valley years ago, lived many resident agents at way points along the track. Today, only one remains. His name is Marden G. Nelson, B. C. Electric's resident agent at Chilliwack.

End of track at Chilliwack is a large, circling loop which turns the trains back, facing the west and home. On the outside edge of the loop, is the station, over which the Nelsons live and which they keep polished and painted like any wayside station on the main line railroad. Tradition with resident agents is the upkeep of the property they have in their charge, with special attention being put on the grounds.

B. C. Electric's Chilliwack station with its surrounding grounds is no exception. The Nelsons have done a good job. Nelson has been resident agent in Chilliwack since 1927. He started with the B. C. Electric in 1919 as assistant agent in New Westminster. Spent seven years from 1920 at Clayburn and when that spot was closed, moved to the top of the line at Chilliwack. He is slender, white headed and deliberate in his speech, direct opposite to his assistant agent, big, tanned, broad shouldered Alex Purvis.

He joined as a motorman in 1910 on the interurban trains, Milner agent in 1912; agent at Huntington in 1914 until '26; two years at Clayburn and then to Chilliwack. Alex was born on the island of Java where his father was a tea and coffee planter. By way of England, the family came to Vancouver when the lad was eight where they lived for years at the corner of Richards and Robson. His years with the B. C.

Electric total thirty-five."

On May 15, changes were made to the mode of storing interurban cars at Carrall Street yard. The 1200-class St. Louis cars (for the Burnaby Lake line) were to occupy track 5, the 1300s track 6, and the Central Park rush hour-only 1000s track 8, the last limited to a maximum of four cars. The storing of cars on tracks 9 and 10 was henceforth forbidden.

War time became grimly tangible on May 22 for fifteen minutes from 10 p.m. with the imposition of the city of Vancouver's first blackout, a successful experiment all around. With typical professional care, the company had even given authority for all regular interurban and freight trains to occupy the main line for the fifteen-minute period without rear end protection.

For the commencement of the horse racing season at Lansdowne Park on June 28, the concern about Granville Bridge's stamina was pointedly raised, as were procedural matters:

New Westminster, B. C.
June 20th, 1941.

TO TRAIN CREWS & ALL CONCERNED, DIS-TRICT 2:

It will be noted that four (4) cars will be generally used on Race Trains this year as opposed to 3-car trains of previous years. The following procedure will govern operation of Race Trains to and from Davie Street.

All Race Trains North from Car Barns or Race Track to Davie Street will proceed via Kitsilano Bridge. At Davie Street the train will be split; A Conductor and Motorman will take the first two cars and a Conductor and Motorman will take the second two cars to 4th Avenue and District Two Interurban intersection and at that point trains will be consolidated, proceeding thence to the Race Track. In the evening follow the same procedure and take train to Kitsilano Barn.

Some remarshalling of trains will no doubt be necessary at the Race Track for the return trip to take care of the trailer situation in each train.

A barn man will be at 4th Avenue at noon and in the evening to assist in coupling trains.

Vancouver City Motormen have been requested not to cut in between the two sections of Race Trains at Pacific and Granville Streets to obviate any possible delay thereby.

Your co-operation is requested to facilitate the various movements required.

J. B. MOUAT,
Superintendent.

On June 21, the C.P.R.'s annual summer schedule for the Steveston-Sidney run of the ferry *Motor Princess* went into effect, and would continue as a special factor for the crew of the 7 p.m. interurban train from Steveston until September 7. As always, a watchful wait was being kept for a further five minutes, or more if connecting passengers were in sight.

The P.C.C.s having proven so popular on the Kitsilano line, the fourth car was placed in regular service throughout the day beginning on July 17, rather than being saved for only the afternoon rush. Commencing August 18, Ash Street, approximately 750 feet east of Heather Street, became a station on the Marpole-New Westminster line. The work of the Powell Street line was aided on December 7 with the elimination of the C.N.R.'s semaphore and derail at its crossing near Campbell Avenue, replaced by a new wig-wag signal.

December 7 virtually plunged Pacific Coast residents of Canada and the United States into the war — what foreshadowing the blackout had been! — with the attack that day on Pearl Harbour. A full blackout went into effect on December 8 for three nights with no street lights, house, or building lights, and transit vehicles on reduced schedules. Their curtains were tightly drawn, inside lighting reduced to one bank of lights when possible; on the ninth and tenth, street cars, interurbans, and buses kept out for the length of their schedules, though running slower times and spaced by specially-assigned employees at all terminals. The blackout was lifted on the eleventh.

As a temporary measure to reduce traffic congestion (the company hoped the change could be permanent), Grandview-Fourth Avenue street cars began operating on Richards Street between Hastings and Pacific streets, rather than just between Hastings and Robson, on December 8.

A further nineteen street cars had been rebuilt at Kitsilano during 1941, boosting the number refurbished since late 1937 to ninety-nine. The curved-side, rounded-front Narragan-set street cars still to be dealt with would now have their front and rear ends reworked to make them conform to those of the Brill cars. In Vancouver, the track of the short line, and its spurs, from Main Street west on Thirty-third Avenue to Little Mountain had been removed during the year, but in North Vancouver, two sidings had been added to help the system cope with increased travel, one for two cars on the Lonsdale line at Twenty-third Street, another on the Lynn Valley line on Grand Boulevard at Ninth Street.

As 1941 closed, the B. C. Electric had reason to be deeply concerned about the efficacy of its transportation system. During the last six months of 1941, the war had turned its worries upside down: the number of passengers carried was up to 83,996,509, and freight tonnage hauled had reached an unprecedented 723,000. The upsurge was due to the establishment of war industries, a factor completely absent during World War I. Shipyards, steel fabricating plants, machine shops, foundries, and an aircraft factory: all were engaged on war contracts. In addition, the coming introduction of gasoline rationing and the difficulty of getting new tires, combined with the atmosphere of conservation, had only increased the company's transit emergency.

The B. C. Electric thus began promoting a three-point program for relief: the number of stops had to be reduced to increase service efficiency, street car-delaying automobile parking had to be curtailed, and hours of work had somehow to be staggered to enable the same number of transit vehicles to carry more passengers.

As 1942 got under way, rush hour crowds were getting larger, but additions and adjustments were continually being made by the B. C. Electric to its transit services. At the depot in New Westminster, interurban trains were dispersing crowds almost as soon as they congregated, and at Main Street and First Avenue in Vancouver, street cars were stopping

A westbound Burnaby Lake line train crosses Victoria Drive at Second Avenue, having dropped eighty feet in the last four-tenths of a mile. (V.L. Sharman photo)

Car 136, having safely arrived at the foot of Fraser Street south, prepares to wye on Marine Drive. (Geoff Meugens collection)

35137 S	From	To	Fare Collected
Form No. T 2 Vancouver			Dollars
New West'r			
So. West'r			1.00 2.00
Hjorth Road			3.00 3.35
Scott			
Kennedy			Cents 5
Craigs			
Hunt Road			10 15 20
Kings			
Newton			25 30 35
Hyland			
Sullivan			40 45 50
McLellan			
Meridian			55 60 65
Cloverdale			70 75 80
Hall's Prairie			85 90 95
Anderson			
Hunter			Jan. Feb.
Langley Pr're			
Norris			Mar. Apr.
Milner			
Jardine			May June
Harmsworth			
Sperling			July Aug.
Warwhoop			
Coughlan			Sept. Oct.
County Line			
Beaver River			Nov. Dec.
Jackman			Days
Lombard			1 2 3
Rand			
Bradner			4 5 6
Dennison			
Mt. Lehman			7 8 9
Gifford			
Glover			10 11 12
Clayburn			13 14 15
St. Nicholas			
Abbotsford			16 17 18
Delair			
Vye			19 20 21
Huntingdon			
Whatcom Rd.			22 23 24
Upper Sumas			
Norton			25 26 27
Vedder Mt'n			28 29 30
Kidd			
Bellerose			31
Sinclair			
Yarrow			1942 1941
Woodroofe			Half fare
Lichman			
South Sumas			Sin.
Evans			
Sardis			Return
Knight Rd.			Special Return
Chilliwack			

Jan.	Feb.	Mar.	Apr.	May	June	
July	Aug.	Sept.	Oct.	Nov.	Dec.	EAST
1 2 3	4 5 6	7 8	9 10 11			
12 13	14 15 16	17 18	19 20 21			WEST
22 23	24 25 26	27 28	29 30 31			

A Chilliwack line receipt from the early forties. (Ken Hodgson collection)

every thirty seconds to take on, or let off, shipyard and industrial workers from the frantically busy False Creek area.

Meanwhile, all street cars and interurban cars were being equipped with metal restricting devices for use on headlights in the event of a blackout, these taking the place of the cardboard covers currently available. One of these new covers would be kept in a vestibule on each car.

On the Chilliwack line, the interchange track east of Abbotsford with the old Great Northern line to Kilgard was placed out of service from January 15, the brick company at Kilgard having abandoned the movement of its materials and products by rail in favour of highway transport, at least for this five-mile short haul. Within a short time the rails were lifted and the trestles levelled.

The Lulu Island line, at Arbutus Street where it intersected Broadway West, had acquired a

The Dominion census for 1941 revealed the following population statistics:	
Vancouver	275,353
Victoria	44,068
Burnaby	30,328
New Westminster	21,967
Saanich	20,535
Surrey	14,840
Richmond	10,370
Oak Bay	9,240
North Vancouver (city)	8,914
Chilliwhack	7,787
Langley	7,769
North Vancouver (municipality)	5,931
Matsqui	5,601
Esquimalt	3,737
Chilliwack	3,675
Sumas	2,473
Abbotsford	562

flagman at the day's busiest times to assist the heavy street car and interurban traffic to function safely and efficiently. In addition there was a daily, electric locomotive-hauled, four-car, C.P.R. train from Steveston to Vancouver, evacuating Canadians of Japanese background to internment camps in the interior of B. C., subsequent to the Pearl Harbour-inspired announcement of intent to evacuate on February 26 by Prime Minister Mackenzie King.

On April 1, gas rationing went into effect across Canada, and in Vancouver alone, the number of passengers carried in the first week thereafter was up twenty-seven percent over the same week in 1941! Easter Sunday was one of the heaviest Sundays ever experienced in Vancouver, 161,000 being carried, most to Stanley Park, whose twenty extra street cars were inadequate for the task. That comprehensive input from a separate source was necessary was manifest in the appointment by Canada's federal transit controller, George S. Gray, of S. Sigmundson, formerly with the Winnipeg Electric, to the newly-created post of regional transit controller for British Columbia, with jurisdiction over all street railway and bus operations in B. C.

In March, the company had placed an order for twenty new P.C.C.'s for the Grandview-Fourth Avenue line at a cost of $31,000 each, an order authorized by the Public Utilities Commission. However, the Greater Vancouver Community Council, representing fourteen communities, offered its full support on April 21 to Alderman Jack Price in his opposition to the acquisition of more one man cars.

For the twelve-month period ending on April 30, only 476 cars of freight had been handled on the Stave Falls line, a meagre total for a railway line whose times of frenzied activity had been many; sad that they were all in the past, the line's questionable trestles as well. Not so Huntingdon, where the growth of freight interchange traffic had caused the company to install a freight agent, W. G. Homewood, in the handsome depot there.

In Victoria, that times were changing was emphasized by the closure of the Japanese tea gardens at Gorge Park in May. On Saturday, May 16, 269 street cars were giving service in Vancouver, fifty more than on the same day in 1941. And on June 13 and 14, for the convenience of employees of the B. C. Plywoods and Canadian White Pine plant on the Marpole-New Westminster line, the B. C. Electric inaugurated special interurban runs, every Saturday from Marpole at 11:30 a.m. to Boundary Road, leaving on the return trip at 12:12 p.m., and every Sunday from Marpole at 11:30 p.m., and from Boundary Road at 12:12 a.m. In addition, an extra interurban train operated every Saturday from Marpole at 3:30 p.m., from Boundary Road at 4:12 p.m.

Needless to say, the summer-only Kitsilano Beach and Stanley Park swim buses did not operate in 1942, but the annual Dominion Day interurban run to the Cherry Carnival in Chilliwack drew more people than ever — extra cars and second, even third, sections of trains were run, the loop at Chilliwack a veritable carnival itself of vintage interurban passenger equipment.

During the summer months the company, the city of Vancouver, and the province discussed the double tracking of three stretches of single track, Forty-first Avenue between Larch and Dunbar streets, Sasamat Street between Fourth and Tenth avenues, and Victoria Road between the wye at Forty-fourth Avenue and the terminus at Fifty-fourth, all in an effort better to expedite hard-pressed car movements.

The Vedder River Logging Company's railroad having been abandoned, and the diamond with the Chilliwack line at its crossing near Woodroofe having just been removed, the positive stop by all company passenger and interurban trains, in both directions, at that point was eliminated on August 3. Thus the last physical link with logging — so crucial once to the line's very existence — disappeared, the discarded right of way a reminder for a time.

On the same day, the shops on Pembroke Street in Victoria set about getting another street car, 257, into optimum operating condition, overhauling its trucks and field coils and installing vestibule braces, all at a cost of $522. Transit controller Sigmundson had instructed both Vancouver and Victoria systems to initiate a "skip stop" system, a viable idea out of the past to speed up service. In Victoria, this order meant the discontinuation of approximately one-third of its current street car stops, as well as the erection of

Published by the British Columbia Electric Railway Company

A war-time, lower mainland Buzzer *with the masthead still widely recognized today. (Ken Hodgson collection)*

about one hundred and fifty new signs and the repainting and re-erection of about sixty existing signs. By the end of August, Victoria's skip stops were in service.

In Vancouver on August 31, skip stops went into effect on the Broadway West, Dunbar, Fourth Avenue, Kerrisdale, and West Point Grey lines, and on September 14, Fraser Street, Grandview, and Hastings East followed suit. Street car crews were instructed courteously to pick up patrons at the eliminated stopping places for the first two days after the changeover, but not thereafter. In the downtown core, stops continued to be made at all the usual stopping places.

In Victoria upgrading continued, for example, with the emerging from Pembroke Street on October 7 of Birney 402 with four new British rolled steel wheels — the old ones were worn out after 125,000 miles — and the renewing of 550 ties by November 15 under the tracks on Fairfield Road between Stannard Avenue and Lillian Road. Bay Street substation, as other company installations, was well guarded and well lit by night.

All of Vancouver's street car lines were operating on the skip stop scheme by October 19; and on the thirty-first of the month, the post office at Dominion Mills on the Marpole-New Westminster line was closed. At Steveston on November 16 at 8:45 a.m., a significant change came into effect, the passing track becoming the main line, with a new platform and shelter south of Moncton Street becoming Steveston station. The original main

August 14, 1942　　　　　　　　*The Buzzer*

TRAVEL BETWEEN 10 AND 4

LEAVE RUSH HOURS FOR WAR WORKERS

This card, now in the street cars, has been produced and displayed by the Transit Controller of Canada, as will be seen by the inscription at the bottom. We have heard from time to time insinuations that the relief of the transit problem is simply for the benefit of the B. C. Electric, but here is convincing evidence that transit is a national problem.

26   *Vancouver Street Car Timetables*

North Vancouver Street Car Lines

1   LONSDALE
Leave Ferry Wharf

2   LYNN VALLEY
Leave Ferry Wharf

3   CAPILANO
Leave Ferry Wharf

WEST VANCOUVER BUS SERVICE
Operated by Pacific Stage Lines

Vancouver Street Car Timetables   27

INTERURBAN LINES
156 MILES OF INTERURBAN ELECTRIC LINES ON MAINLAND

CENTRAL PARK LINE
VANCOUVER TO NEW WESTMINSTER

Comprehensive public timetables were readily available to riders; this one dates from November 16, 1942. (author's collection)

† *The Vancouver Sun*, 25 November 1942, p. 6.

---

line was relegated to spur track status with accommodation for ten freight cars.

Heavy passenger traffic — the Hastings East line was operating on a three-minute headway until after midnight — and the heavy use of vehicles brought the company to the point of doing anything possible to alleviate the situation. Since three combines were not necessary for interurban operations, number 1400 was rebuilt into a "1300," emerging from the shops on September 16 as 1321, the baggage-express compartment having given way to seating. In November, spare observation car 29 was rebuilt into street car 136, a near look-alike for its neighbour-numbered cars (the original 136 had been destroyed twenty years earlier); and interurban coaches 1009 and 1230, dormant wrecks for a number of years, were repaired and reactivated.

In late November and early December, the Street Railwaymen's Union was campaigning strongly in the public press against one man street cars. The following is an extract from a statement released at that time:

"The Street Railwaymen realize the need for new equipment, and we recognize the efficiency of the P.C.C. car. However, we need merely to point out that the efficiency of the P.C.C. car must only be increased by the use of a conductor to add to safety, speed, and individual attention to the travelling public." †

The statement further stressed that one man cars meant a fifty per cent reduction in the number of jobs available and the loss of about $100,000 in wages, should the ordered P.C.C.s go to work on Grandview-Fourth Avenue.

Federal transit controller Gray announced on December 2 that the twenty-car order had been reduced to seventeen because the priorities board of the U. S. government had cut a total Canadian order of one hundred new P.C.C.s (fifty-five for Toronto, twenty-five for Montreal, and twenty for Vancouver) to fifty (seventeen for Toronto, eighteen for Montreal, and seventeen for Vancouver).

One week later, Vancouver's voters voted "no" to one man cars in a highly-publicized plebiscite. Here was a dilemma indeed! Vancouver needed street cars, the only ones being built were P.C.C.s, and all 512 built in 1941 had been one man cars. Victoria alderman W. L. Morgan jumped in quickly, his transportation committee drafting a recommendation to Victoria city council to bid for the seventeen street cars. But clearly, these P.C.C.s were still Vancouver's to fight over.

In Victoria, the operation of the Haultain bus line had been discontinued for the duration, and passengers carried by the complete system during the year had totalled 11,125,795, close to double 1934's low. In Vancouver two new spurs had been laid from the Kitsilano line into the installation of the Royal Canadian Air Force, and twelve more

street cars had been completely reconditioned. Freight hauled was up to an astonishing 845,000 tons, 100,000 of these increases in lumber and shingle movements, another gain of 22,000 in other commodities from eastern Canada and the United States. When the numbers had all finally been stirred in, everyone was only too ready to believe that ridership was up 27.45% to 107,052,564. The B. C. Electric's extraordinary transportation system had been stretched to its very limits in 1942, but it and its employees had performed magnificently.

To help 1943 along the way with more efficiency, thirty-two of Vancouver's street cars began making Kitsilano barn their home on January 16; the transfer of these East Boulevard (fourteen cars), Oak Street (eight), Powell Street (six), Hastings Extension (two), and Nanaimo Street (two) rush-hour-only cars helped relieve congestion and simplify movements at Mount Pleasant and at Prior Street.

Almost beyond belief was the foot of snow which greeted lower mainland residents as they groped for early coffee on Tuesday, January 19. Every piece of snow sweeping and clearing equipment was in use, but all Vancouver schools and shipyards were closed, and on hills such as Granville south, Dunbar, Tenth Avenue, and Davie Street, street cars would actually ride up on the ice packed in the track and slither off the rails. By Thursday, at least a dozen street cars had been immobilized by broken axles, and maintenance-of-way, transportation, and shop men were working around the clock.

The Davie Street-Marpole line was the first interurban line to get well behind in its schedule, Kerrisdale and the area of Vancouver to its southwest being cut off from the rest of the city by the snow. And while Vancouver battled creature discomfort and industrial paralysis, farmers in the Fraser Valley dumped their milk onto the snow because blocked side roads made milk delivery impossible. There were thirty inches of snow at Abbotsford, and drifts up to ten feet between there and Chilliwack: veteran crew members on the Chilliwack interurban line described conditions as the worst they had ever seen.

On Thursday, an extra baggage-express car was added to a Chilliwack interurban train for the purpose of bringing milk into Vancouver to avert a milk famine, and farmers who were able to get their milk to the railway line throughout the time of the storm had their milk loaded, whether at a station or in the middle of a snowbound nowhere. In addition, all trains picked up people at any point they could reach the track and delivered feed to farmers along the line.

Service was interrupted on the Chilliwack line on Thursday evening when the 5:25 p.m. interurban from Vancouver was smothered by a five hundred-foot snow bank near Gifford. Al-

twenty-six passengers spent the night in the train, a special train from New Westminster on Friday morning returning them to New Westminster. On the same morning, a line car headed out from New Westminster to attempt to cut through the ice which had built up solidly in the tracks near Huntingdon because of the flooding there, caused by blocked drainage systems. The enthusiastic line car ran up on the ice, lost all sense of rail, and came to a stop across the right of way, blocking the evening interurban train from Chilliwack which waited at Huntingdon all night before returning to Chilliwack on Saturday morning. New Westminster- and Vancouver-bound Chilliwack residents found themselves travelling by Canadian National, the only open transportation route in the Fraser Valley south of the river. By late Saturday, the interurban line was clear once again, and the reincarnated milk train continued to accomplish its mission with such aplomb that the Fraser Valley Milk Producers Association, in a letter to the B. C. Electric, was moved to the following words:

> "We feel that we must express to you and your organization our appreciation of the help given to us in the past two weeks, enabling us to keep supplies of milk coming into Vancouver.
>
> Our thanks are due in a very special manner to Mr. Burchell and to his staff, whether office or train crew. All the men under his direction, often at great inconvenience themselves, have been most helpful and obliging, and Mr. Burchell himself has cooperated with us by his suggestions as well as by his actual supervision of the special trains run for our benefit, helping the farmer and serving the Vancouver public.
>
> May we ask you to pass on to those concerned our sincere thanks." †

With the rebuilding of Vancouver's street cars an ongoing project, fewer and fewer of the old, projecting Watson fenders were still to be seen on Vancouver's streets, and those only on a few single-end cars. What was observed was another new 1300-type interurban, car 1322, rebuilt from trailer 1603 car "Ladner" in February, using the motors from departed baggage-express car 1708. The 1322, as the earlier 1312 (both, of course, originally "name" interurbans), gave great joy to its motormen, the big motors and heavier trucks with its lighter body making a peppy vehicle, an excellent powered addition to the interurban fleet.

The crossing of the C.P.R. line at Clayburn by the Chilliwack line necessitated specific instructions for the operation of the interlocking plant at that point, and as all B. C. Electric Railway directives, the one for this diamond crossing was precise:

> "If no trains are approaching the diamond on the C.P.R., the Operator will first close the cabin door, put levers Nos. 3 and 5 to the normal position, then put lever No. 8 back to the first

notch, and let time lock run down, which will take about one minute. Then complete the movement of lever No. 8 by putting it to the full normal position. Pull lever No. 1, which will clear the signals for the B. C. Electric train to pass over the diamond. After the B. C. Electric train has passed through and is clear of diamond, put lever No. 1 back to normal and reverse levers Nos. 8, 5 and 3 in the order mentioned.

> NOTE:
> A lever is normal when it is in the position farthest away from the Operator, and the latch is down. A lever is reversed when it is in the position nearest to the Operator, and the latch is down. Great care must be exercised in putting lever No. 8 back toward normal to not allow it to go past the first notch until clock has run down.

> In the operation of these signals there must be no variation from these rules." ‡

By the end of February, the Victoria system had taken a simple step to disentangling congestion on Douglas Street from the north. The Burnside, Esquimalt, Fernwood, and Gorge street cars, inbound, all approached Victoria's busiest intersection, Douglas and Yates streets, on the same track, truly with good reason as Douglas was the principal commercial thoroughfare. Asked by the regional transit controller's special transportation committee to improve the situation, the company responded by routing Burnside and Gorge street cars on Government Street, inbound. This had necessitated the installation of electrical switch mechanisms at the corners of Bay and Government, Yates and Government, and Yates and Douglas, but as the company itself noted, service on all four lines was greatly improved.

As traffic was increasing on all areas of the

† J.B. Mouat, Superintendent, "Bulletin," 1 February 1943.

‡ J.B. Mouat, Superintendent, "Bulletin," 11 February 1943.

A train order for operations on the Steveston line segment of the Lulu Island branch, March 23, 1943. (Ken Hodgson collection)

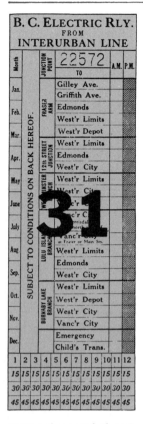

An interurban transfer from the early forties, Fraser Arm now playing the connecting role with buses that Highland Park did with street cars. (Bob Webster collection)

Car 157 on the Capilano line's McKay Creek trestle. (V.L. Sharman photo)

system, ticket offices at depots helped out by instituting new hours on March 22, Saturday being included as a weekday, an obvious indicator of the intensity of wartime's work force: both Carrall Street and Davie Street offices were open from 6:30 a.m. to midnight on weekdays, New Westminster from 5:40 a.m. All three kept 7 a.m. to midnight hours on Sundays, while Marpole's ticket office opened on weekdays only between 7 a.m. and 6:30 p.m. The Chilliwack line's trains 7 and 8 on Saturday evenings had become so overcrowded that a supplementary service was begun on Saturday, March 20, leaving New Westminster for Langley Prairie at 6 p.m., and departing on the return trip at 7:35 p.m.

By April-end, the siding at the foot of Dewdney Avenue on Victoria's Uplands line, disused and in disrepair, was removed, the company only too pleased to salvage the steel for use elsewhere. Much the same impulse must have been engendered in the company by the Stave Falls line's report on April 30 that it had hauled but 312 cars in the last twelve-month period.

May 9 brought news of further organization for the busy yard at Carrall Street, now rather cluttered with interurban cars. Numbers from 1 to 11 had been hung above their respective tracks, and all interurban cars were to be spotted on track 3, with the following exceptions: Central Park's trains 25 and 31 went to tracks 8 and 9, Fraser Valley line trains 3 and 8 went to track 10, and its trains 4 and 7 went to track 11. The outside track to the coal yard became "the wharf track," the inside track, "the bunker track."

In Vancouver, special early morning and late "owl" street cars were in operation every day of the week, and on the regular five weekdays, 297 street cars were at work during the afternoon rush; in a twenty-four-hour weekday, Vancouver's street cars were operating 39,586 miles. On May 16, the Davie-Main line commenced running on Powell, Carrall, and Cordova streets rather than on Hastings Street, thereby helpfully reducing traffic density on Hastings. From all its transit vehicles, the company was removing the blue and white lights, replacing them with yellow lights, which could be left burning during a precautionary blackout, as could the yellow stop lighting and the yellow-lit destination signs.

By the middle of July, the Esquimalt line's terminus had a new loop, toward which Canada's Department of National Defence had contributed $900, in addition to carrying out the grading required, supplying ballast, removing trees, and building platforms. This effort was necessitated by the navy's expropriation and enclosure into its dockyard area, fifteen months earlier, the former terminus and the track reaching to it. What the company lost was 750 feet of track, only 200 feet of it used by the double end street cars. The remaining track, consisting of a wye, had not been

used or kept up for over twenty years. Ties were completely gone, rails were badly corroded, switches and tailtrack had been robbed, and much of the trolley had not been replaced when it had been taken down at the time of pole renewal. The company was relatively pleased; the new loop provided a safe and commodious terminus and facilitated the use of single end street cars.

In July, B. C. Electric "Guides" appeared, women who sold tickets and dispensed information before riders boarded the street cars, and on October 12, eleven women were engaged as street car "conductorettes," Canada's Selective Service Board having ruled that only women would do as conductors, and only men over 45 as motormen.

On September 20, the Chilliwack line having almost become the freight hauler of the company's dreams, yards were established, officially, at twelve locations: South Westminster, Kennedy, Cloverdale, Langley Prairie, Milner, Bradner, Gifford, Clayburn, Abbotsford, Huntingdon, Sardis, and Chilliwack. Part of the wartime approach to operating the Chilliwack line was the new policy of allowing Vancouver-bound passengers to alight on Central Park line territory at the following ten locations between New Westminster and Vancouver: Central Park, Cedar Cottage, Broadway and Commercial Drive, Commercial Drive and Sixth Avenue, Charles Street, Commercial Drive and Venables Street, Clark Drive and Venables Street, Hastings Street and Clark Drive, Campbell Avenue and Hastings Street, and Hastings Street and Main Street. It was, however, still the rule to lock the toilets on Chilliwack line interurban trains between New Westminster and Vancouver.

In North Vancouver, September 30 was the last full day of operations by Capilano line street cars to their terminus. The large wooden trestle across McKay Creek having been condemned, the 3.176-mile line had been forced to cut back 1.014 miles from its outer end to a new terminus at Hamilton Avenue and Twentieth Street, thereby eliminating one of the most picturesque stretches of track anywhere on the B. C. Electric. (A new shuttle bus run from Marine Drive and Fell Avenue to cover some of the street car's territory began service on the following day.) The trestle could not really have been deemed a priority in wartime, especially since the last mile of the line was only sparsely settled and buses, which could run through an even more settled area to the former street car terminus, were available.

With wartime shipbuilding a prominent feature of Vancouver's False Creek east of Cambie Street on the south side, the disruption of traffic on Connaught Bridge, Granville Bridge, and the Kitsilano trestle became a regular feature of Vancouver life as each completed vessel was towed out from its snug confines into less protected water. Opening the two steel bridges was a fairly simple matter, not so Kitsilano trestle. Typical was the case with newly completed S.S. *Tecumseh Park*. All traffic across the trestle ceased at 7:30 a.m. on October 21 to allow its Howe truss span to be completely removed, while street cars detoured, as usual, over Granville Bridge, along Fourth Avenue, north on Fir Street, and through the Kitsilano barn and shop area; the vessel having laboriously been inched through the narrow passage, the trestle was available for traffic again, but not until 2 a.m. on October 22. As can be imagined, the trestle suffered repeated damage from these close encounters.

Despite the new street car loop at Esquimalt, the situation there had reached the point at which the B. C. Electric could barely cope with the continually increasing numbers of navy personnel at H.M.C.S. *Naden* training station and workmen employed at Yarrows' number two shipyard at Esquimalt. These men depended almost entirely on the bus service between Esquimalt and Victoria which the company had inaugurated in 1940, and which in late 1944 consisted of three decrepit Yellow twenty-three seaters (each with 600,000 miles), two broken-down Ford twenty-one seaters (secondhand from Vancouver), and four fairly new Ford twenty-one seaters. It was generally believed that when Great Britain's war activities would be transferred from Europe to the Far East, Esquimalt would become a strategically important naval base, increasing the personnel count of both *Naden* and *Givenchy* stations. The buses the company would acquire to improve this important bus link were vitally necessary, but the very nature of this point-to-point service would make the Esquimalt end of the street car service redundant.

During November as well, the condition of the track on certain Victoria lines was approaching the intolerable, none as run down as the Mount Tolmie line. Realizing that replacement track on this line, still after so many years providing only half-hour service, would scarcely be deemed a priority, the company started giving thought to replacing it with a bus service.

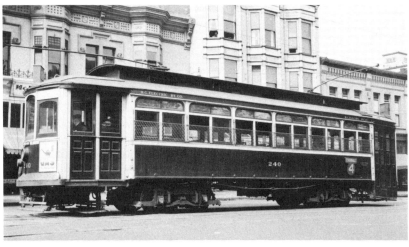

Esquimalt car 240, on Douglas Street, north of Yates, carries a sign over its head light indicating that it meets the bus that continues farther into Esquimalt. (Fred Hall photo)

Car 22, once the hope of the Saanich line, has a change of trolley poles at the terminus of the Mt. Tolmie line. (Geoff Meugens collection)

The Stave Falls line's figures for 1943 hardly augured well for its future:	
EXPENSES	
Maintenance of way and structures	*$7,644.29*
Maintenance of equipment	*265.31*
Traffic and transportation	*3,054.04*
Depreciation	*14,197.83*
General and miscellaneous	*180.00*
Total	*$25,341.47*
EARNINGS	
Passengers	*$25.40*
Freight	*5,429.61*
Total	*$5,455.01*

By December 1 in Vancouver, the operation of Grandview-Fourth Avenue street cars on Pacific and Richards Street was a permanently accomplished fact, thereby necessitating two fewer cars on the line, releasing them for rush hour work and causing considerable anger in the union.

During 1943 on the Chilliwack line, the east leg of the wye at Clayburn had been removed, as had the interchange track at Abbotsford with the Kilgard line.

Eleven more street cars had been rebuilt in Vancouver in 1943, and the number of passengers carried on the whole system was up 22.95% from the previous year (83.98% over 1939!) to another unpreceddented figure, 131,619,270. In Victoria, 1,186,916 had been carried in December alone, a striking contrast with 1939's 632,649; during this, the peak year for street car travel in Victoria, 13,026,857 had ridden the thirty-nine one man

An interurban lines receipt, familiar throughout the forties. (Ken Hodgson collection)

(Right)
A weekly pass for Vancouver city lines, 1944; two street cars are there, but they seem to be going precipitously downhill. (Ted Clark collection)

cars, 843,002, the buses.

Interurban railway freight traffic was up to 890,137 tons, increases in export lumber and other traffic offsetting a falling off of 170,000 tons in domestic and U. S. lumber and shingles. The interurban system had handled over 26,000 carloads of freight in 1943, including 400 carloads (ten million feet of lumber) each month to Atlantic ports for overseas delivery, hundreds of carloads of canned fish, and thousands of tons of steel, aluminum, alcohol, and peat for munitions, and war vehicles. Add to all this about 1,700 carloads of material (100,000 tons) for the construction of the Alaska (Alcan, then) Highway.

In 1943 preliminary planning for transportation modernization and conversion to buses in the post-war period had begun with the formation by president Murrin of "The Committee on Post-War Construction," covering all activities of the B. C. Electric.

Despite the fact that the British Columbia Electric Railway Company was not for sale, leaders of twenty-nine municipalities, encouraged by what B. C. Premier John Hart called "a five-point program for debate," met in Vancouver on February 9, 1944 under the chairmanship of Acting Mayor George Miller (Mayor J. W. Cornett was in Montreal on business) to discuss converting the B. C. Electric into a publicly-owned utility. Though all fifty municipal leaders present unanimously endorsed the principle of taking over the rights and assets of the B.C. Electric, nothing came of the idea at the time.

Four of the seventeen new P.C.C.s arrived on February 19, three more on the twenty-first, at the Kitsilano barn, having travelled by C.P.R. from Montreal on flat cars, each street car wrapped in ropes of excelsior. After inspection, cleaning, and polishing, the cars were moved to the Prior Street barn for breaking in. The union still insisted that they be used on existing one man car lines, not on Grandview-Fourth Avenue, as had been the company's intention, and to work they went on the Joyce and Victoria Road runs, existing one man operations. Three more had arrived by February 26, the remaining seven on March 6. Colourful company billboards all around Vancouver proclaimed their coming.

By mid-March, in Vancouver, the Fairview line was operating on a three-minute headway, but main line services were still incredibly overloaded at rush hours, street car delays beginning to be caused by deteriorating track conditions.

On the Marpole-New Westminster, at the entrance to the Alaska Pine Company Plant. At almost the same time on the same route, the Main Street passing track extension was completed, its 1,640-foot length capable of accommodating thirty-six-foot freight cars. As a safety measure for the freight operation's intrepid crews, the end sills and footboards on all the locomotives and line

cars had been painted white during March.

The Chilliwack line's new three thousand-foot-long interchange track at Huntingdon, increasing the company's interchange facilities with the C.P.R., N.P., and Milwaukee Road there to eighty-six cars, went into operation on April 14, although the runway beside the track for the use of train crews was not yet ready. As good planning would have it, freight cars moved with more intensity than ever through Huntingdon, particularly cars headed north and east via Chilliwack and the C.N.R.; in fact, two B.C. Electric freight trains hauled eighty-eight cars from Huntingdon to Chilliwack on May 8 alone.

The three interurban trailers, 1600-1602, found themselves always in the middle of trains, and invariably by the mid-1940s used only on weekends to augment a normally two- or three-car train. Mid-April was the time of changeover from storm windows to screens for all the Chilliwack line's passenger equipment, and whenever the transition had been completed on only one side of the car, trainmen were alive to the fact that the windows on the devil strip side must not be opened on the close-quarters running of the Central Park line.

The year ending April 30 had been a bad one for the Stave Falls line. With no more power plants to build and a good road paralleling it, the line had experienced falling revenue in each of the last ten years. The crusher had come, however, during the last twelve months with the shutting down of the last sawmill the railway serviced, halfway between Ruskin and the Ruskin power plant, which had still managed to ship out 202 cars of lumber during its abbreviated year. A further 190 cars had consisted of firewood cut by the B. C. Electric for shipment out over line to augment Vancouver's winter fuel supply. Certainly there was little reason for the company to continue operating the beautiful little line.

The heavy passenger business on the Central Park line had forced an increase of five minutes' running time for the eastbound trains, which on May 1 began leaving at five, twenty-five, and forty-five minutes after the hour.

Beginning with two street cars in May, six of Victoria's cars were sent across Georgia Strait in 1944 to the Kitsilano shop for rebuilding, cars 188

On an average day during April, the following number of passengers rode each of Vancouver's street car lines:

Number of Route	Name of Route	Route Length (Miles)	Passengers Per Day
1	Fairview (outer & inner)	5.6	34,006
3	Davie-Main	6.5	31,755
4	Grandview-Fourth Avenue	7.7	36,464
5	Robson-Broadway East	5.2	30,079
6	49th & Fraser — East Boulevard	9.6	40,132
7	Fraser & Marine — Kerrisdale	12.0	
9	44th & Victoria — Post Office	5.2	15,633
10	54th & Victoria — Stanley Park	7.2	
9	Joyce Road — Post Office	5.7	12,588
11	Joyce Road — Stanley Park	7.0	
12	Kitsilano	2.4	4,792
13	Hastings East — Broadway West	7.3	
14	Hastings East — Dunbar	10.4	
15	Hastings East — Sasamat	9.4	65,206
16	Hastings East — West Point Grey	10.2	
	Trafalgar — Hastings East	3.2	
17	Oak Street	6.3	9,003
19	Powell St. — Commercial	2.1	6,928
20	Powell St. — Hastings Park	3.7	
—	16th Ave.	1.6	632
—	Nanaimo St.	1.9	2,109
—	Main St. South	1.2	766

When riders encountered route numbers other than the above, a specific downtown routing was indicated, as the company delineated in its public timetables:

EASTBOUND

21 Used by cars from Kerrisdale, Broadway West (including Dunbar and West Point Grey) and 4th Avenue when routed via Granville Street to Post Office, then via Hastings Street to Richards and Hastings.

23 Used by cars from Kerrisdale, Broadway West (including Dunbar and West Point Grey) and 4th Avenue when routed via Granville Street, Robson Street and Richards Street, to Richards and Hastings.

25 Used by cars from Kerrisdale, Broadway West (including Dunbar and West Point Grey) and 4th Avenue when routed via Granville Bridge, Pacific Street and Richards Street, to Richards and Hastings.

27 Used by cars from Fairview, Kerrisdale, Broadway West (including Dunbar and West Point Grey) and 4th Avenue when routed via Granville Street to Post Office, then via Hastings Street, Cambie Street, to Cambie and Robson.

29 Used by cars from Fairview, Kerrisdale, Broadway West (including Dunbar and West Point Grey) and 4th Avenue when routed via Granville Street, Cordova Street and Powell Street to Powell and Main.

WESTBOUND

22 Used by cars from Hastings East and Grandview, when routed to Main and Hastings.

24 Used by cars from Hastings East, Grandview, Broadway East, Fraser, Kingsway, Main Street and Fairview Outer, when routed via Hastings Street, Cambie Street, to Cambie and Robson.

26 Used by cars from Hastings East, Grandview, Broadway East, Fraser, Kingsway, Main Street and Fairview Outer, when routed via Hastings Street, Richards Street, to Richards and Robson.

28 Used by cars from Hastings East, Grandview, Broadway East, Fraser, Kingsway, Main Street and Fairview Outer, when routed via Hastings Street to Granville Street.

In April, the interurban lines had carried 1,076,172 passengers, 573,446 on the Central Park line; 328,052 on the three lines of the Lulu Island line; 34,551 on the Chilliwack (Fraser Valley) line; and 140,123 on the Burnaby Lake line.

and 259, both becoming single enders in the transformation, and 381, 383, 387, and 389. (This was great luck for 381 and 387 which had recently had $1,148 spent on repairing the heavy damage they had received in a grinding collision with each other on February 9, 1943 at the corner of Fairfield Road and Memorial Avenue.) Recently-rebuilt Vancouver cars, 200 and 201, both with

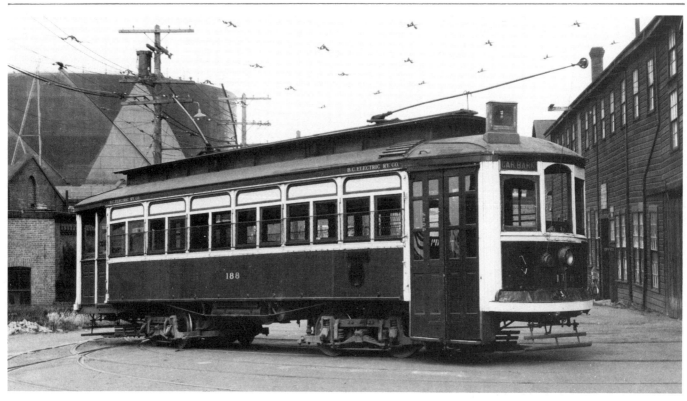

Victoria's car 188, before and after rebuilding at Kitsilano shops in 1944. (Bob Webster collection)

rear treadle exits such as the six would acquire, were sent over to Victoria, fresh and beautifully painted to present Victorians with a revised image of street cars; and when the six, refurbished, would return to Victoria, 200 and 201 would still be allowed to stay. The little Birneys found themselves ever less frequently used as Victoria's street car system moved into, then past, the mid-1940s. The nine "new" street cars (one more would be sent to Kitsilano in the following year) became the desired vehicles, the cars which reminded every rider of just how thoroughly delightful a street car ride could be. On the unrebuilt cars, the traditional, green, destination-and-number plaques, inimitable to Victoria, were still hung next to the entrance and at the back.

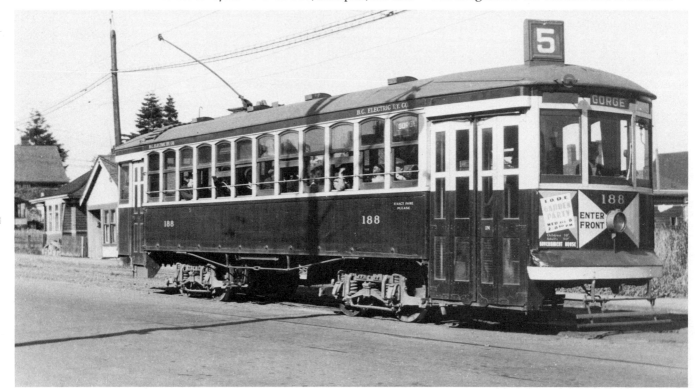

In a wartime step based on priorities and the availability of materials, the company discontinued service on Victoria's Mount Tolmie line, a move similar to its abandonment of the outer end of North Vancouver's Capilano line. The track of the Mount Tolmie line by now in execrable shape, buses took over the route's operation on June 1. The track remained in place on Richmond Road, while the Burnside line now fended for itself, running into downtown on Government Street, and returning via Yates and Douglas streets. Thus, the last street car line initiated in Victoria became the first one to be abandoned, preparing the way psychologically on a variety of fronts for the elimination of all Victoria street car lines.

Street car ridership in Vancouver had begun to level off, with July's increase over 1943's July figure a mere five percent; even June's increase had been ten percent, January's, fifteen.

On August 28, the Board of Transport Commissioners for Canada, meeting at Vancouver, granted authority for the abandonment of the Stave Falls line. No one had appeared at the meeting to oppose the abandonment application, and chief commissioner Cross expressed the opinion that the needs of Stave Falls could be reasonably served by highway transportation, and that there did not appear to be much, if any, prospect of traffic for the railway line. Plans began to be made immediately for the line's disappearance.

September was a banner month for passenger and freight traffic on the interurban lines. On the Chilliwack line, three sections of train number 7 had carried 762 passengers on Labour Day, September 4. Freight traffic had set a record for a twenty-four-hour period, between 4 a.m., Sunday, September 24 and 4 a.m., Monday, September 25, when the B. C. Electric had handled fifty-two cars of livestock from the C.N.R., C.P.R. and P.G.E., all designated for the

A Victoria acquisition in May 1944 from Vancouver, car 200 services the grassy reaches of the Gorge line. (W.C. Whittaker photo)

Fraser Street and Marpole stockyards. The month had climaxed on its final day: 47,303 passengers, a record, were carried on all the interurban lines together on that day.

On the same day, the B. C. Electric announced a fifty-million-dollar, ten-year, postwar development plan, fourteen of those millions earmarked for transportation. The basic design for the elimination of most rail passenger travel was ready on the day of the interurban system's greatest triumph, though Murrin did point out that street cars on main arteries would stay, the older cars to be replaced by P.C.C.s.

Even the Burnaby Lake line had been almost inundated with passenger business, necessitating a variety of adjustment during the last day of October. First, the registering point at Douglas Road was eliminated, Sapperton, Commercial Drive, and Carrall Street sufficing. Second, spring switches were to be installed at Hill, westbound trains taking the siding, and at Douglas Road and Sapperton, spring switches were to be removed, the switches set for the main line. Third, in the case of two-car trains from Vancouver, the second car was to be cut

The Fernwood car, 407, on Caledonia Avenue. (W.C. Whittaker photo)

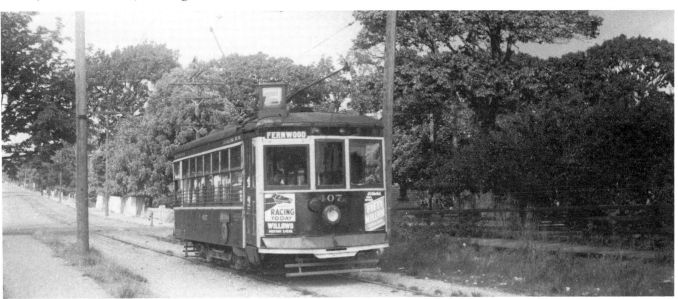

A view to the east up Thirteenth Street from Bewicke Avenue in North Vancouver along the Capilano line. (V.L. Sharman photo)

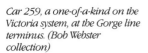

Car 259, a one-of-a-kind on the Victoria system, at the Gorge line terminus. (Bob Webster collection)

off at Douglas Road, lying there in charge of the brakeman until the westbound train arrived to couple to it and bring it back into Vancouver. At Carrall Street, an effort was obviously made to load passengers for points east of Douglas Road into the forward car. At Horne-Payne, eastbound trains would continue to take the siding, westbound trains holding the main line. The complete interurban system was maintained at this time by thirteen section gangs and one bridge gang, each with a complement of between four and six men.

By the end of October in Victoria, the street car system's pre-World War I end-of-line waiting rooms at Esquimalt, Gonzales (Foul Bay), Mount Tolmie, Oak Bay, Outer Wharf, and Willows were demolished by the company. With the frequent street car service in effect, they had grown quite redundant and their physical condition by this time left a lot to be desired.

Only the Gorge terminal building remained in use to the end of street car service, despite the fact that the original Gorge Park buildings, except for the park-keeper's home, had also recently been razed by the company, their destruction hastened by the departure of the former Japanese tenants and subsequent damage by vandals.

In Vancouver from November 16, the afternoon rush used a record 301 street cars. To maintain a service with that number of vehicles, one man cars were often operated on two-man lines, using two men. With the beginning of special Christmas schedules on December 15, a new record was set with 305 of the 319 at work during the afternoon rush period.

Its last runs having been made, the Stave Falls Railway (as the company officially designated it) was abandoned on December 4, its tracks to be torn up and sold for scrap during the coming year. Locomotive 950 was brought to storage outside the barn in New Westminster; locomotive 980 was already in operation on the interurban system, having been brought to Vancouver on March 4; and interurban express car 1802 became a private cabin alongside the line's right of way, its trucks sold for scrap, and its motors, gear cases, governor, brake valve, and pump sent to company stores in Vancouver, one pair of wheels to the shop at Kitsilano. The old truck too had been abandoned, some said pushed into the river. As the line to Ruskin was stilled, the Vancouver-Steveston interurban line had two extra trains added to its operation, creating a half hourly service southbound between 2 p.m. and 7 p.m., northbound between 3 p.m. and 8 p.m.

Nineteen forty-four had been the greatest year

in the company's history! Five Vancouver street cars, in addition to Victoria's six, had been rebuilt; and on Vancouver Island, the third unit, of 10,720 horsepower, had been placed into service at Brentwood. Statistics for 1944 depict the B. C. Electric's extraordinary wartime successes:

	Gross Revenue
Railway	$10,776,412
Electricity	10,533,385
Gas	2,257,318
Buses, Taxis, and Motor Freight	1,222,853
Miscellaneous	417,104
	$25,207,072

Victoria's street cars had carried 12,284,039 riders, down from 1943's peak, its buses 1,174,483. Across the whole system, however, ridership was up almost eight percent to 144,272,508, only 2,826,544 of those on buses, and freight tonnage

Express car 1802 at Stave Falls in December 1944. (E.L. Plant photo)

hauled also reached another record figure, 911,091.

At 4 a.m. on January 9, 1945, motormen, conductors, operators, shopmen, trackmen, etc., went on strike for higher wages. (The Lulu Island and Chilliwack lines were naturally not affected.) Though the walkout was declared illegal by authorities of the Canadian government, the men did not go back to work until the nineteenth, the company and the men agreeing to a four and a half cents per hour increase on February 24. At this time, 303 street cars were handling afternoon rush hour service in Vancouver. On January 15, the company had a new station platform, Jellicoe, ready for use on the Marpole-New Westminster interurban line at the foot of Jellicoe Street; interurban trains had already been handling passengers at this stop, known locally as Red Cedar or Minto, after the names of the industries there. In January as well, the company, to promote postwar development in British Columbia, had formed an industrial development department, its slogan "Business is Moving to B.C." quickly becoming ubiquitous.

To the B. C. Electric, it seemed clear that practically total electrification of the Fraser Valley would be an attainable goal within five years of the end of the war. Poultry and dairy farmers were almost completely committed to electricity

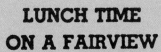

LUNCH TIME
ON A FAIRVIEW
By G. A. ROOTS
(Inspired by a Bottle of Milk)

Did you ever try to eat your lunch
While working a Fairview Run?
Well, brother, if you haven't,
You've missed a lot of fun.

When the morning rush is over,
You've really worked, and how,
Then you reach for the good old lunch box,
To see what you have for chow.

'Tis then the shoppers begin to move,
From the north, east, west and south,
And, my boy, you find you have a time
To get any food into your mouth.

You punch the clock at Granville,
Two bells and you leave with a lurch,
But before you can get at that lunch box,
You have to stop at Birch.

Two bells again, you're on your way,
You wind her up full juice,
Make a grab for a sandwich, then start to swear
Cause you have to stop at Spruce.

From there to Oak, as you all know,
Is only just a hop,
So before you get her wound up full,
Again, you have to stop.

Across the tracks at Oak Street,
You hear the breaker blow,
You bang her in, the bell goes "Ding,"
The next stop is Willow.

Heather Street, the Hospital
Is the next stop that you make,
The sandwich in your hand, you find,
Is a piece of mushed-up cake.

You get two bells and away again,
You close the vestibule door,
Then with a bump, a sway and a jump
Your coffee's over the floor.

Past Cambie, Alberta, Columbia, too,
And still no chance to eat,
Of all the gol-darned places to stop,
Is the one called Quebec Street.

Main Street at last, now you can eat,
Your sandwich, coffee and cake,
But with a groan, you look at your watch,
And find you're three minutes late.

Away you go around and around,
With many a curse and groan,
So boys, my tip to you is this,
Try eating your lunch at home.

Ruskin station of the Stave Falls line, north from near the line's C.P.R. connection, at the end of its operational life, December 1944. (E.L. Plant photo)

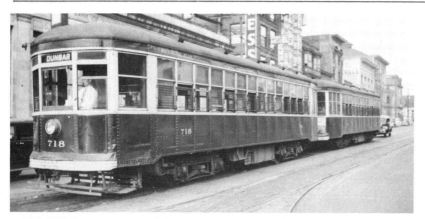

A multiple unit street car, 718 and 719, on Hastings Street, about to cross Main Street, westbound. (E.L. Plant photo)

Lulu Island branch employees timetable from March 1, 1945. (author's collection)

number 3 and 4 only, for the convenience of school children from that locality travelling to and from the schools at Whatcom Road or Abbotsford.

British Columbia's regional transit controller, S. Sigmundson, was appointed B. C. Electric's transportation assistant on April 16. Exactly one week later, a new street car, number 391, made its first appearance in Vancouver; it was actually the rebuilt version of old near side car, 501. Meanwhile, six more P.C.C.s had arrived on April 18. On the last day of the month, the further deterioration of Granville Bridge was attested to by a new company order, making it imperative to move any 1300 type interurban car between Carrall Street and Kitsilano shops through the C.P.R.-B. C. Electric interchange at Drake Street, or, preferably, via Marpole from the barn in New Westminster.

On May 7, the final nine P.C.C.s arrived, giving the company thirty-six, but this event was overshadowed by another: May 7 was the day the war in Europe ended. May 8 was declared a Dominion-wide holiday in celebration of the long-awaited end to hostilities there, but still the war dragged on in the Pacific.

Contentiousness in the matter of the P.C.C.s and the company's desire to operate them on Grandview-Fourth Avenue achieved focus on May 28, 29 and 30 in Vancouver with a hearing at which both the union and the company presented

already, and coolers, household pumps, and refrigerators were becoming more popular. Bulb growing, a comparatively new industry in the Bradner area, was starting to make requirements, and eight cold storage lockers were already in operation. Extensions were installed free when costs did not exceed $82.50, and postwar plans called for the extension of lines to the remaining unserved areas for a minimum monthly charge of two dollars per customer.

Commencing Sunday, March 11, the Marpole ticket office would be closed on Sundays. But two days later on the Chilliwack line, a new station platform, Marion Road, at mile 48.8, midway between Arnold and Vedder Mountain stations, was placed into service as a flag stop for trains

evidence to the Public Utilities Commission, the body which in 1942 had authorized the company to purchase P.C.C.s for this very route.

The Chilliwack line's Hyland station demolished by the company, two new stations four-tenths of a mile on either side of it, Burkhart Road to the west and Archibald Road to the east, went into service on June 13 to serve a growing number of residents better. The long, climbing grade would continue to be known as Hyland hill, Bear Creek hill, officially. On the Central Park line, a new crossover had been installed at Fraser Arm to enable interurban trains to switch ends and run back to Vancouver, should such a movement be necessary. (Fraser Arm was, of course, the busy meeting point with New Westminster buses, as Highland Park had been with New Westminster street cars.) Wells, a fixture on the Chilliwack line's timetable for so many years as a typical

shelter station, but latterly simply the short siding west of Knight Road station, was obliterated from June 23, the siding itself now named after its nearby station.

The Public Utilities Commission ruled on July 13 that the Grandview-Fourth Avenue line was to get its one man Presidents' Conference Committee street cars. The Street Railwaymen's Union countered immediately with a refusal to operate them there. President Murrin stated that the displaced two-man cars from that line would immediately be transferred to two-man routes to alleviate heavy loads. Stalemated, the company and union were together brought to an amicable solution only by the end of the war in the Pacific on August 15 with Emperor Hirohito ordering the cessation of fighting. One week later, the company and the union in a joint application to the P.U.C. asked it to suspend its ruling regarding

Interiors of six different passenger vehicles. Top: car 69, car 70; middle: car 370, car 389; bottom: car 1001, car 1307. (Lawton Gowey photos)

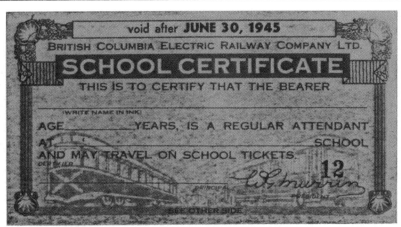

A modified P.C.C. street car graces this school certificate from 1945. (author's collection)

substation, transmission, and distribution facilities would be completely reorganized. Ingledow stressed that the program's completion would give the Fraser Valley a rural electric distribution system unrivalled in Canada.

Three days later, interurban 1304, the former "Connaught car," caught fire near Cloverdale while making its way west from Chilliwack, the last car of an empty three-car train. Only a virtually destroyed shell was left by the time the train's crew realized what was happening behind them and a brave, though futile, attempt was made to extinguish the blaze. It was not to languish long as a bizarre floor on wheels outside the company's Kitsilano complex; since passenger vehicles were still in great demand, the shops, busy with street car refurbishing and rebuilding, got to work, constructing a beautiful, new interurban car, its exterior patterned after the 1309-1311 series. Dark leather, foam-filled, flip-over seats were installed; walls of dark varnished mahogany and a cream painted ceiling clinched its unique handsomeness. For the second time in its career, car 1304 was an attention-getter. Its return to action on December 29 was an unqualified triumph, denizens of Carrall Street viewing with some amazement and pleasure a prime example of the car builders' art at its best, something the company's shops might have turned out in 1910, and could still do thirty-five years later. "Built at Kits. Shops Jan. 1946" proudly lettered over a vestibule door, 1304 quite possibly was the last wooden interurban car built in North America.

In September, W. C. Mainwaring succeeded A. T. Goward as vice-president, B. C. Electric operations on Vancouver Island. A staff member of the National Electric Tramway in 1891, Goward had been manager of the Victoria system since the coming of the B. C. Electric, vice-president since 1923. Mainwaring had been with the company since 1932, its vice-president in charge of sales since 1944.

Grandview-Fourth Avenue. The reason for the request was predicated on the ending of the war, and the fear of unemployment in the offing. To relieve pressure on the two-man street car lines, the company announced a plan to convert fifteen one man street cars to two-man operation, the identical number of P.C.C.s waiting to go into service. On August 27, the P.U.C. agreed to the joint application, ruling that the order in regard to one man P.C.C.s on Grandview-Fourth would be suspended until the postwar transition period was past. Thousands were being thrown out of work with the curtailment of night work in factories and shipyards, and by September 6, the Boeing plant near the airport on Sea Island and those at Georgia West and Terminal Avenue were shut down.

Earlier in the summer, commencing Friday, July 27, the Chilliwack line's Friday market train had had its run lengthened eleven and a half miles from Jardine to Mount Lehman, arriving there one hour after departure from New Westminster at 6:30 a.m., and leaving Mount Lehman at 7:35 a.m. to arrive back in New Westminster for its market at 8:50 a.m.

On September 13, B. C. Electric vice-president and chief engineer Thomas Ingledow announced a one million-dollar five-year program of electrical development for the Fraser Valley. To service the projected population expansion and agricultural and industrial development, the

During October, a trolley coach was brought over to Victoria from Seattle and free rides were offered for a few days over a route specially laid out and equipped for the experiment, on Douglas Street north to Queens Avenue, east to Quadra Street, south to Pandora Street, and back to Douglas. Those rides were not only the first, but also the last, on a trolley coach in Victoria.

The Burnaby Lake line entered the realm of big league interurbaning on October 11 with the inauguration of three-car passenger trains on three runs, the 7 a.m. westbound from Sapperton, and the 5 p.m. and 5:30 p.m. trains out of Carrall Street. The 5 p.m. run cut off one car at Douglas Road, the 5:30 p.m. two. An extra conductor was provided for these Monday-to-Friday three-car operations.

By the end of October, ten — not fifteen — Vancouver street cars, 300-309, had been rebuilt

Reborn 1304 leads a Chilliwack line train inching into the passing siding at Sperling. (E.L. Plant photo)

to two-man cars, pursuant to the company's agreement with the union vis-à-vis not operating P.C.C.s on the Grandview-Fourth Avenue line. The cars presented a singularly attractive appearance, retaining their wide one man entrance doors at the front, even with the addition of similarly wide two-man car entrance doors at the rear. After fourteen years as one man cars, 300-309 returned to their original mode of operation, albeit in 1945 fashion.

Two slides of mud and rock, precipitated by an extraordinary fall of rain and the diversion of a mountain stream, played havoc with the Chilliwack line's operations between October 24 and 26. The October 24 evening trains from Vancouver and Chilliwack, blocked by a slide three to four feet deep and a hundred feet long

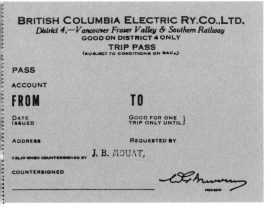

alongside Vedder Mountain near Reclaim, had to transfer passengers, gingerly and with difficulty, and return to their respective points of departure. Fifteen sectionmen of the company's Abbotsford, Vedder Mountain, and Chilliwack gangs successfully cleaned up the mess, only to see an equally large slide cover the right of way on the following night. At the same time, the water level had risen to the point where the bridge over the Vedder River was in some danger, and the outfit cars, at Huntingdon, were rushed to Woodroofe, just east of the bridge, so that a skeleton track could be cribbed up to allow trains to cross over the soggy area. The first train over was the 6:25 p.m. interurban train out of New Westminster on Friday, October 26.

Significant changes in the carrying of mail by the interurban system came into effect on November 1, and there were some major losses. The Central Park line would no more carry mail, and the Lulu Island line would cease its mail deliveries between Davie Street, Marpole, and Brighouse. However, two trains each way daily still carried mail between Davie Street and Steveston, with one train in each direction transporting mail between Davie Street and North West Cedar Company at Kerr Road. Mail on the Burnaby Lake line still moved on one run in each direction daily, on the Chilliwack line on two

trains each way daily. November was also the month in which the last rails were ripped from the right of way of the already forgotten Stave Falls line.

Vancouver had its ten days with the Seattle trolley coach in early December, wires having been strung over its route, from Burrard and Hastings streets, along Burrard, Pender, Georgia, Bidwell, Alberni, Cardero, Pender, Thurlow, and Hastings streets. The public rode free, and famed B. C. Electric observation car conductor, Teddy Lyons, was one of the guides; everyone, including Vancouver's city council, seemed impressed.

In New Westminster, a special Christmas Market was held on Christmas eve, prompting the B. C. Electric to run its market train on that day, operating the same schedule used by the regular Friday market train. During 1945, the Guides had sold nearly four million tickets, 375,000 of those alone in December (for a total of $24,000), the month whose last days broke all records for passenger traffic. On the interurban system eight new freight spurs had been laid during the year, and in addition to the ten 300s, Victoria street car 238 and six Vancouver street cars had been rebuilt in the company's ongoing program. Cars 171, 172, and 177 looked especially dashing in the steel sheathing molded to their Narraganset sides, a new touch in 1945. The company had decided

Flower pots at Hudson's Bay on Douglas Street, with car 235 headed deeper into downtown, then to Gonzales. (K. Hodgson photo)

(Left)
A trip pass for the Burnaby Lake line, designated here not only as District 4 but also as the Vancouver, Fraser Valley & Southern Railway. (Burnaby Village Museum)

On the roof at Mt. Pleasant barn. (author's photo)

At year's end on the complete B. C. Electric system, 327.858 miles of forty- to ninety-three-pound track (sixty- and seventy- on the interurban system) were operational, including 214 sidings and passing tracks (195 on the interurban lines). Seventy-two interurban cars, including the three remaining 1700s, were in service, as were 398 street cars, distributed in the following fashion:

	North Vancouver	Vancouver	Victoria
two-man, single end	—	227	—
two-man, double end	4	12	—
one man, single end	—	62	12
one man, double end	7	23	29
multiple unit		20	
observation		2	
Totals	11	346	41

One hundred and seven buses were working in New Westminster (thirty), North Vancouver (three), Vancouver (fifty-seven), and Victoria (seventeen).

Rush hour at the foot of Lonsdale Avenue. The cross on the face of 150 declares that it's a one man car. (V.L. Sharman photo)

during the year not to scrap 190 worn out freight cars, but rather to salvage everything possible from each of these cars, and rebuild a smaller new fleet of freight and service rolling stock.

A new record of 144,376,774 passengers had been carried in 1945. After the high of 1943 in Victoria, street car travel had dropped off slightly again, as in 1944, although the buses had picked up some of the losses. During the height of the war effort, the Victoria street cars that for years had carried 25,000 people daily had averaged up to 60,000. The armed forces training centres and the heavy movement of armed forces personnel between the city and wartime centres such as the naval barracks, the navy yard, and Work Point contributed massively, using blue and red tickets marked "ARMY and NAVY only." As in Vancouver and North Vancouver, the shipyards had been major employers, the two major Victoria yards together employing ten thousand more people than they would in peace time.

Freight tonnage was down eight and a half percent to 833,017, the dip largely attributed to the return of some lumber shipments to the sea lines after the end of the war. Nonetheless, the five 970-type locomotives handling most of the main line interurban freight traffic continued to perform feats of strength and endurance literally unheard of in electric motor equipment of their vintage. The shop at Kitsilano was peerless in these matters as well.

Car 274, a Fairview-type car, is southbound to Broadway on Granville Street, having just left Granville Bridge. (E.L. Plant photo)

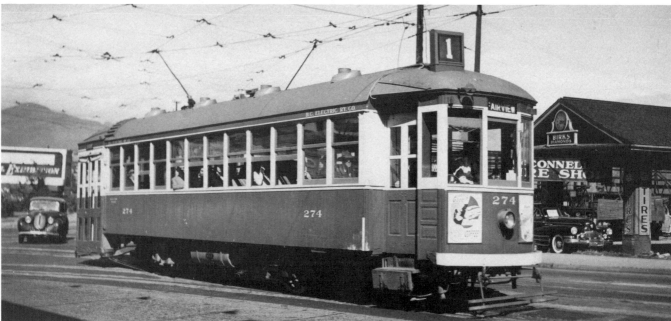

VII

1946-1958:

Ultimate Renewal

On Quebec Street, just south of
Thirteenth Avenue, car 120 waits
at the entrance to the second
deck of Mt. Pleasant barn.
(Williams Bros. photo)

The company's postwar push to modernize, particularly the Vancouver transit system, had gathered momentum during the year. The Beeler Organization of New York, engaged in 1944 to survey the B. C. Electric's operations and to make recommendations, had sent representatives during 1945, as they already had the previous year. A consulting engineer from Toronto, Norman D. Wilson, had also been engaged, first visiting the B. C. Electric in 1945, and then in the two following years presenting reports on his findings. Another consultant, J. D. Ong, of Cincinnati, had also been involved. In addition, the company had had discussions with the Vancouver Town Planning Commission and its consultants in both 1944 and 1945, the Commission reviewing the plan for the city which Harland Bartholomew and Associates of St. Louis, Missouri had drawn up for Vancouver in 1929.

Harland Bartholomew's new preliminary transit report, issued June 29, 1945, praised the exemplary fashion in which Vancouver's street car lines traversed the downtown business district, but it was critical of the locations of the two Vancouver interurban depots:

> "The most serious objection to the present transit routes within the business district is that the interurban lines stop at the outskirts. Persons using these routes and desiring to reach the centre of the shopping district must transfer to another transit line. As indicated later, the operation upon these interurban lines might be by street cars rather than interurbans so that they could continue to and through the business district. It would be neither economical nor desirable to rebuild the terminals nearer the centre of the district."

With the advent of the first war-free year since 1938 came some not unexpected adjustments on the Chilliwack line. On January 21, 1946 the interurban train which had operated from Vancouver to Sardis every Sunday night, "The Soldiers' Special," was discontinued. On February 1, the company's Pacific Stage bus service ended its use of the depot in Abbotsford, preferring to halt at the Ravine Lunch instead. The old gravel pit spur at Sullivan was removed by February 25 (part of it had already been pulled up in 1945), though the passing track at Sullivan was being extended.

Fortunately, a trip on the Chilliwack line by journalist Neville C. Curtis stimulated a report, filed in Cloverdale on February 6:

A unique pass, restricted to use on the Central Park line between Carrall Street Station and Boundary Road (Park Avenue). (Norman W. Williams collection)

A new masthead for Vancouver Island's Buzzer! *(author's collection)*

> "It's a wise old 'owl' that leaves Carrall Street B. C. Electric station at Vancouver at 11:25 Saturday night, and there's a distinct difference in personality between the two old cars that make the midnight run up the Fraser Valley as far as Mount Lehman every week.
>
> The New Westminster car that services way points to the Royal City has rather a cold look, very business-like and is filled with inter-city passengers coming from shows mostly, as well as people who have visited folks in Vancouver.
>
> It is old car 1306 that has the wise, benign look. Within this swaying carriage the people of the Fraser Valley return to their quiet country homes after a 'day in the cities.'
>
> The conductors change at New Westminster where the city crew goes 'off' at midnight. The 'owl' then takes on a more protective look. Its headlight warns it is bringing a precious load of young people from dances, shows and ice rink.
>
> See the conductor coming through the cars? He's been on the run 11 years and knows almost everyone personally.
>
> 'Hi'yer, Jean. Good dance? Many there. Have a good time?' he asks with a smile, stuffing tickets into his side pocket. On he passes, a cheery nod and smile for everyone.
>
> 'Archibald Road? Yes! I'll call you,' he tells a sleepy couple.
>
> Now the hill is passed and the train gathers speed, rushing through the dark countryside. Houses and farms dimly seen in the distance — a winking light. The cars are emptying at each stop.
>
> 'Yes! They're the same sort of passengers each Saturday night,' muses the conductor. 'They're a grand bunch of kids though, and we keep our eye on them in a general sort of way,' he added.
>
> 'Cloverdale,' he calls out. On round the curve, through the grove of trees to Langley Prairie, Milner, Sperling, Coghlan, County Line, Bradner to its destination goes the train.
>
> Wartime transportation restrictions revived the traffic on this 35-year-old line of B. C.'s interurban railway company. Freight, too, rumbles day and night, connecting American lines between Huntingdon and Vancouver, and it may be some time yet before highway stage and freight lines supersede entirely this friendly valley line.
>
> Streamlined, air-conditioned cars may push the relics into the discard, but in the meantime old 1306, groaning and creaking in all its joints, sighs its way into the barn Sunday morning to rest its weary springs before being called out for the next run 'up the Valley.'"

In Victoria, effective February 1, the number 4 street car line, Esquimalt, transferred its Esquimalt-bound passengers at Head Street, its new cut back terminus, directly to feeder buses that connected in both directions with the street cars between 9 a.m. and 11:10 p.m., providing twenty- to thirty-minute service. In Vancouver, the company's transportation and gas divisions took over the newly-added top floor of the head office building at Carrall Street on the last day of

February.

President of the company for more than seventeen years, Gerorge William Murrin retired from that post on April 25, though remaining with the directorate, to be replaced by Albert Edward "Dal" Grauer, the sixth company head, following managing director Frank S. Barnard, general managers Johannes Buntzen and Rochfort Henry Sperling, and presidents George Kidd and Murrin.

My First "300" On Fairview
By *John Gould*

Well, Tuscon, you want a story,
  I guess this coffee can wait.
Did I ever tell ya about the time
  I'm jabbed by the finger of fate?

I'm workin' a "Fairview Inner"
  With old "Charley the Cook",
I tell him we got a "300",
  All he did was give me a look.
And, believe me, brother, I'm sayin'
  It contains more than is written in a
  book!

How we got from Mount Pleasant to Broad-
  way
  Is a story not meant for tender ears.
We learned that our fears were well
  founded,
  I tore up about eight sheets of "red"
That "300" would stand on her snozzle,
  How I wished I was home in my bed.

The grass is green in the valley,
  Now the sky is blue overhead,
About those eight revolutions on Fairview
  The words will be better unsaid.

North Vancouver and the B. C. Electric came to an agreement on May 14 to eliminate its three street car lines. Ratification by the city's voters was still necessary before the street cars could be forced off the steep, broad, undulating north shore mountainside.

On May 31, the Chilliwack line's interurban trains began making stops, if necessary, at the new platform and shelter erected at Stewart Road. Old Sinclair station, a thousand feet west, was discontinued as a stop, its station soon removed.

Since there had for some years been more freight business than the locomotives could comfortably handle, and since the company had ascertained that an order for new ones would cost a wait of more than two years, it decided to investigate the possibility of purchasing second-hand locomotives, a search which proved successful. The Oregon Electric's line between Portland and Eugene was recently de-electrified, and four General Electric-American Locomotive Works products, numbers 21-24, were up for sale in Portland. Number 22, brought to Vancouver in early June on a trial basis, performed admirably, emerging from Kitsilano shop (whose staff of 183 must have delighted in seeing new motive power) brilliantly painted and renumbered 960 on June 27, entering service three days later. Locomotives 21 and 23 quickly arrived, commencing their efforts for the B. C. Electric as 961 on August 8 and 962 on September 9, respectively. Though they

Wrecking car F.4, only two months old, stands ready to assist with the dire plight of street car 183 at Sasamat Street and Fourth Avenue — always a difficult corner — on April 2, 1946. (E.L. Plant photo)

*(Left)
(B.C. Electric Employees Magazine, March 1946)*

Two Lonsdale street cars, double teamed for the rush hour, wait at the line's upper terminus, Windsor Road, in 1946 before returning to the ferry to fetch more commuters. (Ted Clark collection)

Lynn Valley car 162 drifts down Grand Boulevard in June 1946 to meet yet another ferry. (Stan Styles photo)

It's Cherry Carnival time in Chilliwack and nine of the big 1300s hug the loop. (Geoff Meugens photo)

had gone into immediate use, new control equipment had been ordered, necessary since the B. C. Electric operated its interurban system on 600-volt lines, not 1200-volt, as the Oregon Electric had.

New provincial regulations affecting street car operations came into effect on June 22: the maximum allowable speed in business areas was raised from twelve to eighteen miles per hour; during nonrush periods, the number of standees was not to exceed fifty percent of a street car's seating capacity; street cars were to reduce speeds on downgrades, and be kept under instant control (therewith eliminating the regulation of stopping one hundred and fifty feet behind another street car on a downgrade); and all unauthorized persons were banned from riding in the vestibule with the motorman.

Vancouver's diamond jubilee celebrations were off to a colourful, noisy start on July 1 with one of the best parades its citizens had ever witnessed. And in addition, there were the races at Lansdowne and the Cherry Festival at Chilliwack, all this excitement combining to create the day of record passengers-carried statistics.

The Burnaby Lake line's postal service between Carrall Street and Buena Vista post office, near the line's Cariboo Road station, was discontinued, the final mail dispatch eastbound on train number 406 on June 29, the last westbound on train number 413 on July 1. Otherwise on the interurban system, this was the summer all the Burnaby Lake, Central Park, and Lulu Island line stations glistened again in their fresh coats of red and cream paint, and double-length billboards stylishly advertised, "TRAVEL BY INTERURBAN — fast, frequent, economical." It was also the summer the company acquired Victoria's Blue Line Bus Company, a logical step in the company's wish to create in Victoria and vicinity an integrated, larger scale — and competition-free — transit layout.

In North Vancouver, free bus rides between 6:30 p.m. and 9:30 p.m. to the public for one week beginning September 3, following the routes of the street car lines, preceded the voters' ratification on September 11 of a new twenty-year accord, to go into effect October 1, calling for buses to supplant street cars within sixty days. September 24 was the last day of service for the No. 1-Lonsdale line and its four two-man street cars, 153, 155, 156, and 159, just a little over forty years since the first street car had struggled up the hill. And car barn foreman Bert Giffen, who had been there at the very beginning, was one of those riding car 156 on its final journey on Lonsdale, completed at 12:55 a.m. on the twenty-fifth.

Buses went into service later that day, their run on Lonsdale extended three blocks to Carisbrooke Road, two buses running in tandem during rush hours between the ferry wharf and Twenty-third Street. Normally, the Lynn Valley street cars would have had the east track at the ferry wharf, formerly shared with the Lonsdale line, to themselves, the Capilano street cars, as always, the sole occupant of the paralleling west track. However, the buses found it convenient to

The Buzzer

Published by the British Columbia Electric Railway Co.
Vol. 31   VICTORIA, MONDAY, OCTOBER 7, 1946   No. 19

(Victoria Archives)

A view to the west at Huntingdon station on a late summer's day in 1946. The state of Washington lies immediately behind the immaculate depot. (E.L. Plant photo)

use vacant track space. Tearing up of the 2.055 miles, including two passing tracks, of the abandoned Lonsdale rails was undertaken immediately.

The company had begun its first Burnaby bus route, Smith-Rumble, on September 16 as a gesture of good faith to the municipality during negotiations for a new transportation franchise. In Richmond meanwhile, the company had purchased the Airport and Grauer-Miller bus service from Richmond Transportation, commencing its own bus runs on October 1.

In Victoria, Pembroke barn and shop received a new coat of whitewash during October, and a concerted program of body repair and painting commenced on the 230- and 250-class street cars. Special attention was given cars 255, 256, and 258 whose rear vestibule casing over the rear bumper was missing, a dangerous defect. On October 7, route adjustments for two of the lines went into effect: street cars on the Head Street route began entering and leaving the downtown area via Government and Yates streets, and street cars on the Burnside route began entering and leaving the downtown area via Douglas and Yates streets.

On October 29 a daily inspection of signals on the Chilliwack line was begun. Motormen of the first passenger train of the day, in both directions, stopped at the southern crossing of Scott Road and at Newton, their duty to check and inspect the operation of the automatic signals at these points where Scott Road and the King George Highway crossed the Chilliwack line. This order of the Board of Railway Commissioners in addition necessitated the daily reporting on a specific form of the signals' condition. Throughout the years, there were always the B. C. Electric's orders to train crews of specific trains, varying with the natural light available, in regard to turning on, and off, the lights of the stations along the Burnaby Lake, Central Park, and Lulu Island lines. (As example on November 4, the crew of the 4 p.m. Burnaby Lake interurban from Vancouver turned on all the station lights east to Murrin, the 4 p.m. from Sapperton all the lights west to Douglas Road, and the 1:30 a.m. train eastbound from

17489	4 P.M. STUB 24

ISSUED FROM	17489	
LONSDALE		1946
LYNN VALLEY		
CAPILANO		
Jan	Feb	Mar	NORTH VAN.
Apr	May	June	DELAY
Jul	Aug	Sept	CHILD'S Transfer
Oct	Nov	Dec	VAN. CITY

Car left punched terminus at latest time shown below

FERRY Ter.	OUTER Ter.

From 4 P.M. Stub must be attached at top.

4	Subject to Conditions on back hereof	0
5	DO	10
6	NOT	20
7	FOLD	30
		40
		50
8		0
9		10
10		20
11		30
		40
		50

The transfer form used by all three North Vancouver street car lines, this one dated September 24, 1946, the Lonsdale line's last day. (Bob Webster collection)

(author's collection)

Uplands car 257 proceeds east on Fort Street, across the tracks of the Gonzales line at Cook Street. (Bob Webster collection)

Vancouver extinguished them.)

On November 17, B. C. Electric buses replaced the company's Pacific Stage Lines highway buses on the North Vancouver-Vancouver operation via Lions Gate Bridge. It was the same day the

company inaugurated a bus service on Capilano Road running north of Woods Drive to the upper end of Capilano Road, the way for this operation having been prepared by the company's purchase of the Canyon bus service which had been operated by Mr. J. Roy Henry, using automobiles.

The Steveston interurban line acquired yet another station on November 21 with the initiation of Gilbert Road between Brighouse and Lulu Island. As the interurban system approached the hectic Christmas season, orders went out to all motormen to reduce to series operation only, if the power demand on the general distribution system between 3 p.m. and 6:30 p.m. should be so great as to cause a power interruption. Beginning on December 23, the double track on Fir Street north of Fourth Avenue was off-limits to all interurban cars, necessitating awkward, traffic-blocking movements on Fourth Avenue, should an interurban car travel to Kitsilano shops via Granville Bridge.

Victoria voters went to the polls on December 12 — Esquimalt's and Oak Bay's on the fourteenth — to decide the fate of the new by-law, to authorize Victoria to join with Esquimalt and Oak Bay in granting the B. C. Electric an inter-municipal transportation franchise. Needing a three-fifths majority, it missed by fewer than seven hundred votes. Mainwaring was mystified and disappointed by the desire for street cars, the rejection of buses. (Saanich too voted, but in regard to another carrier, Vancouver Island Coach Lines.) The buses already ordered for Victoria were sent to North Vancouver instead. In Burnaby, voters followed the recent precedent by turning down on December 14 the company's request for a twenty-year bus franchise.

FORM T 1625

BRITISH COLUMBIA ELECTRIC RAILWAY CO., LTD.

FOG HEADWAY DISPATCH CARD

Line .... Date .... A.M.
P.M.

Starting Terminus ....

Approx. Headway between Cars:

Other than Rush Hours .... minutes

Rush Hour Period .... minutes

Dispatcher ....

CAR NO.	RUN NO.	TIME LEFT	CAR NO.	RUN NO.	TIME LEFT

[continued over]

A headway dispatch card used in Vancouver during times of particularly heavy fog. (Barrie Sanford collection)

Stanley Park-bound P.C.C. 423 rounds westward onto Cordova Street. This view north on Carrall Street shows the old zig-zag approach for the overpass to Union Steamships. (V.L. Sharman photo)

(Nonetheless, the Smith-Rumble bus kept running.)

During 1946, the B. C. Electric had, after so many years, discontinued the sale of electric and gas appliances. The city of Vancouver's setting up of a special committee in regard to the company's ten-year transit plan had culminated in a transportation franchise agreement, dated December 30, and effective on the first day of 1947. Victoria's Birney 402, wrecked, had been run out of service during the year, and a big job, the renewal of the substructure of the Jordan River flume, had been completed.

The last eight street cars to be rebuilt by the company made their appearance on Vancouver's streets in 1946, car 298 the last. Car 175 had been given steel sheathing for its curved sides, a refinement instituted in the previous year for the last few Narragansets treated. Many new spurs had been laid during the year, particularly on the Lulu Island line, but the passing track in North Vancouver on Grand Boulevard at Ninth Street on the Lynn Valley line had been removed. By the end of the year, the company had 184 buses in city service, 116 on rural and interurban routes. Never in a previous year had as many passengers been carried on the B. C. Electric's street cars, interurbans, and buses on the lower mainland as in 1946 — 141,387,914 — nor would this figure ever be passed! Victoria's street cars having carried 10,726,480 passengers, the total number of riders (including Victoria's bus passengers) during the year was 156,091,301. Freight tonnage hauled was down somewhat to 786,099, a laudable figure nonetheless considering that wartime exigencies were things of the past.

Many street cars had been rebuilt, not so the interurban cars, which had performed with reliability and aplomb through the war years and after, continuing to be heavily used, seemingly indestructible. Much credit for their longevity went to the thirty-five men of the New Westminster barn who had fifty of the cars to tend (Kitsilano had the rest), handling most of the routine work

and repairs that did not require the ministrations of Kitsilano.

January 1, 1947, though the first day of a new year, was the last day for the outer end (Grand Boulevard and Nineteenth Street to Lynn Valley and Dempsey roads) of North Vancouver's No. 2 Lynn Valley line. Cars 160-162 predominated on the final day of the complete operation of the line to Lynn Valley, across the North Vancouver system's other trestle just east of Mountain Highway over Hastings Creek.

Electric derrick (and snow plow and flanger) B.5 menaces Vancouver's streets. (K. Hodgson photo)

Car 175, smart in its new steel sheathing, waits in the wye at Fiftieth Avenue and Main. (Ken Hodgson photo)

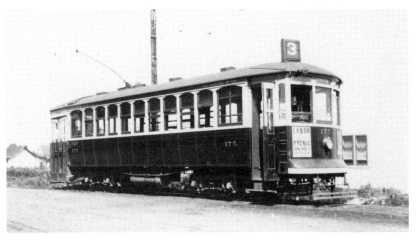

Robson car 213 is eastbound on Robson at Howe Street, Vancouver's court house — art gallery today — lending lustre to the street's north side. (Ted Clark collection)

In Richmond, a new bus franchise for the company went into effect on January 20. By the end of the month, all locomotives at work on the Chilliwack line had received new Kahlenberg air horns. Motormen on both the Chilliwack and Lulu Islands, to comply with a rule in their new agreement regarding payment for motormen for handling mail, began submitting on February 10 a wage ticket which indicated the number of sacks of mail handled. The new agreement itself was entered into by the B. C. Electric and the Locomotive Engineers and the Order of Railway Conductors on February 12, a wage increase of twelve and a half percent being its principal feature.

Three more of Victoria's Birneys were out of service by the beginning of February, stripped of their parts for potential further use on the remaining cars; the three bodies were for sale. By mid-February, North Vancouver Lonsdale cars 153, 155 and 156 had been sold for housing units in the Chilliwack area, 159 had become a home in North Vancouver's Lynnmour area, and 154 had been withdrawn from service.

What many believe to have been one of the strangest traffic accidents in Vancouver history occurred at 10 p.m. on February 24. It was touched off when a Central Park interurban train,

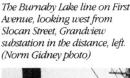

The Burnaby Lake line on First Avenue, looking west from Slocan Street, Grandview substation in the distance, left. (Norm Gidney photo)

car 1000 leading car 1007, barreled furiously out of the Carrall Street depot, derailing eastbound Fairview street car 274, knocking over westbound Dunbar street car 350, sending a taxi flying, and flattening a second automobile. Sixty people were injured, thirteen being taken to hospital, and damage to property was estimated at five thousand dollars. The fortunate absence of serious injury spoke well for the construction of the street cars and interurbans.

The accident, which had brought the imposing, year-old wrecking car, F.4, to the scene, had been generated by the motorman's failure to put the interurban car's air cocks to the open position before starting the train. The motorman had received a shock from the reset switch. Though the brake valve handle had been found in application position, the train would have stopped had the air cock not been closed.

All mail service on the Burnaby Lake line ended on the last day of February, trains 406 and 413 carrying the last sacks of mail between Vancouver and Burnaby Lake. At Huntingdon, the B. C. Electric agent began handling all interchange details at that point, the freight conductors no longer having to leave icing records and switch lists for cars handled between Abbotsford and Huntingdon. On March 7, the fourth of the Oregon Electric locomotive quartet, number 24, arrived at Kitsilano where use of its parts to keep the other three healthy was its fate. (To that end, no customs duty had been paid by the company upon 24's entry into Canada.)

In North Vancouver, car 151 had been withdrawn from service in March, leaving 150, 157, and 160-162 to handle the service on both remaining truncated lines. While the company in mid-April was carefully preparing for another pro-bus plebiscite in Victoria, it had decided that the use of locomotive 905, in need of some repair, would be discontinued, its occasional work

henceforth to be dealt with by line car L.5.

In North Vancouver, the end of a remarkable street car system was mourned in the early hours of April 24, the last full day of service having been Wednesday, April 23. Residents near Fell Avenue were chagrined at losing their Capilano street cars, knowing only too well that buses would never venture up their narrow dirt road. Not only was No. 3-Capilano gone, car 150 providing the last service until 1:15 a.m., but also No.2-Lynn Valley. The car barn, consisting of a two-track metal shed accommodating six street cars, and several outdoor tracks, was located on the Lynn Valley line, at Third Street and St. David's Avenue. Storage was mainly outdoors, the shed used mostly for servicing and repairs; the substation was adjacent to the barn. The Lynn Valley line had partaken of centre-of-street, side-of-road, and private right of way operation, its grade approaching the old terminus at Dempsey Road relatively steep. This fact, in addition to the low power at this remote end of the system, had always slowed the street cars to a crawl, making it almost impossible to run two cars together on this portion.

The final trip on the Lynn Valley line to the top of Grand Boulevard, its terminus of less than four months, was operated by car 161, operator Bill Cochrane in charge. Once again, Bert Giffen was aboard, as was a crowd of hilarious passengers singing old-time songs and ripping off souvenirs, including seats.

On Sunday, April 27, some thirty members and friends of the Lower Mainland Railroad Club gathered in North Vancouver under the direction of club leader, Kitsilano shop employee, and B. C. Electric photographer *par excellence,* Ernie Plant. White flags in place on car 157, they made the final street car trip in North Vancouver, the last stretch covered reaching from the northern extremity of Grand Boulevard to the car barn.

Purchased by H. P. Blanchard, street cars 150, 151, 154, 157, 160, 161, and 162 were hauled by flat-bed truck to Ruskin, and set up, brick chimneys attached, as the Ruskin Hideout Auto Camp. Their trucks and miscellaneous equipment were taken to Kitsilano shop. (Car 160 was found in bush near Gibson's Landing many years later.)

A dozen street cars work Main Street, south from Hastings, in this 1947 view from the Ford Building. (B.C. Transit)

L.2 was scrapped in North Vancouver, its metal salvaged, and S.55 was returned to Vancouver in June for a few more years of snow sweeping. By May most of the track and trolley wire were removed, the streets repaved; a bus garage was in place by May, the adjacent car barn about to be demolished.

A sure sign of summer was the resumption of the C.P.R.'s Steveston-Sidney ferry service on May 2, together with the B. C. Electric's careful orientation of interurban train times from Davie Street and from New Westminster to connect deftly with the ferry's movements. But the thirtieth day of April had brought something atypical of Vancouver's summers, or of any seasons, the last day of service for two lengths of street car line. Fraser Street between Forty-ninth Avenue and Marine Drive; Forty-first Avenue between East Boulevard and Dunbar Street: these were the first street car lines — both of them single tracked (Fraser from Fifty-third south) — to be abandoned as part of the B. C. Electric's modernization program. Buses made their first appearances on these streets on May 1.

On the thirty-first of May, Fraser Street saw its last street cars between Forty-ninth Avenue and Kingsway. The Kerrisdale end of this line was run in its shortened form as No. 8-Kerrisdale from downtown to Forty-first Avenue and East Boulevard, commencing June 1, the same day thirty-two large capacity buses began service on Fraser, supplanting the ten two-car multiple unit city trains and several single street cars used in rush hours. The multiple unit equipment went to work on the busy Hastings East line.

The cessation of street car service on Fraser between Forty-ninth and Kingsway had not been part of the company's plan for 1947; it was a step forced by the city, which in turn had been forced by merchants and property owners on Fraser Street who had initiated a petition for the paving of their street. When faced with the prospect of laying permanent tracks in the new pavement, the

A system-wide pass for the last full year of operation by Victoria's street cars. (Tom Cronk collection)

B. C. Electric chose rather to withdraw its street cars, and rails.

An inspection of the Vancouver system's track by company, city, and provincial officials on June 17 revealed Main Street between Pender Street and First Avenue, and south of Nineteenth Avenue; Kingsway between Main and Fraser; and Powell Street between Campbell Avenue and Templeton Drive to be in very poor condition, particularly the last named. Broadway from Kingsway to Alma; Main Street from First Avenue to Broadway; Fourth Avenue from Granville Street to Alma Road; Hastings Street from Campbell Avenue to Renfrew Street; the Powell Street line east of Templeton, and between Carrall Street and Campbell Avenue; and both the Joyce Road and Victoria Road lines east of Fraser were all deemed to be in poor shape. In best condition was the rarely used section on Alma between Fourth Avenue and Broadway.

With the horse racing season under way again at Lansdowne, on weekdays between June 27 and July 12, and between July 16 and August 2, special three-car interurban trains once more crowded the available street space in front of Davie Street station, running five special trips daily, six on Dominion Day, and seven on Saturdays. The trains were splitting, as in the recent past, for the crossing of Granville Bridge, but a new procedure for return journeys was instituted: upon reaching Fourth Avenue, the trains, rather than breaking into two, operated through the Kitsilano barn area and across the trestle on their way to Davie Street. In the midst of the racing hurly-burly, interurban car 1201, one side painted green, took time off to star in a B. C. Electric-produced movie, "Dinner for Miss Creeden."

In Victoria, the Greater Victoria Transportation Committee's advertisements in local newspapers urged: "The old street cars are to be removed once and for all. This is the requirement of the new Franchise agreement. Vote 'Yes'." Voters in Victoria, Esquimalt, Oak Bay, and Saanich indeed voted "yes" on June 19 for the new twenty-year franchise, to go into effect on November 1, which offered them a "unified transportation system." The inclusion of Saanich municipality in the proceedings and the partnership with the B. C. Electric this time of the Vancouver Island Coach line in the new transportation plan gave this plebiscite a more attractive, comprehensive character than the earlier one; there would even be a universal transfer within a three and a half-mile limit.

The B. C. Electric agreed to pay, toward the estimated $600,000 cost of track removal, $250,000 to Victoria, $35,000 to Esquimalt (the Esquimalt line west of Head Street was ready for removal), and $25,000 to Oak Bay. The withdrawal of street car service — the new agreement allowed the B. C. Electric eighteen months for this

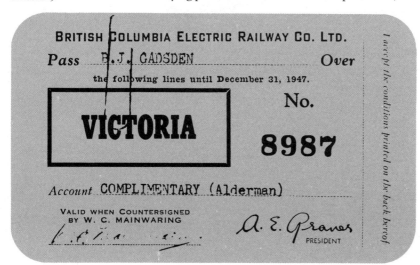

BRITISH COLUMBIA ELECTRIC RAILWAY CO. LTD.

Pass B. J. GADSDEN   Over

the following lines until December 31, 1947.

No.

VICTORIA

8987

Account COMPLIMENTARY (Alderman)

VALID WHEN COUNTERSIGNED
BY W. C. MAINWARING

A. E. Graves
PRESIDENT

I accept the conditions printed on the back hereof

— would depend largely on the delivery of new buses, seven having, in fact, been delivered only a few weeks earlier. The company announced immediately that the street cars would be offered for sale, $150 for the large ones, $100 for the Birneys. Styled "The Jolly Trolley," Birney 401 was already part of the playground equipment as a projection theatre at the Garden Library of Mrs. W. W. McGill, Tattersall Drive, in Saanich.

Otherwise as well, transportation seemed to have Victoria in its grip. The much-loved C.P.R. steamship, *Princess Kathleen,* having served bravely in the war, was now completely reconditioned and made her first peace time voyage, with 700 passengers, to Seattle on June 21. Just five

Uplands-bound 189 leaves Government Street for east-reaching Fort Street. (Stan Styles photo)

Birney 408 moving out on the Burnside line. (Bob Webster collection)

days later, the Black Ball Line's new, streamlined M. V. *Chinook* caused as great a stir on her first entry into Victoria's inner harbour from Seattle.

But it was on June 30 that the destruction of Victoria's street car system commenced. This was the last day of operation for the No. 5-Gorge and No. 4-Head Street lines, signifying the abandonment of all street car tracks west of the intersection of Bay and Government streets, as well as the tracks on Bay from Government to Douglas Street. In addition, the outer seven-tenths of a mile of the Uplands line was abandoned (north of Estevan Avenue), a beautiful section on private right of way to the delightfully landscaped loop at Midland Circle. As if there was something to be festive about, special street cars were running in the afternoon of the same day to the Willows fairgrounds. On Dominion Day, the Burnside line (having lost its Mount Tolmie run three years earlier) was connected with the shortened Uplands line, the street cars showing no change in numbering, 9 to Estevan and 10 to Burnside. On July 14, the first street car tracks were removed to facilitate bus use, those composing the loop (on company property) at the Gorge terminus.

The B. C. Electric's Burnaby transportation services, comprised of the Hastings Extension street car, the Smith-Rumble bus, and three interurban lines, took on more of a bus aspect on

July 1, the company commencing on that date the operation of the just-purchased bus services of Neville Transportation. In Vancouver, the Kitsilano street car line was to have ceased operating at the same time the McDonald bus line was extended downtown through its territory, July 15. Since permission had not been received to abandon the line, street cars stayed on, providing service only in rush hours.

A record freight car load having arrived earlier in the summer, a 176-ton transformer, the B. C. Electric had become keenly aware of the inadequacy of its 100-ton scale. At a cost of nearly $40,000, a new scale for weights up to 150 tons was constructed during the summer on a spur

Car 1308 with green flags at Kitsilano shops, motorman V.L. Sharman at the controls. Burrard Bridge crosses in the background to downtown Vancouver on the right. (V.L. Sharman photo)

line at the foot of Sixteenth Street in New Westminster. The installation of the scale, including its sixty-two-foot by ten-foot concrete pit, was handled by C.P.R. crews, as any such work on the leased V. & L. I. line would be.

While the B. C. Electric was also going ahead with the construction of new bus depots in Abbotsford, Chilliwack, Cloverdale, and Langley Prairie (and Haney and Mission on the north side of the river), New Westminster's famous market opened at its new location, 1051 Columbia Street, on Friday morning, August 22, necessitating particular caution by interurban and freight train motormen as they worked their way through the traffic congestion surrounding the market. August was also the month of the opening of Vancouver's new $440,000 bus depot on the site of Larwill Park, at Cambie and Dunsmuir streets.

In Victoria, buying street car bodies was all the rage, so much so that voices in Oak Bay municipality railed vigorously against any incursion of these wheel-less instant homes into its precincts. Car 254 perhaps went the farthest afield, being purchased in late August by the Summit Lumber Company for use as a camp bunkhouse between Duncan and Cowichan Lake. It was hauled, as most of the street cars seemed to be, by the ubiquitous Heaney Cartage.

An extra interurban train was added to the Marpole-New Westminster line's work on September 2 with the addition of a run to provide transportation for the workers of Canadian White Pine and B. C. Plywoods as they came off their shift at 12:30 a.m. On the Chilliwack line, all mail bound for, and received from, Aldergrove from October 1 was routed via Jackman station (and dispatched to *The Aldergrove Courier*) instead of Langley Prairie.

Vancouver's observation cars, 123 and 124, enjoyed a record season, as of September 14 having carried 35,000 passengers. Since the loss of the track on Forty-first Avenue had necessitated time-consuming travelling from two different

directions to reach both Kerrisdale and Dunbar, the loop to English Bay had been lopped off the two-hour excursion, which would still operate for one more year from the corner of Richards and Robson streets.

In Victoria, October 9 was the day of the first removal of track from city streets. The Gorge line's Henry Street, between Esquimalt Road and Catherine Street, had the dubious honour of being a test case to determine more precisely what costs would be involved in such work.

On October 20, all B. C. Electric transportation lines, except the Chilliwack and Lulu Island interurban operations, were shut down as transportation employees went on strike for higher pay. As the strike continued, the passenger and freight equipment running on the two operating lines began to evince a variety of problems, a condition due to their not being able to receive proper maintenance.

The interurban cars most frequently employed on the Chilliwack run in 1947 were 1301-1303 and 1309-1311, and 1700; 1709 was at Chilliwack, as was locomotive 970. Locomotives 960, 972, 974, 980, 991, 992 were those most closely associated with the Fraser Valley line.

A fifteen-cent an hour wage boost having ended the strike at 4 a.m. on November 18, a number of adjustments followed. On the lower mainland, a seven-cent fare became ten cents cash on November 30; three tickets for twenty-five cents replaced four, and weekly passes were abolished. In Victoria, the new franchise, and fares, would come into effect on December 1, the planned November 1 start having been postponed by the strike. The fare would be seven cents, or four tickets for twenty-five cents, with a weekly pass available for $1.25. Transfers, as agreed, were interchangeable within a three and a half-mile circle between B. C. Electric and Vancouver Island Coach Lines vehicles.

The last day of the old franchise, November 30, was also the last day for the No. 6-Gonzales-Hillside line, the No. 9-10-Estevan-Burnside line, and the Cloverdale line. Sixteen street cars — no Birneys — on three street car lines were still in operation when the sun rose on December 1: No. 1-Oak Bay, No. 3-Beacon Hill-Fernwood, and Willows-Outer Wharf, a new combination. Government Street between Yates and Pembroke streets was now used only by street cars travelling to and from the car barn, and all track on Douglas Street north of Pandora Street was abandoned, including that at the Cloverdale car barn. During the year 21.257 miles of Victoria's track (13.242 route miles) had been abandoned, leaving 18.28 miles (10.09 route miles).

Vancouver's imposing new Murrin substation had gone into service on November 24. On the Central Park line, foggy weather again brought into effect the procedure of interurban conduc-

Former Oregon electric locomotive, 961, both poles up, pushes caboose A.9 and its train on the Chilliwack line. This locomotive is still in service today for Edmonton Transit. (V.L. Sharman collection)

tors registering their trains at Central Park westbound, Cedar Cottage and Fraser Arm eastbound, and maintaining a five-minute block. As had been the case at Highland Park in street car days, doors of both interurban cars were always thrown open at Fraser Arm, an often hectic connection with New Westminster-bound buses.

In Victoria, Bay Street substation had undergone complete modernization during the year, and there was some agitation to have street car 22, a veteran of a million and a half miles of service, presented to the city as an historic artifact. In Vancouver, the three blocks of street car track on Commercial Drive between Hastings and Powell streets had been torn up during the year.

Consulting engineer Norman D. Wilson, in a report to the company during the year, had made a number of significant statements in regard to the interurban system. Though he had made no

Just a few blocks from its terminus, Gonzales car 387 makes a brief stop at Wildwood Avenue, with Hollywood Park to the north. (B.C. Hydro)

Main Street South shuttle car 317 passes Fifty-ninth Avenue, nine blocks from its northern terminus, whence it appears to be destined (16-Main) for Mt. Pleasant.(Ted Clark collection)

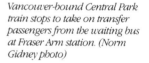

Vancouver-bound Central Park train stops to take on transfer passengers from the waiting bus at Fraser Arm station. (Norm Gidney photo)

specific recommendations for its long range use, Wilson felt the Central Park line to be an especially valuable asset for the future, and further suggested the Vancouver-Marpole line might be appropriate for rapid transit operation. The Burnaby Lake line he would dismantle.

By the end of the year, the company was operating 348 street cars and 317 city buses, and a record 156,416,742 passengers had been carried despite the strike; freight tonnage was down, but eminently respectable, to 723,896.

Another street car line loss initiated 1948, Vancouver's Main Street South line running its last complete day fromn Fiftieth Avenue south on January 15; its bus replacement would not reach to the interurban line at Main Street station as the street car had. In Victoria, trolley wire on the abandoned street car lines was being removed, and on the last day of January, the Willows street car line operated its last complete day, car 232 its last street car. Beginning on February 1, the orphaned Outer Wharf line was connected with the Oak Bay line to form No. 2 line, No. 3-Beacon Hill-Fernwood stoically maintaining its service. (It was announced on the same day that thirteen diesel locomotives would take over the duties of all the Esquimalt & Nanaimo Railway's steam locomotives.) No. 2 car, 231, ran its last on March 2, a collision with a gravel truck on Oak Bay Avenue at Rockland Avenue damaging it to the degree that repairs, in view of the approaching end of service, were not carried out.

On February 28, New Westminster got its fare increase, North Vancouver on March 28. A new Chilliwack substation had gone into operation in February, and on April 15 Vancouver street cars ceased using Kitsilano barn as a base of operations, all cars reverting to Prior Street and Mount Pleasant. In March, Francher & Francher, a California company skilled at track removal, with its own specially-developed equipment, was awarded the contract for ridding Victoria's streets of abandoned tracks and ties. By the end of April, new Westinghouse equipment had been installed on locomotives 960-962, enhancing their

flexibility as switchers or road engines.

The next to last step of the stuttering march into oblivion by Victoria's street cars occurred just past the midnight of Saturday, May 15, when the last Fernwood and Oak Bay street cars hummed their way along Government Street to the car barn. On Sunday, the Beacon Hill and Outer Wharf lines, alone, began an integrated service, running on Government Street — oddly, it now regained regular street car service, having lost it five and a half months previously — to their respective termini. Each line operated a ten-minute service, overlapped carefully to provide a five-minute service between Government and Pembroke streets and the junction at Superior and Menzies streets.

Not without warning, the most devastating flood in British Columbia's recorded history ravaged the Fraser Valley between May 25 and June 15, covering over 50,000 acres of Canada's best farm land. The Fraser River's flood of 1894 had been the yardstick, but any records set during that spring were obliterated by 1948's. At the height of the flood, Vancouver was isolated from the rest of Canada except by air. The interurban line to Chilliwack had been the only railway running through the valley during the flood's early stages, both C.N.R. and C.P.R. lines being completely submerged, but on Monday, May 31, the Fraser smashed through the dyke north of Gifford (the Gifford post office closed permanently two days later!), its angry, muddy waters flooding Matsqui prairie, covering the houses of Clayburn and Matsqui to their eaves. B. C.'s Premier Byron Johnson declared a state of emergency. Navy minesweepers and landing craft swept in across the prairie almost to Abbotsford in their rescue efforts.

The five miles of interurban line between the base of Mount Lehman and south of St. Nicholas were under four to eleven feet of water, the stations at Gifford, Glover, and Clayburn having floated away off their foundations, the roadbed washed out in many places. Though freight service could not be maintained, passenger and mail were kept up by the expedient of running a bus link over high ground between Mount Lehman and Abbotsford, another between Sardis and Chilliwack. At the Vedder River crossing, an electric locomotive with box cars stood watch from June 7, should a dyke breakthrough necessitate the speedy evacuation of residents. In New Westminster the company's trains kept moving despite the deep cover of water all across the area where Twelfth Street meets Columbia Street.

Thousands had assumed the status of refugees, evacuees who had lost everything they owned, devastated by this "80-mile-long Valley of Misery." Drowned animals were even washing up on the beaches of Oak Bay and Victoria. Over 35,000

A view to the south on Nanaimo Street at Fourth Avenue, cars 89 and 99 passing at the Nanaimo line's midpoint. (Bob Webster collection)

volunteer workers and reserve army, navy, and air force personnel were able to rest from their labours only on June 15, when a cooler spell in the mountains slowed the Fraser's rampage at its peak. New dikes would be built, both stronger and higher than those which sandbaggers at their most intense had been unable to keep from collapsing.

It was also on the fifteenth of June that street car service ended on Davie Street between Granville and Denman streets, and on Denman between Davie and Robson streets. On June 16, the No. 5-Robson line began running west on Robson to Denman, and then via Denman and Georgia streets to its new terminus at the Stanley Park loop, returning over the same route. In addition, No. 3-Main Street merged with the No. 8 route to form the Main-Kerrisdale line.

The company announced the stationing of an

Car 1307 has just brought a four-car race track special onto the special spur at Lansdowne track. (K. Hodgson photo)

operator at Lansdowne for 1948's horse racing season. All northbound trains were to stop and acquire a clearance from him before proceeding, the operator maintaining a red flag in position to call the attention of train crews. On the Chilliwack line, about fifty men were at work between Gifford and St. Nicholas, repairing the crazily-buckled track, ruined roadbed, shattered culverts, and scattered stations, when the word came from the district post office inspector that July 3 would be the last day of mail drop-off and pick up at Coghlan. (This post office would not close for another eight years.)

Saturday, July 3 (actually the first minutes of Sunday morning) was the final day of street car service in Victoria, fifty-eight years of street cars coming to a close with the shutting down of the Beacon Hill line and the Outer Wharf line, one of the original operations. On Monday, there was a ceremony befitting the loss of street cars in one of the first communities to have them. Company, government, and civic officials and leaders met at 5:15 p.m. at the B. C. Electric's offices for a brief observance, vice-president Mainwaring passing among the nearly one hundred guests "to fittingly observe the tragic occasion" of the passing of "this monument of public transportation." The "mourners" were then bussed to Niagara and Douglas streets, the Beacon Hill street car's

(Left)
Near Glover, B.C. Electric's Ernie Plant works to photograph the devastation wrought by the flooding of the Fraser in 1948. (E.L. Plant photo)

The Chilliwack-bound morning train has just crossed the Fraser River bridge at New Westminster, Canadian National's line to the right, Great Northern's to the left. (E.L. Plant photo)

Victoria's last street car, 383, heading for Pembroke Street barn, barely nosed out by a '48 Ford in front of the Empress Hotel, July 5, 1948. (B.C. Hydro)

terminus, where car 383 was waiting, tricked out in black crepe paper, inside and out, and bearing a sign on each side reading "The Last Trip of Victoria's Last Street Car." With the B. C. Electric's senior Victoria operator, Walter Peddle, in control, 383 ran back to the Pembroke barn with all the guests aboard, for the very last time on Niagara, Menzies, Superior, and Government streets, for the very last time around the Parliament Building and in front of the Empress Hotel. "Interment" at the car barn meant the stripping of anything removable from the street car, including the operator's stool.

On July 12, after a service disruption of six weeks, the Chilliwack line was back to normal service, though a speed restriction of ten miles per hour was imposed on all trains between Gifford and St. Nicholas. Since the C.P.R.'s line from Mission to Abbotsford and Huntingdon was still not ready for service, the B. C. Electric line was handling the C.P.R.'s freight loads. For the next few weeks, a work train would be hauling gravel from Huntingdon to ballast the rebuilt Gifford-St. Nicholas stretch.

On Friday, the thirteenth of August, company officials and Vancouver and area civic dignitaries and officials were taken by the B. C. Electric's new trolley coaches, leaving the city hall at 3:15 p.m., first over the new Fraser Street line, and then on the new Cambie Street line, before heading west along Forty-first Avenue to the company's new bus and trolley maintenance facilities, Oakridge Transit Centre. One of the honoured guests for the ceremonial beginning of this new direction in the company's half century of transit was Rochfort Henry Sperling, B. C. Electric's general manager

from 1905 to 1914. President Grauer's address did not overlook the company's difficulties with getting rid of its street cars and interurbans:

"At this stage I must say that we ran into an unexpected snag. With our eyes fixed on modernizing our system, we had overlooked the fact that our transportation franchises, drawn up in the early part of the century, did not cover trolley coaches. A sharp-eyed municipal solicitor pointed this out and the result was that all our municipal transportation franchises, which we had thought to be perpetual subject to the periodic rights of municipalities to purchase, were thrown into the pot for re-negotiation. These re-negotiations, with their attendant alarms and excursions, took the better part of two years to accomplish on the Lower Mainland. We ended up with new 20-year franchises all right but we found that we had to pay sums in annual taxes averaging about 4% of our gross revenues for the privilege of modernizing. Knowing the real need of municipalities for revenues, we have no objection to this situation as long as citizens understand that, on a cost of service basis such as we are working under, any addition to costs must be met out of rates and fares."

The company's first trolley coach line, Fraser-Cambie, commenced its operation on Monday, August 16. On the previous day, street cars had run for the last time on Robson Street between Granville and Denman streets, the No. 5-Robson street car line disappearing, its mate, the Broadway East line, now looping via Hastings, Granville, Robson, Richards, and Hastings streets. On August 18, the Oak Street line at its Marpole terminus was cut back almost a block to allow for the paving of Marine Drive in conjunction with the building of a new bus loop.

All summer long, the Central Park line's Gladstone trestle was being given new life by a rebuilding process. Beginning on September 22, the Chilliwack line became even more heavily involved in the transport of school children, arrangements having been made with the Abbotsford-Mission School District to carry students between Huntingdon and Abbotsford on trains No. 3 and 4.

Not all of Victoria's street cars ended up as cottages and coops, a singularly happy fate compared with that of the leftovers. On October 9, an Esquimalt & Nanaimo 0-6-0 switcher backed across the Johnson Street Bridge, passed its newly refurbished depot, and trundled, in reverse, up old Store Street to the Pembroke barn to hook up the remaining street cars, including 383, melancholy last day signs still intact. The steam locomotive then towed them across the bridge to the E. & N.'s Victoria West yards; pushed onto their sides there and torched, as were the various work vehicles, the destruction of these cars was the immediate precursor of the carnage to be wreaked on Vancouver's distinguished array of street cars and interurbans, begun in earnest on the very next day.

On October 2, the Public Utilities Commission authorized an increase in fares in greater Victoria, and on the tenth, the Central Park line, Burnaby, and Richmond became heirs to the fare increase, the last areas so blessed. The first unit, 62,000 horsepower, of the company's new power development at Bridge River, over one hundred and thirty miles north of Vancouver, was officially opened and put into operation on October 23. By the end of October, all damage done to the Chilliwack line was repaired, the track and roadbed fitter than ever.

In November, the B. C. Electric presented a new plan for transportation to the municipality of Burnaby, calling for a significant increase in bus route coverage and for the simultaneous abandonment of the Hastings East Extension street car line. The company expected that the latter thrust would clinch the deal. In the Fraser Valley, Sperling's post office worked its last day on November 30, mail for the community henceforth to be forwarded through Milner.

The city of Vancouver's decision during 1948 to build a new Granville Bridge had thrown the B. C. Electric's rubber-tired transit plans into a tizzy. The company's original conversion plan had not contemplated the scrapping of all the street car lines in the western portion of the city (old Point Grey), but the building of a new bridge forced a decision. The proposed bridge could be a double deck structure with rails on the lower deck, or a single deck structure with buses and trolley coaches operating over it. After much consulta-

tion, the latter option was selected, the company therewith shifting its rails-to-rubber emphasis to those street car lines using the current bridge.

During the year, not only had old steeple-cab locomotive 950 been scrapped, but the unthinkable had begun: Vancouver's street cars, one by one, were being stripped, thrown over onto their sides, and burned, adjacent to the Kitsilano shop and barn. Accident-damaged 97 had been the first, and already nine more had been destroyed.

On Vancouver Island, the renewal of the flume at Jordan River had been undertaken, the modernization of Victoria's Bay Street substation continued, and the conversion of Pembroke car barn into a centre for bus repair and painting began. On November 3, the Garbally Road service garage, little more than half a mile to the north, had become the home of Victoria's buses.

By year's end, 327 street cars, 69 interurban cars, 350 buses, 82 trolley coaches, and 106 highway buses had carried 155,880,307 riders. Freight hauled topped the million mark for the first time with 1,021,368 tons!

Regular service already in its past, the Kitsilano line completed its work on January 15, 1949, the last day of rush hour operation. W. W. Anderson was the operator of the last street car, number 205, the other two cars on the line, 310 and 315, run by F. E. Way and A. Isherwood, respectively. Within the year, the four blocks of private right of way, and the loop, between Chestnut and Yew streets would be removed.

Burnaby municipal council having accepted the B. C. Electric's transit proposal, the Hastings East Extension street car line also ceased operating on January 15. Operator C. O. Owen brought the last car home at 1:45 a.m., January 16, Bill Magee operating the other final street car, number 83. Though the company had given up a perpetual franchise to operate street cars in Burnaby, it had decided its best interests and those of the municipality lay in such a direction: the bus franchise was instituted on January 16.

February, after January's cold weather, turned into a particularly snowy month, especially in the Fraser Valley, where snow plow-equipped locomotive 980 was kept busy all through the Bradner-Mount Lehman-Clayburn section of the Chilliwack line. It was also during February and March that considerable discussion by company officials and in the press highlighted the interurban system's dilemma: should a new, more central depot in the heart of downtown Vancouver be built, or should the interurban trains vanish, just as the street cars were vanishing?

In mid-March, the B. C. Electric publicly announced that it intended to replace the Chilliwack line's passenger service with extended bus services. Vice-president and general manager of Pacific Stage Lines, Ivor W. Neil, was making his way through the Fraser Valley, discussing the

Victoria city street car transfers, 1944. (Bob Webster collection)

The intersection of Hastings and Main streets with its "grand union" track layout made any routing gambit possible. (V.L. Sharman photo)

company's intention with municipal officials. Neill stressed that fares on the interurban line would have to be doubled if its passenger service were brought up to date, and that the company's freight operation would be improved by the elimination of the interurbans from the line.

Two more street car lines operated their last full day of service on April 15. The early hours of April 16 saw street car 339, with motorman E. J. Christian and conductor S. M. Jenue, cover the No. 8-Kerrisdale line for the last time, the track on

Granville Street from Broadway to Forty-first Avenue and on Forty-first to the loop at East Boulevard abandoned. On the same evening, the No. 5-Broadway East line also succumbed, the track on Broadway between Main Street and Commercial Drive operated over for the last time by motorman R. C. Tollepen and conductor T. E. Currie. With the loss of the Kerrisdale line, No. 3-Main Street cars looped in downtown Vancouver. In Victoria, Francher & Francher had returned to begin removal of the remaining track.

Beginning on April 16, Vancouver-bound interurban trains from New Westminster, Steveston, and Marpole ceased making a passenger stop on Granville Street before turning onto Davie Street. Conductors now made certain, after leaving Fourth Avenue station, that the vestibule door of the rear car was closed, with the trap door down. In addition, they and the brakemen positioned themselves in the vestibule to prevent anyone from opening any doors before the loading zone in front of the depot on Davie Street was reached.

On May 6, the second Bridge River unit was placed into operation, and on May 24, Vancouver's two observation street cars commenced their penultimate year of activity, operating from their new loading point at Victory Square on Cambie Street, facing south from Hastings Street — adults fifty cents, children half fare. Until June 30, and between September 7 and 18, four trips were run daily, double headed if necessary, at 10 a.m., 2 p.m., 4 p.m., and 7 p.m. From Dominion Day until Labour Day, the sightseeing trips left at 10 a.m., 11 a.m., 1 p.m., 2 p.m., 3 p.m., 4 p.m., 6 p.m., and 7

Though the mail-carrying work of the interurban system had been cut back, and some post offices along its right of ways had closed, the line to Chilliwack in 1949 was still the mail route for many Valley communities:

Community Addressed	Chilliwack Line Dispatching Point
Aldergrove	Jackman
Bridal Falls	Chilliwack
Cheam View	Chilliwack
Cultus Lake	Sardis
Flood	Chilliwack
Fort Langley	Milner
Glen Valley	Milner
Kilgard	Abbotsford
Laidlaw	Chilliwack
Lindell	Sardis
Matsqui	Clayburn
Murrayville	Langley Prairie
Straiton	Abbotsford
Surrey Centre	Meridian
Vedder Crossing	Sardis
Walnut Grove	Milner

p.m. The route of 123 and 124 followed along Cambie Street to Robson Street, and then via Robson, Richards, Hastings, Granville, Robson, Connaught Bridge, Cambie, Broadway, Alma, and Dunbar streets to the wye at Forty-first Avenue. On the return, they proceeded north on Dunbar and Alma to Broadway, and then along Broadway, Granville, Pacific, Richards, Hastings, Granville, Pender, and Georgia streets to Stanley Park, whence the starting point was again attained, via Georgia, Pender, Granville, and Hastings streets. Of the Lulu Island interurban line's two traditional summer services, the connections with the Sidney-bound *Motor Princess* at Steveston and the extra trains to the races at Lansdowne, only the former would operate in 1949, Lansdowne Park being shut down. Horse racing was held at Exhibition Park (formerly Hastings Park) in Vancouver. The 11 a.m. and 6 p.m. trains from Davie Street and from New Westminster (travellers transferred at Marpole) brought passengers to the outbound ferry at Steveston on weekdays; the one ferry run on Sundays was met by the 11 a.m. trains. As always, the appropriate trains waited for passengers arriving in Steveston from the inbound ferry.

In the city of Nelson, 513 miles east of Vancouver on the C.P.R.'s Kettle Valley line, British Columbia's only other street car system, the three-car Nelson Street Railway Company, ceased operations on June 20 after half a century of service.

Two more Vancouver street car lines terminated many years of service in the early morning of July 16, the No. 20-Powell Street line, including all track east of Powell and Main streets, as well as the single track on Renfrew Street between Eton and Cambridge streets, and the west track of the passing siding on Renfrew between Cambridge and Oxford Street; and the Fourth Avenue leg,

west of Fir Street, of the No. 4 line, including track on Alma Street north to Broadway. Street cars 201-206 had performed most of the runs on the Powell Street line during its last weeks of operation.

A new street car loop had actually been placed into operation on July 16, the same day transit operators moved from a forty-six to a forty-four-hour week. Millar loop, as it was named, had been constructed at the western entrance to Exhibition Park, on the east side of Dundas and Renfrew streets, four blocks north of Hastings Street, nicely terminating this side-of-the-road double tracked street car route. The fact that single track was still in place for two blocks north beyond the loop to Cambridge Street, adjoining Callister Park, enabled special street cars to serve the park's soccer fans in an efficient manner: running north

Granville Street, north from Sixteenth Avenue: the time of rails in streets was past. (B.C. Hydro)

Car 205 on Quebec Street at Thirteenth Avenue, having backed off the roof section of Mt. Pleasant barn. St. Patrick's School forms the backdrop. (Bob Webster collection)

Car 192, on the Sixteenth Avenue line, moves past Simon Fraser School on its way to Main Street on an August 1949 morning. (Stan Styles photo)

on Renfrew, a special would circle Millar loop, counter-clockwise, and, when on the verge of heading south, would stop and run backwards north up Renfrew to Callister Park; when it was loaded after a game, the street car could proceed straight ahead along Renfrew without any further manoeuvres. The Millar loop would ease traffic congestion during the forthcoming exhibition, six of the two-car multiple unit trains using it on a regular basis at that time.

Since the beginning of the year, twenty-three street cars had been torched at Kitsilano shop, including almost all of the double-enders. Multiple unit second units 703, 705, 707, and 715 were out of service at Kitsilano, while 304 and 305 were boarded up there, with 300-303 and 306-309 in storage at Mount Pleasant. The P.C.C.s were on the No. 9-10-Victoria-Stanley Park and No. 11-Joyce-Stanley Park runs, 364-378 assisting in the rush hour periods.

Beginning July 25, ten cents cash became the only fare in Vancouver, ticket deals being abolished; and on August 7, the Nanaimo street car line ran its last full day on Broadway between Commercial Drive and Nanaimo Street. That part of Broadway, as well as the section west of Commercial, was slated to have its rails torn up, new pavement set in, and trolley coach overhead wire strung. The remaining section of the Nanaimo street car line was designated No. 18. The B. C. Electric approached the city of Vancouver on August 10, requesting that it be allowed to discontinue its Sixteenth Avenue street car service; only 3.2 passengers were being carried per trip.

September 15 was the last complete day of service on yet another street car route, the far west reaching runs of the No. 15 and No. 16 cars, from Tenth Avenue and Alma Street, on Tenth, Sasamat Street, and Fourth Avenue to Drummond Drive. On the following day, the Dunbar line, the only remaining street car operation west of Granville Street, was connected with the Main Street line, the combination designated as No. 3-7, Main-Dunbar. Its route through downtown took Hastings, Richards, Pacific, and Granville streets.

Otherwise still in operation were street car lines 1-Fairview, 4-Grandview, 9-10-Victoria-Stanley Park, 11-Joyce-Stanley Park, 13-Hastings East-Exhibition Loop (Millar loop), 14-Hastings East, 17-Oak Street, and 18-Nanaimo. The two Hastings East lines looped through downtown via Hastings, Granville, Robson, and Richards streets, the Grandview via Hastings, Cambie, Robson, and Granville streets, and the short run 9-Post Office via Cordova, Cambie, Hastings, Granville, and Cordova streets. The 10 and 11 lines continued to operate over the original waterfront route, Main, Powell, Carrall, Cordova, and Granville streets, and the Fairview car on Hastings Street.

New operating procedures went into effect on the Burnaby Lake line on September 23, the practice of dropping an interurban car on the main line at Douglas Road being discontinued in favour of doing the same at Hill station. The eastbound train now pulled past the west switch at Hill and cut off the second car on the main line, after which the westbound interurban pulled out of the passing track, the brakeman coupling the car left behind by the eastbound.

The company's wish regarding its No. 19-Sixteenth Avenue street car line having been granted, the one double ender terminated its shuttling on October 15. The rails and trolley wire stayed in place, however, as the route was still a valuable, less crowded alternative for street cars running to and from Mount Pleasant barn.

Diesel locomotives had arrived in September, three of them from the General Electric company, engined by Cooper-Bessemer. Numbered 940-942, the new seventy-ton, 660 horsepower units would be able to haul between 350 and 400 tons on the Mount Lehman and Kennedy grades, somewhat more than the 300 the electrics regularly dealt with, thereby justifying their price of more than $86,000 each. Painted in the B. C. Electric's bus-and-trolley-coach all-cream colour scheme, with red highlighting, including the company's new totem emblem, the three diesels worked through a lengthy trial operating period, the company not taking them over officially until late November. The electric locomotives would not be replaced at this time, but their existence was surely threatened by an electric company's excursion into diesel motive power on a great interurban operation, the Chilliwack line.

Meanwhile, Chilliwack standby 1709 had been brought into New Westminster to lie and wait quietly outside the barn, and on October 27, the B. C. Electric filed with the Public Utilities Commission an application for permission to cease passenger service on the Chilliwack line, and to add, beginning on January 1, 1950, bus routes to its Pacific Stage Lines services in the areas formerly served by the interurban. The B. C. Electric's seeming haste would go unrewarded, the interurban trains continuing to operate past the proposed final date.

On November 16, the second step was taken toward the progressive introduction of a forty-hour-week for all transit operating employees with the establishment of a forty-two-hour week. By the end of November, five P.C.C.s, 400, 404, 426, 427, and 428, had been repainted in the company's new all-cream reversal of the previous colour scheme — none of the older street cars, or interurbans, would fall heir to it — at $350 per street car. With the inception on December 7 of the third 62,000 horsepower unit at Bridge River, the B. C. Electric became one of North America's first utilities to achieve a surplus of electric power.

For street cars, 1949 had been a devastating year. New Westminster's had slipped away in 1938, North Vancouver's in 1947, Victoria's in 1948, and Vancouver, the bastion of street cars for almost sixty years, had been reduced precipitously to eight lines, only four — Fairview, Victoria-Stanley Park, Joyce-Stanley Park, and Oak Street — still adhering to their traditional routings. An astonishing total of forty-eight street cars had been cremated at Kitsilano during 1949, often at the rate

The yellow cardboard public timetable for the Lulu Island branch, December 15, 1949. (author's collection)

of one every two or three days; and the promise by Vancouver's city engineer that the new Granville Bridge would be ready before the end of 1952 had prompted the company to end service on the East Boulevard, Fourth Avenue, and West Point Grey lines earlier than it had planned. Altogether, 16.35 route miles of street car operation had been abandoned in 1949. With the loss of 4.46 route miles in 1947 and 3.54 in 1948, the transportation modernization program had eliminated over twenty-four miles of street car line, most of it double track, and all of it in Vancouver, with the exception of the Hastings East Extension line's 1.89 miles.

One hundred and two fewer street cars were active at the end of 1949 — 225 — than at 1948's close. On the whole system, 381 city and 105 intercity buses were operating, in addition to Vancouver's 168 trolley coaches. Ridership continued its downward trend, with 148,746,411 passengers carried. Freight tonnage hauled, though down 6.71%, had been a healthy 952,784. But it was the poor health of the Chilliwack line's passenger operation that sadly jarred: serving an area, laced by roads, with a population of 72,900, its 1949 revenue from passenger service was $83,597, its deficit from passenger operations,

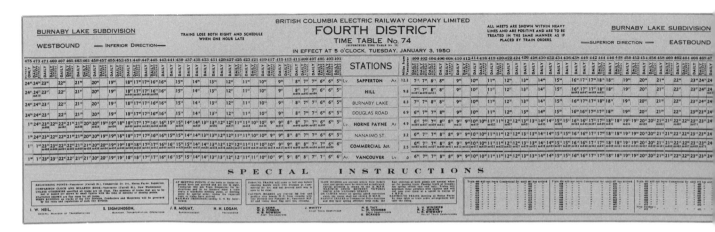

Burnaby Lake line employees timetable from 1950. (Ted Clark collection)

J 133206

B. C. ELECTRIC RAILWAY CO. LTD.
FRASER VALLEY BRANCH

(Above and next page)
Two types of receipts used by conductors on the Chilliwack line during its last year. (author's collection)

$323,168.

The Burnaby Lake line had never been able to fulfil the hopes some had initially dreamt for it, and 1950 began with the cutting back on January 3 of its base service to an hourly one, half hourly between Carrall Street and Horne-Payne. Electric power plans were entering their final stages in the Fraser Valley, with new substations having been constructed and the company ready to close the Chilliwack line's original substations as soon as the interurbans ceased operating. Meanwhile nine of the Chilliwack line's passenger and freight motormen had already taken and passed a twelve-hour course to receive certificates of competency with respect to the operation of the diesel locomotives.

And yet January almost reminded everyone of old times in the valley, thirty-seven inches of snow falling during the month. The B. C. Electric's milk train was reactivated, bringing hundreds of cans of milk into Carrall Street from diverse points all along the line, especially Evans, Upper Sumas, Mount Lehman, and Bradner. An interurban special, consisting of a passenger car and two baggage-express cars loaded with food for residents along the line, left New Westminster on the morning of Friday, January 13, and headed into a snow storm. Two snow plows, one at either end, were attached at Bradner, but to little avail, the train embedding itself in a twelve-foot-high, one thousand-foot-long snow drift at Vye. The passenger coach was taken back to Abbotsford, New Westminster was telephoned for assistance, and the three diesels with a caboose, as well as again the interurban train's rear snow plow, arrived in the early evening at Vye, thirteen men in all to do battle with the snow and a fierce gale in freezing weather.

After the snapping of a towing cable, the breaking of the train line of the leading diesel, and furious shovelling, the train was finally freed at 1 a.m. But then remained more shovelling and plowing through the thousand-foot drift, a grueling task not accomplished until sun-up. On

its way again, the entourage experienced yet another tribulation at Yarrow where water from a small creek had coursed across the tracks, covering them for sixty feet with six inches of ice which had set to a concrete consistency. Shovels, picks, and a sledge hammer created an early morning cacophony, the last vigorous act in a twenty-four-hour drama: the Chilliwack line was again a viable supply link, the special train and the diesel locomotives embracing Chilliwack's loop at 9:30 a.m., Saturday.

The company's snow sweepers in Vancouver had their last great hurrah when snow struck with awesome decisiveness on January 23, paralyzing the transit system. To get, and keep, street cars moving, six snow sweepers, at a cost of $225 an hour, wore out eighty heads of bamboo cane in their first twenty-four hours of operation.

February 15 was yet another black day for street cars, the last full day of operation for the Victoria portion of the No. 10 line and for the Joyce portion of the No. 11 line. Abandoned was the track from Main and Hastings streets via Main, Powell, Carrall, Cordova, and Granville streets to Hastings; the track on Cambie Street between Cordova and Hastings; the track on Kingsway between Main Street and Joyce Road, and on Victoria Drive between Kingsway and Fifty-fourth Avenue, the last two sections well ahead of the company's schedule. Property owners on Victoria Drive, having seen the transformation of Fraser Street, had petitioned the city for new pavement. The city acquiesced, and the B. C. Electric felt it might as well do away with the whole Kingsway-Victoria system.

The Grandview and Stanley Park lines were linked, No. 4 shown in the Grandview direction, No. 10 in the Stanley Park; through the downtown area, the street cars of this new line followed Hastings, Granville, and Pender streets. Both lines fell heir to the P.C.C.s, cars 364-368 aiding both in rush hours, the Hastings East line at peak times also getting help from 200- and 300-class Brills, and even some two-man cars in the afternoon. As a result of the closure of street car running on Kingsway and Victoria Drive, the barn at Prior Street was closed on February 16, the remaining street cars from that date emanating from Mount Pleasant. On the same day, all transit operating employees entered the world of the forty-hour week.

By the end of February, P.C.C.s 419, 429, 432, and 435 had been painted in the new colour scheme, but on April 5, car 705 was the first of the steel multiple unit street cars to be scrapped. After its body had been set afire, burning out the woodwork, torches had been used to cut up the steel frame and sides for a waiting scrap dealer.

The B. C. Electric had targeted July 1 as the last day of interurban trains on the Chilliwack line, but the company was to be disappointed. Public Utilities Commission hearings at the end of March on their wish to replace interurbans with buses were uncovering much opposition from the municipalities of Surrey, Langley, Matsqui, Sumas, and Delta and certain Chilliwack organizations, though Chilliwack's board of trade and New Westminster's city council supported the company's application. The argument against buses centred mainly around the question of maintenance of bus schedules on poor quality Fraser Valley roads. Meetings protesting the ending of interurban service were everywhere. On March 30, the Newton Co-operative Association and the Newton Ratepayers Association even presented a brief to the hearings suggesting that interurban train service be operated only as far east as Langley Prairie from New Westminster, the interurban cars to be replaced by Vancouver's P.C.C. street cars.

On May 2, the B. C. Electric made the move that ended the interurban to Chilliwack: it offered Surrey, Langley, Matsqui, Sumas, and Chilliwack $40,000 each toward the maintenance of roads to be used as bus routes. Matsqui accepted immediately, Sumas and Chilliwack following, but Surrey and Langley held out for $50,000, which

they got. The changeover to buses was thus ratified by the Public Utilities Commission which approved the $220,000 agreement reached between the company and the local governing bodies. The company had already sold the still-active Chilliwack substation in April to a private citizen.

At the end of May, the substation at the corner of Union and Main Street was shut down, having provided electricity for the downtown operations of the street cars and interurbans for forty-six years and for the trolley coaches latterly. Its replacement was next door — the new Murrin substation annex, with completely automatic equipment. The conversion cost had been $400,000. New too was diesel locomotive 943, identical to 940-942, placed in service on June 13.

The Stanley Park street car line operated its last complete day of service on August 24, as did the Nanaimo Street line; track abandoned included Nanaimo Street between Broadway and Hastings Street, and the complete trackage between Granville Street and Stanley Park, including Pender, Georgia, Chilco, Alberni, and Denman streets, as well as the loop at the park. The wye at Boundary Road and Hastings Street at the end of the Hastings east line was used for the last time on the same date, a new combined street car and bus terminus, Kootenay Loop, coming into operation slightly more than a block west on August 25. The loop's track was the last new "line" laid by the B. C. Electric. The Grandview street car line, alone again, once more made its way through downtown using Hastings, Granville, Robson, and Richards streets.

The end of street car operations to Stanley Park made it a certainty that 1950's summer would see the last of the observation cars; there simply was not enough track left for running a viable sightseeing circuit. (After the closure of the Stanley Park line, the observation cars had included Exhibition Park in their peregrinations.) Sunday, September 17, was the last day, with car

B. C. Electric Railway Co., Ltd.
Fraser Valley Branch

ADULT FARE PAID
Five Cents

Good only on date and between stations indicated by punch marks.

94592

JAN FEB MAR APR MAY JUN		Station Nos.
JUL AUG SEP OCT NOV DEC		
1 2 3 4 5 6 7 8		1 2
9 10 11 12 13 14 15 16		
17 18 19 20 21 22 23 24		55 57
25 26 27 28 29 30 31		

Car 123 on one of its last trips. Observation car guide Dick Gardner leans on the brake wheel, while B.C. Electric president A.E. "Dal" Grauer and observation car guide Teddy Lyons link arms. (B.C. Hydro)

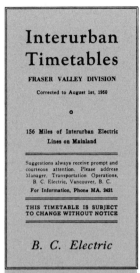

124 the only one of the two in service, 123 having run its last tours on the previous weekend. After the final Sunday trips, at 10 a.m. and 2 p.m., from Cambie and Hastings streets, car 123 did appear, decorated for the occasion, to take a party of company and civic officials at 4 p.m. for a thirty-minute excursion through the downtown area.

After the final ride, a reception at president Grauer's home — Vancouver mayor Charles Thompson attended as well — honoured the popular guides of the two cars, Teddy Lyons, almost as famous locally as the cars themselves, and Dick Gardner. (Teddy Lyons and motorman Jimmy Hope had run the last trip.) Lyons had been an observation car guide for forty years, with consummate showmanship having created a veritable travelling variety show, aided and abetted by resident performers of all ages along the cars' route. Gardner, a magician and musician, had conducted the cars for twenty-five years, the two men together having travelled 600,000 miles on the two observation cars.

Columnist Jack Scott, in a nostalgic piece in the *Vancouver Sun,* later recalled his observation car summers:

> *"Looking back on those pre-war years now I seem to have spent a remarkable amount of time riding Teddy's observation car.*
>
> *For one thing it was a therapeutic journey and so simple were my tastes that when the old car ground around the corner off Robson and into Granville Street with the north shore mountains ahead down the canyon of business blocks I fairly tingled with anticipation.*
>
> *There was, too, the fact that Teddy's vaudeville-style patter was the cheapest entertainment around.*
>
> *Teddy was a slight, leathery man whose insouciant manner and a large red rose in his buttonhole gave him a theatrical look in spite of his shiny blue conductor's uniform.*
>
> *He captivated his audience right from the beginning. 'If your shoes hurt, girls, take 'em off,' he would advise the ladies, speaking like a side-show barker through a red megaphone. 'Those without hat pins — gone with the wind.'*
>
> *His motorman, Ted Clampitt, would give a shave-and-a-haircut toot, crank the old monster into action, and the show, as the saying goes, was on the road.*
>
> *The trip was not so much a sightseeing run as it was a tour of personal triumph for Teddy and, for the passengers, a sharing in the reflected glory.*
>
> *Pedestrians and cops on the corner waved their greetings. Motorists thumbed their klaxons in salute. Small children and large dogs ran alongside.*
>
> *Teddy got everybody into the act.*
>
> *Outside a bank a fat woman harangued her husband. 'There's Mrs. Jones getting her alimony,' he might remark.*
>
> *He would tilt his megaphone up at a window cleaner high on an office building ledge. 'How's*

the weather up there?' — then, turning back to us, 'A man fell from that floor last week,' he would say. 'He didn't hurt himself, though. He was wearing his light fall suit.'

> *So it went and before you'd gone a mile you were bathed in a glow of goodwill, fellowship and the wonder at what appeared to be the friendliest town — and certainly the most beautiful — of any in the wide world."* †

"*The Buzzer* immediately set to sponsoring a contest to allow the public to decide how and where car 124 would be preserved. Closing date was October 14 — the prize for the best suggestion, $25. Would the car go to Stanley Park, perhaps the exhibition grounds, or even next to C.P.R. locomotive 374 at Kitsilano? The contest would determine 124's destiny, for president Grauer had decided that the beautiful big red and gold car would not be scrapped.

This had also been the last summer for the C.P.R.'s *Motor Princess* to ply between Steveston and Sidney. The reconstruction necessitated by new regulations imposed in the wake of the tragic burning of the *Noronic* — one hundred eighteen lives had been lost — on the night of September 16, 1949 in Toronto's harbour required an expenditure the C.P.R. did not wish to lavish on an aging vessel. A fascinating interurban-ship connection had been severed.

Saturday, September 30, began as any other Saturday on the Chilliwack line: Chilliwack-bound passenger train No. 2, car 1302, had left Carrall Street at 8:25 a.m., and would leave Chilliwack as No. 5 on the return trip at 1:30 p.m. (As always, the baggage-express car, 1700 that morning, had left at 8 a.m. to allow it time to load at New Westminster.) Train No. 4, with cars 1402 and 1304, would leave Carrall Street at 1:20 p.m., and Chilliwack at 6:10 p.m., as train No. 7. The final run from Vancouver, No. 8, at 5:30 p.m., would consist of cars 1309 and 1300, the latter dropped at New Westminster.

There was, however, an enormous difference to the day: car 1309 was the last interurban car ever to reach Chilliwack with passengers. It departed from Chilliwack at 9:55 p.m., motorman Jim Lester deadheading it back to New Westminster, arriving at 12:55 a.m. Veteran Chilliwack agent Marden G. Nelson had received the line's last running orders, for car 1309, over the telephone in the Chilliwack depot. Car 1304 was, however, the very last interurban car in regular service carrying passengers, running the "owl" from Vancouver at 11:35 p.m., arriving at Mount Lehman at 1:45 a.m. on Sunday, October 1, and leaving there at 1:50 a.m. for the 2:50 a.m. termination at New Westminster barn of almost precisely forty years of passenger service on the greatest interurban line in Canada.

While regular service was being run on that Saturday, much special activity was occurring,

The last public timetable of the Chilliwack line. (author's collection)

† "Jack Scott," *The Vancouver Sun,* 19 January 1960, p. 17.

Car 1310 leads 1307 from New Westminster, bound for last-day festivities, September 30, 1950, at Langley Prairie. Bert Johnson is at the controls. (E.L. Plant photo)

adroitly stage-managed by interurban superintendent Mouat and chief dispatcher D. W. Stearman. Car 1311, bannered, beflagged, and beribboned, left Chilliwack in the morning, bound for Langley Prairie with forty civic and municipal leaders and guests, many picked up at stops along the way; at 10:52 a.m., a similarly colourful and festive train, cars 1310 and 1307, left New Westminster with one hundred and fourteen company and civic officials, old-timers, and retired Chilliwack line employees, also bound for Langley Prairie. President Grauer rode the latter train. At noon, the trains touched cowcatchers in the centre of Langley Prairie in front of the depot to the skirl of piper Tommy Farquhar's bagpipes, the blowing of whistles by the interurbans, and the shaking of hands through the end vestibule doors of the two facing trains by president Grauer and Langley reeve, George Brooks. Motorman Art Young and conductor "Red" Lowry had brought the special train from Chilliwack, motorman Frank Wolgemuth and conductors A. V. Mortison and Bob Straw the train from New Westminster.

Four Pacific Stage Lines buses took the complete last day party to Newlands Golf and Country Club for a ceremonial luncheon and reception. Among the many distinguished guests were Chilliwack line luminaries, seventy-one-year-old Bert Johnson, with the line from the beginning as motorman until his retirement in 1947, and seventy-year-old Ernie Tait who had helped survey its route. The climax of the luncheon was reached with the presentation of cheques totalling $220,000 by Ivor W. Neil to the reeves of the municipalities for their bus-assisting road improvement programs. With the cheques went engraved gavels, fashioned from wood taken from the still-operating interurban cars which had made the first trip to Chilliwack, 1700, 1401, and 1301. Similar gavels were presented as well to

Abbotsford's commissioner and New Westminster's mayor. The two trains having been coupled together, 1307, 1310, and 1311, in that order, deadheaded back to New Westminster, while all the officials and guests were returned to their destinations by the four buses.

Within a week, Chilliwack's dignified depot was torn down to make way for bus driveways of the new, $75,000, combined Pacific Stage Lines depot and company general offices, opened October 10. (Cloverdale's bus depot had already been in operation since September 23.) With a view to the possibility of their giving longer-term service on the Central Park line, should that be necessary, the two "newest" interurban cars, 1304 and 1321, had their toilets removed in favour of seating space.

Since the B. C. Electric had agreed to maintain a special express service for the shipment of bulbs, flowers, and other perishable commodities, and to maintain a passenger coach for emergencies, trailer 1600 had been fitted up for these purposes, with 1602 languishing in the wings as a possible alternate. To provide for express space, the seats were removed from

Line car L.6 works the track along New Westminster's Front Street on a warm August day in 1954. Fifty-year-old Fraser River Bridge in the distance beckons the B.C. Electric for the run to Chilliwack. (George Bergson photo)

1600's smoking section; all electric lighting was extracted, replaced by kerosene lamps affixed to alternate window posts, and a stove was installed at each end of the car and storm windows on all the window frames. Newly added M.C.B. couplers and air hoses allowed it to be operated, as intended, with any of the four diesels, which replaced the electrics on October 1, 970, 973 and 974 among the latter having been those most in use on the Chilliwack line during the last months of electricity. Car 1600 was seen most often behind one of the diesels on its way to pick up bulbs at Bradner, British Columbia's daffodil and tulip capital.

The de-electrification of the line followed almost immediately after passenger service ceased. Before the removal of the trolley wire, the substation at Vedder Mountain, which had been supplying current for the interurban trains, had been shut down, its task, as that of the other four already dormant pioneer substations, taken over by recently built automatic substations. One of the original interurban cars, 1401, spent its last days pulling flat cars for the wire removal crew of line car L.6. The 7.6-mile stretch from New Westminster up the hill to Kennedy and east to Newton remained electrified so that the electric locomotives could assist the diesels on the long climb; prior to the end of passenger service, car 1706 had assisted in wire renewal work on this section.

Cars 1401, 1402, 1601, 1700, and 1706 were slated for immediate retirement, 1402, in fact, partly dismantled at Kitsilano by December. The 1300s went to work on the Central Park line, a scene they already thoroughly knew, but gone forever was an assortment of routines and practices unique to the Chilliwack line. Chilliwack line crews had worked the interurban trains only between New Westminster and Chilliwack, never into Vancouver on the Central Park line; Doc Watson, the baggage man, had been the only exception, a special arrangement having been made to allow him to carry out his duties from Vancouver right through to Chilliwack.

Conductors wore regular railroad conductors' uniforms, and were members of the Order of Railway Conductors; motormen, belonging to the Brotherhood of Locomotive Engineers, always dressed the part. Many motormen possessed their own distinctive whistle which they installed on the car prior to every trip and removed as they came off duty. Residents up and down the Fraser Valley knew the motorman of a particular interurban train by the call of his whistle. Some motormen even sat on their own specially upholstered chairs.

Normally, the Chilliwack line interurbans had not entrained or detrained passengers between New Westminster and Vancouver, the same track along which urban sensibilities had been protected by the locking of toilet cubicles. (Drinking water was always available, barring the unavailability of paper cups.) A baggage-express car was generally not operated on Sundays, its place taken by one of the 1400s, which did, however, not run ahead separately to New Westminster as the 1700s did on weekdays.

The fares at the cessation of service for the 76.3 mile ride between Vancouver and Chilliwack had been $2.10 one way, $3.85 return. The sixty-one stations along the line, with the exceptions of Coghlan, Bellerose, and Huntingdon, had been situated on the north side of the line, but with the end of passenger service, many found themselves scattered across the countryside in new guises as chicken coops, storage sheds, and the like. Riders will perhaps always remember the bouncy roadbed near Craigs, a situation which even the most diligent of crews never managed to correct permanently. While the interurban trains were still running, seventeen of the stations had also been served by Pacific Stage Line buses.

Most of the five feeder bus lines that extended into areas once served by the interurban trains offered twice-daily service on weekdays, with no Sunday service. Lombard, Bellerose, and Stewart Road were a mile away from a bus line, Beaver River and Rand three quarters of a mile, and fifteen other stations half a mile. Furthermore, the poor quality of mail service by truck had residents all through the valley in a state of discontent. Package freight and express had, of course, been eliminated with the demise of passenger service, but the company had arranged for trucks to work in this area of endeavour.

Arriving by interurban train in Chilliwack had always been an occasion to be noted with interest. First, the train travelled in a clockwise direction on the double-tracked loop, most often using the outside track. (As many as fourteen interurban cars had been seen on the loop at one time during Dominion Day's Cherry Carnival.) Second, upon the train's arrival, a switch was pulled in the adjacent substation, permitting just enough power to reach the train to prevent the line switches from cutting out. This practice allowed the crew to be away from the train without the fear that an unauthorized person might tamper with it. Third, if the weather was cold, the governors were prevented from freezing up by draining the air tanks, a procedure followed especially if an interurban car was left out overnight. After the interurban service had ended and the station had been demolished, one of the loop's two tracks was lifted, the loop having lost the operational importance it once held.

At the cessation of passenger service, the largest communities on the line, after Chilliwack and Abbotsford, were Huntingdon (including Sumas, its U. S. neighbour) with about 1,000 inhabitants, Langley Prairie with 900, and Cloverdale with about 650. Following these in size were South Westminster (500), Milner (425), Yarrow (400), Mount Lehman (361), Bradner (349), Newton (320), Coghlan (320), Sullivan (270), Clayburn (148), and Sperling (144). Other communities of significance were those at County Line, Gifford, Kennedy, South Sumas, Upper Sumas, and Whatcom Road.

A unique feature of the 1:30 p.m. trip from Chilliwack had been the neck-and-neck competition with the C.P.R.'s steam-powered mixed train for close to seven miles between Huntingdon and Clayburn. The C.P.R. left Huntingdon for Vancouver at 2:20 p.m., two minutes after interurban train no. 5 had passed through Huntingdon, clattering over the switches of the line's one wye, on its way to Abbotsford, where it arrived at 2:26 p.m., four minutes ahead of the C.P.R. The interurban arrived at Clayburn at 2:33 p.m., inching over the diamond crossing with the C.P.R. three minutes before the arrival of the mixed train. (Oddly enough, both trains were scheduled to arrive at their respective terminals at 5 p.m.)

The destruction of the interurban cars began immediately with the scrapping of demotorized 1701 on October 4; 1709 on October 26; and 1700, the first car on the first train to Chilliwack, on November 6. Better news was the inauguration of a third 47,000 horsepower unit at Ruskin on October 25, and the opening of the rebuilt Horne-Payne substation, the principal receiver of new Bridge River power, on November 15.

But it had, indeed, been a terrible year for street cars and interurbans, seventy-four of them destroyed by the inferno outside the once-friendly shop at Kitsilano. (Time had somehow been found to cut up Oregon Electric locomotive 24 for scrap.) Over nine more route miles of street car line, all of it double track except for 1.3 miles, had been abandoned in 1950; of Vancouver's 801 transit vehicles, only 165 were street cars. Freight tonnage hauled was strong at 1,015,864, but ridership continued its downward trend to 138,279,028, over seven million of those on the interurban system.

Lulu Island substation, at Cambie on the Steveston line, was the next substation to bow out, in January 1951 ending the work it began as the impressive power supplier when the V. & L. I. was electrified almost forty-six years earlier. On the Burnaby Lake line, service was cut back further, with hourly service in the evening and short runs to Horne-Payne eliminated. The spreading Burnaby bus network was largely to blame for the line's loss of patronage.

The rebuilding of the Steveston line's bridge over the Fraser River was begun on February 5. It was closed for about one month on weekdays, freight moving only at night when the bridge was available for rail traffic. Six interurban cars were

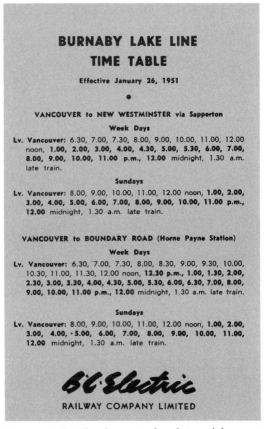

BURNABY LAKE LINE
TIME TABLE

Effective January 26, 1951

●

VANCOUVER to NEW WESTMINSTER via Sapperton

Week Days

Lv. Vancouver: 6.30, 7.00, 7.30, 8.00, 9.00, 10.00, 11.00, 12.00 noon, 1.00, 2.00, 3.00, 4.00, 4.30, 5.00, 5.30, 6.00, 7.00, 8.00, 9.00, 10.00, 11.00 p.m., 12.00 midnight, 1.30 a.m. late train.

Sundays

Lv. Vancouver: 8.00, 9.00, 10.00, 11.00, 12.00 noon, 1.00, 2.00, 3.00, 4.00, 5.00, 6.00, 7.00, 8.00, 9.00, 10.00, 11.00 p.m., 12.00 midnight, 1.30 a.m. late train.

VANCOUVER to BOUNDARY ROAD (Horne Payne Station)

Week Days

Lv. Vancouver: 6.30, 7.00, 7.30, 8.00, 8.30, 9.00, 9.30, 10.00, 10.30, 11.00, 11.30, 12.00 noon, 12.30 p.m., 1.00, 1.30, 2.00, 2.30, 3.00, 3.30, 4.00, 4.30, 5.00, 5.30, 6.00, 6.30, 7.00, 8.00, 9.00, 10.00, 11.00 p.m., 12.00 midnight, 1.30 a.m. late train.

Sundays

Lv. Vancouver: 8.00, 9.00, 10.00, 11.00, 12.00 noon, 1.00, 2.00, 3.00, 4.00, 5.00, 6.00, 7.00, 8.00, 9.00, 10.00, 11.00, 12.00 midnight, 1.30 a.m. late train.

BC Electric

RAILWAY COMPANY LIMITED

The pink cardboard public timetable for the Burnaby Lake line, January 26, 1951. (author's collection)

kept on Lulu Island, serviced and stored there on the main line, while shuttle buses worked between Marpole and Bridgeport to create a temporary connection.

Nothing having come of efforts to save at least one of the observation cars, both were destroyed in late February, as were Chilliwack line combine 1402 and snow sweeper S.57, among numerous street cars.

Snow came again to the lower mainland, burying it under two and one-quarter feet in March. Since bus transportation was tied up, interurban trailer 1600, behind one of the diesels, reactivated passenger service to Chilliwack on

Snow came also to Jordan River in 1951, necessitating sturdy equipment. (J.M. Elliott photo)

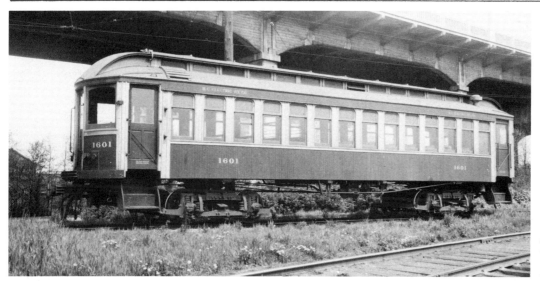

Trailer 1601, the Ottawa-built prototype "Westminster" for the B.C. Electric-built 1200-series, awaits scrapping at Kitsilano shops. (E.L. Plant photo)

Receipts used on the interurban lines during the final years. (author's collection)

March 10, following complaints by the Public Utilities Commission about the absence of Pacific Stage Lines bus transport to and from Chilliwack. By this time, much trolley wire had already been removed from the line, particularly around Cloverdale and Langley Prairie. (In Vancouver, Nanaimo Street presented an unusual sight, all tracks long since removed and the surface newly paved, but street car trolley wire still intact.)

May 20 was the final complete day of service on the Dunbar street car line, the double track on Broadway from Granville to Alma Street, and south along Dunbar Diversion, Sixteenth Avenue, and Dunbar Street, to Forty-first being abandoned, as well as the downtown section on Richards Street between Robson and Davie streets. On the following day, the transit personnel still at the offices at Prior Street moved to Mount Pleasant barn and Oakridge. Only Fairview, Grandview, Oak Street, Hastings East, and Main Street lines remained, and only the Fairview route and the Lulu Island interurban line still used Granville Bridge. The dispossessed Main Street line was connected in an unusual way with the Fairview line, the latter thereby losing its belt mode of operation. This new concoction was No. 3-Main, operating from Sixteenth Avenue and Main Street, via Main, Broadway, Granville, Hastings, and Main to Fiftieth Avenue; and No. 5-Fairview on the return, through downtown, to Sixteenth and Main.

Grandview and Hastings East had the thirty-six P.C.C.s, with help in rush hour from the 310-class and 364-378. All of the Fairview line's trademark cars, 260-274 (actually known as "Fairview" class), had been destroyed at Kitsilano in 1950; in service now on 3-5, Fairview-Main, the only two-man line, were the 275-class Brills, the similar 326-class Prestons, and steel cars 356-363. Oak Street used one man double end cars, usually 78, 79, 80, 83, 89, 90, 91, 316, 317, 319-324, and 382. The nineteen remaining 700-class multiple unit cars

were all out of service, and the second storey of Mount Pleasant barn was used for storing street cars not in service, as well as for street cars employed only in rush hour duty.

In May, locomotive 980, long familiar in winter with its attached snow plow, began a complete transformation at Kitsilano shop. It reappeared on October 9 as a fullfledged, double ended, railway nose snow plow — unpowered — for use with the diesel locomotives on the Chilliwack line. Numbered S.102, it was the piece of special equipment the line had badly needed.

Another Chilliwack line veteran, locomotive 991 — used latterly most often on the Queensborough line — was scrapped on July 12, followed by interurban cars 1401, 1206 (somewhat swaybacked, the first of the 1000s or 1200s to be destroyed, and in 1905 the first interurban coach to operate on the Lulu Island line), 1601, and 1602 in September and October. Even at the end of a career that stretched back to 1899, car 1601 was still elegantly attractive, with the letters B, C, E, and R etched in monogram form into the glass of the upper half of each window, and still displaying distinctive vestiges of its Ottawa Car Company heritage; 1601, as car "Westminster" and then 1200, had, after all, been the pattern for the "name" interurban cars.

An unusual sight on the New Westminster-Marpole-Vancouver interurban line on September 29 was a train chartered by the National Model Railroaders Association, consisting of three coaches (one each from the C.N.R., C.P.R., and G.N.), a P.G.E. business car (formerly an Oregon Electric observation car), and two C.P.R. open-air observation cars, all of them wooden. They had reached New Westminster from Vancouver, drawn by a 4-4-0 steam locomotive, over the C.P.R., but from New Westminster, B. C. Electric locomotive 962 had taken over this colourful assemblage for the journey back to C.P.R.'s Drake Street yards, on the way passing the Kitsilano shop and crossing over False Creek on Kitsilano trestle. A photo stop on a siding in Kerrisdale had caused great local excitement.

In mid-October, the B. C. Electric let it be publicly known that it wanted an end to Marpole-Steveston passenger interurban service by January. In its stead, it would introduce an eight-route bus system, but freight service would continue. Richmond municipality's transportation committee sat later in the month to discuss the B. C. Electric's proposal.

The order having been given on November 28 to prepare recently idle Central Park line interurban car 1322 as a demotorized replacement for car 1600, the shop crew at Kitsilano fitted 1322 up in a fashion very similar to that of 1600, ready for whatever winter would offer, and 1600 was prepared for scrapping.

During the year, the Burnaby Lake line's Murrin station, demolished by a truck, had been replaced by a new, but nameless, shelter. Thirty-seven more street cars and interurban cars had been destroyed in 1951, 4.7 route miles of street car line abandoned; freight hauled set a new record at 1,126,659 tons, though ridership across the system was down farther to 131,430,857. Only 118 street cars and 54 interurban cars were in service at the end of 1951.

With the new year came the installation of speed test boards, placed two thousand feet apart, on each of the interurban lines, their purpose being to assist motormen to acquire a better appreciation of train speeds. The Central Park line's were set up between Leeside and the Connaught gravel pit; the Lulu Island line's adjacent to Quilchena Golf Course, between Twenty-second and Twenty-ninth avenues; the Chilliwack line's between Anderson and Hunter; and the Burnaby Lake line's between Douglas and Sprott.

A completely new system of fares in the greater Vancouver area was introduced in 1952; Sunday, April 6, was the day for the complex change-over. Cash fare in Vancouver became thirteen cents, and tickets at four for fifty cents, and even "slacks" at four for forty-five cents, were available. A system of fare zones which included North Vancouver, Burnaby, New Westminster, Richmond, and Coquitlam was also established at this time.

On April 16, the body of multiple unit street car 712, purchased for $200 by a Jack Lawrence, was hoisted onto a flat car at Kitsilano shop for shipment to Penticton, where it rested on the west side of Main Street for a number of years as a diner, "The Red Racer." During the first few months of the year, baggage-express 1706 had already been scrapped, as had the first of the St. Louis interurban cars, 1226, and the second of the company-built 1200s, 1215.

The 6.34-mile, number 17-Oak Street line had become through the years the quintessential

street car line. First contact with it took one with ease back to what the imagination knew turn-of-the-century street car operations were like: double ended cars, the trolley poles switched at each terminus; lots of single track, middle of the street south of Sixteenth Avenue, but soon along the east side of the road; four passing sidings on Oak Street, passengers craning their necks at each turn to make certain that one motorman passed the staff to the other; unpaved, open track, not in the best condition, causing street cars to "nose" heavily from side to side at anything resembling speed; an infectious friendliness indulged in by all the line's participants; and bush, forest, and relative paucity of settlement that contrived to carry one into a Vancouver of some earlier time.

Its last full day of service, April 17, brought a flood of nostalgia and reminiscences, widely disseminated by the media. The company insisted that the line had in its lifetime carried fifty-one and a half million riders. Early morning, 4:04 a.m., of Friday, April 18 had witnessed the last street car rolling north on Oak Street and to the barn, car

This view shows the Carrall Street station — head office building from the Pender Street side with 1302, 1316, and 1220 waiting their next assignment. (B.C. Transit)

The station on the Vancouver-Marpole line for now-disappeared Quilchena Golf Club, 29th Avenue. (E.L. Plant photo)

Marpole station, with the terminus of the Oak Street line on its back side, here with car 324. (E.L. Plant photo)

† Les Armour, "Old 'No. 17' Blunders Off to the Boneyard," *Vancouver Daily Province,* 18 April 1952, p. 17.

EAST TER.	LAST SECT'N	WEST TER
0 1 2 3	4 5 6 7	8 9
0 1 2 3	4 5 6 7	8 9

THU. APR.
17

| TO DEPOT |
| FROM DEPOT |
| SHORT |
| SPEC |

OAK

CAMBIE & HAST	DN		A
		CAMB HAST	36	
D	9	CAMB BDWY	27	B
	24	41st OAK	19	C
E	36	MARPOLE		
F				MAR-POLE
			UP	

| 00811 | N D | A M |

THU. APR. 17

LEFT PUNCHED TERMINUS AT LAST TIME SHOWN BELOW

12	Subject to Conditions on back hereof	0
1		10
	DO NOT	20
2	FOLD	30
3		40
		50
4		0
5		

Transfer issued on the last full day of service of the once-famous No. 17 — Oak Street line, April 17, 1952. (author's collection)

316, with motorman James "Scotty" Daisley, and F. W. McKee, the last paying passenger. Daisley could not resist telling his favourite story, the one about the inebriated logger who got on a crowded Oak Street car late one night in 1944: "He sat down, nice and dignified like and proceeded to take off all his clothes. He was bigger than me, so I just let him sit there. And nobody said a word. They just acted like it happened every night. Couldn't have happened on any other line!" †

On Saturday, two hundred guests, mostly oldtimers and company and civic officials, participated in one final Oak Street journey. Draped with banner and bunting, the oldest Oak Street cars, 78, 79, 80, 89, 90, and 91, left Mount Pleasant barn at 2:10 p.m. for the corner of Cambie and Hastings, via Main, Broadway, Cambie, and the Connaught Bridge, where the guests boarded; many, including the motormen, Jim Crookall, Joe Griffiths, Tom Howatson, Charles McCaughey, J. B. McKay, and Charles Morrison, were suitably "moustached." With song leaders and accordionists also on board, the procession left at 2:35 p.m., car 78 leading, west on Hastings to Granville Street, up Granville to Robson Street, and then east on Robson to Connaught Bridge and the line's regular route via Cambie, Broadway, and Oak to Marpole, the entire route lined by onlookers relishing the colourful parade.

At Forty-seventh Avenue the cars were brought to an abrupt halt by members of the Vancouver Gun Club who "terrorized" the ceremonial riders

with the firing of ear-splitting blanks. Upon their 3:25 p.m. arrival at Marpole, the guests were transferred to waiting buses and taken to the Oakridge Transit Centre for tea. The six street cars

```
         SELF-ALIGNING SWITCHES

    THE LINE DEPARTMENT WILL CHANGE OVER THE
FOLLOWING ELECTRIC SWITCHES FOR SELF-ALIGN-
MENT, COMMENCING AT 8:00 A.M., MONDAY,
JUNE 11, 1951.  THIS WORK WILL BE COMPLETED
MONDAY.
    SEE BULLETIN FOR FURTHER DETAILS.
                              SWITCH WILL
   LOCATION          DIRECTION   SELF-ALIGN FOR


MAIN & HASTINGS      WESTBOUND   HASTINGS STREET

CAMBIE & HASTINGS    WESTBOUND   HASTINGS STREET

RICHARDS & HASTINGS  WESTBOUND   HASTINGS STREET

GRANVILLE & PACIFIC  SOUTHBOUND  GRANVILLE BRIDGE

BROADWAY & MAIN      SOUTHBOUND  MAIN STREET

CAMBIE & ROBSON      SOUTHBOUND  BRIDGE


    SELF-ALIGNING SWITCHES REMAIN SET FOR
THE MAIN LINE, AS LISTED ABOVE, REGARDLESS
OF WHETHER POWER IS APPLIED OR NOT, WHEN
CROSSING UNDER CONTACTOR.


    ALL OTHER SWITCHES WILL OPERATE AS AT

PRESENT.
```

Even during the final street car years, refinements of an operational nature were still instituted. This notice was masking-taped to one of the bulkheads of the Oak Street line's last car, 316.

April 19, 1952, and six of the
oldest street cars make a
ceremonial last run on the Oak
Street line. (B.C. Hydro)

Published by the British Columbia Electric Railway Company, Limited

Vol. 37   Vancouver, Friday, May 30, 1952   No. 1

deadheaded back to Forty-first Avenue, their
motormen joining the celebration at Oakridge,
after which the cars were run directly to Kitsilano
for scrapping. With the cessation of street car
service on Oak Street came the end as well for the
once invaluable track on Sixteenth Avenue
between Oak and Main streets.

That spur track at Lansdowne, so long the
domain of the race track extras, was removed by
early May. This year's racing season, as succeeding
ones, would see no special interurban trains, only
regularly scheduled ones, augmented by an
additional car, if necessary. (Special buses would
run from Marpole and from Fraser Street.) Along

the Central Park line, a near-stampede by real
estate agents to acquire property for future
industrial development had been generated by
the B. C. Electric's announcement that passenger
service on the line would soon be a thing of the
past.

On June 2, a large ad appeared in Vancouver
newspapers, placed by the "Team Passenger
Committee," urging readers who wanted the
interurbans to continue running between Davie
Street and Steveston to sign the coupon section
and send it to the Board of Transport Commissioners. Over in New Westminster, interurban
trailer 1600 was scrapped on June 24, having
avoided Kitsilano, but not demolition.

In the early morning of Friday, June 18,
Granville Bridge was free of street car and
interurban traffic forever; the Fairview-Main street
cars and the Davie Street-Marpole interurban cars
would never come that way again. The last street
car over the bridge northbound had left
Broadway and Main at 3:06 a.m., the last one
southbound to cross the bridge had departed
from Robson and Granville at 3:13 a.m. The final
interurban train from the station on Davie Street,
car 1223, had left at 12:30 a.m.; leaving Marpole at
1:30 a.m. on the return trip, it was back to Davie

Interurban transfer used on the
interurban lines during the final
years. (author's collection)

Cedar Cottage-bound, P.C.C. 409 crosses the Great Northern cut at Commercial Drive and Eighth Avenue. (B.C. Hydro)

STATIONS	MILES
VANCOUVER (Carrall St.)	0
CEDAR COTTAGE	3.5
LAKEVIEW	3.7
GLADSTONE	3.8
NANAIMO ROAD	4.1
BEACONSFIELD	4.5
EARLS ROAD	4.8
COLLINGWOOD WEST	5.1
COLLINGWOOD EAST	5.4
PARK AVENUE	5.9
CENTRAL PARK	6.1
PATTERSON	6.5
McKAY	6.8
WEST BURNABY	7.0
DOW ROAD	7.1
JUBILEE	7.4
ROYAL OAK	7.8
McPHERSON AVE.	8.1
HIGHLAND PARK	8.3
FRASER ARM	8.7
PRENTER	8.9
McGREGOR	9.1
LEESIDE	9.7
CONNAUGHT HILL	10.1
ELSONA	10.4
MEAD	10.8
NEW WESTMINSTER	12.5

Central Park line 1951. (Lloyd Price collection)

by 2 a.m., having joined forces at Marpole with the inbound train from Steveston. There remained then one further crossing of Granville Bridge for a few hours of rest at Kitsilano barn.

Street car tracks out of commission were those on Fourth Avenue from Granville to Fir Street and north on Fir to the interurban right of way; Cambie Street and Connaught Bridge, from Broadway to Robson and Cambie; Granville between Fourth Avenue and Broadway; Broadway between Granville and Main; Richards Street between Davie and Pacific streets; Davie between Granville and Richards; and Pacific between Granville and Richards. In addition, the roof portion of Mount Pleasant barn was closed down, rendering the track on Thirteenth Avenue and on Quebec Street superfluous.

The 3-Main street car line, alone again, looped now through downtown in a counter-clockwise direction, using Hastings, Richards, Robson, and Cambie streets. Both Hastings East runs — no. 13 to the Exhibition Park (Millar) loop and no. 14 to the Kootenay loop — and the Grandview line, now numbered 1, rather than its historic 4, continued to loop counter-clockwise via Hastings, Granville, Robson, and Richards Streets.

The B. C. Electric had moved quickly to dispense with passenger service on the interurban line to Marpole — authorization to discontinue it had been given by the Board of Transport Commissioners only seven days previously! (Permission had, however, not been received to pull off service on the Marpole-Steveston leg.) A parade in Kerrisdale and a public luncheon at its

arena marked the demise of forty-seven years of interurban service though the cars would run "extra" on the stretch between Kitsilano and Marpole to provide service on the lines from Marpole to New Westminster and Steveston.

The company's office at the Davie Street station was shut down on July 27 and relocated in the trainmen's quarters at Kitsilano barn, the site henceforth of time sheets, the booking-off book, the bumping sheet, and payroll cheques. On Thursday, July 31, Granville Street between Robson Street and Fourth Avenue was finally closed to all rail traffic, necessitating the routing of interurban cars between Carrall Street and Kitsilano via New Westminster. Rail and trolley wire removal on the five-block Commercial Drive connector, between Venables and Hastings streets, commenced on August 6, though sufficient track and overhead was left on Commercial at Venables to permit emergency wyeing of interurban trains.

The B. C. Electric had wanted to end the Steveston line's passenger service in January, but then had settled on April, at the request of Richmond's municipal council, spring being deemed a less hazardous time than winter for a major transportation changeover. On September 19, the Board of Transport Commissioners made public its refusal to grant the company permission to end service, on grounds that buses would aggravate traffic congestion on the two bridges connecting Marpole with Sea Island and the latter with Lulu Island. In late November, loading and unloading platforms, for the use only of

Richmond Junior High School pupils carried by special school interurban trains, were constructed at the south end of the long passing track at Brighouse.

In 1952, the company's various transportation services had carried 123,922,915 passengers, a 5.7% drop from 1951's total. Though freight tonnage hauled, at 1,126,960, was virtually unchanged from 1951, an increase in freight rates had meant a gross revenue increase from freight of 7.4%. Six more interurban cars had been scrapped since June, 1218, 1300, 1301, 1307, 1704, and 1705, part of 1952's total of eighty-one street cars, interurban cars, and snow sweepers burnt at Kitsilano. Though nine and a half route miles of street car line had been abandoned in 1952, eighty-five street cars were still in operating fettle as the year came to an end, and Vancouver's seventeen trolley coach lines and eighteen bus lines had been given numbers — just like those the street car lines had displayed for years, signs of respectability indeed.

The last remains of the passing siding at Hall's Prairie, regularly used as a meeting place by the Chilliwack line's morning passenger trains, were removed on January 22, 1953. In late April, the New Westminster interurban depot was put up for sale: price, $185,000; possession, March 1, 1954.

The final Main Street car — the last of the two-man street cars — made its run from the wye at Fiftieth and Main Street at 4:05 a.m. on Friday, May 8, bound for Mount Pleasant barn. Billy Arnold, Jr. was the last paying passenger on the street car piloted by motorman Billy Nicols and conducted by Billy Arnold, Sr. Fifty-three minutes later, the first bus left Forty-Ninth and Main; two street cars — the lead one 350 — hung on during the day to take ninety-six students and three teachers from General Brock elementary school at Thirty-third Avenue and Main to Fiftieth Avenue and back. City crews almost immediately were at work ripping out the track on Main Street between Sixteenth and Fiftieth avenues, a $37,000 job. The single track rail on Thirty-third Avenue between Main and Fraser streets, its trolley wire pulled down, remained in place for a number of years.

A curious situation now prevailed. The nearly one and three-quarter miles of double track on Main Street between Hastings Street and Sixteenth Avenue were busy with street cars making their way to Grandview and Hastings East service from the barn, but none was allowed to engage in passenger service along this stretch. The cross-street wye on Sixteenth remained in position, and a lonely wye west-turning at Prior Street was all that had survived the network of track formerly at the barn there. Street cars left redundant by the termination of Main Street line service were simply run off Hastings Street into Carrall Street yard, coupled together at the end of the trolley wire, and towed by a C.P.R. steam locomotive through the C.P.R. yard, past the Drake Street interchange, and by an electric locomotive across Kitsilano trestle on their way to a fiery finale.

One adjustment in the 1-Grandview line's downtown routing went into effect on May 8: it took over the Main Street line's routing, Hastings, Richards, Robson, and Cambie streets.

In New Westminster, the B. C. Electric's new, $400,000 combined office building and Pacific Stage Lines bus depot (replacing the bus loading shed across Front Street from the interurban depot) at Sixth Street, just north of Royal Avenue, was opened on Wednesday, June 10.

Despite automobiles and the encroachment of buses, special interurban movements still came to the rescue of special occasions, one of the last affecting the Central Park line being the series of evangelistic camp meetings held by Oral Roberts in an enormous tent at Central Park. Typical of the specials run for this occasion was one consisting

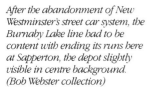

After the abandonment of New Westminster's street car system, the Burnaby Lake line had to be content with ending its runs here at Sapperton, the depot slightly visible in centre background. (Bob Webster collection)

of interurban cars 1321 (leading), 1304, and 1319, Vancouver-bound from Central Park at 10:05 p.m. on September 1; all seats were filled and both 1321 and 1304 had their rear trolleys to the overhead as the train eagerly pulled away for its twenty-six minute journey.

Labour Day, September 7, marked the last time a passenger train operated all the way to Chilliwack, albeit a fan train, sponsored by the P.G.E. and Rail Travel Boosters, Ernie Plant, president. Pulled by one of the electric locomotives, this train of vintage C.P.R. coaches and observation cars left from Fourth Avenue, half a block west of Granville Street, and proceeded on the interurban line through Kerrisdale to Marpole, and then to New Westminster, where one of the company's diesels took over for the run to Chilliwack. Since the coaches would have negotiated the loop with extreme difficulty, the locomotive was instead switched to the opposite end of the train for the return journey.

The guiding of a 125-ton transformer into Horne-Payne substation gave rise to a rare occasion: an electric locomotive putting in an appearance on Commercial Drive to enter the Burnaby Lake line's precincts for completing the job of hauling the eight-axle depressed flat car and its forbidding load. During September as well, the company had taken delivery of E.60, a twelve-ton, four-wheeled, diesel-powered, caboose like vehicle, built in Vancouver by Hayes Manufacturing Company for use by line crews on the Chilliwack line in maintaining and inspecting the transmission lines along the right of way. However, the scrapping of interurban car 1322 on October 13 did close a three-year standby service chapter for the Chilliwack line.

Who possibly would have predicted a few years previous that both the Burnaby Lake and Central Park lines, especially the bustling latter, would ever quit running between New Westminster and Vancouver, and both at precisely the identical scheduled time, 1:30 a.m. from Carrall Street on Friday, October 23? True, the 5.9 miles of the Central Park line between Vancouver and Park Avenue station, the city's eastern boundary, would continue to operate passenger service for a while, but the entire 9.637-mile private right of way of the Burnaby Lake line was abandoned on that Friday. It had been suggested in some quarters that the adjacent area around Renfrew Street and Boundary Road might develop industrially, necessitating at least a portion of the line, connected perhaps to the Great Northern's main line. Other speculation ventured nearer the ultimate truth: an expressway would be built over portions of the line.

On Wednesday, October 21, the second to last complete day of service, the writer rode both lines, departing from Carrall Street at 4 p.m. on a Burnaby Lake train composed of cars 1236

(leading) and 1224. (One "traditional," three-car Burnaby Lake train still left at 5 p.m.) Beginning with nineteen passengers, the train added to them enroute, acquiring one at Gore Avenue, two at Heatley Street, seven at Clark Drive and Hastings Street (4:08 p.m.), one at Clark and Venables Street, one at Commercial Drive and First Avenue, and seventeen at the start of the line's own right of way, just north of Sixth Avenue, at 4:13 p.m. Arriving at Horne-Payne station at 4:25 p.m., the train pulled into the spur to the north of the line just past the station. Car 1224 was dropped, a crew member staying with it, and Vancouver-bound 1220, waiting on the main line, immediately coupled itself to it, and headed west for Carrall Street. Car 1236 then backed onto the main line at 4:28 p.m. and continued its eastward journey, crossing the heavily-protected Great Northern main line at 4:32 p.m. and passing Buranby Lake station at 4:38 p.m. On the siding to the north of the line just before reaching Hill, Vancouver-bound 1228 lay, waiting for 1236 to pass. Sapperton, 12.3 miles from Vancouver, was reached at 4:47 p.m., ten passengers having travelled the distance.

At 5:23 p.m. on the same afternoon, the writer departed from the depot in New Westminster on a Vancouver-bound Central Park train consisting of cars 1321 (leading) and 1305, three minutes behind schedule, both cars well filled. Stops were made at virtually every station, Highland Park being reached at 5:38 p.m., Park Avenue (Boundary Road) at 5:47 p.m., Cedar Cottage at 5:55 p.m., and Broadway at 5:58 p.m., whence the train carried on to Carrall Street. One way fare on either line was twenty-six cents, or twenty-eight with transfer privileges.

Shortly after 1:30 a.m. on Friday, B. C. Electric crewmen placed detonators on the track at Carrall Street station, giving a noisy, rousing sendoff to both final Burnaby Lake and Central Park runs, the latter with thirteen passengers aboard car 1317, motorman George Flett and conductor Norm Carson in command. It had been this same car and crew that had departed from New Westminster at 12:40 a.m., the very last scheduled run out of New Westminster on the Central Park line, concluding over sixty-two years of continuous service.

A little later in the morning — 5:20 a.m. — the interurban cars would be back at work on the Central Park line, but only between Park Avenue and Carrall Street,. delivering a twenty-minute base service, ten-minute in rush hours. A crossover had been installed at the east end of Park Avenue station, with yard limit boards in place eight hundred feet east and west of the crossover. Interurban trains between the barn in New Westminster and Park Avenue were run as extras, and were restricted to a speed of twenty miles per hour over that stretch.

On Friday, all regular Burnaby Lake trains

Car 1231 led a four-car, last run train from Douglas Road to Sapperton, and return, on October 23, 1953. (B.C. Hydro)

having made their final runs, four hundred students, with teachers, parents, and Burnaby's reeve, boarded a special train of four interurban cars, 1229, 1236, 1232, and 1231, at Douglas Road station, bound for Sapperton. Everyone had taken care to dress in gay nineties garb, with "moustaches" suitably attached, and wing collars on the fly; the four cars too were decorated, with banners reading: "Goodbye trams — Douglas Road School." From Sapperton, the assembly walked over to nearby Hume Park, where songs were sung and speeches served. Once back on the train, conductor Alvin Burtch, motorman Alex Stewart, brakemen Carl Doan and Charlie Martin, and all the last day celebrants rolled back over the 5.3 miles of abandoned rail to Douglas Road. For the last time, a Burnaby Lake line train rolled through smash-board territory (the always careful crossing of the G.N.-C.N.R. main line) and westward in the centre of First Avenue before diving down the steep hill to Victoria Drive and out onto Commercial.

Most of this Burnaby end of the line looked much the same as it had when it had started out life so bravely, forty-two years earlier. Every door to the car barn at Sapperton was already locked; the car repairer, on duty seven days a week, and the car cleaner, serving a four-hour half shift, both at night, had left early Friday morning, their jobs done.

The last stop added to the interurban system was Meadow Avenue, between Byrne Road and Trapp Road on the Marpole-New Westminster line, graded, finely-gravelled, and ready for service on December 8.

During 1953, heavier rail had been laid on a few sections of the Chilliwack line, all overhead wire had finally been removed between Newton and

Abandoned Sapperton car barn, the derelict main line of the Burnaby Lake line running to the right for a few more yards to its terminus. (George Bergson photo)

Chilliwack, and the bridge over the Vedder River had been strengthened. To provide more seating space, the lavatories had been removed from interurban cars 1302, 1305, 1306, and 1308-1311. (Ironically, 1302 had been scrapped shortly after.) As in 1952, eighty-one pieces of rolling stock had been destroyed; in 1953, this total included the two snow flangers, two snow sweepers, and twenty-five interurban cars, including all nine of the 1000 series.

Only fifty-seven street cars (310-315, 364-378, and 400-435) and thirty-two interurban cars remained. Two and two-thirds route miles of street car line had been lost during the year; only two street car lines and three interurban lines were operating. Passengers carried had amounted to 118,016,163, another drop from the previous year, but freight tonnage hauled had reached a record 1,129,313.

Though its main approaches awaited completion, the new trackless Granville Bridge was

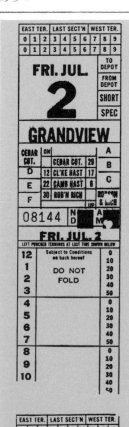

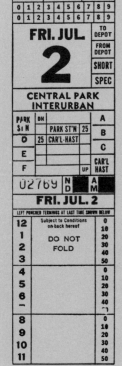

Grandview street car line and truncated Central Park line transfers near the end of service. (author's collection)

Operator Shuttleworth's terminal clearance for the 11:30 a.m. passenger train to Steveston from Marpole on April 20, 1954. (author's collection)

CENTRAL PARK SERVICE

Carrall Street to Park Avenue Only

Effective December 25th, 1953

WEEKDAYS

LV. PARK AVENUE
5.20, 6.00, 6.10, 6.20, 6.30, 6.40, 6.50, 7.00, 7.10, 7.20, 7.30, 7.40, 7.50, 8.00, 8.10, 8.20, 8.30, and 8.50 a.m. Then every 20 minutes at 10 - 30 - 50 minutes past the hour until **3.30 p.m.** Then 3.45, 3.55, 4.05, 4.15, 4.25, 4.35, 4.45, 4.55, 5.05, 5.15, 5.25, 5.35, 5.50, 6.10 and 6.30 p.m. Then every 20 minutes at 10 - 30 - 50 minutes past the hour with the last car at 12.50 a.m.

LV. VANCOUVER
5.50, 6.30, 6.50, 7.00, 7.10, 7.20, 7.30, 7.40, 7.50, 8.00, 8.20, 8.40 and 9.00 a.m. Then every 20 minutes on the hour and 20 - 40 minutes past the hour until **3.00 p.m.** Then 3.10, 3.20, 3.30, 3.40, 3.50, 4.00, 4.10, 4.20, 4.30, 4.40, 4.50, 5.00, 5.10, 5.20, 5.30, 5.40, 5.50, 6.00, 6.10 and 6.20 p.m. Then every 20 minutes on the hour, 20 - 40 minutes past the hour until 1.00 a.m., with a late car at 1.30 a.m.

SATURDAYS

LV. PARK AVENUE
5.20, 6.00, 6.30, 6.40, 7.10, 7.30 and 7.50 a.m. Then every 20 minutes at 10 - 30 - 50 minutes past the hour until **3.10 p.m.** Then 3.20, 3.40, 4.00, 4.20, 4.40, 5.00, 5.20, 5.50 p.m. Then every 20 minutes at 10 - 30 - 50 minutes past the hour with the last car at 12.50 a.m.

LV. VANCOUVER
5.50, 6.30, 7.00, 7.20, 7.40 and 8.00 a.m. Then every 20 minutes on the hour, 20 - 40 minutes past the hour until 1.00 a.m. with a late car at 1.30 a.m.

CENTRAL PARK SERVICE

Carrall Street to Park Avenue Only

Effective December 25th, 1953

SUNDAYS

LV. PARK AVENUE
6.30, 7.00, 7.30, 8.00, 8.30, 9.00, 9.30, 10.00, 10.30, 11.00, 11.30, 11.50 a.m. Then **12.10 p.m.** and then every 20 minutes at 10 - 30 - 50 minutes past the hour with the last car at 12.50 a.m.

LV. VANCOUVER
7.00, 7.30, 8.00, 8.30, 9.00, 9.30, 10.00, 10.30, 11.00, 11.30 a.m. and **12.00 Noon.** Then every 20 minutes on the hour until 1.00 a.m. with a late car at 1.30 a.m.

HOLIDAYS

Sunday service all day with an early car from Park Ave. at 6.00 a.m.; from Carrall Street Depot at 6.30 a.m.

B. C. ELECTRIC

opened for traffic at 11 a.m. on February 4, 1954. The company's transit vehicles began operating over it on the following day.

Within a week's time, the Canadian National Railway, already having purchased the National Harbours Board waterfront railway system in Vancouver, the track on Second Narrows Bridge, and the harbour front trackage in North Vancouver, announced that it had taken a one-year option to buy the abandoned right of way of the Burnaby Lake line through a section of Burnaby that had heavy industry potential.

On the Chilliwack line in February, line car L.4, usually the spare one in deference to L.6, pulled down the 7.6 miles of trolley wire which had been left for electric locomotive helper purposes between New Westminster and Newton. The interurban depot in Langley Prairie had been maintained as the B. C. Electric's freight office until the opening of the new office building and bus depot there on April 26, after which it was torn down. In New Westminster on June 2, a five-car freight train jumped a switch as it pulled out of the depot into the middle of the intersection of Columbia and Eighth streets. Though the locomotive had stayed on the rails, four cars had jumped the track, tying up traffic for hours. This accident merely strengthened the city's inclination to see this brief stretch of traffic-defying rail finally removed. In Abbotsford, June 7 was the day on which the new office-bus depot officially opened.

The last full day of passenger service on the historic Central Park line, the old Westminster & Vancouver Tramway, with both the short-lived Park Avenue interurban run and the Grandview street car operation succumbing, came on July 15. At 3:53 a.m. on July 16, the last Grandview street car pulled away from its comfortable spot on Findlay Street, just north off the Central Park line, and made its way with five passengers on board along the time-honoured, pioneering route through Grandview to the intersection of Hastings and Main streets, then north to Mount Pleasant barn.

At 1:30 a.m., the last interurban train to enter, and leave, the big station at Carrall Street had pulled out onto Hastings, whistle wailing, bell clanging, for the final journey to Park Avenue, reached at 2:10 a.m., and on to the barn at New Westminster. Motorman R. E. Barrett and conductor O. Smith had been in charge of the train, cars 1316 (leading) and 1304. William Inkster, the depot master, had gone home at the end of his shift two hours earlier, but Gordon Crichton had been there at the ticket window to the very end, selling tickets and dispensing transit information. The sixty-three years of passenger service on the Central Park line is a mark exceeded by only one other line in all of Canada and the United States, that between Portland and

Oregon City. †

At the end, the interurban service had been run by cars 1304-1306, 1309-1311, and 1313-1320. Car 1321 would have numbered itself among this elite if an electric locomotive of the 970-class had not rolled down the grade from the entrance to the barn at New Westminster in late June, causing considerable damage and leading to 1321's incineration at Kitsilano on July 13. Car 1304, the pride of a dwindling fleet, would avoid scrapping by being pronounced the system's official standby coach.

Carrall Street's waiting room was closed, and the trolley wire over the two depot tracks was soon removed. The track against the depot's outside eastern wall would remain energized, a necessary connector between the rails of Hastings Street and those of Carrall Street yard. The street-run trackage from Clark Drive and Hastings Street to Cedar Cottage, including that on Findlay Street and Fifteenth Avenue, would soon be torn up, as would the rails on Robson Street between Richards and Cambie streets, and on Cambie between Robson and Hastings. Before long, the line would be cut back over half a mile from Cedar Cottage to Nanaimo Road, eliminating the bridge at Nanaimo as well as Gladstone trestle. Freight would continue as a significant force on the remaining 8.3 miles of the Central Park line, but as double track was no longer necessary, the line gradually returned to being a single tracked one, only the westbound rails in use.

Service on the two remaining interurban lines was a mere shadow of its glory days, the interlacing of new bus routes having gradually sapped much of their vitality, and necessity. Nevertheless, sixteen interurban cars were still servicing the two legs of the Lulu Island line: 1201, 1202, 1203 (the car with the strange brakes), 1207, 1208, 1216 (in the best shape, everyone's favourite), 1217, 1220, 1222, 1223, 1225, 1231, 1232, 1233, 1235, and 1236. On the Marpole-New Westminster line, service was every two hours, with four additional runs on weekdays to create a semblance of rush hour activity. The base hourly service on the Marpole-Steveston line increased to half-hourly during peak times. Line cars L.4 and L.6 and snow plow S.103 were still available for use on the fading interurban system.

On July 31, the interurban depot in New Westminster was locked up for the last time, and on Monday morning, August 2, B. C. Electric city transit and freight headquarters moved into a new $150,000 building on Twelfth Street at Third Avenue. By August 7, the remaining tenants in the old depot had vacated their rented premises, and less than two weeks later, Wosk's Limited, a Vancouver furniture store firm, purchased it. Nonetheless, the B. C. Electric had made an agreement with Wosk's whereby the Marpole-New Westminster interurban cars and the freight trains could continue to use track 3 under and through the building.

Car 1311 was fortunately saved from the scrapper's torch by two of Vancouver's active clutch of railfans, Ernie Plant and John A. Wood. Purchased in August, 1311 was boarded up and shipped in October by barge to Squamish, then

†John F. Due, *The Intercity Electric Railway Industry in Canada* (Toronto, Ontario: University of Toronto Press, 1966), p. 50.

A train from Steveston has just crossed the Fraser River and will be over at Marpole in a few seconds. The line to New Westminster from Marpole begins at this point, heading east in the centre of the picture. (George Bergson photo)

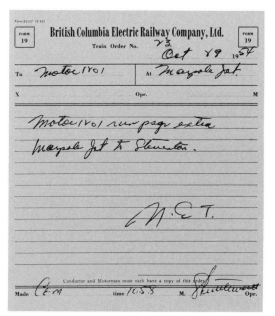

(Right)
A train order for an extra passenger run to Steveston from Marpole on October 28, 1954. Operator Shuttleworth again had the final word. (author's collection)

(Far right)
An interesting train order issued at Marpole, again on October 28, 1954. (author's collection)

the southern terminus of the Pacific Great Eastern Railway. It was subsequently moved four miles north to Mamquam, where its smoking compartment was fitted with tables, ready to display such articles as old whistles, bells, and photographs of railway equipment. Before the year was out, Plant and Wood saved the old salt car, formerly single truck street car number 53, acquiring it from the B. C. Electric.

Transit fares took a further hike on September 7, Vancouver's cash fare becoming fifteen cents (tickets at five for seventy-five cents, "slacks" at four for fifty). Though rail removal in Vancouver made detours commonplace, some sections — Granville Street between King Edward and Forty-first avenues was a highly visible example — still lay with their steel, as they so long had. As part of its franchise agreement, the company notified the city whenever a stretch of track was abandoned, sending along a cheque, computed at roughly $15,000 per mile. After the city had removed the rails and paved the street, the company strung wire for the trolley coaches and installed poles to

support it, charging the city a small proportion of the cost of the poles in return for their use by the city for street lighting.

By the end of October, the demolition of a large section of the New Westminster barn was complete, the once-necessary grand spaces made superfluous. The interurban cars were huddled at Kitsilano. In December, the company borrowed a 1200 horsepower E.M.D. diesel locomotive from the Great Northern with an eye to augmenting its little four-diesel fleet; it took a freight drag to Huntingdon, and brought another back to New Westminster.

During the year, two three-ton gasoline locomotives and smaller passenger cars had been provided for the railway at Jordan River. At Carrall Street yard, wooden locomotive 951 had been supplanted by steel 981, the Chilliwack and Saanich lines veteran. Two and three-quarter route miles of street car line had been abandoned; fifty-seven street cars had fended off the inferno, but ten interurban cars had found no escape from the fires of Kitsilano: 1305, 1306, 1309, 1310, 1312, 1313, 1314, 1318, 1320, and 1321. Both ridership and freight tonnage hauled were down somewhat in 1954, 111,656,285 and 1,088,537, respectively.

On January 24, 1955, Vancouver's city council approved in principle the B. C. Electric's transit conversion plan for Hastings East, the last street car line. That it seemed to have some kind of freight plans for the abandoned Burnaby Lake line seemed apparent to Burnaby's municipal council; in addition, the tracks were all still in place, even after fifteen months of railway inactivity.

A cloudy morning in late January brought the startling sight of street cars 310-315, each showing a destination long out of service, parading in a tight row from Mount Pleasant barn down Main

Two of the B.C. Electric's first four diesel locomotives, 940 and 943, cozy up to New Westminster barn in October 1954. (George Bergson photo)

Street to Hastings, and through to Carrall Street yard on the remaining track by the depot. There they were hooked together and towed by a C.P.R. locomotive to the Drake Street interchange, where a B. C. Electric locomotive took over, hauling them to the Kitsilano shop for scrapping, the last of the wooden cars. Interurban cars 1315, 1316, 1317, and 1319 were also scrapped during the month of January.

Teddy Lyons, the B. C. Electric's most distinguished emissary, its best-known employee, died in his sleep on February 27 at the age of 67. His two-hour sightseeing trip performances through nearly four decades had charmed and delighted thousands, to the extent that he is still fondly remembered today.

The Jordan River railway line acquired a smart, completely closed, eight-passenger speeder in March. Powered with a gasoline motor, it was custom built and outfitted at Victoria's Pembroke Street garage (formerly car barn) as a replacement for a veteran speeder of significantly less sophistication. In mid-March, fast-growing Langley Prairie was incorporated as a city, rejecting the "Prairie" part in the process.

The end of street cars had been a threat of ten years' duration, and always, after the death of one line, there was yet another, somehow filled with more life than any of the vanished lines seemed ever to have possessed. But now, it was serious. When retired Joe Briggs, for so many years the depot master at Mount Pleasant barn — the same Joe Briggs who had dispatched the first street car out of the same barn in 1907 — dispatched the last street car ever to leave the barn for its work on Hastings Street, illusions were in tatters. The other necessary cars were already out on the line as operator Doug Kemp nudged his sleek P.C.C. out of the barn at 4:47 p.m. on Thursday, April 21, slipped northward across a plethora of track work defining the barn, and crept almost imperceptibly across Broadway, against Kingsway, and one more time down the steep slope of Mount Pleasant hill, a veritable barrier once, now hugged by a transit vehicle that could go anywhere, any time, as long as there were rails.

The last street car to run from downtown Vancouver on the 14-Hastings East line, P.C.C. 424, left Robson and Granville streets at 3:05 a.m. on April 22 with eighteen passengers and operator, Vyv Saundry, following its route, via Robson, Richards and Hastings streets, to Kootenay loop. As it stopped, members of the P.G.E. and Rail Travel Boosters ran ahead of the car, placing signal torpedoes on the track. Their explosive blasts at Robson at Granville, Cambie and Hastings, and Hastings and Main attracted police from all directions who joined in the festivities with siren screams. Jung Sing, waiting for his street car at Hastings and Nanaimo Street, as he had done every morning, was the last paying rider

Westbound extra 1225 has no intention of stopping at Main Street as it heads for Marpole from Boundary Road during the late afternoon of March 2, 1955. (George Bergson photo)

B. C. ELECTRIC
TIME TABLES

Vancouver Street Car Timetables   1

14   HASTINGS EAST

No. 14—From Kootenay Loop via Hastings, Granville, Robson, Richards, Hastings, and return.

No. 13—To Exhibition Park only when eastbound.

Leave Kootenay Loop—Weekdays

5.06	5.21	5.36	1.11	1.18ᴴ	1.29	1.39ᴴ	1.51
5.51	6.01	6.07	2.11	2.19ᴴ	2.41	3.00ᴴ	3.34

Saturdays

5.06	5.21	5.36	1.17	1.31	1.38ᴴ	1.51	1.58ᴴ
5.51	6.01	6.09	2.11	2.22ᴴ	2.41	3.00ᴴ	3.34

Sundays

5.30	5.55	6.20	12.35ᴴ	12.47	1.00	1.20	1.25ᴴ
6.34	6.48	7.02	1.38ᴴ	1.55	2.15ᴴ	2.49	3.37

Leave Robson and Granville—Weekdays

4.48*	5.01	5.02*	12.48	1.00	1.12	1.24	1.37
5.30	5.32*	5.45	1.54	2.16	2.35	3.05	3.56ᴴ

Saturdays

4.46*	5.01*	5.01	1.02	1.12	1.22	1.32	1.42
5.30	5.31*	5.45	1.56	2.16	2.35	3.05	3.56ᴴ

Sundays

5.12*	5.37*	5.52	12.16	12.26	12.41	12.56	1.11
6.16*	6.19	6.44	1.24	1.44	2.19	3.12	3.59ᴴ

ᴴ To Main and Hastings only.

* From Main and Hastings only.

The early and late cars of the B.C. Electric's last street car line. (author's collection)

to board a B. C. Electric street car, doing so appropriately to a camera's flash at 3:30 a.m. Scheduled to leave the loop for the return at 3:34 a.m., car 424, operator Saundry, and railfans left late on the return, to the explosion of more torpedoes, arriving at Mount Pleasant barn at 4:22 a.m., five minutes late, welcomed by a film crew.

But there was one more time, "Rails-to-Rubber Day." On Sunday, April 24, twenty-nine of the

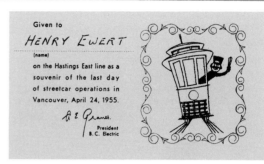

Vyv Saundry, at the controls of B.C. Electric's last street car, P.C.C. 424, welcomes aboard Jung Sing, its very last passenger, in the early morning of April 22, 1955. (B.C. Hydro)

April 24, 1955 featured four hours of free street car riding on the last day of B.C. Electric street cars. Two P.C.C.s move east on Hastings Street to the Kootenay Loop, while Empire Stadium, built to host the British Empire and Commonwealth Games of 1954, crouches importantly in its natural bowl. (George Bergson photo)

Kootenay Loop, the eastern turn-around for B.C. Electric's last street car line, on the last day, April 24, 1955. Car 425 takes on one passenger, at least. (George Bergson photo)

P.C.C.s travelled up and down the Hastings East line, providing celebratory free rides to everyone who wished, between 1 and 5 p.m. Two extra transit supervisors at Kootenay loop, one at Hastings at Main, five maintenance men at Carrall Street, and one at Kootenay loop: all stood by to assist as an estimated 13,700 people travelled the line, many congregating at Exhibition Park for a ceremony at 3 p.m. at Exhibition Gardens. The Fireman's Band played outside, and inside company and civic officials and oldtimers gathered for presentations and speeches. Many of Vancouver's pioneers had boarded three special street cars at 2:15 p.m. at Victoria Square to be brought to the ceremony.

The B. C. Electric's choirs sang, and there was community singing. President Dal Grauer's address centred on the company's ten-year, thirty-million-dollar transit program on the lower mainland, slated to be brought to completion by June. Ernie Plant presented car 53 to the Pacific National Exhibition for display on the exhibition's grounds, P.N.E. president J. S. C. Moffitt presenting Plant with a certificate of ownership of the car. Grauer presented Vancouver mayor Fred Hume with the controller handle from car 53 for inclusion in the city's archives, and both Grauer and the mayor were presented with book ends made from street car rail.

The cloud cover had scattered, the light snow had disappeared and the sun was bright as the

Good-bye Street Cars: Your Last Ride

PIONEERS ONLY

The B. C. Electric invites you to board a special street car for pioneers only. Car will await you at
THE CENOTAPH, CAMBIE STREET

Sunday, April 24th, at 2:15 p.m.

•

Please present this card to the operator.

Two souvenirs of the last day of street car operation. (author's collection, George Bergson collection)

Gardens emptied; gleaming in its fresh, turn-of-the-century, green-with-filigree paint was car 53, within hours catapulted from forgotten salt car to glorious symbol. The P.C.C.s still had a little time, scooting along Hastings Street only a few hundred feet away, but by 7:15 p.m., all thirty-six were clustered around the incinerator at Kitsilano shop. They had one by one run by the Carrall Street depot into the yard, there to be coupled, then drawn by a C.P.R. locomotive to the north side of False Creek; under trolley wire again, a B. C. Electric locomotive had pulled the cars in batches over the trestle to the beginning of a long wait. P.C.C. 415 had been the very last street car in operation. Cars 364-378 were already at Kitsilano, waiting for the P.C.C.s.

Trolley wire removal on Hastings was begun on Sunday evening, track removal Monday morning. Including the track on Main and Renfrew streets, the final seven and a quarter route miles of street car line were redundant. It had been a profoundly exciting day, one that had the aura of renewal about it — but the street cars were really gone this time. Strange how their passing had generated such a profusion of happy talk, hearty laughter, and cheerful hustle and bustle.

Interurban car 1304 had not been out on the Chilliwack line for almost five years, but when Yarrow teacher Miss J. E. Fowlie wondered in a letter to president Grauer if her grade three students might not have a train ride to round off a study unit on transportation, it was as good as done. One of the diesels hauling a freight train brought 1304 to Chilliwack, where the thirty-eight students, with their teacher, boarded it for a forty-five minute ride to Yarrow. After the students had inspected the train's caboose, the freight train continued on its way to New Westminster, leaving behind a class of bubbly, still wide-eyed children.

The lightweight steel street cars 364-378 were scrapped by the end of May, but the P.C.C.s were for sale as a fleet, not piecemeal — South America was rumoured, and so was Vienna. (A new P.C.C. in 1955 cost $48,000.) In mid-October, the company would sign a contract with B. C. Brokerage Company Limited, a Granville Island

(author's collection)

scrap-jobber, to take over the ownership of the thirty-six streamliners. Victoria's street cars may have disappeared seven years earlier, but they were still extremely visible in various guises all around the Victoria area, on Tattersall Drive, in the

Steveston-bound 1207 and 1208 (once named "Steveston" and "Burnaby," respectively) halt momentarily in the late evening sun at Bridgeport. (George Bergson photo)

Looking west across Glen Lyon station on the Marpole-New Westminster line, the bogginess of which is clearly evident. (E.L. Plant photo)

Fernwood district, out at Luxton, at Langford (as the truck stop "Nite Owl"), on Mount Newton Cross Road, and points north and west.

With yet another ceremony on June 17, the B. C. Electric Railway's transit conversion program was complete. Paving of Granville and Hastings streets carried out, trolley coaches inaugurated a Hastings East service on June 21 (a few buses were still operating the route as well), and on June 24, the B. C. Electric's head office — Carrall Street station to some fifty million people to have passed through the depot since its opening — was put up for sale. Automobiles were parking where the big interurban trains used to wait, and the longest magazine rack in town had been boarded up. (The B. C. Electric would open its new, six-storey, glass and steel Victoria headquarters building on Pandora Street on August 31.)

Late in the year, a 900-horsepower G.M.D. diesel locomotive numbered 900, outshopped in June, arrived in New Westminster for use on the Chilliwack line. Freight tonnage of 1,362,554 and gross revenue from freight, $4,249,915 (up 26.1%), set new records in 1955. Two factors contributed heavily to these healthy figures, a 32% increase in the number of cars of forest products moving over the B. C. Electric's system, and flood damage on July 24 to the C.P.R.'s bridge over the

Fraser River at Mission, handing the B. C. Electric the C.P.R.'s flow to and from Huntingdon. The number of passengers carried had come close to regressing to eight figures — 104,561,631.

As 1956 asserted itself, the same sixteen interurban coaches were still toiling over the remaining lines, Marpole-Steveston and Marpole-New Westminster, but New Westminster's city council was eager to have the short section of track on Columbia Street into, and through, the depot building removed. These six "name" cars and ten St. Louis vehicles would be the final steel-wheeled standardbearers of the B. C. Electric Railway's once-magnificent fleet.

In March, one end of the last of the baggage-express cars, 1707, was badly battered in an accident (it would be scrapped later in the year), and on the last day of the month, Coghlan, relatively isolated now from the main traffic routes (all roads) lost its post office.

Vancouver's city council approved on May 7 an application by the company to discontinue its interurban passenger service between Marpole and New Westminster. City engineer John Oliver had found that a mere twenty-five riders had alighted from or boarded the interurban car between 6:30 a.m. and 9:15 p.m. on a particular day at the three stations which were more than normal walking distance from the Marpole-New Westminster bus line on Marine Drive.

The B. C. Electric announced on May 16 that its head office building at Hastings and Carrall streets had been sold for redevelopment purposes to a syndicate headed by two San Francisco businessmen for $700,000. Nonetheless, the company would stay put until its new head office at Burrard and Nelson streets was ready for occupancy. The centre of Vancouver's downtown had long ago slipped westward and away from Carrall Street, but the new building seemed unusually far south of Granville and Georgia streets, actually creating a new focal point in the downtown area.

The death of Rochfort Henry Sperling on July 5, general manager after Buntzen and before Kidd during nine glory years, 1905 to 1914, struck a particularly melancholy note in a discord of change and abandonment.

On a cloudy July 6 the author boarded Marpole-bound car 1216 at 3:05 p.m. at 16th Street in New Westminster, riding with the motorman until leaving the train at 3:27 p.m. at Main Street, a thirty-cent journey. Twenty riders were aboard from New Westminster. A downpour at Dominion Mills preceded a spirit-shattering track torpedo just east of Victoria road, enough to divert 1216 onto a siding to allow locomotive 974 to hustle east with a freight, caboose A. 12 trailing. No one knew for certain yet, but the end of passenger service to New Westminster was, in fact, little more than four months away.

Looking west to Number 3 Road with Brighouse station prominent in this 1955 view. (George Bergson photo)

Old Marpole Line

And it seemed increasingly possible that the thirty-six P.C.C. street cars, so vigorously sought and fought for, were unable to find further life elsewhere. B. C. Brokerage Company Limited, having purchased the cars to sell them to another transit line, had seen its most recent attempt at a deal, with a Vienna, Austria company, fall through. Accordingly, B. C. Brokerage announced on August 21 that the thirty-six cars had been sold to Active Trading Company Limited for scrap. One by one, they were trucked from the storage tracks at Kitsilano to a vacant yard off Gilmore Avenue in Burnaby, where they were lined up, side to side, facing north toward the Great Northern Railway's main line, very close to the roadbed of the Burnaby Lake line, waiting.

All the while, B. C. Electric's freight operations were expanding, the spur from the Queensborough line to the new industrial park on Annacis Island ceremonially inaugurated on November 1, provincial railway minister Lyle Wicks at the throttle of a diesel locomotive. (Trackage on Annacis Island would be considerably extended in 1957 to accommodate the expansion of industry.) The arrival of 901 and 902, two 900-horsepower SW900 RSes, from G.M.D. during the year had enabled District One to be dieselized. (On October 31, a new bridge across the Fraser River between Rosedale and Agassiz had rendered the ages-old ferry obsolete, making travel in the Valley even swifter.)

It was at 12:30 a.m., early Sunday morning, November 18, that sixty-five years of interurban service in New Westminster and Burnaby came to an abrupt halt with the departure from New Westminster of car 1203, conductor Lawrence Love and motorman Tom Pritchard in charge.

Motorman Frank Bernard had left Marpole for New Westminster on the last eastbound run at midnight with car 1223. The thirteen trips each way daily — ten on Sundays — had to be cancelled, the company proclaimed, "owing to lack of patronage."

Later in the morning, the company bus line on Marine Drive began detouring on Willard Street and Trapp Avenue to service an area the interurban line reached so handily, and on Monday morning a connecting "shuttle taxi" service went into weekdays-only operation for Byrne Road area residents. On December 10, a newspaper advertisement placed by the B. C. Electric's disposal section indicated that "offers will be received for the demolition and removal of 21 platforms and 15 shelters between 13th Street New Westminster and Heather Street Vancouver." The freight trains finally had this busy route all to themselves, and the one line which still tunnelled through the otherwise reconstructed New Westminster depot could now be blocked off and the track through it and on Columbia and Front streets lifted, replaced by a new line on the adjacent C.P.R. right of way.

Freight tonnage for 1956 was up a gratifying 15.8% to 1,578,127, for a gross revenue of $5,232,587, largely a result of higher revenue per car and greater volume in pool cars and pipe, westbound. For eastern Canadian soap and fertilizer manufacturers, Steveston alone had delivered six hundred carloads of fish oil. Passengers carried by a system totally rubber-tired, with the exception of the Marpole-Steveston interurban line, numbered 104,869,133. The B.C. Electric operated Canada's largest fleet of trolley coaches, 327.

As 1957 opened, city workmen began the task of removing the street car tracks on Main Street between Hastings and Seventh Avenue. And in mid-March, close to one thousand B. C. Electric employees from the old head office, from the company's general sales division office building at Dunsmuir and Granville streets, and from the bus depot began trekking to their new, twenty-one storey head office building at 970 Burrard Street, the most imposing structure to rise in downtown Vancouver in more than two decades, officially opened on March 28.

Doubtless because the opening of the Oak Street Bridge on June 29 between Marpole and Richmond guaranteed the cessation of the interurban to Steveston, the October 4 lower mainland edition of *The Buzzer* unleashed the following bitter-sweet encouragement:

> *"How long is it since you rode on an interurban tram?*
>
> *They have an appeal all their own.*
>
> *Time was when young sports of Vancouver and New Westminster would take their best girls for a Sunday round-trip on the interur-*

(Left)
The issue of The Buzzer *announcing the end of the Marpole-New Westminster interurban line service. (author's collection)*

ban ... not a bad idea as many a heart was won on such outings.

There are just a few trams left today — and they operate on the Marpole-Steveston line — so why not take a ride? If you're an oldtimer around these parts, riding the trams will bring back many memories; if you're a newcomer, you'll enjoy the ride almost as much, for you will be taken through interesting Delta farmlands and attractive new residential developments on Lulu Island.

From downtown Vancouver take a Granville (No. 20) or Oak (No. 17) trolley coach to Marpole on the north arm of the Fraser River. There you will make connections with the interurbans, leaving every hour on the half hour, for Steveston. We're sure you'll enjoy the trip and be surprised at the rapidly changing face of Lulu Island. At the fishing community of Steveston, you can look around for an hour then board a return interurban to Marpole. Then transfer to a Fourth Avenue (No. 4) or Victoria (No. 25) trolley coach and return to downtown Vancouver. The trip each way will take an hour, with another hour to look around Steveston. Round trip cost per person is 60¢."

(Far right)
Lawrence Love, 1225's conductor on the B.C. Electric's final rail passenger trip, February 28, 1958. (Bob Webster photo)
(Right)
The official announcement of the termination of rail passenger service by the B.C. Electric. (Burnaby Village Museum)

It's 1:30 a.m., February 28, 1958. Car 1225 has just arrived at Marpole, having completed its journey from Steveston, the last scheduled run of rail passenger service. In a few minutes the crew will make its last trip, to Kitsilano shops. (Bob Webster photo)

NOTICE

THE LAST FULL DAY OF RAIL PASSENGER SERVICE BETWEEN MARPOLE AND STEVESTON WILL BE THURSDAY, FEBRUARY 27, 1958.

THE LAST TRIP FROM MARPOLE WILL LEAVE AT 12:30 A.M., FEBRUARY 28, AND THE LAST TRIP FROM STEVESTON WILL LEAVE STEVESTON AT 1:00 A.M., FEBRUARY 28.

A BUS SERVICE IS BEING INAUGURATED FEBRUARY 28, 1958, REPLACING THE RAIL SERVICE.

FULL INFORMATION ABOUT THE BUS SERVICE AND ROUTE MAPS WILL BE AVAILABLE AT MARPOLE TICKET OFFICE UP TO AND INCLUDING FEBRUARY 27.

FOR FURTHER INFORMATION TELEPHONE KErrisdale 7500.

FEBRUARY 21, 1958. British Columbia Electric Railway Company Limited

By year's end, the line between Marpole and New Westminster was dieselized, and two more locomotives, 903 and 904, had increased the company's fleet of diesels to nine. Freight tonnage fell back to 1,364,838, whereas the number of passengers carried increased slightly to 106,912,144.

The Buzzer of January 10, 1958 one last time urged its readers to ride the interurban: "We will be saying goodbye to the Marpole-Steveston interurban passenger cars early in February. Yes, this historic line — last of our interurban services — will soon pass into history, being succeeded by an integrated all-bus system for Richmond municipality. So we're urging you to not delay taking a last run on the historic line that began operating back in 1905." Weekday service consisted of 27 trips each way over the eight-mile run, with hourly service on Sunday and a late train on Saturday "nights" at 1:30 a.m. from Marpole, 2 a.m. on the return from Steveston.

It was early Friday morning, 12:30 a.m., February 28, when the final scheduled run of a B. C. Electric interurban train, car 1225, departed from Marpole with 68 passengers, mostly railfans, and conductor Lawrence Love and motorman Bert Hall. Among those on board were company security police and assistant superintendent L. R. Stewart. Having left Steveston at 1 a.m. on the return journey, the last train — delayed by the opening of the Fraser River bridge on both trips — released all its passengers at 1:30 a.m. at the Marpole depot, and continued its final, lonely trip with only its crew through darkened Kerrisdale and on the line's best speedway, alongside Quilchena Golf Course between Twenty-ninth and Twenty-second avenues, to the suddenly unnecessary barn at Kitsilano.

There was to be one last hurrah, but without

The ceremonial last run is for invited guests only. The
. will leave Marpole at 11 a.m. sharp, proceedin
brighouse, to pick up guests, continuing on to Steveston,
and then back to Brighouse. Following the luncheon
guests will be returned to their points of boarding either
by train or bus.

SPECIAL TRAIN SCHEDULE

Marpole	Lv.	11:00 a.m.
Brighouse	Ar.	11:15
	Lv.	11:20
Steveston	Ar.	11:30
	Lv.	11:45
Brighouse	Ar.	11:55

Train may be boarded at Marpole, Brighouse or Steveston,
whichever is most suitable.

THE PRESIDENT AND DIRECTORS OF THE
BRITISH COLUMBIA ELECTRIC COMPANY LIMITED
REQUEST THE COMPANY OF

at a last ceremonial run of the Marpole-Steveston
Interurban Passenger Trains, to be
followed by a luncheon in the Brighouse United Church Hall,
816 Granville, Richmond, B. C.
on February 28, 1958

R.S.V.P.
Miss S. Gray
970 Burrard Street
MU 3-8711, Local 3251

Last Run—See Attached
Timetable
Luncheon—12:15

car 1225 — the "last ceremonial run of the Marpole-Steveston Interurban Passenger Trains." At 11 a.m. on Friday, a sunny winter's day, two trains, colourfully hung with flags, bunting, and signs with period lettering, left Marpole for a final journey over the line with invited guests taken aboard at Marpole, at Brighouse, and at Steveston; the 225 celebrants, including company and municipal officials, broke their return trip at Brighouse for a luncheon hosted by the B. C. Electric. The first train from Marpole consisted of a St. Louis-built duo, cars 1231 and 1222, with conductor Charlie Martin, motorman Barney Kadey, and brakeman Roy Cameron. The second section followed closely, an old name car pairing from the line's very first days, cars 1208 (ex-"Burnaby") and 1207 (ex-"Steveston"), with conductor Jim Moffat, motorman Jim Metcalf, and brakeman Lawrence Love. Chief dispatcher Joe Whitty sent both trains on their way from Marpole.

At the luncheon, a presentation was made to Tom Leslie, B. C. Electric's agent at Steveston for more than thirty years, and four distinguished guests were introduced. First was Mrs. E. F. Robinson, who had made the trip on the first official run to Steveston as the guest of George Dickie, a friend of her father. Second was George Boston, who, on his retirement on the last day of 1949, had been 44 years and four months on District 2, and who had met his wife-to-be on his first day on the job as a passenger conductor. Boston had served more years on the Steveston line than any other employee, capping his career as number one motorman. Third to be introduced was William Deagle, a crew member on the first run who had gone on to serve District 2 for many years, and currently a resident of Steveston. The last to be introduced was Steve Manning, the youngest son — himself a B. C. Electric bus operator — of the conductor on the first train to Steveston, Ed Manning.

The address, by B. C. Electric's general manager of transportation (and luncheon chairman) S. Sigmundson, focussed on the company's close association with Richmond and the municipality's steady growth, especially since the end of the war. Only in his second paragraph did he make reference to the wider historic significance of February 28, 1958:

"You in this Municipality are experiencing a tremendous development in all aspects of community growth, and we of the B. C. Electric are striving with you to make our contribution towards keeping pace with that expansion. During the past twelve years since the end of World War Two the transportation system of our Company has experienced very extensive growing pains as we sought to keep pace with the development of the Lower Mainland of British Columbia. Today that program reaches a significant stage as we finally abandon our last piece of steel railway to be used for the hauling of passenger traffic."

"God Save the Queen" having been chorused, the guests boarded the two waiting trains for the three and a half-mile jaunt to Marpole — 1207 appropriately leading the procession — whence they dispersed by bus and trolley coach. Having travelled for the last time as well over the Marpole line — even making a photo stop at Forty-first Avenue — the four cars rolled onto the storage tracks at the Kitsilano barns at 3 p.m. looking blatantly, inappropriately festive. Car 1231 had been the last rail passenger vehicle to roll on B. C. Electric track. Sixty-eight years of electric railway passenger service in British Columbia came to a close with the stripping of decorations from the bodies of four proud interurban coaches. The double tracked line from Marpole to Kitsilano was soon single track again, the northbound line ripped up.

(Above left)
All guests received this final timetable for the ceremonial runs. (B.C. Hydro)

(Above right)
The invitation to the last rites for B.C. Electric passenger rail services. (B.C. Hydro)

VIII

After 1958: Epilogue and Dreams

Acquisitions of the mid-1950s, 900 and 903 idle at New Westminster in early spring of 1958. (Harold K. Vollrath collection)

Eleven new bus routes commenced operating in Richmond on February 28; in addition, a new express service to downtown Vancouver had begun from Richmond's new main terminus, the Sexsmith Loop, at 6:35 a.m.

All the while, the company continued with its six-year project, initiated in 1953, of replacing the Chilliwack line's 70-pound rail with 85-pound. Similar upgrading of the Vancouver-Marpole-Steveston and Marpole-New Westminster line had already been accomplished, preparing them as well for the heavier diesel locomotives and larger hauls to come.

When summer came, the way was cleared for the city of Vancouver to become the owner of interurban car 1232 — B. C. Electric offered it as a gift to the city or any group which would display it, perhaps alongside car 53 at the Pacific National Exhibition. New Westminster too expressed an interest, but Vancouver architect Raymond Harrision beat B. C. Electric's end-of-August deadline by a few days, securing 1232 with the help of member of parliament John Taylor. Federal transport minister George Hees drove it from Kitsilano to the adjacent Royal Canadian Air Force station, defense minister George Pearkes having been persuaded by Taylor to give permission for its temporary storage there. The subsequent refusal by Vancouver's park board to give 1232 a home ensured that Vancouver would never be able to display so much as a remnant of the interurban system.

Burnaby fared better. The municipality's final project to celebrate British Columbia's centennial was the acquisition of car 1223, set in place with fanfare and ceremony by the Burnaby Historical Society on Sunday, November 30, at the corner of Edmonds and Kingsway, very near the site of long since dismantled Edmonds station. Replying to a brief, warm speech by Burnaby reeve Allan Emmott, B. C. Electric executive vice-president Harry L. Purdy presented a plaque on behalf of the company to society president Barry Mather, while praising the men who had built up the interurban system.

Car 1207, acquired by the Puget Sound Railway Historical Association at Snoqualmie, Washington, was the only "name" interurban car to survive; 1220 and 1235 became the nucleus of a small, well-kept collection of traction vehicles called Trolleyland Electric Railway, seven miles north of Centralia, Washington on the west side of Interstate 5; 1225 joined the Orange Empire Railway Museum at Perris, California; and 1304, the prize, went to Glenwood, Oregon, to what is today "The Trolley Park" of the Oregon Electric Railway Historical Society. (Car 1311 was still at Mamquam, B. C., car 53 at the Pacific National Exhibition.)

By the end of 1958, four more diesel locomotives of the same class as 900 - 904, numbered 905-908, had arrived, increasing the diesel fleet to thirteen. Unluckily for the B. C. Electric, they would purchase no more motive power.

Freight tonnage hauled in the company's last rail passenger carrying year amounted to 1,258,151, a 7.8% decrease, which nonetheless brought in a gross revenue of $4,927,687. The B. C. Electric's buses and trolley coaches together with the two months of Marpole-Steveston interurban traffic carried 104,157,370 riders, an increase of 2.6%.

By the end of March 1959, all trolley wire had been removed from the Marpole-New Westminster line, as well as throughout the New Westminster terminal, barn, and Sixteenth Street yard areas. Within months, the line from Steveston through Marpole to Kitsilano barns would see the last of its overhead wire as well. The Company had decided to retain only 960 - 962 of the electric locomotives, and those for only a short time in the False Creek area and at Carrall Street.

Despite complaints from merchants and motorists, street car tracks were still in place in many areas of Vancouver, their removal considered a low priority, especially if the provincial highways department or a district renewal plan could save the city the expense. Four years after the last street cars had disappeared, the tracks still remained on Hastings between Renfrew and Boundary Road, on Venables between Clark and Commercial, on Georgia between Main and Campbell, on Templeton between Dundas and Eton, on Alma between Fourth and Broadway, and on Thirty-third between Main and Fraser, as well as on Quebec Street near Mt. Pleasant barns. In New Westminster the entire Queen's Park track system from Sixth Street and Fourth Avenue to Park Row, including the line to First Street (with its wye at Arbutus) and much of the double track on Carnarvon, was still capable of moving flanged-wheel vehicles after more than two decades of street car inactivity.

Car 1231 was sold in August 1959 to Trolleyland Electric Railway, joining cars 1220 and 1235. Altogether, but one street car, 53, and eight interurban cars — 1207, 1220, 1223, 1225, 1231, 1235, 1304, and 1311 — had been saved from destruction. Purchased in autumn from Ernie Plant by the Montreal-based Canadian Railroad Historical Association, car 1311 was vandalized on location before its move to eastern Canada and subsequently scrapped at the Pacific Great Eastern Railway's facilities at nearby Squamish.

Horse racing in Richmond, once so exciting a feature of the interurban system's success, was brought to an end with the shutdown of Lansdowne track at the conclusion of the 1960 summer season. Out in the Fraser Valley, interurban line-created County Line post office closed on August 3, a further small testament to changing patterns of rural focus and mobility.

On December 29, H. L. Purdy became the B. C. Electric's fourth (and last, as 1961 would prove) president, with A. E. "Dal" Grauer appointed chairman of the board, a newly created office. Whereas the president was the chief operating officer of the company with direct responsibility for its business operations, the chairman would be not only the chief policy-making officer, but also the chief executive officer with general control over the entire business and all the affairs of the company.

Culminating a process initiated nine years earlier, the 1897-incorporated B. C. Electric Railway Company Limited was placed in voluntary liquidation during the last month of 1960, and on January 2, 1961, its assets were purchased by the British Columbia Electric Company Limited, in fact a simple and efficient merging of properties and operations. Shortly after, debenture and preference stocks of the B. C. Electric Railway held by the public were paid off.

Within seven months, B. C. Electric's chairman was dead, and the company itself had ceased to exist! Grauer died on July 26, 1961, six days before the expropriation of the company, under the Power Development Act, by the British Columbia Social Credit government of Premier W.A.C. Bennett. Overnight the B. C. Electric was publicly owned, a Crown corporation, but the legal turmoil generated by the take-over would take twenty-seven months to resolve.

Prophetically, the P.C.C. street cars had been scrapped just a couple of months earlier, their six years of forlorn travail finally past. Their motors and trucks disposed of elsewhere, including P.C.C.-rich Toronto, they had even suffered the indignity of having their door motors and dome lights removed to replace identical fittings in trolley coaches the company had purchased in Alabama.

To crown the government takeover, the B. C. Electric Company Limited and B. C. Power Commission were amalgamated by the provincial legislature on March 30, 1962 in accordance with the B. C. Hydro and Power Authority Act, thereby creating British Columbia Hydro and Power Authority. The railway freight service achieved its own identity, B. C. Hydro Rail, both letterhead and box cars, however, bearing the pertinent reminder to shippers, "the BCE route." There would, however, be a new logo.

An opportunity to relive the old interurban days was offered by West Coast Railfan Association on August 25, when a B. C. Hydro Rail locomotive hauled a number of C.P.R. coaches from Kitsilano barns through Marpole to New Westminster, whence Pacific Coast Terminal's 0-6-0 steam locomotive 4012 took over for the longer run to the U.S. border at Huntingdon. On the ascent immediately after crossing the Fraser River, it became apparent that the romance of steam was about to leave the enthusiastic excursionists in the lurch. Insufficient power was the problem, but a call to B. C. Hydro Rail in New Westminster had a diesel locomotive soon at the train's rear, and on

For 1960, the B. C. Electric's last complete year of existence, gross revenues from operations amounted to $103,297,019, an increase of 6.6% over 1959, to which the company's various services contributed as follows:

Electricity	
Canadian	*$64,058,918*
Export	*23,816*
Gas	*19,283,393*
Passenger transportation	*14,052,072*
Rail freight	*5,043,057*
Miscellaneous	*835,763*
	$103,297,019

to Huntingdon and back. A vintage B. C. Electric crew masterminded this long, hectic, but exciting trip into the past — engineer George Martin, engineer's helper Bill Perfonic, conductor A. J. Baker, and trainmen Bill Boston (son of George Boston) and J. Colloton.

Despite urgings in September from a group called the Central Park Committee — it consisted of Burnaby and Vancouver park board members — B. C. Hydro Rail was not about to tear up its Central Park line to make way for automobile parking space. In fact, the company installed new facilities during the year in Burnaby on this very line for unloading automobiles from multi-level freight cars.

On another front, B. C. Hydro Rail had concluded an argument with the Pacific Great Eastern Railway (today's B. C. Rail) for handling its United States-bound lumber loads between New Westminster and Huntingdon. (The P.G.E. had completed its new forty-mile line into North Vancouver from Squamish six years earlier.) Meanwhile, interurban car 1223 continued to deteriorate on its wind-swept plot at Edmonds, set to survive yet another winter, its roof swathed in a protective coating of plastic.

During the first year of B. C. Hydro Rail, ending on March 31, 1963, 1,567,000 tons of freight had been moved over its 155.5 miles of main line, sidings, and yard tracks for its 1,400 freight customers all across Canada and in the western United States. Hydro's fifteen locomotives (thirteen diesels and two electrics) had helped generate a gross revenue of $5,325,286, up 6.2% over the previous corresponding period. The yard at Sixteenth Street in New Westminster had become unequal to "the BCE route's" expanding work load; its 240-car capacity was occasionally asked to process up to 700 freight cars in a twenty-four-hour period. And in August, B. C. Hydro Rail handled its initial piggy-back trailer shipment, two Southern Pacific trailers on an 85-foot flat car from California.

The company pursued an aggressive industrial development program, already having assembled Van Horne, Marine Drive, Kingsway-Boundary, McPherson Avenue, South Westminster, Newton, and Langley Industrial Centres, as well as Annacis Industrial and Langley Park Estates. During 1964, the company added a necessary diesel, 909.

The opening in June 1964 of the swooping, four-lane Port Mann Bridge across the Fraser River, four miles upstream from the railway bridge at New Westminster, signalled the completion of a freeway system from Vancouver east beyond Chilliwack. The construction of the section between Vancouver and the new bridge, begun in 1960, had obliterated much of what still had remained of the Burnaby Lake line's right of way. At Chilliwack, the company's rail line was flown across the freeway on a new bridge, while between the former stations of Jardine and Harmsworth, the freeway burrowed through fill under the railway.

Downtown New Westminster once again displayed street car tracks in April 1965; those buried beneath pavement on Columbia Street between Fourth and Sixth streets were finally removed in a flurry of roadway construction. Late 1965 saw two substantial improvements achieved for Hydro Rail. Four and a half miles of the Marpole-Steveston line were abandoned, and a new route, four-fifths of a mile shorter, was opened on September 13 between the south end of the Fraser River crossing and the ninety degree curve just north of former McCallan Road station, now renamed Railway Avenue. The Vancouver & Lulu Island Railway's parent, the C.P.R., had undertaken the relocation, and Richmond municipality, having taken over the old right of way, would widen adjacent Garden City Way and Granville Avenue into major thoroughfares. A railway not only had been plucked out of a fast-developing urban area, but also had been re-established close to the Fraser River through municipal land which would be developed for light industrial purposes.

On October 28, B. C. Hydro opened the much-needed Trapp yard about a mile east of the Sixteenth Street yard on the line to Marpole. At a cost of $1.25 million, the company had constructed on filled, boggy land a twenty-one acre

The railway division of British Columbia Hydro and Power Authority was organized in the following manner, its four main line subdivisions totalling 95.35 miles:

Central Park Subdivision (New Westminster at Columbia and
Eighth Street to Nanaimo — 8.3 miles)
Queensboro and Annacis Island Branch
Edmonds Branch (6,265 feet)
Vancouver Subdivision (from the junction with the Central
Park Sub. in New Westminster via Marpole to
Kitsilano Bridge — 16.15 miles)
South Shore line
Steveston Subdivision (Marpole Jct. to Steveston — 7.1 miles)
Fraser Valley Subdivision (New Westminster to Chilliwack — 63.8 miles)

marshalling yard consisting of twenty-five storage tracks (7.4 miles) capable of holding 540 freight cars. The two contiguous yards enabled B. C. Hydro Rail freight hauling muscles to flex freely for the first time. At Carrall Street yard, the last electric locomotive in revenue service in Canada, 960, had everything under control, though 961 waited on standby at Kitsilano.

Old electric snowplow S.103 (once locomotive 952) was finally rescued by the Puget Sound Railway Historical Association for $1,200, arriving at Snoqualmie on a Northern Pacific flat car on March 6, 1966 to rejoin interurban coach 1207 after a seven-year hiatus. At Edmonds by the following month, a peaked wooden roof supported by eight steel poles had been erected over 1223, and first cleaning, refurbishing, and painting since the car's placing almost eight years ago had been initiated by a vigorous team of Rover Scouts.

Once-important Sullivan Station was the last of the Chilliwack line-instigated post offices to close, concluding almost fifty-four years of continuous service on May 4, 1967.

By summer, a large automobile loading-unloading facility on Queensborough had been completed, and the newest industrial areas of Brighouse, Stride Avenue (Burnaby), and Matsqui (Abbotsford) were coming into full flower as B. C. Hydro continued to be active in promoting industrial development along its routes to generate more traffic. By year's end, the freight tonnage hauled had breached the two million mark for the first time (2,011,000), another 900-class locomotive had been added (910), and a new repair and service centre had been erected at Trapp yard, rendering Kitsilano's facilities both obsolete and redundant. Locomotive 961 was moved to Carrall Street to keep 960 company there. Sixty- to seventy-car freight trains hauled by four diesels were commonplace on the Fraser Valley Subdivision as far as Huntingdon, two daily through trains on this run being augmented by nighttime operations to collect and deliver cars along the route.

As 1968 began, B. C. Hydro Rail needed to effect some rapid adjustments at Langley. The city had grown to the point where its main street, old Trans-Canada Highway, at its busiest intersection hardly needed the annoyance and danger of heavy freight trains crossing. Nor did Hydro need the slow running. In addition, the Roberts Bank superport just south of Ladner, scheduled to open within two years, promised massive trains of coal through Langley from southeastern British Columbia for reloading onto Japan-bound vessels.

The location of a new rail route from the B. C. Hydro line west of Langley to Roberts Bank having been established in late July, a decision was made to continue Hydro Rail's Langley Industrial Centre

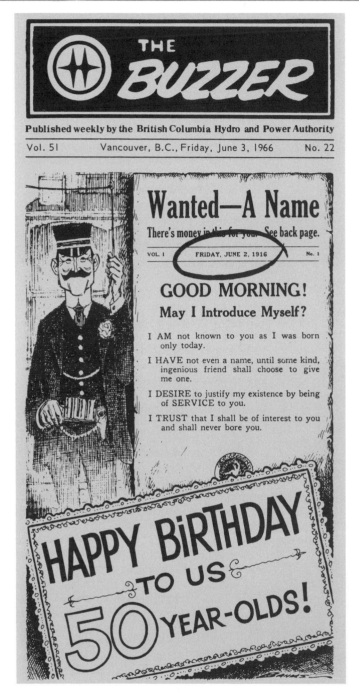

spur — it curved from the main line west of Langley in a northeasterly direction along Production Way — a short distance eastward to reconnect with the main line northeast of Langley, thereby creating a new main line which avoided the city's centre. (To this end, Hydro had already moved its loading dock from near the city hall to a new site on Production Way earlier in the year.)

Across the Fraser River at Stave Falls, the post office had closed on March 30; and at Edmonds, the Royal Canadian Mounted Police vacated its old quarters adjacent to car 1223, making it more vulnerable to vandalism. Termed an eyesore and a white elephant, battered 1223 was deemed by

New logo, new company, same friendly Buzzer. *(author's collection)*

many Burnaby council aldermen to be worthy only of being torched; furthermore, its location was to be the site of a senior citizens' high-rise development.

On November 2, the route of the new 23.3-mile railway line to Roberts Bank (four-fifth of a mile on existing Great Northern trackage) was approved by provincial order-in-council, and B. C. Hydro set about acquiring the necessary right of way. (Ownership of this line was expected to be shared with other principal railways; in the event, it became the provincial British Columbia Harbours Board Railway, managed by the British Columbia Railway, formerly Pacific Great Eastern Railway.) The new line would swing away from the Fraser Valley Subdivision at Pratt, 0.85 mile east of Cloverdale. To give the coal trains access to the line, a two-mile railway connection was to be constructed between Livingstone (just east of old Harmsworth station) and the main line of the Canadian National east of Fort Langley.

Diesel locomotive 931 arrived in July 1969, a thirteen-year-old G.M.D. SW 900 which had laboured on the Midland Railway of Manitoba, and the 900-class was completed during the year with the arrival of 911.

Single-truck street car 53 seemed to be sharing most of 1223's woes. Still at Vancouver's Pacific National Exhibition, it was open to the elements, deteriorating rapidly, a candidate, many opined, for scrapping. Owners Ernie Plant and John A. Wood (Plant would later buy out Wood) accordingly signed an agreement with the owners of The Old Spaghetti Factory Restaurant on Water Street in Vancouver's historic Gastown area. Here the street car would achieve a heaven of sorts in early 1970 as a much admired centrepiece.

Though the car barn building at Prior Street had outlasted the street cars by almost fifteen years, planning for the new twin-bridge Georgia Viaduct had dictated its demolition in February

1970. In October, electric locomotives 960 and 961 were supplanted by a 940-class diesel (usually 942) at nearby Carrall Street yard, where much of the overhead wire was an impediment to construction work on the new viaduct and to the pulling down of the old. Simply, without drama, yet less than a block's distance from the Vancouver terminus of Canada's greatest interurban railway operation, eighty years of electric operation had come to a close. Who now could remember the excitement of that cold February morning in Victoria when horse cars and cable cars were old and electric trolley traction was the world exquisitely revealed.

The Langley by-pass line was opened in April, and trains were on their way from the C.N.R. main line (having earlier crossed the Fraser River from the C.P.R. at Mission) to Roberts Bank. More than two miles of the original Chilliwack line had been abandoned from former Anderson Station east, part of the stretch becoming a footpath, the portion south of the highway in Langley a parking lot. B. C. Hydro was reimbursed by the B. C. Harbours Board Railway for expenditures incurred on the Pratt-to-Roberts Bank railway line. During 1970, B. C. Hydro Rail hauled a record 2,466,000 tons of freight; its line was now laid with 115-pound rail all the way to Huntingdon, 85-pound from there to Chilliwack.

Burnaby celebrated British Columbia's one hundred years of confederation with Canada in

(Right)

No tram went as far as Chilliwack on April 10, 1910, but The Buzzer's intentions are admirable. (author's collection)

Birney 400, discovered near Cowichan Lake in 1970. (John Smyly photo)

THE BUZZE[R]

Published weekly by the British Columbia Hydro and Power

Vol. 55   Vancouver, B.C., Friday, April 17, 1970

MUSKEG MAUDE

[VA]NCOUVER-CHILLIWACK
APRIL 10, 1910

"HOLD 'ER, GEORGE — THIS MUST BE THE LO[CAL] DELEGATION SENT OUT TO MEET US"

1971 by rescuing car 1223. In May, the interurban coach was moved to municipally-operated Burnaby Village Museum and set up on rails not too far from preserved Burnaby Lake line Vorce station. To the surprise of many, and the delight of some, car 1223 was painted in its original green livery rather than in the latterly so-familiar red.

Since the old foundry at Nanaimo Street on the Central Park line had closed in April, there was no need for the line to exist west of Rupert Street, former Collingwood West station. Consequently, by June, the one mile of track between Rupert and Nanaimo streets had been pulled up, the concrete overpass-supporting pillars at Rupert slated for removal.

The thirty million-dollar redevelopment begun three years earlier at Jordan River virtually complete, the flume-hugging railway was shut down in early August. The flume-forebay-penstocks-to-powerhouse system was about to be supplanted by a new one: 430-foot wide, 117-foot high Elliott Dam; a three and a half mile-long, sixteen-foot wide power tunnel; a single penstock; and a new powerhouse six times as powerful as the phased-out plant. J. M. Elliott had arrived at Jordan River in 1916, allowing him time to ride the little narrow gauge railway on countless occasions. He was B. C. Electric's superintendent of stations and power houses for Vancouver Island at retirement and the new dam was given his name. Jack Elliott turned a switch on December 20, putting Jordan River's new 150,000-kilowatt generating station into operation. One of the gasoline engines and the snow plow were acquired by B. C. Forest Museum for display at its site just north of Duncan.

At Carrall Street, de-electrification had been completed in September with the pulling down of the trolley wire yet remaining over the 2.1 miles of industrial trackage. Before 1971 was complete, diesel locomotive 381 arrived from E.M.D.; at two thousand horsepower, it was the largest yet for the company.

When the B. C. government changed the name of its other railway, the Pacific Great Eastern, to B. C. Railway on April 1, 1972, it played a trick on both: B. C. Rail, B. C. Hydro Rail — the public was confused. Fortunately, those who needed to know did. And when two more of the large diesels, 382 and 383, had arrived, there was indeed reason to gaze at Hydro Rail with some awe. Yet, beginning April 1, Hydro Rail's traffic operations were actually entrusted to the control of B. C. Rail, which had been awarded a management contract.

Extraordinarily, the very smallest had its day on May 1, 1973, when refurbished Victoria Birney, car 400, was presented to the B. C. Provincial Museum for display. Its battered body had been rescued from the bush along the Lake Cowichan subdivision of the E. & N. Railway in 1970, and money was donated by B. C. Hydro. Fifteen months of work on the car inside an airplane hangar at Patricia Bay, under the direction of Paul Class of Glenwood, Oregon, had enabled 400 to be brought back, almost to life.

To carry lumber for customers along its routes, B. C. Hydro Rail had leased ten box cars during 1973. Since the B. C. Railway's management of Hydro Rail had not been especially successful, Hydro Rail regained control of its operations in May 1974. The arrival in 1974 of a fourth large diesel locomotive, 384, completed Hydro Rail's 381-class, and with the purchase of three 1,500 horsepower, snow plow-equipped diesels, 151 - 153, from E.M.D. in 1975, the company completed its fleet of diesel locomotives, twenty-four in all.

The British Columbia government announced in mid-August of 1975 its purchase for $5,000 each of two of the three interurban cars, 1220 and 1231, which had formerly been at Trolleyland Electric Railway, more recently in storage at Olympia, Washington. Their acquisition from a Seattle collector, and the purchase of a quantity of spare parts, had been handled by the Provincial Museum, the plan being for the B. C. Transportation Museum in Richmond to take one, Burnaby Village Museum the other. Both cars languish in a warehouse on the former Dominion Bridge property in Burnaby, accompanied by locomotive 960, which was secured by B. C. Transit employee and transit enthusiast Brian Kelly, and the shell of former North Vancouver street car 153, brought in from Ryder Lake Road, southeast of Chilliwack.

On November 13, Hydro Rail moved its first unit train, twenty-seven carloads of mobile homes hauled by locomotives 384 and 909, from Huntingdon to the docks on the Surrey side of the Fraser. In Chilliwack, Hydro's track from the C.N.R. into the centre of town had been removed during the year, making the C.N.R. connection Hydro's eastern railway terminus. During 1975 as well, the National Museum of Science and Technology in Ottawa, Ontario, Canada's capital city, had purchased interurban car 1235, the third of the Trolleyland trio.

On January 28, 1976, a $150,000 Siemens-built street car, ordered in September by the B. C. government, arrived in Vancouver from West Germany. Though this thirty-one-ton, seventy-foot-long, articulated tramcar was to have been tested on the Central Park line, Hydro officials found that it was built too low for local operation, and that its wheels were too small — twenty-six inches high rather than the normal forty-two — and too narrow — two inches wide rather than the normal four. Rounding a bend, the car could leave the rails with astonishing ease. After a spell in storage at New Westminster, the car was moved to Dominion Bridge, a companion for the four B.C. Electric vehicles, but nonetheless an attractive, attention-getting opener for the very idea of rapid transit.

Hydro Rail took the first step toward eliminating the pioneering 940-series of diesel locomotives, now superfluous, by selling the newest, 943, on May 31 to Andrew Merrilees Limited, Toronto.

After years of study and debate, the Greater Vancouver Regional District (G.V.R.D.) announced in early 1977 that its transit priorities called for the restoration of the Central Park line to accommodate an LRT — Light Rapid Transit — system. When B. C. Hydro followed with plans for a feasibility study, the Vancouver area reacquainted itself with a reasonable reality: the old B. C. Electric interurban lines might well have been the best transit idea of all, and any hope for relief from chronic congestion lay in a return, somehow, to those passages.

Early in the year, Hydro Rail removed the snowplows from locomotives 151 - 153 for the greater safety of its crews, and in September it leased a further batch of fifty blue-painted box cars. In December, street car 400 was transferred to the B. C. Transportation Museum in Richmond for closer care, some modifications, and future display.

In a preliminary LRT study done by the city of Vancouver in autumn, the suggested route tunnelled from Victory Square in downtown Vancouver to the Burlington Northern (formerly G.N.) yard, then along that railway's cut to a point north of John Hendry (Trout Lake) Park, near Cedar Cottage, whence it ran to New Westminster over the Central Park line. Three downtown stations — Victory Square, C.P.R. station, and Bentall Centre — were proposed, along with five more in Vancouver, four in Burnaby, and four in New Westminster. Prophetically, Hydro's railway

† Holly Horwood, "Preview Run on Section of Proposed LRT Route Shows Some Quirks," *The Vancouver Sun*, 9 February 1978, p. D.1.

(B.C. Hydro Rail)

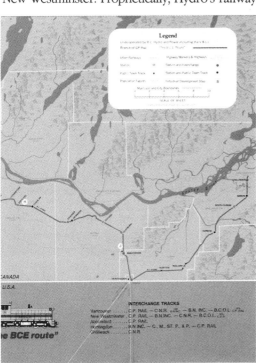

manager Gerry Stevenson sounded a pivotal concern in February 1978: "If LRT is dropped on us, we want to make darn sure that our freight customers don't get sold short." †

The introduction of the computer to Hydro Rail's operation in May 1979 enabled the Company to achieve greater success in improving customer service, in preparing customers' bills, and in dispatching and locating rail cars. That the very last regular passenger train to pull out of Vancouver's C.P.R. station did so on October 27 must not go unrecorded, particularly in the context of the gradually unfolding LRT mystery. On December 12, locomotive 941 was sold to Eurocan Pulp and Paper Company Limited at Kitimat, B.C.

Out in the yard between Hydro Rail's freight office at Vye and the U. S. border at Huntingdon on March 7, 1980, three freight cars of machinery from the company's C.N.R. connection at Chilliwack and two cars from Hydro customers in Abbotsford comprised the last interchange with the Milwaukee Road's line to Bellingham, and south. No cars had been received on that day from the ailing Milwaukee, whose 4,600 miles of western trackage had been ordered shut down on March 1. The loss to Hydro Rail was negligible, the bulk of its healthy work at the border still with the old Burlington Northern — formerly Northern Pacific — line.

Electric locomotive 961 had experienced a second life with B. C. Electric and B. C. Hydro, and beginning with its arrival in Edmonton on March 15, it began its third incarnation. Restoration and updating was completed by September, 961 glamorously repainted as Edmonton Transit's 2001. Its work was to carry away to new E. T. sites and trackage the earth and gravel excavated from the tunnel of the LRT's westward extension under Jasper Avenue. Shuttling with dump cars kept 961 busy refashioning its reputation, and when the bore was ready, other occasional work was entrusted to it.

On April 1, British Columbia Hydro and Power Authority, in accordance with the provisions of the Urban Transit Authority Act and the Metro Transit Operating Company Act (as well as with the written direction of the province's Minister of Municipal Affairs), discontinued bus and trolley coach services, transferring them to the newly-created Urban Transit Authority and Metro Transit Operating Company, the owner and the operator. (Responsibility for Hydro's interurban bus service had been transferred to Pacific Coach Lines Limited exactly one year previously.) Operating losses on the urban transit services for the year ending March 31, 1980 had been almost fifty-six million dollars; the loss on disposal of B. C. Hydro's passenger transportation operations amounted to thirty-seven million dollars.

The gradual transfer of 2,900 B. C. Hydro transit

employees began immediately; the 662 buses, 311 trolley coaches, and two 400-passenger SeaBus catamarans (shuttling on Burrard Inlet between Vancouver at the C.P.R. station and North Vancouver, one block west of Lonsdale, since June 17, 1977) together had carried 104.7 million riders during the previous twelve-month period. B. C. Hydro could now concentrate on providing electric, gas, and rail freight services, in addition to distributing natural gas in greater Vancouver and the Fraser Valley and butane-air gas in greater Victoria. B. C. Hydro Rail's freight revenue for the year had amounted to twenty-four million dollars, its tonnage handled a record 2,869,000.

Fully as daring as the Westminster and Vancouver Tramway's notion of running an interurban line through remote, difficult, lightly populated terrain in 1891 was the astonishing shape the Vancouver area's rapid transit project would take, and using the old Tramway right of way at that! No light rapid transit, the Urban Transit Authority had decided. Vancouver and New Westminster were once again to be linked by sophisticated transit, but this time by a revolutionary rail travel concept — Advanced Light Rapid Transit, ALRT. B. C.'s minister of municipal affairs, also responsible for transit, William Vander Zalm, made the historic announcement on December 6, 1980.

On May 29, 1981, U.T.A. signed a contract with Urban Transportation Development Corporation of the province of Ontario to build a 13.2-mile system between the two cities, U.T.D.C. to operate it for two years before turning it over to its owner, Urban Transit Authority. The signatories were Larry Miller, general manager of U.T.A.; Kirk Foley, president of U.T.D.C.; William Vander Zalm, the instigator of the use of the Ontario-developed ALRT concept; James Snow, Ontario's minister of transportation and communications; federal government cabinet minister Ray Perrault (the financial aid of Canada's government was essential to the project); B. C.'s premier Bill Bennett; and Ontario's premier William Davis.

The ALRT system employs continuous welded standard gauge track. Electrically-powered (third rail) and completely grade-separated from all traffic, it is laid on a concrete guideway, nine miles of it elevated monorail fashion and the rest at grade level. From Vancouver's SeaBus terminal at the C.P.R. depot, the ALRT line uses the C.P.R. tunnel under the city, swings high above Main Street and east along the north rim of the Burlington Northern cut, parallels slightly to the east Commercial Drive, joining the Central Park line's grade — where else? — at Cedar Cottage. The B. C. Electric's old dreams of unimpeded access into downtown Vancouver for its great interurban line have finally been realized! From Cedar Cottage eastward, the guideway follows the old Tramway line right into New Westminster, swooping over its surroundings the whole

Edmonton Transit's 2001 is former B.C. Electric 961, photographed here on June 15, 1983. (George Bergson photo)

distance except for two sections run on the old line's right of way itself, from Nanaimo Street almost to Rupert Street, and alongside the ALRT's maintenance centre at Connaught Hill.

B. C. Hydro Rail's line obviously accompanies the ALRT line, albeit at ground level, from Rupert Street to New Westminster. In addition to this use of B. C. Hydro-owned land, eight of the ALRT line's fifteen stations are situated on Hydro property.

Operating on their own guideway, safely oblivious to the swirl of road and Hydro Rail traffic about them, the 114 Canadian-built cars each seat forty riders and carry an additional thirty-five standees. Measuring 8 feet in width and 41.7 feet in length, each car, of aluminum construction, with fibreglass end caps, weighs 29,500 pounds — two tons less than even the P.C.C. street cars — and cruises at 47-50 miles per hour. Each car is equipped with two linear induction motors which function magnetically, eschewing any connection with the axles or wheels and obviating the necessity of a transmission or gear system. Yet another unique attribute of each vehicle is its steerable axle trucks, designed to cut back on wheel and rail wear.

The slim, delicately-tapered cars are automated. Although two-way radio-equipped employees will be present on each car — at least for a time — a computerized system, developed in the German Federal Republic by Standard Electrik Lorenz AG, directs every aspect of train movements over the ALRT operation.

The ALRT concept eliminates the danger of grade crossing competitions, espouses the risk of a commercially untried technology, requires the expenditure of 854 million dollars, and promises wonders, not least of which are a twenty-seven-minute terminus-to-terminus travel time and exhilarating vistas, especially westbound from Broadway and Commercial and eastbound from the maintenance centre. Not without reason would the ALRT system officially be dubbed "SkyTrain."

In October of 1981, the eastern 4,605 feet of the line to Edmonds from Highland Park were

B.C. Hydro Rail's 903 (ex-B.C. Electric 903) crosses Number Two Road in late February of 1982. (George Bergson photo)

abandoned, tracks torn up. Part of the original Tramway route, this segment's use for freight had declined to the vanishing point. The 1,660-foot section of the spur still intact ends now at the western side of Gilley Avenue, though the track still glistens in the street it once crossed.

The commencement of ALRT construction was symbolized by a ground-breaking ceremony in Vancouver at Main Street and Terminal Avenue on March 1, 1982; and before the balmy warmth of summer at its west coast best, Urban Transit Authority was blessed by the provincial government with a new name, B. C. Transit, and Vancouver Regional Rapid Transit became its term for ALRT.

August 15 was the date by which the C.P.R. was ordered by the Canadian Transportation Commission to relinquish its under-downtown tunnel to ALRT work. It would be heightened to accommodate two tracks, one on top of the other. The C.P.R. had agreed to the elimination of all its tracks and facilities between Carrall Street and the Kitsilano trestle, including the tunnel. This had transpired in 1980, through their sale of this historic property for $27.4 million to B. C. Place for the construction of a domed stadium and the development of the world's fair, to be held in 1986, the year of Vancouver's centenary.

C.P.R.-owned Kitsilano trestle was similarly ordered vacated by October 31, effectively isolating B. C. Hydro's yard tracks at Carrall Street. To ensure access to the Carrall Street yard, a new connecting rail was laid from the south shore line just west of Main Street to the Hydro track which already crept south from Carrall along the eastern shore of False Creek.

The one train daily each way across the Kitsilano trestle swing-span ran for the last time on rainy October 21. The ceremonial train consisted of Hydro locomotive 910 and two Tourism B. C. vehicles, power car "Cheakamus River" and lounge car "Britannia." In fact, the little train made two return trips across the trestle, backing from the Kitsilano shops area across to a point beneath Granville Bridge, and return, twice. Appropriately, the crew represented lifetimes invested in the efficient operation of B. C. Electric's District 2, the C.P.R.-owned Vancouver & Lulu Island Railway. Both conductor Bill Boston and engineer William George Moffat had come out of retirement to honour a water crossing once absolutely essential to the Vancouver area's welfare and economy. A brother of each had also worked District 2, and their fathers, George Boston and William James Moffatt, were pioneers on the line, employees widely acknowledged to have established the superb standard of railway operating associated with the Lulu Island line.

The dismantling of the trestle was given over to the demolition division of Arrow Transportation Systems Inc., and on December 6, the steel centre spans were removed and sold for further bridge use. The barn and shops at Kitsilano, long derelict, were crashed to the ground, their above-ground evidence obliterated, only their concrete pits still holding out. The former Kitsilano street car line track between the trestle and Chestnut Street remains in place, offering a wye function to the main line track from Marpole which splits yet for the shops and for the trestle.

The False Creek area, once the very industrial hotbed of all of British Columbia, entered its final transformative phase with the destruction of the trestle, barn, and shops. B. C. Hydro's south shore line still patrolled one side of False Creek, effecting the old connection with the Burlington Northern near Main Street (interchanging there, as always, with the C.N.R., and now the C.P.R., and pointing the new way to the company's customers at Carrall Street. But its water edge industrial base has disappeared, replaced by row upon row of townhouses and crowned, indeed, by a seawall walk. Even Granville Island was out of bounds to the railway, laced as it now was by boutiques, theatres, and the federally-funded Granville Island Public Market. Now attention turned to the north and east shores of False Creek. The stadium, ALRT, and Expo 86 (for a time termed "Transpo") would combine to create a vista so new that the remembrance of World War II merchant ship launchings in False Creek's waters would seem faulty, a bizarre impossibility.

In early March of 1983, North Vancouver's city council, anxious to lure casual SeaBus riders up Lonsdale to the shopping core around Fifteenth Street, began to consider the idea of rebuilding former North Vancouver street car 153, to run on track that would have to be laid once again on Lonsdale. Such a concept would fit into Expo's transportation theme and at the same time play a positive role in the revitalization of lower Lonsdale.

At the end of the month came the shocking news that B. C. Hydro Rail had sustained an operating deficit of three million dollars during the past twelve months, the first time in its history that the rail freight service had incurred a loss. The 1,966,000 tons hauled were far removed from 1980's peak figure; even since the previous year, revenue from freight hauling had declined from twenty-seven to twenty-two million dollars. Recessionary times could well be blamed — many fewer domestic vehicles had been carried and the demand for B. C.'s forest industry products was markedly down.

The last two of the first four diesel locomotives, 940 and 942, had been sold on March 21 to the Weyerhaeuser Company at Springfield, Oregon, ridding Hydro Rail finally of a type of power which had begun to be outmoded long before the 900-series was even complete.

Concluding a process begun in December 1960, the British Columbia Electric Railway Company Limited was formally dissolved on May 10, more than eighty-six years after its registering in London, where its winding-up was conducted in accordance with "The Companies Act 1948 to 1981." At liquidation — whose costs were to be borne by B. C. Hydro — the sole asset of the B. C. Electric Railway consisted of the right to require B. C. Hydro and Power Authority to surrender its remaining issued share capital of the B.C.E.R. valued at $18,653,599.55, being $4.85 to the £ upon request. Liabilities there were none: Horne-Payne's vision had proliferated even beyond his magnificent horizons.

Later in the month, B. C. Hydro was awarded a $1.8 million grant by the federal government toward repositioning the Queensborough ("Queensboro," to Hydro) line from its side-of-the-road location along Ewen Avenue for almost a mile between Stanley and Jardine streets (and along Jardine itself) to a new right of way to the north, close to the Fraser River. The provincial government and the city of New Westminster together contributed the necessary additional $1.9 million. This project would enhance the basically residential character of Ewen Avenue, at the same time placing B. C. Hydro Rail in a better position to develop the line's industrial potential.

For five months, June 27 to November 27, ALRT was a reality, but only on the first-constructed, seven-tenths of a mile, demonstration segment from the station at Main Street over Terminal Avenue east to the temporary end of the guideway. At the station itself was a twenty-six-foot working model of the ALRT system, but the real attraction was the mile-and-a-half ride along the guideway on the two ALRT cars, BC 1 and BC 2; 291,000 people took B. C. Transit's advice to "take a ride into the future. Free." It would require still more than two years for ALRT construction to be complete, for the Vancouver area to possess a transporting device second to none anywhere in the world, for Expo 86 to be companioned by a railway system without precedent.

By February 1984, it was time for B. C. Hydro Rail to forsake Carrall Street. No argument was possible. Expo 86 needed the north and east shores of False Creek, something Hydro had known all along. It lost some customers, but new facilities for others were organized near Trapp Road-Willard Avenue adjacent to the Marpole-New Westminster line.

While Hydro was tearing out its seventeen-month-old connection from the south shore line to Carrall yard, as well as all trackage there, the provincial government was making a stunning announcement at Surrey Place Mall on March 12: a four and a quarter-mile extension of the ALRT system would be built from New Westminster across the Fraser on a new bridge to Surrey, terminating near the mall, on 104th Avenue,

(B.C. Transit)

Birney 400 in 1984, almost completely back to its original condition. (Monte Wright photo)

between 134th and 135th streets. This $270 million Surrey extension allows Fraser Valley passengers to embark on their ALRT journey without first braving the combative constrictions of Pattullo or Port Mann Bridges to reach New Westminster. In the minds of many, the line to Surrey assuredly guarantees an easy success for the whole ALRT concept.

The end of March brought the expected report that Hydro Rail had performed much better in the past twelve months than it had during the previous year. There was still a loss, but it was one million dollars, not three, and tonnage hauled had climbed, in spite of the effects of labour disputes, to 2,210,000.

The lease about to expire on B. C. Hydro Rail's headquarters building on Twelfth Street in New Westminster, a decision had been made to utilize existing company property in Langley, and on June 18, Hydro Rail stepped into its new head office at 5935 Glover Road, eighteen miles east of New Westminster. Not altered, of course, were the locations of the two freight agencies at Trapp Road and just north of Huntingdon.

On August 21, the "16 o'clock peddler" made its way out across the span to Queensborough and its last run down the old line, once graced by towering St. Louis interurban cars. On the day following, the same freight swung right onto the new line, completed only one week earlier, at

Furness Street, just after crossing the bridge, and worked its way west over a different Queensborough line. Since the track to Annacis Island bends south at Stanley Street, the old line along Ewen from Furness Street, three-tenths of a mile, remained in place. The tracks along Ewen and Jardine beyond Stanley were quickly removed. The "Queensborough Rail Relocation Ceremony" was celebrated at 1:30 p.m. on November 14 at the intersection of Ewen Avenue and Furness Street by company, civic, provincial, and federal officials and dignitaries.

Vancouver's Connaught Bridge, carrying Cambie Street across False Creek, so ceremonially opened so long ago, it seemed, was ceremonially closed on a Sunday of driving rain, November 18. Quite thoroughly out of date, the Connaught was hardly a fitting arch, let alone approach, for the stadium and the burgeoning site of Expo.

The minister responsible for B. C. Transit, Grace McCarthy, announced on November 29 that a twelve-mile-long park of varying width, B. C. Parkway, would be constructed under and adjacent to the ALRT guideway between Vancouver and New Westminster. The five million-dollar development encompasses a jogging track, bicycle path, and fitness stations, in addition to playgrounds, cultural displays, water slides, and even benches. Neighbourhood parks already in place are to be entwined with the Parkway. Two weeks later Flora MacDonald, Canada's employment and immigration minister, presented the B. C. government with a $1.8 million-dollar contribution toward the Parkway project (expected to provide approximately 3,800 man-weeks of work) which, when added to B. C.'s commitment of two million dollars, left $1.2 million to be raised from private, group, and corporate donors.

June 1, 1985, brought the creation by B. C.'s government of an expanded B. C. Transit, an organization with complete responsibility for all public transit in the province. Amendments to the British Columbia Transit Act merged the Metro Transit Operating Company, which had operated transit services centred in Vancouver and Victoria, into B. C. Transit, the provincial authority which operates transit in other cities and purchases equipment for all transit systems.

A month later, ALRT enticed the public with free rides, and on October 21, Premier Bennett announced a three million-dollar engineering study into the feasibility of extending the ALRT line from New Westminster into Coquitlam municipality. Unable in years past to acquire the services of an interurban line, Port Moody may yet be rewarded for its patience with an ALRT branch.

In the midst of ALRT excitement, happily the West Coast Railway Association remembered and celebrated the seventy-fifth anniversary of the B.C. Electric's interurban line to Chilliwack by running a special train from New Westminster to Abbotsford and return on Sunday, September 29. B. C. Hydro locomotives 382 and 383 drew eight ex-C.P.R. coaches of the Royal Hudson Steam Train Society, comfortably filled with 450 passengers.

On November 21 came the formal announcement of the ALRT system's name, "SkyTrain." Grace McCarthy stressed that "a rapid transit system that is unique and technologically advanced by world standards deserves a name that is different and reflects and enhances the service. I think it's most suitable, as it does glide over traffic without delays for signals or traffic tie-ups."

SkyTrain service was officially opened by Premier Bennett on December 11. Free rides were offered all day, as well as on December 12, 13, 14, 20, 21, 27, and 28, the only days upon which

Cloud-swathed mountains above West and North Vancouver form the backdrop for a New Westminster-bound SkyTrain, composed of cars 064 — 067. Such four-car units are the regular pattern. Here, the red-white-and-blue trainset flashes across the Burlington Northern's (once Great Northern) line into Vancouver (used also by Canadian National and VIA Rail). In a minute, the SkyTrain will arrive at Commercial Drive and Broadway, from there to speed effortlessly over and beside the old Central Park line all the way to New Westminster. (B.C. Transit photo)

the system operated for the public in December. More than 450,000 riders travelled free during these eight days of trial running! Regular SkyTrain service commenced on Friday, January 3, 1986, with an estimated 35,000 riders using the system on this first official day of operation.

On New Year's Day, the Canadian Pacific Railway had recommenced operating the Vancouver & Lulu Island Railway segments of B. C. Hydro Rail's system after an eighty-year hiatus. This was the result of the inability of the two companies to arrive at a new lease agreement.

B. C. Electric's rail legacy exists in B. C. Hydro Rail operations and in SkyTrain. And for the determined seeker, concrete traces can still be found of that once-magnificent transportation system. The roadbeds of the Saanich, Stave Falls, Jordan River, Alouette, and Port Moody-Coquitlam lines can be found even today, at least in part, with confidence. But the right of way of the more urban Burnaby Lake line defies the searcher, revealing itself only rarely, somewhat at Glencairn Drive near Sperling Avenue and at the eastern extremities of Burris and Mayfield streets, although an adjacent substation just east of Nanaimo Street still stands. What's left of the magnificent Central Park and Marpole lines may be merely single track rather than double, but both reveal substations, the former, Earles Road, the latter, at Arbutus and King Edward Avenue and at Fir Street and Fifth Avenue. On the Chilliwack line, the substations at Coghlan and Vedder Mountain still dourly stand guard, creating an impressive interurban ambience, at least for their immediate surroundings. Both the Carrall Street station and old head office and the New Westminster station are still in place.

Of all the interurban station shelters, only Vorce has been preserved. Harmsworth, Sullivan, and Upper Sumas grace farmers' fields; the original Sardis depot still functions, as someone's home; most of Vedder Mountain station still exists, a little east, as a section house; and at nearby Langley, the track of the abandoned main line through the town centre can still be seen crossing its main street's blacktop, just as two sets of track still persist at the rear of Carrall Street station.

Power line inspection car E.60 has left Hydro Rail's New Westminster (where it latterly indulged in occasional switching — even movements on Annacis Island) to continue in service for a nearby salvage firm. Snowplow S.102 (in its previous incarnation locomotive 980, one of the Chilliwack line originals) still awaits the next snowfall, surrounded by members of Hydro Rail's stable of twenty diesel locomotives at Trapp Road. Down the road a piece, at the corner of Twelfth Street and Queens Avenue, a section of once-mighty New Westminster barn and shops yet stands, somewhat altered, its north side still revealing a faded coat of B. C. Electric red paint. Behind

Queen's Park Arena, the grade of the street car line into Queen's Park (and once, down to the brickyard) is easily visible.

In Victoria, the car barn on Pembroke Street can be found in a trice, as can the track in the middle of Store Street and the old power house farther up the street near where rickety Rock Bay bridge leapt northward gingerly. Bay Street substation still dominates the upper end of Government Street, and the old head office building at Langley and Fort Street still poses handsomely. As far east as possible on the Victoria system, the Midland Circle terminus of the Uplands line, a careful search of the grassy boulevard on the southern edge reveals both the track going to and coming from the loop.

Vancouver allows for less. The newer southern portion of the Mount Pleasant street car barn has been rebuilt into a supermarket, appropriately complete with rooftop parking. Yet, on adjacent Quebec Street, north from Thirteenth Avenue, the track of the wye for the streetcars that parked on the roof is sparklingly intact. At Main and Georgia Streets, the imposing substation and, surprisingly, the remnants of the former viaduct's street car tracks survive.

Grant to B. C. Hydro Rail its vital role as a successful interchanging-terminating railway, "the BCE route." Bow to the chutzpah of the anti-conservative SkyTrain. That done, gaze westward from the top of the hill on Frances Street in east Vancouver just below Victoria Drive. The brick pavement and stone blocks are still there to define a street car line abandoned decades ago, but even with the steel itself gone, could not the distant, still evocative downtown send one more street car clanging between the tall houses up the long hill?

Appendix A   A Roster of Equipment

This roster is founded completely on the B.C. Electric Railway's own records. Each of B.C. Electric's predecessor companies in the three original operating areas — New Westminster, Vancouver, and Victoria — had its own car numbering system. At the creation of the B.C. Electric Railway in 1897, all cars from the three systems kept their numbers, with the exception of the seven New Westminster-based interurban coaches (10, 12, 13, 14, 15, 16, 17), five of which did keep them for somewhat more than a year before being integrated into the Vancouver street car numbering scheme (30, 32, 34, 36, 38), the other two acquiring names ("Burnaby" and "Richmond").

This roster includes all of the B.C. Electric Railway's electrically-powered vehicles, grouped for convenience into five lists: early street cars, modern street cars, interurban coaches, locomotives, and auxiliary (and support) equipment. A sixth list deals with the diesel locomotives acquired by the B.C. Electric. Not listed are the company's box cars, cabooses, flat cars, dump cars, and seemingly myriad other types of rolling stock that jostled for space on the company's variegated rail system.

Though many of the modern street cars were rebuilt during the late 30 s and 40 s, not a few of the early cars also experienced rebuilding, in many cases frequently, and on an extensive scale. An apt example is Vancouver's 24, bearing scant resemblance to its first form when it was operating in the early 1900's in New Westminster, and even less after its preparation for North Vancouver work in 1906, by which time its end-rounded sleekness made it an attractive miniature version of the 70-series. Victoria's first nine cars, further examples, underwent such transformations, including lengthening, to seem finally almost twins to the lower mainland's 50-series.

Despite the unusual case of car 21, very few of the early street cars strayed from their designated rounds, those not marked "Victoria" working on the three lower mainland operations, New Westminster, North Vancouver, and Vancouver. Since for the modern street cars movement between Victoria and the lower mainland was relatively common, the roster indicates only the operation on which they ultimately performed.

In the listing of early street cars, length is that of the car body alone — exclusive of platforms (vestibules) — upon the vehicle's arrival for service. For each of the modern street cars, length is an over-all measurement, and that in the car's final form. All of the early street cars were double-ended, with the exception of 29 as an observation car. For the modern cars, however, the following symbols indicate their varied types: 1MDE (one man, double end), 1MSE (one man, single end), 2MDE (two-man, double end), and 2MSE (two-man, single end),

in each case in the car's final configuration. Seat material — L (leather), R (rattan), W (wood) and roof type — A (arch), D (deck), M (monitor) — also is that of each vehicle's final condition. For the interurban coaches, separate seating figures are displayed, one for the smoker, one for the saloon.

All of the modern street cars were double trucked, with the exceptions of the single truck Birneys, 400-409, and all passenger vehicles except these Birneys, 356-378, 500, 400-435, 700-719, and 1217-1244 (includes 1313-1320) were of wood construction. During the decade of the rebuilding of the wooden street cars, from 1937, only the following cars were not rebuilt: 69, 74-97, 99, 100, 102-104, 109-129, 150-162, 164, 183-185, 187, 189-194, 200, 202, 203, 207-213, 215, 216, 218, 223, 226-229, 231-237, 239, 240, 244, 248, 250-258, 260-274, 284, 291, 293, 311, 313, 314, 316-318, 388, and 390.

Though the builder's name is indicated for each of the locomotives and the auxiliary vehicles — GE motors are General Electric, WH, Westinghouse, and D-K, Dick-Kerr — the following key clarifies the builders of the street cars and interurban coaches:

1 — American Car Company
2 — J.G. Brill
3 — British Columbia Electric Railway
4 — Canadian Car & Foundry Co., Ltd.
5 — Canadian General Electric
6 — G.C. Kuhlman Car Company
7 — Newburyport Car Mfg.
8 — Niles Car & Mfg. Company
9 — Ottawa Car Company
10 — Patterson & Corbin
11 — Preston Car and Coach Company
12 — Pullman
13 — St. Louis Car Company
14 — John Stephenson Company

Street car numbering spanned 1 and 501, with the multiple unit street cars utilizing 700-719, the odd-numbered ones the trailing units.

By 1943, the following class designations (which did not include all street cars) had evolved:

Big Brills — 166-169, 241-249, 275-355, 381-390
Birneys — 400-409
Boulevard type — 70-73, 98, 101, 105-108
Fairview type — 260-274
Grandview type — 69, 74-97, 99, 100, 102-104, 109-122, 125-149, 170-182, 195-199, 230
Hastings East cars — 356-363
Hobble skirt car — 500
M.U. trains — 700-719
Near side car — 501
Observation cars — 123, 124
P.C.C.'s — 400-435
Small Brills — 150-164, 200-229
Victoria type — 183-194, 231-240
Victoria Road cars — 364-378

In 1920, the company's official classification for its lower mainland street cars took the

following form (all were P.A.Y.E. — pay as you enter — cars with the exceptions of 117-122):

Open Air, Centre Entrance — 29
Closed, Rebuilt from Open — 31, 33, 35
Narragansett Closed Convertible — 74-77, 84-87, 93-96
Narragansett Closed, Drop Platform — 103
Narragansett, Brill Type — 109, 127, 129, 141
Narragansett, Detroit Platforms — 117-122
Narragansett, Seattle Platforms — 111-116, 130-140, 142-149, 170-182
Narragansett, Drop Platforms — 195-199, 230
Brill, Semi-convertible — 200-229
Brill, Semi-convertible, Arch Roof — 241-249, 275-299, 325-355
Closed, Steel Frame — 250-259
Closed, Steel Frame, Arch Roof — 260-274
Stepless & Nearside Cars — 500, 501
Sightseeing - Open — 123, 124

Interurban coach numbering was a model of simplicity:

Light interurbans — 1000-1009, 1011, 1012
Standard interurbans — 1200-1244
Heavy interurbans — 1300-1322
Combines (passengers and express) — 1400-1402
Mail cars (passengers and mail) — 1500, 1501
Trailers (non-motored) — 1600-1603
Baggage-express — 1700-1709
Express — 1800-1803

EARLY STREET CARS

No.	Builder	Year Built	Type of Car	Motors*	Number of Trucks	Length	Remarks
1	10	1889	Closed	Edison 14	1	16'	Victoria
2	10	1889	Closed	G.E.1000	1	16'	Victoria
3	10	1889	Closed	WH 3	1	16'	Victoria
4	10	1889	Closed	G.E.1000	1	16'	Victoria
5	13	1890	Closed	G.E.1000	1	16'	Victoria
6	10	1891	Closed	G.E.1000	1	16'	Originally W.&V.T.; first briefly 1.
6	13	1890	Closed	G.E.1000	1	16'	Victoria
7	10	1891	Closed	G.E. 800	1	16'	Originally W.&V.T., first briefly 2.
7	10	1890	Closed	G.E.1000	1	16'	Victoria
8	10	1891	Closed	G.E. 800	1	16'	Originally W.&V.T.; first briefly 3.
8	10	1890	Closed	G.E.1000	1	16'	Victoria
9	10	1890	Closed	WH101B2	1	16'	Victoria
10	14	1890	Closed	G.E. 800	1	16'	
10	13	1891	Open	Edison 14	1	16'	Victoria
11	14	1890	Closed	?	1	16'	
11	13	1891	Open	Edison 14	1	16'	Victoria
12	14	1890	Closed	WH 12	1	16'	
12	2	1891	Closed	WH 49	2	24'6"	Victoria
13	14	1890	Closed	?	1	16'	
13	2	1891	Closed	G.E.67	2	24'6"	Victoria
14	14	1890	Closed	WH 12	1	16'	
14	13	1891	Closed	G.E.1000	1	16'	Victoria
15	13	1891	Closed	G.E.1000	1	16'	Victoria
16	14	1890	Closed	WH 12	1	16'	
16	7	1892	Closed	WH 49	6 wheels	27'	Victoria
17	14	1890	Closed	?	1	16'	
17	12	c.1890	Closed	G.E.1000	1	16'	Victoria (acquired in 1894 from Port Townsend, Washington system)
18	14	1890	Closed	WH 12	1	16'	
18	12	c.1890	Closed	G.E.1000	1	16'	Victoria (acquired in 1894 from Port Townsend, Washington system) Rebuilt to S.60
19	3	1905	Closed	?	1	16'	
19	12	c.1890	Closed	G.E. 67	1	16'	Victoria (acquired in 1894 from Port Townsend, Washington system)
20	14	1890	Closed	WH 12	1	16'	
20	5	1896	Open	G.E. 800	1	21'6"	Victoria
21	5	1897	Convertible	G.E.1000	1	21'6"	
21	9	1901	Closed	WH 49	2	29'6"	Although initially sent to Victoria, operated on Westminster branch as interurban coach Gladstone until wrecked, 1908
22	14	1890	Closed	WH 3	1	16'	
22	9	1901	Closed	WH 49	2	29'6"	Victoria; listed again in roster below
23	5	1897	Convertible	G.E.1000	1	21'6"	
23	9	1901	Closed	WH 49	2	29'6"	Victoria; listed again in roster below
24	14	1890	Closed	G.E. 67	1	16'	
24	3	1903	Closed	WH 49	1	22'	Victoria
25	5	1898	Convertible	G.E. 800	1	21'6"	
25	3	1903	Closed	G.E.1000	1	22'	Victoria
26	14	1890	Closed	G.E.1000	1	16'	
26	9	1899	Convertible	G.E.1000	2	30'	Renumbered 29. Rebuilt to observation car,1914, and to 136, 1942
26	3	1904	Semi - convertible	G.E.1000	1	22'6"	Victoria; car type, later closed
27	5	1896	Convertible	G.E.1000	1	21'6"	
27	3	1905	Semi-convertible	WH 101B2	1	20'	Victoria; car type later closed
28	2	1899	Convertible	G.E. 67	2	26'	
29	9	1899	Convertible	G.E. 67	2	30'	Renumbered from 26; rebuilt to observation car, 1916, and to 136, 1942
30	2	1891	Closed	G.E.1000	2	24'6"	Formerly W. & V.T. 10
30	3	1905	Semi-convertible	G.E. 67	1	20'	Victoria; car type, later closed
31	9	1899	Convertible	G.E. 67	2	29'9"	
32	2	1891	Closed	G.E. 67	2	24'6"	Formerly W. & V.T. 12
33	9	1900	Convertible	G.E. 67	2	26'9"	
34	2	1891	Closed	G.E. 67	2	24'6"	Formerly W. & V.T. 14
35	9	1900	Convertible	WH 101B2	2	26'9"	
36	2	1892	Closed	G.E. 67	2	24'6"	Formerly W. & V.T. 16
37	2	1891	Closed	G.E. 67	2	24'6"	Formerly W. & V.T. 13; then interurban car Richmond until 1905
38	2	1892	Closed	G.E. 67	2	24'6"	Formerly W. & V.T. 15
39	2	1892	Closed	G.E. 67	2	24'6"	Formerly W. & V.T. 17; then interurban car Burnaby until 1905
40	5	1905	Closed	G.E. 67	1	21'6"	
42	5	1899	Closed	G.E. 67	1	21'6"	
44	5	1899	Closed	G.E.1000	1	21'6"	
46	9	1900	Closed	G.E.1000	1	21'6"	
48	9	1900	Closed	G.E. 67	1	21'6"	Became supply car G.1
50	3	1903	Closed	G.E. 67	1	22'	
50	3	1909	Semi-convertible	G.E. 67	1	22'6"	Victoria
51	3	1904	Closed	G.E. 67	1	22'	
52	3	1903	Closed	G.E. 67	1	22'	
53	3	1904	Closed	G.E. 67	1	22'	On display in Vancouver restaurant
54	3	1903	Closed	G.E. 67	1	22'	Became supply car G.2
56	3	1903	Semi-convertible	G.E. 67	1	22'	
57	3	1904	Semi-Convertible	G.E. 67	1	22'	
58	3	1903	Closed	G.E. 67	1	22'	
59	3	1905	Convertible	G.E. 67	1	20'	
60	3	1904	Convertible	G.E. 67	1	20'	
61	3	1904	Convertible	G.E. 67	1	20'	
62	3	1904	Convertible	G.E. 67	1	20'	
63	3	1904	Convertible	G.E. 67	1	20'	

* In each case, the type of motor is the last one to inhabit the car. Single truck cars had two motors, double truck cars had four, although Victoria cars 10 and 11 each had only one motor while Victoria car 16 had four.

The horsepower rating of each motor type is as follows:

Edison 14	- 20
G. E. 67	- 38
G. E. 800	- 30
G. E. 1000	- 35
WH 3	- 25
WH 12	- 20
WH 49	- 35
WH 101B2	- 40

G.E. = General Electric; WH = Westinghouse

MODERN STREET CARS

No.	Builder	Year Built	Type of Car	Roof	Seats	Length	(Pounds) Weight	Remarks
22	9	1901	IMDE	M	40R	40'10"	46,000	Victoria; also listed in above roster
23	9	1901	IMDE	M	40R	40'10"	46,000	Victoria; also listed in above roster
69	3	1905	2MDE	D	38W	43'4"	46,220	
70	3	1906	2MSE	A	42L	42'2"	45,000	
71	3	1906	2MSE	A	42L	42'2"	45,360	
72	3	1905	2MSE	A	42L	42'2"	44,660	
73	3	1907	2MSE	A	42L	42'2"	44,020	
74	3	1905	2MSE	D	41W	43'4"	44,400	
75	3	1905	2MSE	D	41W	43'4"	43,450	
76	3	1906	2MSE	D	41W	43'4"	43,450	
77	3	1906	2MSE	D	41W	43'4"	43,450	
78	3	1906	1MDE	D	48W	43'4"	46,300	
79	3	1906	1MDE	D	48W	43'4"	46,300	
80	3	1906	1MDE	D	48W	43'4"	46,300	
81	3	1906	2MSE	D	41W	43'4"	45,000	
82	3	1906	1MDE	D	48W	43'4"	46,300	Rebuilt to interurban 1011, 1911, and then back to 82, 1926
83	3	1906	1MDE	D	48W	43'4"	46,300	Rebuilt to interurban 1012, 1911, and then back to 83, 1926
84	3	1906	2MSE	D	41W	43'4"	44,400	
85	3	1906	2MSE	D	41W	43'4"	44,400	
86	3	1906	2MSE	D	41W	43'4"	44,400	
87	3	1907	2MSE	D	41W	43'4"	43,450	
88	3	1907	2MSE	D	41W	43'4"	46,300	
89	3	1907	1MDE	D	48W	43'4"	46,300	
90	3	1907	1MDE	D	48W	43'4"	46,300	
91	3	1907	1MDE	D	48W	43'4"	46,300	
92	3	1907	1MDE	D	48W	43'4"	46,300	
93	3	1907	2MSE	D	41W	43'4"	43,450	
94	3	1907	2MSE	D	41W	43'4"	43,450	
95	3	1907	2MSE	D	41W	43'4"	43,450	
96	3	1907	2MSE	D	41W	43'4"	43,450	
97	3	1907	2MDE	D	38W	43'4"	43,040	
98	3	1908	2MSE	A	42L	43'4"	47,400	
99	3	1908	1MDE	D	48W	43'4"	46,300	
100	3	1908	2MDE	D	48W	43'4"	45,120	
101	3	1908	2MSE	A	42L	43'4"	45,000	
102	3	1908	2MDE	D	48W	43'4"	43,040	
103	3	1908	2MSE	D	41W	43'4"	44,960	
104	3	1908	2MDE	D	38W	43'4"	43,040	
105	3	1908	2MSE	A	42L	43'4"	44,920	
106	3	1908	2MSE	A	42L	43'4"	45,300	
107	3	1908	2MSE	A	42L	43'4"	44,920	
108	3	1908	2MSE	A	42L	43'4"	44,920	
109	3	1908	2MSE	D	41W	43'4"	43,000	
110	3	1908	2MDE	D	38W	43'4"	43,040	
111	3	1908	2MSE	D	41W	43'4"	43,450	
112	3	1908	2MSE	D	41W	43'4"	43,450	
113	3	1909	2MSE	D	41W	43'4"	43,450	
114	3	1909	2MSE	D	41W	43'4"	43,450	
115	3	1909	2MSE	D	41W	43'4"	43,450	
116	3	1909	2MSE	D	41W	43'4"	43,450	
117	3	1909	2MSE	D	42R	43'4"	43,450	
118	3	1909	2MSE	D	42R	43'4"	43,450	
119	3	1909	2MSE	D	42R	43'4"	43,450	
120	3	1909	2MSE	D	42R	43'4"	43,450	
121	3	1909	2MSE	D	42R	43'4"	43,450	
122	3	1909	2MSE	D	42R	43'4"	43,450	
123	3	1909	2MSE		52W	43'8"	36,500	Observation car - no roof
124	3	1909	2MSE		52W	43'8"	35,200	Observation car - no roof
125	3	1909	2MSE	D	41W	43'4"	43,600	
126	3	1909	2MSE	D	41W	43'4"	43,600	
127	3	1909	2MSE	D	41W	43'4"	45,300	
128	3	1909	2MSE	D	41W	43'4"	43,600	
129	3	1909	2MSE	D	41W	43'4"	45,300	
130	3	1909	2MSE	A	42L	43'4"	45,200	
131	3	1909	2MSE	A	42L	43'4"	45,380	
132	3	1909	2MSE	A	42L	43'4"	45,380	
133	3	1909	2MSE	A	42L	43'4"	45,200	
134	3	1909	2MSE	A	42L	43'4"	45,380	
135	3	1909	2MSE	A	42L	43'4"	45,380	
136	3	1909	2MDE	D	42W	43'4"	44,000	Destroyed in collision with a G.N. locomotive, 1922
136	3	1942	2MSE	A	42L	48'8"	45,500	Rebuilt from observation car 29. Originally 26.
137	3	1909	2MSE	A	42L	43'4"	45,380	
138	3	1909	2MSE	A	42L	43'4"	45,380	
139	3	1909	2MSE	A	42L	43'4"	45,390	
140	3	1909	2MSE	A	42L	43'4"	45,380	
141	3	1909	2MSE	A	42L	43'4"	43,000	
142	3	1910	2MSE	A	42L	43'4"	45,380	
143	3	1910	2MSE	A	42L	43'4"	45,380	
144	3	1910	2MSE	A	42L	43'4"	45,380	
145	3	1910	2MSE	A	42L	43'4"	47,180	
146	3	1910	2MSE	A	42L	43'4"	47,100	
147	3	1910	2MSE	A	42L	43'4"	46,840	
148	3	1910	2MSE	A	42L	43'4"	45,380	
149	3	1910	2MSE	A	42L	43'4"	45,380	
150	2	1908	1MDE	D	36R	39'1"	44,520	North Vancouver
151	2	1908	1MDE	D	36R	39'1"	44,520	North Vancouver
152	2	1908	2MSE	D	36R	39'1"	43,380	
153	2	1908	2MDE	D	36R	39'1"	44,520	North Vancouver; in storage in Burnaby
154	2	1908	1MDE	D	36R	39'1"	44,520	North Vancouver
155	2	1908	2MDE	D	36R	39'1"	44,520	North Vancouver
156	2	1908	2MDE	D	36R	39'1"	44,520	North Vancouver
157	2	1908	1MDE	D	36R	39'1"	45,520	North Vancouver
158	2	1908	2MSE	D	36R	39'1"	43,380	
159	2	1908	2MDE	D	36R	39'1"	44,520	North Vancouver
160	14	1910	1MDE	D	36R	41'1"	48,950	North Vancouver
161	14	1910	1MDE	D	36R	41'1"	48,950	North Vancouver
162	14	1910	1MDE	D	36R	41'1"	48,950	North Vancouver
163	14	1910	2MSE	D	33L	41'1"	48,950	
164	14	1910	2MSE	D	33R	41'1"	46,100	
165	9	1910	2MDE	D	40W	44'10"	47,200	Destroyed in collision with a runaway box car, 1915
166	9	1910	2MSE	A	38L	44'10"	45,980	
167	9	1910	2MSE	A	38L	44'10"	45,980	
168	9	1910	2MSE	A	38L	44'10"	45,980	
169	9	1910	2MSE	A	38L	44'10"	45,980	
170	3	1910	2MSE	A	41L	43'4"	45,380	
171	3	1910	2MSE	A	41L	43'4"	45,380	
172	3	1910	2MSE	A	41L	43'4"	45,380	
173	3	1910	2MSE	A	41L	43'4"	45,380	
174	3	1910	2MSE	A	42L	43'4"	45,700	
175	3	1910	2MSE	A	41L	43'4"	45,380	
176	3	1910	2MSE	A	41L	43'4"	45,380	
177	3	1910	2MSE	A	41L	43'4"	45,380	
178	3	1910	2MSE	A	41L	43'4"	45,380	
179	3	1910	2MSE	A	42L	43'4"	45,380	
180	3	1910	2MSE	A	42L	43'4"	45,980	
181	3	1910	2MSE	A	42L	43'4"	45,380	
182	3	1910	2MSE	A	42L	43'4"	45,380	

Modern Street Cars - continued

No.	Builder	Year Built	Type of Car	Roof	Seats	Length	(Pounds) Weight	Remarks
183	3	1910	2MDE	D	38R	44'6"	46,600	
184	3	1910	1MDE	D	38R	44'6"	49,820	
185	3	1911	2MDE	D	38R	44'6"	46,600	
186	3	1911	2MSE	A	40L	44'6"	46,300	
187	3	1910	2MDE	D	38R	44'6"	45,500	
188	3	1910	1MSE	A	53L	45'8"	48,850	Victoria
189	3	1910	1MDE	D	44R	44'6"	46,600	Victoria
190	3	1910	2MDE	D	38R	44'6"	46,600	
191	3	1910	2MDE	D	38R	44'6"	46,600	
192	3	1910	1MDE	D	38R	44'6"	47,000	
193	3	1910	2MDE	D	38R	44'6"	46,600	
194	3	1910	1MDE	D	38R	44'6"	47,000	
195	3	1911	2MSE	A	42L	43'	46,720	
196	3	1911	2MSE	A	42L	43'	46,720	
197	3	1911	2MSE	A	42L	43'	46,720	
198	3	1911	2MSE	A	42L	43'	45,380	
199	3	1911	2MSE	A	42L	43'	45,380	
200	2	1911	1MSE	D	47L	40'6"	47,500	Victoria
201	2	1911	1MSE	D	47L	43'	49,540	Victoria
202	2	1911	1MSE	D	47L	40'6"	47,500	
203	2	1911	1MSE	D	47L	40'6"	47,500	
204	2	1911	1MSE	D	47L	43'	47,500	
205	2	1911	1MSE	A	47L	43'	48,440	
206	2	1911	1MSE	A	47L	43'	48,440	
207	2	1911	2MSE	D	36R	40'6"	47,500	
208	2	1911	2MSE	D	36R	40'6"	47,500	
209	2	1911	2MSE	D	36R	40'6"	47,500	
210	2	1911	2MSE	D	36R	40'6"	47,500	
211	2	1911	2MSE	D	36R	40'6"	47,500	
212	2	1911	2MSE	D	36R	40'6"	47,500	
213	2	1911	2MSE	D	36R	40'6"	47,500	
214	2	1911	2MSE	D	36L	40'6"	47,500	
215	2	1911	2MSE	D	36R	40'6"	47,500	
216	2	1911	2MSE	D	36R	40'6"	47,500	
217	2	1911	2MSE	D	36L	40'6"	47,500	
218	2	1911	2MSE	D	36R	40'6"	47,500	
219	2	1911	2MSE	D	36L	40'6"	46,280	
220	2	1911	2MSE	D	36L	40'6"	46,280	
221	2	1911	2MSE	D	36L	40'6"	46,280	
222	2	1911	2MSE	D	36L	40'6"	46,280	
223	2	1911	2MSE	D	36R	40'6"	46,280	
224	2	1911	2MSE	D	36L	40'6"	46,280	
225	2	1911	2MSE	D	36L	40'6"	46,280	
226	2	1911	2MSE	D	36R	40'6"	46,280	
227	2	1911	2MSE	D	36R	40'6"	46,280	
228	2	1911	2MSE	D	36R	40'6"	46,280	
229	2	1911	2MSE	D	36R	40'6"	46,280	
230	3	1911	2MSE	A	42L	43'	46,720	
231	3	1911	1MDE	D	38R	44'	46,000	Victoria
232	3	1911	1MDE	D	38W	44'	46,000	Victoria
233	3	1911	1MDE	D	38R	44'	46,000	Victoria
234	3	1911	1MDE	D	38R	44'	46,000	Victoria
235	3	1911	1MDE	D	38R	44'	46,000	Victoria
236	3	1911	1MDE	D	38R	44'	46,000	Victoria
237	3	1911	1MDE	D	38R	44'	46,000	Victoria
238	3	1911	1MDE	A	48W	47'	48,550	Victoria
239	3	1911	1MDE	D	38R	44'	46,000	Victoria
240	3	1911	1MDE	D	38R	44'	46,000	Victoria
241	2	1912	2MSE	A	42L	42'8"	45,720	
242	2	1912	2MSE	A	42L	42'8"	45,720	
243	2	1912	2MSE	A	42L	42'8"	45,720	
244	2	1912	2MSE	A	42W	42'8"	45,720	
245	2	1912	2MSE	A	42L	42'8"	45,720	
246	2	1912	2MSE	A	42L	42'8"	45,720	
247	2	1912	2MSE	A	42L	42'8"	45,720	
248	2	1912	2MSE	A	42W	42'8"	45,720	
249	2	1912	2MSE	A	42L	42'8"	45,720	
250	3	1912	1MSE	D	48R	44'	48,000	Victoria
251	3	1912	2MSE	D	42R	44'6"	48,500	
252	3	1912	1MSE	D	48R	44'	48,000	Victoria
253	3	1912	1MSE	D	48R	44'	48,000	Victoria
254	3	1912	1MSE	D	48R	44'	48,000	Victoria
255	3	1912	1MSE	D	48R	44'	48,000	Victoria
256	3	1912	1MSE	D	48R	44'	48,000	Victoria
257	3	1912	1MSE	D	48R	44'	48,000	Victoria
258	3	1912	1MSE	D	48R	44'	48,000	Victoria
259	3	1912	1MSE	A	48R	46'	48,000	Victoria
260	3	1912	2MSE	A	47R	44'6"	44,500	
261	3	1912	2MSE	A	47R	44'6"	44,500	
262	3	1912	2MSE	A	47R	44'6"	44,500	
263	3	1912	2MSE	A	47R	44'6"	44,500	
264	3	1912	2MSE	A	47R	44'6"	44,500	
265	3	1912	2MSE	A	47R	44'6"	44,500	
266	3	1912	2MSE	A	47R	44'6"	44,500	
267	3	1913	2MSE	A	47R	44'6"	44,500	
268	3	1913	2MSE	A	47R	44'6"	44,500	
269	3	1913	2MSE	A	47R	44'6"	44,500	
270	3	1913	2MSE	A	47R	44'6"	44,500	
271	3	1913	2MSE	A	47R	44'6"	44,500	
272	3	1913	2MSE	A	47R	44'6"	44,500	
273	3	1913	2MSE	A	47R	44'6"	44,500	
274	3	1913	2MSE	A	47R	44'6"	44,500	
275	2	1912	2MSE	A	40L	42'8"	45,720	
276	2	1912	2MSE	A	42L	42'8"	45,720	
277	2	1912	2MSE	A	42L	42'8"	45,720	
278	2	1912	2MSE	A	42L	42'8"	45,720	
279	2	1913	2MSE	A	42L	42'8"	45,720	
280	2	1913	2MSE	A	40L	42'8"	45,720	
281	2	1913	2MSE	A	40L	42'8"	45,720	
282	2	1913	2MSE	A	40L	42'8"	45,720	
283	2	1913	2MSE	A	42L	42'8"	45,720	
284	2	1913	2MSE	A	40W	42'8"	45,720	
285	2	1913	2MSE	A	42L	42'8"	45,720	
286	2	1913	2MSE	A	40L	42'8"	45,720	
287	2	1913	2MSE	A	42L	42'8"	45,720	
288	2	1913	2MSE	A	42L	42'8"	45,720	
289	2	1913	2MSE	A	42L	42'8"	45,720	
290	2	1913	2MSE	A	40L	42'8"	45,720	
291	2	1913	2MSE	A	40W	42'8"	45,720	
292	2	1913	2MSE	A	42L	42'8"	45,720	
293	2	1913	2MSE	A	40W	42'8"	45,720	
294	2	1913	2MSE	A	42L	42'8"	45,720	
295	2	1913	2MSE	A	42L	42'8"	45,720	
296	2	1913	2MSE	A	42L	42'8"	45,720	
297	2	1913	2MSE	A	42L	42'8"	45,720	
298	2	1913	2MSE	A	40L	42'8"	45,720	
299	2	1913	2MSE	A	42L	42'8"	45,720	
300	2	1912	2MSE	A	44L	43'2"	49,400	
301	2	1912	2MSE	A	44L	43'2"	48,600	
302	2	1912	2MSE	A	44L	43'2"	48,600	
303	2	1912	2MSE	A	44L	43'2"	48,600	
304	2	1912	2MSE	A	44L	43'2"	48,600	
305	2	1912	2MSE	A	44L	43'2"	48,600	
306	2	1912	2MSE	A	44L	43'2"	48,600	
307	2	1912	2MSE	A	44L	43'2"	48,600	
308	2	1912	2MSE	A	44L	43'2"	48,600	
309	2	1912	2MSE	A	44L	43'2"	48,600	
310	2	1912	1MSE	A	51L	43'2"	48,600	

Modern Street Cars - continued

No.	Builder	Year Built	Type of Car	Roof	Seats	Length	(Pounds) Weight	Remarks
311	2	1912	1MSE	A	51L	43'2"	48,600	
312	2	1912	1MSE	A	51L	43'2"	48,600	
313	2	1912	1MSE	A	51L	43'2"	48,600	
314	2	1912	1MSE	A	51L	43'2"	48,600	
315	2	1912	1MSE	A	51L	43'2"	48,600	
316	2	1912	1MDE	A	42L	43'2"	48,600	
317	2	1912	1MDE	A	42L.	43'2"	48,600	
318	2	1912	1MDE	A	42L	43'2"	48,600	
319	2	1912	1MDE	A	42L	43'2"	48,600	Before rebuilding in 1931 was car 324
320	2	1912	1MDE	A	42L	43'2"	52,180	
321	2	1912	1MDE	A	42L	43'2"	50,400	
322	2	1912	1MDE	A	42L	43'2"	49,000	
323	2	1912	1MDE	A	42L	43'2"	51,980	
324	2	1912	1MDE	A	42L	43'2"	49,000	Before rebuilding in 1931 was car 319
325	2	1913	2MSE	A	42L	42'8"	45,600	
326	11	1913	2MSE	A	42L	42'8"	45,600	
327	11	1913	2MSE	A	42L	42'8"	46,100	
328	11	1914	2MSE	A	42L	42'8"	45,600	
329	11	1914	2MSE	A	42L	42'8"	45,600	
330	11	1914	2MSE	A	42L	42'8"	45,600	
331	11	1914	2MSE	A	42L	42'8"	46,300	
332	11	1914	2MSE	A	42L	42'8"	45,600	
333	11	1914	2MSE	A	42L	42'8"	45,600	
334	11	1914	2MSE	A	42L	42'8"	45,600	
335	11	1914	2MSE	A	42L	42'8"	45,600	
336	11	1914	2MSE	A	42L	42'8"	45,600	
337	11	1914	2MSE	A	42L	42'8"	45,640	
338	11	1914	2MSE	A	42L	42'8"	45,440	
339	11	1914	2MSE	A	42L	42'7"	45,600	
340	11	1914	2MSE	A	42L	42'8"	45,600	
341	11	1914	2MSE	A	42L	42'8"	45,600	
342	11	1914	2MSE	A	42L	42'8"	45,460	
343	11	1914	2MSE	A	42L	42'8"	45,600	
344	11	1914	2MSE	A	42L	42'8"	45,600	
345	11	1914	2MSE	A	42L	42'8"	45,600	
346	11	1914	2MSE	A	42L	42'8"	46,160	
347	11	1914	2MSE	A	42L	42'8"	45,600	
348	11	1914	2MSE	A	42L	42'8"	47,320	
349	11	1914	2MSE	A	42L	42'8"	45,600	
350	11	1914	2MSE	A	42L	42'8"	45,600	
351	11	1914	2MSE	A	42L	42'8"	45,600	
352	11	1914	2MSE	A	42L	42'8"	45,600	
353	11	1914	2MSE	A	42L	42'8"	45,600	
354	11	1914	2MSE	A	42L	42'8"	45,600	
355	11	1914	2MSE	A	42L	42'8"	45,600	
356	4	1926	2MSE	A	50R	48'8"	44,900	
357	4	1926	2MSE	A	50R	48'8"	44,900	
358	4	1926	2MSE	A	50R	48'3"	44,900	
359	4	1926	2MSE	A	50R	48'8"	44,900	
360	4	1926	2MSE	A	50R	48'8"	44,900	
361	4	1926	2MSE	A	50R	48'8"	44,900	
362	4	1926	2MSE	A	50R	48'8"	44,900	
363	4	1926	2MSE	A	50R	48'8"	44,900	
364	4	1929	1MSE	A	52L	46'2"	39,000	
365	4	1929	1MSE	A	52L	46'2"	39,000	
366	4	1929	1MSE	A	52L	46'2"	39,000	
367	4	1929	1MSE	A	52L	46'2"	39,000	
368	4	1929	1MSE	A	52L	46'2"	39,000	
369	4	1929	1MSE	A	52L	46'2"	39,000	
370	4	1929	1MSE	A	52L	46'2"	39,000	
371	4	1929	1MSE	A	52L	46'2"	39,000	
372	4	1929	1MSE	A	52L	46'2"	39,000	
373	4	1929	1MSE	A	52L	46'2"	39,000	
374	4	1929	1MSE	A	52L	46'2"	39,000	
375	4	1929	1MSE	A	52L	46'2"	39,000	
376	4	1929	1MSE	A	52L	46'2"	39,000	
377	4	1929	1MSE	A	52L	46'2"	39,000	
378	4	1929	1MSE	A	52L	46'2"	39,000	
381	11	1914	1MDE	A	42W	44'2"	48,000	Victoria
382	11	1914	1MDE	A	42L	44'2"	50,400	
383	11	1914	1MDE	A	42W	44'2"	48,000	Victoria
384	11	1914	2MSE	A	42L	44'2"	45,680	
385	11	1914	2MSE	A	42L	44'2"	45,680	
386	11	1914	2MSE	A	42L	44'2"	45,680	
387	11	1914	1MSE	A	42W	44'2"	48,000	Victoria
388	11	1914	1MSE	A	42W	44'2"	48,000	Victoria
389	11	1914	1MSE	A	42W	44'2"	48,000	Victoria
390	11	1914	1MSE	A	42W	44'2"	48,000	Victoria
391	2	1945	2MSE	A	48L	46'6"	44,000	Rebuilt from "near side" car 501
500	2	1913	2MDE	A	51R	44'	36,000	"Stepless"(or "hobble skirt") car
501	2	1913	2MSE	A	44W	45'	44,000	"Near side" car
400	11	1922	1MSE	A	28W	28'	16,600	Victoria; on display in Richmond
401	11	1922	1MSE	A	28W	28'	16,600	Victoria
402	11	1922	1MSE	A	28W	28'	16,600	Victoria
403	11	1922	1MSE	A	28W	28'	16,600	Victoria
404	11	1922	1MSE	A	28W	28'	16,600	Victoria
405	11	1922	1MSE	A	28W	28'	16,600	Victoria
406	11	1922	1MSE	A	28W	28'	16,600	Victoria
407	11	1922	1MSE	A	28W	28'	16,600	Victoria
408	11	1922	1MSE	A	28W	28'	16,600	Victoria
409	11	1922	1MSE	A	28W	28'	16,600	Victoria
400	13-4	1938	1MSE	A	54L	46'	34,400	
401	13-4	1940	1MSE	A	53L	46'	34,700	
402	13-4	1940	1MSE	A	53L	46'	34,700	
403	13-4	1940	1MSE	A	53L	46'	34,700	
404	13-4	1944	1MSE	A	53L	46'	34,400	
405	13-4	1944	1MSE	A	53L	46'	34,400	
406	13-4	1944	1MSE	A	53L	46'	34,400	
407	13-4	1944	1MSE	A	53L	46'	34,400	
408	13-4	1944	1MSE	A	53L	46'	34,400	
409	13-4	1944	1MSE	A	53L	46'	34,400	
410	13-4	1944	1MSE	A	53L	46'	34,400	
411	13-4	1944	1MSE	A	53L	46'	34,400	
412	13-4	1944	1MSE	A	53L	46'	34,400	
413	13-4	1944	1MSE	A	53L	46'	34,400	
414	13-4	1944	1MSE	A	53L	46'	34,400	
415	13-4	1944	1MSE	A	53L	46'	34,000	
416	13-4	1944	1MSE	A	53L	46'	34,000	
417	13-4	1944	1MSE	A	53L	46'	34,400	
418	13-4	1944	1MSE	A	53L	46'	34,400	
419	13-4	1944	1MSE	A	53L	46'	34,400	
420	13-4	1944	1MSE	A	53L	46'	34,400	
421	13-4	1945	1MSE	A	53L	46'	34,400	
422	13-4	1945	1MSE	A	53L	46'	34,400	
423	13-4	1945	1MSE	A	53L	46'	34,400	
424	13-4	1945	1MSE	A	53L	46'	34,400	
425	13-4	1945	1MSE	A	53L	46'	34,400	
426	13-4	1945	1MSE	A	53L	46'	34,400	
427	13-4	1945	1MSE	A	53L	46'	34,400	
428	13-4	1945	1MSE	A	53L	46'	34,400	
429	13-4	1945	1MSE	A	53L	46'	34,400	
430	13-4	1945	1MSE	A	53L	46'	34,400	
431	13-4	1945	1MSE	A	53L	46'	34,400	

No.	Builder	Year Built	Type of Car	Roof	Seats	Length	(Pounds) Weight	Remarks
432	13-4	1945	1MSE	A	53L	46'	34,400	
433	13-4	1945	1MSE	A	53L	46'	34,400	
434	13-4	1945	1MSE	A	53L	46'	34,400	
435	13-4	1945	1MSE	A	53L	46'	34,400	
700	4	1925	2MSE	A	48R	48'8"	45,800	
701	4	1925	1MSE	A	55R	48'8"	45,800	
702	4	1925	1MSE	A	48R	48'8"	46,400	
703	4	1925	1MSE	A	55R	48'8"	45,800	
704	4	1925	2MSE	A	48R	48'8"	46,400	
705	4	1925	1MSE	A	55R	48'8"	45,800	
706	4	1925	2MSE	A	48R	48'8"	46,400	
707	4	1925	1MSE	A	55R	48'8"	45,800	
708	4	1925	2MSE	A	48R	48'8"	46,400	
709	4	1925	1MSE	A	55R	48'8"	45,800	
710	4	1925	2MSE	A	48R	48'8"	46,400	
711	4	1925	1MSE	A	55R	48'8"	45,800	
712	4	1926	2MSE	A	48R	48'8"	46,400	
713	4	1926	1MSE	A	55R	48'8"	45,800	
714	4	1926	2MSE	A	48R	48'8"	46,400	
715	4	1926	1MSE	A	55R	48'8"	45,800	
716	4	1926	2MSE	A	48R	48'8"	46,400	
717	4	1926	1MSE	A	55R	48'8"	45,800	
718	4	1926	2MSE	A	48R	48'8"	46,400	
719	4	1926	1MSE	A	55R	48'8"	45,800	

INTERURBAN COACHES

No.	Builder	Built	Type of Car	Roof	Seats	Length	(Pounds) Weight	Remarks
Burnaby	2	1892	2MDE	D	36R	37'7"		- Originally W.&V.T. 17. Rebuilt to street car 39, 1905
Richmond	2	1891	2MDE	D	36R	37'7"		- Originally W.&V.T. 13. Rebuilt to street car 37, 1905
Gladstone	9	1901	2MDE	M	44R	40'		- Originally intended for service in Victoria as 21. Wrecked 1908.
1000	11	1910	2MDE	M	36R-12R	45'4"	63,000	
1001	11	1910	2MDE	M	36R-12R	45'4"	63,300	
1002	11	1910	2MDE	M	36R-12R	45'4"	63,000	
1003	11	1910	2MDE	M	36R-12R	45'4"	61,000	- Destroyed by fire, 1914
1004	11	1910	2MDE	M	36R-12R	45'4"	63,000	
1005	11	1910	2MDE	M	36R-12R	45'4"	62,100	
1006	11	1910	2MDE	M	36R-12R	45'4"	63,300	
1007	11	1910	2MDE	M	36R-12R	45'4"	63,300	
1008	11	1910	2MDE	M	36R-12R	45'4"	62,100	
1009	11	1910	2MDE	M	36R-12R	45'4"	63,300	
1011	3	1906	2MDE	D	32R-16R	43'10"	60,500	- Rebuilt from street car 82, 1911, and then back to 82, 1926
1012	3	1906	2MDE	D	32R-16R	43'10"	60,500	- Rebuilt from street car 83, 1911, and then back to 83, 1926
Westminster	9	1899	2MDE	M	36R-20W	c. 50'		- Rebuilt to 1200, 1912, and to 1601, 1913
Vancouver	9	1899	2MDE	M	36R-20W	c. 50'		- Destroyed by fire, 1904
1200	9	1899	2MDE	M	36R-20W	50'4"	71,000	- Rebuilt from Westminster, 1912, and to 1601, 1913
1201	3	1904	2MDE	M	36R-20W	50'4"	71,550	- Rebuilt from Vancouver (the second car of this name, built in 1904), 1911
1202	3	1904	2MDE	M	36R-20W	50'4"	71,550	- Rebuilt from Langley, 1912
1203	3	1903	2MDE	M	36R-20W	50'4"	71,550	- Rebuilt from Delta, 1911
1204	3	1903	2MDE	M	36R-20W	50'4"	71,550	- Rebuilt from Surrey, 1913
1205	3	1905	2MDE	M	32R-24W	50'4"	71,550	- Rebuilt from Richmond, 1912
1206	3	1905	2MDE	M	32R-24W	50'4"	71,550	- Rebuilt from Eburne, 1912
1207	3	1905	2MDE	M	32R-24W	50'4"	71,550	- Rebuilt from Steveston, 1912; on display at Snoqualmie Falls, WA.
1208	3	1905	2MDE	M	32R-24W	50'4"	71,550	- Rebuilt from Burnaby, 1912
1209	3	1906	2MDE	M	32R-24W	50'4"	71,550	- Rebuilt from Coquitlam, 1910; to 1500, 1913; and to 1312, 1929
1210	3	1907	2MDE	M	32R-24W	50'4"	71,550	- Rebuilt from Chilliwack, 1912, and to 1602, 1913
1211	3	1908	2MDE	M	32R-24W	50'4"	71,550	- Rebuilt from Cloverdale, 1911
1212	3	1908	2MDE	M	32R-24W	50'4"	71,550	- Rebuilt from Abbotsford, 1912
1213	3	1908	2MDE	M	32R-24W	50'4"	71,550	- Rebuilt from Ladner; to 1603, 1913; and to 1322, 1943
1214	3	1908	2MDE	M	32R-24W	50'4"	71,550	- Rebuilt from Sardis; and to 1600, 1913
1215	3	1909	2MDE	M	32R-24W	50'4"	71,550	- Rebuilt from Matsqui, 1912
1216	3	1907	2MDE	M	32R-24W	50'4"	71,550	- Rebuilt from Sumas, 1910; to 1501, 1913; and back to 1216, 1928
1217	13	1913	2MDE	A	42R-18W	51'	70,800	
1218	13	1913	2MDE	A	42R-18W	51'	70,800	
1219	13	1913	2MDE	A	42R-18W	51'	70,800	
1220	13	1913	2MDE	A	42R-18W	51'	70,800	- In storage in Burnaby
1221	13	1913	2MDE	A	42R-18W	51'	70,800	
1222	13	1912	2MDE	A	42R-18W	51'	70,800	
1223	13	1912	2MDE	A	42R-18W	51'	70,800	- On display at Burnaby Village Museum
1224	13	1913	2MDE	A	42R-18W	51'	70,800	
1225	13	1912	2MDE	A	42R-18W	51'	70,800	- On display at Perris, CA
1226	13	1912	2MDE	A	42R-18W	51'	70,800	
1227	13	1913	2MDE	A	42R-18W	51'	70,800	
1228	13	1913	2MDE	A	42R-18W	51'	70,800	
1229	13	1913	2MDE	A	42R-18W	51'	70,800	
1230	13	1913	2MDE	A	42R-18W	51'	70,800	
1231	13	1913	2MDE	A	42R-18W	51'	70,800	- In storage in Burnaby
1232	13	1913	2MDE	A	42R-18W	51'	70,800	
1233	13	1913	2MDE	A	42R-18W	51'	70,800	
1234	13	1913	2MDE	A	42R-18W	51'	70,800	
1235	13	1913	2MDE	A	42R-18W	51'	70,800	- In storage in Ottawa, Ontario.
1236	13	1913	2MDE	A	42R-18W	51'	70,800	
1237	13	1913	2MDE	A	42R-18W	51'	70,800	- Remodelled to 1320, 1931
1238	13	1913	2MDE	A	42R-18W	51'	70,800	- Remodelled to 1319, 1931
1239	13	1913	2MDE	A	40R-18W	51'	70,800	- Remodelled to 1313, 1930
1240	13	1913	2MDE	A	40R-18W	51'	70,800	- Remodelled to 1314, 1930
1241	13	1913	2MDE	A	40R-18W	51'	70,800	- Remodelled to 1315, 1929
1242	13	1913	2MDE	A	40R-18W	51'	70,800	- Remodelled to 1316, 1929
1243	13	1913	2MDE	A	40R-18W	51'	70,800	- Remodelled to 1317, 1929
1244	13	1913	2MDE	A	40R-18W	51'	70,800	- Remodelled to 1318, 1929
1300	1	1910	2MDE	M	42R-18R	54'0"	84,000	- Renumbered from 400, 1913
1301	9	1910	2MDE	M	42R-18R	55'	81,200	- Renumbered from 402, 1913
1302	9	1910	2MDE	M	42R-18R	55'	81,200	- Renumbered from 404, 1913

No.	Builder	Year Built	Type of Car	Roof	Seats	Length	(Pounds) Weight	Remarks
1303	3	1911	2MDE	M	42R-14R	55'2"	81,720	
1304	3	1911	2MDE	A	40L-20L	55'2"	84,480	- Rebuilt after fire, 1945, in operation at Glenwood, Oregon
1305	3	1911	2MDE	M	42R-18R	55'2"	80,205	
1306	6	1911	2MDE	M	42R-16R	53'4"	85,300	
1307	6	1911	2MDE	M	42R-16R	53'4"	85,300	
1308	6	1911	2MDE	M	42R-16R	53'4"	85,300	
1309	3	1914	2MDE	A	38R-20R	55'3"	81,820	
1310	3	1914	2MDE	A	38R-20R	55'3"	81,820	
1311	3	1914	2MDE	A	38R-20R	55'3"	81,820	
1312	3	1906	2MDE	M	3ER-20R	50'4"	75,400	- Rebuilt from 1500, 1929. Formerly was Coquitlam; 1209, 1910; and 1500, 1913
1313	13	1913	2MDE	A	42R-18W	51'	73,890	- Remodelled from 1239, 1930
1314	13	1913	2MDE	A	42R-18W	51'	73,880	- Remodelled from 1240, 1929
1315	13	1913	2MDE	A	42R-18W	51'	73,880	- Remodelled from 1241, 1929
1316	13	1913	2MDE	A	42R-18W	51'	73,880	- Remodelled from 1242, 1929
1317	13	1913	2MDE	A	42R-18W	51'	73,880	- Remodelled from 1243, 1929
1318	13	1913	2MDE	A	42R-18W	51'	73,880	- Remodelled from 1244, 1929
1319	13	1913	2MDE	A	42R-18W	51'	73,880	- Remodelled from 1238, 1931
1320	13	1913	2MDE	A	42R-18W	51'	73,880	- Remodelled from 1237, 1931
1321	1	1910	2MDE	M	44R-20R	55'4"	84,600	- Rebuilt from 1400, 1942
1322	3	1903	2MDE	M	30R-24W	50'4"	75,440	- Rebuilt from 1603, 1943. Formerly was Ladner; 1213, and 1603, 1913
1400	1	1910	2MDE	M	30R-18R	55'4"	82,000	- Renumbered from 401, 1913; rebuilt to 1321, 1942
1401	9	1910	2MDE	M	30R-18R	55'4"	81,000	- Renumbered from 403, 1913
1402	9	1910	2MDE	M	30R-18R	55'4"	81,000	- Renumbered from 405, 1913
1500	3	1906	2MDE	M	30R	50'4"	75,400	- Rebuilt to 1312, 1929. Formerly was Coquitlam; 1209, 1910 and 1500, 1913
1501	3	1907	2MDE	M	30R	50'4"	70,000	- Rebuilt to 1216, 1928. Formerly was Sumas; 1216, 1910; and 1501, 1913
1600	3	1908	DE	M	30R-24W	50'4"	46,000	- Unmotored. Rebuilt from 1214, 1913; formerly was Sardis
1601	9	1899	DE	M	34R-20W	50'4"	46,000	- Unmotored. Rebuilt from 1200, 1913; formerly was Westminster, 1912
1602	3	1907	DE	M	30R-24W	50'4"	46,000	- Unmotored. Rebuilt from 1210, 1913; formerly was Chilliwack, 1912
1603	3	1908	DE	M	30R-24W	50'4"	46,000	- Unmotored. Rebuilt from 1213, 1913; formerly was Ladner. Rebuilt to 1322, 1943
1700	1	1910	DE	M		55'4"	81,100	- Renumbered from 300, 1913
1701	1	1910	DE	M		55'4"	81,100	- Renumbered from 301, 1913
1702	3	1911	DE	M		45'3"	69,280	
1703	3	1911	DE	M		44'10"	69,280	
1704	3	1911	DE	M		54'3"	76,500	
1705	3	1911	DE	M		54'3"	76,500	
1706	8	1912	DE	A		54'3"	83,700	
1707	8	1912	DE	A		54'3"	83,700	
1708	8	1912	DE	A		54'3"	83,700	
1709	8	1913	DE	A		54'3"	83,700	
1800	3	1902	DE	A		41'1"	58,700	- Renumbered from 505; formerly 105; originally 5
1801	3	1903	DE	A		41'	57,300	- Renumbered from 507; formerly 107; originally 7. Stock car at Kitsilano, 1925-1946
1802	3	1905	DE	M		44'	57,310	- Renumbered from 501; originally 102
1803	3	1910	DE	M		45'3"	59,000	- Renumbered from 502. Converted to wrecking car, F.4, 1920

ELECTRIC LOCOMOTIVES

No.	Builder	Year Built	Body	Length	(Pounds) Weight	Motors	Remarks
503	B.C.E.R.	1899	Wood				- Formerly 101. Originally W.&V.T.3, "Flying Dutchman". Rebuilt to S.61
901	B.C.E.R.	1907	Wood	36'8"	50,000	G.E.73(4)	- Rebuilt to S.100, 1937
902	B.C.E.R.	1905	Wood	26'11"	50,000	WH.101-B2(4)	- Renumbered from 103
903	B.C.E.R.		Wood	36'	50,000	G.E.73(4)	- Renumbered from 3 (not W.&V.T.3!)
904	B.C.E.R.	1909	Wood	36'	50,000	G.E.73(4)	- Renumbered from 104. Rebuilt to S.101, 1937
905	B.C.E.R.	1909	Wood	28'10"	40,500	WH.101-B2(4)	- Victoria
906	B.C.E.R.	1909	Wood	37'10"	50,000	WH.101-B2(4)	- Victoria
907	B.C.E.R.	1925	Wood	11'	28,000	G.E. 73(2)	- Single truck shunter at Kitsilano until scrapped in 1935
915	B.C.E.R.	1900	Wood	20'	20,000	G.E. 67(4)	- Rebuilt to S.62, 1910. Formerly 504; originally 4
950	B.C.E.R.	1907	Wood	36'1"	72,600	G.E. 73(4)	- Renumbered from 900. Originally 108
951	B.C.E.R.	1909	Wood	34'4"	76,900	WH.112-B2(4)	- Renumbered from 916
952	B.C.E.R.	1911	Wood	32'10"	60,200	WH.112-B2(4)	- Rebuilt to S.103, 1951
953	B.C.E.R.	1911	Wood	29'3"	79,140	WH.112-B2(4)	- Saanich
960	American Loco Wks.	1912	Steel	37'7"	125,400	G.E.212A(4)	- Acquired from Oregon Electric Railway, 1946; in storage in Burnaby
961	American Loco Wks.	1912	Steel	37'7"	124,300	G.E.212A(4)	- Acquired from Oregon Electric Railway, 1946; sold to Edmonton Transit, 1980
962	American Loco Wks.	1912	Steel	37'7"	127,000	G.E.212A(4)	- Acquired from Oregon Electric Railway, 1946.
970	Baldwin	1913	Steel	35'	110,000	WH.308-D3(4)	
971	Baldwin	1913	Steel	35'	106,650	WH.308-D3(4)	
972	Baldwin	1913	Steel	35'	112,000	WH.308-D3(4)	
973	Baldwin	1913	Steel	35'	111,300	WH.308-D3(4)	
974	Baldwin	1913	Steel	35'	111,000	WH.308-D3(4)	
980	Baldwin	1911	Steel	31'1"	95,800	WH.301-D2(4)	- Rebuilt to S.102, non-motored, 1951
981	Baldwin	1911	Steel	31'1"	96,340	WH.301-D2(4)	
990	Dick-Kerr	1909	Steel	34'	123,000	DK-12A(4)	- Renumbered from 911
991	Dick-Kerr	1909	Steel	34'	116,600	DK-12A(4)	- Renumbered from 912
992	Dick-Kerr	1910	Steel	34'	120,700	DK-12A(4)	- Renumbered from 913
No Number	B.C.E.R.	1924	Wood	19'		G.E. 67(2)	- On Stave Falls line until scrapped in 1937 (Single truck)

AUXILIARY VEHICLES

No.	Builder	Year Built	Function	Length	Weight	Motors	Remarks
B.1	Marion	1902	Steam Shovel	35'		None	
B.2	Marion	1902	Steam Shovel	35'		None	
B.3	Industrial Works Bay City, Mich.	1911	Steam Derrick	40'		None	
B.4	Thews Shovel	1910	Electric Shovel	40'		None	
B.5	Browning Hoist	1912	Electric Derrick	40'		G.E.57(4)	
B.6	Thews Shovel	1897	Steam Shovel	25'		None	- Not equipped to move on rails
F.1	B.C.E.R.	1911	Wrecking Car	36'2"	51,290	G.E.67(4)	- Originally "numbered" simply F
F.2	Hicks	1910	Maintenance Car	40'7"		None	- Originally numbered W.1; a converted box car
F.3		1900	Maintenance Car	41'	23,000	None	- A flat car
F.4	B.C.E.R.	1910	Wrecking Car	45'3"	59,000	WH.101-D2	- Converted from express car 1803, 1920. Originally 502
F.4	B.C.E.R.	1946	Wrecking Car	36'	70,760	WH.101-D2	- Completely new body for F.4 above
F.5		1951	Maintenance Car			None	- A converted box car
G.1	Ottawa	1900	Supply Car	21'6"		G.E.67(2)	- Formerly street car 48
G.2	B.C.E.R.	1903	Supply Car	22'		G.E.67(2)	- Formerly street car 54
G.10	B.C.E.R.	1904	Supply Car	20'		G.E.67(2)	- Formerly street car 61
L.1	B.C.E.R.	1900	Line Car	19'	18,300	G.E.67(2)	- Renumbered from 530
L.2	B.C.E.R.	1902	Line Car	32'5"	51,700	G.E.57(4)	- Renumbered from 500; originally 100 (initially single trucked)
L.3	B.C.E.R.	1910	Line Car	40'	59,600	G.E.57(4)	- Renumbered from 532
L.4	B.C.E.R.	1912	Line Car	42'3"	68,000	G.E.57(4)	
L.5	B.C.E.R.	1912	Line Car	42'	68,500	G.E.57(4)	- Victoria
L.6	B.C.E.R.	1914	Line Car	45'	69,280	G.E.57(4)	
S.1							
S.2							
S.3			Snow Plow			None	- Small, non-electrical snow plows in use prior to 1912 (Single truck)
S.4							
S.5							
S.50	B.C.E.R.	1905	Sprinkler Car	25'9"	28,000	G.E.57(2)	- Renumbered from 550; originally 188
S.51	Brill	1910	Sprinkler Car	19'	24,000	WH.101-B2(2)	- Renumbered from 551
S.52	B.C.E.R.	1907	Sprinkler Car	20'5"	28,000	G.E.57(2)	- Victoria
S.53	Ottawa	1912	Sweeper	28'1"	28,000	G.E.57(2)	
S.54	Ottawa	1912	Sweeper	28'1"	36,500	G.E.57(2)	
S.55	Ottawa	1913	Sweeper	28'1"	36,500	G.E.57(2)	
S.56	Ottawa	1912	Sweeper	28'1"	36,500	G.E.57(2)	
S.57	Ottawa	1913	Sweeper	28'1"	35,320	G.E.57(2)	

Auxiliary Vehicles - continued

No.	Builder	Year Built	Function	Length	Weight	Motors	Remarks
S.58	Ottawa	1913	Sweeper	28'1"	35,320	G.E.57(2)	- Victoria
S.59	Ottawa	1913	Sweeper	28'1"	35,320	G.E.57(2)	- Victoria
S.60	B.C.E.R.	1905	Motorized flat car	25'9"	20,500	G.E.67(2)	- Rebuilt from Vancouver street car 19
S.61	B.C.E.R.	1899	Wrecking car	35'8"	36,000	G.E.67(4)	- Victoria - Rebuilt from 503; formerly 101. Originally W.&V.T.3, "Flying Dutchman"
S.62	B.C.E.R.	1900	Wrecking car	20'	18,000	G.E.67(2)	- Rebuilt from 915; formerly 504. Originally 4
S.63	B.C.E.R.	1923	Sweeper	28'1"	36.500	G.E.57(2)	
S.64	B.C.E.R.	1923	Sweeper	28'1"	36,000	G.E.57(2)	
S.65	B.C.E.R.	1935	Sweeper	28'1"	36,000	G.E.57(2)	
S.66	B.C.E.R.	1935	Sweeper	28'1"	36,000	G.E.57(2)	
S.100	B.C.E.R.	1907	Snow flanger	42'	50,000	G.E.57(4)	- Rebuilt from 901, 1937
S.101	Kopple	1912	Dump car	34'6"	26,000	WH.112-B2(4)	
S.101	B.C.E.R.	1909	Snow flanger	42'	50,000	G.E.57(4)	- Rebuilt from 904, 1937
S.102	Canadian Car & Foundry	1912	Dump car	35'6"	26,000	WH.112-B2(4)	- Victoria
S.102	Baldwin	1911	Snow plow			None	- Rebuilt from 980, 1951: at Trapp yard, New Westminster
S.103	B.C.E.R.	1911	Snow plow	32'10"	66,800	WH.112-B2(4)	- Rebuilt from 952, 1951; on display at Snowqualmie Falls, WA

DIESEL LOCOMOTIVES

No.	Builder	Year Built	Builder's Model	Horse Power	Weight	Remarks
900	General Motors Diesel Ltd.	1955	SW900RS	900	240,100	
901	"	1956	"	"	"	
902	"	1956	"	"	"	
903	"	1957	"	"	"	
904	"	1957	"	"	"	
905	"	1958	"	"	"	
906	"	1958	"	"	"	
907	"	1958	"	"	"	
908	"	1958	"	"	"	
940	General Electric/Cooper-Bessemer	1949	70-ton	660	139,000	
941	"	1949	"	"	"	
942	"	1949	"	"	"	
943	"	1950	"	"	"	
E.60	Hayes Manufacturing	1953				- A Cummings diesel powered, single truck line car.

WIDTH (FEET AND INCHES)

Only listed are those street cars and inter-urban coaches for which information is available.

7'6"	-	12,13 (both Victoria)
7'8"	-	400-409 (Birney cars)
8'2"	-	500
8'3"	-	364-378
8'3 3/8"	-	400-435 (P.C.C. cars)
8'4"	-	356-363, 700-719
8'5"	-	250-255
8'6"	-	1306-1308
8'7"	-	7, 26 (both Victoria); 1000-1009, 1200-1244, 1312-1320, 1322, 1500, 1501, 1600-1603
8'8"	-	165-169
8'9"	-	123, 124, 160-164, 183-194, 200-229, 231-240, 300-324, 381-390, 1300-1305, 1309-1311, 1321, 1400-1402, 1700-1705
8'10"	-	22, 23 (both Victoria)
8'11"	-	69-122, 125-149, 170-182, 195-199, 230, 1011, 1012
9'2"	-	1-6, 8, 9, 27, 30 (all Victoria)

NON-MOTORIZED ROLLING STOCK AT THE END OF ELECTRIC OPERATION

Box cars - 6012, 6222, 6292
Cabooses - A.5, A.7, A.9 - A.15
Flat cars - 6509, 6585, 8047
Hopper cars - 3000-3003, 3005-3007, 3009, 3010, 3014
Maintenance - X.48, X.50, X.51, X.61 - X.64, 8035
Sprinkler - X.53

MOTORS

In the case of each street car and interurban coach, the type of motor is the last to inhabit the car. Each piece of rolling stock contained four motors, with the exception of the single truck Birneys and car 500 which operated with two.

E.E. DK 83-B (60 horsepower) - 700-719

G.E.57(50 horsepower) - 500, 1002, 1003, 1008, 1012, Westminster, 1200, 1209, 1210, 1213, 1214, 1800-1803

G.E.67(38 horsepower) - 72-116, 118, 120-122, 124-126, 128, 130, 133, 136 (second car), 141, 150-159, 181, 187, 212, 214, 221, 241, 251, 260-274, 337, 345, 349, 382, 391, 501.

G.E.204A(75 horsepower) - 1201-1208, 1211, 1212, 1215-1244, 1501, 1702, 1703.

G.E.1000 (35 horsepower) - Burnaby, Richmond, Vancouver

WH.49 (35 horsepower) - Gladstone

WH.101B2 (40 horsepower) - 22, 23, 69-71, 117, 119, 127, 129, 131, 132, 134, 135, 137-140, 142-149, 160-180, 182-186, 188-211, 213, 215-220, 222-240, 242-250, 252-259, 275-336, 338-344, 346-348, 350-355, 381, 383-390.

WH. 101D2 (50 horsepower) - 123, 1011

WH. 112B2 (75 horsepower) - 1000, 1001, 1004-1007, 1009

WH. 333C2 (125 horsepower) - 1300-1322, 1400-1402, 1500, 1700, 1701, 1704-1709

WH. 508A (25 horsepower) - 400-409 (Birneys)

WH. 510A2 (40 horsepower) - 364-378

WH. 533T4 (53 horsepower) - 356-363

WH. 1432 (55 horsepower) - 400 (P.C.C.)

WH. 1432D (55 horsepower) - 401-435(P.C.C.)

Sign Rollers

Interurban Coaches

VANCOUVER
WESTMINSTER
CENTRAL PK
HIGHLAND PK
BURNABY LK
DOUGLAS RD
STEVESTON
MARPOLE
LIMITED
SPECIAL
RACE TRACK
HORNE PAYNE
CARRALL ST
PARK AVE
CAR BARNS

Vancouver Street Cars

GRANDVIEW
4th AVE.
FAIRVIEW
BROADWAY E.
ROBSON
DAVIE
33 - MAIN
50 - MAIN
RICH - HAST
DUNBAR
STANLEY PK
JOYCE
POW' - MAIN
49 - FRASER
FRASER
KERRISDALE
SHA'NESSY
OAK ST.
WEST PT. GREY
RENFREW ST
POST OFFICE
54 - VICTORIA
44 - VICTORIA
BROADWAY W.
HASTINGS E.
EXHIBITION PK
KITSILANO
16th AVE.
16 - MAIN
10 - SASAMAT
BOULEVARD
CAMBIE ST
NANAIMO
PRIOR ST.

Victoria Street Cars

OAK BAY
OUTER WHARF
CLOVERDALE
BEACON HILL
FERNWOOD
ESQUIMALT
GORGE
GONZALES
HILLSIDE
UPLANDS
BURNSIDE
MT.TOLMIE
WILLOWS
JOSEPH ST.
SPECIAL

Appendix C

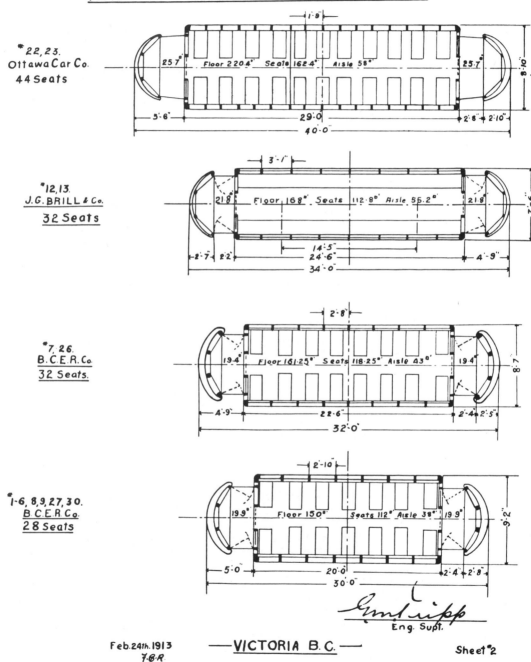

B.C. ELECTRIC RAILWAY Co. LTD.
FLOOR PLAN AND SEATING ARRANGEMENT
OF CITY CARS INCLUDING PLATFORMS ALSO
AREA IN SQUARE FEET IN EACH CASE.

#22,23.
Ottawa Car Co.
44 Seats

#12,13.
J.G. BRILL & Co.
32 Seats

#7,26.
B.C.E.R.Co.
32 Seats.

#1-6, 8,9,27,30.
B.C.E.R.Co.
28 Seats

Feb. 24th. 1913
7.B.R.

VICTORIA B.C.

Eng. Supt.

Sheet #2

308

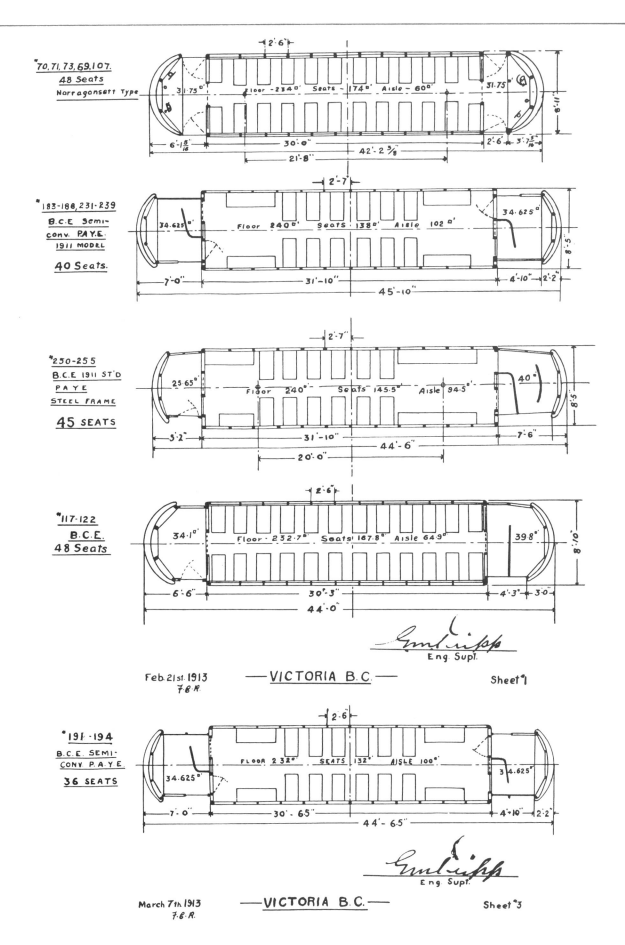

70, 71, 73, 69, 107.
48 Seats
Narragansett Type

Floor - 234ᵈ⁰ Seats - 174ᵈ⁰ Aisle - 60ᵈ⁰

183-188, 231-239
B.C.E. Semi-
conv. P.A.Y.E.
1911 Model
40 Seats.

Floor 240ᵈ⁰ Seats 138ᵈ⁰ Aisle 102ᵈ⁰

250-255
B.C.E. 1911 ST'D
P A Y E
STEEL FRAME
45 SEATS

Floor 240ᵈ⁰ Seats 145.5ᵈ⁰ Aisle 94.5ᵈ⁰

117-122
B.C.E.
48 Seats

Floor - 232.7ᵈ⁰ Seats 167.8ᵈ⁰ Aisle 64.9ᵈ⁰

Feb. 21st 1913
7·B·R.

— VICTORIA B.C. —

Eng. Supt.

Sheet #1

191-194
B.C.E. SEMI-
CONV. P.A.Y.E.
36 SEATS

FLOOR 232ᵈ⁰ SEATS 132ᵈ⁰ AISLE 100ᵈ⁰

March 7th 1913
7·B·R.

— VICTORIA B.C. —

Eng. Supt.

Sheet #3

309

B. C. ELECTRIC RAILWAY CO., LTD. —TYPES OF CARS OPERATING ON CITY LINES.

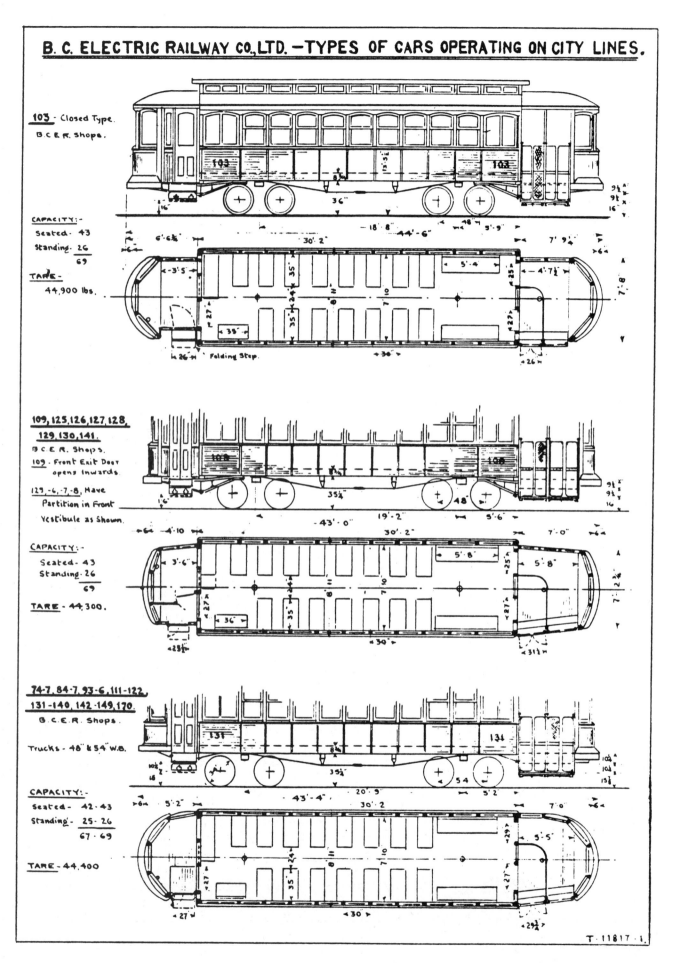

103 - Closed Type.
B.C.E.R. Shops.

CAPACITY:-
Seated - 43
Standing - 26
⎯⎯
69

TARE -
44,900 lbs.

Folding Step.

109, 125, 126, 127, 128,
129, 130, 141.
B.C.E.R. Shops.
109 - Front Exit Door
opens inwards.
129, -6, -7, -8, Have
Partition in Front
Vestibule as Shown.

CAPACITY:-
Seated - 43
Standing - 26
⎯⎯
69

TARE - 44,300.

74-7, 84-7, 93-6, 111-122,
131-140, 142-149, 170.
B.C.E.R. Shops.

Trucks - 48" & 54" W.B.

CAPACITY:-
Seated - 42-43
Standing - 25-26
⎯⎯⎯⎯
67-69

TARE - 44,400.

T-11817-1

310

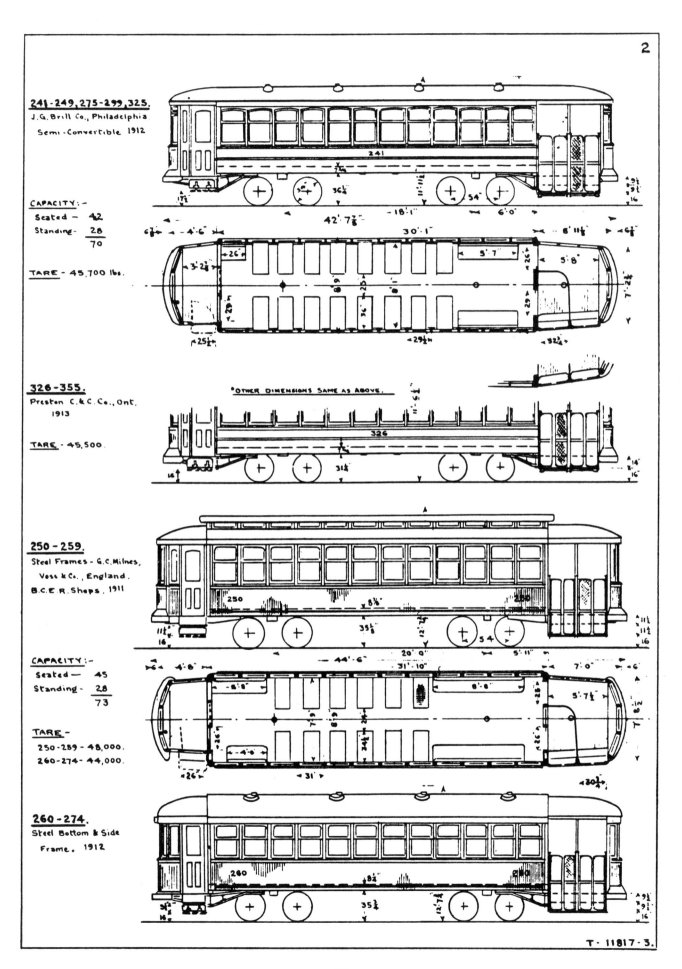

241-249,275-299,325.
J.G.Brill Co., Philadelphia
Semi-Convertible 1912

CAPACITY:-
Seated — 42
Standing — 28
              70

TARE - 45,700 lbs.

326-355.
Preston C.&C.Co., Ont.
1913

TARE - 45,500.

250-259.
Steel Frames - G.C.Milnes,
Voss & Co., England.
B.C.E.R.Shops. 1911

CAPACITY:-
Seated — 45
Standing — 28
              73

TARE -
250-259 - 48,000.
260-274 - 44,000.

260-274.
Steel Bottom & Side
Frame. 1912

*OTHER DIMENSIONS SAME AS ABOVE.

T-11817-3.

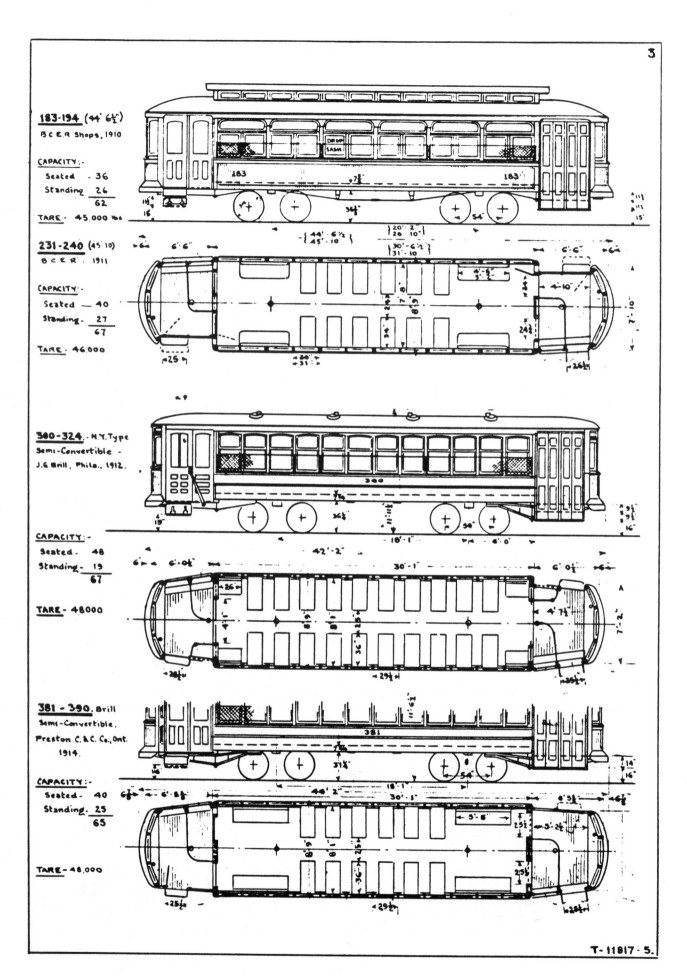

183-194 (44' 6½")
B.C.E.R. Shops, 1910

CAPACITY:-
Seated - 36
Standing 26
       62
TARE - 45,000 lbs.

231-240 (45' 10")
B.C.E.R. 1911

CAPACITY:-
Seated — 40
Standing - 27
        67
TARE - 46,000

300-324 - N.Y. Type
Semi-Convertible -
J.G.Brill, Phila., 1912.

CAPACITY:-
Seated - 48
Standing - 19
        67
TARE - 48000

381 - 390. Brill
Semi-Convertible.
Preston C. & C. Co., Ont.
1914.

CAPACITY:-
Seated - 40
Standing - 25
        65
TARE - 48,000

T - 11817 - 5.

3

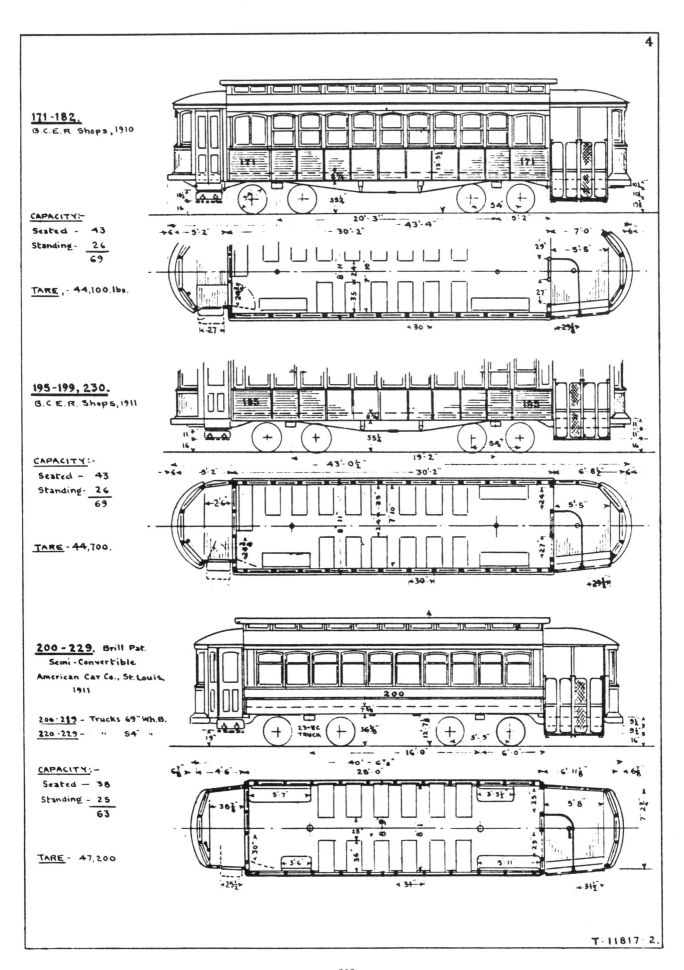

171-182.
B.C.E.R Shops, 1910

CAPACITY:-
Seated - 43
Standing- 26
──
69

TARE,- 44,100.lbs.

195-199, 230.
B.C.E.R. Shops, 1911

CAPACITY:-
Seated - 43
Standing- 26
──
69

TARE - 44,700.

200-229. Brill Pat.
Semi-Convertible
American Car Co., St.Louis
1911

200-219 - Trucks 69" Wh.B.
220-229 - " 54" "

CAPACITY:-
Seated — 38
Standing - 25
──
63

TARE - 47,200

T·11817·2.

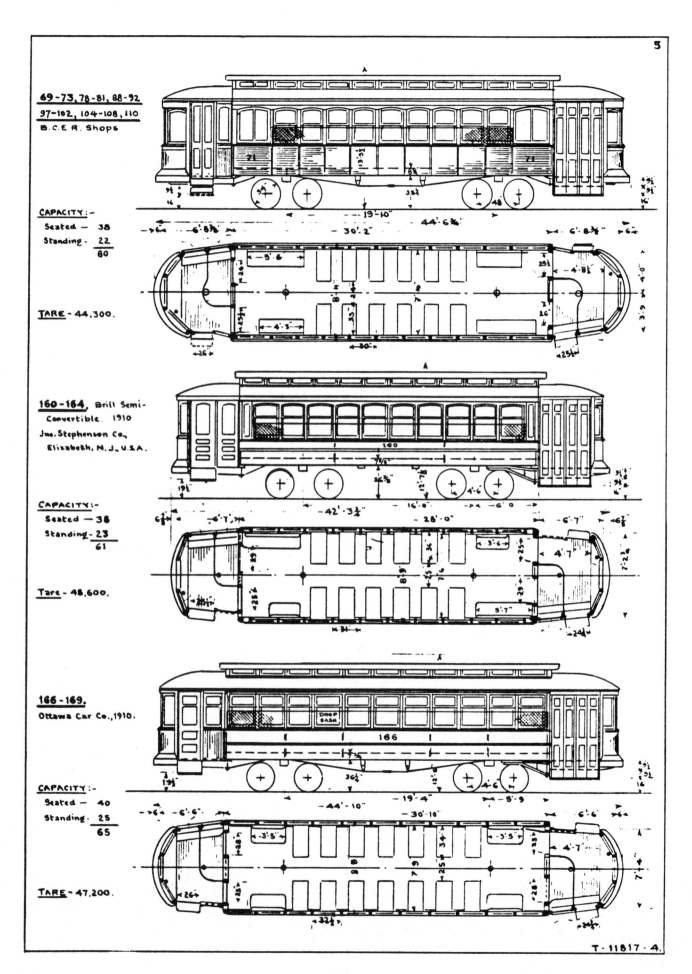

69-73, 78-81, 88-92
97-102, 104-108, 110
B.C.E.R. Shops

CAPACITY:-
Seated — 38
Standing - 22
80

TARE - 44,300.

160-164, Brill Semi-
Convertible. 1910
Jno. Stephenson Co.,
Elizabeth, N.J., U.S.A.

CAPACITY:-
Seated — 38
Standing - 23
61

TARE - 48,600.

166-169.
Ottawa Car Co., 1910.

CAPACITY:-
Seated — 40
Standing - 25
65

TARE - 47,200.

T-11817-4.

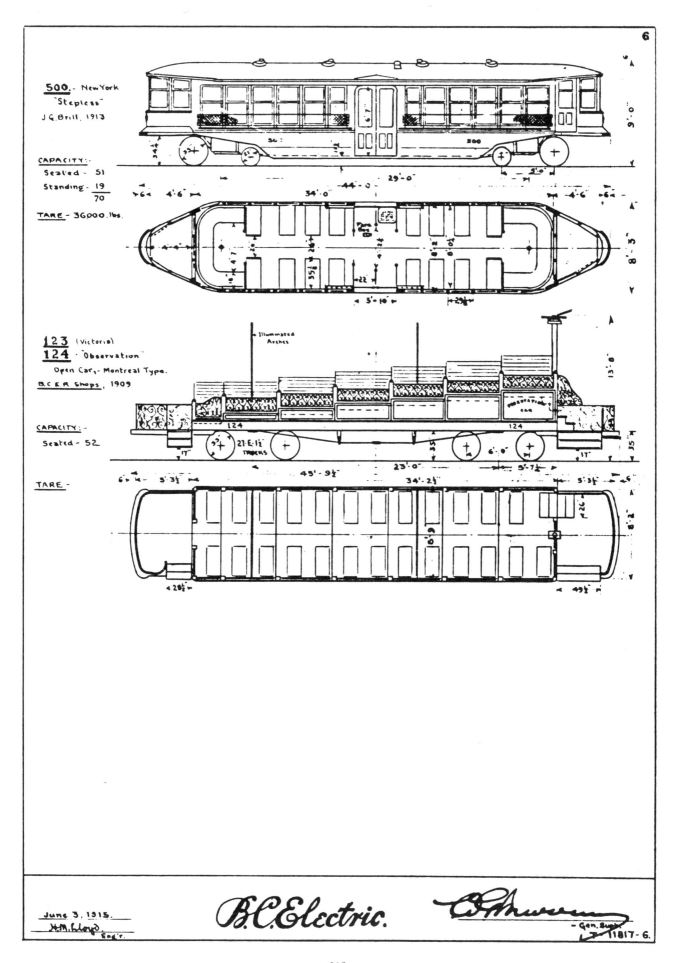

500. - New York
"Stepless"
J.G. Brill, 1913

CAPACITY:-
Seated - 51
Standing - 19
—
70

TARE - 36,000 lbs.

123 (Victoria)
124 - "Observation"
Open Car - Montreal Type.
B.C.E.R. Shops, 1909

CAPACITY:-
Seated - 52

TARE -

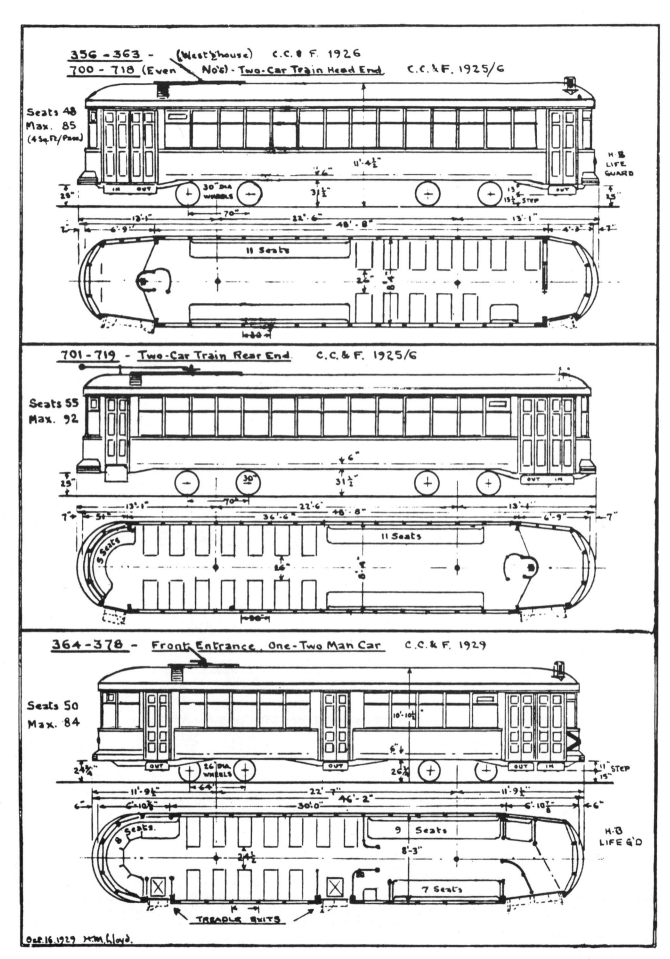

356 - 363 - (West'ghouse) C.C. & F. 1926
700 - 718 (Even No's) - Two-Car Train Head End   C.C.&F. 1925/6

Seats 48
Max. 85
(4 Sq.Ft./Pass)

H.B LIFE GUARD

11 Seats

701 - 719 - Two-Car Train Rear End   C.C. & F. 1925/6

Seats 55
Max. 92

11 Seats

364 - 378 - Front Entrance, One-Two Man Car   C.C. & F. 1929

Seats 50
Max. 84

8 Seats
9 Seats
7 Seats
H-B LIFE G'D

TREADLE EXITS

Oct.16.1929 H.M.Cloyd.

INTERURBAN PASSENGER & EXPRESS EQUIPMENT.

— MULTIPLE UNIT CARS. —

1000 CLASS ÷-

No's 1000-2, 1004-9

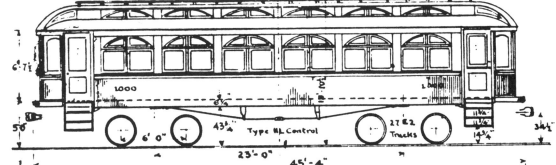

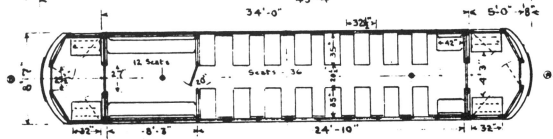

Built by PRESTON CAR & COACH Co., 1910; Platforms Rebuilt at N.W. Shop, 1911. Capacity 48
STANDARD EQUIPT:- Type "HL" Control; #112-B-2 (75 h.p. 500v) Motors; "AMM" Air Brakes;
Air Signals; Watson Wheel Guards. Weight 63,300 lbs.
EXCEPTIONS:- #1002, 1012:- GE 57 (50hp) Motors; 1905, 08, 09, 11:- W.101-D (55 hp) Motors

No. 1011, 1012

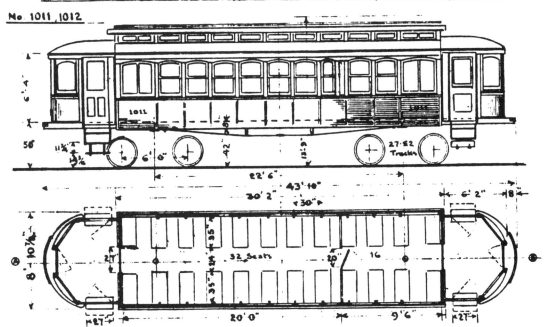

REBUILT, 1911 from City Cars 82, 83. Weight (Approx) 60,500 lbs.

T-11855-1

1200 CLASS :-

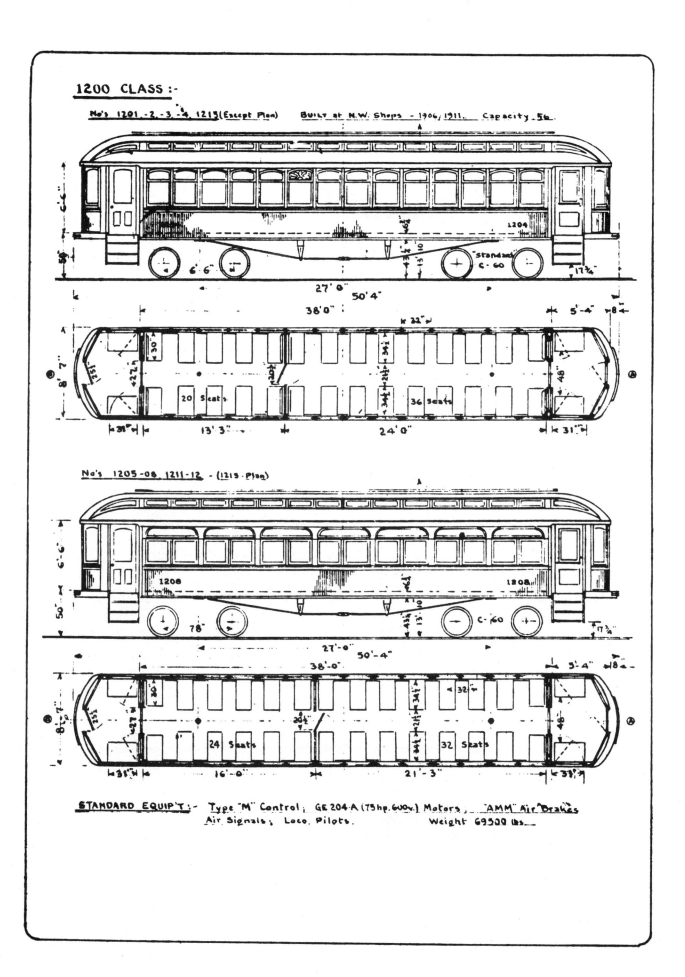

No's 1201 -2.-3.-4, 1215 (Except Plan) Built at N.W. Shops - 1906/1911. Capacity 56.

1204

Standard C-60

20 Seats   36 Seats

No's 1205-08, 1211-12 - (1215 Plan)

1208   1208

C-60

24 Seats   32 Seats

STANDARD EQUIP'T :- Type "M" Control; GE 204-A (75hp. 600v.) Motors, "AMM" Air Brakes
Air Signals; Loco. Pilots.   Weight 69500 lbs.

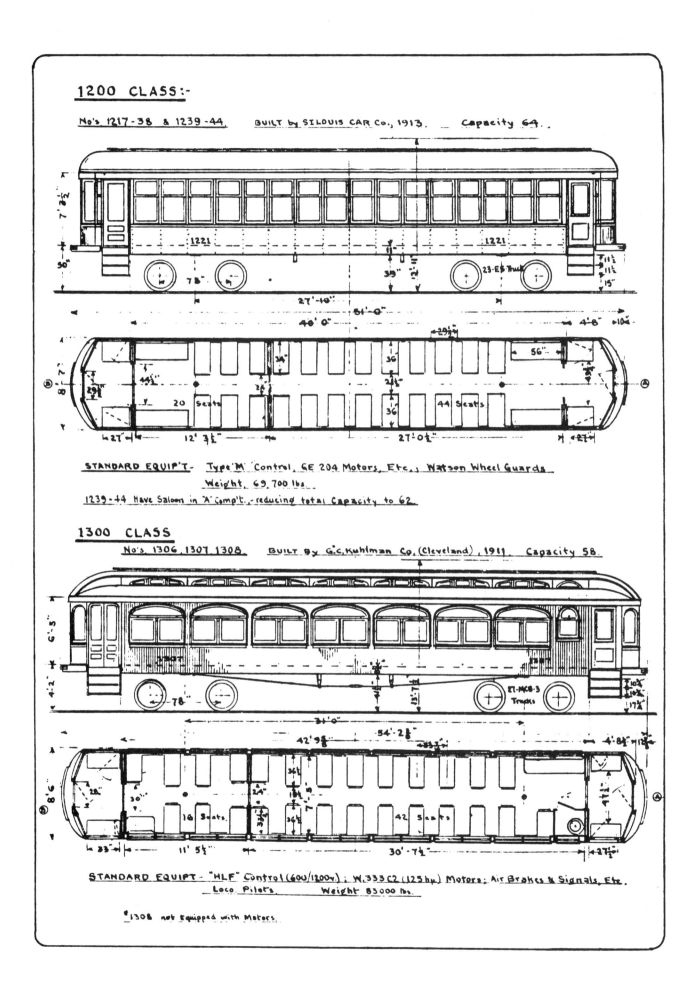

1200 CLASS:-

No's 1217-38 & 1239-44.   BUILT by ST LOUIS CAR Co., 1913.   Capacity 64.

STANDARD EQUIP'T- Type 'M' Control, GE 204 Motors, Etc.; Watson Wheel Guards
Weight 69,700 lbs.
1239-44 Have Saloon in 'A' Comp't.-reducing total Capacity to 62.

1300 CLASS

No's 1306, 1307, 1308.   BUILT By G.C. Kuhlman Co. (Cleveland), 1911.   Capacity 58.

STANDARD EQUIPT- "HLF" Control (600/1200v); W.333 C2 (125 hp) Motors; Air Brakes & Signals, Etc.
Loco. Pilots.   Weight 83,000 lbs.

*1308 not equipped with Motors.

1300 CLASS:-

No's 1300 to 1305.

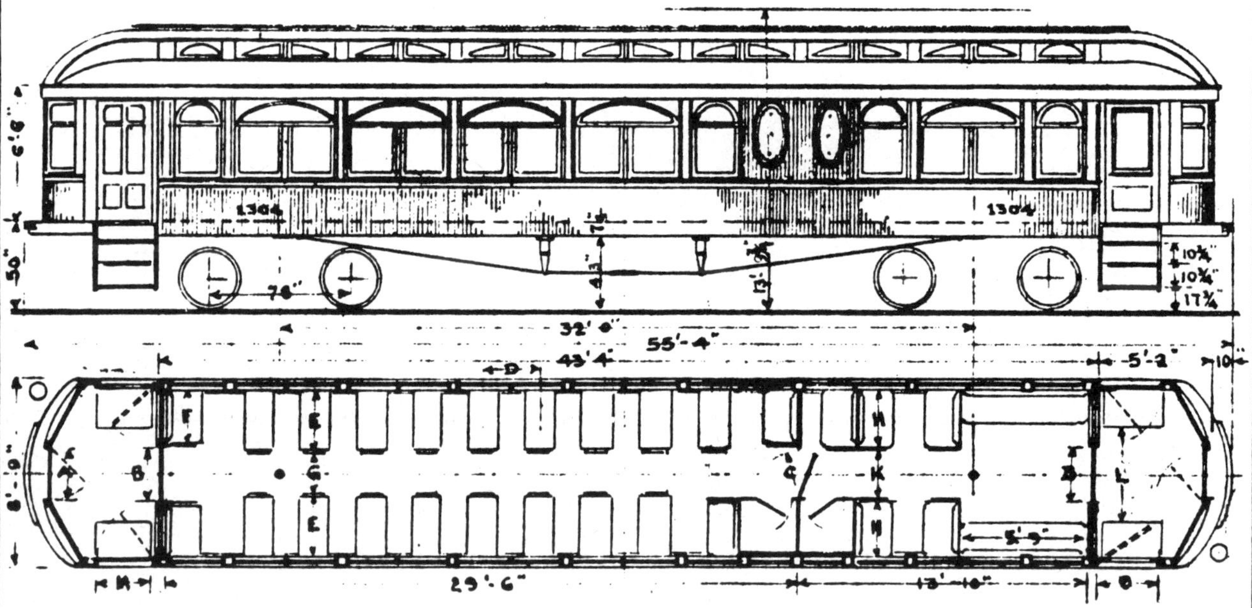

EQUIPMENT:- "HLF" Control; 333 C2 Motors; Etc., . Pilots. Weight 81,000 lbs.

CAPACITY - (42+18) - 60.

CAR No.	BUILT By	Year	TRUCKS -Type	VARIABLE DIMENSIONS.											
				A	B	C	D	E	F	G	H	K	L	M	O
1300	American Car Co.	1910	27-E3	25"	29½"	27"	32"	35½"	30¼	19½"	34½"	20½"	49½"	29½"	28"
1301	Ottawa Car Co.	"	27-MCB-3	20¼"	30"	20¼"	31½"	35"	29¾"	19"	34½	20"	67¼"	29½"	29½"
1302	" "	"	27-E3	20¼"	30"	20½"	31½"	35"	29¾"	19"	34½	20"	67¼"	29½"	29½"
1303	B.C.E.R	1911	27 E3	20¼"	30"	20½"	31½"	34¾"	28¾"	18½"	34½"	19½	49½"	29½"	29½"
1304	"	"	27 MCB 3	20¼"	30"	20¼"	31½"	34¾"	28¾"	18½"	34½"	19½"	49½"	29½"	29½"
1305	"	"	27 E3	20¼"	30"	20½	31½"	34¾"	28¾"	18½"	34½"	19½"	49½"	29½"	29½"

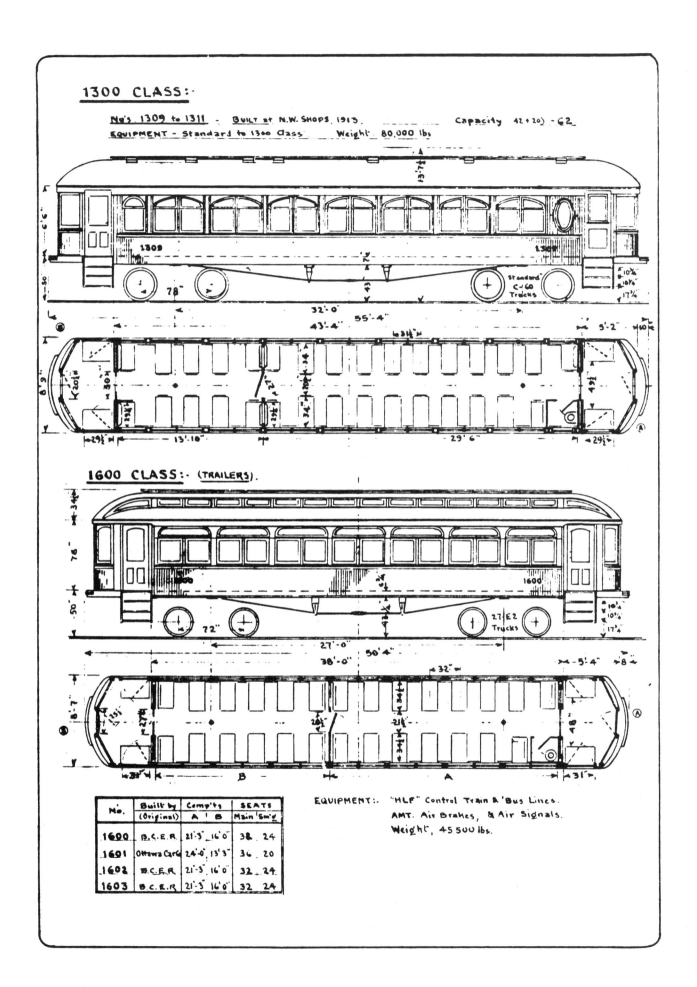

1300 CLASS:-

No's 1309 to 1311 - Built at N.W. Shops, 1913.   Capacity 42+20) - 62

EQUIPMENT - Standard to 1300 Class   Weight 80,000 lbs

1309

1300

Standard
C-60
Trucks

1600 CLASS:- (TRAILERS).

1600

1600

27 E2
Trucks

EQUIPMENT:- "HLF" Control Train & 'Bus Lines.

AMT. Air Brakes, & Air Signals.

Weight, 45,500 lbs.

No.	Built by (Original)	Comp'ts A	B	SEATS Main	Sm'g
1600	B.C.E.R.	21'-3"	16'-0"	38	24
1601	Ottawa Car Co	24'-0"	13'-3"	36	20
1602	B.C.E.R.	21'-3"	16'-0"	32	24
1603	B.C.E.R.	21'-3"	16'-0"	32	24

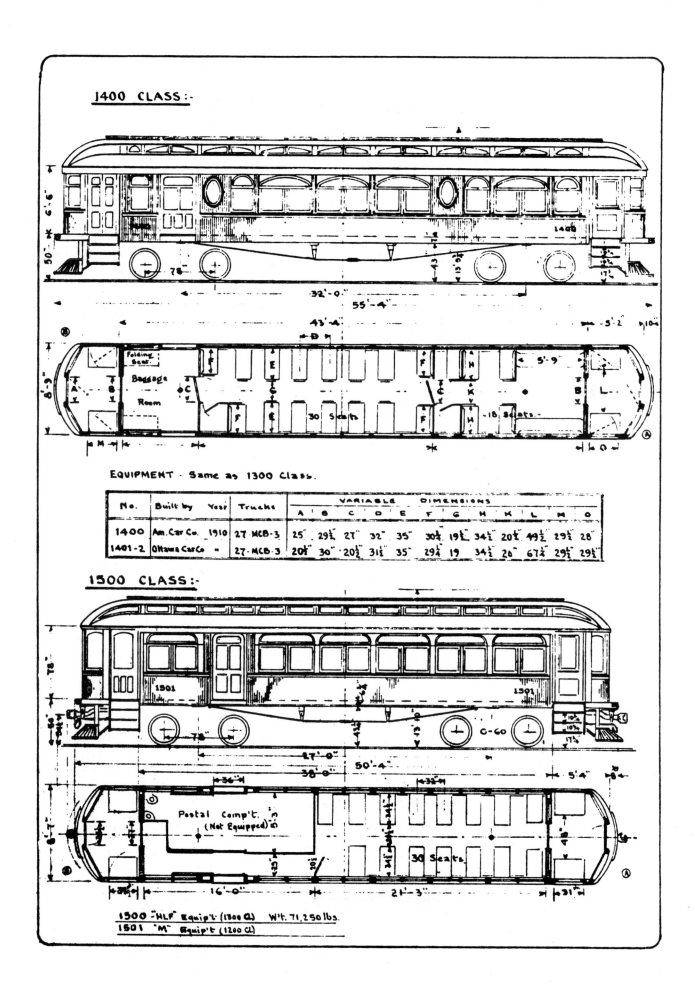

1400 CLASS:-

EQUIPMENT - Same as 1300 Class.

No.	Built by	Year	Trucks	VARIABLE DIMENSIONS											
				A	B	C	D	E	F	G	H	K	L	M	N	O
1400	Am. Car Co.	1910	27·MCB-3	25"	29½"	27"	32"	35"	30¼	19½	34½	20½	49½	29½	28
1401-2	Ottawa CarCo	"	27·MCB-3	20½	30	20½	31½	35"	29¼	19	34½	20	67¼	29½	29½

1500 CLASS:-

1500 "HLF" Equip't (1300 Cl)   W't. 71,250 lbs.
1501 "M" Equip't (1200 Cl)

1700 CLASS :-

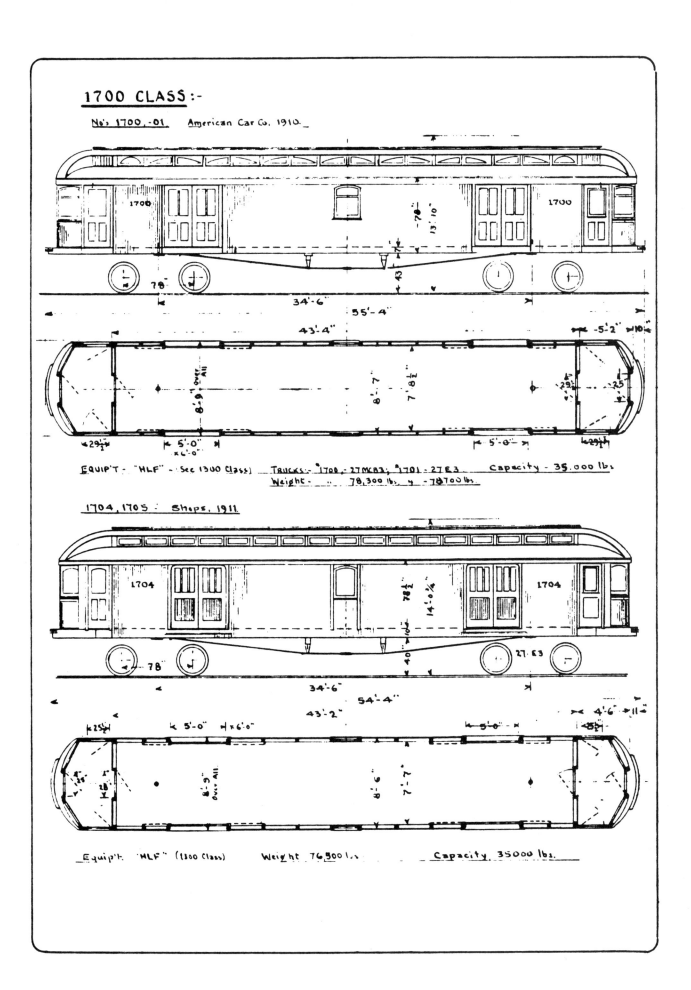

No's 1700, -01.   American Car Co. 1910.

1700

1700

13'-10"

-78"

7¼

43

78"

34'-6"

55'-4"

43'-4"

-5'-2"→10

8'-9" over All

8'-7"

7'-8½"

29½

25

29½

5'-0"
×6'-0"

5'-0"→

29½

EQUIP'T - "HLF" - See 1300 Class.   TRUCKS - 1700 - 27 MKA3; 1701 - 27 E3   Capacity - 35,000 lbs.
Weight -   78,300 lbs,   4 - 78700 lbs.

1704, 1705 : Shops, 1911

1704

1704

78½

14'-0¾"

10½

40

34'-6"

27 E3

78"

54'-4"

43'-2"

4'-6" →11

25½

5'-0"   ×6'-0"

5'-0"

8'-9" over All

8'-6"

7'-7"

Equip't "HLF" (1300 Class)   Weight 76,500 lbs.   Capacity 35000 lbs.

1700 CLASS :-

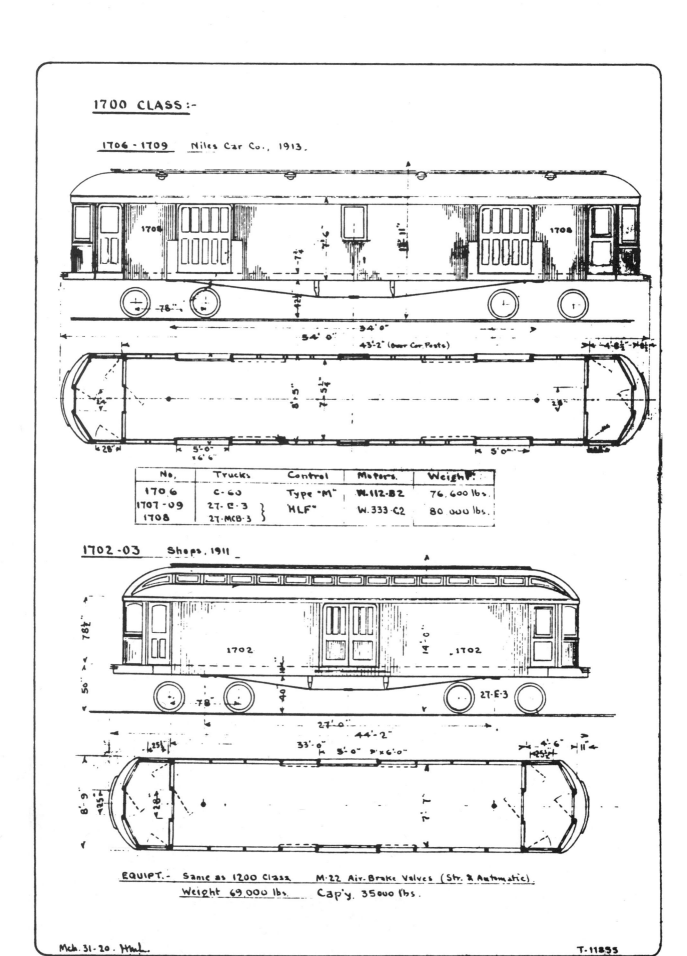

1706 - 1709   Niles Car Co., 1913.

No.	Trucks	Control	Motors.	Weight.
1706	C-60	Type "M"	W.112-B2	76,600 lbs.
1707-09	27-E-3 }	"LF"		
1708	27-MCB-3 }		W.333-C2	80,000 lbs.

1702-03   Shops, 1911

EQUIPT.- Same as 1200 Class   M-22 Air-Brake Valves (Str. & Automatic).
Weight 69,000 lbs.   Cap'y. 35000 lbs.

Mch. 31-20. HmL.   T-11835

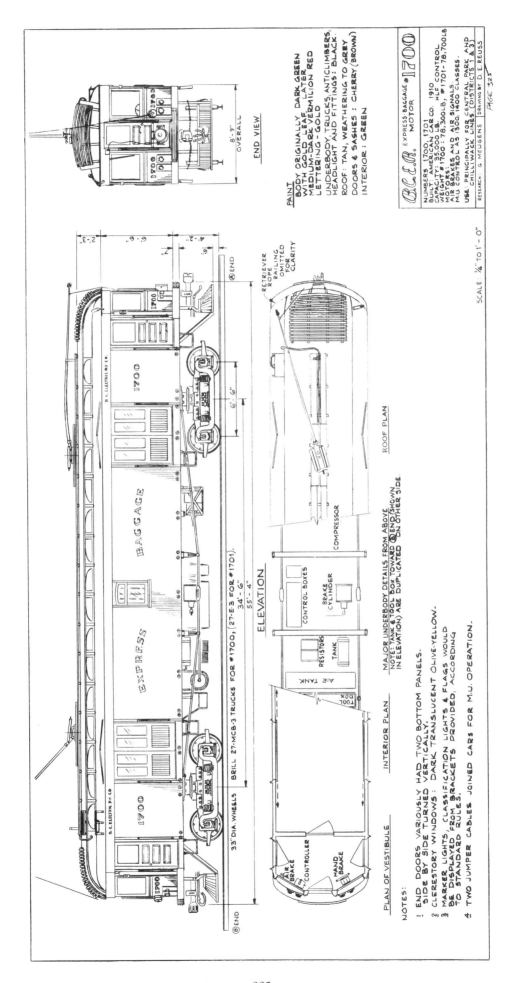

END VIEW

8'-9" OVERALL

PAINT

BODY ORIGINALLY DARK GREEN WITH GOLD LEAF. LATER MEDIUM-DARK VERMILION RED. LETTERING-GOLD.

UNDERBODY, TRUCKS, ANTICLIMBERS, HEADLIGHT AND FITTINGS: BLACK.

ROOF: TAN, WEATHERING TO GREY

DOORS & SASHES : CHERRY (BROWN)

INTERIOR : GREEN

B.C.E.R. EXPRESS-BAGGAGE **#1700** MOTOR

NUMBERS. 1700, 1701
BUILT: AMERICAN CAR CO. 1910
CAPACITY: 35,000 LB.   HLF CONTROL
WEIGHT:#1700:78,300LB, #1701-78,700LB
MOTORS:
AIR BRAKES AND AIR SIGNALS.
M.U. CONTROL AS 1300,1400 CLASSES.

USE: PRINCIPALLY FOR CENTRAL PARK AND CHILLIWACK LINES (DISTRICTS 1 & 3)

RESEARCH: G. MEUGENS DRAWING BY D. E. REUSS

PAGE 325

SCALE: ¼" TO 1'-0"

1700

EXPRESS

BAGGAGE

1700

B.C.ELECTRIC RY. CO

33' DIA. WHEELS   BRILL 27-MCB-3 TRUCKS FOR #1700, (27-E-3 FOR #1701).

2'-3"
6'-9"
4'-2"
7"
6"

(A) END
(B) END

55'-4"
34'-6"
6'-6"

ELEVATION

RETRIEVER ROPE RAILING OMITTED FOR CLARITY

COMPRESSOR

ROOF PLAN

CONTROL BOXES

BRAKE CYLINDER

RESISTORS

TANK

AIR TANK

TOOL BOX

AIR BRAKE

CONTROLLER

HAND BRAKE

MAJOR UNDERBODY DETAILS FROM ABOVE NOTE: TANK & TOOL BOX TOWARD (B) END SHOWN IN ELEVATION) ARE DUPLICATED ON OTHER SIDE.

PLAN OF VESTIBULE   INTERIOR PLAN

NOTES:

1 END DOORS VARIOUSLY HAD TWO BOTTOM PANELS.
   SIDE BY SIDE TURNED VERTICALLY.

2 CLERESTORY WINDOWS: DARK TRANSLUCENT OLIVE-YELLOW.

3 MARKER LIGHTS, CLASSIFICATION LIGHTS & FLAGS WOULD
   BE DISPLAYED FROM BRACKETS PROVIDED, ACCORDING
   TO STANDARD RULES.

4 TWO JUMPER CABLES JOINED CARS FOR M.U. OPERATION.

325

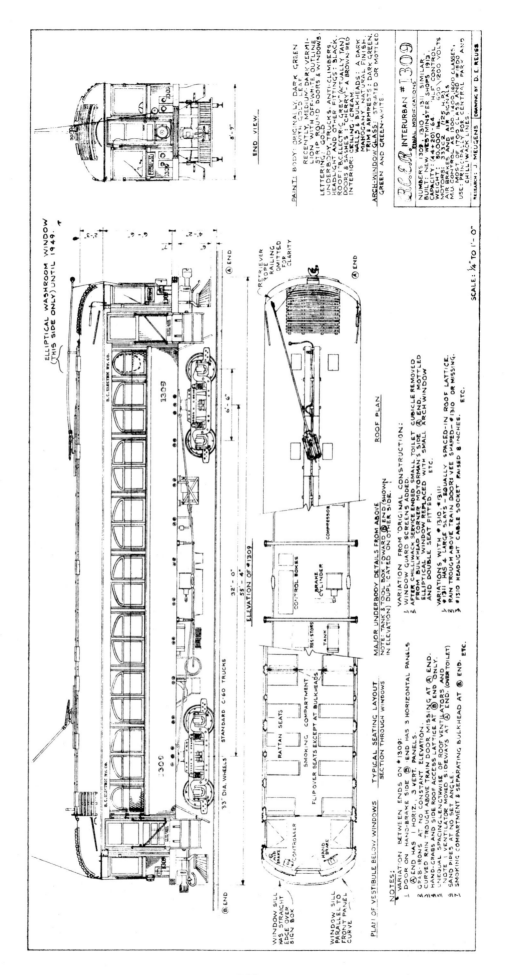

BCER INTERURBAN #1309

END VIEW

PAINT: BODY: ORIGINALLY DARK GREEN WITH GOLD LEAF. RECENTLY, MEDIUM DARK VERMILION WITH OFF-WHITE OUTLINE STRIP ROUND DOORS & WINDOWS. LETTERING & SIGNS: GOLD. UNDERBODY, TRUCKS, ANTI-CLIMBERS, HEADLIGHT AND OTHER FITTINGS: BLACK. ROOF: B.C. ELECTRIC GREY (ACTUALLY TAN). DOORS & SASHES: CHERRY - A BROWN-RED. INTERIOR: CEILING & DREAMS - A DARK MAHOGANY NATURAL FINISH. WALLS & BULKHEADS: A DARK TRIM & ARMRESTS: DARK GREEN.

ARCH WINDOW GLASS: STRIATED OR MOTTLED GREEN AND GREEN-WHITE.

NUMBERS: 1309. 1310. 1311 SIMILAR.
BUILT: NEW WESTMINSTER SHOPS 1912.
CAPACITY: (44+20)-64. H.P. CONTROL.
WEIGHT: 80,000 lbs. 600 /1200 VOLTS
MOTORS: 4x 125 H.P.
AIR BRAKES 3x C2 AIR SIGNALS.
MU CONTROL AS 1300, 1400, 1600 CLASSES,
USE: MOST OF 1700 & 1725 AND #1300
CENTRAL PARK AND CHILLIWACK LINES.

RESEARCH: J. MEUGENS   DRAWING BY D.E. REUSS

ELLIPTICAL WASHROOM WINDOW (THIS SIDE ONLY) UNTIL 1949.

1309

B.C. ELECTRIC RY. CO.

ELEVATION OF #1309

55'-4"
32'-0"

33' DIA. WHEELS   STANDARD C-60 TRUCKS

RETRIEVER
ROPE
RAILING OMITTED FOR CLARITY

A END

ROOF PLAN

SCALE: ¼" TO 1'-0"

WINDOW SILL HAS STRAIGHT EDGE OVER SIGN BOX

WINDOW SILL PARALLEL TO FRONT PANEL. CURVE

RATTAN SEATS

SMOKING COMPARTMENT

FLIP-OVER SEATS EXCEPT AT BULKHEADS

CONTROLLER

HAND BRAKE

PLAN OF VESTIBULE BELOW WINDOWS   TYPICAL SEATING LAYOUT
SECTION THROUGH WINDOWS

CONTROL BOXES

RESISTORS

BRAKE CYLINDER

TANK

COMPRESSOR

MAJOR UNDERBODY DETAILS FROM ABOVE
NOTE: TANK & TOOL BOX TOWARD ⒷEND (SHOWN IN ELEVATION) DUPLICATED ON OTHER SIDE.

NOTES:
VARIATION BETWEEN ENDS ON #1309:
1 DOOR ON HAND-BRAKE SIDE Ⓑ END HAS 3 HORIZONTAL PANELS
ⒶEND HAS 1 HORIZ. 3 VERT. PANELS.
2 GRAB-IRONS AT NO CONSTANT ELEVATION.
3 CURVED RAIN TROUGH ABOVE TRAIN DOOR MISSING AT Ⓑ END.
4 HAND-GRABS AND SIDE ROOF ACCESS LATTICE AT Ⓑ END ONLY.
5 UNEQUAL SPACING LENGTHWISE OF ROOF VENTILATORS AND
NOTE 1 VENTILATOR MOVED SIDEWAYS AT Ⓐ END. (OVER TOILET)
6 SAND PIPES AT NO SET ANGLE.
7 SMOKING COMPARTMENT & SEPARATING BULKHEAD AT Ⓑ END. ETC.

VARIATION FROM ORIGINAL CONSTRUCTION:
1 WINDOW GUARD SCREENS ADDED
2 AFTER CHILLIWACK SERVICE ENDED SMALL TOILET CUBICLE REMOVED FROM BULKHEAD CORNER. MOTORMAN'S SIDE Ⓐ END. MOTTLED ELLIPTICAL WINDOW REPLACED WITH SMALL ARCH WINDOW AND DOUBLE SEAT FITTED. ETC.

VARIATIONS WITH #1310, #1311:
1 #1311 HAS 4 LARGE SLATS - EQUALLY SPACED-IN ROOF LATTICE.
2 RAIN TROUGH ABOVE TRAIN DOOR: VEE SHAPED - #1310 OR MISSING.
3 #1310 HEADLIGHT CABLE SOCKET RAISED 8 INCHES. ETC.

326

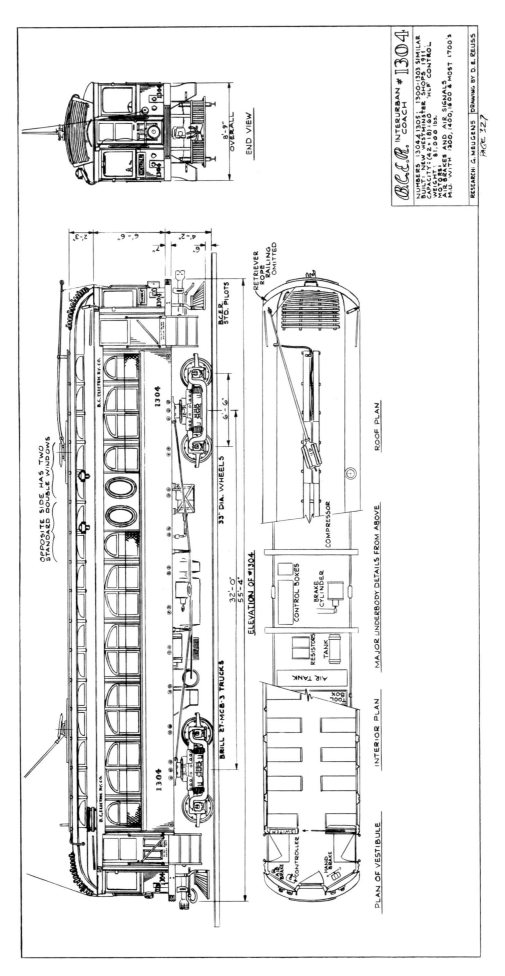

B.C.E.R. INTERURBAN #1304 COACH

NUMBERS 1304,1305; 1300-1303 SIMILAR
BUILT: NEW WESTMINSTER SHOPS 1911
CAPACITY:(42+18):60   "HLF" CONTROL
WEIGHT: 81,000 lbs.
MOTORS:
AIR BRAKES AND AIR SIGNALS
M.U. WITH 1300,1400,1600 & MOST 1700's

RESEARCH: G.MEUGENS   DRAWING BY D.E.REUSS

PAGE 327

OPPOSITE SIDE HAS TWO STANDARD DOUBLE WINDOWS

1304

B.C. ELECTRIC RY. CO.

1304

B.C. ELECTRIC RY. CO.

BRILL 27-MCB-3 TRUCKS

33" DIA. WHEELS

6'-6"

32'-0"

55'-4"

B.C.E.R. STD. PILOTS

ELEVATION OF #1304

END VIEW

8'-9" OVERALL

RETRIEVER
ROPE
RAILING OMITTED

ROOF PLAN

COMPRESSOR

CONTROL BOXES

BRAKE CYLINDER

RESISTORS

TANK

AIR TANK

TOOL BOX

MAJOR UNDERBODY DETAILS FROM ABOVE

INTERIOR PLAN

SWITCH

AIR BRAKE

CONTROLLER

HAND BRAKE

PLAN OF VESTIBULE

327

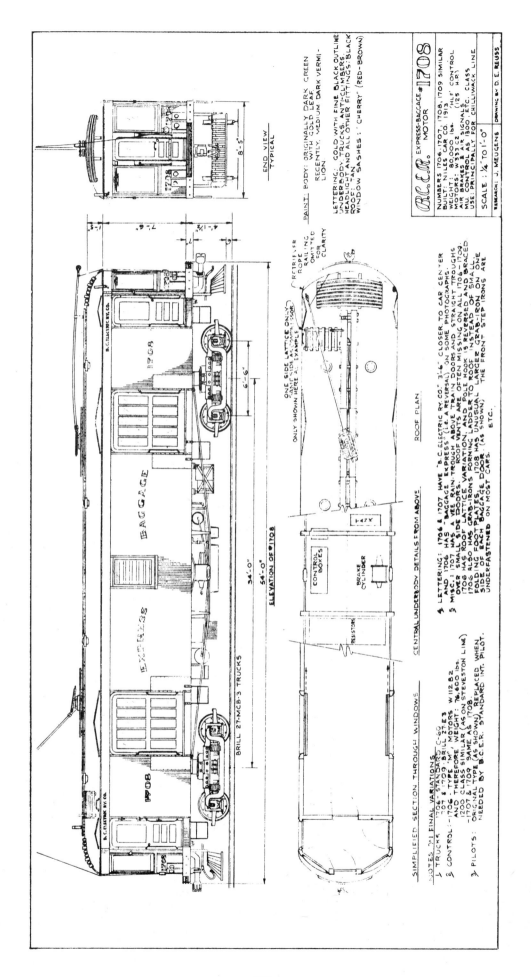

First row of transfers:

00558 — 4 P.M. STUB — Fri. Dec. 11
Outer	TRAVEL TIME	Inner	MAR-POLE L.I.	JUB-ILEE
0	Broadway & Main	35		
7	Main & Hastings	28		
16	Robson & Granville	19	MAGEE	PARK AVE.
26	Broadway & Gr...	9		
35	Main & Broadway	0		

FAIRVIEW — FRI. DEC. 11 — BWAY. & MAIN — Inner / Outer — STAN. PARK 00558

01084 — 4 P.M. STUB — Fri. Jan. 8
Outer	TRAVEL TIME	Inner	MAR-POLE	JUB-ILEE
0	Broadway & Main	35		
7	Main & Hastings	28		
16	Robson & Granville	19		PARK AVE.
26	Broadway & Gran.	9		
35	Main & Broadway	0		

FAIRVIEW — FRI. JAN. 8 — BWY. & MAIN — Inner / Outer — STAN. PARK 01084

06240 — 4 P.M. STUB — Fri. Dec. 11
Down	TRAVEL TIME	Up	MAR-POLE	JUB-ILEE
0	50th Avenue	37		
3	Broadway & Main	24		
20	Main & Hastings	17		PARK
29	Robson & Granville	8		
37	English Bay	0		

DAVIE-MAIN — FRI. DEC. 11 — 50th AVE. / ENG. BAY — STAN. PARK 06240

10616 — 4 P.M. STUB — Fri. Dec. 11
Down	TRAVEL TIME	Up	MAR-POLE	JUB-ILEE
0	Cedar Cottage	43		
11	Clark & Hastings	31		
15	Main & Hastings	27		PARK AVE.
24	Robson & Granville	18	MAGEE	
32	4th & Granville	8		
43	4th & Alma	0		

G.V.-4th Ave. — FRI. DEC. 11 — CED. COT. / 4th. ALMA — STAN. PARK 10616

09968 — 4 P.M. STUB — Fri. Dec. 11
Down	TRAVEL TIME	Up	MAR-POLE	JUB-ILEE
0	Commercial Drive	32		
8	Broadway & Main	24		
15	Main & Hastings	17	MAGEE	PARK AVE.
24	Robson & Granville	8		
32	English Bay	0		

ROB. BWAY. E. — FRI. DEC. 11 — BWAY & COM. / 'G. BAY — STAN. PARK 09968

15706 — 4 P.M. STUB — Fri. Dec. 11
Down	TRAVEL TIME	Up	MAR-POLE	JUB-ILEE
0	Marine & Fraser	67		
20	Broadway & Kingway	47		
27	Main & Hastings	40		PARK AVE.
47	Robson & Granville	30	MAGEE	
47	Broadway & Gran.	20		
67	41st & Dunbar	0		

FRA.-KERR. — FRI. DEC. 11 — MAR. DR. / 41st. DUN. — STAN. PARK 15706

Second row of transfers:

02575 — 4 P.M. STUB — Fri. Dec. 11
Down	TRAVEL TIME	Up	MAR-POLE	JUB-ILEE
0	Hastings Park	21		
15	Powell & Main	6	MAGEE	PARK AVE.
21	Post Office	0		

POWELL ST. — FRI. DEC. 11 — HAST. K. / P.O. — STAN. PARK 02575

03108 — 4 P.M. STUB — Fri. Dec. 11
Down	TRAVEL TIME	Up	MAR-POLE	JUB-ILEE
0	54th & Victoria Rd.	38		
8	Victoria & Kingsway	30		
17	Broadway & Kingsway	20	MAGEE	PARK AVE.
25	Main & Hastings	13		
32	Post Office	6		
39	Stanley Park	0		

VICTORIA RD. — FRI. DEC. 11 — 54th / S.PK. VIC. / P.O. — STAN. PARK 03108

04673 — 4 P.M. STUB — Fri. Dec. 11
Down	TRAVEL TIME	Up	MAR-POLE	JUB-ILEE
0	Joyce Road	37		
7	Victoria & Kingsway	20		
17	Broad'y & Kingsway	17	MAGEE	PARK AVE.
24	Main & Hastings	13		
31	Post Office	6		
37	Stanley Park	0		

JOYCE RD. — FRI. DEC. 11 — JOY. / S.PK. RD. / P.O. — STAN. PARK 04673

01289 — 4 P.M. STUB — Fri. Dec. 11
Down	TRAVEL TIME	Up	MAR-POLE	JUB-ILEE
0	Kitsilano	15		
8	Robson & Granville	6	MAGEE	PARK AVE.
15	Richards & Hastings	0		

KITSILANO — FRI. DEC. 11 — RICH. / K'TS. HAST. / BCH. — STAN. PARK 01289

20121 — 4 P.M. STUB — Fri. Dec. 11
Outer	TRAVEL TIME	Inner	MAR-POLE	JUB-ILEE
0	Boundary Road	55		
16	Main & Hastings	38		
26	Robson & Richards	30	MAGEE	PARK AVE.
34	Broadway & Gran.	21		
44	Alma & Broadway	11		
55	41st Ave.-W. Pt. G.	0		

Hast E-Bway W — FRI. DEC. 11 — B'DRY. / 41st KU. / W.P.G. — STAN. PARK 20121

Third row of transfers:

00908 — 4 P.M. STUB — Fri. Dec. 11
Down	TRAVEL TIME	Up	MAR-POLE	JUB-ILEE
0	Cambie & Hastings	35		
11	Broadway & Oak	24		
14	16th & Oak	21	MAGEE	PARK AVE.
17	King Ed. & Oak	18		
35	Marpole	0		

OAK-M'POLE — FRI. DEC. 11 — HAST. ST. / MAR...E — STAN. PARK 00908

00094 (16th AVE.)
Down	TRAVEL TIME	Up	MAR-POLE	JUB-ILEE
0	16th & Main	19		
5	16th & Oak	14		
8	Broadway & Oak	11	MAGEE	PARK AVE.
19	Cambie & Hastings	0		

16th AVE. — SUN. FEB. 21 — 16th / BWAY. MAIN / HAST. — STAN. PARK 00094

01219 (HAST. EXT'N.)
Down	TRAVEL TIME		DELAY
0	Ellesmere Avenue		TO BARN
10	Boundary Road		FROM BARN
27	Main & Hastings		

HAST. EXT'N. — THU. JAN. 14 — BDY. RD. / ELL'R AVE. — STAN. PARK 01219

00121 (MAIN SOUTH)
Down	TRAVEL TIME	Up	MAR-POLE	JUB-ILEE
0	50th & Main	5		PARK AVE.
5	Lulu Island Rly.	0	MAGEE	

MAIN SOUTH — SAT. MAY 22 — 50th / L.Is. MAIN / Rly. — STAN. PARK 00121

00592 — 4 P.M. STUB — Fri. Dec. 11
Down	TRAVEL TIME	Up	MAR-POLE	JUB-ILEE
0	Hastings & Nanaimo	10		PARK AVE.
10	Broadway & Coml.	0	MAGEE	

NANAIMO — FRI. DEC. 11 — HAST. / BWAY. ST. / COML. — STAN. PARK 00592

(Ken Hodgson collection)

329

Appendix E

Bibliography

A. *British Columbia Electric Railway Company Limited Papers.*

These papers are a major source for this book. They are housed in four separate locations: in the B.C. Hydro Building, Vancouver; in the Fir Street Substation, Vancouver; in the Library of the University of British Columbia (Special Collections Division); and in Victoria, under the aegis of the B.C. Provincial Archives, including the extraordinary materials held until 1983 in the B.C. Electric's former electric meter shop in Vancouver.

This collection of the B.C. Electric's records, as well as those of predecessor and associated companies, is exhaustive in its completeness, an ultimate challenge to the researcher.

B. *Books, Articles, Government Publications, and Theses*

Adams, Norris. "The Late Kitsilano Railway Trestle 1886–1982." *Canadian Rail*, March-April 1983, pp. 40-64.

Adams, Norris. "The Big Boys Little Helper in the British Columbia Lower Mainland." *Canadian Rail*, January-February 1985, pp. 11-25.

Bannerman, Gary. *Gastown: The 107 Years.* Vancouver, B.C.: Lagoon Estates Ltd., 1974.

Barr, Capt. James. *Ferry Across the Harbor,* Vancouver, B.C.: Mitchell Press Limited, 1969.

Barrett, Anthony A., and Rhodri Windsor Liscombe. *Francis Rattenbury and British Columbia: Architecture and Challenge in the Imperial Age.* Vancouver, B.C., University of British Columbia Press, 1983.

Bartholomew, Harland et al. *A Plan for the City of Vancouver British Columbia Including Point Grey and South Vancouver and a General Plan of the Region 1929.* Vancouver, B.C.: Vancouver Town Planning Commission, 1929.

Bartholomew, Harland and Associates. *A Preliminary Report Upon Transit (Mass Transportation) Vancouver, British Columbia.* Vancouver, B.C.: Vancouver Town Planning Commission, 1945.

Bell, Betty. *The Fair Land, Saanich.* Victoria, B.C.: Sono Nis Press, 1982.

Binns, R.M. "The Point Ellice Bridge Disaster." *Canadian Rail*, April 1969, pp. 98-107.

Bourdon, Donald J. *The Boom Years.* North Vancouver, B.C.: Hancock House Publishers, 1981.

Boyd, Denny. *History of Hockey in B.C.* Vancouver, B.C.: Canucks Publishing Ltd., 1970.

Breen, David and Kenneth Coates. *The Pacific National Exhibition: An Illustrated History.* Vancouver, B.C.: University of British Columbia Press, 1982.

Brown, Spike. "When the British Columbia Electric Was Young." *The Dispatcher,* July-August 1964, pp. 14-21.

Burnes, J. Rodger. *Echoes of the Ferries.* North Vancouver, B.C.: Carson Graham Secondary School, 1974.

Burnes, John Rodger. *North Vancouver, 1891-1907.* North Vancouver, B.C.: Carson Graham Secondary School, 1971.

Canada Department of Mines. *Transcontinental Excursion C1, Part III.* Ottawa, Ontario: The Geological Survey, 1913.

Carstens, Harold H., ed. *Traction Planbook.* 2nd ed. Fredon, N.J.: Carstens Publications, Inc., 1975.

Cavin, Ruth. *Trolleys.* New York, N.Y.: Hawthorn Books, Inc., 1976.

Cheevers, Bruce Bissell. "The Development of Railroads in the State of Washington 1860 to 1948." Unpublished thesis, Western Washington College of Education, 1949.

City and Interurban Cars. San Marino, California: Pacific Railway Journal, 1961.

Cross, W.K., C.F. Goulson, and A.E. Loft, eds. *The British Columbia Source Book.* Victoria, B.C.: Printer to the Queen's Most Excellent Majesty, 1966.

Cummings, Douglas E. "Railway Entrances to Vancouver 1887-1969." *Canadian Rail*, May 1970, pp. 142-163.

Davies, David L. *Historical Summary — Railways in British Columbia.* Vancouver, B.C.: Canadian Railroad Historical Association, Pacific Coast Branch, 1973.

Davies, David L. *English Bay Branch, C.P.R., Vancouver.* Vancouver, B.C.: Canadian Railroad Historical Association, Pacific Coast Branch, 1975.

Dorman, Robert. *A Statutory History of the Steam and Electric Railways of Canada 1836-1937.* Ottawa, Ontario: Canada Department of Transport, 1938.

Downs, Art. *Paddlewheels on the Frontier.* Seattle, Washington: Superior Publishing Company, 1972.

Due, John F. *The Intercity Electric Railway Industry in Canada.* Toronto, Ontario: University of Toronto Press, 1966.

Edwards, Graham Morison. "The Lynn Valley Tramline Extension, 1908-1911." Unpublished thesis, Capilano College, 1971.

Effle, Mark, ed. *I.N.L.: The Early Interurban Newsletters 1943-1944.* Glendale, California: Interurbans Publications, 1978.

Evenden, L.J., ed. *Vancouver: Western Metropolis.* Victoria, B.C.: University of Victoria, 1973.

Forward, C.N., ed. *Residential and Neighbourhood Studies in Victoria.* Victoria, B.C.: University of Victoria, 1973.

The Fraser Valley of British Columbia, Canada. Victoria, B.C.: Printer to the Queen's Most Excellent Majesty, 1953.

Gosnell, R.E. *The Year Book of British Columbia.* Victoria, B.C.: British Columbia Legislative Assembly, 1911.

Green, George. "Some Pioneers of Light and Power." *British Columbia Historical Quarterly,* July 1938, pp. 145-162.

Green, George. *History of Burnaby and Vicinity.* North Vancouver, B.C.: Shoemaker, McLean & Veitch (1945) Ltd., 1947.

Gregson, Harry. *A History of Victoria, 1842-1970.* Vancouver, B.C.: J.J. Douglas Ltd., 1970.

Gross, Joseph. *Trolley and Interurban Lines of the United States and Canada,* rev. ed. Spencerport, N.Y.: Joseph Gross, 1977.

Gunn, Angus M. *Vancouver, British Columbia: Profile of Canada's Pacific Metropolis.* Vancouver, B.C.: Smith Lithograph Company Limited, 1968.

Gutstein, Donald. "Peril on the Slopes." *Vancouver,* February 1983, pp. 32-34.

Hacking, Norman R., and W. Kaye Lamb. *The Princess Story.* Vancouver, B.C.: Mitchell Press Limited, 1974.

Hamilton, Reuben. *Mount Pleasant Early Days: Memories of Reuben Hamilton, Pioneer, 1890.* Vancouver, B.C., City Archives, 1957.

Harker, Douglas E. *The Woodwards.* Vancouver, B.C.: Mitchell Press Limited, 1976.

Harvey, R.D. *A History of Saanich Peninsula Railways.* Victoria, B.C.: Department of Commercial Transport, Railways Branch, 1960.

Hatcher, Colin K., and Tom Schwarzkopf. *Edmonton's Electric Transit.* Toronto, Ontario: Railfare Enterprises Limited, 1983.

Hearn, George and David Wilkie. *The Cordwood Limited.* Victoria, B.C.: British Columbia Railway Historical Association, 1966.

Henson, Fred C. "Tote 'em Railroad." *The Railway Conductor,* April 1950, pp. 104-108.

A History of the Municipality of Richmond. Richmond, B.C.: Crown Zellerbach Canada Limited, 1958.

Hoffmeister, John E. "The Far-West Trolley." *Canadian Rail,* September 1973, pp. 277-284.

Hoffmeister, John E. "Car 400 Comes Home!" *Canadian Rail,* February 1974, pp. 53-56.

Hull, Raymond, Gordon Soules, and Christine Soules. *Vancouver's Past.* Vancouver, B.C.: Gordon Soules Economic and Marketing Research, 1974.

Hutchison, Bruce. *The Fraser.* Toronto, Ontario: Clarke, Irwin & Co., 1950.

Ireland, Willard E. *New Westminster: The Royal City — The First 100 Years.* New Westminster, B.C.: The Columbian Co. Ltd., 1959.

Johnson, Norman K. "B.C. Electric Today." *ERA Headlights,* November 1954, pp. 1-2.

Johnson, Patricia M. *Canada's Pacific Province.* Toronto, Ontario: McClelland and Stewart Limited, 1966.

Jones, David C. "The Strategy of Railway Abandonment: The Great Northern in Washington and British Columbia, 1917-1935. *The Western Historical Quarterly,* April 1980, pp. 141-158.

Jones, Roy Franklin. *Boundary Town.* Vancouver, Washington: Fleet Printing Co., 1958.

Jordan, W. *Statistics for the B.C. Railway Historian.* Vancouver, B.C.: Canadian Railroad Historical Association, Pacific Coast Branch, 1973.

Jorgensen, Birgette. "A City Back on Track." *Beautiful British Columbia,* Winter 1984, pp. 16-21.

Kalman, Harold. *Exploring Vancouver 2.* rev. ed. Vancouver, B.C.: University of British Columbia Press, 1978.

Kelley, C.C., and R.H. Spilsbury. *Soil Survey of the Lower Fraser Valley.* Ottawa, Ontario: Dominion of Canada — Department of Agriculture, 1939.

Klassen, Agatha E., ed. *Yarrow, A Portrait in Mosaic,* rev. ed. Clearbrook, B.C.: A. Olfert & Sons, 1980.

Kloppenborg, Anne, Alice Niwinski, Eve Johnson, and Robert Gruetter, eds. *Vancouver's First Century: A City Album 1860-1960.* Vancouver, B.C.: J.J. Douglas Ltd., 1977.

Kluckner, Michael. *Vancouver: The Way it Was.* Vancouver, B.C.: Whitecap Books Ltd., 1984.

Knight, Rolf. *Along the No. 20 Line.* Vancouver, B.C.: New Star Books Ltd., 1980.

Lai, Chuen-yan David. *Arches in British Columbia.* Victoria, B.C.: Sono Nis Press, 1982.

Lamb, Chris, ed. *Bradner Flower Show, 1928-1978.* Abbotsford, B.C.: Hacker Press, 1978.

Lewis, Donald C. *Rail Canada: Volume 2.* Vancouver, B.C.: Launch Pad Distributors Ltd., 1977.

Lind, Alan R. *From Horsecars to Streamliners: An Illustrated History of the St. Louis Car Company.* Park Forest, Illinois: Transport History Press, 1978.

Luce, P.W. "Fraser Valley Goes Electric." *The Country Guide,* April 1954, pp. 60-61.

Lyons, C.P. *Milestones on the Mighty Fraser.* Vancouver, B.C.: The Wrigley Printing Company, Limited, 1950.

MacDonald, Norbert. "A Critical Growth Cycle for Vancouver, 1900-1914." *B.C. Studies,* Spring 1973, pp. 26-42.

McGeachie, Pixie. *Bygones of Burnaby: an Anecdotal History.* Burnaby, B.C.: Century Park Museum Association, 1976.

McGregor, D.A. *They Gave Royal Assent.* Vancouver, B.C.: Mitchell Press Limited, 1967.

Maclachlan, Morag. "The Success of the Fraser Valley Milk Producers' Association." *B.C. Studies,* Winter 1974-75, pp. 52-64.

Maguire, Stephen D. "The Hobble-Skirt Car." *Railroad Magazine,* February 1944, pp. 74-77.

Maiden, Cecil. *Lighted Journey.* Vancouver, B.C.: British Columbia Electric Company Limited, 1948.

Mather, Barry. *New Westminster, the Royal City.* Toronto, Ontario: J.M. Dent & Sons (Canada) Limited, 1958.

Mathews, W.H., C.E. Borden, G.P.V. Akrigg, and J.E. Gibbard. *The Fraser's History.* Burnaby, B.C.: The Burnaby Historical Society, 1977.

Melvin, George E. *The Post Offices of B.C., 1858-1970.* Vernon, B.C.: Wayside Press, 1972.

Meugens, Geoff. "The British Columbia Electric in Miniature." *The Dispatcher,* July-August 1964, pp. 28-31.

Meyers, Leonard W. "When the Horseless Carriage Came to Vancouver." *Heritage West,* Fall 1983, pp. 6-9.

Middleton, William D. *The Interurban Era.* Milwaukee, Wisconsin: Kalmbac Publishing Co., 1961.

Middleton, William D. *The Time of the Trolley.* Milwaukee, Wisconsin: Kalmbach Publishing Co., 1967.

Miller, Charles A. *Valley of the Stave.* Surrey, B.C.: Hancock House Publishers Ltd., 1981.

Modern Types of City and Interurban Cars and Trucks, John Stephenson Company. Felton, California: Glenwood Publishers, 1972.

Monk, H.A.J. and John Stewart. *A History of Coquitlam and Fraser Mills, 1858-1958.* [New Westminster, B.C.: Jackson, 1958?]

Montgomery, R.H. *Altitudes in Southern British Columbia*. Ottawa, Ontario: Canada Department of Mines and Resources, 1948.

Morgan, Roland. *Vancouver: Then and Now*. Vancouver, B.C.: Bodima Publications, 1977.

Morgan, Roland and Emily Disher. *Victoria, Then and Now*. Vancouver, B.C.: Bodima Publications, 1977.

Morley, Alan. *Vancouver — From Milltown to Metropolis*. Vancouver, B.C.: Mitchell Press, 1961.

Morton, James W. *Capilano, the Story of a River*. Toronto, Ontario: McClelland and Stewart Limited, 1970.

Myers, Thomas R. *Ninety Years of Public Utility Service on Vancouver Island: A History of the B.C. Electric*. Victoria, B.C. B.C. Electric, 1954.

Nelson, Denys. *Place Names of the Delta of the Fraser*. Vancouver, B.C.: n.p., 1927.

Neuberger, Richard L. "British Columbia Electric Rolls On." *Railroad Magazine*, March 1948, pp. 90-98.

Newell, Gordon, ed. *The H.W. McCurdy Marine History of the Pacific Northwest*. Seattle, Washington: The Superior Publishing Company, 1966.

Nickols, Sheila, ed. *Maple Ridge: A History of Settlement*. Maple Ridge, B.C.: The Fraser Valley Record, 1972.

Nicol, Eric. *Vancouver*. Toronto, Ontario: Doubleday Canada, Limited, 1970.

O'Kiely, Elizabeth, ed. *Gastown Revisited*. Vancouver, B.C.: Community Arts Council, 1970.

Our First 50. Vancouver, B.C.: Fraser Valley Milk Producers Association, 1968.

Paetkau, Walter, ed. *Our Town*. Abbotsford, B.C.: M.S.A. Community Services, 1977.

Parker, Douglas V. *No Horsecars in Paradise*. Toronto, Ontario: Railfare Enterprises Limited, 1981.

Plant, Ernie Les. "Old Days in Vancouver." *Bank of British Columbia's Pioneer News*, October-November 1981, pp. 7-10.

Plant, Ernie Les. "Getting There Was All The Fun." *The Coupler*, July-August 1984, p. 5.

Porzig, Jack. *The Fraser River Railway Bridge, New Westminster, B.C.* Mankato, Minnesota: Great Northern Railway Historical Society, 1982.

Province of British Columbia. *Manual of Provincial Information, 1930*. Victoria, B.C.: Provincial Bureau of Information, 1930.

Pugsley, Edmund E. "Electric Lines of British Columbia." *Railroad Magazine*, October 1946, pp. 99-106.

Railway Department, Province of British Columbia. *Annual Report, Year Ended December 31, 1953*. Victoria, B.C.: Printer to the Queen's Most Excellent Majesty, 1954.

Ramsey, Bruce. *Five Corners: The Story of Chilliwack*. Chilliwack, B.C.: Chilliwack Historical Society, 1975.

Reid, Glen and Alan Lysell, eds. *The Days Before Yesterday in Cedar Cottage*. Vancouver, B.C.: Gladstone Secondary School, 1968.

Reksten, Terry. *Rattenbury*. Victoria, B.C.: Sono Nis Press, 1978.

Reuss, David E. "The Royal Interurban You Can Ride." *Traction & Models*, July 1970, pp. 8-12.

Robinson, Lewis J., ed. *British Columbia*. Toronto, Ontario: University of Toronto Press, 1972.

Ross, Leslie J. *Richmond, Child of the Fraser*. Richmond, B.C.: Historical Committee of the Richmond '79 Centennial Society, 1979.

Roy, Patricia E. "The British Columbia Electric Railway Company, 1897-1928; A British Company in British Columbia." Unpublished Ph.D. thesis, The University of British Columbia, 1970.

Roy, Patricia E. "Direct Management from Abroad: The Formative Years of the British Columbia Electric Railway." *The Business History Review*, Summer 1973, pp. 239-259.

Roy, Patricia E. *Vancouver: An Illustrated History*. Toronto, Ontario: Lorimer, 1980.

Sanford, Barrie. *The Pictorial History of Railroading in British Columbia*. Vancouver, B.C.: Whitecap Books Ltd., 1981.

Sebree, Mac. "Light Rail in the West." *Pacific News*, June 1984, pp. 8-10.

Sharman, Vic. "B.C.E.R. Notes." *Interurbans*, May 1947, p. 55.

Siemens, Alfred H., ed. *Lower Fraser Valley: Evolution of a Cultural Landscape*. Vancouver, B.C.: Tantalus Research Limited, 1966.

Sochowski, David. "The Granville Island Switching Operations of the British Columbia Hydro and Power Authority Railway." *The Dispatcher*, July-August 1964, pp. 6-13.

Stevens, G.R. *Canadian National Railways. vol. 2*. Toronto, Ontario: Clarke, Irwin and Company Limited, 1962.

Swett, Ira L. "Commuting in British Columbia." *Rail Classics*, May 1973, pp. 40-45, 76-79.

Till, Harold. *Vancouver's Traffic History*. Vancouver, B.C.: B.C.E.R., 1946.

Treleaven, G. Fern. *The Surrey Story*. Cloverdale, B.C.: Surrey Museum and Historical Society, 1969.

Treleaven, G. Fern. *The Surrey Story*. vol. 2. Cloverdale, B.C.: Surrey Museum and Historical Society, 1970.

Treleaven, G. Fern. *Rivers, Roads and Railways*. Cloverdale, B.C.: Surrey Museum and Historical Society, 1981.

Turner, Robert D. *Vancouver Island Railroads*. San Marino, California: Golden West Books, 1973.

Turner, Robert D. *The Pacific Princesses*. Victoria, B.C. Sono Nis Press, 1977.

Vancouver, City of. *Municipal Year Book 1950*. Vancouver, B.C.: City of Vancouver, 1950.

"Vancouver, Victoria and Eastern Railway and Navigation Company." St. Paul, Minnesota: Great Northern Railway, 1949.

Waite, Donald E. *The Langley Story Illustrated*. Maple Ridge, B.C.: Waite, 1977.

White, George B. "Development of Eastern Fraser Valley." *British Columbia Historical Quarterly*, October 1948, pp. 259-291.

White, James. *Altitudes in the Dominion of Canada*. Ottawa, Ontario: Commission of Conservation Canada, 1915.

Wilson, Robert S. "British Columbia Electric Ry." *Electric Railroads*, April 1949, pp. 1-13.

Wilson, Robert S. *Trolley Trails Through the West: Trolleys of Western Canada*. Yakima, Washington: Wilson Brothers Publications, 1979.

Woodland, Alan. *New Westminster: The Early Years, 1858-1898*. New Westminster, B.C.: Nunaga Publishing Company, 1973.

Woods, J.J. *History and Development of the Agassiz Harrison Valley*. Agassiz, B.C.: n.p., 1941.

Woodward-Reynolds, K.M. "A History of the City and District of North Vancouver." Unpublished M.A. thesis, The University of British Columbia, 1943.

Wright, Monte J. *The Birney Car: 1921-1948*. Victoria, B.C.: British Columbia Provincial Museum, 1974.

Wright, Monte J. *Street Railways in Victoria, 1888-1948*. Victoria, B.C.: British Columbia Provincial Museum, n.d.

C. *Newspapers and Journals*

Abbotsford, Sumas, and Matsqui News
Beautiful British Columbia
Brill's Magazine
B.C. Electric Employees' Magazine (also B.C. Electric Employees Magazine, and B.C.E. Family Post)
British Columbia Historical Quarterly
B.C. Studies
Burnaby Advertiser
Burnaby Courier
The Business History Review
The Buzzer
Canadian Car & Foundry Bulletins
Canadian Electrical News
Canadian Rail
Canadian Railway and Marine World
Canadian Transportation
Chilliwack Progress
The Country Guide
The Coupler
The Courier (Vancouver)
The Dispatcher
Electric Railroads
ERA Headlights
Fraser Valley Record
The Guardian
Heritage West
Intercom
Interurbans
Juan de Fuca News-Review
Kerrisdale Courier
The Mirror (Sooke)
The Mining Record
New Westminster Columbian (also New Westminster British Columbian, British Columbian Magazine, the British Columbian, and the Columbian)
North Shore Express
North Shore News
The Official Guide of the Railways
Pacific News
Pioneer News (Bank of B.C.)
Progress
Rail Classics
Railroad Magazine
The Railway Conductor
Richmond Review
The Sandhouse
Traction and Models
Trains
Urban Reader
Vancouver
Vancouver Daily News-Advertiser (also The Weekly News-Advertiser)
The Vancouver Daily Province (also The Daily Province, and The Province)
The Vancouver News-Herald (latterly The Herald)
The Vancouver Sun (also The Sun)
Vancouver World
The Victoria Daily Colonist (also The Daily British Colonist, The Daily Colonist, and The Colonist)
The Victoria Standard
The Victoria Times
W.C.R.A. News
The Western Historical Quarterly

D. *Miscellaneous*

Ministry of Railway (files in the collection of B.C. Provincial Archives)
Railway timetables
    Canadian National
    Canadian Northern
    Canadian Pacific
    Great Northern
Statistics Canada records

Index

332

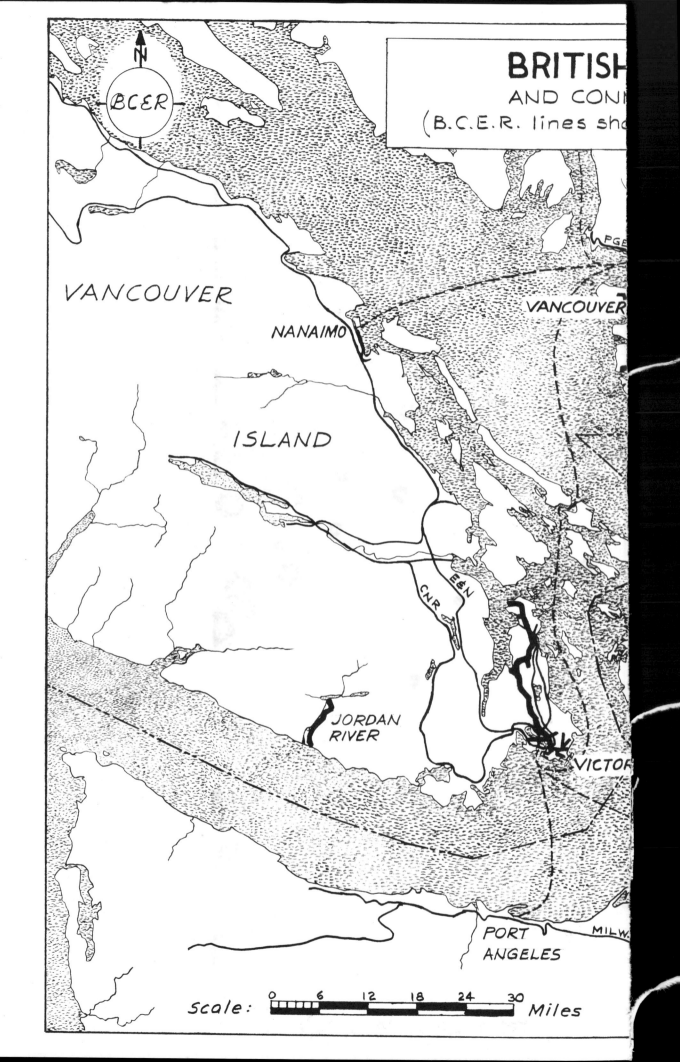